INCOME AND WEALTH

Acknowledgements

The original book, *Income and Wealth*, was published in Japanese by Iwanami Shoten in 1991. Widely acclaimed as a new classic on distribution theory, it won the prestigious Nikkei Shimbun Economics Book Award the same year. Tsuneo Ishikawa started working on the English translation of his own book soon after its publication but he became seriously ill and, by the time he died in 1998, left half of it unfinished. His untimely death brought his friends, colleagues, and students together to establish the Ishikawa Tsuneo Fund to commemorate his life and work, and by the end of 2000 as many as five hundred people had contributed to the Fund. One of the Fund's missions was to publish the English translation of *Income and Wealth*. That so many of his former students, Takahisa Dejima, Kyota Eguchi, Yuji Genda, Mikinari Higano, Hidehiko Ishihara, Mamiko Ishihara, Susumu Imai, Shinsuke Kambe, Tomoko Kishi, Hideaki Murase, Nobuko Nagase, Naoko Nishimura, Hiroshi Teruyama, Atsushi Tsuneki, Kaoru Ueda, Shigeru Wakita, and Akiko Yoshida, volunteered to participate in the translation project is a testament to Ishikawa's stature as a teacher and a scholar. Without their devotion, the book would not have come to life. Yuji Genda coordinated the project and he was assisted by Shinsuke Kambe, Naoko Nishimura, and Hiroshi Teruyama. Asami Tokuda compiled references, Takehisa Shinozaki and Yoko Takahashi proofread, and the Daido Life Foundation provided financial assistance. Rebecca Bryant, Toyoshi Onji, and Andrew Schuller of Oxford University Press provided important advice and encouragement during the book's long gestation period.

The Board of Ishikawa Tsueo Fund
Katsuhito Iwai (Co-chair)
Masahiro Okuno-Fujiwara (Co-chair)
Konosuke Odaka
Yukihiko Kiyokawa
Toshiaki Tachibanaki
Yuji Genda

Income and Wealth

TSUNEO ISHIKAWA

*This publication was supported by a generous
donation from The Daido Life Foundation*

OXFORD
UNIVERSITY PRESS

Great Clarendon Street, Oxford OX2 6DP

Oxford University Press is a department of the University of Oxford.
It furthers the University's objective of excellence in research, scholarship,
and education by publishing worldwide in

Oxford New York

Auckland Bangkok Buenos Aires Cape Town Chennai
Dar es Salaam Delhi Hong Kong Istanbul Karachi Kolkata
Kuala Lumpur Madrid Melbourne Mexico City Mumbai Nairobi
São Paulo Shanghai Singapore Taipei Tokyo Toronto

with an associated company in Berlin

Oxford is a registered trade mark of Oxford University Press
in the UK and in certain other countries

Published in the United States
by Oxford University Press Inc., New York

SHOTOKU TO TOMI by Tsuneo Ishikawa

British Library Cataloguing in Publication Data
Data available

Library of Congress Cataloging in Publication Data
Ishikawa, Tsuneo, 1947–
[Shotokū to tomo. English]
Income and wealth / Tsuneo Ishikawa.
p. cm.
Includes bibliographical references and index.
1. Economics—Mathematical models. 2. Income—Mathematical models.
3. Wealth—Mathematical models. I. Title.
HB135 .I8313 2001 339.2—dc21 2001021787
ISBN 0-19-828862-X

1 3 5 7 9 10 8 6 4 2

Typeset by Newgen Imaging Systems (P) Ltd., Chennai, India
Printed in Great Britain
on acid-free paper by
Biddles Ltd., *www.biddles.co.uk*

Contents

Contents

List of Figures

List of Figures

List of Tables

1

Introduction

1.1. THE PURPOSE AND ORGANIZATION OF THE BOOK

Income and wealth, these are the fruits of our economic activities and, in turn, are the foundation of future economic activities. The aim of this book is to explain systematically how income and wealth are produced and distributed, a subject which is of fundamental importance in economic theory.

The distribution of income and wealth is determined in a market economy as a part of price formation. Given the varied abilities and preferences and also physical resources that people possess, we may conclude that income is merely a reflection of market equilibrium and may not require further discussion. Yet economists have long been interested in the study of income and wealth as an independent field, because they have wanted to answer the following basic questions that arise in our daily lives.

Why do workers who work equally hard obtain different incomes? Is this fair?

Why do people make different levels of effort? Is it a matter of preference? Is it possible that difference in job content influences the motivation of workers?

Through their experience of work, people expect to obtain many intangibles: they acquire new knowledge and new skills, find out who they are, establish confidence in themselves, and receive trust and respect by fulfilling social responsibilities. How does the market economy provide the jobs that meet the above expectations? Also, is it possible that the market does not provide the opportunity for these jobs equally among workers?

Does economic efficiency necessitate the uneven distribution among workers of the jobs that are desirable in the sense described above?

What is the relationship between economic efficiency or economic growth and income distribution?

If workers sometimes engage in co-operative and collective activities without competing with each other, what is their reason for doing so? Moreover, what consequence does such action have on the allocation of economic resources and income distribution?

Why do people save?

If those who have more income save more than those who have less income, does the difference in wealth not increase in a cumulative way and does not an extremely unequal society emerge?

Similarly, is it not possible that inequality is increased over generations by means of inheritance and education? Is there any force in the market that restrains this tendency? If so, what is it?

The setting of asset prices is strongly influenced by how people forecast future events, which is the characteristic feature of the asset market. Thus, how much information people possess about the future is a crucial factor in determining the distribution of wealth. The theory states that all investors can learn from asset prices what other people know and that the disparity arising from informational difference does not persist. Should we trust this theory?

In this book, I systematically examine and evaluate the arguments that have been advanced in relation to these questions, citing the results of my own research. The main characteristic of this book is that it not only analyses income distribution as the consequence of economic activities, but also focuses on the process of obtaining income, especially the nature of various jobs, and examines how different jobs influence employment and income distribution.

In the real market economy, in addition to the market distribution process, income redistribution is operative, through the tax system, social welfare, and the provision of public goods. Income redistribution modifies the consequences of the distribution process and changes (or distorts) it. Many people are interested in the burden and benefits of the process of social redistribution but this topic is beyond the scope of this book. In order to study income redistribution we need to understand how the market economy produces differences in income and wealth. An understanding of this process, this book claims, is of great significance in its own right.

This book does not attempt to address the problem of the inequalities in income and wealth among nations. Since the 1970s, inequalities in the per capita income between the countries of South Asia, Africa, and Latin America, and the developed countries, have continually increased. What measures can be taken to alleviate this situation? Those who think this issue to be of paramount importance may find the scope of this book to be too narrow. However, knowledge of the kinds of problems that arise in developed market economies can be useful in dealing with problems in developing economies. Moreover, an understanding of how income and wealth are generated and distributed can increase the interest of people in general in international redistribution of income and wealth.

This book has eight chapters. Since each chapter is discrete, the chapters can be read in any order.

The rest of Chapter 1 provides an overview of the current labour participation structure and the structure and distribution of income and wealth in Japan. It also draws attention to the pitfalls that may arise in interpreting the data on these issues.

Chapter 2 examines what distribution system is just. Naturally, there are many views about what is just. There is, however, no doubt that each view has universal applicability since it is concerned with ethical evaluation. This chapter looks at several representative views on just distribution. It is hoped that the findings of this examination may be useful in the analysis of the problems of the distribution of income and wealth later in this book.

Chapters 3 to 6 explain the neo-classical theory of the labour market and its alternative, the dual labour market theory, present the results of empirical studies, and try to integrate the two theories.

In Chapter 3, I describe how neo-classical economics explains the supply of labour resources to various jobs from the viewpoint of rational choice of economic individuals. Factors specific to the labour market such as time-variable resources and incomplete information about the quality of resources mean that there are situations that cannot be explained by the simple logic of market equilibrium. I also point out here theoretical developments in this area.

Chapter 4 surveys the empirical studies on the theoretical framework of neo-classical economics. Focusing especially on the relationship between educational level and income distribution, it examines the extent to which educational level increases income, how much the inborn ability of individuals and/or socio-economic background influences the choice of educational level or the formation of income, and why educational level increases productivity.

In Chapter 5, I explain the theoretical as well as the historical background of the dual labour market approach, discuss the theoretical background and the conditions under which the involuntary division of the labour market emerges, and, moreover, analyse its implication for the distribution of income. I point out the possibility that the dual labour market theory and the neo-classical theory may eventually be integrated as a theory of employment and income distribution. In this sense, this chapter constitutes the central chapter of the book.

In Chapter 6, I examine the applicability of the dual labour market theory and/ or the integrated theory in the Japanese labour market. I analyse why a two-tier wage system based on firm sizes has emerged and examine the degree of competitiveness between large firms at the point of entry to the internal labour market, in order to examine whether the dual structure persists through time.

In Chapter 7, I treat the accumulation of wealth as a physical asset. First, I look at various motives for saving and examine the effect of different motives on wealth distribution and the long-term effect on wealth distribution of inheritance of physical assets and education from parents to children. Then, I analyse price fluctuations in the asset market and the role of information for future capital gain.

In Chapter 8, I summarize the arguments made in previous chapters and present my conclusions. I also list topics for future research.

1.2. INCOME AND WEALTH IN JAPAN

This discussion begins by assembling the basic facts on the composition and distribution of income and wealth in Japan. Using income and asset statistics at the macro level it first looks at how income and wealth are distributed over major institutional sectors of the economy such as households, firms, and the public sector. Later, there is discussion of the distribution of income and wealth among households or individuals based on the micro data of individual employment surveys and household surveys. There is also description of the employment structure, which is central to the process of generating income. Since this book is mainly concerned with the income and wealth generation process, it focuses on the distribution of pre-tax income, ignoring any evaluation of the redistributive mechanism through taxation and the social security system.

Composition of National Income and National Net Worth

The national income (total value-added) of Japan for 1985 was estimated as 251.2 trillion yen. This is 4.3 times the figure for 1970, which was 59.2 trillion yen. Since consumer prices have grown by 2.6-fold over the course of these years, real national income has increased by 1.6-fold, or has on average grown at 3.3 per cent annually.

How is national income divided between economic agents and between factors of production? We divide economic agents into three institutional sectors, households, private firms and the public sector. The public sector is a consolidation of government and public firms. For the sake of convenience, private non-profit organizations which provide households with services in such areas as education, health, and medicine are integrated in the household sector. The income of the household sector is decomposed into employment income (or earnings) consisting primarily of wages and salaries, self-employment income, and asset income. The change in the composition of national income over the period 1970 to 1988 is summarized in Table 1.1.

Towards the end of that period employment income constituted almost 70 per cent of national income, asset income in the broad sense (which is the sum of asset income that directly accrues to households and the post-dividend private firm income) constituted 25 per cent, and self-employment income, which is an intermediate category between the other two categories of income, made up a little less than 8 per cent. The public sector's income share is negative, reflecting the losses of the public firm and interest payment on public debt. The trend decline in the share of self-employment income is partly due to a decline in the weight of the agricultural sector, and partly due to the fact that self-employed concerns increasingly obtained corporate status. Their income was thereby gradually absorbed into the categories employment income and private firm income. Another notable feature is the rise in the share of household dividends and interest income. This reflects a large increase in household ownership of financial assets over the period. Dividend income remained almost unchanged at 0.7 per cent, however and it was only interest income that rose.

An overall picture of who owns wealth and in what form, is given by the national balance sheet prepared as a part of the national account statistics. The estimated market values of the real assets as well as the detailed composition of

Table 1.1. *Movement in the Distributional Composition of National Income (1970–1988, per cent)*

	1970–74	1975–79	1980–84	1985–88
Household sector income				
(1) Employment income	59.2	67.1	68.8	69.4
Wages and salaries	(54.3)	(60.4)	(60.4)	(59.9)
Other benefits	(4.9)	(6.6)	(8.4)	(9.5)
(2) Self-employment income	15.8	13.3	9.1	7.6
Agriculture, forestry, and fishing	(4.3)	(3.5)	(1.8)	(1.3)
Non-agricultural	(11.5)	(9.7)	(7.4)	(6.4)
(3) Asset income	12.1	12.5	14.6	14.2
Dividends and interest	(8.1)	(9.1)	(11.5)	(10.8)
Rent	(0.6)	(0.8)	(0.7)	(0.7)
Imputed rent on owner-occupied housing	(3.5)	(2.6)	(2.4)	(2.7)
Private firm sector income	12.4	7.7	9.1	10.6
Public sector income	0.5	−0.7	−1.9	−1.9
Total	100.0	100.0	100.0	100.0

Notes
1. All income figures are before tax.
2. 'Other benefits' as an item of 'Employment income' refers mainly to contribution of employers to social security and retirement benefits.
3. 'Private firm income' refers to income after receipt and payment of dividends.
4. 'Public Sector' refers to 'general government' and 'public firm' combined.
5. The asset income of private non-profit organizations has been added to the interest and dividend income of the household sector. For any period its proportion (to total) is less than 0.2%.
6. Household disposable income as a percentage of total household income (= employment income + self-employment income + asset income) for each period is 94.4%, 96.7%, 95.7%, and 95.1%, respectively.
7. Private firm disposable income (profit) as a percentage of total private firm income for each period is 51.0%, 31.4%, 36.8%, and 32.1%, respectively.

Source: Calculated from Economic Planning Agency, *Annual National Economic Accounts* 1990.

financial assets and debts are listed for each institutional sector. Table 1.2 shows the composition of wealth at the end of 1985 (before the sharp rise in land and stock prices). For financial assets and debts, we have separated out corporate shares and pension reserve assets from other forms of loan–debt relationship, for which only the total is listed. Corporate shares are evaluated at current market values both on the credit side and the debit side.[1]

---

[1] As in Table 1.1, private non-profit organizations are included in the household sector. The 'social security account' which forms a part of the 'general government' sector is simply the account for pension reserve assets. Therefore, its real asset is attributed to the public sector, while its net financial asset is attributed to the household sector, its ultimate claimant. Furthermore, the (qualified) pension assets originally treated as an asset of the private firm sector in the national accounts are transferred to the household sector, which is where they belong. A more detailed account of the procedures employed in preparing this table is given in Ishikawa (1990).

Table 1.2. *Sectoral Composition of Net National Wealth (end 1985, trillion yen)*

	Household sector		Private firm sector		Public sector		Domestic total		Foreign sector	
	Asset	Debt	Asset	Debt	Asset	Debt	Asset	Debt	Asset	Debt
Real assets	914.7	—	562.6	—	340.1	—	1,817.4	—	—	—
Residential houses							159.2	—	—	—
Net fixed assets (non-residential)	192.0	—	243.3	—	252.8	—	528.9	—	—	—
Land	682.4	—	259.8	—	73.5	—	1,015.7	—	—	—
Other resources	31.0	—	3.4	—	10.3	—	44.6	—	—	—
Inventories	9.2	—	56.2	—	3.5	—	68.9	—	—	—
Financial assets	671.2	212.9	1,150.5	1,332.1	297.2	540.8	2,118.9	2,085.9	78.2	111.2
Corporate stocks	66.0	—	174.3	253.2	1.6	0.1	241.9	253.3	11.4	—
Pension reserves	92.3	—	—	18.9	—	73.4	92.3	92.3	—	—
Other financial assets	512.9	212.9	976.2	1,060.0	295.6	467.3	1,784.7	1,740.3	66.8	111.2
Net worth (wealth)	—	1,373.0	—	381.0	—	96.5	—	1,850.4	—	−33.0
Addendum: Consumer durables	49.8	—	—	—	—	—	49.8	—	—	—

Notes: The sectoral breakdown is based on the tables for 'private sector' and 'public sector' given as Supplementary Table 2 in the *National Accounts*. Therefore, the 'private firm' sector refers to the sum of 'non-financial corporate firms' and the private financial institutions, and the 'public' sector refers to the sum of 'general government', public enterprises, and the public financial institutions. 'Non-profit organizations serving households' are absorbed into the 'household' sector. The 'foreign' sector is obtained from Supplementary Table 4 in the *National Accounts*.

Source: Calculated from Economic Planning Agency, *Annual National Economic Accounts* (cited as *National Accounts* hereafter). For a detailed description of how the figures were derived, see Ishikawa (1990).

The net national wealth (aggregate net worth) of Japan at the end of 1985 is estimated as 1,850.4 trillion yen. It is worth 7.4 times the national income of that year. Since it was 296.4 trillion yen at the end of 1970, it has increased 6.2-fold in nominal terms and 2.4-fold in real terms over the course of fifteen years. Recalling that an annual increase in the net national wealth is the sum of the annual savings flow defined as the residual of goods consumed from the annual product of the economy and the revaluation of already existing assets (that is, capital gains), the fact that net national wealth increased much faster than national income implies that the element of asset revaluation has been particularly important. Capital gains are naturally concentrated in land and corporate stocks.

Net national wealth is the sum of domestic real assets (1,817.4 trillion yen) and the net debt outstanding of the foreign sector (33.0 trillion yen, also called the net external credit). Net national wealth is also the sum of the net worth of the three domestic sectors. The largest wealth holder is the household sector (1,373.0 trillion yen). Yet fairly large amounts of wealth are also accumulated in the private firm and public sectors (381.0 trillion yen for the former and 96.5 trillion yen for the latter). In particular, the private firm sector has net worth equalling about 20 per cent of net national wealth or almost 30 per cent of household net worth. Such an amount of wealth is not reflected in the valuation of their corporate stocks.

In each sector that part of real assets which is not matched by the net worth becomes dependent on outside funds, while that part of net worth which exceeds the value of real assets becomes the fund supplied to other sectors. The household sector is the sole net supplier of finance, which amounts to 458.3 trillion yen. Of that amount 39.6 per cent is used by the private firm sector, 53.2 per cent by the pubic sector, and the remaining 7.2 per cent is used by the foreign sector.

Cross-country Comparison of Wealth Composition

We now compare the net national wealth of Japan with that of other mature capitalist economies, the United Kingdom and the United States. Because there are differences among the three countries in the composition of the assets included and the manner of evaluation, rigorous comparison cannot be hoped for, but we have tried to standardize the classification of sectors and asset items as far as possible. (The balance sheets of the UK and the USA are given as Tables 1A.1 and 1A.2, respectively, in the Appendix to this chapter.)

First, we look at the ratio of total real assets owned by the private sector (households and private firms) to national income and also at the composition of real assets in the three countries. In terms of the ratio of private sector assets to national income, the figures during the years 1985–7 rose from 4.5 to 5.0 in the UK, remained constant at 3.4 in the USA, and rose from 5.9 to 7.9 in Japan. Once the value of land is deducted, however, the figures become closer, with

2.6 for the UK, 2.5 for the USA, and 2.1 for Japan. Moreover, these figures remain remarkably constant over time. Thus the differences in the ratios of private sector real assets to national income and their changes over time in the three countries can be explained mostly by the size of land values and their change over time. The remaining difference is explained by the ratio of housing assets to income; more specifically, its very low value in Japan. Once adjustments are made to land values and housing, there remains little difference among the three countries in the holding of real assets.

Second, we turn to the ratio of household net worth to household disposable income, and its composition. While this ratio stayed constant at 4.0 in the USA over the three-year period 1985–7, it rose in both the UK and Japan, from 4.8 to 5.7 in the former and from 6.3 to 8.5 in the latter. Here again, the largest factor was land value; 0.4 of the 0.9 increase in the UK and 1.6 of the 2.2 increase in Japan was due to large capital gains on land during this period.

Another important difference between the three countries, however, lies in the household ownership of net financial assets. The ratio of *disposable net financial assets* (that is, excluding pension reserve assets) to household disposable income in 1.1–1.4 for the UK, 0.9 for the USA, and 1.7–2.2 for Japan. (The ratios of pension reserves to disposable income are 0.7 for the UK and the USA and 0.5 for Japan; Japan's ratio is only slightly below those of the other two countries.) The major reason for the rise in the figures for the UK and Japan is, of course, the rise in the price of corporate stocks. In particular, there was a sharp rise in the ratio of stock holding to disposable income in Japanese households, which reached 0.67 at the end of 1987. It is also noteworthy, however, that the figure for financial assets other than corporate stocks is also higher in Japan than in the UK and the USA.

In sum, the relatively large ratio of the Japanese private sector net worth to national income is seen to be explicable by relatively high land values. Similarly, the relatively large ratio of household net worth to household disposable income is partly explicable by high land values, but there is another factor, a relatively large disposable net financial asset holding, that is also important. Japanese households seem in the period under discussion to have owned both in absolute and relative (to income) terms larger disposable net financial assets than those in the UK and the USA.

Distribution of Income among Households

The foregoing has provided an overview of the composition of income and wealth at the macro level. We turn next to look at the size distribution of income.

If we take the view that each individual has different endowments, and determines his or her economic activity on the basis of his or her own will and responsibility, what we have to evaluate is the distribution of income among individuals. This concept is the main focus of the theoretical discussion in this book.

On the other hand, given the fact that households contain plural members whose needs are reasonably similar, once such observable attributes as the size, age composition, and physical health of the household are controlled, there is perhaps more practical meaning to the evaluation of the distribution of income among households. In fact, because statistical surveys of consumption, income, and assets normally take the household as a unit of observation, research on the size distribution of income in Japan, with a few exceptions, has been concerned with that among households.

When we look at the characteristics of the size distribution of income we must always keep in mind the fact that every survey contains several sources of bias that may quite easily affect the overall appraisal. In particular, it is necessary to examine (a) whether or not households sampled in the survey cover the entire population of households, (b) whether or not samples can reasonably be regarded as random, and (c) whether or not income is reported correctly.

The accuracy with which income is reported varies greatly depending on whether the figures have been recorded in an expenditure diary or have simply been recalled from memory. On the other hand, because maintaining an expenditure diary requires an enormous amount of time and effort the number of households that refuse to take part in a sample using diaries is high. Economists familiar with survey statistics suggest that households at both the high and the low ends of income distribution generally tend to be omitted from samples. Furthermore, the asset incomes reported in surveys tend to fall short of the asset income shown in the national accounts basis by a wide margin, and seem therefore to be clearly under-reported.[2]

---

[2] Taxation statistics are limited in that, first, they are restricted to actual taxpayers, so that households below the taxable income level are omitted, and second, there are several sources of under-reporting biases in income, and the fact that interest income is taxed at the source. Three conditions referred to in the text are thus not met.

Household surveys such as the *Family Income and Expenditure Survey* and the *Family Saving Survey* (both conducted by the Statistics Bureau, Management and Coordination Agency), which give convenient annual time series and are therefore widely used are limited in that the population of the survey is restricted to non-agricultural, plural member households. Moreover, it is frequently pointed out that there are significant numbers of households who refuse to co-operate in such surveys, making it difficult to ensure the randomness of the samples. The problem is said to be acute in urban areas and also at the low and high ends of the distribution of income. There is the further restriction that those for whom the composition of income is observable are non-managerial workers (for the remainder, only the total annual income is reported), and also that even for this group the reported interest and dividend income is almost nil.

The larger-scale *National Survey of Family Income and Expenditure* (Statistics Bureau, Management and Coordination Agency) whose questionnaire items are similar to those of the two surveys referred to above, and which is conducted every five years, has since 1984 enlarged its sampling base to cover all households, including agricultural households. Nevertheless it still must deal with the second and third difficulties discussed in the text.

The *Basic Survey on the Living Conditions of the Nation* (Ministry of Welfare, formerly called the *Survey on the Living Conditions of the Nation*), because it employs different survey methods, is said to be better able than the afore-mentioned surveys to include high-income households in its sample, though other sources of bias remain.

For these reasons, the figures on income distribution must always be considered jointly with the assumptions incorporated in such figures. Special care must be taken when inequalities of income distribution are compared across countries or across time within the same country, especially during periods, as in the latter 1970s in Japan, in which households accumulate financial assets rapidly (see Table 1.1).

The works of Ishizaki (1983: ch. 1) and Mizoguchi and Takayama (1984: ch. 1) may be adduced as recent, representative research incorporating critical examination of the data. The former, based on the *Employment Status Survey*, and the latter, based on the *Family Income and Expenditure Survey* and the *Survey on the Living Conditions of the Nation*, investigated the nature of changes in the size distribution of income among households over time by cross-examining the consistency of figures with various other surveys. The former work also attempted to correct the under-reporting bias in asset income by allocating total financial asset income (on the national accounts basis) to different income strata.

Despite differences in the database and methodology of appraisal the two studies present almost the same qualitative picture of the movement in the distribution of income. The size inequality of income in post-war Japan is characterized by the following cycles; namely, (a) movement towards equality at the very beginning of the post-war period (up to the early 1950s), (b) movement towards inequality during the next decade (up to the early 1960s), (c) significant movement towards equality during the next decade (up to the early 1970s), and then (d) movement towards inequality again since the first half of 1970s.

The first movement towards equality obviously reflects the outcome of various post-war reforms (including agricultural land reform, the wealth levy and the dissolution of the *zaibatsu*, the monopolistic organizations). The reverse movement in the 1950s has mainly to do with a rise in the distribution of earnings between firms of different sizes that arose by way of bonus income. Significant equalization since the early 1960s is mainly explained by the tightening of the labour market that accompanied rapid economic growth, and which significantly reduced the distribution of wages among individuals of different age groups or to firms of different sizes. The movement towards inequality since the first half of the 1970s is due to the fact that the reduction in wage distribution has come to a stop and also to a reduction in the share of the low-income group as well as a rise in the share of the high-income group for each of the categories: self-employed income, corporate managers' income, and asset income. Moreover, factors such as an increase in the number of single

---

Another large-scale survey that includes all households is the *Employment Status Survey* (Statistics Bureau, Management and Coordination Agency). Since 1979, however, the survey questionnaire has asked only the income bracket to which the principal source of income belongs. For a more detailed discussion of the sources of income distribution statistics in Japan, see Economic Planning Agency (1975: 4–10) and Ishizaki (1983: 9–11).

person households (especially among the elderly) and an increase in the number of households with both husband and wife at work (reflecting women's increasingly active participation in the labour market) seem to have gained increased importance in explaining the size distribution of income among households.

The foregoing statements refer to studies of data to the early 1980s, and detailed investigation of the data since that period awaits execution.[3,4]

The Employment Structure and the Distribution of Earnings

According to the *Employment Status Survey* conducted in October 1987, 36.37 million males and 24.13 million females were employed, out of a total population aged 15 and over of 47.24 million males and 50.10 million females. These figures amounted to 77.0 per cent of males and 48.2 per cent of females. Among women who work, those who work full-time comprise 31.0 per cent and the remainder, 17.2 per cent, work part-time, combining employment with housework or studying. (The latter group is very small among men, amounting to only 1.7 per cent.) Among the non-employed population are those who wish to be employed, who amount to 5.6 per cent of the male population and 16.0 per cent of the female population.

The composition of the workforce, classified by occupation and employment status, is shown in Table 1.3. Professional, technical, or managerial workers (that is, upper-tier workers, see section 5.3) constitute one in every six males and one in every eight females. While managers and regular employees constitute nearly three-quarters of the entire male workforce, they comprise less than half of the female workforce. Because many women work part-time, most women workers are family workers in the self-employed sector and home-workers.

The composition of the workforce by size of firm is shown in Table 1.4. Those who work for large (private) firms with 1,000 or more employees or public offices constitute 26 per cent of males and 17 per cent of females. Those who work in tiny firms with fewer than 10 employees constitute 33 per cent of males and 44 per cent of females. Furthermore, if we add together all firms with fewer than 100 employees the figures rise to 57 per cent of men and 68 per cent of

---

[3] That a tendency towards inequality has continued since the 1980s is indicated by Economic Planning Agency, *Annual Report on the Economy 1990* (White Paper): 267–77, especially Fig. 3.1.5.

[4] International comparison of the size distribution of income is an extremely difficult task. Sawyer (1976), in comparing the statistics of OECD countries, judged Japan to have one of the most equal distributions. However, Ishizaki argues that the *National Survey of Family Income and Expenditure*, used by Sawyer, has a serious defect (with respect to under-reporting) and that the conclusion should be reversed: Ishizaki argues that Japan's income distribution is one of the most unequal among the OECD countries. The problem here is that, as Ishizaki himself admitted, under-reporting of asset income is expected to hold for other countries as well, and it is only after a correction is made for each country that a suitable comparison becomes possible. Such a comparison is left to future researchers.

Table 1.3. *Composition of the Workforce by Occupation and Employment Status (1987)*

Type of occupation	Private firm managers (%)		Regular employees (%)		Part-time (%)		Others (%)		Self-employed (%)		Total (%)		Total no. of workers (million)	
	Men	Women	Men	Women	Men	Women	Men	Women	Men	Women	Men	Women	Men	Women
Professional, technical, and managerial workers	4.1	0.8	9.6	8.2	—	0.7	0.6	1.0	1.7	1.6	16.1	12.3	5.86	2.97
Office workers	0.3	1.0	12.1	16.7	—	3.5	0.6	1.9	0.2	2.8	13.2	25.9	4.79	6.26
Sales workers	1.1	0.4	9.9	4.7	—	2.4	0.4	0.8	3.4	5.1	15.0	13.5	5.44	3.25
Agricultural, forestry, and fishery workers	—	—	0.7	0.1	—	0.2	0.2	0.2	6.4	9.2	7.4	9.6	2.69	2.33
Transportation and communication workers	0.1	—	5.3	0.4	—	0.1	0.4	—	0.5	—	6.2	0.5	2.25	0.12
Skilled workers and production process workers	0.9	0.2	22.1	7.6	0.2	6.5	2.3	0.8	5.7	6.3	31.3	21.3	11.39	5.13
Manual labourers	0.1	—	2.9	1.2	0.1	2.2	0.8	0.6	0.3	0.7	4.2	4.8	1.54	1.16
Service and security workers	0.1	0.1	4.0	3.8	0.1	2.9	0.8	1.3	1.6	3.9	6.6	12.1	2.41	2.91
Total	6.8	2.6	66.7	42.7	0.6	18.5	6.1	6.7	19.8	29.5	100.0	100.0	36.37	24.13

Notes: 'Self-employed' includes the heads of self-employed concerns as well as family workers and home-workers. 'Regular employees', 'part-time', and 'others' refer to classifications as made in the workplace. 'Others' includes temporary workers, consultants, and catering services personnel.

Source: Calculated from Statistics Bureau, Management and Coordination Agency, *Employment Status Survey*, 1987, Table 6.

Table 1.4. *Composition of the Workforce by Size of Firm (1987, per cent)*

Type of organization	1–9 persons		10–99 persons		100–999 persons		1,000– persons		Total	
	Men	Women	Men	Women	Men	Women	Men	Women	Men	Women
Self-employed										
Agricultural, forestry, and fishery	6.0	9.0	—	—	—	—	—	—	6.0	9.1
Non-agricultural	18.0	27.6	1.6	3.3	—	—	—	—	19.6	30.9
Private corporations	8.5	7.6	22.5	20.2	17.5	14.6	16.5	10.3	65.0	52.7
Public office	—	—	—	—	—	—	9.3	7.1	9.3	7.1
Total	32.5	44.2	24.2	23.6	17.5	14.6	25.8	17.4	100.0	99.8

Notes
1. The total employed population is 36.37 m. men and 24.13 m. women.
2. In the table, a blank indicates non-existence, and '—' indicates magnitude of less than 0.05%.
3. The figures in the 'self-employed' sector refer to the sum of head of concern, family workers, and the employed. The figures for 'private corporations' refer to the sum of managers and workers.
4. While the original size classifications for the self-employed sector are '1–9 persons' and '10 persons and over', we have assumed that the latter group falls entirely in the '10–99 persons' group. Also, we have assumed that all 'public office' employees fall in the '1,000 persons and over' group.
5. The total may not add up to 100.0% because of rounding errors and the existence of samples in which the firm size is not known.

Source: Calculated from Statistics Bureau, Management and Coordination Agency, *Employment Status Survey*, 1987, Table 5.

women. Workers in the self-employed sector (or non-corporate firms) constitute 26 per cent of all male workers and 40 per cent of all female workers. Thus roughly 60 per cent of Japanese workers are employed in small firms.

Information concerning the size distribution of income is recorded in the same survey, by means of histograms of pre-tax annual principal earnings (that is income from main occupation) as classified by sex, status of employment, and size of firm. Using this information we have calculated the proportions of low-income workers (with annual earnings of less than one million yen) and high-income workers (with annual earnings of 10 million yen or more) in the work-force categories described above. The results are shown in Table 1.5. In order to illustrate how the frequencies of low income and high income differ between groups, we have taken male regular employees as the reference group and calculated the frequency of each group relative to the frequency of this reference group. The resulting numbers are referred to as the 'multiplication factor' in the table. Four points are to be noted in this table.

First, low-income earners are obviously concentrated in 'part-time' workers and 'other types' of workers. Also the smaller the size of the firm, the higher the proportion of low-income earners.

Second, even if we confine ourselves to 'regular employees', the smaller the size of the firm, the higher the proportion of low-income earners and the lower

Table 1.5. *Characteristics of Earnings Distribution by Employment Status and Size of Firm*

Employment status and size of firm	No. of workers (million)		Ratio of regular employees (%)		Low-income earners ratio (%)		Multiplication factor of the same		High-income earners ratio (%)		Multiplication factor of the same	
	Men	Women	Men	Women	Men	Women	Men	Women	Men	Women	Men	Women
Total employees	29.15	17.00	—	—	3.8	32.0	3.94	33.1	2.6	0.2	1.71	0.12
Workers	26.68	16.38	—	—	3.9	32.4	4.07	33.6	1.4	0.1	0.92	0.06
Managers	2.47	0.62	—	—	2.4	19.1	2.52	19.8	15.9	2.7	10.2	1.77
Regular employees	24.26	10.31	83.2	60.6	1.0	8.5	1.00	8.85	1.6	0.1	1.00	0.08
Part-time and others	1.17	5.39	—	—	52.3	76.7	54.2	79.5	0.0	0.0	0.00	0.00
Head of self-employed	6.27	2.80	—	—	16.8	67.8	17.4	70.3	3.9	0.6	2.50	0.37
Regular employees by size of firm												
1–9 persons	2.87	1.64	60.4	44.8	3.7	23.7	3.86	24.6	0.1	0.1	0.07	0.04
10–99 persons	6.79	3.22	78.7	57.6	1.3	10.4	1.34	10.8	0.4	0.1	0.26	0.06
100–999 persons	5.67	2.34	89.2	66.3	0.4	4.4	0.42	4.51	1.2	0.0	0.76	0.03
1,000 persons and over	5.70	1.80	94.8	72.3	0.2	2.5	0.20	2.60	4.4	0.3	2.86	0.22
Public office	3.20	1.30	95.2	76.0	0.2	0.8	0.19	0.88	0.8	0.1	0.54	0.05

Notes
1. 'Income (earnings)' refers to before-tax annual income on customary basis from the primary occupation. For employed workers it includes wages, including bonus payments and other benefits. For the self-employed, it refers to annual operating profit (total sales − cost).
2. The 'ratio of regular employees' in items 'regular employees' and 'regular employees by size of firm' refers to the ratio of the number of regular employees to the total employees (including managers) of either the overall economy or the corresponding firm size.
3. 'Part-time and others' is the sum of 'part-time' and 'other' workers in Table 1.3.
4. 'Low-income earners ratio' refers to the ratio of individuals earning less than one million yen to all individuals in the same group. The 'high-income earners ratio' is calculated in the same way, in relation to those earning ten million yen or more.
5. The 'multiplication factor' refers to the relative frequency of occurrence of this group when the frequency of the male regular employees in this income category is normalized to unity.

Source: Calculated from Statistics Bureau, Management and Coordination Agency, *Employment Status Survey*, 1987, Tables 13, 14, and 15.

that of high-income earners. (The effect on earnings of firm size is discussed further in section 6.1.)

Third, among private sector 'managers' and 'self-employed', the proportions of low-income earners and high-income earners are both high. This is due to the fact that these two groups contain a particularly wide spectrum of occupations. Thus managers include those who are only nominally so, as well as those who are genuinely entrepreneurial managers. Similarly, the self-employed include petty home workers as well as professionals such as doctors and lawyers. Another possible reason for the high frequency of low-income earners among the self-employed is that there exists a significant degree of leeway in measuring costs; in particular, the omission of self-consumed items, thus resulting in a significant under-reporting of earnings.

Fourth, there is a great disparity between the incomes of men and women. As already remarked, this is partly explicable by the fact that the employment of women tends to assume a more subsidiary character than that of men. Yet even if we focus on 'regular employees', the proportion of low-income earners is far higher than that of men. Differences in experience and training or differential access to employment opportunities are the putative causes for such a distribution.

Distribution of Wealth among Households

Despite severe limitations on the availability of data various attempts have been made to estimate the distribution of wealth among households in Japan. (Pioneering works include Economic Planning Agency (1975: 35–104), Togashi (1979), Takayama (1980: ch. 2).) The limitations on data consist of the following. First, there are no comprehensive published statistics on the distribution of real assets. Second, large wealth owners are likely to be under-represented in household surveys. Third, there is a clear under-reporting of financial assets held. The last point is related to the under-reporting of asset income discussed earlier.

As to the holding of real assets no official survey has taken place since the *National Wealth Survey* of 1970. Therefore, it was a massive task to estimate the value of assets from the information available on the area of owner-occupied residential land, the area, age, and building materials of houses, and the attributes of the surrounding environment. Economic Planning Agency (1975), Takayama *et al.* (1989), Togashi (1979). Togashi, using data from a non-government survey, also verified the self-evaluation of the sampled households by independently estimating the real asset values using similar information to that referred to above.

Among these studies, the estimates of Takayama *et al.* (1989), based on the *National Survey of Family Income and Expenditure* of 1984, are by far the most carefully conducted study so far made on the subject. Their study revealed the distributions of real wealth and net worth (that is, the sum of real wealth

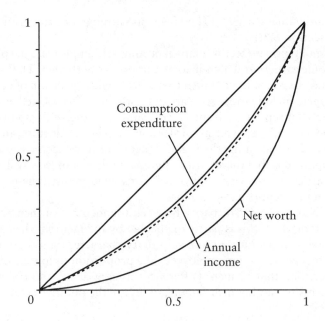

Figure 1.1. *Lorenz Curves for Consumption Expenditure, Income, and Net Worth (1984)*

Source: Takayama *et al.* (1989: 24, Fig. 1.3.3 and related supplementary tables).

and net financial wealth) among plural-member households. The evaluation of real assets included owner-occupied residential land and houses, properties for rent, and consumer durables.

Figure 1.1 shows the Lorenz curves for consumption expenditure, (pre-tax) annual income, and net worth (excluding consumer durables) among plural-member households, that were obtained by Takayama *et al.* (1989). The features such as income being more unequally distributed than consumption expenditure and net worth being more unequally distributed than income are common to many countries. The Gini coefficients are 0.26 for consumption expenditure, 0.30 for annual income, and 0.55 for net worth. The Lorenz curve for consumption expenditure is closer to the 45° line than that for annual income because the former is likely to be determined independently of fluctuations in annual income.

As seen from the figure, the degree of concentration for net worth is much higher than that for annual income. The top 5 per cent of households owns 26.4 per cent of total net worth, while the top 10 per cent owns 38.9 per cent. (When consumer durables are included, the corresponding figures become 24.9 per cent and 37.0 per cent, respectively, and the Gini coefficient becomes 0.52).[5]

---

[5] The *Lorenz curve* is defined as the locus of points (x, y) where the x coordinate expresses the cumulative frequencies of households (where households are assumed to be ranked in ascending

From Takayama *et al.* (1989) we find that (i) the amount of real assets held is far larger than the net financial assets, (ii) the Gini coefficient of real asset holdings is 0.57, and (iii) the Gini coefficient of net worth (including net financial assets) is 0.55, which, together with (ii), indicates that the distribution of financial assets and debts mitigates somewhat the dispersion in real asset holdings. (Similar results were reported by Togashi (1979).)

Findings (i) and (ii) imply that the most significant explanatory factor of cross-household dispersion in net worth is the dispersion of real assets. In fact, Takayama *et al.* (1989: Table 1.2.1) showed that the median value of real asset holdings (including consumer durables) is 22.94 million yen and that of net financial assets is 2.90 million yen for plural-member households resident in owner-occupied housing (76.4 per cent in the sample); the corresponding figures for households not resident in owner-occupied housing (23.6 per cent) are 1.48 million yen for real assets and 2.31 million yen for net financial assets. They also decomposed the Gini coefficient for net worth to discover that more than 80 per cent of explanatory power comes from the Gini coefficient of real assets, and, in particular, a little more than half is contributed by that of the residential land.

What about the distribution of household wealth by age? If savings out of annual income flows were the sole source of wealth formation, then much of the variation in household wealth would be explained by differences in the age of the household head. Also the variance of asset holding within each age group is expected to rise as the household head's age increases.

Table 1.6 provides the summary statistics of the distribution of net worth by age of household head. From this table, we see (a) that the median (and average) level of wealth holding rises with the age of the household head, but (b) that the dispersion of wealth holding as measured by the Gini coefficients for each age group is similar in magnitude to that for the entire household, and moreover, (c) that the Gini coefficients for the age groups of young household heads tend to be higher than that for the entire household. Findings (b) and (c) tell us that saving out of annual income flows (called life-cycle savings in section 7.1) is not the only source of wealth formation, but rather that many households acquire real assets via bequests (or *de facto* bequests)[6] from their parents.

order in terms of the variable concerned, e.g., net worth) and the y coordinate expresses the cumulative frequencies of the variable (e.g., net worth) held by the corresponding households. The 45° line corresponds to the case of perfect equality. The *Gini coefficient* is the ratio of the area of a region between the 45° line and the Lorenz curve to the area of the triangle formed by the 45° line and the horizontal axis. It is used as a representative indicator of degree of inequality.

[6] '*De facto* bequest' is a term used in connection with a situation where a young household head lives with an elderly, house-owning parent or parents. (See discussion in section 7.1.) In Japan, just about half of the elderly population (aged 65 or over) live with their children (see, footnote 10 of Chapter 7). Because household head is defined, in household surveys, as the major earner in the household, when retired elderly parents live with children, their assets are included in total household assets. An attempt to disaggregate parents' assets from those of the total household has been made by Hayashi, Ando, and Ferris (1988).

Income and Wealth

Table 1.6. *Characteristics of Wealth Distribution by Age of Household Head*

Age group	Number of samples	Estimated number of households (million)	Real assets			Net worth (wealth)		
			Median	Mean	Gini coeff.	Median	Mean	Gini coeff.
			(million yen)			(million yen)		
–24	339	0.22	0	4.12	0.858	1.03	5.08	0.823
25–29	2,081	1.36	0	5.72	0.795	2.34	6.91	0.703
30–34	5,465	3.48	0	10.89	0.669	6.26	12.22	0.617
35–39	7,579	4.73	13.15	16.27	0.578	12.03	17.58	0.564
40–44	7,345	4.51	16.26	20.32	0.516	16.90	22.29	0.506
45–49	6,360	3.91	17.46	23.26	0.506	19.43	26.65	0.494
50–54	5,761	3.50	18.31	25.07	0.502	22.30	30.33	0.474
55–59	5,064	3.05	20.20	30.06	0.507	26.85	38.16	0.479
60–64	3,170	1.95	21.99	32.48	0.513	30.32	42.19	0.468
65–69	2,057	1.30	23.18	35.15	0.534	30.70	44.46	0.485
70–74	1,234	0.75	22.11	32.65	0.510	30.15	41.34	0.463
75+	716	0.43	23.38	34.29	0.518	29.54	43.00	0.482
All ages	47,171	29.18	15.74	21.72	0.567	17.63	25.80	0.550

Notes
1. The sample includes all plural-member households (including agricultural households).
2. 'Real assets' refers to the sum of 'residential land for owner-occupied housing', 'residence (buildings only)' and 'real assets for rental purposes'. It does not include 'consumer durables'. 'Net worth (wealth)' refers to the sum of real assets (excluding consumer durables) and net financial assets.
3. Characteristics of distribution are calculated by including households with zero holdings of the asset in question.

Source: Takayama *et al.* (1989: Table 1.2.1 and the related supplementary table).

These statistics on household wealth distribution must be qualified, however. The major qualifications concern the omission of large wealth from the sample and the under-reporting of financial assets discussed earlier. There is a clear evidence that various household surveys including the *National Survey of Family Income and Expenditure* (upon which the Takayama *et al.* (1989) estimates are based) underestimate holdings of financial assets. Indeed, the financial assets of the entire household sector, estimated on the basis of holdings reported in the survey (for both plural- and single-member households), comprise (taking the average of the figures for the different elements of financial assets) only 45 per cent of the corresponding figures in the national balance sheet (where the data on financial assets are derived from the operating accounts of financial institutions). In particular, this ratio is lowest for corporate stock holdings, which is only 28 per cent (Ishikawa 1990: 235, Table 1).

There has been critical appraisal in the UK and the USA to the effect that ordinary household surveys can never succeed in capturing the assets of large-income and wealth-holding households (Atkinson and Harrison (1978), Wolff (1987)). That this appraisal also applies to Japan seems well attested by the fact that the gap between the estimated aggregate value of assets on the basis of household surveys and that of the national balance sheet is much the largest for corporate stock holdings, which are believed to be most heavily concentrated among large wealth owners. This means that if the sampling and under-reporting biases are corrected, the Lorenz curves of income and net worth shown in Figure 1.1 would move further from the 45° line. Instruments to correct for such biases include the estate multiplier method adopted by the Central Statistical Office of the United Kingdom, on the one hand, and complementing household sample survey data with the tax return data of large income earners. (The former method classifies annual numbers of deaths, by sex and age group, and by assuming them to be a random sample representing each group, uses bequest figures to estimate the wealth distribution of the population. It is believed that this method represents more accurately wealth holding at the high end of the scale.) At present, neither method is used in Japan, and further improvements in the wealth distribution statistics must certainly be high on the agenda.[7]

A surprising feature of the distribution of wealth statistics in the UK and the USA is its extreme skewness. According to the 1983 Federal Reserve Bank survey, 35.1 per cent of all household net worth (excluding consumer durables) is held by a mere 0.5 per cent of households. If we take the top 10 per cent of households, we find that they hold 71.7 per cent of total household net worth (Smith 1988: 24, Table 2). On the other hand, in the UK, the top 1 per cent of individuals (*not* households) hold 22 per cent of total individual net worth (including consumer durables), while the top 10 per cent holds 53 per cent (UK, Central Statistical Office *Inland Revenue Statistics* 1987, Table 7.5). There clearly exists an extremely wealthy class in both countries.

[7] We provide have some additional time-series information concerning wealth distribution in Japan. Because of a lack of data only the movement in the distribution of financial assets can be discussed here. The differences between income groups in financial asset holdings tended to reduce significantly from the end of the 1950s to the early 1970s. From then until 1985 the differences remained almost the same (Economic Planning Agency, *Annual Report on the Economy 1988* (While Paper), Table IV.1.20). However, the range of variation in income is known to be far less than that of assets, and therefore, variations in average asset holding by income class do not necessarily represent distribution of asset holdings themselves. In fact, since the latter half of the 1970s there is some indication that the distribution of financial asset holding among households has grown over time. (Even allowing for the problem of under-reporting that affects the ratio of the upper limit of gross financial wealth for the top decile to that for the bottom decile, there is a trend towards gradually increase in asset accumulation for households where the head is aged 45–49, 50–54, and 55–59, respectively). (Although what we really wish to know is the movement in the distribution of net financial wealth, data limitation does not allow this. However, since as we proceed from the group with lower gross financial assets to one with more assets, the average amount of debt holding increases but at a decreasing pace, it seems that the movement in the distribution of net financial assets has a similar tendency to that of gross financial assets.)

If we compare the concentration ratios in Takayama *et al.* (1989) (see Figure 1.1) with those of the UK and the USA, it appears that wealth is far more equally distributed in Japan than in either the UK or the USA. It is, however, not appropriate to make such a comparison since in the UK and the USA there have been stringent attempts to correct the under-representation of large wealth owners in surveys.[8] Although casual observation suggests that there is no evidence of an extremely wealthy class in Japan (which would mean a broader upper tail in the distribution), it would be premature to conclude that Japan is far more equal with regard to wealth distribution than the UK or the USA. On the other hand, there are two specific characteristics to the structure of wealth inequality in Japan. First, there are huge differences in wealth between households with owner-occupied land (especially in three major metropolitan areas) and those without owner-occupied land. Second, a relatively far larger proportion of wealth than in the USA or the UK is held in the private firm sector, a feature whose implications seem to require further investigation.[9]

[8] Furthermore, note that only limited categories of real assets were evaluated in Takayama *et al.* (1989). More specifically, information on land holdings other than the place of current residence, second homes, and forests and woodlands must also be collected and evaluated. These items would increase the concentration in real asset holdings.

[9] Noguchi (1989) discusses the first of these characteristics, which he sees as an important policy issue. He proposes various ways to ameliorate it. As to the second feature, see the discussions in Chapter 8 and Ishikawa (1990).

Appendix 1.1

Table 1A.1. Sectoral Composition of Net National Wealth, United Kingdom (end 1985, billion pounds)

Year end, 1985	Private firm sector		Public sector		Household sector		Domestic total		Foreign sector	
	Assets	Debt	Assets	Debt	Assets	Debt	Assets	Debt	Assets	Debt
Real assets	471.7	—	342.4	—	726.6	—	1,540.7	—	—	—
Residential houses	6.1	—	59.8	—	242.3	—	308.2	—	—	—
Net fixed assets (non-residential)	315.8	—	268.5	—	43.2	—	627.5	—	—	—
Land	74.2	—	7.0	—	325.1	—	406.3	—	—	—
Tenancy rights	0	—	0	—	107.3	—	107.3	—	—	—
Inventories	75.6	—	7.0	—	8.7	—	91.3	—	—	—
Financial assets	1,501.1	1,722.4	145.7	270.6	629.3	204.2	2,276.1	2,197.2	520.6	599.6
Corporate stocks	185.1	280.5	14.9	0.2	66.5	—	266.1	280.7	14.2	—
Pension reserves	—	156.4	—	—	156.4	—	156.4	156.4	—	—
Other financial assets	1,316.0	1,285.5	130.8	270.4	406.4	204.2	1,853.6	1,760.1	506.4	599.6

Table 1A.1. (Continued)

Year end, 1985	Private firm sector		Public sector		Household sector		Domestic total		Foreign sector	
	Assets	Debt	Assets	Debt	Assets	Debt	Assets	Debt	Assets	Debt
Net worth (wealth)	—	250.4	—	217.5	—	1,151.7	—	1,619.6	—	−79.0
Addendum:										
Consumer durables	—	—	—	—	113.2	—	113.2	—	—	—

Notes:

1. 'Household sector' corresponds to 'Personal sector' (Table 11.2), and includes non-incorporated firms and non-profit organizations serving households. 'Private Firm sector' is a consolidation of 'Industrial and Commercial Companies' (Table 11.3), 'Monetary sector (Table 11.4), and 'Other Financial Institutions' (Table 11.5). 'Public sector' is a consolidation of Public Corporations (Table 11.6), Central Government (Table 11.7), Local Authorities (Table 11.8). The figures for the 'Foreign sector' are given in Table 11.1.

2. Because the original tables only report the consolidated value of land and buildings (called Residential Buildings), the land value was separated by subtracting the current replacement value of the Dwellings portion of the Net Capital Stock as reported for each sector in Table 13.7 from the aforementioned total. This corresponds to Revell's (1967) implied land value'. The value of Non-Marketable Tenancy Rights as reported in Table 11.2 is also listed in the above table.

   A difficulty encountered in the above procedure is that, in subtracting the housing value from the total, the net capital stock value of Dwellings of Local Authorities (a part of the 'Public sector') in Table 13.7 consistently exceeded the value of Residential Buildings (land included) in Table 11.8, rendering the implied value of residential land negative for the 'Public sector' as a whole. Therefore, a convention was used, admittedly for want of a better measure, to attribute the entire figure for Residential Buildings (as obtained from Tables 11.6 to 11.8) for the 'Public sector' to 'Residential Houses' in the table, with the residential land component of the public sector being treated as zero. The table thus refers to land for non-residential purposes.

3. The item 'Net Fixed Assets (Non-residential)' in the table does not include military facilities and equipment (*Sources and Methods*, p. 7, Item 1.48).

4. As to 'Pension reserves', because the National Accounts, Table 11, gives only the sum of pension and life insurance reserves (called Life Assurance and Pension Funds) and not its decomposition, the figure for 'Pension reserves' is taken from the current market value of the assets owned by pension funds as of year-end, 1985, as reported in *Financial Statistics*, Table 14.

Sources: Compiled from: Central Statistical Office (CSO), *United Kingdom National Accounts*, 1988, Tables 11.1–11.8, 13.7; CSO, *UK National Accounts, Sources and Methods*, and CSO, *Financial Statistics*, No. 320, Dec. 1988, Table 7.14.

Table 1A.2. *Sectoral Composition of Net National Wealth, United States (end 1985, billion dollars)*

Year end, 1985	Private firm sector		Public sector		Household sector		Domestic total		Foreign sector	
	Assets	Debt	Assets	Debt	Assets	Debt	Assets	Debt	Assets	Debt
Real assets	4,224.0	—	1,914.5	—	6,861.7	—	13,000.2	—	—	—
Residential houses	51.1	—	71.8	—	3,431.8	—	3,554.7	—	—	—
Net fixed assets (non-residential)	2,878.2	—	1,842.7	—	893.5	—	5,614.4	—	—	—
Land	536.5	—	n.a.	—	2,431.1	—	2,967.5	—	—	—
Inventories	758.2	—	—	—	105.3	—	863.5	—	—	—
Financial assets	8,606.9	11,498.3	1,507.5	2,999.5	7,992.9	3,643.3	18,107.3	18,263.4	714.6	558.5
Corporate stocks	775.3	2,544.4	—	—	1,685.3	—	2,460.6	2,544.4	123.7	39.9
Pension reserves	—	1,652.8	—	148.8	1,801.6	—	1,801.6	1,801.6	—	—
Other financial assets	7,831.6	7,301.1	1,507.5	2,850.7	4,506.0	3,643.3	13,845.1	13,795.1	590.9	518.6
Unallocatable assets	—	—	—	—	—	—	—	122.3	—	—
Net worth (wealth)	—	1,332.6	—	422.5	—	11,211.3	—	12,844.1	—	156.1
Addendum: Consumer durables	—	—	—	—	1,397.7	—	1,397.7	—	—	—
Military facilities	—	—	416.8	—	—	—	416.8	—	—	—

Sources: Because the US national balance sheet is not prepared in a unified form including the private, government, and foreign sectors, the following three materials were combined to prepare the table: Bureau of Statistics, US Dept. of Commerce, *Survey of Current Business*, August 1988; Board of Governers of the Federal Reserve System, *Balance sheets for the US Economy 1948–1987*, October 1988, and *Flow of Funds Accounts: Financial Assets and Liabilities, Year-End, 1964–1987*, September 1988.

2

The Concept of Distributive Justice: Ideas for Equality

One of the most fundamental problems for any society to solve is how to distribute the economic resources and the outputs of economic activities. The scheme of distribution a society chooses in practice is inevitably connected with its political structure. Who decides what kind of distribution is desirable? How does this agent justify his or her idea of desirable distribution in a whole society, and implement it in practice? Where does the source of implementing power come from? These are indeed fundamental political questions. It is safe to say that throughout history, every social reform movement, radical or not, aimed to make a change in the idea of desirable distribution or in the domain of agents who could implement the idea effectively.

In this chapter we discuss what scheme of distribution, within the current democratic regime, is desirable in terms of justice. There should be various points of view, since the idea of justice naturally depends upon individual value judgements. However diverse the opinions may be, since these opinions are of an ethical nature, each of them must assert, to a greater or lesser extent, its universal applicability—which is independent of the position of each member of society. This observation provides us with a basis from which to classify and assess the various views on distributive justice.

A passage in John Stuart Mill's *Utilitarianism* (1863) illustrates the dichotomy of views on distributive justice:

In a co-operative industrial association, is it just or not that talent or skill should give a title to superior remuneration? On the negative side of the question it is argued, that whoever does the best he can, deserves equally well, and ought not in justice to be put in a position of inferiority for no fault of his own; that superior abilities have already advantages more than enough, in the admiration they excite, the personal influence they command, and the internal sources of satisfaction attending them, without adding to these a superior share of the world's goods; and that society is bound in justice rather to make compensation to the less favoured, for this unmerited inequality of advantages,

The author gratefully acknowledges the detailed comments of Ryuzo Sato (Soka University), Susumu Sato (Niigata University), Tatsuo Hatta (Ohsaka University), and Konosuke Odaka (Hitotsubashi University) on a draft of this chapter (Discussion Paper, Department of Economics, University of Tokyo, September 1985).

than to aggravate it. On the contrary side it is contended, that society receives more from the more efficient labourer; that his services being more useful, society owes him a larger return for them; that a greater share of the joint result is actually his work, and not to allow his claim to it is a kind of robbery; that if he is only to receive as much as others, he can only be justly required to produce as much, and to give a smaller amount of time and exertion, proportioned to his superior efficiency.   (Mill 1879: 86)

Readers are invited to decide which of these two views, distribution according to one's effort and distribution according to one's contribution, they favour. Perhaps many, including the author himself, would tend to agree with both. Nevertheless, in order to continue with our discussion, we have to extend our consideration beyond the confines of everyday life.

Economics as a discipline, developed in England since Adam Smith, maintained an essential tie to moral psychology or utilitarianism all the way through Mill and Marshall, until Pigou (especially in the early 1930s). It then defined itself as moral science.[1] Naturally, such problems as fairness of income distribution and redistribution, equal opportunities for education, and so on occupied the central themes of economics. The inclination of British economics toward practical ethics can be traced even to Marx, who departed from British economics in making the radical assertion of the abolition of private ownership. After the 1930s, however, under the strong influence of the positivism movement advocated mainly by Lionel Robins, the research of economics as a moral science (especially welfare economics) rapidly diminished. The stoicism of natural science was imposed on economists, making them extremely cautious about making any value judgement. The idea of distributive justice was not supposed to be the object of economic research. It was *A Theory of Justice* (1971) by the American philosopher, John Rawls, that warned and urged economists to give fundamental reconsideration to the nature of the intellectual environment in which they were working. He confronted the issue of distributive justice based on the critical study of utilitarianism, and proposed new principles of justice. In response to this discourse, there began a critical re-examination of welfare economics, which had been established by Marshall and Pigou. Using new theoretical tools scholars proceeded to develop the field of applied economic analysis, in such areas as the theory of optimum income taxation. It is no exaggeration to say that the principles of justice proposed by Rawls brought about a renaissance not only in philosophy but also in theoretical economics.

The purpose of this chapter is to examine the logical foundations of typical views of distributive justice. Significant in its own right, this study will provide us with a basic point of view from which to investigate, in each of the later chapters, how the distribution of income and wealth is determined.

---

[1] Economics and moral psychology or utilitarianism gradually became one, over time. Adam Smith regarded these fields as a single discipline, but Mill recognized the difference between economics as science and economics as practical art. For further discussion of this matter in the field of history of economics, see Hutchison (1964: ch. 1).

In this chapter section 2.1 explains the marginal productivity hypothesis as the principle which determines income distribution through markets, and then proceeds to examine where within this mechanism the problem of justice arises. In section 2.2, we present various conventional criteria of distributive justice that have been proposed in the past. While all of these criteria are intuitive, they provide an important starting point for our investigation. In section 2.3, we state Mill's theory of utilitarianism, which was intended to satisfy diverse criteria, and then examine the theories of the material welfare school, in particular those of Marshall and Pigou, who taking as their basis the spirit of utilitarianism, further developed economic analysis. Section 2.4 deals with the Rawls's principles of justice, providing in-depth coverage of the method of moral philosophy—which is the foundation of the principles as well as its implications. The final section presents our conclusions.

2.1. THE DISTRIBUTIVE FUNCTION OF THE MARKET MECHANISM AND ITS FAIRNESS

In a state of equilibrium under the fully functioning market economy, the markets simultaneously determine all resource allocations to the various production processes and income distribution among individuals through pricing each of their resources. It is one of the most fundamental theorems in microeconomics that the resource allocation thus attained is efficient in the sense that there is no resource inefficiently employed in the production process and no room to raise individuals' utilities from consumption. On the other hand, we rarely pursue the question whether the resultant income distribution is socially fair or not. Such investigation is generally avoided because any definition of fair distribution depends upon individuals' value judgements and cannot be discussed objectively. This is not to say that investigation is impossible. On the contrary, some insist that the income distribution generated by markets is fair, whereas others will see it as unfair. Before continuing, we must first clarify the grounds of such conflicting arguments.[2]

The Marginal Productivity Principle

The most basic logic of distributive procedure through markets is known as the marginal productivity principle. It stems from the fact that the conditions for the rational behaviour of producers (or agents who demand factors of production), are satisfied in the market equilibrium. That is, a producer tries to minimize cost by equating each factor's marginal physical productivity per unit cost (that is, marginal productivity divided by factor price). (When each value of the marginal physical productivity per unit cost is not equated, the producer

---

[2] This discussion does not deal with the problems of imperfect markets. For the distributive implications of the imperfect labour market, see sections 5.1, 5.4, and 5.5.

can further reduce the cost by decreasing the input amount of a particular factor whose value is relatively lower, and increasing the input amount of a factor with a relatively higher value.) The inverse of this equated value is equivalent to the minimum increase in cost required to produce one more unit of output, that is, the marginal cost of production (due to the law of proportion). In a competitive market without economies of scale, the production level is determined at the point where the marginal cost coincides with the market price. The marginal productivity principle states that, as a result of producers' rational behaviour, for every input resource, the value of marginal productivity multiplied by the product price (called marginal value product) equals the price of input.[3]

Some argue that the marginal productivity principle should be understood as satisfying the moral criterion of distributive justice on the basis of equality of prices for services provided by each resource and its productive contribution, more precisely, the productive contribution to what is valuable to the society, which is measured by the product market price. It follows that a market economy is an efficient and just system as long as it functions perfectly. Those who advocate this view believe in a free market economy, and include Friedrich Hayek (1960) and Milton Friedman (1962).

The idea that fair distribution is defined in terms of contributions to what is valuable for society has been around for a long time. And we must admit that the product market price is one possible measure of the value to society of the resource in production. Yet, we can argue against this view.[4]

First, demand for a product depends upon such factors as each individual's preference, the distribution of purchasing power among individuals, and whether there is any substitute for the product or not. These factors are basically unrelated to intrinsic social value. Hence, though the price determined in a market represents some social usefulness, what it really reflects is the mere aggregation of individual wants.

Second, granted that the above criticism could be invalid, whether the income distribution resulting from the marginal productivity principle is fair

---

[3] Where the economic agents who demand the factors of production (resources) are heterogeneous, even if the factors of production themselves are homogeneous (e.g., the degree of heterogeneity may be the extent to which each agent faces uncertainty caused by product demand or productivity), the different factor prices are determined to reflect the heterogeneity among the agents who demand the factors of production (so as to offset the difference), and different income is generated. This is called the principle of equalizing differences. While the marginal productivity principle reflects the conditions required by the demand side for input resources, the principle of equalizing differences reflects the conditions required by the supply side of resources. In market equilibrium, the income difference is explained by both principles combined. Even in this complex situation, however, the marginal productivity principle continues to hold for each agent that demands input resources. Consequently, the argument that follows is still applicable. For more detail of the principle of equalizing differences, see section 3.1.

[4] Knight (1923) is typical of those who opposed this view. A similar argument is that of Inada (1977: 170–5).

or not depends to a large extent upon how fair the distribution of the initial resource endowment (wealth) it at each point of time. Recall that the distribution of purchasing power among individuals influences the formation of market prices. Aggregating individual demands in a market can be regarded as a voting (monetary voting) process whereby one's right to vote is proportionate to one's purchasing power. Consequently, the more wealth one possesses, the more voting power one can exercise. It follows that more of the resources of the whole economy will be allocated in such a way as to accommodate the preferences of the holders of large initial endowments, and under such resource allocation, the marginal physical productivity of each resource will be determined. Thus, the distribution of initial wealth has a powerful influence upon the determination of income distribution through markets.

The distribution of initial wealth can be ultimately attributed to three factors; inheritance, luck, and effort (in the past). The problem is how to evaluate the admissible weight attached to each of these three factors, and therefore it is not straightforward to judge how just the distribution of initial endowment is.[5] At least we can find no logic, within the market economy itself, to justify the distributive justice of initial endowment. This means that there can be no logic in the market economy either to assert the fairness of income distribution generated by the marginal productivity principle.

2.2. VARIOUS CRITERIA OF JUSTICE

There are two ways to approach the problem of defining the 'justice' of distribution. One focuses on procedural justice, the other on consequential justice. The former discusses what sort of institutions should facilitate justice, and does not provide any independent criterion for evaluating the consequences. The latter discusses literally what sort of distributive consequences should be regarded as just.

Typical of the former is the 'fair gamble'. If the gain expected from a probability calculation is totally offset by the expected loss, such a gamble is said to be fair, and whatever changes there are in the income distribution after the resolution of the probability process do not interfere with the notion of fairness. Of course, no matter how 'fair' the gamble may be in the sense described above, if the loss involves a threat to one's life, then this gamble can hardly be considered a fair alteration of the distribution. Another example may be the criterion of 'equal opportunity'. In relation to the latter concept, various ideas have been proposed as criteria for justice such as 'distribution according to one's contribution', 'distribution according to one's need', and 'distribution according to one's effort'. We now look at each of these criteria in turn.

---

[5] It is the historic entitlement principle of justice proposed by Nozick (1974) that asserts acceptance of all three factors as just. This view is regarded as the most right-wing of the arguments about distributive justice.

Equality of Opportunity

The idea of equality of opportunity aims to remove the obstacles and circumstances that stand in one's way to equal job opportunities or responsible social status. It takes the form of practical proposals to abolish discrimination based upon individual attributes such as race and gender, or to organize assistance in the form of scholarships and educational loans to provide equality to the disadvantaged.

Obviously, it is not at all easy to judge what is equal opportunity. The concept of equal opportunity is often likened to the starting line in a running race which represents human life. But it is not clear what sort of starting line is fair because some of the participants in the race are inherently talented, others may be handicapped. Some are situated in an advantageous environment and others are in a disadvantaged environment because of such factors as the size of their parents' income and wealth, or occupation and social status. (Differences of this sort are inevitable as long as we retain the family system.)

One way of coping with this problem is termed the 'formal equality of opportunity', the purpose of which is to eliminate all kinds of artificial obstacles preventing individuals in a society from climbing a social ladder (for example, by abolition of privileges accorded to certain social classes), and impartially to provide national policy measures or facilities for promoting the individual's position (for example, by enforcing compulsory public education). This corresponds to the world that the European liberalism movement tried to achieve in the nineteenth century with its slogan 'career open to talents', which still receives support from believers in the free market economy today. The important characteristic of this idea is that state interference should be impartial and kept to the minimum.

A contrasting view advocates not merely formal equality of opportunity but stronger state interference. It says the government should intervene to eliminate all differences in the life prospects of individuals who, whatever their abilities and motivations may be handicapped by differences in social environment, historical and cultural background, or natural properties such as gender and race—in other words, the government should give appropriate handicaps to each individual at the starting line to ensure equality for all. This is the concept that lies at the basis of liberalism, and it is reflected in the current educational and social institutions of many modern societies to varying degrees. (Rawls called this concept the principle of 'fair equality of opportunity' to distinguish it from the concept discussed above.) The matter still ignored under this concept is the problem of how to deal with the differences in opportunities among individuals endowed with different abilities.[6]

---

[6] For an excellent discussion of equal opportunity, see Okun (1975: ch. 2).

Distribution According to One's Contribution and Distribution According to One's Needs

One of the most typical conflicts of views regarding distributive justice may be between the concept of distribution according to one's contribution and of distribution according to one's needs. The concept 'distribution according to one's contribution' takes a position that the distribution is fair if each individual is paid a price in proportion to the amount of social benefit generated from his or her services. This view corresponds to the second argument of Mill quoted at the beginning of this chapter. The idea of distribution determined by the marginal productivity principle of the market economy, examined earlier, is a typical example of this. It sounds entirely natural and reasonable that a hard worker will get paid and a lazy one will not, indeed is just like a story from Aesop's Fables. On the other hand, it is also reasonable to regard it as fair that when one is in difficulties one's needs should be met by society. For instance, we cannot apply Aesop's Fables to people who are out of a job against their will. In this way, these two concepts are as opposed as oil and water.

The major problem of the criterion of distributive justice based mainly on one's needs is twofold. First, it is difficult to obtain general agreement on a definition of what human beings need. Second, unless labour itself is recognized as a part of human needs, this criterion is not necessarily compatible with ensuring work incentives.

As regards the first problem, on one hand, there have been some attempts to define the meaning of 'needs' so as to include 'necessities' (as used by the material welfare school) and Rawls's 'social primary goods'. These attempts, and their limitations, will be discussed later. On the other hand, there is an approach which tries to define justice based upon each individual's sense of needs and yet at the same time avoids giving an absolute definition of 'needs', since the substance of 'needs' should be considered a matter for each individual. One example of this approach proposes regarding distribution as fair if no one envies anyone, after every individual has evaluated others' consumption of goods and services by reference to his or her own preference (Varian 1974, 1975). This is called the criterion of 'no envy'. This criterion, however, does not avoid the problem of defining 'needs', because it requires each individual's desire (preference) to be absolutely inviolable, and as a result it is unable to reject even a preference that is totally incompatible with society's values.[7]

___

[7] If we were to follow this view, it would be possible to make the obviously unreasonable argument that a distribution system that ensured that most drugs and alcohol was consumed by drug addicts and alcoholics was actually fair. Furthermore, as regards a more fundamental aspect, it is not appropriate for a consideration of fairness to presume that one would feel envy towards others from the very beginning (this is just the opposite of Rawls's criticism, stated later, of classical utilitarianism for presuming altruism). We should understand that what a rational individual aims to realize is the value of himself or herself, and only where society cannot mediate conflicts among individuals which arise in the process of realization of their values, would an individual envy

It was Marx who clearly pointed out the second problem. In the following short extract from his *Critique of the Gotha Programme*, Part I, he crystallized the principle of distribution in the ideal communist society:

after the enslaving subordination of the individual to the division of labour, and therewith also the antithesis between mental and physical labour, has vanished; after labour has become not only a means of life but life's prime want; after the productive forces have also increased with the all-round development of the individual, and all the springs of common wealth flow more abundantly—only then can the narrow horizon of bourgeois right be crossed in its entirety and society inscribe on its banners: From each according to his abilities, to each according to his needs!   (Marx 1875).

The expression 'the narrow horizon of bourgeois right' means the distributive criterion according to one's contribution, against which Marx presented the criterion according to one's needs as the ultimate criterion for just distribution. What should be noted is that Marx conceived a qualitative change in the concept of need itself to bring about an increase in productive incentives and abilities and make it possible to implement a distribution based on the new criterion, as he stated that the complete reorganization of division of labour led people to recognize labour itself as a part of needs. Though often misunderstood, his statement does not imply that an unlimited growth of productivity would fulfil the immutable needs to the point of satiation.

Distribution According to One's Effort

Earlier, we referred to three factors that determine individuals' initial endowments, namely, inheritance, luck, and past effort. Employing the criterion of distribution according to one's contribution implicitly assumes that these three factors are all recognized as fair. On the other hand, there is a view that perceives the initial endowment obtained through luck and inheritance as an asset to be socially shared. This idea is called the criterion of 'distribution according to one's effort'.

It states that the emergence of individual differences in natural talents is purely a matter of luck, and consequently it can be hardly be fair that a lucky person demands a large share of the social product just because he or she possesses a fortune. This argument corresponds to the first viewpoint of Mill quoted at the beginning of the chapter. A similar argument applies to inheritance, that is, it is a matter of luck that a person inherits an asset. In short, this

---

others. People have feelings of envy a posteriori, not a priori. Pazner and Schmeidler (1974, 1976) which examine the implication of this criterion point out that the criterion of no envy is not necessarily compatible with the criterion of efficient production. The reason is that it is rational for production efficiency to allocate a higher income to a person with higher ability in order to give him or her a proper incentive to work more. If a person with relatively lower ability has a weak preference for leisure, then he or she may envy the person with higher ability.

view recognizes only one's effort and diligence as valuable elements. Many gradual social reformers support this view.[8]

Thurow, who looks at distributive justice by means of empirical studies in the field of sociology and labour economics, also indicates that people have a strong sense of relative deprivation, a sense most likely derived from the fact that people tend to see fairness as being close to the criterion of effort (Thurow 1973, 1975: ch. 2). Further explanation may be needed. The concept of the reference group plays a role in one's judgement and evaluation of people. In other words, when one considers the material and non-material cost (effort, hard work, education, training, etc.) required to achieve one's current occupation and status, one perceives people who incurred a similar level of cost as belonging to the same reference group. On the basis of that judgement, one is inclined to regard the return as fair if two conditions are met, namely that: (a) the economic rewards earned by the members of a reference group should be equal, and (b) the difference in rewards between two reference groups should be proportional to the difference in the cost incurred by members of the groups. So, if either of the conditions is not met, a sense of relative deprivation results. It follows that in the industrial sector where an organization such as a labour union can exert an influence over wage determination independent of market competition, wages are set at levels that accord with such a sense of fairness. And we can think of this sense as being mirrored in the finding of labour economists that there exists a wage contour which is stable in the long term (which is consistent with the relative wage hypothesis—proposed by Keynes to explain the phenomenon of the downward rigidity of money wages).

However, this criterion, too, presents several difficulties. First, it is generally quite difficult to trace individuals' wealth back to the three factors. It is especially difficult to find an objective test of which part of one's acquired ability is attributable to natural talent and which to past endeavour, or, if one's educational cost is subsidized by parents (a kind of inheritance), to what extent such help from parents may contribute to one's ability. With no objective means, we must rely on subjective judgement, which in turn creates the problem of whose judgement this should be (Hayek 1960: 92–100). To further complicate the matter, the factor of effort is not necessarily independent of the other factors. The better endowed with natural talents or favorable environment are in general more likely to strive conscientiously than the less (Rawls 1971: 312).

Second, as regards inheritance, there is no effective refutation of the following counter-argument: from the point of view of a person who wants to

---

[8] It was Knight who most clearly articulated this point of view (Knight 1923, 1935: 54–8). According to Mill, by 'a limitation of the sum which any one person may acquire by gift or inheritance to the amount sufficient to constitute a moderate independence' and by a system of economically alleviating inequality generated by chance, such as the differences in one's natural talents, the diversity among individuals would be fully recognized and properly evaluated. Knight's account is close to Mill's. Mill's philosophy had a pronounced influence on Tawney, Titmuss, and Rawls. See Tawney (1920: ch. 5, 1952: 48–9), and Titmuss (1952).

pass his or her wealth on to his or her children, instead of the view of a person who inherits it, he or she is fully entitled to choose to leave some wealth (part of which is in the form of education) to his or her posterity by refraining from using his or her income extravagantly (Friedman 1962: 164). As long as we follow our instincts, the argument whether to regard it as luck on the part of the person receiving an inheritance or free choice on the part of the person leaving the wealth does not get us anywhere.

Third, the exclusion of benefits attributable to luck is likely to deter people from taking risks. The most problematic example of such effect may be the investment of resources in inventions and research (Hayek 1960: 95–6). If there are institutional restrictions preventing someone who has made a successful investment of this sort from sharing the fruits of the investment with other people who made the same effort for the same purpose (which is difficult to verify), then he or she might not have made the first effort to begin with. The same comment applies to the innovative activities of entrepreneurs. Furthermore, in the invention and discovery of new knowledge, since there is no cost for reproducing the knowledge obtained, the economic rewards to the inventors and discoverers could be quite small. In many countries, it is concern for this negative effect on incentives that provides the ground for setting up the patent system which permits inventors and discoverers to benefit from the rewards for a limited time. Of course, such concern may be unnecessary, since the incentive to invent and make discoveries is present whenever a person has a propensity or spontaneous drive to surpass the business or achievement of others (termed the emulation propensity).[9]

Need for a Principle of a Higher Order

So far, we have outlined some of the criteria for distributive justice. Each criterion has its own shortcomings, but the biggest problem is all three criteria for justice based on consequences merely exhibit the head-on clash between conflicting value judgements, and cannot further the discussion. In order to move forward, we need some arbitrating principle of a higher order. We need to find some social agreement upon what sort of social conditions can be imposed on the distributive decision process so that the resulting distribution is

---

[9] See Hindle (1981). Using examples from the history of the steamboat, he argued that the patent system was not necessarily indispensable for ensuring incentives for invention. He also pointed out that there had been doubts as to the necessity of a patent system at its very introduction. For instance, in the mid-eighteenth century, 'the Society for the Encouragement of Art, Manufactures and Commerce' (known as the Society of Arts) established in London offered cash premiums for inventions and offered medals for achievements. Its founder thought the Society's endorsement such as offering medals would be sufficient to encourage invention and research. The Society of Arts method was adopted progressively in the countries of Europe and the United States (through the influence of Benjamin Franklin) (*op. cit.*: 14–23). It follows that we cannot accept Hayek's assertion without reservation, though we must admit that the cost of workers and facilities needed for current research and development is incomparably greater than in the eighteenth century.

recognizable as just, upon admitting that each individual is subject to different circumstances and has a different sense of values. We investigate the proposed criteria from such a point of view, in the next two sections.

2.3. UTILITARIANISM AND THE MATERIAL WELFARE SCHOOL

J. S. Mill's Utilitarianism

The utilitarianism that Mill advocated can be described as follows. In his *Utilitarianism*, he started by declaring that the basis of his idea lay in pure teleological ethics, as he states that 'all action is for the sake of some end, and rules of action [including moral and law], it seems natural to suppose, must take their whole character and colour from the end to which they are subservient' (Mill 1879: 3). The judgement of whether an action is right or wrong should be guided by how much that action promotes happiness—which is defined as pleasure and lack of pain. The sources of pleasure must be examined. There are bodily pleasures and mental pleasures (which are of the intellect, of the feelings and imagination, and of the moral sentiments). Mill ranks the latter as qualitatively superior, on the basis of the introspective judgement of a person who has experienced both kinds of pleasure. The superiority of mental pleasures is also due to their externality, that is, one's high mental capacities (nobleness) give pleasure to others as well (*op. cit.*: 10–17). Measuring quality against quantity is left to 'the preference felt by those who, in their opportunities of experience, to which must be added their habits of self-consciousness and self-observation, are best furnished with the means of comparison' (*op. cit.*: 17), namely impartial observers. Mill calls the degree of people's 'happiness' thus quantified 'utility' and the aggregation of each person's utility 'social utility'. Thus he presents the theory of utilitarianism, which prescribes choosing the action that maximizes social utility, by following the principle of the greatest happiness—the greatest happiness of the greatest number—advocated by Bentham.

Mill proceeds to adopt utilitarianism as a criterion of higher order that arbitrates among various criteria of distributive justice, including the two views referred to earlier in this chapter. In contrast to the arguments discussed in the previous section, he does not propose a single criterion for determining the weights of contributions, needs, and effort in ensuring fair distribution—a task that we have already found impossible. Instead, Mill wished to determine the weights according to Bentham's principle. As a result, he argued, a society will be able to establish a practical procedure of fair distribution where that society redistributes income and wealth according to needs, while it increases the size of the pie by considering contribution and effort. Mill held that the fairness of this procedure would be fully justified by the fact that it aims at the greatest happiness of the greatest number.

We would like to mention two points, which are relevant to the argument of Marshall and Pigou, which will be referred to later. First, Mill points out that the occupation to which each person (especially a young person) devoted him- or herself and the society into which he or she was thrown have a significant effect on his or her aspiration to attain a higher capacity for noble feelings, since such aspiration is easily killed by mere want of sustenance (*op. cit.*: 15). Second, as an aspect of utilitarianism, Mill emphasizes reduction of pain as much as (or more than) increase of pleasure (*op. cit.*: 18–22).[10]

The Material Welfare School

It was the next generation rather than Mill himself, including Marshall, Cannan, Fisher, and Pigou, who undertook the task of analysing the implications of utilitarian ethics in detail. In the process of their analysis, however, an important change was made in the object for examination. Although Mill considered that the concept of 'utility' was equated with subjective pleasure and lack of pain, the next generation defined the concept more narrowly, as things that had use-value for people's physical health and material needs. They focused their interest on the level of people's material welfare.[11] As a matter of course, the source of material welfare is limited to goods whose value is measurable in money terms (economic goods). Furthermore these goods are arranged in a hierarchical order that proceeds from necessary goods for survival to luxury goods which are not necessary for ordinary living.

What sort of prescription for distributive justice is derived from restricting the objects of study? First, by defining utility as material welfare, we find that the increment of individual utility caused by additional income—marginal utility—decreases as income rises. The reason is that, the higher one's income, the greater is the share of one's income expended on non-necessary goods. Second, we can think of material needs as being common to almost all people (whether wealthy or not). If there is little difference among individual abilities to transform material goods into utility (which would not be the case for general desire), the difference among individual utility functions will not be so substantial. As for the average utility functions, the difference between wealthy people and poor people must be very small. Meanwhile, the material welfare of the whole society attains its maximum when the marginal utility of individual income is equalized.

---

[10] Mill emphasizes this point in order to defend utilitarianism from the argument by Thomas Carlyle, who was strongly critical of the epicurean aspect of utilitarianism.

[11] As opposed to the concept of utility proposed by the Material Welfare School, Pareto calls general desire 'ophelimity'. The latter is used as the concept of utility in current economic theories. Mill himself adopted the broad concept of utility and explicitly disagreed with restricting it to material welfare (Mill 1879: 8). Refer to Cootner and Rappoport (1984), which reconfirms a new understanding of the significance of the material welfare school for modern economics. I am greatly indebted to them for the argument in this section.

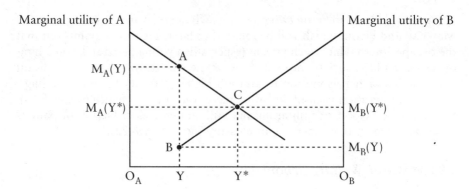

Marginal utility of A | Marginal utility of B

$M_A(Y)$ ----- A

C

$M_A(Y^*)$ ----- $M_B(Y^*)$

B ----- $M_B(Y)$

O_A Y Y^* O_B

Figure 2.1. *The Welfare Maximizing Condition of the Material Welfare School*

Figure 2.1 illustrates the discussion. For simplicity, suppose there are two people, A and B, in the economy.[12] The income of A is measured to the right from O_A and that of B to the left from O_B. The line $O_A O_B$ reflects the amount of total income generated in the economy. The marginal utility of each person is represented by a straight line, which declines with a rise in his or her income. The area of the trapezoid formed between this line and the horizontal axis $O_A O_B$ expresses the level of each person's utility. Suppose that the level of A's income is $O_A Y$ and that of B's income is $O_B Y$, determined in the market, and the difference between them reflects a difference in their initial endowments. In this economy A is considered to be poor and B to be wealthy. Since the marginal utility of A, $M_A(Y)$, is higher than that of B, $M_B(Y)$, the economy as a whole does not maximize its material welfare. With fixed total income, social material welfare will be maximized when the total income is divided at Y^*, where $M_A(Y^*) = M_B(Y^*)$. When the economy realizes such income distribution, the total welfare will increase by the area of $\triangle ABC$. Since the marginal utility

---

[12] Figure 2.1 is based on the figure in Sen (1973: 17). It should be noted that since he argues that utility is equivalent to general needs, his interpretation differs from that presented here. For instance, suppose person A derives less utility than person B from any given level of income, since A is physically handicapped. Then A's marginal utility curve shifts down. The utilitarian rule of distribution gives more income to B in order to maximize the sum of social utility, instead of transferring income from B to handicapped A to reduce the social inequality. Therefore Sen argues that utilitarianism implies egalitarianism only when individuals' utility functions are equal, which is a very special case. He considers that utilitarianism generally brings inequality to society (*op. cit.*: 18). Since Sen emphasizes the differences between individuals in their ability to transform goods into utility, he does not view equality of goods (or income) as a criterion. (Likewise he does not attach importance to the concept of primary goods, advanced by Rawls, and mentioned later.) In spite of the above criticism by Sen, the author considers that the approach where needs are defined in terms of goods is meaningful. It seems that Sen's criticism stems from directly connecting the concept of needs and that of utility. It is possible to compare the utility of the normal individual and the handicapped individual (who is unfortunate as regards natural primary goods, as Rawls terms them), provided that the goods with which the handicap is compensated (such as care services) have already been redistributed.

functions of A and B are considered to be almost identical, as mentioned above, the total income is almost equally divided at point Y^*. The economy can realize this income distribution by transferring the amount of $Y^* - Y$ from B to A.

However, this argument is valid with an important reservation. The economy can achieve its object of maximizing social welfare by redistributing income, only because the total income is assumed fixed. We need to ask which transfer method (such as poll tax or income tax) should be adopted in order to maintain the assumption of fixed income and so as not to damage the incentive of both wealthy and poor people to produce. Usually it is inevitable that wealthy people's incentive to produce is to some extent spoiled by such redistribution. On the other hand, it is possible that the simultaneous increase in the income of poor people may promote society's productivity if that increase results in improvements in children's nutrition, health, and education. In fact, Pigou emphasizes this scenario and the possibility of an increase in net total income. That is to say, efficiency can be compatible with fairness.

Thus, the Material Welfare School narrows the definition of utility from the fulfilment of desire in general to the fulfilment of material needs for everyday life, and this limited definition enables them to make interpersonal comparisons of utilities and to obtain approximate similarities among people's utility functions. This ultimately makes the principle of utilitarianism manœuvrable. Although the Material Welfare School focuses on material welfare, it is not the case that they have no interest in nobler mental pleasure, which Mill regarded as so important. As Marshall mentions at the beginning of his *Principles of Economics* (1920), the fulfilment of material needs is considered to be an essential prerequisite for cultivating people's higher mental capacities.

The introspection of the fully experienced observer appears at important stages of the logic in both Mill and the Material Welfare School.[13] It shows in that they regard mental pleasure as superior to material pleasure, and that they presume one yen is worth more to a poor person than to a wealthy person. They primarily consider that the intrinsic ethical nature of a human being lies in his or her acceptance of the judgement of an impartial observer as a moral instruction. However, each person does not necessarily come to the same conclusion regarding the introspective judgement of the ideal observer. What the Material Welfare School attempted to do may be summed up as an attempt to minimize the occurrences of such difficulties by restricting the objects of introspective judgements to phenomena which can be grasped objectively, such as material destitution and wealth richness.

---

[13] In his letter to Harrod, Keynes indicates the importance of introspection by mentioning that 'economics is essentially a moral science and not a natural science. That is to say it employs introspection and judgments of value'. Refer to Moggridge (1976: 14). In this sense Keynes is also a faithful successor to the classical economics which he attacked.

Criticisms of the Material Welfare School and its Contemporary Significance

In the 1930s the positivists, represented by Robbins (1932), and behaviourism, embodied in the theories of ordinal utility and revealed preference formulated by Hicks and Samuelson, extended the object of economics to the encounter between general desire and general scarcity. At the same time they rejected moral norms, interpersonal comparison of utilities, and introspective methods as unscientific and completely rewrote welfare economics. As a result, economists have since that time almost completely ignored the concept of distributive justice in their analysis. Arrow used ordinal utility to find social preference ordering by democratically aggregating individual ordinal preference ordering. However, this approach is incapable of ordering different social situations beyond the criterion of Pareto optimality. After all, interpersonal comparison of utilities based on some introspection is essential for obtaining a concrete criterion of equality (Sen 1973: Theorem 1.1; Hammond 1976: 268, Theorem).

It is quite unreasonable to require economic theory to be falsifiable as natural science is, for the lack of strict falsifiability of the introspective method. After all one cannot say how strict falsifiability should be and that is a matter of degree. It is not proper to reject as meaningless the Material Welfare School's method of introspective judgement with its carefully restricted objects of study. As a matter of fact, redistribution of income and other welfare policies have been effective in many countries in improving people's nutrition and physique, lowering disease rates and death rates, and raising levels of education. Although the focus of economics has moved on to other fields, it is clear that the Material Welfare School has not lost its systematic and theoretical consistency as part of economics.

2.4. RAWLS'S PRINCIPLES OF JUSTICE

Starting with criticisms of utilitarianism, John Rawls, a modern American philosopher, has developed new principles of justice that cover the fields of politics, psychology, and economics. His work, *A Theory of Justice* (1971), is an epoch-making masterpiece which declares the resurrection of substantial and practical philosophy, in contrast to the extremely abstract mainstream contemporary philosophical thoughts, such as logical positivism and analytic philosophy. One may say that it revivifies the tradition of English classical empiricism—represented by Hume, Adam Smith, Bentham, and J. S. Mill—which aims to make a political and practical proposal on the basis of broad social and moral scientific thought.[14] Rawls reformulates individualistic

---

[14] Rawls's work reflects the extremely strained political situation of the times when it was written—from the latter half of the 1960s to the early 1970s. In West European countries and Japan, a fierce anti-Establishment movement had broken out under the leadership of universities. People cast strong doubts on the fairness of the Establishment. They considered that the existing

liberalism, which lies in the tradition of European democratic societies, by clarifying the principles of justice on which liberalism stands. Though Rawls's argument ultimately defends liberalism, it by no means accepts all existing institutions. It is intended as a critical approach for evaluating any political, economic, and social institutions—whatever system they are situated in, such as capitalism or socialism.[15]

Criticisms of Utilitarianism

In order to characterize Rawls's principles of justice, it is necessary to launch our investigation by looking into his criticisms of the utilitarianism of Bentham, Mill, and Sidgwick, where he began his argument. Rawls in fact constructed his argument on the basis of these criticisms. His three major criticisms of utilitarianism may be summarized as follows.

First, there are only weak grounds for choosing the principle of the greatest happiness as the ultimate goal for social institutions. Although the ultimate goal is supposed to be selected by 'the impartial observer', he or she is a kind of entity with no character other than impartiality. There is no reason for him or her to exclude all other principles.

Second, if we assume that all people are empathetic to each other, that is, all people are altruistic, we can impose a 'benevolent' character above the 'impartiality' upon the ideal observer, and then achieve the choice of the principle of the greatest happiness. A principle of justice that crucially depends on a transcendental altruism, however, cannot be said to have a firm foundation. The true need for the principles of justice arises when there is a conflict to be arbitrated which inevitably emerges through each individual's rational effort to realize his or her own value under the constraint of scarce resources. Since one's own value is invaluable to oneself, one should put the highest priority upon its realization. Thus, we must suppose in the first place that people are mutually disinterested in each other and each other's value.

Third, the criterion of maximizing the sum of each person's utility is not sufficient in the choice of a fair social institution. There is always the case, that a certain thing must be given priority over others, which could be incompatible with the implicit assumption of the interpersonal substitutability of utilities and

---

political and social institutions went against the idea of democracy by allowing concentration and unjust exercise of powers, and promoting racial and sex discrimination and distributive inequality. Rawls's work can be interpreted as an attempt by a philosopher to give an answer to the movement by offering a fundamental critical re-examination of the ideological foundation of existing institutions, liberalism.

[15] Daniels (1975) is a collection of the leading articles by philosophers discussing Rawls's *A Theory of Justice*. Daniels's excellent commentary is also referred to in the present evaluation of Rawls's argument. Shionoya (1984, in Japanese) explains and examines Rawls's argument in detail.

the substitutability of one source of utility for another within an individual.[16] For example, the principle of the greatest happiness admits the possibility that some individuals might obtain very few utilities, even where the total sum of utilities is maximized. Such a situation, however, will never be fair. Or it may not be permitted to restrict fundamental human rights—we have only to consider the slavery that existed in the past or military organizations past and present—even if such restriction might be efficient. We much give careful consideration to the order of priorities.

The Social Contract and the Concept of the Original Position

To deal with the first and second difficulties referred to above, Rawls adopted the concept of the social contract which originated with Hobbes, Locke, and Rousseau. That is, the fundamental principle of justice which defines the social institutions and organizations is chosen and forms the subject of a contract with the agreement of all members of the society, as a consequence of each member's rational behaviour. He calls the initial status quo where people make the choice and the contract, the original position (which corresponds, in the traditional theory of one social contract, to the state of nature where people make a mutual agreement on the rights of the civil society). The restrictions which Rawls imposes upon the original position indicate what he thinks of as the conditions of fairness (justice). The restrictions are threefold:

1. *Equal participation.* All human beings (including unborn generations) are equally entitled to participate in the procedure of social contracting.[17]
2. *Limitation of knowledge.* People are limited, in that: (a) they know only that there exist natural endowments ('natural primary goods', which will be mentioned later), or that people are different in their senses of value and their life goals, and (b) they have only general knowledge of natural and social science. People do not know what type of persons they may be, with what particular attributes (such as their endowments and goals in life).
3. *Restrictions on motives.* People (irrespective of their personal attributes) have a preference for obtaining, to the extent that is possible, such goods as are rationally expected to be needed. We call these goods, which include liberties, opportunities, positions of authority, income, and wealth, 'social primary goods'.

Conditions 1 and 2 jointly produce an effect equivalent to that of the concept of 'the ideal impartial observer', introduced in the previous section.

---

[16] Of course in purely formal terms, it is possible to express the situation where a certain factor is given priority over others via assuming discontinuous (lexical) utility functions.

[17] The unborn generations are mentioned here because of the problem of justice in distribution of income among generations. However it is shown that the application of Rawls's difference principle to intergenerational distribution is clearly not appropriate since it leads the optimal savings rate to fall to zero (Arrow 1973a, Dasgupta 1974). Therefore the question of intergenerational distribution should be looked at separately and omitted from the discussion that follows.

That is, these two constraints render people's moral decisions independent of their particular circumstances, values, and aims.[18] Condition 3 implies that all individuals, who are subject to the same limitation of knowledge implied by condition 2, possess the same preferences which determine their motives. As long as we take the theoretical approach of the social contract, which requires agreement by all members as a consequence of condition 1, it is critical that all members demand the same set of primary goods. Condition 3 corresponds to the benevolence assumption additionally imposed upon the impartial observer in the utilitarianism approach. In contrast to the altruism assumed in utilitarianism, each individual's motives are in conflict with those of others because of the restrictions imposed by the fixed quantity social resources (in a broader sense). This is the most distinctive feature of contract theory, as previously mentioned.

The original position is a purely hypothetical situation. Therefore there is scope for questioning the actuality of the principles; even if people who start from the original position agree upon certain principles of justice, there is no guarantee that they will adopt and apply the principles in actual situations. Yet, we can think of human beings as having an innate moral skill (or 'a sense of justice') that enables them to judge what is just or not, so that the original position can be understood as a schematic expression of the mental process where this moral skill really comes into play. With this understanding, they may be no need to worry about the hypothetical aspect of the original position.

Now, what is this moral skill or, equally, the sense of justice? These are the basis of people's ethical sense. In utilitarianism, the ultimate feature of ethics is that everyone accepts the goal of maximizing social welfare based upon sympathy. This is why utilitarianism is said to be teleological. It is this ethical sense that requires the impartial observer whose function is the same as the original position of Rawls. In Rawls's theory, ethics does not have its basis in any kind of goals, nor in an obligation to accept transcendental values—this is the so-called ontological view. The basis of this view is that people have a natural right to equal concern and respect in a society regardless of their natural talent and social status (Dworkin 1975: 50, 51). The original position realizes the right to 'equal concern and respect' in a very natural manner.

---

[18] Such a thought is common to all ethical analyses. Kant characterized the nature of human beings as embodying freedom, equality, and rationality and called the state of having a will capable of adequately expressing this nature, autonomy. Then Kant postulated that an autonomous person follows a categorical imperative as the ultimate ethical norm. The categorical imperative in Kant's sense requires that people should choose the maxim for their own will that prompts their actions, to be the appropriate maxim for others as well. The implications of this are twofold. First, ethical value exists in the person's will itself but not in its result. Kant said that if the will were a jewel, its results would correspond to the setting in which the jewel was to be mounted (Kant 1785). Second, individual autonomy requires a person's will to be independent of his circumstances or contingent factors. To behave in a way that is contingent upon one's own circumstances is heteronomous and goes against categorical imperatives. Autonomy and categorical imperatives are expected to bring about an effect equivalent to that of the original position or the impartial observer. See Kant (1785, 1793).

The Concept of Primary Goods

Together with the original position, the concept of primary goods is the main component of Rawls's theory. With the help of this concept, he attempts to differentiate human needs from the utilitarian concept of utility and define them more precisely. This view may be interpreted as an extension of the concept of 'necessary goods' of the Material Welfare School.

Rawls starts by considering an ideal person who tries to ensure the maintenance of a just society and at the same time makes an effort to realize his or her own value. While able and willing to understand the principles of justice and to act in accordance with them, a person also has the ability and will to find his or her goal (good) in life, to change it if necessary, and to pursue it rationally. Rawls calls this individual 'a moral person'. It is the 'primary goods' that are essential for fulfilling a moral person's needs.[19]

There are two kinds of primary goods. One consists of 'natural primary goods' such as life, health and vigour, intelligence, and imagination, the possession of which depends on the structure of the society in question. The other is 'social primary goods', which depend heavily on the basic structure of the society. The structural elements include the following:

(i) Fundamental human liberty, including freedom of thought, conscience, and expression.
(ii) Open opportunities and freedom of movement and choice of occupations.
(iii) Authority and responsibility associated with position and office.
(iv) Income and wealth.
(v) Social bases for a sense of one's own worth (self-respect).

Freedom of types (i) and (ii) is obviously necessary for moral persons as defined above. The open opportunities of types (ii) and (iv) are the 'maximally elastic' goods that support a moral person socially and economically. Type (iii) enables a moral person to act with self-discipline and perform social duties. Type (v) is included because self-respect makes the individual stronger as a moral person and drives him or her to gain self-confidence and make further efforts.

Rawls introduces the concept of primary social goods into the original position that precedes his 'well-ordered society'. The primary social goods are regarded as giving people the fundamental motives for choosing and agreeing on the principles of justice. That is, people in the original position are supposed to be able to rationally predict the goods that will be needed by moral persons in the future. In other words, primary goods must pass the test of the veil of ignorance—that is, they must be commonly needed by all people, irrespective

---

[19] In compiling this summary I consulted Buchanan (1975), Rawls (1980), and Shionoya (1984).

of circumstances and values that they may possess in the future. Therefore, in order to specify the composition of primary goods, people in the original position can only refer to the most general knowledge about human psychology, the conditions and technology of life, and the natural and social environment of human beings.

There arises a trade-off of the following sort. While detailed specification of the precise content of primary goods would make the principles of justice more substantial, the principles might not stand the test of the veil of ignorance, so that a social agreement could not be achieved. On the other hand, if the content of primary goods is left quite general, then a social agreement on the principles of justice can easily be reached, but at the cost of less substantial principles. Let us consider the case of food. If we specify the contents of primary food according to nutritional requirements alone, we can easily reach agreement, but we cannot distinguish a gourmet dinner from the 'cheapest meal providing a good nutritional balance'. In contrast, if we try to specify a menu for a meal, we cannot avoid differences in individual tastes and religious taboos. Thus the task of prescribing the contents of primary goods bears the heavy burden of making marginal choices that meet both of above constraints.

The concept of primary goods raises another problem, a quantitative one. Is it true that the greater the quantity of primary goods consumed, the better the result? Rawls assumes that people have a common preference for greater consumption when they are in the original position (restriction 3, mentioned above). (Of course people also have the general knowledge that the unlimited consumption of primary goods is impossible because of the constraints on resources in society as a whole, and consequently the principles of just distribution are necessary.) Too great a quantity of primary goods does no harm, and one can refuse to accept them afterwards if necessary. Therefore such an assumption about preferences does not contradict the postulate of the rational person. This is why Rawls adopts such preferences. However, this assumption precludes the existence of a suitable amount of each primary good for each person. Moreover, it may be desirable for some of the primary goods to be shared socially, though Rawls regards all primary goods as being possessed privately. These points are especially important when we consider income and wealth (point 4 on Rawls's list). The concept of income and wealth here does not merely refer to material of pecuniary riches. Rather it refers to a higher mentality as it reflects the flow and stock of purchasing power for acquiring the materials necessary for a moral person to realize his or her own value. However this property of wealth does not necessarily imply that people prefer to own wealth privately, or that they have an unlimited desire for wealth.[20]

---

[20] On these points, see Teitelman (1972) (to which Rawls responded (Rawls 1972)), and Schwartz (1973).

In fact, economic anthropologists such as Karl Polanyi tell us, as a historic or synchronic fact noted in various regions and over a long period of time, that people had (and still have) observed the value of owning wealth in common and of owning a proper amount of wealth as a notion embodying the idea of justice particular to society.[21] The painful history of modern socialist states started from their desire to make amends for various evils which had been brought about by the private ownership of wealth. These facts indicate that Rawls's assumption of a preference for income and wealth is in conflict with the concept of the original position which should be independent of particular historical stages or value concepts. In other words, at least some part of his list of primary goods cannot pass the test of the 'veil of ignorance'. This is the most decisive reason why his argument is sometimes recognized as providing a theoretical basis for only one particular system of thought, liberal democracy, contrary to his intention.

The above discussion does not reduce the value of the idea of primary goods itself. It may be too naïve for economists to include income and wealth as one of the items comprising primary goods. We must examine in detail such matters as the material goods considered necessary by the Material Welfare School, compensation for differences in the distribution of natural primary goods among people (for example, the provision of care for handicapped people), and the proper supply of public goods. But these are problems to be solved in the field of economics. Rawls's approach has another significance, in that he places preference for economic goods on an equal footing with preference for social goods or social status goods such as authority and responsibility associated with position and office. This means that he perceives human beings not only as consumers but also as producers of and participants in social activities. We discuss this point later when we examine self-respect as a primary good.

Rawls's Principles of Justice

Within the framework described above, Rawls argues that people would rationally choose and agree on the following two principles of justice.

The first principle is the priority of liberty:

Each person is to have an equal right to the most extensive basic liberty compatible with a similar liberty for others.

The second principle is the difference principle:

Social and economic inequalities are to be arranged so that they are both: (a) to the greatest benefit of the least advantaged and (b) attached to offices and positions open to all under conditions of fair equality of opportunity.

---

[21] See Polanyi (1968, 1977: chs 6 and 7). Refer, in particular, to the former, which argues for Aristotelian fair exchange among the family communities of polities (city-states).

Individuals in the original position choose the principles that provide the fundamental foundation of the political, economic, and social structure, and they agree on these unanimously. Rawls considers that the principle of people's choice, as the most general idea, should reflect the view that 'all social primary goods—liberty and opportunity, income and wealth, and the bases of self-respect—are to be distributed equally unless an unequal distribution of any or all of these goods is to the advantage of the least favored' (the generalized difference principle). Further measuring of and allocating priorities among primary social goods leads him from this general view to the above two principles.

The first principle implies that fundamental human rights and liberty (the first of his list of primary social goods) must be given higher priority than the other economic and (social) status goods, provided the material welfare of the whole society exceeds the minimum level required. Rawls represents the priorities among primary social goods in the form of 'lexical order'. That is, people consider it most important to retain political liberty and refuse to regard it as a freedom that may be traded off against economic and social benefits. Consequently, a social system will never be adopted if it contravenes political rights, however economically efficient that system may be.

The second principle deals with the distribution of economic and social-status goods, that is, what sort of offices and positions people may occupy, what powers and responsibilities they may exercise, and what income and wealth they may obtain. The second part of the second principle (b) requires the guarantee of 'fair equality of opportunity'. In order to correct any remaining inequality, the first part of this principle (a) provides for consideration of the share of unfortunate people. As already explained (in section 2.2), the equality of opportunity requires that social institution should provide a guarantee of no difference in expectation of life, especially in terms of job opportunities, for people with the same ability. Such differences among people should not be brought about by social contingencies such as gender, race, parents' social and economic position, or other differences in family circumstances. Preventing certain groups of people from taking some jobs means not only that they are excluded from certain economic rewards and social functions associated with the jobs, but also that they are debarred from 'experiencing the realization of selves which comes from a skillful and devoted exercise of social duties'. Thus Rawls always considers the distribution of jobs as primary goods together with its psychological implication—self-respect, a more fundamental primary good dealt with later. In this respect, his idea is similar to that of Marx.

Even if equality of opportunity is realized, it is only realized subject to given talents. A person is gifted by natural chance. Thus this factor is no more appropriate for justifying the inequality than social contingencies. The difference principle plays an important role in eliminating a meritocratic bias which inevitably occurs under conditions of equal opportunity. It is not necessarily true that a man of great gifts is entitled to obtain by right to a higher position and income. Rather the difference principle implies that the benefit from each individual's natural talents must be shared in a society as if the talents themselves were collective assets in that society. According to this principle, determination of the distribution of social primary goods such as offices and positions, income and wealth must be done independently of one's inherent abilities, and then those goods should be distributed so as to maximize the share of the least advantaged. The principle is often called the maximin principle due to this last postulate.

The following two statements show more concrete implications of the difference principle. First, perfect equality among people in terms of their social status, income, and wealth must be pursued in society where the aggregate social dividend (the size of the total pie) cannot be significantly altered and the share of the least advantaged cannot be raised, no matter how the distribution of those goods may be adjusted. Second, if a change in the distribution results in raising the share of the least advantaged, that distribution should be permitted. In other words, as long as the system satisfies the priority of liberty and equality of opportunity, it must also fulfil the criterion of efficiency. Rawls suggests that the second implication is valid to some extent since any social system has a property of 'close-knittedness', which he defines as follows:

For as we raise the expectations (expected shares) of the more advantaged the situation of the worst off is continuously improved. Each such increase is in the latter's interest, up to a certain point anyway. For the greater expectations of the more favored presumably cover the costs of training and encourage better performance thereby contributing to the general advantage.   (Rawls 1971: 158)

Criticisms of Rawls's Difference Principle

As we have observed above, Rawls's principles of justice have a hierarchical structure which accords first priority to political liberty and the second to fair equality of opportunity, and at the same time insists on egalitarianism to counteract the effect of natural contingencies on the distribution of economic and status goods. As mentioned earlier, people in the original position face the task of choosing a fair social system, which is different from the usual economic problem of choosing the most preferable among various social states given the basic institutional structure of the society. Such a formulation of the problem reflects Rawls's emphasis that distributive justice can only be discussed appropriately as a problem of procedural justice.

Then what sort of social institutions can satisfy Rawls's principles? Let me cite his statement:

Suppose that law and government act effectively to keep markets competitive, resources fully employed, property and wealth (especially if private ownership of the means of production is allowed) widely distributed by the appropriate forms of taxation, or whatever, and to guarantee a reasonable social minimum. Assume also that there is fair equality of opportunity underwritten by education for all; and that the other equal liberties are secured. Then it would appear that the resulting distribution of income and the pattern of expectations (of life) will tend to satisfy the difference principle. In this complex of institutions, which we think of as establishing social justice in the modern state, the advantages of the better situated improve the condition of the least favored. Or when they do not, they can be adjusted to do so, for example, by setting the social minimum at the appropriate level.   (*op. cit.*: 87)

The words 'social minimum' appear twice here. We can say that the main practical role of Rawls's difference principle is to provide a rational foundation for the concept of social minimum, which utilitarianism failed to generate.

Problems remain. Rawls says nothing about what constitutes the social minimum and at what level it should be decided. (In particular the difficulty and complication of deciding the minimum level of status goods such as authority and responsibility associated with jobs bears no comparison with the task of deciding the minimum income level.) If all that was required was the satisfaction of a certain social minimum, then a much weaker principle than the 'difference principle' would do. In that case, the weaker principle might be called the 'principle of social insurance'—to provide social aid only when one's share falls below a certain level. In order literally to satisfy the difference principle, it is necessary to show exactly how to decide the level of social minimum. We must go beyond the scope of pure procedural justice and proceed to compare the consequences of different distributions (the social states) possible within a given social institution. The ultimate choice of social institution cannot be done without such consideration. In this case, the maximin rule functions as an independent criterion to evaluate the social state. Only then does the difference principle, except for the priority accorded to political liberty and fair equality of opportunity, become comparable with the utilitarian criterion of maximizing the sum of utilities.

So far this subsection has examined Rawls's interpretation of the difference principle. As regards the difference principle itself, there have been a number of criticisms by philosophers and economists. Let me examine three of these.

The first concerns why people choose the difference principle. Rawls presumes that people, lacking knowledge, behave in a quite risk-averse fashion, fearing that they may fall into a worse situation. Let w_i denote the index of individual i's share of primary social goods (i is the index for individual $1, 2, \ldots, n$). Then people are assumed to choose the social institution maximizing the minimum value of w_i, $\min\{w_i\}$. The source of information about w_i for each i is limited to the general knowledge available to people in the original position.

The following question has been raised. Suppose that people assign an equal prior probability, $1/n$, to the event that a person happens to be an individual i for each i. Then, in so far as we identify the index w_i as individual i's utility, the criterion of people's choice corresponds to the rule of maximizing the expected utility, which is consistent with (average) utilitarianism. In fact, this argument was proposed by economists such as Vickrey and Harsanyi in order to give utilitarianism a contract theoretical basis (Vickrey 1945, 1960; Harsanyi 1953, 1955). Even within their framework, however, there is an extreme case where the maximin rule is chosen. In this case people exhibit infinite risk aversion. Arrow gives two reasons why people become infinitely risk averse. First, in the original position, people are confronted with a very serious problem of choice, which determines the whole prospect of their lives. The kind of risk they face there must be different from the risk assumed under the expected utility hypothesis involving gains and losses of economic wealth. Second, whether one can assign a prior probability of $1/n$ behind a veil of ignorance or not is a controversial problem in the theory of probability and therefore it is not obvious (Arrow 1973: 256–7).

The second criticism is that, contrary to its egalitarian basis, the difference principle may induce the making of a choice that is the opposite of the intuitive view of equality. Since the maximin rule focuses on the welfare of the least advantaged people, a tiny rise in their welfare level may result in a large loss by other people (Sen 1970: 138–40). Paradoxically, however, the maximin rule may also justify a small increase in the welfare of the least advantaged causing a rise in the share of others (and thereby widening the income difference) gets wide. The latter case is closely connected with Rawls's assumption (of 'close-knittedness'), mentioned above, that for any society, pursuing efficiency to some extent and enlarging the whole pie for society benefits the least advantaged. In reality, however, there is no assurance that a society satisfies this assumption and realizes a distribution with reasonable intuitive appeal. In other words, this assumption is too fragile as the knowledge referred to in the original position. Sen generalizes these critiques as follows: the maximin rule does not tell us how to compare one's gain with others' loss. In contrast, utilitarianism focuses on interpersonal comparison of gains and losses and pays no attention to the level of people's welfare. Starting from these critiques, Sen pursues his search for the moral axiom integrating these two viewpoints (Sen 1974).[22]

The third of the criticisms is directed to the inadequacy of Rawls's argument on the formation of the index of primary social goods (w_i). Rawls himself considers that income could be the proxy of w_i since the level of status goods such as powers and responsibilities associated with jobs is 'correlated' with income. The reason for this seems to be attributed to his assumption (quoted above) that the abilities and skills which deserve powers and responsibilities

---

[22] In addition to 'the Namelessness (or the Symmetry Preference) Axiom' which corresponds to the assumption of the impartial observer, Sen proposed the weak interpersonal comparison of utility ('the Weak Equity Axiom' in (1973) and (1974)—which allowed income to function as the mean of compensating other handicaps than income—and 'the Joint Transfer Axiom' in (1974)— which showed that a kind of transfer of income led to a fairer situation among more than three individuals). In introducing this axiom, he attempted to make the concept of equality the criterion and to generalize the argument of Atkinson's measure of inequality (1970) based on the utilitarian viewpoint.

can be obtained only at a cost and that a proper reward is necessary to meet that cost. However there are other sources of abilities such as natural talents, the cost of which we do not need to consider. In this connection, we may even suppose that a high position and authority can substitute for economic rewards to some extent, as is implied by Mill's ideas quoted at the beginning of this chapter.

In short, more discussion is still needed in order to construct the index. Even if primary social goods can be divided into two groups, status goods and economic goods, it is necessary to examine whether these two are substitutes—if they are, an increase in economic goods can compensate for a decrease in status goods—or whether they are complements. Furthermore, if their substitutability or complementarity depends on the situation, the rule which tells when they are substitutes or not should be discussed. This remains as a significant problem for establishing the materiality of Rawls's principles of justice. Designing real social institutions seems to depend greatly on how this problem is dealt with.

Self-Respect as a Primary Good

To conclude our discussion of Rawls, we must examine the concept of 'self-respect' that he regards as the most important social primary good. Rawls's self-respect consists of two kinds of confidence. The first is confidence in one's own value and one's life plan (which includes one's preparations for revising the plan in the future) which embodies one's self-value. And the second kind of confidence lies in one's ability to fulfil one's intentions so far as it is within one's power. Two factors enable one to maintain confidence in one's life plan. First, one's life plan should be rational in the sense that it satisfies the most fundamental feature of human desire, which will be mentioned later. (Rawls terms this idea 'the Aristotelian Principle'.) Second, one must find oneself and one's deeds appreciated and recognized by the people whom one regards with high esteem. Therefore self-respect is a social concept, not a concept of aloofness.

What is the fundamental feature of human desire assumed here—in other words, the source of happiness? Rawls defines it as follows: 'other things equal, human beings enjoy the exercise of their realized capacities (their innate or trained abilities), and this enjoyment increases the more the capacity is realized, or the greater its complexity'. He introduces this psychological assumption as a part of the general knowledge and the axiom to which people refer when in the original position.[23] It is obvious why complex activities are more enjoyable.

---

[23] Like Rawls, Scitovsky (1976: Part I) regards as important the pleasures resulting from activities that challenge one's intellect and psychology. However he also points out, referring to the results of research in psychology, that these activities could cause pain if there is a marked disparity between the ability required and one's own ability.

Complex activities allow variety and novelty of experience, invite feats of ingenuity and invention, and permit individuality of expression. Thus the activities that display one's intricate and ingenious talents are appreciated by both oneself and people around one. We can understand that self-respect is deeply involved in the distribution of status goods such as the duties, authority, and responsibility associated with jobs.

The most important effect of self-respect in social life is that it generates in one's mind the sense of recognizing another person's value and appreciating that person's deeds. That is, the sense of self-respect creates in one's mind a capacity for respecting other people. Each person's self-respect brings about a reciprocal relationship in society. This is where Rawls finds the moment of emerging social empathy and co-operation. As mentioned earlier, people in the original position are defined as selfish. Empathy directly shared among people through altruism and philanthropy is a priori precluded. It was Rawls's theory that originally demanded the construction of this assumption in order clearly to institute the situation of interpersonal confrontation in which the criteria for justice are required. More positively indeed, he could have insisted that true empathy among people is made possible only when all individuals have a sense of self-respect. Here emerges Rawls's utopia—'a well-ordered society' that exists in the social union of 'moral persons' supported by a sense of self-respect. This clarifies the difference between Rawls's approach and that of classical utilitarianism. With a little exaggeration, we may say that it is the choice of the egalitarian social institutions that generates the social empathy. The logic is not that the a priori social empathy creates the inclination toward egalitarianism. The greatest significance of Rawls's theory lies in the fact that it prompts us fundamentally to re-examine the problem of justice through its novel viewpoints and logic.

2.5. SUMMARY AND CONCLUSION

This chapter has discussed the basic concepts of distributive justice. After discussing such well-known and intuitive concepts as distribution based on contribution, need, and effort, it examined the ideas of utilitarianism and Rawls's principles of justice as the higher-order principles to arbitrate between these intuitive norms.

The economic implications of utilitarianism were considered by Marshall, Pigou, and others (designated the Material Welfare School) who restricted the domain of the notion of utility narrowly to refer to fulfilling the basic material needs for living, rather than fulfilling wants (or pleasures) in general. Such a restriction not only made it possible to allow for interpersonal comparisons of utility, but also to suppose further that they were almost identical. The pursuit of equality follows from this. Although Bentham's principle of the greatest happiness of the greatest number, taken as the ultimate objective by utilitarianism, requires the equality of marginal utility of income among all individuals, this condition reduces to that of income equality when every individual's utility function is identical. The latter, of course, becomes realizable when income is redistributed among individuals.

Of course, the Material Welfare School was not blind to the possibility that redistribution of income might discourage work incentives. Rather, they emphasized the tendency of the global effects of redistribution—through improvements in the nutrition, health, and education of the children of the poor, thereby raising labour productivity—to overcome the incentive obstruction effect, and argued that the pursuit of fairness and efficiency were mutually compatible.

On the other hand, Rawls's principles of justice are based on the idea that human beings, irrespective of the circumstances in which they are born, have a natural right to receive attention from and be respected equally by society. This idea leads people to suppose a hypothetical original position as the place for social choice, and to accept the results of choice made there as being applicable as a normative rule in the real world.

According to Rawls, the question of justice arises because there is bound to be conflict among individuals over the distribution of social primary goods. He then argues that as a result of individual rational behaviour in the original position, the principle according priority to political liberty as well as equality of opportunity, and the difference principle concerning the distribution of economic and status goods, are adopted.

The difference principle (or the maximin principle) is a standpoint from which to approve the pursuit of efficiency and the occurrence of inequality only in so far as it improves the welfare of the least advantaged individual. Rawls himself suggests that the pursuit of efficiency and a call for equality will be reasonably harmonious, as society has some degree of 'trickle-down' (or in his own words, *close-knittedness*)—where a rise in the income of the relatively more advantaged will also help increase the income of the less advantaged.

Rawls's social primary goods are defined as the goods that are expected to be necessary for human beings whatever their circumstances and whatever their values. As with the 'goods needed for living' of the Material Welfare School, this concept approaches the judgement of fairness from the viewpoint of 'needs'. It naturally includes the 'goods needed for living', but is more comprehensive than that. Thus it includes other economic goods in general (income and wealth), political freedom, basic human rights, opportunities, and furthermore, the 'status goods' consisting of power and responsibility associated with jobs and social status.

In particular, the power and responsibility associated with jobs must conform to the difference principle, as with economic goods. This raises the question of how to arrange the organization of work as a field of production and social activity and how to enrich each individual's work processes. The enrichment of the activity and an increase in social responsibility are believed to be important bases for people's sense of self-respect. Having a sense of self-respect is a driving force for individuals to expend further effort, and simultaneously, it is expected to become a source of empathy and reciprocal altruism among people.

Rawls's concept of social primary goods, however, leaves many important problems unresolved; in particular, their content and their precise specifications, the relative weights placed on such constituents as economic and status goods (which are important for the construction of an aggregate index), and the suitability of private versus public ownership. These limitations, however, do not immediately lead us back to the world of pure deontology, nor to the world of the epicurean utility concept encompassing want in general—or the world of pure teleology. Nor are we led back to the pursuit of a purely formal procedure to aggregate individual values that has developed since the work of Arrow.

We all know, from our inherited wisdom, that the more a deontological ethic tries to purify itself, the less substantive are its contents and its concrete guidelines for human life; the more idiosyncratic objectives and values of individuals that a teleological ethic addresses, the more difficult the comparison and weighing of utility among individuals (tasks that are essential for discussing the problem of fairness) become; on the other hand, trying to obtain an aggregation procedure for social choice within the confines of formal logic, and lacking information on individual values, would not succeed.[24] It is by regarding untying of the knots of those unresolved questions as an important intellectual challenge to economists that we can further substantiate the notion of distributive justice.

---

[24] For Arrow's procedures of aggregating values and his impossibility theorem, refer to the explanations by Arrow (1963*a*) and Suzumura (1982) and critical evaluations by Sen 1977, 1979).

3

The Labour Market and the Distribution of Income: The Neo-Classical Approach

The marginal productivity principle was introduced in the previous chapter (section 2.1) as a general rule governing how the market economy rewards each material resource put into production, in particular, labour power. The reward, according to this principle, represents the value of contribution that the last unit of each resource makes in the production of socially useful goods and services.

This principle is deduced only from the demand side of the picture, and remembering that price is determined at the level where demand and supply are equilibrated in the labour market, it is not yet complete as a theory of market rewards. In fact, how much contribution the last unit makes depends on the amount of resource supplied to the market. Hence, the more scarce the resource is, the higher the reward becomes, and vice versa. Therefore, each individual's income depends not only on how much resources he or she owns but also how scarce those resources are in the market.

It is therefore necessary to clarify the logic of the supply side. This chapter addresses the question of how the resources of labour power are supplied to alternative uses from the neo-classical viewpoint of individual rational choice, and further explains various modifications made to the framework of analysis. The modifications are designed to cope with the circumstances that are peculiar to the labour market; such as the resource itself being modified over time or the information on the quality of the resource being imperfect or coming to be improved gradually over time. These circumstances cannot be handled well in a standard framework of market clearing. The outline for this chapter is as follows.

Section 3.1 formulates the theory of general equilibrium for an economy with heterogeneous abilities and heterogeneous jobs, and derives some fundamental properties governing the distribution of income. In particular, it answers the supply-side questions of how people's diverse abilities are allocated to different job types and how people's preferences for types of job affect such a process, and discusses implications of these on the size distribution of income. The answers are summarized in terms of the principle of *comparative advantage* and the principle of *equalizing difference*.

Section 3.2 discusses the possibility that each person's ability might change over time, in particular that it might be modified into a more valuable one at the expense of economic resources. Investment in human capital, as it is called, includes school education, with complete specialization in learning, and on-the-job training in which learning takes place in parallel with labour supply. In the latter case, the market changes from being a *simple commodity exchange* into a *joint exchange* where labour service and *learning opportunity* as an intangible good are jointly traded. There is also a proposal for an accounting framework in which learning-by-doing, a form of learning requiring no input of economic resources, can still be understood as a form of human investment.

Section 3.3 discusses the types of labour market equilibrium that obtain when each person's ability is imperfectly revealed; to be more specific, asymmetry of information exists between the workers and the employer in that every worker knows his or her ability perfectly well while the employer cannot observe it directly. It is on such informational grounds that an economic value is attached to workers' observable attribute that is statistically correlated with the invisible ability, even though the attribute itself does not enhance productivity. Such an attribute is called a *signal*. Employers pay rewards to a signal in order to provide each worker with an incentive to reveal his or her own ability. The type or length of schooling obtained by a worker clearly has such a signalling property. A serious possibility that remains to be examined is that such a signalling role for education might lead to social over-investment in schooling.

Section 3.4 again discusses the implications of informational imperfection, but this time imperfection falls equally (or symmetrically) on workers and employers. Indeed, it is perhaps more natural to suppose that both parties, employers and workers alike, come gradually to learn what ability each worker owns. Workers may even invest their time in taking different jobs so that information can be more advantageously obtained. In such a world, allocational efficiency of labour resources is achieved with a greater degree of approximation over time. A further interesting possibility is that, whenever employers have more opportunity for risk taking than their employees, workers might be willing to enter into an insurance contract characterized by a long-term minimum wage guarantee so as to avoid having their ability revealed as unexpectedly low. Under such an arrangement, workers' income might still rise as the ability is found to be high and/or ascertained more precisely. In this way, the labour market may become a place where labour service and insurance are jointly exchanged.

3.1. LABOUR MARKET EQUILIBRIUM WITH HETEROGENEOUS ABILITIES AND HETEROGENEOUS JOB PREFERENCES

Human beings are diverse in terms of the abilities they own. They are also diverse in terms of their preferences about different jobs (i.e., types of work). How does a market economy combine these diverse human beings and different jobs types? How does employment get allocated, and how is income distributed as a consequence? To answer these questions from the viewpoint of individual choice behaviour (both for those who demand and those who supply labour power) lies at the heart of the neo-classical approach. This section constructs a simple general equilibrium model and analyses these most basic questions, thereby also preparing the ground for the discussions that follow. In the course of this analysis we derive two principles that are inherent in the workings of the labour market; one, the principle of *comparative advantage* concerning the allocation of workers to each job type and the other, the principle of *equalizing difference* concerning how workers' job preferences become reflected in the level of income. It will be assumed throughout this section that each worker's ability does not change over time.

A Two-Sector General Equilibrium Model with Multiple Types of Job

Consider a market economy where inputs of labour power into two different job types are necessary to carry out production. What is the mechanism that determines who works where and what does the resulting income distribution look like? What are the factors generating income disparity? These questions are answered by means of a two-sector general equilibrium model. Such a two-sector model is by now familiar in the areas of economic growth and international trade (Uzawa 1961, Jones 1965). The present model differs from the original formulation in that each individual who differs in ability and tastes chooses the job type endogenously. The analysis thus focuses on the supplier's behaviour. For the labour demand side the marginal productivity principle applies throughout this discussion. First it is supposed that all workers have identical preferences and then differences in job preferences are introduced.

More specifically, assume a closed economy with two goods and two factors of production. Two types of work, called job A and job B, constitute the factors of production. Also for the sake of simplicity suppose that (i) the production of two goods 1 and 2 occurs, each under the technology characterized by constant returns to scale and smooth factor substitutability, (ii) the ratio of labour power input on job B to that on job A is uniformly higher for one good (without loss of generality this is supposed to be good 2—see below) than for the other over the entire range of the relative wage ratio—known as the case of no factor intensity reversal, (iii) the economy-wide demand for goods 1 and 2 is neutral with respect to the distribution of income, and can be represented by a single homothetic utility function. The assumption of constant returns to scale in production can be interpreted as showing that our model is implicitly positioned in the long run, whereby the input of other hidden factors such as capital equipment varies proportionately.

Suppose further that the goods as well as the labour markets are perfectly competitive. This assumption implies that information concerning the ability of each individual and the content of each job is perfectly known to all the parties concerned. Consequently the wage of each worker for each job equals his or her value marginal product.

The foregoing presents the basic framework of the economy. The general equilibrium for the case when the supplies of labour power for job A and job B are respectively fixed exogenously, say (L_A^0, L_B^0), is expressed by Figure 3.1. The figure depicts the labour power space in the first quadrant, and the commodity space in the third quadrant. In the labour power space a box diagram is drawn with horizontal and vertical sides of length L_A^0 and L_B^0, respectively. Also depicted are the isoquants of goods 1 and 2 with O and O′ as the origin, respectively. The curve connecting O and O′ is the efficiency locus of production. Because of the assumptions concerning the relative factor intensity and constant returns to scale ((ii) and (iii) above) the efficiency locus becomes convex downward and the lengths of the line segments PO and PO′ (where P is an arbitrary point on the efficiency locus) respectively become proportional to

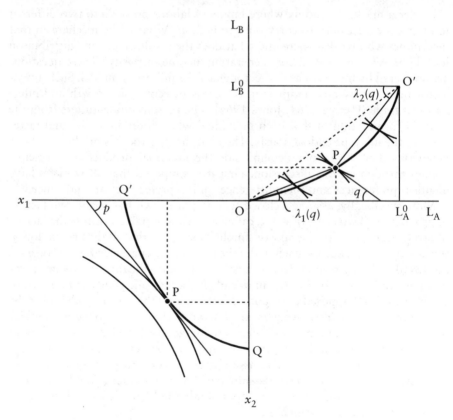

Figure 3.1. *General Equilibrium of a Closed Economy when the Labour Supply to Each Job is Exogenously Given*

the amount of output. Furthermore, the slope of the two isoquants that are tangential to each other at P represents the relative wage ratio w_A/w_B. Hereafter this is expressed by q.

Corresponding to the efficiency locus of production OO' in the labour power space there is an efficient production frontier QQ' in the commodity space. P on the frontier QQ' corresponds to P on the efficiency locus OO'. The slope of the tangent on the QQ' curve at P represents the relative commodity price ratio p_1/p_2. Hereafter this is denoted by p. Because of this correspondence, there exists a monotonically increasing relationship between p and q. As p rises, it enlarges the production of good 1, but since good 1 uses job A more intensively, the relative demand for job A increases, thereby raising the relative wage ratio q. The general equilibrium of this economy is established at a point where the efficient production frontier and the social indifference curve become tangential to each other. The slope of the tangent is the equilibrium relative commodity price ratio. In Figure 3.1 such a circumstance occurs coincidentally at point P. Under the constant returns to scale technology the wage levels w_A and w_B as well as the relative wage ratio q depend only on the ratio L_A^0/L_B^0, and not on the levels of L_A^0 and L_B^0 separately.

Heterogeneity of Ability and the Principle of Comparative Advantage

We now turn to the question of endogenous labour supply. Suppose that the diversity of workers' ability can be expressed by a circle as depicted by Figure 3.2. Each worker occupies a single point on the circle. The proximity of diverse abilities is measured by the smallest arc distance between two points on the circle. (By choosing the radius of the circle to be $1/\pi$, the smallest arc distance between any two points on the circle always falls between 0 and 1.) All individuals are located here symmetrically with each other in terms of the spectrum of ability that surrounds their own.[1]

For job A and job B we suppose that there exists a particular ability that is most well matched to performing each job, and that as one moves away gradually from this most well-matched ability the efficiency with which the job is carried out (called *productive efficiency*) declines correspondingly. Two cases will be discussed below.

Case I supposes that the most well-matched points for job A and job B are located at diammetrically opposed positions, as O for job A and O' for job B in

---

[1] With regard to the device employed here to represent quality differences among individuals, see Vickrey (1964: ch. 8) and Helpman (1981). Even when ability can be ranked from inferior to superior, the analysis presented here holds. The reason is the existence of a well-known one-to-one correspondence between the set of points on the circle and the set of points on the real line. To see this, it is only necessary to choose a point (any point) and draw a tangent to the circle at that point, then draw a line from the point diametrically opposed to this initial point to the tangent cutting through the circle. The two points, one on the circle and the other on the multiple dimensions, then the (hyper-)sphere of the corresponding order must be considered.

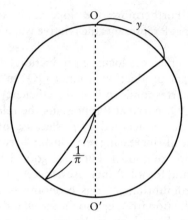

Figure 3.2. *Diversity of Ability among Individuals*

the figure. Case II, on the other hand, supposes that the most well-matched point for each job is located at an identical position, O in the figure. Case I is later interpreted as a situation where distributions of both ability and jobs are mutually *congenial*, while Case II is interpreted as a situation where some general ability dominates the scene. For Case II it will further be supposed that the manner in which the productive efficiency declines as the ability moves away from the most-well matched position differs between the two jobs A and B.

To be more specific, we express the productive efficiency of the ability located with distance x from the most well-matched point for job i by $k_i(x)(0 \leq x \leq 1)$. This function is assumed to satisfy

$$k_i(0) = 1, \quad k_i'(x) < 0, \quad k_i''(x) \leq 0 \qquad (i = A, B),$$

and for Case II it is further assumed that, for any $x > 0$,

$$k_B(x) > k_A(x),$$

and that

$$\frac{k_B(x)}{k_A(x)}$$

increases monotonically as x increases. (Using the terminology introduced later, the latter assumption implies that the index of comparative advantage between jobs varies monotonically.) Hence the value marginal product at position x is $k_i(x)$ times the value marginal product measured at the most well-matched point for each job $(x = 0)$, which is still expressed by w_A and w_B, respectively.

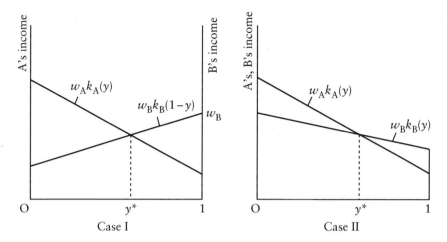

Figure 3.3. *Choice of Job by Workers of Different Ability*

The foregoing assumptions are illustrated by Figure 3.3 for Cases I and II separately. In Case I, the origins for job A and job B are far apart, and the value marginal product curve for job A is downward sloping, while that for job B is upward sloping. On the other hand, in Case II, the origins for both types of job are identical and the value marginal product curves for both job A and job B are downward sloping. Furthermore, the slope of the value marginal product curve for job A is steeper than that for job B.

Under the current premise of no differences in preferences for alternative job types, an individual worker's choice of job depends solely on the income that each job brings. It is, of course, independent of other workers' choices. The criterion for choice is expressed in Figure 3.3, namely choice of the job whose level of value marginal product is higher than that of the other.

This criterion can alternatively be expressed as follows. The productive efficiency of a worker who is located at distance y from the leftward origin (corresponding to O in Figure 3.2) is $k_A(y)$ for job A regardless of whether Case I or Case II applies. For job B, it is $k_B(1 - y)$ in Case I and $k_B(y)$ in Case II. Hence if we define for this worker the ratio of productive efficiency between two types of jobs as:

$$\theta(y) \begin{cases} = k_B(1 - y)/k_A(y) & \text{Case I,} \\ = k_B(y)/k_A(y) & \text{Case II,} \end{cases} \tag{3.1}$$

then the earlier criterion becomes equivalent to:

$$\theta(y) \lesseqqgtr q = \frac{w_A}{w_B} \iff \begin{cases} \text{job A} \\ \text{job A and job B indifferent} \\ \text{job B.} \end{cases} \tag{3.2}$$

The left-hand side of this expression is designated as the index of *comparative advantage* at the ability position y. The right-hand side is the relative wage ratio, which is common to all individuals. The borderline ability position, denoted by y^*, for which job A and job B become indifferent, is determined uniquely. The criterion (3.2) has become known as the *principle of comparative advantage*. The rationale for the use of the term 'comparative advantage' is than, in Case II, even though every worker, regardless of ability position, is uniformly more efficient in job B than in job A in absolute terms, only those workers who are relatively more efficient in job B (that is, with relatively high y) are advised to choose job B.[2] It can easily be verified that when each worker adheres to the principle of comparative advantage the economy-wide labour resources are efficiently employed in the sense that national income is maximized for given w_A and w_B.[3]

The General Equilibrium of the Economy under Conditions of Heterogeneous Ability

What does the general equilibrium with endogenous choice of job types look like? We first normalize the entire work population to be unity, and for the sake of simplicity suppose that the distribution of ability within the population is given, and moreover that its density is symmetric with respect to the diameter OO'. Then the amount of labour supply to each job measured in efficiency units, and denoted by L_A and L_B, defines a downward sloping locus in the labour power space as the relative wage ratio q ($= w_A/w_B$) changes. This locus will be called the *labour supply frontier*. It can easily be verified that the slope at each point of the frontier (i) equals the index of comparative advantage at the borderline ability position for job choice $\theta(y^*)$ and (ii) becomes steeper as it moves from left to right (reflecting the assumption that the index of comparative advantage increases monotonically as y increases) (see Appendix 3.1, mathematical note 1). Hence, the labour supply frontier is (strictly) upward convex, and for a given market relative wage ratio $q = w_A/w_B$ the combination of actual labour supply (L_A, L_B) is determined at the point where the line with slope q becomes tangential to the frontier. The features just noted are depicted in Figure 3.4.

The correspondence between Figure 3.4 and Figure 3.1 should be evident. We can think of the point O' in the first quadrant of Figure 3.1 as moving gradually around to depict the labour supply frontier in response to changes in q. The production frontier SS' depicted in the third quadrant of Figure 3.4 can be understood as the envelope of an infinite number of production frontiers

---

[2] In Case II, the relative wage ratio $q = w_A/w_B$ determined by the market must be greater than unity. Otherwise, there will be no workers supplying job A. In drawing Figure 3.3, this condition is, in fact, supposed to be satisfied.

[3] On the principle of comparative advantage, the reader is referred also to an exposition by Rosen (1978).

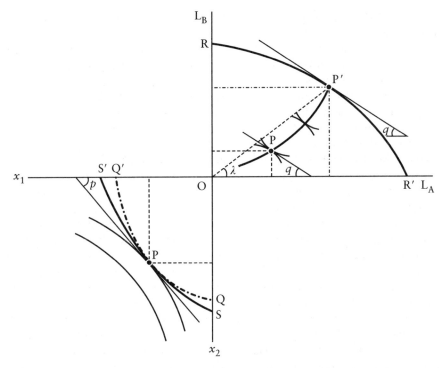

Figure 3.4. *General Equilibrium of an Economy with Diverse Ability
among Individuals*

(one of which is the curve QQ′) generated by each efficiency locus that is
defined for each point on the labour supply frontier RR′. By recalling the basic
property of the envelope that each point on the curve SS′ corresponds to a
single point on the labour supply frontier RR′, we see that there exists a unique
and monotonically increasing relationship between the relative commodity
price p and the relative wage ratio q just as in the case of an exogenously fixed
labour supply (see Appendix 3.1, mathematical note 2). The general equilibrium of the system is established at the point of tangency between the production frontier SS′ and a social indifference curve (P in Figure 3.4). It is clear
from the above discussion that the slope of the isoquants that are tangential to
each other at P in the labour power space (which corresponds to the general
equilibrium point P in the commodity space) and the slope of the labour supply
frontier RR′ at the corresponding point P′ are both equal to the equilibrium
relative wage ratio q.

Determinants of Factor Income Distribution

As a step towards discussing personal income distribution we first discuss the
determinants of the relative wage ratio and the size of employment for each job.

This is called the problem of factor income distribution. In the two-sector general equilibrium model with exogenous factor supply, the properties called the Stolper–Samuelson theorem and the Rybczynski theorem are well known. These familiar theorems are seen to carry over to the world in which factor supplies are endogenous.

In our general equilibrium system the factors (i) production technology, (ii) patterns of commodity demand, and (iii) distribution of abilities are the main determinants of the factor income distribution. Among these, the effects of factors (ii) and (iii) can be stated as follows.

First, when the demand for good 1 which uses job A relatively more intensively increases, the wage rate w_A of, as well as the employment in, job A increases. Therefore, the share of job A's income in national income definitely rises. The reason for this must be clear. An increase in the demand for good 1 raises the relative commodity price ratio p, which, as we have already seen, raises the relative wage ratio $q(=w_A/w_B)$. This result confirms the Stolper–Samuelson theorem for our present model. The rise in the relative wage ratio q raises the borderline ability position y^*, thus increasing the population choosing job A.

Second, when the distribution of ability among workers changes and the proportion of those having comparative advantage in job A increases, then under the homotheticity of social indifference curves the wage rate w_A declines relatively to w_B. Whether or not the size of employment in job A increases depends on whether the increase in population density occurs farther away from or near to the original borderline ability position of comparative advantage. So long as it occurs sufficiently far from the borderline (i.e., at sufficiently small y) then employment will definitely increase.

The foregoing property can be explained as follows. An increase in the population over the ability distribution would shift the labour supply frontier horizontally, maintaining the slope intact, if the increased population is confined in the region of comparative advantage for job A. On the other hand, there would be a shift in the vertical direction, again keeping the slope intact, if the increased population is confined in the region of comparative advantage for job B.[4] When there is no net increase in population and only the density of distribution is changed from the region of comparative advantage in job B to that in job A, the labour supply frontier shrinks in the vertical direction and expands in the horizontal direction at the same time, resulting in a shift towards the right-downward direction, still keeping the slope intact.

---

[4] Suppose there is some addition of density to $f(y)$. This, of course, leads to an increase in the labour supply, but with employment fixed, there should be no change in the slope of the labour supply frontier because this is entirely independent of the density function $f(y)$ (see Appendix 3.1, mathematical note 1). Thus, when addition of density occurs in the region of comparative advantage for job A (or for job B), the frontier shifts outward horizontally (or vertically), keeping its slope intact. When the addition of density occurs in both regions, the shift occurs as the vector sum of horizontal and vertical movements.

There is no change in the relationship between the relative commodity price ratio p and the relative wage ratio q. Therefore, with p maintained constant, an expansionary shift in the horizontal direction would induce an increase in the production of good 1 which uses job A relatively more intensively and a decrease in the population of good 2, and vice versa for an expansionary shift in the vertical direction. Thus, when only the density of the distribution changes in the manner described above the result is an expansion of good 1 and curtailment of good 2 in a reinforced manner. This confirms the Rybczynski theorem for our context. Furthermore, if the social indifference curves are homothetic, then the change in the distribution of ability will result in an excess demand for good 2, lowering the relative price ratio p. Hence, the relative wage ratio q as well as the wage rate w_A will definitely decline.

Diversity of Ability and Personal Income Distribution

Our discussion so far has suggested that the determinant of personal income distribution can be summarized as having two major elements (though they are by no means independent); first, those affecting the choice of job type by each individual, and second, those that affect the wage rate for each job type. It is this second element that has been discussed previously under the name factor income distribution. One of the immediate implications of the first element is that, even among individuals working in the same job, disparities of income appear reflecting the productive efficiency of each individual.

A moment of thought will reveal that such disparities arise out of the purely exogenous circumstance that the two types of work required for production happen to match most closely a particular set of positions in the ability spectrum. (As to the character of differential rents occurring here, there is further discussion of this in section 5.1.)

The shape of personal income distribution is determined by the shape of the value marginal product curves, $w_A k_A(x)$ and $w_B k_B(x)$, and the shape of the ability distribution among individuals. Because each worker's income is uniquely related to his or her ability position, the density of income distribution is derived as the density of ability distribution multiplied by the reciprocal of the (absolute) slope of the value marginal product curve effective at each ability position. That the same density of ability generates more density for income, the flatter the value marginal product curve is, should be intuitively clear.

In view of the correspondence shown in Figure 3.3 between the ability position and income level, we see that personal distribution of income generally has the following two properties. In the first place, as long as the ability distribution is not concentrated at the corners $y = 0$ or $y = 1$, the distribution is positively skewed, with thick densities for low income earners and thin densities for high income earners. This property is common to Case I and Case II.

In the second place, whereas in Case I there is a mixture of those who choose job A and those who choose job B in the strata of low income earners, in Case II

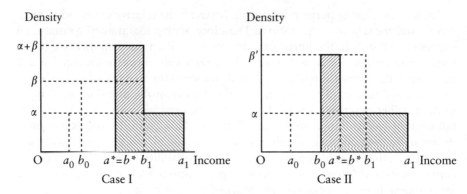

Figure 3.5. *Distribution of Income with Diversity of Ability among Individuals*

there is a perfect separation of income strata according to job type. That is, high-income earners work in job A and low-income earners work in job B. Moreover, holding the proportions of the population working in job A and job B constant between Cases I and II, the range of income distribution is the greater, and the rate at which the density of high income earners diminishes is the slower for Case II than for Case I. In this particular sense, the degree of inequality for Case II is larger than for Case I.

Figure 3.5 depicts the pattern of income distribution under the assumption of uniform ability distribution and under the value marginal product curves depicted in Figure 3.3. The parameter values have been chosen in such a way that the proportion of workers working in job A (or in job B) is the same in Case I as in Case II. The two heavily dotted lines in each figure represent the potential patterns of income distribution for job A and job B had there been only a single job in the economy.

Case I implies that jobs matching fairly well with wide-ranging diversity in ability, given the number of jobs, are offered, and it may be called the case where diversity of ability and the range of ability required by work are *congenial* with each other (or for short, distributions of ability and job types are *congenial*).

Case II, on the other hand, implies that a certain type of ability is commonly needed for all job types. It may therefore be called the case of *dominant* ability. In this case the congeniality between the distributions of ability and job types is certainly low. It may naturally be understood that the degree of inequality, when suitably compared, is higher in the latter case.

At any rate the resulting income distribution has a broad lower tail and a thin upper tail as compared with the potential income distribution to be generated under a single job type. This property arises because each person chooses the job type that maximizes income.

In fact, there is a classic approach to income distribution called the Galton–Pigou paradox. Why is income distribution skewed towards the right despite the fact the distribution of human abilities is perforce symmetrical (this latter supposition itself is not questioned here)?[5]

In response to this query statisticians have offered an interpretation in terms of a proposition stating that, if each person's income is generated by multiplicative application of innumerable and mutually independent random circumstances, then a positively skewed income distribution (such as log-normal or Pareto distributions) among individuals would result in the limit (Gibrat (1931), and subsequent refinements by Kalecki (1945) and Champernowne (1953)). Although there are certainly instances, such as a rare talent helped by enormous effort effecting extraordinary outputs, where various factors operate multiplicatively, it is not convincing to suppose that such a state of affairs is always the rule. Furthermore, there seems to be a difficulty in supposing from the start that income generation is a random process. Our Figure 3.5 provides an explanation of the paradox from the viewpoint of economic theory. This explanation was first given by Roy (1951).

The foregoing discussion can be easily extended to the case where human ability is multidimensional. For instance, one may consider another dimension consisting of personality characteristics besides the dimension of, say, cognitive ability. In such a case, distribution of ability lies not over a circle but over a sphere, and it suffices to locate the two components of ability in terms of latitude and longitude, say (y, z) with similar normalization on radian numbers as before. If the positions of the ability that is most well matched to either job A or job B is located on the sphere, then we can specify the criterion of comparative advantage by assuming the productive efficiency of each job type to be a function of the form $k_A(y, z)$ and $k_B(y, z)$, where y and z represent the latitudinal and longitudinal distances, respectively, from the most well-matched ability position for job A. The rest of the discussion follows exactly the same path as in the single-dimension case.

The new possibility opened up by such an extension is that the performance of some jobs might depend only on one component of ability (hence one of the arguments of the productivity efficiency function becomes redundant). If this discussion is extended further to consider multidimensional ability, then we can simultaneously consider the existence of many jobs that vary in the degree to which any particular component of ability is required. And so long as the distribution of ability among persons is uniform or symmetrical over multiple dimensions, the more components that a job (an occupation) needs simultaneously, the more equal intra-job distribution of income becomes (in the sense of quickly dissipating the density of high income earners), and also that the more such jobs exist in the economy, the more equal the overall distribution of income becomes. It was Mandelbrot (1962) who showed the relationship

---

[5] Pigou himself sought the explanation mainly in terms of (i) the skewed distribution of the wealth that people inherit from their parents, and (ii) the skewed distribution of the level of education and training that are made possible by such wealth. See Pigou (1932: Pt IV, ch. II).

between these properties, by means of rigorous discussion of the shapes of distributional curves.

Diversity of Job Preferences and the Principle of Equalizing Difference

We next introduce people's diverse tastes in relation to types of job. As a matter of fact, work is not simply an expenditure of toil and exhibition of a particular ability. People may value the intrinsic interest and meaning of particular jobs, and also value the physical and social environment that goes with the work. In fact, people's evaluation may extend to such a wide range of qualities as the scope for exhibiting creativity, social responsibility and power (or the feeling of one's own worth), the scope for self-development, amenity of the workplace (e.g., temperature, humidity, noise, and other factors related to pleasantness), the degree of mental tension required, the possibility of physical danger, the extent of co-operation with other persons, the relationship of authority and subordination, the extent of individual control over the operation of tasks, and so on. Even in terms of financial reward, the stability of employment and income as well as the opportunity for future income increase may differ among jobs and they may naturally enter into the evaluation. People seem certain to include such evaluation, as well as income, in deciding the type of work they wish to supply.

Going back to our model, suppose that the satisfaction that each worker (with the ability position y) gets from work can be expressed by a product of income $w_i k_i(y)$ and an index of desirability of work itself, denoted by z_i[6] ($i = A, B$). The ratio of desirability of jobs, z_B/z_A, is expressed by v. Although it may depend very much on an individual worker to decide how the indices of desirability z_A and z_B are constructed, it will be maintained that the ratio of desirability v is a measure that is comparable among different individuals. It designates the extent of income compensation that it is necessary to give to job A in order to make the two jobs equally appealing. The ratio v will be called the *individual measure of equalizing difference*. It therefore becomes a summary index for expressing an individual's preference for jobs.

This measure can be illustrated by a concrete example. Suppose z_i depends on an observable factor called the risk of physical danger at work. More specifically, let t_i denote the degree of risk involved in each type of work and express

---

[6] z_i itself will be regarded as an aggregate measure of the evaluation of various attributes. Some of the attributes, like the extent of risk, can be objectively quantifiable, while other attributes involve such subjective elements as intrinsic interest in work, and are difficult to quantify. Of course, it might be possible to decompose the sources of the intrinsic interest further into objective elements, but such a task is beyond the scope of present analysis. To suppose that an individual has an index of work is admittedly a gross simplification, and, in general, there is a need to consider a utility function of the form $u\ (w_i k_i(y), z_i)$.

its valuation by

$$z_i = t_i^a \qquad a: \text{constant} \quad (i = A, B).$$

Then, v can be expressed as

$$v = \left\{ \frac{t_B}{t_A} \right\}^a.$$

The fact that a differs among people gives variation of v among individuals. Thus people with $a = 0$ do not care about the possibility of physical danger at all, while people with a large negative a are strongly risk averse with respect to physical danger.

A modified criterion of job choice is expressed by Figure 3.6. The horizontal axis measures a worker's ability position y (the arc distance from O) while the vertical axis measures the index v. The downward-sloping curve VV′ represents the locus of points where job A and job B become indifferent, that is

$$\theta(y)v = q.$$

When a worker's (y, v) is located above the VV′ curve, job B is chosen, while if it is located below the VV′ curve then job A is chosen. In the previous framework with no consideration of job preference, it was the point of intersection $y = y^*$ between the VV′ curve and the horizontal line at $v = 1$ that divided the region of choice for job A and job B. Now the borderline has become a downward-sloping curve reflecting the possible diversity in tastes.

What kind of change will the new circumstance bring about? First of all, there should be no change in the criterion for using labour inputs in production so long as the sources that bring about taste difference in job types themselves do not impose any additional constraints on production (other than those

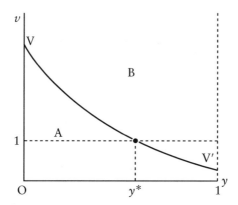

Figure 3.6. *Equalizing Difference and Choice of Job*

already embodied in the production function).[7] Hence, if we suppose that p is given, there will be the same relative wage ratio q, and the same factor input ratio as obtained previously. Any changes that arise in the labour supply side will be absorbed completely, through the operation of the Rybczynski theorem, by the changes that occur in the scale of production of each good.

What is central to the discussion is the change occurring in the labour supply. In view of the fact that the criterion of comparative advantage is not rigorously adhered to in determining the job type, the labour supply frontier generally shifts inward. Moreover, the slope at each point of the frontier equals the relative wage ratio q divided by the average measure of equalizing difference, where the average is taken over all individuals positioned along the VV' curve (whose extent depends on the distribution of individuals over (y, v)), or the effective relative wage ratio, if you will; and therefore, there is no necessity that the shape of the frontier is upward convex. In the special case where all individuals have the same v (say $v = \bar{v}$), the shape of the labour supply curve remains the same as the previous one. However, the choice of job is made in the light of the effective relative wage ratio

$$\frac{q}{v}.$$

(see Appendix 3.1, mathematical note 3).

In any case, because there exists a gap in the prices that the agent of demand and the agent of supply face in making decisions, efficiency in production is deterred and the production frontier shifts inward. The direction in which the production point P shifts under the same given p depends on whether or not the labour supply ratio L_B/L_A rises in consequence. Thus if the preference in favour of job B is strong on average and consequently L_B/L_A rises, the production point moves to the direction such that the ratio of outputs X_2/X_1 rises. Also the

---

[7] Although there is no change in the basic point that the occurrence of equalizing difference is predicated on the existence of tastes about jobs on the labour supply side, what types of jobs are actually offered in the market are determined by the producers, or the labour demand side. Hence producers' behaviour has much to do with the characteristics and the magnitude of the equalizing difference (the *market equalizing difference*, to be discussed below) that appear. Many of the attributes that are associated with the job and that become the objects of people's evaluation can be improved by spending resource costs. For instance, consider the case of improving the physical environment of work. By changing slightly the amount of expenditure on improvement producers can, in fact, generate infinite types of finely differentiated jobs, maintaining the ability position that is best matched to the work in question and the productivity efficiency function $k_i(x)$ intact. Such a type of job differentiation is dealt with quite easily by working with the net output, that is, deducting the cost of improvement from the gross output, and defining the net value marginal product, and then supposing that wages are paid on the basis of net marginal products. We just accept the convention that differentially paid jobs, even though they are otherwise the same, are viewed as different types of jobs. The discussion that follows concerns the case where only two types of jobs are left even after such a possibility of differentiation as has just been described is taken into consideration. The discussion, however, can be easily extended to the demand side and the supply side in generating equalizing differences within a partial equilibrium framework, see Rosen (1974).

size of the inward shift depends on the magnitude of correlation between the variables ability (y) and taste (v). For instance, it is easily seen that, in comparison with the case where the distributions of v and y are independent, the stronger the positive correlation between v and y is (i.e., the more there are people whose job type with comparative advantage is simultaneously the job type that is preferred), the smaller the shift is, while the stronger the negative correlation between v and y, the larger the shift becomes.

The effect on the general equilibrium of the market should now be seen as straightforward. Under our assumption of homothetic social indifference curves, the market acts to eliminate the excess demand for a good whose production has been curtailed relatively more heavily than the other good as a result of the change in labour supply. Therefore, the relative price of that particular good rises. In consequence, the relative wage ratio is adjusted so that the job which is not on average the preferred one (i.e., the job for which relative labour supply has declined) pays a higher wage rate. The market aggregates each person's *individual equalizing difference* into the *market equalizing difference*. The *market equalizing difference*, to be denoted by v_m, can be defined as the ratio of the new equilibrium relative wage ratio, say q_1, over the initial market equilibrium relative wage ratio (with everyone's $v = 1$) q_0, that is,

$$v_m = \frac{q_1^{\,8}}{q_0}.$$

Some remarks on the significance of the principle of equalizing difference are in order.

First, the existence of people's preference for job types limits the working of the principle of comparative advantage, and in so doing it restrains the efficiency of production (the maximization of national income). Nonetheless, there will be no change in the property that the market realizes Pareto optimum once individuals' tastes in relation to desirability of work are taken into account in the calculation of economic welfare.

Second, in forming the shape of personal income distribution, forces that ameliorate the effect of the comparative advantage criterion operate. Figure 3.7 charts the shape of the income distribution on the basis of Figure 3.5 and under the assumption that the job preference index v for any given y is distributed uniformly in the interval $[0, v_{\max}]$. In both Cases I and II, the shape of the distribution expands the tip of its lower-tail, and curtails the positive (or rightward) skewness somewhat. Furthermore, the density at the centre part of the distribution is thicker. In the foregoing sense, equalization of income has taken place. Moreover, the income segregation between the occupational groups seen previously in Case II has disappeared.

---

[8] It is easy to verify that, even when every worker has the same * (the *individual equalizing difference*) the *market equilibrium equalizing difference* realized, v_m, would be a milder one satisfying

$$\bar{v} > v_m > 1 \quad \text{if } \bar{v} > 1 \qquad \text{and} \qquad \bar{v} < v_m < 1 \quad \text{if } \bar{v} < 1.$$

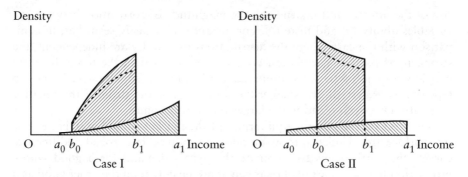

Figure 3.7. *Personal Income Distribution with Diversities in Ability and Job Preference among Individuals*

Third, the market equalizing difference finds it sole expression in the wage rates of existing jobs, and so long as the number of job types is finite, it does not need to go into the detail of each individual's preference to determine the amount of income compensation. Such a limitation is, of course, a common limitation of the market economy.

The principle of equalizing difference is clearly described in Adam Smith's *Wealth of Nations*, and it is therefore a concept that is as old as the study of economics.[9] At the same time, when Milton Friedman argued that the greater part of the inequality in the distribution of income that is observed in the market is to be attributed to the operation of the equalizing difference in maintaining true equality among individuals,[10] he used this concept to justify the free market economic system. Friedman's argument, however, rests

[9] Adam Smith stated (1776, 1904: vol. 1: 89–92) that in a world of free occupational choice and free market competition the wages of labour must be 'either perfectly equal or continually tending to equality' except in some areas of employment, where there are differences and counterbalance based on factors such as: (i) 'the ease or hardship, the cleanliness or dirtiness, the honourableness or dishonourableness of the employment', (ii) 'the easiness and cheapness, or the difficulty and expense of learning the business', (iii) 'the constancy or inconstancy of employment', (iv) 'the small or great trust which must be reposed in the workmen', and (v) 'the probability or improbability of success in [employment]'. The discussion in this section has mainly concerned circumstance (i) above. Other circumstances are discussed in sections 3.2 and 5.5. There is an overview of the results of empirical investigations conducted in the United States in section 5.1.

[10] A quote from Friedman (1962: 162) illustrates his point well.

> Given individuals whom we are prepared to regard as alike in ability and initial resources, if some have a greater taste for leisure and others for marketable goods, inequality of return through the market is necessary to achieve equality of total return or equality of treatment. One man may prefer a routine job with much time off for basking in the sun to a more exacting job paying a higher salary; another man may prefer the opposite.... Much observed inequality is of this kind.

Friedman (1953) also argued earlier that a significant part of the observed disparity in personal income reflects the difference in attitudes toward risk among individuals pointing out that, if all people were risk averse, then they would all wish to mutually insure against the risk of income

squarely on the supposition that the menu of income and quality of work (as objectively measured) faced by individuals does not differ much, or that if there was disparity, it would still tend to disappear as the market economy succeeds in purifying itself.[11] A point worth emphasizing is that as long as this supposition is not empirically validated, Friedman's argument remains at best a tenet of political ideology. Once we recognize the diversity of human ability and the diversity of the degree to which there is a good match between endowed ability and existing types of work, the menus that people face are indeed very different, as we have seen in the model discussed in this section.

3.2. EDUCATION, ON-THE-JOB TRAINING, AND INCOME DISTRIBUTION

Our economic activities are carried out throughout our lifetime. We learn many things through our activities. For example, we devote ourselves to school education, or on-the-job training at workplaces. Of course, some learning may have its own intrinsic purposes and values and such learning never increases our ability in economic activities. However, learning is usually pursued for the accumulation of economic ability, and then it gives high income to learners and a net increase in production resources to society.

At the same time, in many cases, learning is costly. A learner has to sacrifice income opportunities during the learning period and, in addition, has to pay the fees for educational services. In society, numerous resources, such as the potential labour inputs of trainees and the time given by trainers, are used for

disparity), and to that extent it is justified. Furthermore, he argued that redistribution of income through progressive income taxation would obstruct free choice in behaviour on risk and thus diminish the size of the economic pie in society as a whole.

Kanbur (1979) examined Friedman's proposition in a rigorous general equilibrium framework, showing, in contrast to Friedman, that an increase in the degree of risk aversion does not necessarily imply greater equality in distribution, and that when the degree of risk aversion in the society is sufficiently large, progressive, taxation will raise the level of national income.

[11] Friedman's discussion can be understood more clearly by taking a plane with income from each type of work along the horizontal axis and the quality of each job assumed to be a downward-sloping frontier representing the menu of jobs that individuals can choose from. Suppose that this menu is the same for all individuals. Individuals are regarded as maximizing utility by locating the tangency point of this frontier with their indifference curves. Depending on how diverse the shape of the indifference curves is, diversity in job choice arises: some individuals with a high quality of work sacrifice income, and other individuals with greater income sacrifice quality of work, etc. However, everyone is maximizing his or her own utility subject to the same opportunity set (menu), and in this sense the circumstance can be said to be perfectly equal. In our discussion in this section the work menu is confined to two jobs only, and our focus is more on the derivation of the frontier (though consisting of only two points) itself in a general equilibrium setting. In spite of such minor differences, we can essentially make the same arguments as Friedman, if all individuals have identical ability. Divergence from Friedman's arguments arises, however, because people differ in ability, and there exists a significant limitation to how congenial the job and ability distributions are. Hence, it is difficult to maintain that everyone has the same set of menus.

ends other than current production. In this sense, learning can be regarded as a rational investment for society as well as for individuals. Then, it is necessary to consider whether their decision making is rational for the whole of society.

Adam Smith long ago viewed learning as investment: the input of costs and the gain of revenue. However, it was only following the work of Schultz, Becker, Mincer, and others at the University of Chicago in the 1950s that studies on economic activities from this viewpoint became popular. The studies are usually said to embrace 'human capital' or 'human investment' theory. In particular, Schultz (1960, 1971) explicitly points out that the accumulation of human capital is a part of the fundamental social infrastructure in the process of economic development.[12] Becker (1964) and Mincer (1974), measuring the return from human investment and comparing it with the return from other investments, investigate whether human investment is efficient from the view of social welfare, and also point out that human investment is very important and significant in explaining the differences in individuals' incomes. One characteristic of these studies is that theoretical research was done simultaneously with extensive empirical research. We will consider the empirical studies more closely in the next chapter. The main theme in this section is to consider, from the viewpoint of human investment theory, the characteristics of learning by workers and their effects on wages and income distribution.

There is one exception in the field of on-the-job training, in that there is one type of learning that does not require a sacrifice of earnings, unlike formal training at the workplace. This is learning by doing. Even though the original definition of human investment theory, the input of costs and the gain of revenue, does not encompass this type of learning, it is possible to regard it as an activity of human investment in the broadest sense. One of the tasks of this section is to clarify the meaning of human investment.

Determination of Educational Investment Level

Assume that an individual works from 0 to period T. He has the initial endowment of economic ability x_0, and has opportunities for changing x in either direction through education. This implies that he can choose from two different types of school. Denoting s as the periods of schooling, economic ability x after s periods is expressed as follows:

$$|x - x_0| = h(s, a) \quad h_s > 0, \quad h_{ss} < 0 \qquad (3.3)$$

Note that the assumption that $h_{ss} < 0$ indicates the effect of the decreasing return of scale. It is assumed that the effect of two types of school education is symmetry. The parameter a is a shift parameter about investment

---

[12] This point was taken up by Denison (1967: ch. 8) in his discussion of the origin of economic growth and by Jorgenson and Griliches (1967) in their discussion of the measurement of changes in labour quality.

opportunities; this is later interpreted as the individual's innate ability, or his or her social or economic background. Here, consider that it is at the same level among individuals. For simplicity, we pay no attention to direct costs of education such as school fees, or to values as consumer goods provided from learning. Further, we assume that wage rates of job A and B, w_A and w_B, are constant over time, and that a perfect capital market exists: the individual's borrowing is constrained only by the present value of his or her future earnings.

In this situation, to consider how individuals choose various jobs and educational levels, we proceed by two steps. First, they choose an educational level to maximize their present value of future earnings given a job.[13] Second, they compare the maximized present values, and then choose the job that yields the higher value to them.

The optimal educational level is determined by the following principle: for individuals who have been receiving education to date, the increase in the present value of earnings in each subsequent period from additional education in the current period is equal to the income which they would receive in the current period if they were to stop education and start working (see Appendix 3.1, mathematical note 4). If the former exceeds the latter, they can get returns that exceed their loans by borrowing funds equal to the latter in the financial market and investing these funds themselves. On the other hand, if they work in this period and invest their rewards in the financial market, they can receive higher earnings. The value of the latter is called the opportunity cost of education. Even if they pay nothing for education directly, the existence of opportunities for other investments brings them indirect costs in the form of lost rewards. This principle implies that the rate of return on education is equal to the interest rate in the financial market. Note that the interest rate is equivalent to the rates of return of other marginal investments. Hence, in other words, this is the principle which leads to the socially efficient allocation of resources without externality or the value of education as consumption.

How do changes in conditions influence decisions on educational level? Under the assumptions that the only educational costs are lost rewards, and that wages are constant over time, the choice of educational level given a job is independent of the wage rate because both earnings and opportunity costs are proportional to changes in the wage rate. (However, if there are direct costs for education other than lost wages, the increase in the wage rate enhances the educational level. Further, as we mention later, since choice among jobs depends on wage rates, large changes in wage rates lead to reallocation among jobs and affect educational level). Second, take the initial endowment x_0. If we assume that $k_i' < 0$ and $k_i'' \leq 0$, given a job, the same change in x cannot increase the ability of an individual whose ability is more suitable to the job

---

[13] The decision on educational level is often made by parents. If parents have a benevolent interest in the wealth of their children, they choose the optimal educational level for them. Please see section 7.2 for further discussion.

than that of another. Hence, the former will choose a lower educational level. Third, an increase in the life span T encourages an individual to obtain a higher level of education because he or she can receive earnings for more periods at the same cost. Finally, an increase in the interest rate in the financial market lowers educational level as well as physical investment. To sum up, educational level given a job is an increasing function of the life span T, and a decreasing function of the distance between the initial endowment x_0 and the most preferred ability position suitable for the job, and the market interest rate.

The above statement explains the maximization of the present value of future earnings discussed in the first step. The analysis in the previous section is applied in the same way to the maximization (choice of job yielding the highest value) in the second step. Combining these, individuals determine types and levels of education, which in turn determine the jobs they choose in the future. Naturally, in this process, the wage rate is an important factor.

Here, as an extreme case, we suppose that all individuals have an equal initial endowment of ability and identical opportunities for investment.[14] If labour inputs are supplied to every job in the whole economy, the present values of earnings on each job maximized by proper educational choice, denoted as V_A^* and V_B^*, have to be identical. Denoting the optimal educational level of each job as s_A^* and s_B^*, and the allocation of economic ability after education as x_A^* and x_B^*, the following equation holds since $V_A^* = V_B^*$:

$$\frac{w_A k_A(x_A^*)}{w_B k_B(x_B^*)} = \frac{e^{-rs_B^*} - e^{-rT}}{e^{-rs_A^*} - e^{-rT}},$$

where e is the base of the natural logarithm. If we ignore e^{-rT} as it is close to zero, the following equation holds approximately:

$$\ln Y_A - \ln Y_B = r(s_A^* - s_B^*),$$

where Y_A and Y_B are the incomes in each period. In other words, (Y_A, s_A^*) and (Y_B, s_B^*) satisfy the logarithmic linear equation:

$$\ln Y = \ln Y_0 + rs \quad (\ln Y_0 \text{ is constant}), \tag{3.4}$$

where $\ln Y_0$ is a constant. Indeed, this result holds when there are more jobs than just the two jobs A and B. Although the difference in income reflects the difference in education, the utility of each individual in his lifetime is identical, regardless of his income. This illustrates perfectly the statement of Adam Smith that differences in learning costs cancel out differences in income. In this case, the principle of equalizing difference works perfectly.[15]

---

[14] The empirical implications of the following discussion are considered in the first half of section 4.2.

[15] See footnote 9 for the statement by Adam Smith. Mincer (1958) was the first to consider the case explicitly. Mincer identified two results. First, even under symmetric distribution of schooling,

The actual incomes of individuals depend on casual events or slight differences in their tastes.

However, in the real world, there is no doubt that conditions among individuals are not exactly identical. Usually, individuals have different initial endowments of ability and various investment opportunities. At the end of this section, we indicate how these differences affect income distribution. Even in that case, if we suppose that each new generation has exactly identical distributions of attributes, the general equilibrium analysis similar to the one in section 3.1 is feasible through the aggregation over generations about labor supply (see Appendix 3.1, mathematical note 5).

General On-the-Job Training as Joint Exchange

In on-the-job training, labour supply and learning opportunity are exchanged jointly in the market. We now explain what this means.

Here, individuals work for two periods. In the same manner as before, there are job A and job B. As Case I, consider, without loss of generality, the situation in which ability distribution and job distribution are mutually congenial. We study the long-term situation and assume constant wage rates w_A and w_B over time, thus ignoring any uncertainty in the future labour market. Further, in a perfect financial market, firms and workers can lend and borrow funds freely at the constant rate r. Hence, workers will maximize the sum of the present value of incomes from the two periods.

There are various learning opportunities with jobs. In the following discussion, we take the following situation as a benchmark. First, there is no learning opportunity on job A. Hence, the abilities of individuals choosing job A are determined by their initial endowments of ability, and are not changed in the second period. In contrast, variable learning opportunities exist on job B. The learning opportunities are assumed to apply as follows. If workers spend some time on training in the first period, their ability positions are improved in the second period, that is, x is increased. All the consequences of training belong to the trainee alone, and are not affected by the identity of the employer. This is called 'general training', as compared with the firm-specific training mentioned later. The term 'variable' means that individuals choose firms that offer the most appropriate learning opportunity from among the firms offering various opportunities, or that they can induce their employers to change learning densities through different learning opportunities. In other words, it is a characteristic of job B that simultaneous trade between the demand and the

income distribution is positively skewed. In particular, if the former follows a normal distribution, the latter takes a logarithmic normal distribution. (Remember the Golton–Pigue paradox mentioned in section 3.1) Second, equality of distribution of s leads to equality of income distribution.

supply of labour inputs and learning opportunities occurs. This is what we mean when we say that on-the-job training is a 'joint exchange'.[16]

For on-the-job training to function in practice, it must achieve a higher efficiency of learning than that in outside training organizations. Since the labour market is competitive, the price of training is equivalent to the marginal value of products lost in the training. Hence, on equilibria, firms offering learning opportunities gain no excess profits from their workers.[17]

To make the arguments more concrete, we suppose that the amount of learning opportunity in job B is given by a parameter, λ $(0 \leq \lambda \leq 1)$. It is assumed that inputs $\lambda k_B(x)$ in the first period, which is an opportunity cost in the first period, increase x at the rate of $g(\lambda)$ in the second period, that is, the ability in the second period is $k_B(\{1 + g(\lambda)\}x)$. For simplicity, we assume that the rate of increase of ability is independent of the initial endowment x, and is common among all firms; $g(\lambda)$ satisfies the following conditions:

$$g(\lambda) \geq 0, \quad g'(\lambda) > 0, \quad g'(0) > 1, \quad g''(\lambda) < 0 \qquad (0 \leq \lambda \leq 1).$$

Workers' income opportunities during the two periods given x are described in Figure 3.8. The horizontal axis is income in the first period, the vertical one is income in the second period. The choice of job A, expressed by the point A in the figure, gives reward $w_A k_A(x)$ in each period. V_A on the horizontal axis represents the sum of the present value of rewards given the interest rate r. Next, we see what happens when workers choose job B. Then, learning density, λ, needs to be chosen. The learning opportunities are shown by the upward convex curve drawn from B(0) to B(1) in the figure. B(0) means $\lambda = 0$, and B(1) means $\lambda = 1$. At each point on the curve, the sum of the present values of income, V_B, depends on λ. λ^* expressed by $B(\lambda^*)$ in the figure is the learning density that maximizes the sum of the present values of income. When the learning density λ^* is chosen, the cost

$$\overline{B(0)Q} = \lambda^* w_B k_B(x)$$

yields the return

$$\overline{B(\lambda^*)Q} = w_B\{k_B(\{1 + g(\lambda^*)\}x) - k_B(x)\}$$

---

[16] Rose (1972*a*,*b*) first analysed explicitly the joint exchange of labour services and training in the labour market.

[17] Unless a firm provides the learning opportunities desired by its workers, the firm allows other firms to supply the opportunities to obtain the entrepreneurial profits. However, competition among firms eventually leads to zero excess profits (premium) in equilibria because a firm cannot monopolistically supply learning opportunities for general skills which workers can take with them when they go elsewhere. (This differs from the case of firm-specific skills explained later.) When workers have different preferences about density of learning, a spectrum of learning opportunities is always offered, and then the premium remains zero. This is a characteristic of the competitive market.

Second-period income

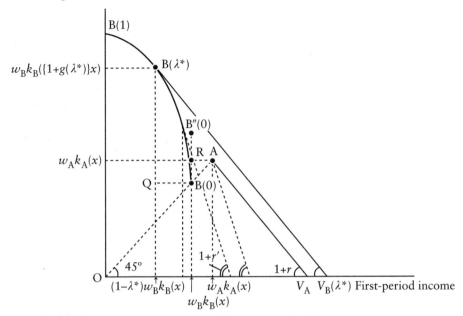

Figure 3.8. *Optimal Investment in General Learning Opportunities*

and the marginal rate of return is identical to the interest rate r.[18] Each worker compares the maximized $V_B(\lambda^*)$ with V_A, and then chooses the job with the higher value. In the figure, it is job B that workers choose. Note that this choice depends on the interest rate. When the interest rate is higher as depicted in the dashed line in the figure, the smaller learning density $\lambda^{*\prime}$ is chosen. Then, $V_B(\lambda^{*\prime})$ may be less than V_A, in which case job A is chosen.

In Figure 3.8 a worker's ability is given as x. If his ability is more suitable to job A, then point A will move in a north-easterly direction on the 45° line

---

[18] Using:

$$\text{Max}_{\lambda} V_B = w_B\left\{(1-\lambda)k_B(x) + \frac{k_B(\{1+g(\lambda)\}x)}{1+r}\right\},$$

the first order condition of the maximization is given by:

$$\frac{xk_B'(\{1+g(\lambda)\}x)}{k_B(x)}g'(\lambda) - 1 = r.$$

The left-hand side means the marginal return of human investment. In general, the optimal density of investment λ^* depends on x.

and point B(0) in a south-westerly direction. Thus, he is likely to choose job A even when learning opportunities are taken into account.

Given the market wage rates w_A and w_B and the interest rate r, workers' choice of jobs and learning opportunities and their income level in each period are characterized as above. In addition, we have found that an increase in the interest rate decreases labour supplies in job B together with learning opportunities. In the same manner as in section 3.1, a general equilibrium becomes attainable in the whole economy, where the equilibrium is a market equilibrium such that the labour supplies are equal to the firms' labour demands determined by the principle of marginal productivity given the wage rates w_A and w_B. In terms of income distribution among individuals, we find the occurrence of an age–wage profile, that is, income change in age due to the cost of learning and its return; this is not considered in section 3.1.

The General Optimal Path of Human Investment

We have considered the optimal level of education at school and general on-the-job training in the workplace separately. These should have been considered simultaneously, in the same framework. A considerable number of theoretical studies have analysed workers' optimal path of learning density in their lifetime (see Ben-Porath 1967; Blinder and Weiss 1974). It is, however, important to note that there are some essential differences between learning in the classroom and on-the-job training in the workplace.

If there is no difference in quality between them, then it is only the difference in accumulation speed that matters. First, there is the effect of decreasing returns of scale to resource inputs, either in each period or over a number of periods. Second, the number of periods during which to recover investment decreases with age. Hence, in the early periods, workers will devote themselves to educational investment for a while. After starting work, they gradually decrease their learning densities. This implies that workers, either in a firm or among firms, move to other jobs with fewer learning opportunities in the same occupation (Rosen 1972*b*). Therefore, the age-wage profile after labour participation is convex upward and gradually increases, which is consistent with observed facts. Further, the assumption of homogeneity between two ways of learning implies that on-the-job training is less effective for workers with higher levels of schooling, since they already have a higher level of ability at the start of the job.

However, the assumption of homogeneity cannot be accepted easily. In practice, the effect of education seems to be universal and general, and is likely to enhance the efficiency of on-the-job training, which we call trainability. If so, even though the age–income curve remains convex upward, workers with higher schooling levels tend to choose higher learning densities of on-the-job training. In this case, the slope of the age–wage profile is steeper for those with the higher schooling levels.

Learning-by-Doing and the Concept of Human Investment by the User Cost Approach

As regards investment in general learning, there is often confusion about how we recognize investment costs. A typical situation is the case of learning-by-doing, which does not require separate training time.[19] In our formulation, the case is expressed by

$$g(0) > 0, \quad g'(\lambda) = 0.$$

Indeed, there are many reports of the occurrence of this type of learning in manufacturing industries, such as the existence of the 'learning curve' in the production of ships and aircraft. It is likely that there is a strong element of learning-by-doing in many specialized, administrative, or technical jobs. The reason is that knowledge or learning in these jobs is derived both from the daily acquisition and analysis of information and the making of decisions, and from the organization and generalization of information by feedback from routine working.

Here, we assume that job B involves the learning effect as stated above, but that job A does not. In this case, point B(0) moves to the point $B''(0)$ in Figure 3.8. As before, each worker compares the sum of the present values of income on each job. In the figure, job B is chosen under interest rate r, but job A is chosen under interest rate r'. Under interest rate r, a worker sacrifices part of current income

$$\overline{AR} = w_A k_A(x) - w_B k_B(x).$$

Thus, in the future, he will increase his income by

$$\overline{B''(0)R} = w_B k_B(\{1 + g(0)\}x) - w_A k_A(x).$$

If we regard the former as a cost and the latter as a return, this action might be regarded as a productive investment, the return rate of which is higher than the rate of interest on financial investments. Indeed, Becker proposes this kind of interpretation (1964: 45–7).

---

[19]   Blaug (1976: 837) and Psacharopoulos and Layard (1979: 489–90) insist that there is no job that does not involve some learning-by-doing, and hence it is impossible to explain the path of income growth (the age-income profile) perfectly from the viewpoint of costs and returns in the human investment theory. However, their criticism lacks an alternative theoretical explanation of how to understand learning-by-doing, so that they then move on to questions of empirical consistency. Thus, their criticisms are not necessarily persuasive. As the present discussion goes on to show, in the opportunity cost approach that regards learning-by-doing as investment, the economic value of learning-by-doing depends on external factors such as the characteristics of other job opportunities, even when learning-by-doing clearly raises workers' productivity. This is the most unsatisfactory point in the opportunity cost approach.

If we follow this interpretation of opportunity costs as investment, the following remarks are obvious: (i) workers who have an ability most suitable for job A make no investment; (ii) also, workers who have abilities sufficiently suitable for job B make no investment because, in the first period, their income on job B is higher than that on job A; (iii) only workers having abilities between (i) and (ii) make an investment.

However, there is a sense of incongruity in this interpretation of investment cost. It is because the size of the input cost and the actual return on learning (i.e., the size of human capital accumulation) do not match well. Consider two examples. First, workers of type (ii) in the above argument can obtain a strictly positive return at no cost. In other words, their rate of return on investment is infinite given the result of learning. However, the infinite rate is merely a mathematical convenience. Second, suppose that learning-by-doing occurs in job A. The workers who have a comparative advantage for job A, who used to give up part of their current income and choose job B to get the return on learning-by-doing, now do not have to do so. Therefore, workers of type (iii), described above, decrease. As a result, a paradox occurs in the economy: the volume of investment decreases in terms of opportunity cost, but the accumulation of workers' economic abilities increases. (In Figure 3.9, shown later, $\triangle PQR$ corresponds to an amount of investment. When there is the same degree of learning-by-doing opportunity in job A as in job B, this triangle disappears.) Therefore, it is not a satisfactory explanation to regard the increased abilities of workers through learning-by-doing as the return brought by the input of opportunity cost.

Is there any alternative way of looking at this? One possibility is to see it from the viewpoint of user cost: the cost is derived from the worker's choice of use (or job) in which to use his productive abilities. In the following discussion, we call this 'the user cost approach', in contrast to the opportunity cost approach. The approach yields a logically consistent definition of human investment and income, which leads to a correct choice criterion for job and learning opportunities (Ishikawa 1988a). Here, we follow Keynes (1936: 53–5) to explain user cost.

The idea of user cost was originally introduced to explain the depreciation in value of the capital equipment used in the production processes of firms. Now, suppose that, when a firm uses its capital equipment in production for one period while it spends an optimal amount on its maintenance and improvement, the value of the capital at the end of the term (i.e. the present value of the future net incomes) becomes G. Suppose that the firm has spent B on the maintenance and improvement of its capital equipment. If the firm had not used the equipment in production during the period, the capital would have been worth G' at the end of the period. Even if the firm had decided not to use the equipment, there is, nevertheless, a certain optimal sum B' which it would have spent on maintenance and improvements. B and B' are regarded as investment expenditure in a narrow sense since real resources including time are used.

$G - B$ and $G' - B'$ are the net value of the capital equipment at the end of the period after the costs of maintenance and improvement are subtracted. The size of the difference between $G - B$ and $G' - B'$ depends on whether the capital equipment has been used in the period. We define this difference $(G' - B') - (G - B)$ as 'the user cost', which we denote by U.

The user cost is a part of the firm's current costs, like other factor costs. The 'investment' by the firm is defined as the net total expenditure A_1 on the capital equipment in this period after the user cost is subtracted. Employing the usual terminology, A_1 and $A_1 - U$ correspond to the gross and net investment respectively. The 'income' of the firm is defined as $A - U$: the value of the products A minus the user cost. Observe that the capital equipment referred to above can be thought of as including capital in a broad sense, such as raw materials, work in process, and inventories.[20,21]

Here, workers can be regarded as producers using their economic abilities as capital, and user cost is defined for them in the same manner as for firms. Recall the previous model. The user cost is measured as the difference in abilities for earnings at the end of the period depending on whether they have engaged in the job or not done so.

When a worker chooses job A in the first period, his user cost is zero, regardless of the ability position x. No matter whether he has engaged in the job or not, his abilities for earnings in the second period are not changed, since there is no learning opportunity.

On the other hand, when a worker chooses job B in the first period, doing the job causes the occurrence of learning-by-doing and changes his ability for earnings in the second period. From the assumption of learning-by-doing, he always uses no resources for the improvement in his economic ability: $B = B' = 0$. Hence, the user cost is $G - G'$. Note that this value is measured in terms of the present value at the beginning of the first period.

The user cost on job B depends on the position of workers' ability position x. See Figure 3.9. In the figure, the following curves are shown: the curve $w_A k_A$ means the marginal value product $w_A k_A(x)$ on job A; the curve $w_B k_B$ means the

---

[20] To help understand these definitions, consider the following case of production and material inventories management at a firm. Wages of $4,000 and materials worth $3,000 are necessary to produce $10,000 worth of output at the firm. Suppose that the optimal stock of materials for smooth production stands at $5,000 at the beginning of production. In this case, $G' = G = \$5,000$, $B' = 0$, and $B = \$3,000$. Then, user cost becomes $U = (G' - B') - (G - B) = \$3,000$. The firm's income is $7,000 (subtracting user cost (U) from outputs (A)). Investment by the firm is zero (deducting user cost $3,000 ($U$) from the firm's expenditure on inventory supply $3,000 ($A_1$)).

[21] The definition of user cost has an important characteristic: it assumes the possibility that the firm does not use some of the capital equipment. When the idea is applied to human investment, as we do below, this corresponds to the possibility of unemployment. Indeed, the user cost approach proposed later has an important merit: the definition is applicable even in an economy with unemployment. On the other hand, the occurrence of unemployment is not considered in the opportunity cost approach. Unfortunately, further investigation of this point is beyond the scope of this book.

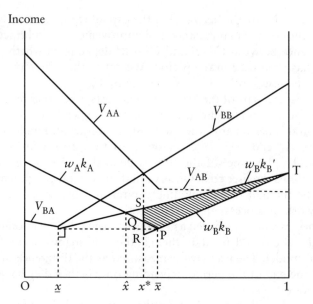

Figure 3.9. *Learning by Doing as Human Investment*

marginal value product $w_B k_B(x)$ on job B before learning; the curve $w_B k'_B$ expressed as a function of x instead of x' means the value $w_B k_B(x')$ after learning. (Note that position x' corresponds to x at which the horizontal line from the point on the curve $w_B k'_B$ crosses the curve $w_B k_B$.) In addition, the curves V_{ij} $(i, j = A, B)$ indicate the sum of the present values of the marginal value product when a worker works on job i in the first period and job j in the second period. Four points of intersection from the left of the figure are as follows: $\underline{x}$ for V_{BA} and V_{BB}, $\hat{x}$ for $w_A k_A$ and $w_B k'_B$, x^* for V_{AA} and V_{BB}, and $\bar{x}$ for $w_A k_A$ and $w_B k_B$. $\bar{x}$ or $\hat{x}$ is the critical value from the principle of static comparative advantage before or after learning respectively. x^* is the critical value of optimal job selection for two periods. (See Ishikawa 1988*a*: 342–4 for the complete proof.) $\underline{x}$ is the critical point such that, in the second period, a worker moves to job A to recover the loss of the first period when he has mistakenly chosen job B instead of job A in the first period.

Using Figure 3.9, the user cost on job B given x is computed as follows. First, in the case of x less than $\underline{x}$, the ability for earnings is $w_A k_A(x')$ in the second period from the definition of $\underline{x}$. On the other hand, if a worker does not work, the ability is $w_A k_A(x)$ since the effects of learning-by-doing do not materialize. Hence, the user cost in this period is

$$\frac{w_A k_A(x) - w_A k_A(x')}{1 + r}.$$

This value is positive. Second, in the case of x between $\underline{x}$ and $\bar{x}$, the ability for earnings in the second period is $w_B k_B(x')$ if he works; otherwise, it is $w_A k_A(x)$. Thus, the user cost is

$$\frac{w_A k_A(x) - w_B k_B(x')}{1+r},$$

and the value becomes negative from positive at $\hat{x}$ in the middle. Third, in the case of x between $\bar{x}$ and 1, the user cost is

$$\frac{w_B k_B(x) - w_B k_B(x')}{1+r},$$

and it is always negative.

The above results are summarized in the user cost column in Table 3.1. In the table, for each case, we show the gross income A in the first period, and the net income (which is the gross income minus the user cost U, and corresponds to income $A - U$ by Keynes's definition). Workers will compare the net incomes of job A and job B and choose the job with the higher value. Therefore, clearly, job A is chosen between 0 and $\underline{x}$, job B between $\bar{x}$ and 1. For values between $\underline{x}$ and $\bar{x}$, job selection depends on the relative sizes of $V_{AA}(x)$ and $V_{BB}(x)$. Hence x^* becomes the critical point of job selection and our user cost approach yields the same job selection standard as the opportunity cost approach.

Investment $(A_1 - U)$ defined by the user cost approach is identical to $-U$, which is the negative user cost because investment expenditure A_1 on outside

Table 3.1. *Learning by Doing and the User Cost*

Ability position	Job	Gross income	User cost	Net income
$0 \leq x \leq \underline{x}$	A	$w_A k_A(x)$	$\dfrac{w_A k_A(x) - w_A k_A(x)}{1+r} = 0$	$w_A k_A(x)$
	B	$w_B k_B(x)$	$\dfrac{w_A k_A(x) - w_A k_A(x')}{1+r} > 0$	$w_B k_B(x) - \dfrac{w_A k_A(x) - w_A k_A(x')}{1+r}$
$\underline{x} \leq x \leq \bar{x}$	A	$w_A k_A(x)$	$\dfrac{w_A k_A(x) - w_A k_A(x)}{1+r} = 0$	$w_A k_A(x)$
	B	$w_B k_B(x)$	$\dfrac{w_A k_A(x) - w_A k_B(x')}{1+r} \gtrless 0$ $\Leftrightarrow \quad x \gtrless \hat{x}$	$\left\{ w_B k_B(x) + \dfrac{w_B k_B(x') - w_A k_A(x)}{1+r} \right\}$
$\bar{x} \leq x \leq 1$	A	$w_A k_A(x)$	$\dfrac{w_B k_B(x) - w_B k_B(x)}{1+r} = 0$	$w_A k_A(x)$
	B	$w_B k_B(x)$	$\dfrac{w_B k_B(x) - w_B k_B(x')}{1+r} < 0$	$\left\{ w_B k_B(x) + \dfrac{w_B k_B(x') - w_B k_B(x)}{1+r} \right\}$

Table 3.2. *Investment under Learning by Doing*

Ability position	Opportunity cost approach	User cost approach
$0 \leq x \leq x^*$	0	0
$x^* \leq x \leq \bar{x}$	$w_A k_A(x) - w_B k_B(x)$	$\dfrac{w_B k_B(x') - w_A k_A(x)}{1 + r}$
$\bar{x} \leq x \leq 1$	0	$\dfrac{w_B k_B(x') - w_B k_B(x)}{1 + r}$

opportunities is zero. We summarize the size of investment on the job actually chosen in Table 3.2. This table also gives a comparison with the opportunity cost approach. Note that, when we assume uniform distribution of abilities, the total sum of investment in the entire economy is equal to the area of the shaded quadrilateral PQST in Figure 3.9 divided by $(1 + r)$. This makes a contrast with $\triangle$PQR, which is the total sum of investment under the opportunity cost approach. However, the problem that the increase in human investment does not always raise productivity, which is encountered in the opportunity cost approach, disappears in the user cost approach.

In general, the approach that regards human investment as a negative user cost can be applied not only to learning-by-doing but also to on-the-job training that requires workers' time. In the same manner as in the previous section, the standards of investment and job selection can be deduced (Ishikawa (1988a: 338–40). In this case,

$$A_1 = B = \lambda^* w_B k_B(x)$$

constitutes a part of the investment expenditure. Therefore, this new approach is a perfect alternative to the opportunity cost approach.

The above argument has shown that learning-by-doing can be regarded as a situation where the user cost is negative. The negative user cost is equivalent to the expenditure on the negative depreciation cost. In this regard, it is no doubt an expenditure on human investment. However, it is important to distinguish it from human investment in the narrow sense, that is, one which increases economic abilities by the input of physical resources like time.

Firm-Specific Skills

It is possible that some skills acquired by workers on the job are of value only in their present firm. For blue-collar and lower-level white-collar workers, the main elements of skills are concrete and routine. Even though they become familiar with the tasks required of them in a particular workplace (such as checking the conditions of pieces of equipment regulated and modified individually), the particular rules of management in a firm (such as methods of contacting another department, and writing out slips and accounting books), or the operations of and relations with the members of a particular team are usually not useful in other firms (see Piore 1975 and section 5.3). Workers in the real economy know that they might be dismissed for such reasons as lay-off, or they might find better jobs in the near future. So they would have no motivation to obtain these firm-specific skills at their own expense.

On the other hand, firms benefit considerably if they can take advantage of these skills. A firm then has an incentive to pay for the training of employees in firm-specific skills, at the risk of losing some of the return on investment through declines in demand or resignations of workers in a subsequent period. Hence we start examining the significance of firm-specific skills from an idealized situation in which a firm has no worries about future demand or resignations.

To begin with, we should note the possibility that opportunities for learning firm-specific skills contain different implications from those for general skills. It has already been pointed out that a firm cannot monopolize the provision of learning opportunities for general skills or collect more than the opportunity cost from employees in the long run. As regards a firm-specific skill, however, the learning opportunity itself can be an element of a scarce managerial resource in the firm. That is, it is impossible in other firms not only to employ the skill but also to duplicate the opportunity to learn it; such skills reflect, for example, idiosyncratic arrangements for the maintenance of equipment, and management of a production process or personnel matters. Of course such properties are not shared by all firm-specific skills. The learning opportunities for some skills can be duplicated easily in other firms even though the result of learning (knowledge) is not portable. For those skills, it is easy to guess that the rent for firms providing the learning opportunities would vanish, as in the case of general skills. From the theoretical viewpoint, only the skills for which the learning opportunities are scarce managerial resources require new treatment. We consider this case in the following discussion. In the real workplace, learning opportunities are available outside firms for some of the skills needed by workers. When learning opportunities are not available outside firms for the majority of firm-specific skills, the following argument becomes more relevant.

Consider the two-period model again. As in the previous analysis of a general skill, only job B is assumed to provide opportunities for learning skills. Figure 3.10 is an adaptation of Figure 3.8 to the case of a firm-specific skill. The initial position of ability of a worker is denoted by x, and the point B(0) on the 45-degree line is the marginal value product $m_B(x)$ in the first and second periods, if the worker acquires no skill. (The reason for expressing the marginal value product in this way will soon be understood.) The curve B(0)B(1) is, as in Figure 3.8, the frontier showing how much the marginal value product in the second period goes up at the cost of that in the first period. In this figure, however, this frontier is relevant only if the worker stays in this firm. Unlike the formation of a general skill, the formation of firm-specific skills occurs as if the worker were lending his body to the firm and permitting unconditional investment in it. This is an important implication of firm-specific skills. In the

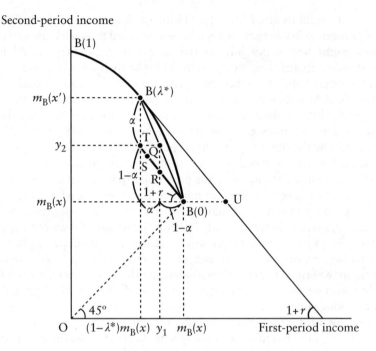

Figure 3.10. *Optimal Investment in Firm-Specific Skills*

idealized situation discussed above, therefore, investment in a firm-specific skill is a purely private matter for the firm.

In this situation, the firm gains all the return on the investment while the worker has the income corresponding to $B(0)$. Then the optimal investment rate λ^* is determined, as in the case of a general skill, at the point where the marginal rate of return on investment is equal to the given market interest rate. This point is $B(\lambda^*)$ on the frontier. The firm attains a higher average rate of return than the market interest rate at this point, because the figure assumes that the learning opportunity is a managerial resource specific to the firm.[22]

But in the real world a firm cannot force an employee to stay until the next period. The worker's employment contract in the situation discussed above does not give the worker a positive incentive to stay. Can the firm in the model find a way to secure the maximum return by preventing the worker from resigning?

One solution is the introduction of a positively-sloped wage profile designed to prevent a worker from leaving (Donaldson and Eaton 1976; Salop and Salop 1976). This is just a seniority wage contract. The logic is simple.

---

[22] For the argument that educational opportunities are not scarce, see the discussion in section 6.1 on the causes of true disparity of wages.

Assuming perfect capital markets, workers are indifferent among income patterns with the same present value. If the contract at point B(0) in Figure 3.10 is acceptable to a worker, any contract corresponding to a point on the line having the slope $-(1+r)$ and passing through B(0) is also acceptable. Suppose that the firm offers a contract on this line, at a point to the left of B(0) (say S). Then it can provide the worker with sufficient incentives to stay, without any loss of return.

However, this solution does not seem to be readily acceptable to a worker in the real economy. This is because the seniority wage is a form of compulsory saving within the firm.[23] In other words, workers lend the firm not only their bodies to invest but also their funds. A worker would not be so naïve as to accept such a contract. Having freer outside opportunities for saving, with the same interest rate, why do employees deposit their funds in the firm? When capital markets are imperfect, this sort of contract becomes more questionable.

Thus we have reached Becker's original idea, that is, proposing an investment partnership to the worker in order to give an incentive for him not to quit. Let the firm pay α $(0 < \alpha < 1)$ of investment cost and the worker pay the residual, $1 - \alpha$ of the cost. The return is also shared in the same ratio. This contract does not change the optimal investment level, but the worker's income in each period becomes

$$y_1 = (1 - (1 - \alpha)\lambda^*)m_B(x)$$

and

$$y_2 = \alpha m_B(x) + (1 - \alpha)m_B(x')$$

respectively. We have another positively-sloped wage profile (a seniority wage). In Figure 3.10, this is the contract at point Q. This seniority wage contract is essentially different from the previous one, compulsory saving, in the sense that the human capital investment directly raises the worker's income via the partnership. These contracts also reduce total employment by the firm, reflecting the fact that the payment to the worker is higher than the competitive level.

Becker does not discuss the determination of the sharing rate α. The larger α is better for the firm as long as it prevents the worker from resigning, while the smaller α is better for the worker as long as it ensures his or her future employment. Because of uncertainty about the future market, however, nothing can guarantee perfect avoidance of resignation or dismissal in the real economy. Taking such risks into consideration, therefore, α and optimum λ will be determined simultaneously. Furthermore, when a firm employs workers

---

[23] In many countries, firms are not permitted to offer workers such compulsory saving as a condition of continued employment. But such regulations are applied only to explicit saving, and do not cover the seniority wage contract referred to above.

for several periods, the group of workers gain bargaining power derived from their local monopoly of firm-specific skills. In the case of bilateral monopoly, determination of α would depend on the relative bargaining power of each side.

These circumstances lead the system of employment and income to depart from the model of pure competitive markets. We will discuss such a system in section 5.4.[24]

The Effects of Uncertainty

The above analysis assumes that future income is perfectly predictable. This assumption is not realistic. Investments in education and on-the-job training are in a sense even more fixed than capital investments, because they are embodied in human beings and such human capital cannot be resold. Thus these investments are sensitive to future uncertainty.

Uncertainty about investments in education and on-the-job training occurs for many reasons, but they are basically of three types. First, it is impossible to be sure of the quality of education and training beforehand. Second, the trainability of a worker, that is, how much the productivity of an individual effectively increases with a given amount of input, is uncertain. Third, a worker does not fully know how the future market will evaluate his or her accumulated economic abilities. The first two types of uncertainty relate to the process of investment, the third to the outcome.

Choosing a combination of risky investments and riskless ones is known as portfolio selection. In the case of education, however, portfolio selection differs from that in relation to financial assets in the sense that the amount of investment itself affects its marginal return and risk. An investment decision is greatly influenced by whether the risk is increasing or decreasing with respect to the investment level. Let us examine this point by using the two-period model on the learning opportunities of a general skill (returning to Figure 3.8). Suppose that the value of $(m_B(x') - m_B(x))$, which is the return on investment of an individual with initial ability x, putting $\lambda \cdot m_B(x)$ into the learning opportunity of job B, depends on an uncertain factor μ. The worker does not know the realized value of μ until the second period. Thus the worker cannot determine the future consumption level, c_2, in advance. Assuming that μ is a random variable with a known probability distribution, each individual determines the current consumption level c_1 and the training investment level λ at the first period to maximize the expected utility $Eu(c_1, c_2)$ of lifelong consumption. Future consumption c_2 is determined at a level to ensure spending of all the budget, when the future income is realized.

---

[24] But it will be shown in section 5.4 that constructing a situation where the rules of competitive markets work fully is possible, even in such a world. In this sense, critical deviations from the principles of competitive markets do not occur even if firm-specific learning opportunities are predominant in learning opportunities as a whole.

The first modification of the model by the introduction of uncertainty is that it is no longer possible to separate the decisions on consumption and investment (the implications of which will be discussed later). The optimum investment condition is given by the equality of the marginal disutility of an additional unit of investment cost in terms of future consumption and the marginal expected utility of the additional return.[25]

As a reference point, let us introduce the certainty case, in which the individual is always paid the expected value of the return at each value of λ irrespective of the realized state. This can be seen as the situation where the individual is able to use complete insurance without any cost. Then, as we have already seen, the condition of optimum investment in education and on-the-job training occurs where marginal expected return equals marginal interest cost.

In the uncertainty case, if the risk is increasing—in the sense that the variance of the marginal rates of return under different states goes up as the investment level rises—the optimum investment level will be lower than in the certainty case. Similarly, if the risk is decreasing—in the sense that the variance of the marginal rates of return under different states goes down as the investment level rises—the investment level will be higher than in the certainty case. The reason for the increasing risk is as follows. Even though a positive shock causes the marginal return on the human investment to go up (while the interest cost is constant) its value is smaller, because of the decreasing marginal utility of consumption. On the other hand, a negative shock causes the marginal return to go down and the loss from it is given a larger value, for the same reason as above. The exact reverse happens in the case of decreasing risk. More intuitively, in the former case, the individual reduces the amount of human investment because the variance of future income rises. On the other hand, in the latter case, the level of investment will be increased, to avoid extremely low income and consumption.

As we have discussed above, the prediction of the model depends on whether the risk is increasing or decreasing. Which case is more realistic? The answer is

---

[25] Levhari and Weiss (1974) treat the theory of human investment under uncertainty in the most transparent style. Our argument here owes much to their analysis. The condition of optimum investment is given by:

$$E\left\{\frac{\partial u}{\partial c_0} - (1+r)\frac{\partial u}{\partial c_1}\right\} = 0$$

and

$$E\left\{\frac{\partial u}{\partial c_1}(-m_B(x)(1+r) + f_\lambda(\lambda, \mu; x))\right\} = 0,$$

where

$$m_B(x', \mu) - m_B(x) = f(\lambda, \mu; x).$$

dependent on the cause of uncertainty. If the uncertainty is of the first or second type that we have discussed, that is, uncertainty about the quality of education and training or about information on trainability, the risk is usually increasing. In the case of the third type of uncertainty, difficulties in forecasting the future market, the risk can be increasing or decreasing.

To see this point, let us return to the original model. Suppose that there exists uncertainty about the future income from job A caused by a market-wide shock (it makes little difference if we assume that opportunities for education and training also exist for job A). We consider a structural shift of demand to be the market-wide shock. That is, there exists a negative correlation between demands for job A and job B. Increasing risk corresponds to the case where both job A and job B require a specific ability. On the other hand, decreasing risk occurs when both jobs use general ability (See the argument in section 3.1). It is evident that the accumulation of specific ability is risky when there are possibilities of demand shifts. We could argue generally that when jobs depending on general ability prevail, higher levels of human investment would be achieved because of decreasing risk. When jobs requiring specific ability prevail, levels of human investment would be lower, because of increasing risk. These are the effects of risk with respect to market conditions. In the case of firm-specific skills, specific disturbances in each firm have an effect, adding to the possibilities of structural shift in the markets. Thus there are more factors reinforcing increasing risk, and workers' incentives to invest would become weaker.

Human Investment and Income Distribution

How can the theory of human investment be used to explain the disparity of personal incomes? Roughly speaking, two viewpoints exist. The first is the human capital hypothesis in the narrow sense, which insists that the main factors that explain the disparity of income are differences in the levels of direct and indirect investment in education and training. The second viewpoint sees the human capital theory as an analytical framework for explaining how differences in the background attributes of individuals, rather than investment levels such as innate ability and the socio-economic background of families, are transformed into differences in earning abilities (the first viewpoint does not ignore differences in background attributes but argues that they affect income distribution independently of human investment and are therefore not so influential).

Thus empirical studies adopting one or other of these viewpoints have different objectives. Researchers who take the first one, such as Becker and Mincer, are interested in how much of variance in personal incomes is explained by differences in years of schooling and years of experience (or years of service with a specific firm, if the possibility of firm-specific skill is taken into consideration), which are treated as proxies of investment in education and on-the-job training. Here the human capital hypothesis is considered more appropriate as it explains more of the variance in income. This line of research measures internal rates of return on investment in education and on-the-job training, and much energy has been denoted to it (see section 4.2). Researchers adopting the second viewpoint have tried to estimate how much each background attribute (directly or indirectly via investment in education and on-the-job training) contributes to disparities of income. These empirical studies estimate earnings functions (see sections 4.3 and 4.4).

As a preliminary step in evaluating the empirical resources, let us examine the theoretical relationship between the two viewpoints. First, consider the case of educational investment. If people have the same background attributes (the initial endowments of ability x_0 and the factors determining the parameter a) and if the capital markets are perfect, as we have already shown, equation (3.4) holds as the relation between income and years of schooling. That is, the disparity of income is equal to the difference in educational cost. This is a case in which the principle of equalizing difference is perfectly realized. The principle also holds in the case where training processes in general skills begin after schooling is completed. Even if various learning opportunities are offered by different jobs and firms, the present values of income over a lifetime, including the period of educational investment, must be equalized. The disparity of income is adjusted in the labour market to reflect the equalization. In this limited case, the principle of comparative advantage ceases to work.

Once we consider differences in background attributes among individuals, however, the principle of comparative advantage starts to work again, and disparity of (the present values of) lifelong income arises. We can directly apply the argument in section 3.1 to see how the disparity occurs. We take into account three differences in the initial conditions of individuals:

1. Differences in initial ability or trainability.
2. Differences in rates of interest for borrowing or in maximum sizes of loans.
3. Differences in quantities of non-human assets.

Differences in trainability vary investment opportunities by shifting the curve of the marginal rate of return on investment. The parameter a in function (3.3) has the same effect. The second factor is the problem known as capital market imperfection. The third includes differences in present values of future inheritances from parents, if capital markets are perfect. Although (3) is closely related to (2), it also works independently. Let us see the working of each item.

Differences in Initial Ability or Trainability
Trainability and initial ability have different effects. A rise in the former implies an improvement in investment opportunities and the level of investment in education and on-the-job training usually goes up. Even if individuals have the same initial abilities, differences in comparative advantage arise eventually, and income inequality occurs. Note that the degree of inequality becomes

smaller if ability distribution and job distribution are more congenial and, related to this, the degree of trainability varies between jobs.

How about differences in initial abilities? Among individuals working at the same job, one with a lower initial ability puts in more investment because of the higher returns to education and training. Differences in lifelong income decrease though the advantage of higher initial ability remains.

Capital Market Imperfection

Capital markets are imperfect for individuals in the real economy. Because slavery is forbidden in modern society, individuals cannot take out a mortgage on themselves. Let us consider the case where the rate of interest for borrowing (denoted by r_b) differs from the rate of interest for lending (denoted by r), as a weaker type of capital market imperfection. Realistically, accessibility to the capital market varies, reflecting the quantity of non-human assets held by each individual, and the borrowing rate is higher for the individual with fewer non-human assets. For simplicity, however, we assume that the borrowing rate is constant independently of asset positions. Needless to say, $r_b > r$ is assumed.

When capital markets are imperfect, it does not hold that the decision on investment in education and on-the-job training is independent of the consumption decision. The investment decision also depends on the quantity of non-human assets. This point can be easily illustrated by using the two-period model on general learning opportunities (we can apply the same argument to the case of educational investment).

Let us examine Figure 3.11. The curve $B_0 B_0'$ is the investment opportunity of the individual whose quantity of non-human assets (denoted by A) is zero (this curve corresponds to the curve $B(0)B(1)$ in Figure 3.8). Denote by $P(r)$ the point at which the curve is tangential to the line having the slope $-(1+r)$, and denote $P(r_b)$ the point at which the curve is tangential to the line having the slope $-(1+r_b)$. The consumption frontier is given by the curve $P_0 - P(r_b) - P(r) - P_0'$. Utility from consumption is represented by indifference curves. The level of investment in training depends on the pattern of these indifference curves. That is, if the consumption frontier is tangential to an indifference curve at a point on the line $P(r)P_0'$, the intensity of investment $\lambda^*(r)$, corresponding to the point $P(r)$, is chosen. If it is tangential at a point on the line $P_0 P(r_b)$, the intensity $\lambda^*(r_b)$, corresponding to the point $P(r_b)$, is chosen. In the intermediate case, where the consumption frontier is tangential to an indifference curve at a point on the curve $P(r) - P(r_b)$, this point directly determines the intensity of investment. Indifference curves in Figure 3.11 are drawn to be tangential to the consumption frontier at the point R on the line $P_0 P(r_b)$. When an individual has a (uniformly) higher rate of time preference, the indifference curves have steeper slopes and the lowest intensity of investment $\lambda^*(r_b)$ becomes more likely.

We can see how the intensity of investment depends on the initial endowment A of non-human assets, by changing its value to a positive. This causes a rightward parallel shift of the frontiers of investment and consumption, by the

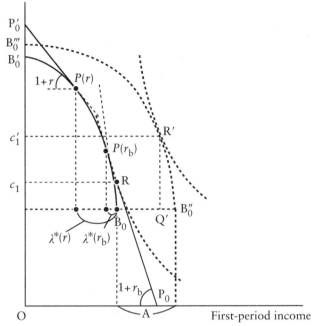

Figure 3.11. *Human Investment under Imperfect Capital Market Conditions*

precise amount of A. If both present and future consumption are normal goods, the point of tangency between the consumption frontier and the indifference curves moves as the value of A goes up, to the phase where the point directly determines the level of investment. And eventually, the point enters into the loan phase. The change in investment as this movement occurs is shown as the real curve in Figure 3.12.

From this figure, we can also deduce other comparative statics. When the rate of interest for borrowings goes up, the intensity of investment in the borrowing phase goes down. When the rate of time preference falls uniformly, the intensity of investment outside the loan phase rises uniformly.

The above argument is easily applicable to the case in which capital market imperfection arises as credit rationing. In the extreme case that a mortgage on future income is impossible, r_b is infinite and the borrowing phase in Figure 3.11 vanishes. Here we can see the significance of the public provision of student loans. This policy will reduce the phase in which an investment decision depends on the individual's initial endowment of non-human assets.

Differences in Quantities of Non-Human Assets

Even in perfect capital markets, levels of investment in education and on-the-job training can still depend on the quantity of non-human assets. First,

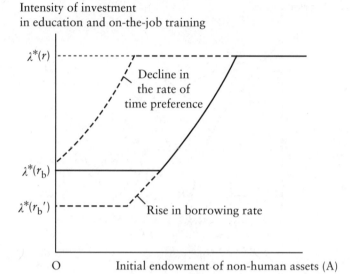

Figure 3.12. *Comparative Statics under Imperfect Capital Market Conditions*

experiences of education and training may not be just the subject of investment, but people may derive utility directly from them. Second, there is the case of uncertainty, which has already been discussed. If people have decreasing absolute risk aversion in their preference to risk, human investment with uncertain return becomes a normal good, and an individual raises the level of investment as the quantity of non-human assets increases.

In the real economy, these three kinds of difference work simultaneously and have composite effects on the distribution of income. Is there correlation between ability factors (1) and financial factors (2) and (3)? And if correlation exists at all, what causes it? These are important questions when we consider equality of income distribution. If a positive correlation exists, that is, an individual with the advantage of ability factors also has the advantage of financial factors, inequality of income will become serious. A negative correlation, however, will mitigate income disparity (see Becker 1967 or 1975: Appendix). It is clear that empirical research on the working of these factors is an important premise in examining policies designed to enhance equality of income. The second viewpoint acknowledge the contribution of the theory of human investment to those empirical studies.

3.3. SIGNALLING EQUILIBRIUM UNDER CONDITIONS OF ASYMMETRY OF INFORMATION

Another direction of theoretical extension is to analyse asymmetric information with respect to the ability of workers. When workers know their own ability to work but the employer does not know, the observable characteristics of individuals that are statistically correlated with the ability acquire economic values via this the informational difference, even when they themselves do not increase productivity. Employers pay higher wages to those with these characteristics and provide an incentive for workers to reveal their true abilities. Let us call these observable characteristics a signal. Schooling has been identified as one characteristic that functions as a signal (Spence 1973; Arrow 1973*b*). This subsection examines the equilibrium in the labour market that involves signalling.

The Labour Market under Conditions of Asymmetry of Information

Consider the situation where a worker knows the position *y* of his own ability, but neither the employer nor the other workers know it either before or after employment. The only thing that the employer knows is the average of marginal productivity among all the employed workers. We assume that the workers know that the employer's information is limited in this way.

Suppose that the distribution of job A and job B and that of ability are mutually congenial (Case I). As before, the wage rates w_A and w_B per efficiency unit are adjusted by demand and supply in the market. Under the above assumption that information is imperfect, the real wage reflects the average ability of the workers who work at a task and thus it is identical among those who do the same task for the same employer. There are two more important properties.

First, on a given task, the wage level tends to be equalized among firms and among workers. Let us imagine that the wage levels set prior to the employment and the average marginal productivities *ex post* do not coincide and that some firms make a surplus and some firms incur a loss. Employees in the firms with productivities higher than the average are wooed away by other firms while those in the firms with productivities lower than the average are dismissed or leave. However, since the group of workers who have been hired by the offer of a high wage cannot be distinguished from the incumbent workers *ex post*, their wage will eventually be reduced. In the same way, those who obtain a job at voluntarily lowered wages will obtain a higher wage that corresponds to the average productivity of both themselves and the incumbent workers *ex post*. In this way, competition equalizes average marginal productivity and wages among firms, and attains zero excess profits.[26]

---

[26] The crucial factor in the above discussion is the supposition that the productivity of the newly employed workers and that of the incumbent workers are not and cannot be distinguished. If they can be, then the employer can infer the quality of each worker by making a comparison with the productivity of the worker group to which the worker belonged before being recruited. However, this situation is inconsistent with the assumption of incomplete information.

Second, the wage for jobs A and B are also equalized. The market does not evaluate the individual ability position and only gives information about which job is paid a higher wage. Hence, as long as there is a wage difference, people keep changing jobs for higher wages. In this case, the relationship between the ability position and the choice of jobs is influenced by chance, and there is a possibility of a low-level equilibrium with extremely inefficient resource allocation. Moreover, though we have implicitly assumed that people work in either job, in reality, they have a reservation wage, which is based on the substitution between labour and leisure, and choose unemployment if the wage does not exceed the reservation wage. Hence, if the reservation wage increases as the worker's ability position y moves close to either 0 or 1, the supply of labour will be from those with a disadvantageous ability position, which is the situation of so-called adverse selection (Akerlof 1970). Even if the workers are allocated in equilibrium to utilize their knowledge to the maximum extent (that is, there is a threshold y such that those whose ability position is below this will work at job A and those whose ability position is above it work at job B), the fact that the wages for two jobs are the same does not change and thus the distortion in resource allocation remains.[27]

Some readers may ask why a worker, when he realizes that he happens to belong to a group that has high productivity, does not refuse to move to another firm since such a move is likely to reduce his income. Certainly, it is better for each worker to obtain from his or her current employer the pay rise that corresponds to their ability (by indicating that he or she might leave), instead of accepting a job offer from another firm. However, these workers cannot prohibit their employer from hiring other workers who are willing to bid down their own wages to obtain a job (which gives excess profits to the firm). Therefore, equalization occurs.

[27] Suppose that the most desirable situation arises and let v denote the boundary between job A and job B. When the distribution density function (the cumulative distribution function) of a worker's y is given by $f(y)$ and ($F(y)$ respectively), then the condition for the incomes from job A and job B to be equal is:

$$\frac{\int_0^v w_A k_A(y) f(y)\, dy}{\int_0^v f(y)\, dy} = \frac{\int_v^1 w_B k_B(y) f(y)\, dy}{\int_v^1 f(y)\, dy}.$$

From this, we obtain:

$$q = \frac{w_A}{w_B} = \frac{F(v)}{1 - F(v)} = \frac{\int_v^1 k_B(y) f(y)\, dy}{\int_0^v k_A(y) f(y)\, dy}.$$

By applying the mean value theorem to both the numerator and the denominator of the right-hand side, we can show that there exist constants λ and λ' (both of which are between 0 and 1) such that:

$$q = \frac{k_B(v + \lambda'(1 - v))}{k_A((1 - \lambda)v)}.$$

By the way, even though $k_B(v + \lambda'(1 - v)) > k_A(v)$ and $k_B((1 - \lambda)v) > k_A(v)$, the ratio between the left-hand sides of these inequalities is not equal to $k_B(v)/k_A(v)$ except coincidentally. Therefore, the principle of comparative advantage is not generally satisfied.

Equilibrium with Signalling

When a worker can inform a potential employer of a variable that is related with his ability position y through his own economic activity, such an economic activity is called signalling, using the term developed by Spence (1973, 1974).

The level of educational investment s is a typical example of a signal. If the cost of educational investment is related to y, we can infer the size of y by looking at how much education a worker has obtained. Let z be the factor that influences the cost of education ($0 \leq z \leq 1$) and suppose that:

$$y = z + u. \tag{3.5}$$

Here, u is white noise, independent of z. It has[28] the expected value of 0 and variance of σ_u^2. The factor z can be interpreted as the expected value of the true ability position y. In the following discussion, z is called the expected ability position. The employer knows that the distribution of y among workers is generated by this structure but does not know either the z or the u of an individual worker. On the other hand, we assume that a worker knows at least the value of his own z. (It does not matter in the following argument whether the worker knows the values of his own u.) In this sense, we assume asymmetry of information. We suppose that different types of education are required for different jobs and that the cost of education for job A is $c_A(z)$ and that for job B is $c_B(z)$. In the following discussion, we assume that these functions are given by:

$$c_A(z) = \frac{1}{1-z}, \quad c_B(z) = \frac{1}{z}. \tag{3.6}$$

Compared with (3.5), this assumption is that the cost of education is counter-proportional to the distance on the circle between the expected ability position and the position most desirable for each job. (This specification is by no means essential.)

On the other hand, if revenue depends on the level of education needed for each job, then workers choose the level of education that will maximize their net income (revenue minus costs), and then choose the job, A or B (and the corresponding level of education), that gives the higher net income. Here, what

---

[28] Because of the constraint that $0 \leq y \leq 1$, strictly speaking, taking the domain of z between 0 and 1 causes a problem at both ends. By considering the symmetry of the circle, it is possible to deal with the problem at both ends rigorously. However, it does not change the nature of the argument and we will ignore this issue in this analysis. Note that, when the variance of z is given by σ_z^2, the correlation coefficient between y and z is:

$$\frac{\sigma_z^2}{\sigma_z^2 + \sigma_u^2}.$$

produces the return on education? In the previous section, we considered the case where education enhances productivity and thus produces the return. There is a completely different reason for the return on education. The employer may pay a premium for education, in order to solicit from workers the information about z which is not directly observable. This is known as signalling by education. In the following analysis, we omit the effect of education on productivity.

The reason why the information about z has value is as follows. Let us imagine, as a starting point, that all the workes receive the same wage (as explained in the previous subsections). In this situation, the workers do not obtain any education. Now, suppose that one firm, taking a new, creative approach, offers to employ those who have an educational level above $\underline{s}$ (which can be small) in either job with a small premium in addition to the current wage. When the premium is small, those who invest to education above $\underline{s}$ will be either those who have a z near to zero (in the case of job A) or those who have a z near to 1 (in the case of job B). However, by equation (3.5) and the law of large number, those workers who apply to work for this firm will have a much higher average marginal productivity than the previous average (= the same wage level) and thus the firm will obtain large excess profits.

The generation of excess profits motivates other firms to follow the same course. Moreover, it may even give other firms an incentive to take other creative initiatives. For example, one firm may hire those who have the education level s', which is a little higher than $\underline{s}$ and is paid a premium that is also a little higher. By doing so, this firm can hire more productive workers. If this type of trial is repeated, then there will be a monotonically increasing relationship between schooling level and wage level, which is called the 'wage schedule', and the worker's expected ability position z becomes informationally distinguishable. To describe what happens ultimately, we examine two different cases: first, where there is only one job and then the case of two jobs, job A and job B.

Informationally Separating Equilibrium with a Single Type of Job

We first study the eventual market equilibrium when there is only job B. The conditions for market equilibrium are, first, each worker chooses his or her level of education rationally, second, no employer wants to change the wage schedule, and, third, demand and supply of labour are in equilibrium. It is obvious that the third condition is achieved by the adjustment of the market parameter w_B (the wage level per efficiency unit). Hence, in the following analysis, we confine our attention to the first and the second conditions by taking w_B as exogenous. The situation where the first and second conditions are satisfied is generally called a 'signalling equilibrium'.

The first condition can be decomposed to two conditions:

(a) the expected net income of educational investment is maximized, and
(b) the maximized expected net income is more than the minimum expected income without educational investment.

As first pointed out by Spence, the second condition (in the previous paragraph) can be decomposed to two further conditions:

(c) the ability position z of each worker can be informationally separated completely, and
(d) each employer obtains zero expected excess surplus.

A signalling equilibrium that satisfies conditions (a), (b), (c), and (d) is called 'an informationally separating equilibrium'. It should be noted that a criticism has been made, to the effect that condition (c) is not appropriate as a condition required a priori for maximization of the employer's expected profit. We will discuss this criticism later.

Using conditions (a) and (d), we can derive the characteristics of the form of the wage schedule. For ease of discussion, we assume in the following that the ability curve $k_B(y)$ takes the linear form,

$$w_B k_B(y) = w_B(1 - k_B + k_B y),\qquad(3.7)$$

where k_B is a positive constant.

When we regard the wage schedule $W_B(s)$ as an unknown function of s from the condition (a), s is chosen so that, for any z,

$$W'_B(s) = \frac{1}{z}\qquad(3.8)$$

$$W''_B(s) < 0.\qquad(3.9)$$

Hence, there is a monotonically increasing relationship between s and z. Moreover, the wage schedule has to be convex upward. On the other hand, condition (d) is equivalent to the situation in which, given any educational level, expected marginal productivity and wages are equal for the group of workers whose educational level is informationally separated. Hence, from (3.5) and (3.7), for any pair (s, z) that satisfies (3.8), it is satisfied that:

$$W_B(s) = w_B(1 - k_B + k_B z).\qquad(3.10)$$

By substituting $z = 1/W'_B(s)$, which we obtain from (3.8), into z in (3.10), we get the first order differential equation that the unknown function $W_B(s)$ should satisfy. The general solution is given by:

$$W_B(s) = \sqrt{2 w_B k_B s + C_B} + w_B(1 - k_B),\qquad(3.11)$$

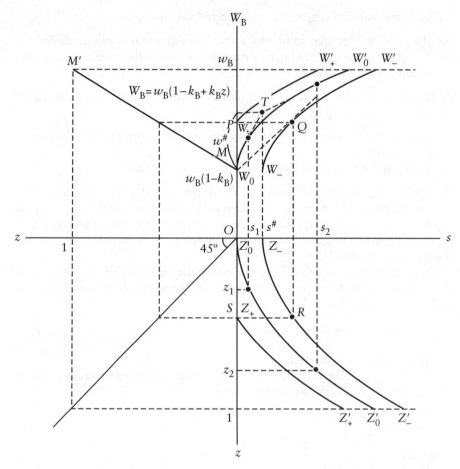

Figure 3.13. *Informationally Separating Equilibrium with a Single Type of Job*

where C_B is a constant. Thus, the wage schedule takes the form of a sideways parabolic curve (which confirms that condition (3.9) is satisfied).[29]

In the first quadrant of Figure 3.13, we give three examples of the solution of (3.11): one for a negative C_B, one for zero C_B, and one for a positive C_B. In the

---

[29] Define $\Omega_B(s) = W_B(s) - w_B(1 - k_B)$. Then, the differential equation in question can be expressed as:

$$\frac{w_B k_B}{\Omega'_B(s)} = \Omega_B(s).$$

(Note that $\Omega'_B(s) = W'_B(s)$.) Since this equation is equivalent to

$$\{\Omega'_B(s)^2\} = 2w_B k_B,$$

we obtain the general solution in the main text immediately.

second quadrant, the line MM' represents the expected marginal productivity that corresponds to each example. Three curves W_+W_+', W_0W_0', and W_-W_-' in the first quadrant, through the above line in the second quandrant and the 45-degree line in the third quadrant, create three images Z_+Z_+', Z_0Z_0', and Z_-Z_-' in the fourth quadrant. These curves describe the correspondence between education level and z for each wage schedule.

From the above, we can identify the shapes of the wage schedule that satisfies conditions (a) and (d). However, we have not solved how the constant C_B is determined. If it can take any value, then it means that there are an infinite number of equilibria. Fortunately, by using conditions (b) and (c), which have not so far been utilized, we can uniquely identify the value of C_B to be zero. The reason is as follows.

First, when $C_B > 0$ as in case of the curve W_+W_+' in Figure 3.13, the corresponding curve Z_+Z_+' has a positive intercept $z = Z_+$ on the z-axis. In this case, those with z below Z_+ are not informationally separated and thus condition (c) is not satisfied. Hence, when $C_B > 0$, it is not in equilibrium.

Next, when $C_B < 0$ as in the case of the curve W_-W_-', it looks as if the value of each z was informationally separated. However, for those with z close to 0, their maximized expected net income from the educational investment would be less than the minimum wage level $w_B(1 - k_B)$, which this system guarantees. Look at the point Q on the curve W_-W_-' in the figure. This point is chosen so that the line tangential to the curve at this point crosses the vertical axis at the point M. Let the point P be the point where the horizontal line from the point Q crosses the vertical axis. (It happens, by coincidence, that it takes the same position as W_+.) From (3.8), the wage that corresponds to the point P is given by the length of the line OP, and the cost of education is given by the length of the line MP. Hence, the net income of education is given by OM, which is equal to $w_B(1 - k_B)$. On the points to the left of point P, the educational investment is clearly not profitable and is not undertaken. Hence, on the points to the left of the corresponding point R on the curve Z_-Z_-' (below point Z_+ on the z axis), the information about z is not separated. Hence, when $C_B < 0$, conditions (b) and (c) are not satisfied and it cannot happen in equilibrium.

The above arguments show that the informationally separating equilibrium does not occur except when $C_B = 0$. In fact, it is easy to see that conditions (b) and (c) are both satisfied when $C_B = 0$. Therefore, the curve W_0W_0' is the only wage schedule that brings about the informationally separating equilibrium. The relationship between z and the level of schooling is represented by Z_0Z_0'. When $z = 0$, the level of schooling is zero and it increases as z increases.

Informationally Separating Equilibrium with Multiple Types of Job

We now consider the informationally separating equilibrium when both job A and job B are present. Here, given the wage schedule of each job, the worker

Income and Wealth

chooses the job, and also the type and level of education, where the information (z) of the expected ability position is separated. There is a possibility that efficient allocation of abilities is achieved, even if it is based on expected values. We have argued that, when there is no signal, the allocation of workers to jobs is affected by chance and the low-level equilibrium with inefficient matches between abilities and jobs may arise. Compared to that, the situation has improved with signalling since the choice of job is made rationally. On the other hand, the other form of inefficiency may arise. When there are multiple jobs, workers may overinvest in education and the allocation may be distorted in equilibrium. We study these issues by using our model. In the following analysis, we denote the level of education for job A by s_A and that for job B by s_B.

The ability curve of job A, like that of job B, is represented by the linear form:

$$w_A k_A(y) = w_A(1 - k_A y), \tag{3.12}$$

where k_A is a positive constant.

When we denote the wage schedule of job A by $W_A(s_A)$, from conditions (a) and (d), the following conditions have to hold:

$$W_A'(s_A) = \frac{1}{1 - z} \tag{3.13}$$

$$W_A''(s_A) < 0 \tag{3.14}$$

$$W_A(s_A) = w_A(1 - k_A z), \tag{3.15}$$

which correspond respectively to (3.8), (3.9), and (3.10) for job B. Hence, the wage schedule for job A is given by:

$$W_A(s_A) = \sqrt{2w_A k_A s_A + C_A} + W_A(1 - k_A), \tag{3.16}$$

where C_A is a constant, and has the same structure as $W_B(s_B)$.

So far, we have assumed that there were no other jobs when we derived (3.11) and (3.16). In practice, each worker chooses a job based on comparison of the expected net incomes given the optimal educational investment for each job. Hence, some part of the wage schedule is not selected. In fact, the level of C_A and C_B are determined by where the boundary between two jobs is located on the scale of z.

In the same way as in the case of the single job, conditions (b) and (c) function as constraints in determining C_A and C_B. However, it is immediately obvious that we cannot determine these values just by adding these extra constraints. The wage schedule of each job does not have to separate information over the entire region of z by itself. For condition (c) to be satisfied, we only need the existence of some value of z such that, for those above this value, the wage schedule for job B separates information, and, for those below this value, the wage schedule for job A separates information of z. (We denote this boundary by $\hat{z}$ hereafter.) Hence, for either positive or negative C_A and C_B within the finite domain, the informationally separating equilibrium that satisfies conditions (a), (b), (c), and (d) exists. In the following, we give examples for two cases. The first example depicts an efficient informationally separating equilibrium, and the second depicts an inefficient informationally separating equilibrium with excessive educational investment.

Figure 3.14 describes an efficient signalling equilibrium. It is defined as an equilibrium where the educational level for either job is zero at the boundary between jobs. From assumption (3.6), we remember, education becomes more costly as z moves further away from the ability position that matches each job best. In terms of the minimization of educational costs, it is desirable that the wage schedule be specified so that the minimum (zero) education is chosen at the boundary. Then, the boundary is given by the z that lies where the expected marginal productivity curves of job A and job B cross. That value is denoted by

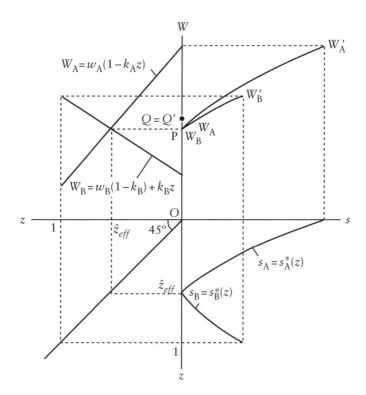

Figure 3.14. *Efficient Informationally Separating Equilibrium*

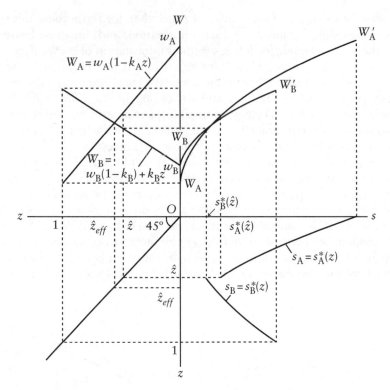

Figure 3.15. *Inefficient Informationally Separating Equilibrium*
Note: $C_A = 0$, $C_B = 0$.

$\hat{z}_{eff}$ (see Appendix 3.1, mathematical note 6). That is, the choice of job made by each individual employs the principle of comparative advantage that is based on the information of expected marginal productivity. Hence, this equilibrium is efficient but, since it is not based on true y and also since the revelation of information is costly, it is the second-best equilibrium.[30]

By contrast, Figure 3.15 illustrates the separating equilibrium where C_A and C_B are both zero. This equilibrium is doubly inefficient since the boundary $\hat{z}$ between jobs is distant from the crossing point $\hat{z}_{eff}$ of the expected marginal productivity curves and since the educational investment is positive at the boundary. From the viewpoint of information revelation, there is clearly overinvestment. In the figure, we are supposing that $w_B(1 - k_B) > w_A(1 - k_A)$. In this case, $\hat{z}$ is smaller than $\hat{z}_{eff}$ and, from the principle of comparative advantage, the supply to job B is excessive (see Appendix 3.1, mathematical note 7). Note that the possibility of excessive educational investment was

---

[30] It is not clear which is the more efficient: the second-best equilibrium here or the situation discussed in footnote 27.

pointed out by Spence (1974) and Arrow (1973b). The above discussion shows that it entails distortion of labour allocation at the same time.

In general, there are a number of inefficient equilibria, as in Figure 3.15. Why is there a counter-force that precludes the emergence of inefficient equilibrium? It is possible if workers who know the system thoroughly recognize the expected marginal productivity $w_A(1 - k_A \hat{z}_{eff})(= w_B(1 - k_B + k_B \hat{z}_{eff}))$ that corresponds to $\hat{z}_{eff}$ as the attainable expected net income, and never make the educational investment that causes the net income to fall lower than that. This is a strengthened constraint of condition (b) where there is perfect foresight on the part of the workers. However, although the assumption of perfect foresight is effective in showing the logical limit, its validity in reality is rather questionable.

Inefficient informationally separating equilibrium can be excluded by an argument that does not assume perfect foresight by workers, as we explain later. However, this argument is a double-edged sword since it causes us to doubt the robustness, as an equilibrium concept of the informationally separating equilibrium defined by conditions (a), (b), (c), and (d).

Limits to the Informationally Separating Equilibrium as an Equilibrium Concept

Whether we can define a separating equilibrium or not is an issue quite different from whether we can reach such an equilibrium. More fundamentally, there is a potential issue about whether the separating equilibrium is in fact consistent with the expected utility maximization of the employer. If it is not, we have the case where Pareto improvements are possible via agreements among employers and employees about a different type of contract. Let us denote the former as an issue of dynamic stability, and the latter as the issue of sustainability.

The Dynamic Stability of the Separating Equilibrium

It is not easy to guarantee the dynamic stability of the separating equilibrium. Let us explain the point by returning to the single job case described in Figure 3.13. As we have already seen, if the wage schedule is either $W_+ W'_+$ or $W_- W'_-$, then the signal is incomplete. The employer will try to adjust his wage schedule for further informational separation. Whether the adjustment is successfully done is determined by whether the current wage schedule is located above the equilibrium schedule $W_0 W'_0$ (as in the case with $W_+ W'_+$) or below the schedule $W_0 W'_0$ (as in the case with $W_- W'_-$). That is because, although the two cases are similar in terms of providing incentives for the worker with low z to acquire education, they are opposite to one another in terms of how the incentive is incorporated. If the schedule is above $W_0 W'_0$, the incentive scheme needs to raise the marginal benefit of education, while lowering the overall level of income. On the other hand, if the schedule is below $W_0 W_0'$, the incentive scheme needs to lower the marginal benefit of education, while raising the overall level of income. If the employer adjusts the wage schedules on the basis of incorrect understanding of the situation, then the allocation moves further away from the equilibrium.

If we assume that the employer knows the relative position of the current wage schedule and the equilibrium schedule $W_0 W_0'$, then that would be equivalent to assuming that the employer has perfect foresight, as we did with respect to the workers at the end of the last section.

But if we do not assume perfect foresight, then the employer is forced to make adjustments by trial and error. In that case, in order for the system to move towards the long-run equilibrium, once the employer realizes that things are moving on the wrong track, he has to decide to start behaving in the opposite way. It is possible that the situation is such that, as long as employers engage in trial and error independently of one another, market forces will start to work, leading to long-run equilibrium in the end. However, it is obvious that convergence to the equilibrium cannot be easily guaranteed.

The Issue of the Sustainability of the Separating Equilibrium

The separating equilibrium is not necessarily stable. Let us explain the point, following Riley (1979). First, assume that for a single job, the wage schedule in the separating equilibrium is $W_0 W_0'$.

The important characteristic of this schedule is that, at each point, it is tangential to the indifference curve of the expected net income. The indifference curve of the expected net income is the combination of signal s and income W_B such that, given z, income W_B would just compensate the additional purchase of signal s. From assumptions (3.5) to (3.7), we can derive that they are straight lines with slopes $1/z$, that is:

$$W_B - \frac{s}{z} = \text{constant.}$$

Needless to say, the expected net income schedule increases towards the top left. The first order condition (3.8) describing the optimal choice of a worker means that the indifference curves defined above are tangential to the wage schedule.

The fact that, for each given z, there is a unique tangency point and that s increases with z can be seen from schedule $Z_0 Z_0'$ in the fourth quadrant of Figure 3.13.

Now, let us assume that the employer offers a contract $(s^{\#}, w_B(1 - k_B) + w^{\#})$ corresponding to point T in Figure 3.13. Then, we can draw two tangential lines from point T to the wage schedule $W_0 W_0'$. For the two tangent points, as the value of s, denote the smaller by s_1 and the larger by s_2. Also, let z_1 and z_2 be the corresponding values of z on the curve $Z_0 Z_0'$. Then, we can show that z_1

and z_2 are related to each other as follows:[31]

$$\frac{w_B k_B}{2}(z_1 + z_2) = w^{\#} \tag{3.17}$$

$$\frac{w_B k_B}{2} z_1 z_2 = s^{\#}. \tag{3.18}$$

The figure tells us that, for any z in between z_1 and z_2, the expected net income of the indifference line tangential to the corresponding wage schedule $W_0 W_0'$ is lower than the expected net income of the indifference curve that goes through the point T, and has the same slope as the above tangent line. That is, a worker with this z would prefer the new contract, $(s^*, w_B(1 - k_B) + w^*)$, to the existing contract.

Does the employer benefit from such a contract? If we assume that z is distributed among workers with density $f(z)$, then the expected profit $E\pi$ for the employer who chooses the above contract is:

$$E\pi = \int_{z_1}^{z_2} (w_B k_B z - w^{\#}) f(z)\, dz.$$

If we substitute (3.17) for $w^{\#}$, then:

$$E\pi = \int_{z_1}^{z_2} w_B k_B \left(z - \frac{z_1 + z_2}{2} \right) f(z)\, dz. \tag{3.19}$$

If z is distributed uniformly, the value of the integral is zero, that is, the employer is indifferent between the new and the old contract and thus there is no incentive for him to offer the new contract. Also, if we have $f'(z) < 0$ on the

---

[31] From (3.11) (given $C_B = 0$) and (3.10), we can derive the following relationships, between s_1 and z_1, and between s_2 and z_2:

$$s_1 = \frac{w_B k_B}{2} z_1^2,$$

$$s_2 = \frac{w_B k_B}{2} z_2^2.$$

Now, the line tangential to point T is the indifference curve that corresponds to the maximum expected net income. Therefore, z_1 and z_2 satisfy:

$$w^{\#} - \frac{s^{\#}}{z_i} = w_B k_B z_i - \frac{s_i}{z_i}$$

$$= \frac{w_B k_B}{2} z_i \quad (i = 1, 2).$$

The second equality is derived by substituting (3.17). By taking the difference of the expressions z_1 and z_2, we derive the equations in the main text. That is, z_1 and z_2 are the two roots of the second-order equations whose sum is $2w^{\#}/w_B k_B$ and whose product is $2s^{\#}/w_B k_B$.

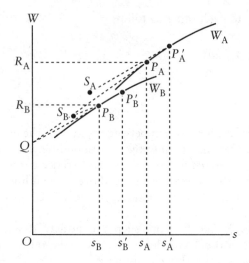

Figure 3.16. *The Collapse of the Inefficient Informationally Separating Equilibrium*

interval of our interest, that is, if it is the case that the higher the productivity, the fewer the people there are that are capable of it, then $E\pi < 0$, and the employer would never offer the contract described above. But in the opposite case, $(f'(z) > 0)$, the employer would adopt the new contract to improve his expected net benefit. More generally, as long as we can find an interval where $f'(z) > 0$, then, through drawing up a contract where $[z_1, z_2]$ is part of the interval, both employer and the employee will be better off.

The above discussion indicates that, depending on the distribution of z among workers, the contract without complete separation would dominate the separating equilibrium in the Pareto sense. We call such a contract the 'pooling contract'. Hence, condition (c), which assumes perfect separation, does not always result in maximization of the employer's expected utility.[32]

Next, let us analyse the case of multiple jobs. First, the employer's deviation from the equilibrium schedule would destroy the inefficient signalling equilibrium shown in Figure 3.15. Let us demonstrate the point using the argument in Riley (1975: section 2). (See Figure 3.16, which is a magnification of the first quadrant of Figure 3.15.)

Let us assume P_A and P_B to be the points on the wage schedule corresponding to the boundary point $\hat{z}$. The fact that, at the boundary point, the expected net revenues for workers from job A and job B are equal means that, on the figure, the lines tangential to P_A and P_B (the slopes are $1/(1 - \hat{z})$ and $1/\hat{z}$, respectively) have the same intercept Q. Let us denote the projection of the points P_A and P_B to the y-axis as R_A and R_B, respectively. And let us now assume that an

---

[32] The above discussion follows Riley (1979: Theorem 4). Notice that, in our discussion, (3.19) is still applicable if we set $z_1 = 0$ when we have the lower bound of $s^{\#}$ at zero.

employer offers, simultaneously, contract S_A within the triangle $\triangle P_A R_A Q$ for job A and contract S_B within the triangle $\triangle P_A R_A Q$ for job B. It is clear that, for all the workers on the boundary point $\hat{z}$, contracts S_A and S_B are preferred to the original contracts P_A and P_B respectively, because they are on indifference curves with higher utilities. At the same time, because of the wage decrease, the new contracts increase the employer's benefits. Furthermore, the employer can hire more productive workers with higher education on interval $[s_A, s_A']$ or $[s_B, s_B']$ for the same wage. Hence, that further increases the employer's profits.[33] Thus, the inefficient separating equilibrium in the figure is destroyed.

The essence of this discussion is that, by exploiting the trade-off between labour income and education cost, the employer can increase his profits while increasing workers' expected net income. The possibility exists as long as the triangles $\triangle P_A R_A Q$ and $\triangle P_B R_B Q$ are non-empty. Those triangles disappear only in the efficient separating equilibrium illustrated in Figure 3.14. Therefore, in the real world where there are multiple jobs, as long as we assume rational behaviour by employers, there is no possibility that overinvestment in education will act as a signalling device.

But the employer's offer of a pooling contract not only eliminates the inefficient separating equilibria, but also destroys the efficient separating equilibrium. First, as we confirm below, in the neighbourhood of the boundary point $\hat{z}_{\text{eff}}$ between jobs A and B, regardless of the distribution of z, there exists a pooling contract which Pareto dominates the equilibrium wage schedule. Second, for z located away from the boundary point, since relations similar (see Appendix 3.1, mathematical note 8) to those in equation (3.19) for the single job case hold for both jobs A and B, there could exist a pooling contract that is Pareto superior to the equilibrium wage schedule for some distribution of z. Now, observe that even though the assumption that the higher-ability workers are scarce makes sense for the single job case, those distributional assumptions become meaningless when there are multiple jobs. That is because, save by pure coincidence, the boundary point $\hat{z}_{\text{eff}}$ would not be equal to the peak of the distribution of z.

To verify the first point, let us consider the pooling contract corresponding to the $\{Q, Q'\}$ pair in Figure 3.14. That is, the employer tries to lure workers around the boundary point by offering a contract with a small wage increase and keeping the required schooling level at zero, and keeping the optimal educational investment level at the boundary point $\hat{z}_{\text{eff}}$. We suppose that the wage is increased by the same amount for jobs A and B, so that the boundary point remains unchanged. (We will discuss the amount of the wage increase later.)

---

[33] The new boundary $\hat{z}$ moves depending on whether the intercept of the line parallel to the line $P_A Q$ and going through the point S_A is larger or smaller than the intercept of the line parallel to the line $P_B Q$ and going through the point S_B. If the former is larger than the latter, then $\hat{z}$ moves up. And if $\hat{z}$ moves up, the result will be that contract S_A will attract workers who are of lower skill than before, but then, by choosing the appropriate combinations of contracts S_A and S_B, the employer can increase his expected profits.

Denote the maximum of the expected net income level of the workers under the wage schedule $W_A(s_A)$, $W_B(s_B)$ in the separating equilibrium by:

$$U_A(z) = W_A(s_A(z)) - \frac{s_A(z)}{1 - z}$$

$$U_B(z) = W_B(s_B(z)) - \frac{s_B(z)}{z}.$$

(Here, $s_A(z)$ and $s_B(z)$ are the optimal level of education given z.) Then, using conditions (3.8) and (3.13) and the fact that $s_A(\hat{z}_{eff}) = s_B(\hat{z}_{eff}) = 0$, we can obtain:

$$U'_A(\hat{z}_{eff}) = 0 \quad \text{and} \quad U'_B(\hat{z}_{eff}) = 0. \tag{3.20}$$

That is, the workers with z in the neighbourhood of $\hat{z}_{eff}$ can only get the expected net income that is approximately equal to the income of workers with $\hat{z}_{eff}$.

Denote by $\underline{V}_A(z)$ and $\underline{V}_B(z)$ the average expected productivities of the workers between $\hat{z}_{eff}$ and the point z in its neighbourhood. Computing the change of the average expected productivity due to the change in z and taking the limit as z approaches $\hat{z}_{eff}$ from the left and from the right, as long as the boundary point remains unchanged, we obtain (see Appendix 3.1, mathematical note 9):

$$\underline{V}'_A(\hat{z}_{eff}) = \tfrac{1}{2} w_A k_A > 0 \tag{3.21}$$

$$\underline{V}'_B(\hat{z}_{eff}) = \tfrac{1}{2} w_B k_B > 0. \tag{3.22}$$

That is, in the neighbourhood of $\hat{z}_{eff}$, regardless of the distribution of z, increasing the pool of workers always results in higher average productivity.

The left-hand side of equation (3.20) is zero while those of equations (3.21) and (3.22) are positive. This gap is the source of the Pareto superior pooling contract. Now, suppose that the employer chooses a point $\hat{z}_{eff}$ sufficiently close to $\hat{z}_0$ ($z_0 > \hat{z}_{eff}$), and offers a wage equal to $\underline{V}_B(z_0)$, which is the average expected productivity of the interval between $\hat{z}_{eff}$ and z_0, to both jobs A and B. Then, we can determine the necessary wage increase, which we have left out of our discussion earlier. In that case,

$$\underline{V}_B(z_0) = \underline{V}_A(z'_0)$$

for some $z'_0 (z'_0 < \hat{z}_{eff})$ and, needless to say, this z'_0 is sufficiently close to $\hat{z}_{eff}$.

From (3.20), it is clear that workers with z in $[z'_0, \hat{z}_{eff}]$, in job A, prefer the new contract and the employer achieves zero profit. Similarly, workers with z in $[\hat{z}_{eff}, z_0]$, in job B, prefer the new contract and the employer again achieves zero profit. In practice, the new contract is not only preferred by workers with z in

$[z'_0, \hat{z}_{\text{eff}}]$, $[\hat{z}_{\text{eff}}, z_0]$, but also by workers with z in larger sets. At the same time, following (3.21) and (3.22), the average expected productivity of the employer exceeds $\underline{V}_B(z_0)(= \underline{V}_A(z'_0))$. This, we can verify that, in the neighbourhood of the boundary point, there exists a contract which is preferred to the one in the informationally separating equilibrium by both the employer and the worker.[34]

In general, a signalling equilibrium with the pooling contract is unstable. If the expected excess profit is zero in the current situation, that is because there always exist some incentives for employers to offer new contracts that enable them to sort out more productive workers, as long as the pooling contract is beneficial. Thus, there is no equilibrium in the Nash sense, which postulates that, for any employer, his actions do not cause any counter-actions from other employers.[35]

One possible case in which the separating equilibrium can be sustained is what Riley (1979) called the reactive equilibrium. That is, even if an employer destroys the separating equilibrium by offering the above pooling contract and thus obtains excess profits, other employers will offer new (either pooling or separating) contracts and will take away the highly productive workers, causing a loss to the employer who destroyed the original contract. The employer, foreseeing such countermoves, would feel reluctant to be the first to offer the pooling contract.

There is another equilibrium concept, suggested by Wilson (1977) (which is called the Wilson equilibrium). It is similar to Riley's reactive equilibrium in the sense that it satisfies conditions (a), (b), and (d), and no employer engages in activities that change the informational structure of the market. But the unique characteristic of the equilibrium lies in the point that it does not assume that the employer decides whether or not to deviate from equilibrium behaviour not only by considering whether it is profitable to do so given all the other conditions to be the same; rather, the employer calculates the profitability of deviation, taking into consideration that, when he deviates, he will deprive other employers of productive workers, making their productivity less than their wages, and thus forcing them out of the market. That, the employer knows, will flood the labour market with unproductive workers, and thus he will eventually be forced to hire those workers under the same contract as before. In other words, the equilibrium concept assumes that the employer has the capability of long-term foresight that correctly analyses the possibility of others exiting the market and the consequences of it. This equilibrium concept is similar to Riley's reactive equilibrium in the sense that it allows the employer

---

[34] The above discussion follow Riley (1979: Theorem 3). In the earlier case with a single job, the educational cost becomes infinite at $z = 0$. Hence this is an exception where the theory cannot be applied.

[35] See Riley (1979: Theorem 5). This property was also shown by Rothschild and Stiglitz (1976). This in essence has the same logic as the result claiming that the Nash equilibrium fails to exist under the assumption of asymmetric information.

to foresee others' reaction to his behaviour, but the reactive equilibrium assumes that the other employers will offer new contracts instead of exiting the market.

Miyazaki (1977) shows that, in the case where there are only two types of worker, there is a unique Wilson equilibrium with a contract informationally separating the low-productivity workers. He argues that since wages and marginal productivity are not equalized for each informationally separated type of worker, but a set of different contracts for workers of different types achieves zero profit in combination, the theory can explain the existence of an organization with various types of workers and the internal wage structure of that organization. This means that the internal wage structure of an organization is a tool for the employer to use to internalize the externality among the workers caused by asymmetry of the information. But Riley (1979) proved that there is no Wilson equilibrium when the quality of workers is assumed to be continuously distributed.

The above scenario is, however, just an example of possible strategic behaviour on the part of employers. The theoretical derivation of the stable signalling equilibrium in a general strategic environment is still unresolved.[36]

Concluding Remarks

As we have shown, the discussions concerning the concept of signalling have advanced well beyond Spence's original model of the labour market, to provide a general characterization of market equilibrium under conditions of asymmetric information. Despite the problem of solving the indeterminacy of equilibrium, this line of research has contributed greatly to economics by clarifying the signalling role of education and by pointing out that some income is the reward for a certain signal.

3.4. ON-THE-JOB INFORMATIONAL LEARNING AND THE INSURANCE CONTRACT

It is possible that both a worker and his employer have imperfect information about the ability of the worker. Indeed, it is perhaps more natural to suppose that both parties, employers and workers alike, come gradually to learn what ability each worker has. This section formalizes a process whereby such information can be obtained, and analyses how such a process influences the allocational efficiency of labour resources and the distribution of income.

---

[36] The reader may refer to Rasmusen (1989: chs 8 and 9) for the game theoretic reinterpretation of the Wilson equilibrium on insurance and education signalling under the asymmetric information. (This reference was suggested by Masahiro Okuno.) The discussion in this section corresponds to Rasmusen's screening model the situation in which the employer offers an employment contract before the employee signals his choice.

The Meaning of On-the-Job Informational Learning

Consider the case where the characteristics of job A and job B are congenial to the distribution of ability (Case I) as in the previous section. Workers are employed over two periods. Learning through education or training (that is, change in the ability position) is ignored. Assume that the wage rates w_A and w_B are constant and unchanged over the two periods.[37] Furthermore, suppose that the ability functions are the same as (3.7) and (3.12). The following three assumptions are peculiar to this section.

First, we assume that the prior probability distribution (in the sense that it is before they take jobs) of each worker's ability position is known. To be more specific, assume that the prior distribution of period $t(t = 1, 2)$ is the normal distribution of the average $\bar{y}_t$ and the variance $\sigma_{y,t}^2$. Needless to say, the values of the parameters here can differ among individuals.

Second, we assume that each worker's income is paid on the basis of observed productive efficiency. The evaluation of productive efficiency inevitably includes observation error, but the probabilistic structure of the error is known. Let $u_{A,t}$ and $u_{B,t}$ denote the observation errors on job A and on job B, respectively. It is assumed that $u_{A,t}$ and $u_{B,t}$ are statistically independent of each worker's y and follow the normal distributions with the average zero and the variance σ_A^2 and σ_B^2, respectively.[38] Among the observation errors in different periods, there is no time-series correlation, irrespective of the job selected. (A later subsection considers the case where $u_{A,t}$ and $u_{B,t}$ refer to the degrees of the ability specific to a job instead of to observation errors.)

Third, we assume that each worker and each employer (including potential ones) knows the prior distribution of y and the probabilistic structure of $u_{A,t}$ and $u_{B,t}$. This assumption implies symmetry of information.

The income obtained from job A and period t, denoted by $W_{A,t}$, and that obtained from job B, denoted by $W_{B,t}$, are determined as follows:

$$W_{A,t} = w_A(1 - k_A y + u_{A,t}) \tag{3.23}$$

$$W_{B,t} = w_B(1 - k_B + k_B y + u_{B,t}). \tag{3.24}$$

Using these equations, we can deduce the valuation of productive efficiency in the period from the level of the income actually paid. That is, if $\hat{y}_t$ denotes the

---

[37] The stationary state where w_A and w_B generate an equilibrium in the labour market over time can be easily created by supposing the situation where a new generation appears in place of an old generation every period. In this section, as in and after section 3.2, the levels of w_A and w_B are assumed to be exogenously given.

[38] The assumption of normal distribution is convenient as a concrete example of training process, but is problematic in the treatment of the end-points of the domain of y (that is, 0 and 1). Such a strict consideration of the end-points is ignored here, for the same reason as in footnote (28).

value of observed efficiency in terms of the ability position, then:

$$\hat{y}_t = \begin{cases} y - \dfrac{u_{A,t}}{k_A} = \dfrac{w_A - W_{A,t}}{k_A} \equiv \hat{y}_{A,t} & \text{(job A)} \\[2ex] y + \dfrac{u_{B,t}}{k_B} = \dfrac{W_{B,t} - w_B(1 - k_B)}{k_B} \equiv \hat{y}_{B,t}. & \text{(job B)} \end{cases} \tag{3.25}$$

Since y, $u_{A,t}$, and $u_{B,t}$ are mutually statistically independent and normally distributed, $\hat{y}_t$ also follows a normal distribution. From (3.25), the average of $\hat{y}_t$, the posterior value of observed efficiency, equals the prior average, $\bar{y}_t$. The variance of $\hat{y}_t$, on the other hand, varies in accordance with the jobs selected by the worker:

$$\sigma_{y,t}^2 + (\sigma_A^2/k_A^2)$$

in job A, and

$$\sigma_{y,t}^2 + (\sigma_B^2/k_B^2)$$

in job B. The correlation coefficient between $\hat{y}_t$ and y can also be calculated as:

$$p_{i,t} = \frac{\sigma_{y,t}}{\sqrt{\sigma_{y,t}^2 + \dfrac{\sigma_A^2}{k_i^2}}} \qquad (i = A, B). \tag{3.26}$$

Without loss of generality, assume that the observation error of ability position in job B is greater than that in job A; that is:

$$\frac{\sigma_B^2}{k_B^2} > \frac{\sigma_A^2}{k_A^2}. \tag{3.27}$$

The correlation between y and $\hat{y}_t$ enables both parties to update the prior probability distribution as to y through the actual experience of work in each job in period t. If $\hat{y}_{i,t}$ denotes the value of $\hat{y}_t$ observed in job i in period t, the posterior distribution of y (this is the same as the prior distribution in period $t+1$) is normal, with the average

$$\bar{y}_{t+1} = \rho_{i,t}^2 \hat{y}_{i,t} + (1 - \rho_{i,t}^2)\bar{y}_t \tag{3.28}$$

and the variance

$$\sigma_{y,t+1}^2 = (1 - \rho_{i,t}^2)\sigma_{y,t}^2. \tag{3.29}$$

That is, the average of the distribution equals the average of $\hat{y}_{i,t}$ and $\bar{y}_t$ weighted with the decision coefficient between $\hat{y}_{i,t}$ and y.[39] Since the assumption (3.27) implies $\rho_{A,t}^2 > \rho_{B,t}^2$, each worker supposes that the smaller the evaluation noise of the job is, the greater the weight of the observed value of that period. (If the observation error does not exist at all, $\rho_{i,t} = 1$ and the true value of y can be found through only one job experience.) On the other hand, the new variance is definitely smaller relative to that of the last period. The decrease of the variance is greater, the smaller the evaluation noise of the job is. That is, the degree of acquisition of information depends on the kind of job.

So far, the process has assumed that workers and employers learn each worker's y through actual job experience. Let us call this learning process 'information learning', to distinguish it from the term 'learning', which usually implies the acquisition of new knowledge or a new skill. From the third assumption above, both workers and employers engage in such informational learning.

Informational Learning and Job Matching

When there is some difference in the density of informational learning among jobs, it is conjectured that workers take into account factors other than the level of expected income in the choice of their jobs. The criterion of comparative advantage is not a criterion for optimality over time, though it is a criterion for static optimality. Under the assumption that workers are risk neutral, consider how the process of job selection by each worker deviates from the criterion of comparative advantage.

It should be noted first that informational learning through job experience in the second period, which is the last period in which workers take jobs, cannot be utilized in the choice of job afterwards and therefore such learning is useless.

---

[39] The prior probability distribution of y and $\hat{y}_{i,t}$ can be written as:

$$\begin{pmatrix} y \\ \hat{y}_{i,t} \end{pmatrix} \sim N(\mu, \Sigma_i), \quad \mu = \begin{pmatrix} \bar{y}_t \\ \bar{y}_t \end{pmatrix}, \quad \Sigma_i = \begin{pmatrix} \sigma_{y,t}^2 & \sigma_{y,t}^2 \\ \sigma_{y,t}^2 & \sigma_{y,t}^2 + \dfrac{\sigma_i^2}{k_i^2} \end{pmatrix} \quad (i = A \text{ or } B),$$

where μ is the average vector and Σ_i is the variance–covariance matrix. It is known to be a fundamental property of normal distribution that the (posterior) conditional distribution of y under a given value of $\hat{y}_{i,t}$ is expressed as follows:

$$y \mid \hat{y}_{i,t} \sim N\left(\bar{y}_t + \frac{\text{Cov}(y, \hat{y}_{i,t})}{\text{Var}(\hat{y}_{i,t})}(\hat{y}_{i,t} - \bar{y}_t), \sigma_{y,t}^2(1 - \rho_{i,t}^2)\right).$$

By substituting each term of Σ_i into the formula above, it is easily verified that:

$$\frac{\text{Cov}(y, \hat{y}_{i,t})}{\text{Var}(\hat{y}_{i,t})} = \rho_{i,t}^2.$$

Hence, the job in this period is selected according to the criterion of comparative advantage. That is, if y^* denotes the critical value of y in which the incomes in the two jobs are the same, the criterion of job selection can be written with the expected value of prior distribution of y in this period, $\bar{y}_2$, as:

$$\bar{y}_2 \begin{Bmatrix} < \\ = \\ > \end{Bmatrix} y^* \Leftrightarrow \begin{Bmatrix} \text{job A} \\ \text{job A and job B indifferent} \\ \text{job B} \end{Bmatrix}. \tag{3.30}$$

The influence of informational learning appears in every period except the last; needless to say, in the two-period model considered here, it does so only in the first period. Now consider workers for whom the average of the prior distribution of the first period, $\bar{y}_1$, equals y^*; that is, workers who are indifferent between job A and job B at least from the viewpoint of expected income. Under the assumption (3.27), which implies that the information from job B includes greater noise, it is intuitively clear that these workers should select job A, which contains more information about their ability. Indeed, the approximate value of the difference in the expected lifetime incomes from job A and job B of the workers for whom $\bar{y}_1 = y^*$ at the beginning of the first period (denoted by $L_A - L_B$ can be written as:

$$L_A - L_B = \frac{1}{1+r}(w_A k_A + w_B k_B)(\rho_{A,1} - \rho_{B,1})\frac{\sigma_{y,1}}{\sqrt{2\pi}}, \tag{3.31}$$

where r is the interest rate (see Appendix 3.1, mathematical note 10). This value represents the difference between job A and job B in the present value of informational learning. The marginal rate of return from the revision of the ability position is $(w_A k_A + w_B k_B)$. On the other hand, $(\rho_{A,1}\sigma_{y,1}/\sqrt{2\pi})$ and $(\rho_{B,1}\sigma_{y,1}/\sqrt{2\pi})$ can be interpreted as the expected degree of workers' revision of their y through job A and job B, respectively.

It is clear from the argument above that the worker for whom $\bar{y}_1$ is smaller than y^* will certainly choose job A. As for the worker for whom $\bar{y}_1$ exceeds y^*, if his $\bar{y}_1$ is sufficiently close to y^*, he will choose job A; the remaining workers, for whom the informational gain from engaging in job A cannot compensate for the loss of the expected income in this period, will select job B. To sum up, the system shows some bias towards job A under the assumption (3.27). The people who take job A in spite of the fact that $\bar{y}_1 \geq y^*$ invest the amount of difference of expected income between job B and job A as an opportunity cost in the informational learning as to their ability.[40]

---

[40] The reason why a worker selects job A as long as $\bar{y}_1$ is sufficiently near y^* even if it is greater than y^* is that (A.7) and (A.8) are continuous in $\bar{y}_1$.

The Case of Job-Specific Ability

It was Johnson (1978) who first formalized the process whereby each worker learns his productive ability through job experience and decides to make a change, by means of a phenomenon he termed 'job shopping'. He shows that workers will first engage in jobs with greater risk of income (1978: Proposition 1). This result seems totally inconsistent with the argument above that workers will first engage in the jobs with smaller risk.

Johnson supposes a world where the accomplishment of a job requires not only general ability, y, but some ability specific to each job which is independent of y, neither of which can be observed in advance. In our model, such a situation can be described by assuming that $u_{A,t}$ and $u_{B,t}$ are permanent noises which take some constant values over periods rather than assuming them to be noises independent in each period. In the following argument, these variables will be rewritten as u_A and u_B. This assumption implies that the job experience in the first period completely proves the value of $y - (u_A/k_A)$ or $y + (u_B/k_B)$. Thus, when this worker engages in the same job in the next period as in the first period, the uncertainty of income will disappear. However, since the true value of y cannot be directly observed, the worker should consider the posterior distribution of y in choosing his job in the next period. As for the posterior distribution, (3.28) and (3.29) hold, as in the previous model.

Consider again the people for whom $\bar{y}_1 = y^*$ in order to examine how informational learning causes a deviation in job selection in the early period from the criterion of comparative advantage. As in the previous model, in job selection in the last period workers adopt the criterion of comparative advantage. The following analysis examines these points in more detail.

Assume that a worker for whom $\bar{y}_1$ equals y^* was engaged in job A in the first period and evaluated as $\hat{y}_{A,1}$. As noted above, $\hat{y}_{A,1}$ is the true value of $y - (u_A/k_A)$, so that in the second period he will acquire the same income as in the first period if he continues with job A. On the other hand, if he moves to job B, his expected income can be calculated on the basis of the average of the new prior distribution, $\bar{y}_2$, which has just been updated by the information $\bar{y}_{A,1}$ and on the basis of the fact that the average of u_B equals zero. Since the criterion of comparative advantage is valid at this stage, the condition for the worker to move to job B can be expressed as follows, from (3.28):

$$w_A(1 - k_A\hat{y}_{A,1}) < w_B[1 - k_B + k_B\{\rho_{A,1}^2\hat{y}_{A,1} + (1 - \rho_{A,1}^2)y^*\}]$$

If we consider the equation

$$w_A - w_B(1 - k_B) = (w_A k_A + w_B k_B)y^*,$$

we can prove that this condition is equivalent to the condition

$$\hat{y}_{A,1} > y^*.$$

This inequality holds when y is sufficiently large that this worker suits job A and/or when he lacks the ability specific to job A. In such a case, turnover takes place. On the other hand, when this condition does not hold, the worker recognizes that it was appropriate *ex post* for him to engage in job A in the previous period, and he will continue with the same job in the second period.

When the worker for whom $\bar{y}_1 = y^*$ chose job B in the first period and was evaluated as $\hat{y}_{B,1}$, it can be shown in the same manner that if $\hat{y}_{B,1} \geq y^*$, he continues with job B as in the previous period and, if not, moves to job A. To sum up, the criterion for the selection of job in the second period can be expressed as follows:

$$\hat{y}_{i,1} \begin{Bmatrix} < \\ = \\ > \end{Bmatrix} y^* \; (i = A, B) \quad \Leftrightarrow \quad \begin{Bmatrix} \text{job A} \\ \text{job A and job B indifferent} \\ \text{job B} \end{Bmatrix}, \quad (3.32)$$

where i is the job in the first period.[41]

Now let us turn to the problem how a job is selected in the first period. Since the criterion for job selection in the second period has been altered from (3.30) to (3.32), the gain from the informational learning in the first period must be valued in a different way from the previous model. In fact, if I_A and I_B denote the present values of informational learning through job A and job B, respectively, they are expressed as follows:

$$
\begin{aligned}
I_A &= \frac{1}{1+r} \frac{\tilde{\sigma}_{A,1}}{\sqrt{2\pi}} (w_A k_A + \rho_{A,1}^2 w_B k_B) \\
I_B &= \frac{1}{1+r} \frac{\tilde{\sigma}_{B,1}}{\sqrt{2\pi}} (\rho_{B,1}^2 w_A k_A + w_B k_B),
\end{aligned}
\qquad (3.33)
$$

where:

$$\tilde{\sigma}_{i,1} = \sqrt{\sigma_{y,1}^2 + (\sigma_i^2 / k_i^2)} \quad (i = A, B). \qquad (3.34)$$

(See Appendix 3.1, mathematical note 11.) The difference in the expected lifetime wage at the beginning of the first period between job A and job B, $L_A - L_B$, equals $I_A - I_B$ and can be calculated by using (3.32) and (3.33) in the

---

[41] Unlike (3.32), (3.33) is the criterion which is valid only for the people for whom $\bar{y}_1 = y^*$. Under a general $\bar{y}_1$ the condition that the worker moves from job A to job B is expressed as:

$$w_A k_A (y^* - \hat{y}_{A,1}) < w_B k_B \{ (\bar{y}_1 - y^*) + \rho_{A,1}^2 (\hat{y}_{A,1} - \bar{y}_1) \},$$

whereas the condition that he moves from job B to job A is:

$$w_B k_B (\hat{y}_{B,1} - y^*) < w_A k_A \{ (y^* - \bar{y}_1) + \rho_{B,1}^2 (\bar{y}_1 - \hat{y}_{B,1}) \}.$$

following expression:

$$L_A - L_B = \frac{1}{1+r}\left(1 - \frac{\sigma_{y,1}^2}{\tilde{\sigma}_{A,1}\tilde{\sigma}_{B,1}}\right)(w_A k_A \tilde{\sigma}_{A,1} - w_B k_B \tilde{\sigma}_{B,1}). \qquad (3.35)$$

The expression between the first parentheses of the right hand side is definitely positive, from (3.34). The expressions $w_A k_A \tilde{\sigma}_{A,1}$ and $w_B k_B \tilde{\sigma}_{B,1}$ in the second parentheses coincide with the standard deviations generated from the uncertainty of ability as a whole (concerning both the common factor and the specific one). For convenience, let us call these expressions the 'income risk'. Then, in the first period, the job with the higher income risk is always selected. That is, the criterion of job selection for the worker for whom $\bar{y}_1 = y^*$ is reduced to:

$$w_A k_A \tilde{\sigma}_{A,1} \left\{\begin{matrix} > \\ = \\ < \end{matrix}\right\} w_B k_B \tilde{\sigma}_{B,1} \quad \Leftrightarrow \quad \left\{\begin{matrix} \text{job A} \\ \text{job A and job B indifferent} \\ \text{job B} \end{matrix}\right\}. \qquad (3.36)$$

Thus, it has been verified that Johnson's proposition is still valid in our model. It should be noted that though assumption (3.27) does imply $\tilde{\sigma}_{B,1} > \tilde{\sigma}_{A,1}$ it does not always imply $w_B k_B \tilde{\sigma}_{B,1} \geq w_A k_A \tilde{\sigma}_{A,1}$. Therefore, the ratio $w_A k_A / w_B k_B$ as well as the ratio $\tilde{\sigma}_{A,1}/\tilde{\sigma}_{B,1}$ influences the direction in which the deviation will take place from the criterion of static comparative advantage.

Now it is clear why the two models produce exactly the opposite results. In the first model, it is only y that contains the information that is effective in the future, so that workers will be inclined to choose the job through which they can acquire more accurate information as to y. On the other hand, in the second model, which considers the ability specific to each job, since y, u_A, and u_B contain equally significant information, workers need not stick to knowing y accurately. They would rather take risks, in the hope of gaining a fairly high income.[42] The two reasons why the selection of the job depends crucially on the degree of risk in either case in spite of the risk neutrality of workers are as

---

[42] Such a situation, where a risk-neutral person selects the job with great risk, is similar to the positive risk-taking behaviour that is involved in the occupational choice of becoming an entrepreneur, formalized by Shorrocks (1988) though his formulation is rather different from that applied to informational learning. Shorrocks assumes a world where a person can work not only as a labourer but also as an entrepreneur whose income involves risk, and considers the problem of occupational choice over a life cycle under risk-neutral preference. To be more precise, he assumes two kinds of risk in the investment opportunities of entrepreneurs: high input, high return and low input, low return. Furthermore, he supposes that (i) the latter type is accessible to all people whereas access to the former is limited to people who have made a success in the latter opportunity and then acquired great capital which is necessary in the former (this implies imperfection in the capital market); (ii) in either case, there is scope for sharing risk among people who undertake the same kind of investment, through the formation of a group of arbitrary size. Then he shows that in the early phase of their life cycle people decide to engage in the entrepreneurial opportunity involving low input and, low return, without sharing any risk with others. He also shows that if they prove to be unsuccessful after a certain period, they return to being workers; on the other

follows. First, the amount of informational learning is dependent on the degree of original risk. Second, the influences of risk on the income of the worker are asymmetric over time, in the sense that he can revise his choice of job if he realizes through informational learning that has made the wrong choice.

It is not easy to verify how Johnson's assumption of job-specific ability has practical significance in the labour process. Indeed, there exist some types of ability such that the talent of a person gives its name to the occupation; examples include pianist, painter, and so on. Such kinds of talent, however, often follow an extremely skewed distribution, so that we can hardly suppose symmetry of distribution of ability as in our model. Thus, however large the income risk may be, such occupations will not in practice be selected by risk-neutral workers. Most people can be supposed to aim at learning their y as accurately as possible through the informational learning process, as in our previous model.

Extension towards the Multiple-Periods Model

Our former model can be extended to the case of multiple periods. In the extended model, the ability position, y, will gradually be learned through the selection of and experience on a job in each period. From consideration of the equations (3.26), (3.28) and (3.29), we can see that $\sigma_{y,t}$ diminishes as time goes by, so that $\rho_{i,t}$ ($i = A, B$), the coefficient of correlation between $\hat{y}_{i,t}$ and y, also declines, whereby the weight of the newly acquired information ($\hat{y}_{i,t}$) in the update of $\bar{y}_t$ becomes smaller. In the limit of $t \to \infty$, $\sigma_{y,t}$, $\rho_{A,t}$ and $\rho_{B,t}$ altogether converge to zero and $\bar{y}_t$ converges to the true value of y.[43] Moreover, the value of informational learning in each period will also decline as time passes owing to the decrease in the amount of new information and in the number of remaining periods in which the information learned through job experiences can be utilized. Thus, the region of the deviation in job selection from the criterion of comparative advantage must gradually be reduced.

hand, once they succeed and acquire the high-return opportunity, it is rational for them to share the risk in as large a group as possible and to try to secure their property. The reason why they take the greatest risk in the early phase of their life cycle is as follows. Since the period during which they can recoup their investment is limited, in the form of finite labour periods, they expect that on average they can move on to the high-return opportunity earlier by taking risk alone and attempting to clear the hurdles through a single great success, rather than by sharing risk in a group and obtaining preparatory resources through gradual entrepreneurial success.

[43] It is clear that $\bar{y}_t$ will converge to some finite value. Contrary to the assertion in the text, suppose that $\bar{y}_t \to y + m$ ($m \neq 0$). Then, when $t \to \infty$ the covariance between $\bar{y}_{i,t}$ and y equals:

$$E\{(\hat{y}_{i,t} - \bar{y}_t)(y - \bar{y}_t)\} = E\left\{ \left(y \pm \frac{u_i}{k_i} - (y + m) \right)(y - (y + m)) \right\}$$
$$= m^2 > 0 \quad (i = A \text{ or } B).$$

This contradicts the property that $\rho_{i,t} \to 0$ as long as $m \neq 0$. Therefore, $\bar{y}_t \to y$ must hold.

Needless to say, it is in the earlier periods of each worker's lifetime that the inferred value of y fluctuates sharply and that changes of job may take place. In some cases, a job change arises in the form of personnel reshuffling within a firm on the initiative of employer; in other cases, it occurs as a voluntary change of job by a worker. Therefore, in the context of informational learning, the dynamic efficiency of resource allocation can be achieved by the reduction of the workers' cost of changing jobs and by making the reshuffling of personnel within a firm more prompt.[44,45]

Risk Aversion and the Insurance Contract

In the process of informational learning, the change in each worker's income can be understood by identifying within that change the following three factors: (i) the change in the ability position perceived in each period $(\bar{y}_t)$,

---

[44] Discussion similar to that developed above can be adapted to the case in which workers learn their own preference among jobs through the experience of actual work. Recall that in section 3.1 the index v expressed the relative degree of preference between job A and job B. If it is supposed that the prior probability distribution of each worker as to v exists and that the *ex-post* evaluation of utility in a job involves some error in each period, the same discussion as above is possible. In this case, the principle of equalizing differences in terms of expected utility holds. Through informational learning as to workers' preferences, workers also move among jobs or among employers.

On the other hand, there are several kinds of arguments that try to explain labour turnover from the viewpoint that workers search labour opportunities by investing their time resource and acquire better matching of their ability and their preference because of the existence of informational imperfection in the job opportunity itself (Mortensen 1978; Jovanovic 1979). These models describe the case of human investment, which involves the input of physical resources, whereas the model developed in the text (section 3.2) describes the case of the learning-by-doing.

In another context, a group of sociologists led by White (1970) point out that the worker's search for or acquisition of information about employment opportunities is strongly constrained by the size of the informational networks or social nexus of individual workers (friendship relations at school, kinship with parents or other relatives, human relations at present job, and so on).

Granovetter (1974) verifies such a hypothesis empirically. Boorman (1975) theoretically formalizes the economic aspect of the investment behaviour in such a social nexus. Granovetter (1974) and Osterman (1980) point out, on the basis of interviews with young people, that it can hardly be suggested that the process of getting or changing jobs by young workers in the United States is conducted with the definite intention of achieving optimality over time, as the present text states. They emphasize instead the importance of the role of the relatively limited social nexus that each individual obtains or of mere accidents. This argument presents doubts about how rational people invest in informational learning, but does not constitute doubts about the existence of informational learning itself. Moreover, even if people do not seem definitely, to plan their own career ahead in the period when they have not yet committed themselves to be professional workers (such periods are regarded as relatively longer in the United States than in Japan), there is still the possibility that they do come to plan ahead in the process of moving to a job that involves commitment. As for young workers in Japan, Tachibanaki (1988) points out on that in recent years the rate of turnover, which can be thought of as based on informational learning, is increasing.

[45] Ohashi (1978) formalizes the process of informational learning and job matching and then stresses, as the reason for the high productivity of Japanese workers, the fact that in Japanese enterprises reshuffles of personnel can take place quite often without much conflict between labour and management.

(ii) the change of job, and (iii) the existence of observation error. As noted above, the effect of factor (ii) is only at work at relatively early stages and, after that, factors (i) and (iii) have a dominant influence on the process. Both of these factors can cause either an increase or a decrease in the income of workers. Given the fluctuation in income, if there are some differences in the attitude towards risk between workers and employers (for instance, if workers are risk averse whereas employers are risk neutral), there is room for employers to provide an insurance contract that guarantees their workers a certain income in the future (Harris and Holmstrom 1982). Suppose that the workers work for T periods. For simplicity, assume there is only one type of job, say, job B. Therefore, the relation between the ability position y and the value of the marginal product of a worker is expressed as (3.24). (As in the analysis above, w_B has the role of adjusting supply and demand in the total labour force.) In what follows, express the value of the marginal product as $m(\hat{y}_t)$ using the same expression as in (3.25). The characteristic of the insurance contract considered here is that the income in a certain period and thereafter is decided in advance of actual job experience on the basis of the information at the beginning of that period ($I_t = (\bar{y}_t, \sigma_{y,t})$). If a worker is evaluated more highly in the future as a result of, informational learning, however, he can move freely among employers; if he wants to do so, the present contract will be replaced by a new one at that time. Such behaviour is possible because of competition among employers. In consideration of such a possibility, the worker should sign the original contract.

When the employer is risk neutral whereas the worker is so risk averse that he wants to avoid fluctuations in income in each period, the optimal contract for both parties is one that guarantees the worker a certain income from the period in which the contract is signed to the last period (period T).[46] The following paragraphs investigate the characteristics of this insurance contract. Let v_t denote the present value of the net expected return that the employer gains from the worker of age t whose information about y is $I_t = (\bar{y}_t, \sigma_{y,t})$ when the employer guarantees the worker a certain wage x from that period. It can be regarded as the value of the labour contract in the t-th period for the employer. Obviously, competition among employers exceeds the value of v_t. The question here is how v_t is evaluated in the actual market. When t is the last period ($t = T$), it is clear that v_T equals the values of the expected marginal product, $m(\bar{y}_T)$, minus the guaranteed wage, x; that is,

$$v_T = m(\bar{y}_T) - x. \tag{3.37}$$

---

[46] This subsection is based on Harris and Holmstrom (1982). The Pareto optimality of the contract referred to in the text makes the following two assumptions: (i) the intertemporal utility function of workers is additively separable and the utility of each period depends on the wage of that period; (ii) workers have the same rate of time preference (discount rate) as employers. For the proof of Pareto optimality, see Harris and Holmstrom (1982: 321–2). In the following discussion, we ignore the possibility that the employer may default on the contract.

In the last period, $\sigma_{y,T}$, the index of the remaining uncertainty about ability position has no influence on the evaluation of v_T.

It is more complicated to evaluate v_t for t in general. In addition to the net expected return in period t, $m(\bar{y}_t) - x$, the present value of the net expected return in the future must be considered. In period $T - 1$,

$$v_{T-1} = (m(\bar{y}_{T-1}) - x) + \frac{1}{1+r} E(v_T \mid I_{T-1}, v_T \leq 0). \tag{3.38}$$

In this equation, v_T is the value defined by (3.37). In the evaluation of the expectation term in the right hand side the fact is taken into account as a restriction that if $\bar{y}_T$ is sufficiently high that v_T becomes positive, the guaranteed wage x will immediately be bid up and v_T will reduce to zero. With $I_{T-1} = (\bar{y}_{T-1}, \sigma_{y,T-1})$ given, v_T follows the normal distribution with the average $m(\bar{y}_{T-1}) - x$ and the standard deviation $w_B k_B \rho_{B,T-1} \sigma_{y,T-1}$.[47] Therefore, it can easily be shown that the value of v_{T-1} depends both on $m(\bar{y}_{T-1}) - x$ and on $\sigma_{y,T-1}$ and that it is monotonically increasing and concave in $m(\bar{y}_{T-1}) - x$. In the following, express this dependence as follows:

$$v_{T-1} = \hat{v}_{T-1}(m(\bar{y}_{T-1}) - x, \sigma_{y,T-1}). \tag{3.39}$$

In the same way, the value of the labour contract in an arbitrary period $t (t \geq 1)$ is defined backwardly through the following recurrence relation of degree one:

$$v_s = (m(\bar{y}_s) - x) + \frac{1}{1+r} E(v_{s+1} \mid I_s, v_{s+1} \leq 0) \quad (s = T - 2, T - 3, \ldots, t) \tag{3.40}$$

Moreover, these relations produce a similar dependence as (3.39):

$$v_t = \hat{v}_t(m(\bar{y}_t) - x, \sigma_{y,t}), \tag{3.41}$$

where $\hat{v}_t(\cdot)$ is a monotonic increasing and concave function in $m(\bar{y}_t) - x$ (see Appendix 3.1, mathematical note 12).

In this function, $m(\bar{y}_t) - x$ is the difference between the expected marginal product in this period (period t) and the guaranteed wage and is the net return to the employer in this period. Let z_t denote this value. It can be correctly expected from the argument above that whenever the labour contract is rewritten in this period, the value of z_t must be decided so as to satisfy:

$$\hat{v}_t(z_t, \sigma_{y,t}) = 0. \tag{3.42}$$

Such value of z_t depends merely on t, the age of the worker, and on $\sigma_{y,t}$, the index of uncertainty. Write this value as $\hat{z}_t(\sigma_{y,t})$. This function, $\hat{z}_t(\sigma_{y,t})$ is a

---

[47] See Appendix 3.1, mathematical note 10, equations (A.9) and (A.10).

non-stochastic function depending only on the worker's age, t, because there is no uncertainty in $\sigma_{y,t}$ (see (3.26) and (3.29)) and the function $\hat{v}_t$ is also a non-stochastic function. Particularly, note that it is independent of the value of $m(\bar{y}_t)$, which varies as time passes. Define $\hat{x}_t$ as follows:

$$\hat{x}_t = m(\bar{y}_t) - \hat{z}_t(\sigma_{y,t}). \tag{3.43}$$

The value $\hat{x}_t$ is the level of the guaranteed wage when a new labour contract is signed. In what follows, call this value 'the market value of the worker'. On the other hand, from the worker's viewpoint, $\hat{z}_t(\sigma_{y,t})$ is interpreted as an 'insurance premium' that he will pay to the employer in order to receive a certain amount of wage over his lifetime. To sum up, the change of the market value of the worker depends on the change of $\bar{y}_t$ and on the level of the insurance premium.

As for the level of the insurance premium, the following three characteristics can be verified. First, it takes a positive value except in the last period (period T); second, it declines with the decrease in uncertainty of y; and third, it declines monotonically with the age of the worker (see Appendix 3.1, mathematical note 13). Because of the second and third characteristics, the market value of the worker will continually be pushed up with his age. In fact, the expected value of $\hat{x}_t$ based on the information in the first period, I_1, is

$$E(\hat{x}_t \mid I_1) = m(\bar{y}_1) - \hat{z}_t(\sigma_{y,t}), \tag{3.44}$$

from the fact that $E(m(\bar{y}_t) \mid I_1) = m(\bar{y}_1)$. This value monotonically increases with the age of the worker. On the other hand, however, the variance of $\hat{x}_t$ based on the information in the first period is

$$\mathrm{Var}(\hat{x}_t \mid I_1) = \frac{(t-1)\rho_{B,1}^2}{1 - \rho_{B,1}^2 + (t-1)\rho_{B,1}^2} \{w_B k_B \sigma_{y,1}\}^2, \tag{3.45}$$

so that it can be seen that the dispersion of the market value of worker also increases with the age of the worker.[48]

How does the actual wage paid to each worker change under such an insurance contract? In the first period, the wage w_1 equals $\hat{x}_1$, the market value of the worker in the period. This value is also the guaranteed wage paid in and after that period. In the second period, the market value $\hat{x}_2$ which can be known at the beginning of the period is compared with the guaranteed wage level, w_1: if $\hat{x}_2 \leq w_1$, w_1 continues to be paid; if $\hat{x}_2 > w_1$, $w_2 = \hat{x}_2$ holds. In the latter case, the contract signed in the first period is actually replaced with a new one. In general, the wage level in period t is determined as:

$$w_t = \max\{w_{t-1}, \hat{x}_t\}. \tag{3.46}$$

---

[48] Equations (3.45) and (3.46) can be derived by calculating the average and the variance from (3.28) under the given I_{t-1} and then by applying recursively the rule of sequential expected value as to the conditional expected value.

From this equality, it can be verified that the actual wage never declines but usually increases with the age of the worker.

Figure 3.17 illustrates the two possible cases of the age-income curve. Figure (a) shows a case when the level of expected ability of the worker in the first period, $\bar{y}_1$, is smaller than true y; and figure (b) describes the case when $\bar{y}_1$ is larger than the true y. Reflecting the observation error in productive efficiency, the expected marginal value product, $m(\bar{y}_t)$, fluctuates stochastically, but was seen at the end of the previous subsection it converges to the true marginal value product, $m(y)$, as time passes. In either case, the insurance premium $\hat{z}_t$ declines and then converges to zero. In figure (a), because $m(\bar{y}_t)$ tends to increase and the insurance premium tends to decline the wage gradually rises with age. In contrast, in figure (b), $m(\bar{y}_t)$ tends to decline, which offsets the effect of the decrease in insurance premium; so that the market value $\hat{x}_t$ can change in either direction though it eventually converges to $m(y)$. Therefore, it is possible for the value of $\hat{x}_t$ to rise temporarily and to determine the level of wages in the long term. This is the case depicted in the figure.

The most interesting implication of the theory of the insurance contract mentioned above is that it explains the seniority-wage curve in a different way from the human capital theory; furthermore, it also explains the widely known fact that the variance of income among individuals increases with age (see section 4.2). This point can be verified from the fact that the expected value and the variance of the wage of the worker given certain initial information (I_1) rises in each period (see Appendix 3.1, mathematical note 14). When we refer to workers given the same initial information we mean the workers whose educational backgrounds are the same, for example. In practice, the two facts noted above can also be verified in each group classified according to the level of education. Above all, the hypothesis of an insurance contract provides a convincing alternative explanation to the empirical that the increase of productive efficiency through continuous training is not always the only source of the increase in wages with seniority.[49]

---

[49] In the United States, this fact is known as the Medoff–Abraham paradox. Medoff and Abraham (1980, 1981) find on the bases of micro-data about the income of and the evaluation of the performance of middle management in the United States that though the income of staff of the same rank increases with length of service or experience, evaluation of performance in the same job by a superior does not increase with length of experience but sometimes decreases. They interpret these facts as evidence that productive efficiency does not always increase with experience and that there exists a pure seniority factor in income. It seems rather hasty to accept their interpretation, because the evaluation of performance that they consider is the subjective evaluation by the workers' superiors, and such evaluation can be distorted in several ways. On the other hand, however, their argument certainly serves as a warning against the naïve view of the school of human investment (see section 4.2) that the increase in a worker's ability through training is a major source of the growth of income. In Japan, Funahashi (1983) insists that improvement in the skill of the worker should not be regarded as the only cause of the increase in wages with seniority. This assertion, however, lacks clear quantitative evidence. In this respect, see also (10) in section 6.1.

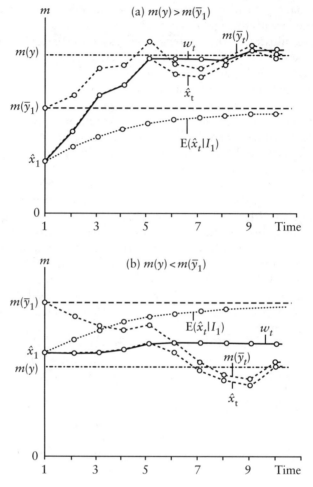

Figure 3.17. *Informational Learning and Insurance Contract*

Appendix 3.1. **Mathematical Appendix**

1. We denote the density of individuals who are positioned with distance y from point O of the circle by $f(y)$. Since there are two sides to the circle as divided by O, we set the convention that $f(y)$ has already added up the densities of the same y on both sides. The normalization made in the text implies that the total number of workers in the economy is

$$\int_0^1 f(y)\, dy = 1.$$

The labour supply frontier is a locus of points (L_A, L_B) defined by the following parametric representation:

$$L_A = \int_0^{y^*} k_A(y)f(y)dy = L_A(y^*) \quad L_A' > 0$$

$$L_B = \int_{y^*}^1 k_B(y)f(y)\,dy = L_B(y^*) \quad L_B' < 0,$$

with y^* satisfying the relationship $q = {}^*(y)$ as the parameter involved. Its slope is given by:

$$-\frac{dL_B}{dL_A} = -\frac{L_B'(y^*)}{L_A'(y^*)} = \frac{k_B(y^*)f(y^*)}{k_A(y^*)f(y^*)} = \theta(y^*),$$

and also:

$$-\frac{d^2L_B}{dL_A^2} = \frac{d}{dy^*}\left\{-\frac{dL_B}{dL_A}\right\}\frac{dy^*}{dL_A} = \frac{\theta'(y^*)}{k_A(y^*)f(y^*)} > 0.$$

Hence its shape is (strongly) upward convex and its (absolute) slope equals the index of comparative advantage at the borderline of job choice, which, in turn, equals the relative wage ratio q.

2. This point holds just as in the standard two-sector model. In fact, by denoting the labour input ratio L_{Bi}/L_{Ai} (which is the factor intensity ratio) by λ_i for each good produced, i ($i = 1, 2$) and the output per L_{Ai} by $g_i(\lambda_i)$, the producer's profit is maximized when the conditions

$$pg_1'(\lambda_1) = g_2'(\lambda_2) = w_B$$
$$p(g_1(\lambda_1) - \lambda_1 g_1'(\lambda_1)) = g_2(\lambda_2) - \lambda_2 g_2'(\lambda_2) = w_A$$

are satisfied. By taking the ratio of these expressions side by side, we observe that there exists a unique and monotone relationship between the factor intensity and the relative wage ratio q, that is,

$$\frac{dq}{d\lambda_i} = -\frac{g_i''(\lambda_i)g_i(\lambda_i)}{\{g_i'(\lambda_i)\}^2} > 0.$$

Hence, we can write $\lambda_i = \lambda_i(q)$. Our assumption in the text implies $\lambda_2(q) > \lambda_1(q)$ for any given q. Nothing that $p = g_2'(\lambda_2)/g_1'(\lambda_1)$ and differentiating this expression logarithmically with respect to q, where use is made of the above expressions for $\{dq/d\lambda_i\}$, we obtain

$$\frac{1}{p}\cdot\frac{dp}{dq} = \frac{1}{\lambda_1(q) + q} - \frac{1}{\lambda_2(q) + q} > 0.$$

What is different from the standard two-sector model is that the factor endowment (L_A, L_B) becomes a function of q. The functional relationship, however, affects the size of employment for the two sectors, yet it does not affected the optimum labour input ratio λ_i at all.

3. In the general case where the density function takes the form $f(y, v)$, the labour supply frontier is defined by the following parametric representation:

$$L_A(q) = \int_0^1 dy \int_0^{q/\theta(y)} k_A(y) f(y, v) \, dv$$

$$L_B(q) = \int_0^1 dy \int_{q/\theta(y)}^{\infty} k_B(y) f(y, v) \, dv,$$

with q being the parameter. By differentiating both sides with respect to q, we get:

$$L_A'(q) = \int_0^1 \frac{k_A(y)}{\theta(y)} f\left(y, \frac{q}{\theta(y)}\right) dy > 0$$

$$L_B'(q) = -\int_0^1 \frac{k_B(y)}{\theta(y)} f\left(y, \frac{q}{\theta(y)}\right) dy < 0.$$

Hence, the labour supply frontier is downward sloping. However, its slope generally depends not only on q but also on the shape of the population density $f(\cdot, \cdot)$ on the (y, v) plane.

If, for any given q, we denote the borderline level of v that corresponds to each y by $v^* = q/\theta(y) = v^*(y; q)$ (which is expressed by the VV' curve in Figure 3.6) the slope at each point of the frontier becomes:

$$-\frac{dL_B}{dL_A} = \frac{\int_0^1 k_B(y) v^*(y; q) f(y, v^*(y; q)) \, dy}{\int_0^1 k_A(y) v^*(y; q) f(y, v^*(y; q)) \, dy}.$$

That is, it is equal to the ratio of average productivity efficiencies between the two jobs, where the average is taken with weights of the population density as well as the strength of preference for job B (or the index of individual equalizing difference) both along the borderline stratum of population. By applying the mean value theorem to the numerator and the denominator of the above expression respectively, there exists a suitable pair of numbers y_1 and y_2 such that:

$$\int_0^1 k_B(y) v^*(y; q) f(y, v^*(y; q)) \, dy = k_B(y_1) \int_0^1 v^*(y; q) f(y, v^*(y; q)) \, dy$$

$$\int_0^1 k_A(y) v^*(y; q) f(y, v^*(y; q)) \, dy = k_A(y_2) \int_0^1 v^*(y; q) f(y, v^*(y; q)) \, dy.$$

Hence, by recalling the definitions of $\theta(y)$ and $v^*(y;q)$:

$$-\frac{dL_B}{dL_A} = \frac{k_B(y_1)}{k_A(y_2)} = \frac{q}{v^*(y_1;q)\dfrac{k_A(y_2)}{k_A(y_1)}}.$$

Namely, the slope equals q divided by a certain positive number that depends on the shape of the distribution. In the text this expression is called the *effective relative wage ratio*.

In the special case where people have the same v all around, say $\bar{v}$, it is easily verified from Figure 3.6 that this case reduces to that of no preference diversity except that all individuals take $q/\bar{v}$, instead of q, as the relevant relative wage ratio. Thus $q/\bar{v}$ becomes the effective relative wage ratio for this special case.

4. Mathematically, the sum of the present values of future income brought by the input of education s_i at job i is expressed as

$$V_i = \int_{s_i}^{T} w_i k_i (x_0 \pm h(s_i, a)) e^{-rt}\, dt.$$

The first order condition for its maximization with respect to s_I is given by

$$\frac{k_i'(x)}{k_i(x)}\{\mp h_s(s_i,a)\}\left(\frac{e^{-rs_i} - e^{rT}}{e^{-rs_i}}\right) = r \quad x = x_0 \pm h(s_i, a).$$

The meaning of the signs in these equations, $\pm$ or $\mp$, are as follows. When x is decreased by learning, that is, for job A in Case I or for jobs A and B in Case II, the first equation takes the negative sign $(-)$ while the second equation takes the positive sign $(+)$. On the other hand, when x is decreased by learning, that is, for job B in Case I, the first equation has the positive sign $(+)$ while the second one has the negative sign $(-)$. The term $(e_i^{-rs} - e^{-rT})/e_i^{-rs}$ is an adjustment term, accounting for a finite lifetime, and we can ignore it if T is sufficiently large. This adjustment term disappears when lifetime is infinite and death occurs with a constant probability μ. In this case, in the right-hand side of the above equations, r is replaced as $r + \mu$. This formulation actually makes mathematical derivation simpler.

5. Here, I show how the labour supply frontier is derived for the case with stochastic death process that we introduced in the mathematical note (1) for simplicity. When s_A^* and s_B^* are the optimal education levels, it holds that

$$\frac{V_A^*}{V_B^*} = \frac{w_A k_A (x_0 - h(s_A^*, a))}{w_B k_B (x_0 \mp h(s_B^*, a))} e^{-(r+\mu)(s_A^* - s_B^*)},$$

where the sign $\mp$ corresponds to the negative $(-)$ in Case I, or the positive $(+)$ in Case II. Both s_A^* and s_B^* are functions of x_0 and a. Hence, given the relative rate of wages $q = w_A/w_B$, on the (x_0, a) plane, let $\Omega_A(q)$ be the set of points where job A is chosen and let $\Omega_B(q)$ be the set of points where job B is chosen. (When the workers are indifferent between the two jobs, the point is included in $\Omega_A(q)$ for convenience.) Under the assumption that each generation is identical, the results obtained are:

$$L_A = \int_{s_A^*}^{\infty} \left\{ \iint_{\Omega_A(q)} k_A(x_0 - h(s_A^*, a)) f(x_0, a) e^{-\mu t} \, da \, dx_0 \right\} dt$$

$$= \frac{1}{\mu} \iint_{\Omega_A(q)} k_A(x_0 - h(s_A^*, a)) f(x_0, a) e^{-\mu s_A^*} \, da \, dx_0$$

and

$$L_B = \frac{1}{\mu} \iint_{\Omega_B(q)} k_B(x_0 \mp h(s_B^*, a)) f(x_0, a) e^{-\mu s_B^*} \, da \, dx_0.$$

When we regard q as a parameter, L_A and L_B make downward-sloping labour supply frontiers on the plane (L_A, L_B). From this, in the same way as in section 3.1, we can study the formation of a general equilibrium.

6. Substituting (3.11) and (3.16) into (3.8) and (3.13) respectively, we can obtain the optimal level of education given z:

$$s_A = \frac{(w_A k_A)^2 (1 - z)^2 - C_A}{2 w_A k_A} = s_A^*(z) \tag{A.1}$$

$$s_B = \frac{(w_B k_B)^2 z^2 - C_B}{2 w_B k_B} = s_B^*(z). \tag{A.2}$$

The boundary $\hat{z}$ of job choice is computed by equating the net incomes of both jobs given optimal investment. Namely, by using (3.10) and (3.15), we get:

$$w_A(1 - k_A \hat{z}) - \frac{s_A^*(\hat{z})}{1 - \hat{z}} = w_B(1 - k_B + k_B \hat{z}) - \frac{s_B^*(\hat{z})}{\hat{z}}. \tag{A.3}$$

The efficient signalling equilibrium is attained by C_A and C_B such that:

$$s_A^*(\hat{z}) = 0 \quad s_B^*(\hat{z}) = 0.$$

Moreover, in this case, by comparing (A.1), (A.2), and (A.3), it holds that:

$$w_A(1 - k_A \hat{z}) = w_B(1 - k_B + k_B \hat{z}). \tag{A.4}$$

The $\hat{z}$ that satisfies this relation is $\hat{z}_{\text{eff}}$. Note that the values of C_A and C_B respectively are the upper limits of those under which informationally separating equilibria exist.

7. By substituting $C_A = 0$ and $C_B = 0$ into (A.1), (A.2), and (A.3) in mathematical note (6), and by rearranging terms, we can determine the value of the boundary point $\hat{z}$ as the solution to

$$w_A(1 - k_A\hat{z}) - w_B(1 - k_B + k_B\hat{z}) = \tfrac{1}{2}\{w_A k_A - (w_A k_A + w_B k_B)\hat{z}\}.$$
(A.5)

The condition that $\hat{z}$ has a solution between 0 and 1 is:

$$w_A - w_B(1 - k_B) \geq w_B(1 - k_B) - w_A(1 - k_A) \geq w_A(1 - k_A) - w_B.$$

(In Figure 3.15, we assume that these inequalities are satisfied.) Moreover, by comparing with the value of $\hat{z}$ ($\hat{z}_{\text{eff}}$) that makes the left-hand side of (A.5) zero, we can easily verify that:

$$w_A(1 - k_A) \underset{>}{\overset{\leq}{\lessgtr}} w_B(1 - k_B) \quad \Leftrightarrow \quad \hat{z} \underset{>}{\overset{\leq}{\lessgtr}} \hat{z}_{\text{eff}}.$$

For Figures 3.14 and 3.15, we assume that $w_A = 7$, $w_B = 5$, $k_A = 0.8$, and $k_B = 0.6$. In this case, $\hat{z}_{\text{eff}} = 0.581$. For Figure 3.14, $C_A = 5.495$, $C_B = 3.042$, and for Figure 3.15, $\hat{z} = 0.512$.

8. We use equations (A.1) and (A.2) in mathematical note (6) to derive the optimal educational level, given z, as:

$$s_A = \frac{w_A k_A}{2}\{(1 - z)^2 - (1 - \hat{z})^2\} \quad (z < \hat{z})$$

and

$$s_B = \frac{w_B k_B}{2}(z^2 - \hat{z}^2) \quad (z > \hat{z}).$$

Using this s_B, and the same logic as in the main text, equation (3.19) can be derived. Using the same method, we can derive the version of equation (3.19) for job A.

9. For the proof, see Riley (1979: 342). Let us discuss equation (3.21). Given $z \geq \hat{z}_{\text{eff}}$, if we denote the density function of z as $f_B(z)$, and the cumulative distribution function as $F_B(z)$, then:

$$\underline{V_B}(z) = \frac{\int_{\hat{z}_{\text{eff}}}^{z}\{w_B(1 - k_B) + w_B k_B v\}f_B(v)\, dv}{F_B(z)}.$$

Now, let us integrate the right-hand side, taking note that $F_B(\hat{z}_{\text{eff}}) = 0$. The above equation can then be rewritten as:

$$\underline{V_B}(z) = w_B(1 - k_B) + w_B k_B z - \frac{\int_{\hat{z}_{\text{eff}}}^{z} w_B k_B F_B(v)\, dv}{F_B(z)}.$$

After taking the derivative of the above and rearranging the terms, we get:

$$\underline{V_B'}(z) = \frac{F_B'(z)}{\{F_B(z)\}^2} \int_{\hat{z}_{\text{eff}}}^z w_B k_B F_B(v)\, dv.$$

We can derive the equation in the main text, by taking the limit as z approaches $\hat{z}_{\text{eff}}$ and by using the L'Hospital rule twice. Equation (3.22) can be derived in the same way.

10. The problem of the maximization of expected lifetime wages can be considered as the problem of stochastic dynamic programming (DP) over two periods. Abbreviate the income functions of jobs A and B defined by (3.23) and (3.24) as $W_A(y - (u_A/k_A))$ and $W_B(y + (u_B/k_B))$, respectively. Such a problem can be solved backwardly. The optimization in the second period is to find

$$v_2 = \max\{W_A(\bar{y}_2), W_B(\bar{y}_2)\} \tag{A.6}$$

under the given $\bar{y}_2$ at that point of time. Let I_1 denote the set of information at the beginning of the first period, that is, the characteristics of the prior probability distribution of y, $u_{A,1}$, and $u_{A,2}$. Then, the expected lifetime income in the first period can be written as:

$$L_A = W_A(\bar{y}_1) + \frac{1}{1+r} E(v_2 \mid I_1, A) \tag{A.7}$$

$$L_B = W_B(\bar{y}_1) + \frac{1}{1+r} E(v_2 \mid I_1, B), \tag{A.8}$$

according to the job selected in the first period. Note that the expected values that appear in the right-hand side of (A.7) and (A.8) are evaluated under the given I_1 and the job in the first period. The optimization in the first period is to find

$$v_1 = \max\{L_A, L_B\}.$$

In order to find the values of L_A and L_B, it is necessary to know the prior distribution of $\bar{y}_2$ at the beginning of the first period. It is obvious that $\bar{y}_2$ follows a normal distribution, and that:

$$E(\bar{y}_2 \mid I_1, i) = \bar{y}_1 \quad (i = A, B). \tag{A.9}$$

On the other hand, the variance can be found by using the following formula:

$$\text{Var}(\bar{y}_2 \mid I_1, i) = E(\bar{y}_2^2 \mid I_1, i) - \{E(\bar{y}_2 \mid I_1, i)\}^2.$$

Substitute (3.28) into $\bar{y}_2$ in the first term of the right-hand side of this formula and calculate it using the equation,

$$E(\hat{\underline{y}}_{i,1}^2 \mid I_1, i) = \sigma_{y,1}^2 + \bar{y}_1^2 + \frac{\sigma_i^2}{k_i^2} \quad (i = A, B).$$

Then,

$$\text{Var}(\bar{y}_2 \mid I_1, i) = \rho_{i,1}^2 \sigma_{y,1}^2 \qquad (A.10)$$

can be obtained. In this case, it may seem paradoxical that the variance of prior distribution of $\bar{y}_2$ is larger in spite of the fact that job A provides more accurate information than job B. The reason is that, in the calculation of $\bar{y}_2$ job A places greater weight than job B on the observed value $\hat{y}_{i,1}^2$ which contains evaluation noise.

Let $n(\bar{y}_2 \mid \bar{y}_1, \rho_{i,1}\sigma_{y,1})$ $(i = A, B)$ denote the density function of normal distribution as to $\bar{y}_2$ with the average $\bar{y}_1$ and the standard deviation $\rho_{i,1}\sigma_{y,1}$. The domain of $\bar{y}_2$ can be regarded as being enlarged to $(-\infty, \infty)$. Substitute (A.6) into (A.7) and (A.8) and use the criterion (3.30). Then, L_A and L_B can be expressed as:

$$L_i \simeq W_1(\bar{y}_1) + \frac{1}{1+r} \left\{ \int_{-\infty}^{y^*} W_A(\bar{y}_2) \cdot n(\bar{y}_2 \mid \bar{y}_1, \rho_{i,1}\sigma_{y,1}) \, d\bar{y}_2 \right.$$
$$\left. + \int_{y^*}^{+\infty} W_B(\bar{y}_2) \cdot n(\bar{y}_2 \mid \bar{y}_1, \rho_{i,1}\sigma_{y,1}) \, d\bar{y}_2 \right\}. \qquad (A.11)$$

In this case, (A.11) is an approximate expression because the domain of $\bar{y}_2$ is enlarged, but the approximation is sufficiently accurate since we are interested in the case where $\bar{y}_2$ is in the middle of the interval $[0, 1]$. In general, the second term of (A.11) cannot be analytically expressed when $\bar{y}_1$ is arbitrary; however, if $\bar{y}_1 = y^*$, it is expressed in a simple form. That is, from the expression

$$\frac{d}{dx} n(x \mid \mu, \sigma) = -\frac{x - \mu}{\sigma^2} n(x \mid \mu, \sigma)$$

the formulae

$$\int_{-\infty}^{\mu} x \cdot n(x \mid \mu, \sigma) \, dx = \frac{\mu}{2} - \frac{\sigma}{\sqrt{2\pi}} \qquad (A.12)$$

$$\int_{\mu}^{\infty} x \cdot n(x \mid \mu, \sigma) \, dx = \frac{\mu}{2} + \frac{\sigma}{\sqrt{2\pi}} \qquad (A.13)$$

can be verified. Therefore,

$$L_i \simeq W_i(y^*) + \frac{1}{1+r} \left\{ \left(\frac{W_A(y^*)}{2} + \frac{w_A k_A \rho_{i,1}\sigma_{y,1}}{\sqrt{2\pi}} \right) + \left(\frac{W_B(y^*)}{2} + \frac{w_B k_B \rho_{i,1}\sigma_{y,1}}{\sqrt{2\pi}} \right) \right\}$$
$$= W_i(y^*) + \frac{1}{1+r} \left\{ W_i(y^*) + w_A k_A + w_B k_B \frac{\rho_{i,1}\sigma_{y,1}}{\sqrt{2\pi}} \right\} \quad (i = A, B) \qquad (A.14)$$

can be obtained. From (A.14), the expression in the main text can be obtained.

11. In contrast to mathematical note (10), it is the prior probability distributions of $\hat{y}_{A,1}$ and $\hat{y}_{B,1}$ at the beginning of the first period that are necessary in the evaluation of L_A and L_B. From (3.25), $\hat{y}_{A,1}$ has a normal distribution with the average y^* and the variance $\tilde{\sigma}_{A,1}^2$ ($i = A, B$). By considering both this fact and criterion (3.32), we can derive the expected lifetime wage at the beginning of the first period:

$$L_A \simeq W_A(y^*) + \frac{1}{1+r} \left\{ \int_{-\infty}^{y^*} W_A(\hat{y}_{A,1}) \cdot n(\hat{y}_{A,1} \mid y^*, \tilde{\sigma}_{A,1}) \, d\hat{y}_{A,1}. \right.$$

$$\left. + \int_{y^*}^{\infty} W_B(\rho_{A,1}^2 \hat{y}_{A,1} + (1 - \rho_{A,1}^2)y^*) \cdot n(\hat{y}_{A,1} \mid y^*, \tilde{\sigma}_{A,1}) \, d\hat{y}_{A,1} \right\}$$

$$L_B \simeq W_B(y^*) + \frac{1}{1+r} \left\{ \int_{-\infty}^{y^*} W_A(\rho_{B,1}^2 + (1 - \rho_{B,1}^2)y^*) \cdot n(\hat{y}_{B,1} \mid y^*, \tilde{\sigma}_{B,1}) \, d\hat{y}_{B,1}. \right.$$

$$\left. + \int_{y^*}^{\infty} W_B(\hat{y}_{B,1}) \cdot n(\hat{y}_{B,1} \mid y^*, \tilde{\sigma}_{B,1}) \, d\hat{y}_{B,1} \right\}.$$

From these expressions and formulae (A.12) and (A.13) in mathematical note 10, the equation in the text can be obtained.

12. In general, v_t depends on I_t, the information in period t, and x, so that it can be expressed as

$$v_t(\bar{y}_t, \sigma_{y,t}, x).$$

From the recurrence relation (3.40), this function can be written as:

$$v_t(\bar{y}_t, \sigma_{y,t}, x) = m(\bar{y}_t) - x$$
$$+ \frac{1}{1+r} \int_{v_{t+1}(\bar{y}_{t+1}, \sigma_{y,t+1}, x) \leq 0} v_{t+1}(\bar{y}_{t+1}, \sigma_{y,t+1}, x)$$
$$\cdot n(\bar{y}_{t+1} \mid \bar{y}_t, \rho_{B,t} \sigma_{y,t}) \, d\bar{y}_{t+1}, \tag{A.15}$$

where $n(\bar{y}_{t+1} \mid \bar{y}_t, \rho_{B,1} \sigma_{y,t})$ is the density function of normal distribution with an average of $\bar{y}_t$ and the standard deviation $\rho_{B,1} \sigma_{y,t}$, which $\bar{y}_{t+1}$ follows under given I_t.

First, let us verify the fact that the function $v_t(\bar{y}_t, \sigma_{y,t}, x)$ is monotonically increasing in $\bar{y}_t$ and monotonically decreasing in x for an arbitrary $t(1 \leq t \leq T)$. In the following proof, the method of mathematical induction as to t will be adopted. In fact, when $t = T$, these properties hold obviously, from (3.37). Then, let us show that when these two properties hold in an arbitrary period $t+1 \leq T$, so they do in period t. Now suppose that $\bar{y}_t$ grows to $\bar{y}_t'$ then along with the increase in the first term of (A.15), the second term also increases because the distribution of $\bar{y}_{t+1}$ moves rightwards and because v_t is monotonically increasing in $\bar{y}_{t+1}$ from the assumption of induction. Therefore, v_t is also a monotonic increasing function in $\bar{y}_t$. On the other hand, when x grows to x', it is clear that if the graph of the function v_{t+1} (as the function of $\bar{y}_{t+1}$) shifts leftwards (which is assured by the assumption of induction), v_t also decreases. (QED.) (This property coincides with Lemma 1 in Harris and Holmstrom (1982).)

Second, let us show that $v_t(\bar{y}_t, \sigma_{y,t}, x)$ can be expressed in the form of (3.41) by using this property (Harris and Holmstrom (1982: Lemma 3).) Again, the method of mathematical induction is adopted. For $t = T$, it holds because of (3.37). For an arbitrary $t + 1 \le T$, assume that $v_{t+1}(\bar{y}_{t+1}, \sigma_{y,t+1}, x) = \hat{v}_{t+1}(m(\bar{y}_{t+1}) - x, \sigma_{y,t+1})$. From the property proved above, $\hat{v}_{t+1}$ is a monotonic increasing function in $m(\bar{y}_{t+1}) - x$. Now let $\hat{z}_{t+1}(\sigma_{y,t+1})$ denote the value of $m(\bar{y}_{t+1}) - x$ with which $\hat{v}_{t+1}$ equals zero. Then, the region of $\bar{y}_{t+1}$ in which $v_{t+1}(\bar{y}_{t+1}, \sigma_{y,t+1}, x) \le 0$ is as follows:

$$\bar{y}_{t+1} \le m^{-1}(x + \hat{z}_{t+1}(\sigma_{y,t+1})).$$

(Note that $\hat{z}_T(\sigma_{y,T}) = 0$) Let y_{t+1}^* denote the value of the right-hand side of the inequality above. Using this notation, (A.15) can be rewritten as:

$$v_t(\bar{y}_t, \sigma_{y,t}, x)$$
$$= m(\bar{y}_t) - x + \frac{1}{1+r} \int_{-\infty}^{y_{t+1}^*} \hat{v}_{t+1}(m(\bar{y}_{t+1}) - x, \sigma_{y,t+1}) \cdot n(\bar{y}_{t+1} \mid \bar{y}_t \rho_{B,t} \sigma_{y,t}) \, d\bar{y}_{t+1}.$$

Furthermore, by the change of variable such that $z'_{t+1} = m(\bar{y}_{t+1}) - x$, this equation can be expressed as follows:

$$v_t(\bar{y}_t, \sigma_{y,t}, x) = m(\bar{y}_t) - x + \frac{1}{(1+r)w_B k_B} \int_{-\infty}^{\hat{z}_{t+1}(\sigma_{y,t+1})} \hat{v}_{t+1}(z'_{t+1} - \sigma_{y,t+1})$$
$$\cdot n(z'_{t+1} \mid m(\bar{y}_t) - x, w_B k_B \rho_{B,t} \sigma_{y,t}) \, dz'_{t+1}. \tag{A.16}$$

The integral value depends on $m(\bar{y}_t) - x$, and from (3.26) and (3.29) $\sigma_{y,t+1}$ can be expressed as a known function of $\sigma_{y,t}$. Hence, $v_t(\bar{y}_t, \sigma_{y,t}, x)$ can also be written as $\hat{v}_t(m(\bar{y}_t) - x, \sigma_{y,t})$. (QED.)

Finally, it is obvious that the function $\hat{v}_t(m(\bar{y}_t) - x, \sigma_{y,t})$ is monotonically increasing in $m(\bar{y}_t) - x$. Its concavity in $m(\bar{y}_t) - x$ is clear when $t = T$. For an arbitrary $t + 1 \le T$, begin with the definition of the following function:

$$\hat{v}_{t+1}^*(m(\bar{y}_{t+1}) - x, \sigma_{y,t+1}) \begin{cases} = \hat{v}_{t+1}(m(\bar{y}_{t+1}) - x, \sigma_{y,t+1}) & (\bar{y}_{t+1} \le y_{t+1}^*) \\ = 0 & (\bar{y}_{t+1} > y_{t+1}^*). \end{cases} \tag{A.17}$$

From the assumption of induction that $\hat{v}_{t+1}$ is concave in $m(\bar{y}_{t+1}) - x$, $\hat{v}_{t+1}^*$ is also concave in the same variable. By the change of variable such that

$z''_{t+1} = z'_{t+1} - z'_t$, (A.16) can be rewritten as

$$v_t(m(\bar{y}_t) - x, \sigma_{y,t})$$

$$= m(\bar{y}_t) - x + \frac{1}{(1+r)w_B k_B} \int_{-\infty}^{+\infty} \hat{v}^*_{t+1}(z''_{t+1} + m(\bar{y}_t) - x, -\sigma_{y,t+1})$$

$$\cdot n(z''_{t+1} \mid 0, w_B k_B \rho_{B,t} \sigma_{y,t}) \, dz''_{t+1}. \tag{A.18}$$

In this expression, $m(\bar{y}_{t+1}) - x$ is replaced with $z''_{t+1} + m(\bar{y}_t) - x$, but from the linearity of the integral operator the concavity in $m(\bar{y}_t) - x$ is preserved when integrated with respect to z''_{t+1}. Because the first term of the right-hand side of (A.18) is also linear, the right-hand side as a whole is concave in $m(\bar{y}_t) - x$. These two properties coincide with Lemma 3 in Harris and Holmstrom (1982). Thus, the assertions in the text have been proved. (The concavity of $\hat{v}_t(\cdot)$ with respect to $m(\bar{y}_t) - x$ will be used in the proof of property (b) in mathematical note 13 below.

13. The value $\hat{z}_t(\sigma_{y,t})$ has the following three properties (Harris and Holmstrom 1982: Theorem 2(ii), Theorem 3(ii)):

(a) $\hat{z}_t(\sigma_{y,t}) > 0, \ 1 \le t \le T-1$.
(b) If $\sigma'_{y,t} > \sigma_{y,t}$, $\hat{z}_t(\sigma'_{y,t}) > \hat{z}_t(\sigma_{y,t})$.
(c) If $t > s$, $\hat{z}_t(\sigma) < \hat{z}_s(\sigma)$.

Proof of (a): The third term of the right-hand side of (A.18) is definitely negative, so that the value of $m(\bar{y}_t) - x$ that satisfies $\hat{v}_t = 0$ must be positive. Hence, $\hat{z}_t(\sigma_{y,t}) > 0$. In this case, t is an arbitrary number other than T.

Proof of (b): When $\sigma'_{y,t} > \sigma_{y,t}$, it is shown that

$$\sigma'_{y,t+1} > \sigma_{y,t+1}$$

and

$$\rho'_{y,t+1} \sigma'_{y,t+1} > \rho_{y,t+1} \sigma_{y,t+1},$$

because

$$\sigma^2_{y,t+1} = \frac{\sigma^2_B / k^2_B}{\sigma^2_{y,t} + (\sigma^2_B / k^2_B)} \sigma^2_{y,t}$$

$$\rho^2_{B,t} \sigma^2_{y,t} = \frac{1}{\dfrac{1}{\sigma^2_{y,t}} + \dfrac{\sigma^2_B / k^2_B}{\sigma^4_{y,t}}},$$

from (3.26) and (3.29). In the same manner, it can be shown that these kinds of inequality also hold as to $\sigma_{y,t}$ and $\rho_{y,t}\sigma_{y,t}$ in any succeeding period.

The fact that $\hat{z}_t(\sigma_{y,t})$ is monotonically increasing in $\sigma_{y,t}$ when $t \le T-1$ is equivalent to the fact that the function $\hat{v}_t(\cdot)$ is monotonically decreasing in $\sigma_{y,t}$.

When $t = T$, $\hat{v}_t(\cdot)$ is independent of $\sigma_{y,T}$. In what follows, let us show that $\hat{v}_t(\cdot)$ is monotonically decreasing in $\sigma_{y,t}$ if $\hat{v}_{t+1}(\cdot)$ is monotonically non-increasing in $\sigma_{y,t+1}$.

From the assumption of induction,

$$\hat{z}_{t+1}(\sigma_{y,t+1}) \leq \hat{z}_{t+1}(\sigma'_{y,t+1}),$$

so that

$\hat{v}_t(m(\bar{y}_t) - x, \sigma'_{y,t}) - (m(\bar{y}_t) - x)$

$$= \frac{1}{(1+r)w_\mathrm{B}k_\mathrm{B}} \int_{-\infty}^{\hat{z}_{t+1}(\sigma'_{y,t+1})} \hat{v}_{t+1}(z'_{t+1}, \sigma'_{y,t+1}) \cdot n(z'_{t+1} \,|\, m(\bar{y}_t) - x, w_\mathrm{B}k_\mathrm{B}\rho'_{\mathrm{B},t}\sigma'_{y,t})\, dz'_{t+1}$$

$$\leq \frac{1}{(1+r)w_\mathrm{B}k_\mathrm{B}} \int_{-\infty}^{\hat{z}_{t+1}(\sigma_{y,t+1})} \hat{v}_{t+1}(z'_{t+1}, \sigma'_{y,t+1}) \cdot n(z'_{t+1} \,|\, m(\bar{y}_t) - x, w_\mathrm{B}k_\mathrm{B}\rho'_{\mathrm{B},t}\sigma'_{y,t})\, dz'_{t+1}$$

$$\leq \frac{1}{(1+r)w_\mathrm{B}k_\mathrm{B}} \int_{-\infty}^{\hat{z}_{t+1}(\sigma_{y,t+1})} \hat{v}_{t+1}(z'_{t+1}, \sigma_{y,t+1}) \cdot n(z'_{t+1} \,|\, m(\bar{y}_t) - x, w_\mathrm{B}k_\mathrm{B}\rho'_{\mathrm{B},t}\sigma'_{y,t})\, dz'_{t+1}$$

$$< \frac{1}{(1+r)w_\mathrm{B}k_\mathrm{B}} \int_{-\infty}^{\hat{z}_{t+1}(\sigma_{y,t+1})} \hat{v}_{t+1}(z'_{t+1}, \sigma_{y,t+1}) \cdot n(z'_{t+1} \,|\, m(\bar{y}_t) - x, w_\mathrm{B}k_\mathrm{B}\rho_{\mathrm{B},t}\sigma_{y,t})\, dz'_{t+1}$$

$$= \hat{v}_t(m(\bar{y}_t) - x, \sigma_{y,t}) - (m(\bar{y}_t) - x).$$

The second-last inequality follows from the assumption of induction; and the last inequality results from the fact that $\hat{v}_{t+1}$ is a concave function in z'_{t+1} and that the mean preserving spread has decreased as to z'_{t+1}.

Proof of (c): Note that it is sufficient to show that

$$\hat{v}_t(z, \sigma) < \hat{v}_{t+1}(z, \sigma) \tag{A.19}$$

holds for an arbitrary $t(t \leq T - 1)$ and an arbitrary set of (z, σ) in order to show that this property is satisfied. (This is clear from the definition of $\hat{z}_t(\sigma)$ and $\hat{z}_{t+1}(\sigma)$ and from the property that $\hat{v}_t(\cdot)$ is monotonically increasing in z.) In the proof of (A.19), the method of mathematical induction is used. As for $t = T - 1$, the inequality holds because

$$\hat{v}_{T-1}(z, \sigma) = z + \int_{-\infty}^{0} z \cdot n(z' \,|\, z, \rho_\mathrm{B}\sigma) < z = \hat{v}_T(z, \sigma),$$

where

$$\rho_\mathrm{B} = \sigma / \sqrt{\sigma^2 + (\sigma_\mathrm{B}^2/k_\mathrm{B}^2)},$$

by considering $\hat{z}_T(\sigma) = 0$. The next step is to show that if

$$\hat{v}_t(z, \sigma) < \hat{v}_{t+1}(z, \sigma)$$

for an arbitrary $t(\leq T-2)$,

$$\hat{v}_{t-1}(z,\sigma) < \hat{v}_t(z,\sigma).$$

In fact,

$$\hat{v}_{t-1}(z,\sigma) = z + \int_{-\infty}^{\hat{z}_t(\sigma)} \hat{v}_t(z,\sigma) \cdot n(z'\,|\,z,\rho_B\sigma)\,dz'$$

$$< z + \int_{-\infty}^{\hat{z}_{t+1}(\sigma)} \hat{v}_t(z,\sigma) \cdot n(z'\,|\,z,\rho_B\sigma)\,dz'$$

$$< z + \int_{-\infty}^{\hat{z}_{t+1}(\sigma)} \hat{v}_{t+1}(z,\sigma) \cdot n(z'\,|\,z,\rho_B\sigma)\,dz'$$

$$= \hat{v}_t(z,\sigma).$$

The first inequality follows from the fact that $\hat{z}_{t+1}(\sigma) < \hat{z}_t(\sigma)$, which results from the assumption of induction and from the monotonic increasing property of $\hat{v}_t$ in z, whereas the second inequality follows from the assumption of induction itself. (QED.)

14. The property asserted in the text corresponds to the fact that both $E(w_t\,|\,I_1)$ and $\mathrm{Var}(w_t\,|\,I_1)$ increase with t. This is equivalent to Harris and Holmstrom (1982: Theorem 4). First, it can be verified that:

$$E(w_{s+1} - w_s\,|\,I_1) = E(E(\cdots E(w_{s+1} - w_s\,|\,I_s)\cdots\,|\,I_2)\,|\,I_1)$$

$$\mathrm{Var}(w_{s+1}\,|\,I_1) - \mathrm{Var}(w_s\,|\,I_1) = E(E(\cdots E((w_{s+1} - E(w_{s+1}\,|\,I_s))^2$$

$$- (w_s - E(w_s\,|\,I_s))^2\,|\,I_s)\cdots\,|\,I_2)\,|\,I_1)$$

for an arbitrary period s. On the other hand, under the given information I_s in period s, it can be shown that:

$$E(w_{s+1}\,|\,I_s) - E(w_s\,|\,I_s) = E\{\max(w_s, x_{s+1}\,|\,I_s) - w_s$$

$$= (1 - \Pr\{x_{s+1} \leq w_s\,|\,I_s\})$$

$$(E(x_{s+1}\,|\,I_s, x_{s+1} \geq w_s) - w_s) > 0,$$

and:

$$\mathrm{Var}(w_{s+1}\,|\,I_s) - \mathrm{Var}(w_s\,|\,I_s) = E\{w_{s+1}^2\,|\,I_s\} - \{E(w_{s+1}\,|\,I_s)\}^2$$

$$= \Pr\{x_{s+1} \leq w_s\,|\,I_s\}(1 - \Pr\{x_{s+1} \leq w_s\,|\,I_s\})$$

$$\cdot \{w_s - E(x_{s+1}\,|\,I_s, x_{s+1} \geq w_s)\}^2 > 0.$$

One of the fundamental properties of the conditional expected value is that the expected value of a positive variable is also positive irrespective of the condition of constraint, so that substituting these inequalities into the previous two equalities generates the following:

$$E(w_{s+1} - w_s \,|\, I_1) > 0$$
$$\mathrm{Var}(w_{s+1} \,|\, I_1) - \mathrm{Var}(w_s \,|\, I_1) > 0.$$

Note that this property does not hold in our previous model in this section where the formation of wage is dependent on the *ex post* evaluation of productive efficiency. In such a model, when workers are relatively younger, turnover may occur and the variance of income tends to decrease with time.

4

Schooling and the Distribution of Earnings: The Development of Empirical Research

Economic theory has two important roles: the first is to offer a framework from which to view and organize real-world phenomena. The second role is to prepare tools for interpreting such organized information. Therefore, the power of economic theory should be evaluated in view of observations of the real world. A vast body of statistical work has been accumulated in the USA on the formation and distribution of income, especially statistics concerning the relationship between schooling, occupation, and earnings. The subject has attracted participation from a wide variety of social science disciplines including sociology and psychology, since it is related with social mobility, ambition, and social status, interests beyond the traditional economic sphere. This chapter focuses on the relationship between schooling and distribution of income. I first provide a survey of the fruits of past empirical research, and then discuss the efficacy and limitation of the theoretical framework given in the previous chapter.

The chapter is divided into four parts. Section 4.1 deals with internal rate of return to educational investment, now a classical concept concerning schooling and earnings. In section 4.2, I study closely Mincer's conclusion that education and other human investments are the major cause of differences in labour earnings. Section 4.3 offers a more generalized framework for the cause of differences in labour earnings, where education is treated as one of a number of factors producing the inequality in earnings. I present a survey of the trials conducted to measure statistically the contribution of different factors to income. This field is called the estimation of earnings function. The model in section 4.3 does not limit the analysis of education merely to the direct productivity-enhancing effect examined in section 3.2. It also studies the role of education as intermediary, as revealing individuals' innate abilities, and reflecting the family and socio-economic background that might limit access to good educational opportunities. Therefore, educational investment is evaluated in section 4.3 not only from the point of view of productivity enhancement as in section 3.2 but also from the point of view of the signalling effect of information as studied in section 3.3. Finally, section 4.4

re-examines the relationship between educational attainment and earnings by addressing a more fundamental question: In what way does education enhance productivity?

4.1. ESTIMATION OF THE INTERNAL RATE OF RETURN TO EDUCATIONAL INVESTMENT

The first, and still important, theme in an empirical analysis of human investment theory is the estimation of the internal rate of return to education. Early works of Hansen (1963), Becker (1964), and Hanoch (1967) intended to investigate whether private returns to education are on balance with other private investment opportunities. Their aim was to test whether an individual effectively utilized his or her investment opportunities.

The internal rate of return on capital is defined as follows when the direct cost of education and training is assumed to be none for simplification. Suppose an individual earns a permanent income flow of $y(s)$ each period when he attended school for s periods. Suppose he earns $y(s+1)$ income when he attended school for $(s+1)$ periods. The internal rate of return (hereafter ρ_s) on this additional investment period from s to $(s+1)$ is defined as a discount rate that exactly equates the additional income flow every period, $y(s+1) - y(s)$, to the opportunity cost $y(s)$.

$$\frac{y(s+1) - y(s)}{\rho_s} = y(s). \tag{4.1}$$

In the same manner, for all the remaining periods $(s = 0, 1, 2, \ldots)$, the rate of return on this additional investment can be defined as $\rho_0, \rho_1, \rho_2, \ldots$ By using (4.1), repeatedly, the following equation is produced:[1]

$$y(s+1) = (1+\rho_0)(1+\rho_1)\cdots(1+\rho_s)y_0. \tag{4.2}$$

This equation relates to the theoretical part elaborated in section 3.2, equation (3.3). If return on capital (the interest rate) is r and if ρ_s is decreasing in s, then the optimal investment rate s^* must be such that $\rho_{s^*} = r$, as we saw in Chapter 3.[2]

---

[1] Equations (4.1) and (4.2) make the following three assumptions: (i) the direct cost of investment is zero; (ii) there is an indefinite lifetime and a permanent flow of income; and (iii) the age–income curve is flat. When these are no longer assumed, the definition of ρ_s as in (4.1) can be expressed as in the following equation. Let $c(s)$ be the direct cost of education for the period s, let the income horizon be T, and the age–income profile for each educational attainment be $y(s,t)$. (t stands for the age. $t = s+1, s+2, \ldots, T$.)

$$\sum_{t=s+1}^{T} \frac{y(s+1,t) - y(s,t)}{(1+\rho_s)^{t-s}} = y(s,s) + c(s).$$

Hanoch's estimation discussed later in this section is based on this definition.

[2] See Chapter 3, Appendix 3.1, mathematical note 4. If T is definite, then this relation stands only approximately.

If $\rho_s > r$ in an individual's actual educational choice, then one is under-investing in schooling. If, on the other hand, if $\rho_s < r$, then one is over-investing in schooling.

Hansen and Hanoch estimated a posterior internal rate of investment at each level of schooling. Hanoch used a 0.1 per cent sampled population in Los Angles in 1959. He divided the population into groups by region (north and south), race (white, non-white), and sex (male). For each group, he calculated the mean before-tax income level by years of education and age category, and estimated the posterior internal rate of return, ρ_s. (The direct costs of education were neglected on the assumption that such cost is evened out by students' part-time jobs.) The estimated result is shown in Table 4.1. The table also contains the results of a study of a Japanese sample (Danielsen and Okachi 1971), which followed a similar estimation procedure.

The table has the following features. First, the internal rate of return on finishing high school (row (3)) is 16.1 per cent in the USA and 10.0 per cent in Japan, while that of graduating from university (row (6)) is 9.6 per cent in the USA and 10.5 per cent in Japan. In the USA, the posterior rate of return on higher education is decreasing, while that of the two educational levels in Japan is about the same. The estimated results on the return to education are considerably higher than market interest rates. The difference in return between education and market interest rates, however, may or may not be high if we consider the risks inherent in education. If we were to answer the first question that was posed, whether the educational investment opportunity is fully utilized or not, we would have to give another independent evaluation of the risk premium required for educational investment. Second, we can point out

Table 4.1. *Estimations of the Internal Rate of Return to Education*

Japan (1966, male, regular workers)		USA (1959, male, white, northern region)	
Schooling (years)	Estimated rate of return (%)	Schooling (years)	Estimated rate of return (%)
(1) 10–11/0–9	6.6	9–11/8	16.3
(2) 12/10–11	11.4	12/9–11	16.0
(3) 12/0–9	10.0	12/8	16.1
(4) 13–14/12	7.8	13–15/12	7.1
(5) 16/13–14	14.3	16/13–15	12.2
(6) 16/12	10.5	16/12	9.6

Notes: The estimation was made by estimating the cross-section earnings function using before-tax earnings for the two countries. The (time-series) trend in earnings was ignored. In the USA, only the opportunity cost of education was included, while for Japan, both the opportunity cost and the direct cost of education—admission fees, education fees, after-school education fees, books, and other school necessities—are included.

Source: For the USA, Hanoch (1967: 332, Table 3); for Japan, Danielsen and Okachi (1971: 395, Table 1).

from the table that, except in a few cases, a higher return was estimated to school graduates than to those who are assumed to have dropped out of school without completion. (Two-year-college graduates were treated as the latter to enable comparison with university graduates.) It shows the possibility that school completion, and not just number of years of education, conveys some specific information about an individual's economic ability.

How are we to interpret the result obtained if we are to be faithful to the theoretical requirement? The theory tells us that for any level of education an individual chooses to attain, the internal rate of return to education must equal the market interest rate. Therefore, if the capital market is perfect, the posterior rate of return to education must be equal for all years of schooling. The fact that ρ_s is decreasing in the USA can be interpreted as an imperfection in the capital market, that high school graduates face a higher interest rate than university graduates.

Another means of interpreting the result is to take the estimated rate of return to education as an 'anterior' return similar to the coefficients of the production function, and not as a posterior rate of return produced by individuals' rational choices of investment in education. One should be careful, however, when following this line of interpretation. First, is it justifiable to assume that an individual faces a time-invariant age–income profile? Hanoch had to make this assumption because he had only one-period cross-sectional data. Expectations of future age–income profiles, however, should be explicitly accounted for. Second, a large income difference was observed even among a group of individuals in the same educational category and age group. Such difference can be interpreted as reflecting differences in innate ability, divergences in the quality of education, or variations in training in the workplace, rather than just random errors. Hanoch's estimation using the mean income of different groups is not assured, in the strict sense, to truly reflect expectations on returns to each educational category when we consider such differences. If, for example, a higher innate ability is positively correlated with higher educational attainment, a higher quality in education, and more training in the workplace, then a group of individuals with more schooling should contain a higher proportion of more able individuals than a group comprising individuals with lower educational levels. Should that be the case, the internal rate of return on education calculated in the above manner would include not only the genuine return on education but also the return to higher abilities. Indeed, tracking such bias in estimation became one of the major issues in the empirical analysis that followed.[3] The possibility of the existence of such bias is present in the results shown in Table 4.1, that a higher return is placed on graduation than

[3] Becker (1964: 70–82) dealt with this aspect using available data, such as the relation between scholastic score during school years and postgraduate earnings, or comparison of returns to schooling between school dropouts and graduates. His conclusion was that the ability bias is rather small (the bias correction reduces the rate of return by 1.5 to 2 percentage points). Blaug

on mere number of years of education. Graduation can be interpreted as playing an information-screening role, showing not only scholastic achievement but also other ability correlated with economic abilities such as patience and upward motivation.

So far, as this section has shown, the estimation of the internal rate of return to education is one of the first empirical analyses based on human capital theory, the results of which were quite useful. The experiment, however, evoked new issues with regard to the interpretation of what was actually estimated through the empirical analysis. The true contribution of the series of experiments, therefore, lay in the fact that they paved the way for the next advance in empirical analysis in this field, and not in the estimation results themselves.

4.2. HUMAN CAPITAL INVESTMENT AND DISTRIBUTION OF INCOME: MINCER'S EMPIRICAL STUDY

Mincer's work is well known for its measurement of the contribution of differences in human capital to the variation of individual earnings. His work is presented in Mincer (1974). Though there are lacunae in the logic, as I will mention later in this section, the work still forms a solid foundation for many empirical works today. The work was based on the same US Census data for 1959 as in Hanoch, but sampled in different manner: males aged 15 to 64, white, non-agricultural population and non-students, on the basis of more than 31,000 observations.

Equalizing Difference with Respect to Educational Opportunity

Mincer's work is based on equation (3.4). In this equation, remember that an individual's ability position (y_0), which represents one's innate ability (a) and initial endowment, is identical throughout the population. Differences in individuals' income are so determined as to fully compensate the schooling investment costs. Since the world in this model assumes that the principal of equalizing differences fully works, individuals' choice of occupation and schooling cannot be determined by a mere economic considerations of costs and returns. The ideal world of the model may be far distant from the real world, as I have already mentioned, yet Mincer considered such a model a useful starting point for his empirical research.

Let us introduce the error term, u_i, into equation (3.4):

$$\ln Y_i = \ln Y_0 + rs_i + u_i \quad (i \text{ stands for individual}).\qquad(4.3)$$

(1972: 227) estimated the school-score-corrected internal rate of return on education using UK data, with the result that the internal return on schooling is 13 per cent and 14 per cent respectively for high school and university graduates. The ability bias problem will be covered again in sections 4.2 and 4.3.

Let such factors influencing one's income—other than education, innate abilities, and social background, for example—be represented in the error term. Suppose that: (i) error terms are mutually independent between different individuals and follow the same random distribution with mean zero and variance $\sigma^2(u)$; and (ii) the error term u_i is independent of the explanatory variable s_i (no correlation between the two). Then by estimating (4.3), the resultant R^2 would represent the contribution of schooling investment in the variation of personal earnings. Mincer's whole work follows this assumption, so let us suppose at this point that the assumption is valid and see the estimation result.

The estimation of equation (4.3) is shown in Table 4.2, row (1). The first point to note is that the estimated coefficient r, the internal rate of return to education, is 7.0 per cent, about a half of that obtained by Hanoch (compare the result in Table 4.1). The main reason for the difference may lie in the following: (a) differences in the controls given to the sample (or the sampling); (b) differences in the estimation method. Mincer did not use the information on

Table 4.2. *Estimation Results using Mincer's Specification*

Sample			R^2
USA 1959	(1)	$\ln Y = 7.58 + 0.070 \cdot s$ (43.8)	0.067
	(2)	$\ln Y = 6.20 + 0.107 \cdot s + 0.081 \cdot t - 0.0012 \cdot t^2$ (72.3) (75.5) (−55.8)	0.285
UK 1972	(1)	$\ln Y = 6.60 + 0.053 \cdot s$ (13.3)	0.031
	(2)	$\ln Y = 5.20 + 0.097 \cdot s + 0.091 \cdot t - 0.0015 \cdot t^2$ (32.3) (45.5) (−37.5)	0.316
Japan 1967	(1)	$\ln Y = 3.68 + 0.047 \cdot s$ (2.59)	0.243
1975	(2)	$\ln Y = -1.80 + 0.072 \cdot s + 0.065 \cdot t - 0.0011 \cdot t^2$ (19.6) (27.4) (−21.7)	0.967
1967	(3)	$\ln Y = 2.17 + 0.113 \cdot s + 0.095 \cdot t - 0.0013 \cdot t^2 - 0.0014 \cdot s \cdot t$ (7.83) (8.72) (−10.4) (−1.89)	0.891

Notes
1. The US result is from Mincer (1974: 92, Table 5.1). The dependent variable is non-agricultural white male, aged 15–64, annual earnings in 1959. The sample size is 31,093.
2. The UK result is from Psacharopoulos and Layard (1979: 493, Table III). The dependent variable is employed male, aged 15–64, and annual earnings. The sample size is 6,873.
3. The Japanese result is from two different papers. The 1967 result is from Shimada (1981: 22, Table A.3(ii)). The dependent variable is aggregated data on hourly salary of regular male employees by industry, with 91 aggregated cells. The 1975 result is from Kaizuka *et al.* (1979: 31, Table 2.2). The dependent variable is the same as in Shimada.
4. The values in parenthesis are the *t* statistics.

the average age–income profile by educational group, which Hanoch used. Instead, Mincer relied solely on the theoretical restriction that the internal rate of return on education is the same for every individual at the chosen educational level. Nevertheless, the difference between the two is substantial. The second point to note is that R^2 is a mere 0.067. This means that differences in schooling account for only 6.7 per cent of the differences in individuals' log earnings variation. From this result, we would have to say that educational difference explains only a very small fraction of differences in individual earnings.

Why is the explanatory power so low? Mincer points out that equation (4.3) is unsatisfactory for two reasons. His first point is that for every educational level, the mean age–income profile is concave: earnings increase by age but the relative rate of increase diminishes with age. The earnings growth lasts longer for the group with the higher level of schooling. While the peak income age is between 35 and 40 years of age for groups with lower levels of schooling, that of university graduates is 50 to 55 years of age. For the group with the lower level of schooling, elementary and junior high school graduates, earnings level off after the peak age to the retirement age of 60 to 65. The earnings profile of high school graduates has intermediate characteristics. At ages 40 to 45, a plateau is reached (Mincer 1974: 66, Chart 4.1). Such facts must mean that the mean expectation of the error term u_i in equation (4.3) varies between different age groups. In other words, the right-hand side of equation (4.3) lacks an explanatory variable that correlates with age.

Second, when we look at the income distribution of different age groups, Table 4.3 shows that the variance of log income increases with age from the age category of 30 and over. However, let us look at equation (4.3). Since the return r is theoretically bound to be equal between individuals, and the error terms are assumed to be mutually independent and are drawn from the same population, the next equation must hold for different groups, however differently the group is composed.

$$\sigma^2(\ln Y) = r^2\sigma^2(s) + \sigma^2(u). \tag{4.4}$$

At the same time, $\sigma^2(u)$ has to be identical in different groups. To put it differently, all the differences among groups in log earnings variance must be fully explained by variance among groups in years of education. Observed facts belie this theoretical requirement. Compare the groups in the top (aged 25–29) and bottom (aged 60–64) rows in Table 4.3. Between the two groups, the difference in the variance in log income is as large as 0.238. On the other hand, the difference in variance in education multiplied by the estimated r^2 is a mere $0.0169 (= (0.07)^2 * (13.69 - 10.24))$. Unless we dismiss the assumption that $\sigma^2(u)$ is identical between the groups, we cannot explain the income variance difference between the two age groups.

The fact that income inequality increases with age is not limited to this sample. It is universally observed when different cohorts born in different years are taken. Schultz clearly illustrates the facts as shown in Table 4.4. (Among the established facts concerning personal earnings distributions are the upward-sloping age–earnings profile and the increase in earnings inequality with age.) Comparison across rows in the table shows earnings variance by age group at one time, while comparison of vertical columns illustrates intra-cohort changes with age. The cross-sectional increase in variance is about the same size as the intra-cohort increase in variance with age, indicating that the age difference in earnings variation is mostly the consequence of changes within the same cohort.

Table 4.3. *Changes in the Distribution of Income and Education across Age Cross-Section Groups*

Age group (years)	Variance of log income σ^2 (ln Y)	Mean years of education ($\bar{s}$)	Standard deviation of years of education $\sigma(s)$
25–29	0.433	12.2	3.2
30–34	0.343	11.7	3.4
35–39	0.388	11.7	3.4
40–44	0.426	11.2	3.4
45–49	0.498	10.5	3.6
50–54	0.506	10.1	3.6
55–59	0.590	9.4	3.7
60–64	0.671	8.8	3.7
Total (14 or more)	—	10.9	3.5

Note: The sample comprises non-agricultural white males.
Source: Mincer (1974: 61, Table 3.5; 112, Table 6.3).

Table 4.4. *Earnings Distribution Change between and within Age-group Cohorts*

Year	Variance in log earnings by age group		
	25–34	35–44	45–54
1948	0.355	0.445	0.585
1958	0.445	0.489	0.727
1968	0.389	0.454	0.567
1949	0.379	0.538	0.680
1959	0.442	0.478	0.692
1969	0.418	0.469	0.572
1950	0.378	0.471	0.642
1960	0.428	0.554	0.719
1970	0.458	0.486	0.585

Source: From an unpublished manuscript of Schultz presented at AEA meetings in 1971, cited in Mincer (1974: 62, Table 6.3). The data used are US, all male, 1948–1970.

Equalizing Difference with respect to the Use of On-the-Job Training Opportunities

Mincer, while recognizing the poor performance of the regression result of equation (4.3), expected to improve the result by augmenting the effect of training in the workplace. He expected that this improvement would cover the above-mentioned two weaknesses and that the true explanatory power of the human capital theory would be shown. His expectation was that the dispersion of earnings distribution with age could be explained by diversification of training programmes with age. He also attributed the upward-sloping concave age–income profile to the finiteness of life and the consequent decline in the optimal training density with ageing. (Training can be either general training or a joint investment by firm and workers in firm-specific training.)

Mincer's idea is explained in Figure 4.1. The vertical axis represents log income, the horizontal axis years of work experience. T is the possible work horizon. I will follow Mincer's assumption that the higher educated have a longer working life while sustaining the assumption that every individual is identical. $L_{10}L_{10}$ and $L_{20}L_{20}$ are income profiles for s_1 and s_2 years of education respectively for work with no post-school training. Both profiles are supposed to satisfy equation (3.4) and the individuals are indifferent between the two options. Now let us introduce work with intensive training (H), with

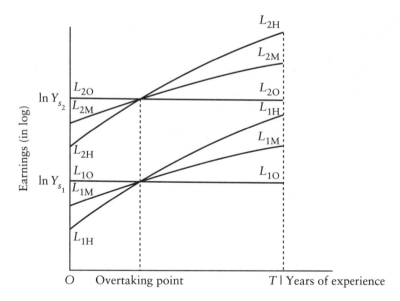

Figure 4.1. *Wide Menu of Training Opportunities at Workplace and their Earnings Profiles*

Source: Derived from Mincer (1974: 17, Fig. 1.2) and Psacharopoulos and Layard (1979: 488, Fig. 1).

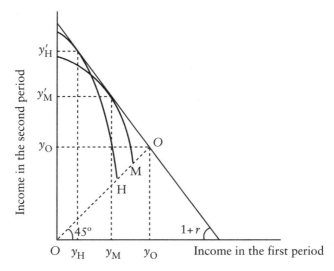

Figure 4.2. *Labour Market Equilibrium with Choice from a Wide Menu of Training Opportunities*

the income profile $L_{1H}L_{1H}$, $L_{2H}L_{2H}$, and work with intermediate training (M), with the income profile $L_{1M}L_{1M}$, $L_{2M}L_{2M}$, as well as work with no post-school training (O). Because training intensity decreases with time, the earnings profiles are both upward sloping and concave for work H and M. If all the jobs are necessary and cannot be perfectly substituted by any other job, at the equilibrium of the labour market the relative wage for the jobs is so adjusted that for every individual, all jobs are indifferent.

Figure 4.2 refers back to Figure 3.8. Labour market equilibrium is portrayed when the time horizon of work (T) is two periods. The level of schooling is fixed and is given. Similar figures can be drawn for different educational groups if the same length of working horizon is assumed.[4] The difference between Figure 3.8, which deals with the optimal investment level of an individual, and Figure 4.2, which deals with a labour market equilibrium when all individuals

---

[4] The labour market equilibrium condition relating to different educational levels s_1 and s_2 is as follows. Let the present value of each job at the start of work years to be $V(s_1)$ and $V(s_2)$ respectively. Under the assumption of no direct cost of education, the present value of lifetime income has to be the same for all schooling levels at the time when each individual made his or her educational investment decision. This means:

$$\frac{V(s_1)}{(1+r)^{s_1}} = \frac{V(s_2)}{(1+r)^{s_2}}.$$

From this equation,

$$V(s_2) = (1+r)^{s_2-s_1} V(s_1).$$

In this way, the same principle of equalizing differences links together all six types of job, with their different educational investments and their different levels of training intensity. If Figure 4.2

are identical, is that different training opportunity curves are tangential to the same market investment opportunity line in the latter. The flow of income for each occupation, (y_O, y_O), (y_M, y'_M), (y_H, y'_H) denotes the income curve $L_{1O}L_{1O}$, $L_{1M}L_{1M}$, $L_{1H}L_{1H}$, or $L_{2O}L_{2O}$, $L_{2M}L_{2M}$, $L_{2H}L_{2H}$ in Figure 4.1.

Let us return to Figure 4.1, and let me explain Mincer's logic. First, unless no overwhelming skewness exists for individuals in their post-school training investment choice, the mean age–income profile will be similar to $L_{1M}L_{1M}$ or $L_{2M}L_{2M}$. This will explain the first stylized facts: the upward-sloping age–income profile. Second, the earnings variation within an educational category by years of experience (or age) can be depicted as follows. A large variation is observed at the starting point reflecting differences in the density of post-schooling investment (the opportunity cost of working hours devoted to training). The variation converges to zero when the three age–income profiles cross, and this is followed by a divergence in earnings reflecting the returns to different levels of training. This logic solves the second stylized fact, that income divergence increases with age. Mincer call this point, where the non-trained and the trained cross, the overtaking point (Mincer 1974: 17). As a matter of course, different crossing points exist for different training opportunities. However, they are thought to be concentrated in a small region, thus Figure 4.1 is simplified to show identical overtaking points for different training intensities and educational levels.

The Regression Equation on Schooling and On-the-job Training

When training in workplaces is accounted for, how much of the inequality in personal income distribution does the human capital accumulation behaviour explain? Suppose work M represents work with mean training opportunities. If one is indifferent between work M and work O, the income difference at each period, that is $y_M(t) - y_O$ $(1 \leq t \leq T)$, must equal the returns on the human capital investment accumulated in the previous period, less the new investment in this period. This relation can be written as in the following equation if the investment amount at t is denoted by $C(t)$ (see Appendix 4.1, mathematical note 1).

$$y_M(t) - y_O = r \sum_{n=1}^{t-1} C(n) - C(t) \quad (t \geq 2). \tag{4.5}$$

The investment cost at the initial period is of course $C(1) = y_O - y_M(1)$. If direct investment cost data for each period are available, by adding up the

denotes the graph for educational level s_2, then the graph demonstrating the lifetime income for s_1 and its tangential curve will be placed inward to the origin by the above relation that defines $V(s_1)$. I did not include this illustration in the figure, as the graph would become too complicated.

accumulated costs and the cost for this period and inserting them as explanatory variables in equation (4.3), one can measure the effect of education and training in the workplace. In practice such data are not readily available. Mincer instead defined the investment rate in each period as the rate of investment in this period $C(t)$ divided by the gross income as shown in the first term of the right-hand side of equation (4.5). He also assumed that the average rate of investment declined linearly with years of experience. Using this assumption he obtained a new regression equation (Mincer 1974: 85–91):

$$\ln Y_i = \ln Y_O + rs_i + b_1 x_i + b_2 x_i^2 + u_i \quad (i \text{ stands for individual}). \quad (4.6)$$

First- and second-order terms of experience in the workplace, x, are new variables, introduced in this equation. The estimate of experience is usually given as ⟨age minus school year minus six⟩ since the actual number of years of experience is not available, though in reality, work experience does not monotonically increase with age, due to people leaving and dismissals.

Row (2) in Table 4.2 shows the estimation results of equation (4.6). A return to education (which theoretically includes returns to investment in the workplace) is now 10.7 per cent. We should note that the estimated result has moved closer to that of Hanoch, and that the coefficient of determination, R^2, has improved markedly, to 0.285. Table 4.2 also shows the results for the United Kingdom, from the research conducted by Psacharopoulos and Layard (1979).[5] The results for the United States and the United Kingdom are admirably similar in both size and effect. The R^2 result of the United Kingdom, including experience, is as high as 0.316.

Mincer's first comment based on the estimation result is that a 30 per cent variation in log income between individuals can be explained by differences in education level and training. If a large divergence in the spectrum of training in the workplace is measured carefully and used instead of the assumption based on mean training rate, he presumes that a larger proportion of the variation in log income can be accounted for by the inequality in human capital of the population.

Mincer's second statement concerns overtaking points. He deduced that if overtaking points between different educational categories are as close to each other as depicted in Figure 4.1, then training differences do not affect income variation at the overtaking points. Therefore, Mincer's view is that by applying equation (4.3) to those members of the population who are at the overtaking points, one can single out the contribution of education to income variation by focusing on the resultant R^2.

---

[5] Figures for males 15–64 years of age, before tax annual income of regularly employed workers from the General Household Survey of 1972 are used for the UK estimation. The sample size is a little below 7,000.

Income and Wealth

The largest difficulty in implementing such an idea is distinguishing the population at the overtaking points. No confirmation is given on the existence of such points, nor any assurance of the closeness of such points between different educational categories. Mincer conjectured that such supposition is valid, and applied regression equation (4.3) to a group of the population with a similar number of years of work experience. He supposed that the number of years of experience where the coefficient of determination attained was maximized was the overtaking point.

The resultant estimation is shown in Table 4.5. If we look at the coefficient of determination of the different categories of years of experience, we see that, it is U-shaped with the peak at seven to nine years of experience. Mincer concluded that overtaking points do exist at around seven to nine years of experience. The variance of estimation residual ($\sigma^2(u)$) is 0.353, which is the variation in log earnings not explicable by the difference in education. From the definition of overtaking points, the figure 0.353 does not include income variance generated by differences in post-school training. If we assume the portion is the same for

Table 4.5. *Estimated Results of the Overtaking Points*

Years of experience	Schooling equations				*h*-index
	Estimated coefficients (r)	Coefficient of determination (R^2)	Variance of estimated residual ($\sigma^2(u)$)	Variance of dependent variable ($\sigma^2(\ln Y)$)	
United States					
4–6	—	0.30	—	—	—
8	0.162	0.306	0.333	0.48	0.501
7–9	0.165	0.328	0.353	0.52	0.472
10–12	—	0.26	—	—	—
13–15	—	0.20	—	—	—
Total	—	0.067	—	0.668	—
United Kingdom					
3–5	0.114	0.236	0.273	0.357	0.374
6–8	0.064	0.068	0.263	0.282	0.397
9–11	0.068	0.105	0.206	0.230	0.528
12–14	0.078	0.151	0.138	0.162	0.683
15–17	0.079	0.182	0.135	0.165	0.690
Total	—	0.031	—	0.436	—

Notes: The figures are based on the application of the regression equation on schooling (4.3) to the group with different years of experience.
— means no data in the original tables.

Source: Calculated from Mincer (1974: 96 and Tables 3.3, 3.4) and Psacharopoulos and Layard (1979: 496, Table VI and 491, Table IIA).

all experience groups, educational differences account for a little less than half the variation in the log earnings variance of 0.668.[6]

$$h \equiv 1 - \frac{\sigma^2(u)}{\sigma^2(\ln Y)} = 1 - \frac{0.353}{0.668} = 0.472.$$

Unfortunately, the evidence for the United Kingdom, as derived from the research conducted by Psacharoupoulos and Layard (1979) does not provide additional support for Mincer's statements. Table 4.5 also shows the estimation result for the United Kingdom. No clear relationship is evident between the categories coefficient of determination, R^2, and years of experience. The R^2 maximizing years of experience is three to five years for the United Kingdom, while the residual variance minimizing years of experience is 15 to 17 years. At any rate, the results are quite different from that obtained by Mincer. It is difficult to find evidence for the existence of overtaking points from the case of the United Kingdom.[7] Therefore, even if the estimation for the United States was satisfactory, further independent evidence is necessary to confirm that the result was not just coincidental.

Let me introduce the results for Japan before we proceed further with a general assessment of Mincer's work. The Japanese data are not yet fully exploited. Shimada (1974) and Kaizuka *et al.* (1979: ch. 2) used cross-tabulated aggregate data of *Chingin Kozo Kihon Chosa* in order to apply Mincer's equations (4.3) and (4.6), as I have already shown in Table 4.2. The estimated coefficient closely follows those of the United States and the United Kingdom. However, because categorized and aggregated data are used for the estimation, Mincer's main question of measuring the contribution of education to income inequality remains unresolved. (Even though the coefficients of determination depicted in the table are quite high, because individual observations are not used, they are not comparable to those of the United States and the United Kingdom.) Kaizuka *et al.* (1979) pointed out that returns to education estimated in this way showed a declining trend in the 1970s.

---

[6] Mincer furthermore states that if permanent income is used for the calculation, estimated by adjusting the temporary shift in income caused by changes in working hours, as much as two-thirds of the variation in log permanent income is explicable by the difference in schooling (Mincer 1974: 96). With regard to adjustments in working hours, Psacharopoulous and Layard (1979: 490) offer a better model for distinguishing between temporary and permanent income variations. Further discussion is beyond the scope of this book, but we should note that working hours also play an important role in income variations.

[7] My assessment differs from that given by Psacharopoulos and Layard (1979), who concluded that the overtaking points were in the 9–11 years of experience range and that investment contributed 0.53 of income variation, a result quite close to that of Mincer. The problem is that they give no clear standard for the choice of the range. Their explanation (*op. cit.*: 496) is not persuasive.

Evaluation of Mincer's Empirical Study

Mincer's work is a splendid example of how well a logically constructed theoretical framework can draw out, from a series of data sets, organized and productive information. Mincer has done a great deal in establishing facts in relation to earnings distribution.

Mincer's work, however, is founded on numerous assumptions both strong and weak. If these assumptions are well founded, his logic in determining the contribution of education to earnings distribution is both clear and interesting. His work, therefore, cannot be persuasive empirical research unless detailed and thorough examination of these assumptions is undertaken. The limitation of his analysis is that he does not follow this important procedure adequately.

Mincer's work seems to contain a few testable hypotheses. The first is the constraint on the size of the estimated coefficients on schooling in the regression equations (4.3) and (4.6). Underlying Mincer's theory is the assumption that income differences between individuals are solely the result of equalizing differences and random noise. Therefore, theoretically, the coefficients should be identical to the opportunity cost or the interest rate. Without the help of any elaborate theory, we can easily guess from our own experience that individual income may increase with education and training. The constraint that the coefficients on schooling be equal to interest rates, however, can only be strictly elicited by the assumption stated above. The estimated return on investment in education in fact is around 0.10, which is roughly equal to the return on real capital investment or the market interest rate of long-term bonds. (Mincer's discussion may have lost reliability if the estimation result is, for example, over 0.5 or below zero.) However, Mincer makes no rigorous attempt to prove whether, and to what extent, the estimation result satisfies the requirement of this testable constraint. He should have conducted an independent analysis to ascertain what opportunity interest rate should be used for comparison.[8] Mincer, moreover, often neglects this theoretical constraint, and allows the coefficient estimates between educational levels to vary.[9] Insofar as the present discussion of the world of equalizing difference is concerned, the theoretical postulation of Mincer has not yet been precisely verified.

---

[8] Mincer's theoretical constraint was derived from the assumption of a world of no uncertainty, or risk-neutral individuals. Therefore, it is not logically consistent if the difference between return on schooling and the market interest rate were interpreted as the risk premium.

[9] For example in Mincer (1974: 56, 93). Mincer's explanation (*op. cit.*: 93) of the interpretation of the estimation result of the coefficient on educational investment, r, is quite astonishing: 'The partial coefficient of schooling is an estimate of the average rate of return to schooling. The marginal rates are approximated in nonlinear formulations,..., which permit the estimation of different rates at different levels of schooling'. This sentence is clearly inconsistent with his theoretical discussion (*op. cit.*: 11). Rosen (1977: 9, 11) has already pointed out that such inconsistency in interpretation causes much confusion in the work of estimating return to schooling. However, there has been no change in interpretation since that time.

The second hypothesis concerns the existence of overtaking points. The theorem predicts that despite a wide variety of intensity of training, the income variation of the population should temporarily narrow at the transition point from training to reaping the rewards of training. However, as we have already seen, this prediction depends on the particular shapes of the earnings profiles, whether a wide variety of different income paths cross at a single point. Various explanations can be given, therefore, even if the predictions do not materialize, so this theorem does not qualify as a testable hypothesis in the strict sense. At any rate, as shown in the evidence, though the estimated result correlates with the theorem in the United States, it does not do so for the United Kingdom: the conclusion derived from this theorem is not yet fully proven.

In order fully to prove Mincer's main statement that differences in schooling and training explain a large part of the earnings inequality in the population, data that measure individuals' actual investment of time and money on training is indispensable.[10] To sum up, Mincer's regression equation and the underlying theory have not yet been verified by the data. Rather, I have two doubts on the way that Mincer approaches this problem.

The first concerns the passiveness or remoteness of his research objective. Mincer's conclusion provides no support or guidance to researchers seeking the cause of the inequalities evident in the real world and the means to rectify these. Mincer concludes that at least 30 per cent of income differences (in variance terms) is explicable by human investment, and 50 per cent by the overtaking points analysis. When difference in working hours is accounted for, moreover, the figure rises to as much as nearly two-thirds of the inequality in the population's earnings, he states. However, in Mincer's underlying model, human capital is given the role only of changing the allocation over time of the same lifetime income. Such a difference does not represent in the context of a whole lifetime. Then which part of Mincer's model is the inequality that truly matters? Mincer deals with such differences only as residuals: no attention is given to analysing the constituents of the residuals. Therefore, as a research scheme to track and focus on the social problem of inequality, his research proposition is very passive in its character. It is not surprising, therefore, that many researchers question his method of approaching this subject: stressing the enormity of the difference in income that theoretically merits no attention, without questioning the various assumptions underlying the theory.

Second, if innate abilities and socio-economic background differ between individuals, the investment opportunity curves differ between individuals. In this case, individuals with more advantageous income opportunities will invest more in education and training, causing a real lifetime income inequality

---

[10] Thurow (1983: 168) criticized Mincer's work as an 'elaborate tortology'. He stated that what Mincer does is only to credit the residual difference in income not explicable by education to the unobserved on-the-job training. He commented that such a procedure provided no proof of the importance of the role of training in the workplace.

between individuals. The estimated coefficients of education in the regression equations (4.3) to (4.6) will not represent a mere return to schooling but also the rents to innate abilities and a good investment environment. If this is the case, the coefficient estimates will be biased upwards, as well as the coefficient of determination, as I have already mentioned. The income distribution difference explicable by the equalizing difference, as a matter of course, will be smaller than in Mincer's estimation. In the next section, I review empirical analyses that have tried to capture the contribution of innate differences and socio-economic background in the generation of income inequalities.

4.3. EARNINGS FUNCTION: INNATE ABILITY, FAMILY AND SOCIO-ECONOMIC BACKGROUND, AND THE DISTRIBUTION OF INCOME

Recognizing that people's initial abilities and socio-economic factors such as family are varied, as also are people's opportunities to invest in human capital, one cannot regard differences in schooling and training in the workplace as reflecting 'equalizing inequality'. The measurement of how such factors influence income distribution is known as the earnings function estimation. The procedure is first to estimate the earnings functions and then to compare the magnitudes of causal effects. We begin with prototypes of empirical models for estimating earnings.

Empirical Models of Earnings Determination

The first equation of the empirical model is the earnings function, as follows. It corresponds to the 'production function' of earnings.

$$\ln Y_i = \alpha + \beta s_i + \gamma A_i + \delta H_i + u_i. \tag{4.7}$$

The suffix i denotes the i-*th* individual. This equation presumes that the basic factors determining earnings are schooling, s, ability after schooling, A_i, and socio-economic factors of the home environment, H_i. The error term u_i expresses all factors independent of these factors. The coefficient β is a marginal rate of return, $(\partial y_i/\partial s_i)/y_i$, brought about by an additional unit of schooling.[11]

The second equation of the empirical model explains how individuals choose schooling. Years of schooling, s_i, depends on one's ability in childhood

---

[11] As the function is linear, the marginal rate of return bears little relationship to years of schooling. This is incompatible with our assumption of diminishing returns. However, the optimal investment level is determined under the assumption of an incomplete capital market in which the interest rate is the increasing function of borrowing.

(denoted by $A_{0,1}$) and family socio-economic factors, H_i. Therefore, we set this out as follows.

$$s_i = aA_{0,i} + bH_i + v_i. \tag{4.8}$$

The error term v_i denotes all factors independent of $A_{0,i}$ and H_i.

Third, as schooling is expected to transform one's initial ability into adulthood abilities, the latter is expressed as follows.

$$A_i = cA_{0,i} + ds_i + w_i. \tag{4.9}$$

The coefficients c and d represent unity and zero, respectively, if the adulthood ability remains constant over a lifetime. w_i is the error term representing all factors independent of the explanatory variables.

Fourth, childhood ability is assumed to be based on genetic factors, G_i, socio-economic factors, H_i, and incidental factors (z_i). This we write as follows.

$$A_{0,1} = eG_i + fH_i + z_i. \tag{4.10}$$

The mutual relationships among the four equations are expressed in Figure 4.3.

The arrows denote predicted causal relationships. First, childhood ability is determined and then schooling, adulthood ability, and income in turn. The symbol attached to an arrow corresponds to the coefficient of each equation. The arrow between the two symbols G_i and H_i expresses the possibility that there exists a correlation between them (no causal relationships are assumed).

It can be presumed that there are no relationships among error terms, as only one variable is determined at a time, one after another. As a result, this system has a special structure, known in econometric terminology as a 'recursive structure'. The ordinary least square (OLS) estimation of this structure leads to

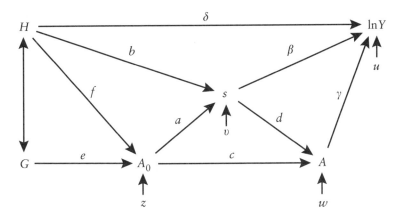

Figure 4.3. *Empirical Model of Income Determination*

unbiased estimates.[12] Regression coefficients estimated by standardizing each variable (dividing the differences between each variable and the average by the standard deviation) are called 'path coefficients'. By using the correlation coefficient between path coefficients and variables, we can compare the magnitudes of various causal relationships with each other. (This method is referred to as 'path analysis'.)

For example, two causal links are assumed between schooling, s, and income, $\ln Y$; one is the direct effect, in which schooling raises income, and the other is the indirect effect, in which schooling raises innate ability, A_i, which in turn raises income. However, there also exists a spurious correlation between s and $\ln Y$, as both are affected by family socio-economic factors, H. Thus we are concerned with the magnitudes of direct effects, indirect effects, and spurious effects. By standardizing each variable in equation (4.7), multiplying it by standardized s_i, and summing up, we get:

$$\rho_{ys} = \mathrm{p}_{ys} + \mathrm{p}_{ya}\rho_{as} + \mathrm{p}_{yh}\rho_{sh}, \tag{4.11}$$

where ρ_{ys}, ρ_{as}, and ρ_{sh} are simple correlation coefficients between $\ln Y$ and s, A, and s, and s and H, and $\mathrm{p}_{ys}, \mathrm{p}_{ya}$, and p_{yh} are path coefficients corresponding to β, γ, and δ. The three terms of the right-hand side of the equation denote the direct effect, the indirect effect, and the spurious effect, respectively.

If people's economic ability is the same as their innate ability A_i, the coefficients for schooling s_i and the socio-economic factors variable H_i as determinants of income, that is β and δ, become zero, and the effects of s_i and H_i will be absorbed into A_i. If they are not so extreme, the true values of β and δ will be small enough that economic abilities have the same effect as initial abilities. In other words, the values of β and δ have upward biases called 'ability biases'.

The problems are to determine the most important element of economic abilities and to measure such ability. Economics has traditionally assumed that the most important factor in determining earnings is cognitive ability, which can be measured by the IQ and test scores. Thus economists have performed analyses which assume $A_{0,i}$ to be a childhood IQ and A_i to be scores received in school or IQ after schooling.

---

[12] To be more precise, it is required that the error term, u_i, which determines income, is not known when one determines what kind of schooling to choose. Then, as the schooling level is chosen, based on the expected income (or additionally considering the risk), the independence of the explanatory variable for income, s_i, and the error term, u_i, is maintained, and the OLS method may be appropriate. However, if the error term is specific to an individual, in the sense that the individual can perceive its value in advance, the independence of s_i and u_i can no longer be maintained, so that the so-called endogeneity bias can occur. See Griliches (1977) and Willis and Rosen (1979) on the procedure for deleting the endogeneity bias. Discussion of the precision of this procedure is beyond the scope of this volume. See Willis (1986) for a survey of the earnings equation.

Cognitive Ability as an Economic Ability

The representative study estimating the earnings function on the assumption that the most important economic ability is cognitive ability is Griliches and Mason (1972). Their sample, from the 1964 Current Population Survey, comprises about 1,500 individuals aged 21 to 34 who were full-time employees with military experience at the time of the survey. The sample was also restricted to individuals for whom there were test scores prior to their military service. As the sample was limited to people who had been admitted to military service, those with extreme scores were excluded and there was a possibility that those at both ends of the sample were not included. However, the data from this survey are invaluable, covering the whole country, which enables us to match income with indices of cognitive ability.

The data used by Griliches and Mason do not include all the variables shown in Figure 4.3. As the study does not have any data on childhood IQ, it offers no answers to the question whether schooling raises adult earnings ability and income independently of childhood ability. However, it supplies the minimum data that enables us to match income with indices of cognitive ability. The military entrance test is a kind of intelligence test that covers vocabulary and mathematics. One complicating factor is that the researcher must distinguish between schooling before and schooling after military service, as some individuals return to school after completing their period of service. The empirical model employed by Griliches and Mason is shown in Figure 4.4. As in Figure 4.3, the error terms are independent of each other. As a result, the model takes the recursive form, as Figure 4.3 does.

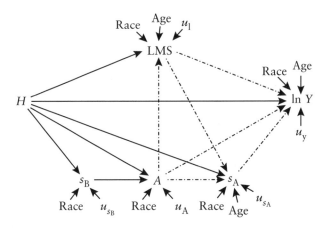

Figure 4.4. *Griliches and Mason Model*

Source: Griliches and Mason (1972).

Income and Wealth

Table 4.6. *Correlation among Income, Schooling, IQ, and Home Environment*

Variables	Average	Standard deviation	Correlation coefficient						
			1	2	3	4	5	6	7
Age	29.0	3.5	—	—	—	—	—	—	—
Race (white = 1, black = 0)	0.96	—	—	—	—	—	—	—	—
Log income (gross income per week)	4.73	0.40	1.0	0.264	0.149	0.329	0.235	0.114	0.229
Schooling before military service (years)	11.5	2.3	—	1.0	−0.70	0.832	0.469	0.283	0.307
Schooling after military service (years)	0.8	1.4	—	—	1.0	0.405	0.098	0.103	0.085
Total years of schooling	12.3	2.5	—	—	—	1.0	0.490	0.321	0.333
Scores on military entrance test (IQ)	54.6	24.8	—	—	—	—	1.0	0.229	0.242
Father's schooling	8.7	3.2	—	—	—	—	—	1.0	0.431
Father's occupational status index	29.0	20.6	—	—	—	—	—	—	1.0

Note: The size of the sample is 1,454.

Source: Griliches and Mason (1972: S78, Table 1; S83, Table 2).

The new variables which were not included in Figure 4.3 are schooling prior to military service, s_B schooling after military services, s_A and the period of military service, LMS. The order of the endogenous variables is: $s_B \rightarrow A \rightarrow$ LMS $\rightarrow s_A \rightarrow \ln Y$. The model allows for the fact that each variable is affected by such factors as race, age, and home environment and there is provision for these to be taken into consideration. The data representing home environment, H, are: father's schooling, professional status (Duncan score),[13] and the characteristics of the region where one spent one's childhood (whether the south or the north, and metropolitan areas or suburbs or non-suburban areas). The reason why we controlled for the influences of age and race is straightforward. The characteristics of the variables and the correlation among them are as shown in Table 4.6.

From Table 4.6 we see that the simple correlation coefficient between years of schooling and the entrance test is 0.47. The partial correlation[14] between them is 0.42, even if we exclude father's schooling and profession. The results are only to be expected, given that the purpose of formal schooling is to select those with high cognitive ability.

---

[13] The Duncan Index is a socio-economic status variable devised by the American sociologist Otis D. Duncan. It is an index, ranging from zero to 100, based on a survey of social prestige. In the United States, architects, judges, doctors, dentists, and chemical engineers compose the highest status group. For details, refer to Blau and Duncan (1967: 119–23, especially Table 4.1).

[14] The partial correlation coefficient here is that of the error terms, derived as follows (Johnston 1972: 61–5, 132–5). We denote the race variable as C and define the correlation coefficient matrix

Table 4.7. *The Effects of Schooling and Cognitive Ability on Income*

Independent variable ln Y	Explanatory variable			Other explanatory variables in an equation	R^2
	s_B	s_A	A		
(1)	0.0502	0.0528	—		0.167
	(0.0042)	(0.0070)		Race, periods of	
(2)	0.0418	0.0475	0.00154	military service, age	0.173
	(0.0045)	(0.0072)	(0.00045)		
(3)	0.0379	0.0496	—	Race, periods	0.213
	(0.0045)	(0.0070)		of military	
(4)	0.0328	0.0462	0.00105	service, age, regional	0.216
	(0.0050)	(0.0071)	(0.00045)	characteristics in childhood, father's schooling years and occupational status	

Note: Figures in parentheses are standard deviations.

Source: Griliches and Mason (1972: S86, Table 3).

What kinds of relationships exist between income and schooling? As mentioned earlier, if cognitive ability lies at the root of economic ability, the effects of schooling will be blurred by variables representing cognitive ability. Let us examine Table 4.7, which shows estimated coefficients of schooling and ability. At the end of each row are other explanatory variables. Rows (1) and (2) are different from rows (3) and (4) in that the latter contain home environment, H. Row (1) and row (2) differ from each other in that (1) contains entrance test scores which are not found in (2). Rows (3) and (4) differ from each other in the same way as rows (1) and (2). All rows have variables such as age, periods of military service, and race in common.

From Table 4.7, we can confirm the following points. The entrance test score pushes up income significantly. If we ignore the scores, the coefficient of

R among A, s_B, H, and C as follows:

$$R = \begin{bmatrix} 1 & \rho_{A,s_B} & \rho_{A,H} & \rho_{A,C} \\ \rho_{s_B,A} & 1 & \rho_{s_B,H} & \rho_{s_B,C} \\ \rho_{H,A} & \rho_{H,s_B} & 1 & \rho_{H,C} \\ \rho_{C,A} & \rho_{C,s_B} & \rho_{C,H} & 1 \end{bmatrix}.$$

If we define $R_{i,j}$ as the cofactor of the (i,j) element, the partial correlation coefficient ρ' is given as follows:

$$\rho' = -\frac{R_{1,2}}{\sqrt{R_{1,1} R_{2,2}}}.$$

If we substitute father's schooling into H, we get $R_{1,2} = -0.376$, $R_{1,1} = 0.920$, and $R_{2,2} = 0.867$. Instead, if we substitute father's occupational status into H, then we get $R_{1,2} = -0.366$, $R_{1,1} = 0.898$, and $R_{2,2} = 0.861$. ρ' is 0.42, after rounding, for both cases.

schooling will have an upward bias. However, the magnitude of the bias is only 17 per cent. The rate of return of the variable s_A is even smaller (10 per cent). This point remains true even if we adopt variables representing home environment. If we compare rows (3) and (4), we find that rates of return are biased upwardly by about 13 per cent for s_B, and only 7 per cent for s_A. To sum up, indices of cognitive ability are not strong enough to blur the effects of schooling.

In order to assess the relationship between entrance tests and income, path analysis is effective. From Table 4.6, the simple correlation coefficient between cognitive ability (A) and log income (ln Y) is 0.235. To what extent are they 'true coefficients' and to what extent are they spurious? In Figure 4.4, the dotted lines represent causal relationships. These relationships are divided as the 'direct effect' in which cognitive ability raises income directly and the 'indirect effect' in which cognitive ability gives rise to income through the effects of the length of military service (LMS) and schooling after military service (s_A). Other relationships are spurious, involving socio-economic factors such as home environment (H), schooling prior to military service (s_B), and race.

The result of the path analysis indicates that 0.065, that is, only one-quarter of the correlation coefficient 0.235, is direct, 0.036 is indirect, and 0.134 is spurious.[15] That is to say, only 0.1 of the correlation coefficient ($R^2 = 0.01$) is due to the causal relationship. Therefore, the assumption that the main component of economic ability is cognitive ability cannot be supported.

This finding was confirmed by other studies based on larger samples, such as Duncan, Featherman, and Duncan (1968: Fig. 6.4.1 and 117), Bowles (1972), Bowles and Nelson (1974: 44, Table 2), and Jencks (1972: Appendix 13). They extrapolated the correlation coefficients among cognitive ability indices, income, and other variables obtained by Griliches and Mason in the path analysis, as their data contained no indices of cognitive ability. Thus there remains the question of the extent to which they are independent of Griliches and Mason.

Fägerlind's study (1975), which was based on a follow-up survey of individuals aged between 10 and 43 (from 1938 to 1971, sample size 700) in a middle-sized city (Malmö) had different results from those of Griliches and Mason. First, as shown in Table 4.8, not only the correlation between years of schooling and income, but also the indirect effect through cognitive ability,

---

[15] The figure 0.065 is obtained by dividing the coefficient 0.00105 by the ratio of the standard deviation of ln Y to A. That is:

$$\sigma(\ln Y) = 0.40, \qquad \sigma(A) = 24.8;$$

$$\frac{0.00105}{0.40/24.8} = 0.0652.$$

For other figures in the text, refer to Griliches and Mason (1972: S89, Note 18). The figures quoted here are not exactly the same as those in Griliches and Mason, due to rounding.

Table 4.8. *Increase in the Economic Effect of Cognitive Ability with Age*

	Malmö Cohort Data (ages)				
	25	30	35	41	43
Influence of schooling years on log income					
Direct root	0.178	0.218	0.297	0.272	0.301
Cognitive ability root	0.017	0.045	0.091	0.078	0.114
Total (correlation coefficient)	0.195	0.263	0.388	0.350	0.415
Influence of schooling type on log income					
Direct root	0.176	0.380	0.427	0.470	0.500
Cognitive ability root	0.000	0.015	0.061	0.028	0.060
Total (correlation coefficient)	0.176	0.395	0.488	0.498	0.560

Note: The direct root represents the correlation of schooling with log income through the direct effect or occupational choice. The cognitive ability root represents the correlation of schooling with log income because schooling raises adults' IQ; it is the sum of the direct effect of IQ on income and the effect of IQ on occupational choice. See footnote 16 for further details.

Source: Fägerlind (1975: Table 10).

grew stronger with age when the effects of schooling on income were split into two: the direct and indirect causal relationships through cognitive ability in one's adulthood[16] (measured by IQ score at age 20). However, the weight of the indirect effect was only one-quarter of the total effects even at the age of 43. Therefore, the study could not support the contention that the effect of years of schooling was erased when cognitive ability was taken into consideration. When he looked at the kind of education instead of number of years,[17] no

---

[16] Fägerlind's model is similar to that in Figure 4.3, but differs from it in that the effects of socio-economic background (*H*) are wholly absorbed in schooling (*s*), and IQ, (A_0) in childhood has effects on income through occupation. The model without the error term is shown as follows:

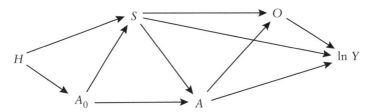

As for the schooling variable, *s*, two kinds of analysis are carried out: one substitutes the length of schooling into *s* and the other uses kind of schooling. If we use the same notations as in equation (4.11) in the text, the relationships between income and schooling are as set out in equations (a) and (b):

$$\rho_{ys} = \rho_{ys} + \rho_{yO} \cdot \rho_{os} + \rho_{ya} \cdot \rho_{as}. \qquad \text{(a)}$$
$$\rho_{os} = \rho_{os} + \rho_{oa} \cdot \rho_{as}. \qquad \text{(b)}$$

tendencies appeared for the weight of cognitive ability to increase, although the relationship between schooling and income grew stronger as the sample became older. The weight of cognitive ability was only 10 per cent of the total correlation. In this respect, his findings were consistent with those of Griliches and Mason. On the other hand, his results differed from theirs, since they concluded that cognitive ability could almost be ignored. As their sample was limited to young people aged from 21 to 34, there remained a possibility that the full effect of cognitive ability was not apparent. Lillard (1977, Figure 1) analysed data on aircraft pilots (NBER–Thorndike data) and found that the contribution of cognitive ability to income increased with age.

Second, the contribution of cognitive ability to income depended on both educational category and occupation. This was especially true at age 43. As for educational category, for people with high school diplomas or less, cognitive ability had almost no bearing on income. However, for people with more than high school diplomas, income increased with cognitive ability. The correlation between income and cognitive ability grew stronger as level of education rose (Fägerlind 1975: 94, Appendix; Table 6). As the data used by Lillard were also limited to those with higher levels of schooling, the effects of cognitive ability were clear. His analysis classified occupations into the following six categories: (1) unskilled manual workers, (2) semi-skilled manual workers, (3) skilled manual workers, (4) foremen, (5) upper-rank clerical workers, (6) managerial, directorial, and professional workers. While for groups (1) to (3), cognitive ability is almost unrelated to income, for groups (4) to (6), the two variables are positively correlated. Especially for group (6), a high correlation is observed (*op. cit.*: 95, Appendix; Table 7). As the sample was small, the tendencies observed here cannot be regarded as decisive. However, it is plausible to conclude that the economic effect of cognitive ability depends on both schooling and occupation.

There is a problem concerning the relationship between cognitive ability and income. This is the possibility that intelligence may be inherited, as shown in Table 4.3. Many researchers have raised this question and many controversies have reappeared in the area of psychology in the past. Although it is recognized

By substituting (b) into (a) and rearranging, we get (c):

$$\rho_{ys} = \{\rho_{ys} + \rho_{yO} \cdot \rho_{os}\} + \{(\rho_{ya} + \rho_{yO} \cdot \rho_{oa})\rho_{as}\}. \tag{c}$$

Table 4.8 shows the decomposition of ρ_{ys} by (c). The 'total' row, the first parenthesis on the right-hand side, and the second parenthesis correspond to ρ_{ys}, the 'direct effect', and 'cognitive ability' respectively.

[17] The kinds of schooling examined here are: (1) the legal minimum elementary schooling, (2) six to seven years of national school (elementary school), (3) vocational training after national school, (4) junior high school or some senior high school, (5) qualification for entering university or teacher training after high school, (6) some university (Fägerlind 1975: 48). Fägerlind numbered the six categories from 1 to 6. Therefore, the numbers reflect quality of schooling as well as years of education.

that genetic factors lie at the root of the intergenerational relationship of ability and income, the magnitude of their effects varies with the researcher (Bodmer 1972: 98–99). It was Jensen (1969) who stressed the importance of genetic factors. He even argued that income differentials between black and white people could be attributed to IQ differentials. One of the important applications of earnings functions is that they can test the validity of extreme assertions. What the above-mentioned analysis indicated was that the effect of IQ on income differentials was limited, except in the case of a few occupational categories, even though intelligence is inherited to a considerable extent. (According to Griliches and Mason, however, inheritance factors are also negligible.) Income differentials between different races cannot be validated by the inheritance of intelligence.

Family Socio-economic Background Factors

Let us examine Table 4.7 again. If we introduce the factor of home environment, the explanatory power of the earnings function increases considerably (rows (3) and (4)). In terms of R^2, the explanatory power rises about 0.04 or 0.05. As R^2 was only 0.17 before adding the factor of home environment, the increase is not negligible. The coefficient of schooling has also changed after home environment has been introduced. Two-thirds of the 35 per cent differential in estimated s_B, the effect of schooling before military service, shown in rows (1) and (4), are attributed to home environment factors. If we compare the estimated coefficients of the test scores A in rows (2) and (4), we find such factors to be so small as to lead to overestimation of the effects of cognitive ability. The estimated coefficients decrease to two-thirds after home environment is taken into consideration. (This point was mentioned previously as a spurious regression.) Thus home environment affects not only schooling and cognitive ability but also income distribution (independently). This point was confirmed by Sewell and Hauser (1975), who conducted a follow-up survey of high school students in the twelfth grade in the State of Wisconsin over a ten-year period. Their data were unique in that they included parents' income as a home environment variable.[18] The parents' income significantly affected income distribution, even if we control for schooling and the cognitive ability of the sample students.

On the other hand, analysis of the data for Malmö leads to the conclusion that both father's schooling and his occupational status when the student was

---

[18] This study followed on from a study of individuals who were in the fourth year of high school in the State of Wisconsin in 1957. The outstanding point of the follow-up study is that it includes detailed information on individuals' ability and home environment, especially income (for three years after graduation from high school). On the other hand, the data have limitations in that they are local, and they are confined to those who have finished at least three years of high school (about one-third of the cohort is excluded). As for the data about home environment and other factors, refer to Leibowitz (1977).

10 years old affect his/her income at the age of 43 through his/her cognitive ability in childhood (at 10 years old). However, when schooling and occupational status were taken into consideration, there was no statistical significance of the variables related to fathers and indices of cognitive ability in childhood (Fägerlind 1975: 71; Table 9). Moreover, occupational status at the age of 43 is mainly explained both by schooling and by cognitive ability in adulthood, with variables related to father and cognitive ability in childhood having little effect. Although it is true that home environment factors affect the type of schooling chosen and cognitive ability in adulthood, they do not have any independent effects. In that respect, the conclusions from the Malmö study differ from those of Griliches and Mason.

The role of home environment may be interpreted as a variable denoting (unmeasured) quality of schooling. It is plausible enough to suggest that there are variations in the quality of schooling and that the upper economic classes tend to have a better home environment.[19] In Fägerlind's study, mentioned previously, home environment has little effect on social status when schooling is measured by type rather than number of years. This result can be interpreted as showing that the kind of schooling is a better measure of the quality of schooling than is the number of years. Interpreted in that way, Fägerlind's results are not totally inconsistent with those of Griliches and Mason.

Sociology and psychology present another way to interpret home environment. This interpretation regards home environment as representing occupational preference, desire to climb social ladders, and willingness to achieve. It is considered that preferences for specific jobs and willingness to achieve help one to gain higher educational qualifications and higher cognitive ability. In fact, from an investigation of varied data, Duncan, Featherman, and Duncan (1968: ch. 7) conclude that, on average, children from families of higher social status prefer occupations of higher social status. On the basis of opinion poles (both national and local) on attitudes to child rearing, Kohn (1969) found that different occupational and social strata had different attitudes. That is, 'middle class' parents engaged in white collar jobs and professional and managerial jobs required 'self-direction' of their children, while 'working class' parents engaged in semi-skilled or skilled production jobs required of their children 'cooperation [with] external prestige' (*op. cit.*: 11). These findings are limited by the fact that the data are cross-sectional and that the analysis does not examine whether children's preferences for jobs and parents' child-rearing attitudes lead to higher social status for the children. However, it is plausible to suggest that such factors have effects on social status through personal ambition or the formation of characteristics.

---

[19] In the United States, the costs of public schools were borne by local government until the 1970s, when the federal government started to support the public schools. Differences in financial aid to public schooling between rich and poor municipal areas intensified differences in the quality of schooling. Wachtel (1975) showed that differences in the quality of schooling led to income differentials.

The Potential Variables Approach

Thus far we have discussed the possibility that parents' socio-economic background affects the occupation and earning ability of children in an unobservable way. It was Griliches and Chamberlin who refined the empirical model presented in Figure 4.3 (or Figure 4.4) in order to check it through data analysis. They measured profitability of schooling by estimating the characteristics, using measurable variables, after defining the ability nurtured in families as a potential variable that cannot be measured directly (Chamberlin and Griliches 1975, 1977; Griliches 1979).

Figure 4.5 is a diagrammatic representation of the theory underlying this approach. The potential variable is presented as L. L affects income $\ln Y$ either directly or through schooling (therefore, it corresponds to the initial ability, A_0). On the other hand L is, by assumption, comprised of home environment factors (denoted as B) and error terms peculiar to each individual (expressed as g). The assumption that cognitive ability scores are measured twice, that is before and after schooling (expressed as T_0 and T_1, respectively) is the same as in Figure 4.3. However, Figure 4.5 differs from Figure 4.3 in that it regards test scores as one of the indices representing ability and returns to schooling, rather than just ability. Therefore, it permits the interpretation that ability includes ambition or 'willingness' (the term used by psychologists), and that such ambitions assists one to get good marks in tests of cognitive ability. In this case, the correlation between income and cognitive ability is spurious.

The background factor B is assumed to include both observed factors (region of origin, father's schooling, number of siblings, number and kinds of books held), and unobserved home environment factors. Parents' values and child-rearing attitudes are, of course, unobserved home environment factors. The question is how to identify the unmeasured home environment and the individual factor g, which is also unmeasured. Personal factors can be identified if we control for common family factors by collecting data of brothers brought up in the same household.[20]

Chamberlin and Griliches (1977) pointed out that overestimation biases were brought about by neglecting potential ability. They also indicated that estimated potential ability included a variable that increased the cognitive ability score and another independent variable. That is to say, the initial ability that parents provide to their sons and daughters is somewhat different from cognitive ability.

This analysis is in some ways a trial. The amount of data was limited and incomplete. For income data, they used the expected mean income of the

---

[20] If brothers have the same home environment, their earnings functions and factors peculiar to each of them can be estimated by calculating the differences in their variables beforehand. However, as genetic factors cannot be regarded as identical, more sophisticated consideration is required (Griliches 1979: S41–S42). To estimate purely genetic factors, it is desirable to use data on monozygotic twins. Such an analysis was conducted by Behrman and Taubman (1976).

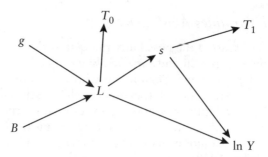

Figure 4.5. *The Potential Variables Approach*

occupations members of the sample were likely to enter in the future, as the sample comprised people who had just started working. For this approach to be fruitful, the data must be improved and observed indices other than cognitive ability test scores must be obtained. Such issues remain to be solved. At present, we cannot say whether cognitive ability is important in itself or whether willingness underlying that ability is more important, nor can we say what effect another ability may have. Even if it is proved that the ability bias on the profitability of schooling is small, we cannot explain what sort of effect schooling has on income.

Conclusion

In this section, we have summarized the empirical results of studies of the earnings function, starting with those of Griliches and Mason. The assumption that the main determinant of economic ability is cognitive ability is, in conclusion, dubious, as the positive effects of cognitive ability on earnings are limited. It was shown that the historically repeated statement that the persistence of income differentials could be explained by the inheritance of intelligence was not valid. In conclusion, the effect of schooling on income is small, even when we hold cognitive ability constant.

However, follow-up studies have revealed that the contribution of cognitive ability grows stronger as one gets older. This point is interpreted theoretically in either or both of the following ways: (i) That cognitive ability is positively related with trainability as we discussed in section 3.2. The effect gradually appears as one gets older, as it leads to better opportunities for on-the-job training. (ii) That, as seen from long-term follow-up studies, the economic ability that is related with cognitive ability gradually appears.

In addition, it is posited that cognitive ability has a strong effect on the determination of occupation, and that the role of cognitive ability tends to vary among occupations. Especially for professional and managerial occupations, cognitive ability not only determines access to such occupations but also becomes an important factor in income distribution. Therefore, equalizing opportunities for schooling is a significant means of income distribution.

With regard to income differentials, differences in home environment also play an important role. However, their effects are mainly through quality of schooling, parents' occupation, and differences in values and feelings of attainment. Whether we can check these points through statistical tests depends on the accumulation of high-quality data. However, in considering equality of opportunity to receive schooling, we must pay special attention to equalizing the quality of schooling.

One important issue that remains to be resolved is understanding the economic effects of schooling for more than half of all occupations, although the role of cognitive ability in certain occupations is clear. Part of the answer lies in the social integrative role that schooling plays. We examine this point in the next section.

4.4. THE SOCIAL INTEGRATIVE ROLE OF SCHOOLING AND THE PRINCIPLE OF CORRESPONDENCE

It is observed in our everyday life that schooling provides children with basic cognitive ability as human beings and, at the same time, conveys social values to them to integrate them into the social system and existing rules. It was a sociologist, Talcott Parsons, who discussed this point in the context of the theory of the social system (Parsons 1959). Building on Parsons' analysis, Gintis (1971) drew attention to the correspondence between the social structure of the production system and that of the education system. In this section, we investigate the studies that developed from Gintis's analysis.

The firm, as a representative contemporary production system, has such features as a hierarchical structure, information management, and decision making. Those in the upper positions have the right to issue instructions to those in lower positions. Hierarchies create relationships based on status and obligations among the people who work there. Of course, the relationship between those in the upper positions and lower positions is not based only on status and obligations. It is possible that those lower in the hierarchy may act collectively. Sometimes they have strong bargaining power. In some cases, bargaining power takes the form of a trade union and in other cases, it is just potential power. However, where bargaining power is exerted, recognizing the basic authority of entrepreneurs and the regulations of workers' activities, to obtain better employment conditions, the hierarchical structure is stable. Moreover, the discipline ensuring the smooth functioning of the organization is established by clear rules of action. Individuals' freedom is thereby sometimes restricted. However, such restrictions are limited as long as every worker has the right to make his or her final decisions and the power of self-control. When there is a conflict between the subordination to authority that the hierarchical structure expects and an individual's self-control, a firm's production process faces a crisis. The production process has to be regarded as involving social relationships as well as technological relationships.

The productivity of a firm and its workers depends not only on individuals' cognitive ability and self-expression, but also on the extent to which each individual accepts the rules and the organization's purposes, and responds to the incentive structure of rewards and punishment, such as opportunities for promotion, and the wage structure. Characteristics such as obedience to rules and discipline, predictability and reliability, and acceptance of obligations, as internal values are desirable. Furthermore, such characteristics (which make up what we call 'spiritual capacity') strengthen the effects of occupational training. That is to say, 'spiritual capacity' is an important factor in what we call 'trainability.'

Of course, the kinds of characteristics that are related to productivity depend on the position that an individual holds in a hierarchy. Obedience to rules and directions is important in lower positions of a hierarchy. Conversely, as one climbs to the higher positions, one requires superior cognitive ability for managing and integrating all elements of the organization, independence and creativity to exert such power, and internal self-discipline. Individuals in middle-level positions require medium levels of both characteristics as well as reliability. This argument has rarely been tested, although as stated it is plausible.

One of the empirical grounds supporting the hypothesis that a worker's personal characteristics are important factors determining productivity is given by a sample survey conducted by Edwards (1977). He selected a sample of workers who held lower-ranking positions in public organizations (mainly clerical), and private enterprises (manufacturing plants, mainly clerical) and classified them into groups of about 15 workers under a common supervisor. He collected data concerning (i) background information on the individuals, such as schooling, (ii) IQ scores, (iii) scores of ratings by colleagues, (iv) scores of achievement, rated by supervisors, and (v) wage differentials within groups (among colleagues) in the case of government organizations. By examining the relationships between these data, Edwards made the following discoveries.

First, characteristics such as 'patient', 'understands basic needs and order', 'accepts obligations', 'consistent job attitudes', 'practical (not necessarily creative)', 'not moody', 'frank', are highly correlated with ratings by bosses and wage differentials among groups in both public organizations and private firms (Edwards 1977: 130, Table 1).

Second, if we control for the variables representing workers' characteristics, the influence of schooling and IQ scores on boss's ratings and wage differentials are not statistically significant (*op. cit.*: p. 133, Table 4, p. 135, Table 6).[21]

---

[21] The magnitude of the correlation coefficient is (as expected), smaller for the coefficient between ratings and wages. The pairs of characteristics are as follows. The first group is composed of the following pairs: 'be on time/not on time', 'demanding rewards/not demanding rewards',

These individual personal characteristics are formed through everyday life and social life, with strong influences from both family and school. Organizations not only select those with such characteristics but also strengthen such characteristics (Kohn and Schooler 1973).

If we look at the school environment, we find a social relationship that reflects what may be seen as a hierarchical production process involving school administration, teacher, and students. Students are required to attend classes regularly, conform to the authority of school administrators and teachers, accept studies inculcating spiritual values, and meet the wishes of teachers. Furthermore, schools give students external incentives, in terms of rewards and punishments, by means of a points system. Such a system evaluates not only scores of cognitive ability but also the development of all personal characteristics (especially the characteristics that are suitable for the social roles that individuals are expected to play in the future). Just as different hierarchical positions in a firm require different characteristics, each stage of schooling has specific requirements of students. In middle school and in high school, acceptance of authority, co-operation with rules, and social co-operation are required, while choice of studies is limited. As one enters junior college or university, independence, self-discipline, and self-control are expected. At the same time, students are allowed to choose from a wide range of subjects. Of course, these differences owe much to the development of mind and body and the growth of cognitive ability. However, these differences correspond to the situation in which people's characteristics are required to suit their own position and role in the production structure of their organization (Gintis 1971; Bowles and Gintis 1976: 131–3).

In fact, Bowles, Gintis, and Meyer (1975) collected data that may be regarded as counterparts of those of Edwards (1977). That is, they gathered data on students' IQs, scores on cognitive ability tests, mutual ratings of characteristics by students, and ratings by teachers in high schools in the United States and found the following results. First, cognitive ability is the most important factor in explaining scores in school subjects. However, even when we control for cognitive ability, students' characteristics and social attitudes (spiritual capacity) have significant effects on scores independently. Thus, schools play a social role of moulding and selecting people who adapt themselves to the hierarchical structure in order to be productive. Bowles and Gintis called such relationships 'principle of correspondence'.

'predictable/unpredictable', 'thoughtful/thoughtless', 'obedient/independent'. These characteristics had positive relationships with bosses' ratings (and with wage differentials, with the exception of 'obedience') in public institutions but not in private enterprises. The second group is composed of the following pairs: 'aggressive/not aggressive', 'interested in wages/not interested in wages'. These had significant positive relationships with bosses' ratings in private firms. Lastly, the factor 'loves to be alone/sociable' was not significant in either type of institution. For evaluating statistical significance, it should be noted that the samples are 340 for public institutions, and 115 for private institutions, the latter being smaller.

Table 4.9. *Correlation between School Ratings and Ratings in the Workplace: A Case Study of Aircraft Manufacturing Plant Workers*

	Ratings in high school				Ratings in the workplace			
	Absence rates	Average scores in 3rd Year	Work habits	Social co-operation	Absence rates	Ability	Ratings of conduct	Ratings of productivity
Average	21.5	2.2	2.1	2.4	11.2	3.4	3.5	3.4
Standard Deviation	19.6	0.6	0.4	0.3	9.2	0.9	0.9	0.9
High school								
Absence rates	1.00	−0.11	−0.28	−0.27	0.30	−0.25	−0.31	−0.21
Average scores	—	1.00	0.78	0.67	−0.16	0.36	0.37	0.34
Work habits	—	—	1.00	0.85	−0.26	0.34	0.44	0.41
Social co-operation	—	—	—	1.00	−0.29	0.30	0.45	0.39
Workplace								
Absence rates	—	—	—	—	1.00	−0.14	−0.31	−0.23
Ratings of ability	—	—	—	—	—	1.00	0.61	0.72
Ratings of conduct	—	—	—	—	—	—	1.00	0.73
Ratings of productivity	—	—	—	—	—	—	—	1.00

Notes: Work habit in high school and social co-operation are rated by high school teachers. Ability in the workplace conduct, and productivity are rated by direct bosses.

Source: Brenner (1968: 30, Table 1).

In order to test whether this principle exists between school and workplace, we need a follow-up survey of an individual. It is hard to obtain such data. However, a quite useful sample is given by Brenner (1968) (Bowles and Gintis 1976: Appendix B). This survey is based on data from a hundred workers, both male and female, in an aircraft company. The data consist of boss's ratings, job records, high school scores, ratings by high school teachers, and high school attendance. Table 4.9 shows the correlation coefficient between high school scores and ratings by bosses. Cognitive ability is reflected in high school 'average scores' and performance ratings. Spiritual capacity, on the other hand, is reflected in high school scores for 'work habits' and 'social co-operation', and in workplace scores for 'job performance and attitudes' in the workplace. Productivity in the workplace, on the other hand, is reflected in bosses' ratings.

From this table we see that (i) cognitive ability in high school and various ratings in the workplace have a relatively high positive relationship, (ii) work habits and social co-operation in high school have a high positive relationship with ratings by bosses, (iii) rates of absence and ratings by bosses are negatively related. The problem is that the scores one got in the high school days are also positively related with work habits and co-operation. (This point is consistent

Table 4.10. *Regression Coefficients of Cognitive Ability on Workplace Ratings: A Case Study of Aircraft Manufacturing Plant Workers*

	Without controls	+Absence rates	+Absence rates + co-operation	+Absence rates + work habits	+Absence rates + co-operation + work habits
Ratings by	0.540	0.505	0.473	0.447	0.447
bosses	(0.141)	(0.139)	(0.188)	(0.226)	(0.227)
R^2	0.13	0.17	0.18	0.18	0.18
Ratings of	0.555	0.510	0.228	0.193	0.183
work habits	(0.141)	(0.136)	(0.179)	(0.217)	(0.216)
R^2	0.14	0.21	0.25	0.24	0.25
Rations of	0.510	0.481	0.238	0.124	0.119
productivity	(0.142)	(0.142)	(0.188)	(0.225)	(0.226)
R^2	0.12	0.15	0.18	0.18	0.19

Note: Figures in parentheses are standard errors.

Source: Regression analysis based on data from Bowles and Gintis (1976: Appendix B) and Brenner (1968).

with the findings of Bowles, Gintis, and Meyer (1975)). Thus it is difficult to find out how spiritual capacity contributes independently to cognitive ability.

In order to answer the question, we follow the same procedure as Gintis and Meyer to test how the correlation coefficient between ratings received in the workplace and scores received at school decreases if we add other indices to the high school material as control variables. Table 4.10 shows how the regression coefficients between high school scores (average scores in the third grade) and bosses' ratings change as we include control factors sequentially. This table also shows the coefficient of determination (R^2) that measures the explanatory power of the regression equation.

From this table we see that 'ratings of ability', 'ratings of work habits', and 'ratings of productivity' are related with cognitive ability in high school in different ways. On 'ratings of ability' by bosses, school scores have significant effects, with constant regression coefficients, even if we control for other factors. Social co-operation and work habits in high school do not have statistically significant effects on ratings made by bosses. On 'ratings of conducts' and 'ratings of productivity', on the other hand, regression coefficients decrease significantly and the statistical significance is lost if we add one's co-operation and work habits in one's schooldays as additional variables. However, 'social co-operation' and 'work habits' are statistically significant.[22]

---

[22] In the regression analysis, including both 'social co-operation' and 'attitudes to study', statistical significance is lost, although both variables have the same sign. As the correlation coefficient is 0.85, information on the two variables is not easily distinguished. Therefore, we cannot tell which variable has the stronger explanatory power.

From the findings mentioned above, we see that productivity in the workplace is related with spiritual capacity such as social co-operation in schooldays and adaptability to jobs, instead of with cognitive ability measured by school scores. These data have limitations in that they are derived from a study of people working in just a few occupations in a plant and a process of selection[23] has already been undertaken, through the investigation of background factors. They are also incomplete in that the standard of ratings by teachers and bosses is not clear.[24] However, it is a fact that people's spiritual capacity raises productivity independently of cognitive ability and that such capacity is evaluated in the process of schooling.

Appendix 4.1. **Mathematical Appendix**

1. The equation was derived mathematically from the following. Let $V_L(t)$ be the present value of income advantage at time t of the work M, compared to the work with no post-school training O. Let us call $V_L(t)$ the 'value of training investment'. $V_L(t)$ should satisfy such recursive relations as (A.1). The income is produced at the end of each period and $V_L(T + 1) = 0$.

$$V_L(t) = \frac{1}{1+r}\{y_M(t) - y_O + V_L(t + 1)\} \quad (1 \leq t \leq T). \tag{A.1}$$

The increment of the value of training from t to $(t+1)$, that is, $V_L(t + 1) - V_L(t)$ must just equal the training cost $C(t)$ for one to be indifferent between the work O and the work M. (If it were not, the relative wage would be so adjusted by arbitraging.) This means:

$$V_L(t + 1) = V_L(t) + C(t) \quad (1 \leq t \leq T - 1). \tag{A.2}$$

By iterating, the following is obtained:

$$V_L(t) = V_L(1) + \sum_{n=1}^{t-1} C(n). \tag{A.3}$$

Another condition that is necessary for job O to be indifferent as regards job M is that the value of the training investment is zero at $t = 1$ when one makes the

---

[23] For this reason, variables from individuals' schooldays do not have large variations. The possibility remains that the estimation is biased.

[24] Workers had to meet the following criteria: (a) graduated from a high school in a school area in Los Angeles, (b) attended the school for at least two years, (c) hired by the firm surveyed (Lockheed Company) within one year of graduation from high school, and (d) worked for at least a year. However, Brenner (1968) gives no detailed explanation of differences in jobs and years of experience. Therefore, it is not clear whether bosses' ratings are based on the average productivity in one job or whether they include productivity differences between jobs. Thus the incompleteness of the data.

occupational decision. Therefore:

$$V_L(1) = 0. \tag{A.4}$$

It is clear that this condition is identical to the following from (A.1):

$$\sum_{n=1}^{T} \frac{y_M(t)}{(1+r)^n} = y_0 \sum_{n=1}^{T} \frac{1}{(1+r)^n}.$$

By substituting (A.4) in (A.3), we get:

$$V_L(t) = \sum_{n=1}^{t-1} C(n). \tag{A.5}$$

The equation shows that the value of training investment $V_L(t)$ is equal to the accumulated sum of the past training investment. If (A.5) is substituted in (A.1) and then compared to (A.2), equation (4.5) in the text is obtained.

For the two-period model (see Figure 4.2), the expression becomes as follows if the training investment cost in the first period is $C = y_0 - y_M$:

$$y_M' - y_0 = (1+r)C.$$

5

The Labour Market and the Distribution of Income: The Dual Labour Market Approach

Labour power, that is, the amount of labour service measured in time units, and simultaneously an object of market exchange, is one of the basic factors of production supporting material production in the economy. At the same time, however, because labour power cannot be separated from the human being supplying it, it exhibits several complex features that are not normally observable for other factors of production.

What makes the circumstances complex are the following factors. (i) Each person possesses different labour *ability* (as distinct from *power*). (ii) Each person has an individual preference regarding the jobs offered in the market; namely, a preference in relation to job attributes. (iii) Each person is able to transform his or her own ability and also to learn more about what ability he or she has in the process of providing the labour service. (iv) Each person has a certain degree of discretion as to how much intensity he or she puts into exhibiting his or her ability within a given amount of time. (v) Each person is potentially able to act collectively and co-operatively with fellow workers in the workplace in order to improve their economic welfare.

Such circumstances tell us that the exchange of labour power cannot be analysed fully by means of the simple textbook tool of market exchange. It is the role of the theory of the labour market proper to show what sort of framework is available.

The neo-classical approach explained in Chapter 3 has extended the analytical framework necessary to deal with factors (i)–(iii). Indeed, we have seen that the principles of comparative advantage and equalizing difference dealt with the problem of diverse individual abilities and preferences, and that the theory of joint exchange facilitated the basic analytical framework by which to deal with the problem of learning ability or skills and the problem of informational learning. Apart from a few anomalies (namely, the market imperfection caused by firm-specific knowledge and asymmetry of information), we have reconfirmed, even in the expanded framework, the efficiency of resource allocation and realization of the full employment characteristic of the competitive market system.

Another approach has taken up factors (iv) and (v) seriously and discussed the circumstances that render labour market imperfections inevitable. This line of discussion, which has a partial lineage in institutional labour economics, is called the *dual labour market* approach. (It is also sometimes called the *segmented labour market* approach, but for our purpose they may be regarded as identical.) This approach argues that the labour market is segmented into two (or possibly more) sectors, one being the internal labour market created within each firm and characterized by a highly organized workplace and by the presence of fairly extensive learning on the part of workers, and the other being the *external labour market* with virtually no learning taking place on the part of workers. It also argues that determination of employment and income in each sector is governed by a different set of principles. While this approach acknowledges the contribution made by the neo-classical approach in developing theories pertaining to factors (i), (ii), and (iii), it simultaneously argues that such factors have only limited influence over the allocation of employment opportunities and distribution of income among people. There has been a significant advance recently in developing a formal analytical apparatus for this approach. Such development has been motivated by the fact that empirical research on earnings distribution along neo-classical lines was not as successful as expected (as explained in sections 4.1–4.3). There has also been a recognition in the field of macroeconomics of the need to explain labour market imperfections within a framework that is consistent with individuals' rational behaviour.

This chapter begins by providing an overview of the basic arguments of the dual labour market approach and of previous attempts to construct a formal analytical framework, and, by drawing attention to some important but neglected points, proposes a synthesis with which to understand the working of the labour market. The outline of this chapter is as follows.

Section 5.1 examines various empirical criticisms of the neo-classical theory, and discusses the need for a new analytical framework as well as the features that must be incorporated into such a framework. This section also serves as an introduction to the theoretical discussion that follows.

Section 5.2 considers the determinants of the division of labour and of technology that are treated as exogenous in the neo-classical theory. It does this from a historical and political-economy point of view, and furthermore, it briefly surveys the historical process which gave rise to the internal labour markets of firms, the key concept in this approach.

Section 5.3 discusses the content of the dual labour market hypothesis. Section 5.4 constructs a model of the economy with dual labour markets and analyses the determinants of earnings distribution in the long run. Furthermore, it highlights and examines points of controversy with the neo-classical approach.

Section 5.5 presents an analytical framework embodying factors (iv) and (v) above, namely the theory of *incentive-dependent exchange*, derives implications on the allocation of employment opportunities and the distribution of earnings, and discusses in what respects this theory competes with the neo-classical theory.

The following points emerge from the considerations in sections 5.4 and 5.5. First, it should not be concluded unequivocally that the labour market either establishes a competitive equilibrium or confronts quantitative rationing, a choice that lies at the centre of the conflict between the neo-classical and the dual labour market theories. Either type of equilibrium can occur depending on the conditions given. Second, there certainly exists a regime in the economy in which co-operative behaviour on the part of workers has a clear influence on the allocation of job opportunities and the distribution of real earnings. Hence, the neo-classical view that workers' social behaviour is nothing more than a façade is to be corrected. These conclusions appear in section 5.6. Throughout this chapter, the word income is synonymous with earnings.

5.1. COMPETING VIEWS OF THE LABOUR MARKET

The main focus of the neo-classical analysis (as set out in Chapter 3) is to distinguish the stock of *labour ability* that people possess from the flow of *labour power* that they provide, and to discuss how people's labour ability is formed and allocated to different types of jobs. It was there supposed that people exhibit such rational supply behaviour as: (1) directing their ability to the economically most advantageous job, (2) accumulating labour ability most advantageously via education and on-the-job learning, (3) accumulating information and possibly taking risk-avoiding measures most advantageously so long as they are partially ignorant of their own labour ability as well as of market opportunities. At the same time, the concept of the labour market has been extended, so that it is treated not just as a market involving simple commodity exchange, but as a market of joint exchange wherein such tangible and intangible goods as the amenity of the workplace, training and learning opportunities, and insurance are jointly traded with labour power. Thus, what people expect as rewards from work are not only wages (as compensation for lost leisure) but also the economic value of jointly exchanged goods.

In spite of these changes, it remains the case, as verified in Chapter 3, that every person's labour ability is allocated to some type of job through competitive adjustment of wage rates, and that, in equilibrium, both the marginal productivity principle and the equalizing difference principle are satisfied with respect to the wage rate for each job. Hence, apart from the operation of uncertainty and the operation of the equalizing difference principle, disparities of income between individuals reflect differences in the labour ability of these individuals. The earnings functions reviewed in section 4.3 have sought the sources of disparity in individuals' labour ability in disparities in individuals' education, experience, and family socio-economic background, regarding the exceptional factors mentioned above as residuals.

Empirical Criticisms of the Neo-Classical Approach

The foregoing view of the labour market is based on the presumption of individual rationality and market competition, and therefore, it can claim universal status, in the sense that it does not require validation in any specific country. In practice, however, observed facts do not live up to the theoretical implications described above in several important respects, even in a country such as the United States where those presumptions are widely believed to be most well met.

In the first place, the explanatory power of the earnings function is very weak. As was seen in section 4.3, the extent of differences in earnings that can be explained by differences in education, cognitive ability, and family socio-economic factors, even after controlling for age and sex, is at most 20 to 30 per cent in terms of the variance explained (or the coefficient of determination). The fact that the major source of the explanation lies in uncertainty (informational imperfections as regards labour ability, demand and supply shocks in the market, etc.), equalizing differences (however, as will be seen in a moment not much can be expected from this source), or pure luck implies that the neo-classical explanation, however consistent it may formally be with the facts, certainly cannot be regarded as an attractive interpretation. It makes us wonder if something important has been omitted from the overall framework.

In the second place, equality of income does not go hand in hand with equality of schooling years. In particular, the economic advantage of highly educated individuals has not diminished. As is clear from section 3.1, the great increase in higher education must have decreased the rate of return to higher education relatively to the rates for primary and secondary education unless accompanied by a large-scale upgrading of the quality of higher education *vis-à-vis* education at other levels (which is not so likely) and/or accompanied by changes in other circumstances. Evidence from the United States, however, suggests the contrary. First, if we compare the years 1950 and 1970, we see there has been a tremendous equalization in the distribution of years of education among white males (aged 25–64), and yet, no equalization in earnings seems to have taken place (Thurow 1975: 62, Table 11). Second, the estimated rate of return on investment in education has shown almost no signs of change (Fallon and Layard 1975: 279–80).[1]

Yet it is premature to reject the marginal productivity hypothesis from these facts alone, for the previous discussion has ignored the fact that the accumulation of capital equipment had been taking place simultaneously.

---

[1] In Japan, the average rate of return to education showed a declining tendency during the 1960s and 1970s (Kaizuka *et al.* 1979: 35, 36, 42). But at the same time, it is shown (*op. cit.*: 56, Table 2.11) that the rates of return calculated separately for junior-high school, high school, and college have declined at about the same pace, and there is no apparent sign that the rate of return to higher education, which spread throughout the population rapidly during the period, declined more sharply than those for other education levels. Hence, we cannot verify the validity of the marginal productivity principle just by looking at the movement of these rates of return statistics.

However, this is not to suggest that once we consider the effect of capital accumulation the problem is resolved. Indeed, if the labour power of highly educated, skilled individuals is relatively more complementary (as a factor of production) with capital equipment than the labour power of the lowly educated, unskilled, then as a result of capital accumulation there will be an increase in income disparity between highly educated individuals and those with a lower level of education.[2] Hence, so long as the relative increase in the number of highly educated individuals occurs simultaneously with the process of capital accumulation, there will be a cancellation of the forces arising from the supply side to decrease income disparity. It is then perfectly possible to see no decline in the returns to highly educated individuals. In fact, Griliches (1969) and Fallon and Layard (1975) have respectively used US time-series data and international cross-section data to estimate the production function involving three factors of production. Their estimation results tended to favour the hypothesis that complementarity between skilled labour and capital equipment was stronger than that between unskilled labour and capital equipment.

So far, so good. Yet, the problem remains. As the latter half of the 1960s saw high rates of capital accumulation occurring in conjunction with the popularization of higher education, it would certainly have invited the

---

[2] The term *complementarity* refers, in rigorous terms, to Hicks's (1970) measure of *q-complementarity*. The production function is linearly homogeneous with respect to three factors of production, capital equipment, v_K, skilled labour, v_S, and unskilled labour, v_U. The corresponding factor prices are denoted by w_K, w_S, and w_U. The marginal cost is denoted by $\lambda (= \lambda(x))$. Then the first-order conditions for cost minimization becomes:

$$w_i = \lambda F_i \quad (i = K, S, U).$$

We now evaluate the (proportionate) change in the i-th factor price (w_i) that would justify a unit (proportionate) increase in the input of factor $j(v_j)$ under the condition that the marginal cost λ is maintained constant. By taking the logarithm of the above first-order condition and differentiating the expression totally, regarding λ as constant, the following relationship is obtained:

$$\frac{\partial \ln w_i}{\partial \ln v_j} = \frac{F_j v_j}{F} \cdot \frac{FF_{ij}}{F_i F_j} \quad (i, j = K, S, U).$$

The first product term of the right-hand side expresses the income share of factor j. Hicks defines the second product term of the right-hand side as *the elasticity of complementality* between factors i and j (to be denoted by C_{ij}), and calls the two factors of production *q-complements* if its value is positive, or *q-substitutes* if its value is negative. The rationale behind this terminology is that $C_{ij} > 0$ corresponds to a situation wherein inputs of v_j and v_i are increased together to maintain the marginal cost constant even if it would lead to a rise in w_i. These notions are neatly explained by Sato and Koizumi (1973). The property referred to in the text can be shown by using the above definition and deriving the relationship

$$\frac{\partial(w_S/w_U)}{\partial v_K} = \frac{F_S F_K (C_{KS} - C_{KU})}{F_U F}.$$

Therefore, if $C_{KS} > C_{KU}$, then:

$$\frac{\partial(w_S/w_U)}{\partial v_K} > 0.$$

expectation of a rapid rise in labour productivity during the same period. Yet what, in fact, occurred was a decline in the rate of increase of productivity as compared with the preceding period.[3] Thus there remains doubt over the validity of the marginal productivity hypothesis. Let the above two points be combined, and be called the *schooling paradox*. Section 5.4 is devoted to a theoretical explanation of this paradox.

In the third place, there is no overwhelming empirical support for the operation of the principle of equalizing difference. According to Smith (1979) who surveyed the results of numerous empirical studies of this issue, the only factor showing consistent support for the operation of this principle was physical danger in the workplace; more specifically, jobs involving risk of death of the worker. Furthermore, even in these cases, the compensation was not more than 3–4 per cent of the wage for jobs involving average risk. For all other potential sources of compensation there was none that clearly supported the operation of the principle.

Table 5.1 summarizes the results of the independent statistical investigations surveyed by Smith. It shows the distribution, in these studies, of the orientation of compensation. There is a danger in such a simple compilation of results, for the data and methods of the studies vary quite widely. Nonetheless, this table shows the general tendency. It should be noted that the table shows that attributes which would normally be expected to attract positive compensation, such as risk of injury, job '*severe or tense*', '*job or income unstable*', in fact, do not receive clear-cut compensation. Also, at least from the viewpoint of the author, the fact that the attribute *manual labour* receives fairly significant negative compensation while the attribute *supervision of other workers* receives significant positive compensation seems the opposite of what would normally be expected. It may rather suggest the existence of different forces working to determine income distribution, and which offset and perhaps more than offset the force of equalizing differences.[4]

In the fourth place, and perhaps the most evident reason, is the existence of unemployment, more specifically involuntary unemployment. It shows that the labour market cannot realize the full utilization of labour ability through flexible price adjustments. Of course, there is vociferous opposition to the view

---

[3] According to Bowles, Gordon, and Weisskopf (1983: 56, Fig. 3.7), the capital stock per labour hour (i.e., capital intensity) in the USA rose by 1.8 per cent during the period 1948–66, 2.5 per cent during the period 1967–73, and 1.2 per cent during the years 1974–9 (all figures refer to the per annum average). The period from the latter 1960s to the early 1970s saw (on average) the most rapid capital accumulation. In contrast, the rates of increase in the real net national income per labour hour (i.e., the average rate per annum) was 2.9 per cent during the years 1948–66, 2.0 per cent during the years 1967–73, and 0.6 per cent during the years 1974–9. These rates exhibit a clear declining tendency.

[4] For a relatively more recent empirical evaluation of the existence of equalizing differences using panel data (which confirms the general conclusion stated in the text), see Brown (1980). Dickens and Katz (1987) and Krueger and Summers (1988) have also come to negative conclusions on the operation of the equalizing difference principle.

Income and Wealth

Table 5.1. *Results of Empirical Studies on Equalizing Differences*

Job attribute	Direction of compensation				Total
	+*	+	−	−*	
Risk of death	8	2	0	0	10
Risk of injury	4	2	4	0	10
Manual labour	0	0	3	2	5
Repetitive	1	0	0	1	2
Rapid pace	1	1	0	0	2
No room for discretion	0	2	2	0	4
Severe or tense	2	1	1	0	4
Job or income unstable	1	1	1	1	4
Machine tasks	1	0	0	0	1
Supervision of other workers	2	0	0	0	2

Notes: + signifies the payment of positive compensation, i.e., an increase in wages for the attribute in question. − signifies negative compensation. * indicates that the compensation (in either direction) is statistically significant.

Source: Compiled from Smith (1979: 3, Tables 1 and 2).

that all unemployment is inevitably involuntary. The *new unemployment theory*, as it was assuredly called, argues that the major part of unemployment can be construed as people voluntarily choosing unemployment while seeking better job opportunities (Phelps 1970). By abandoning the assumption of perfect price information this theory rescues the neo-classical presumptions of economic rationality and market competition, making them compatible with the fact that unemployment actually exists and that it fluctuates over time. In the world described by this theory, the collection of price information involves a cost, and so people set a reserve wage level, which is fixed in the short term, below which they choose not to work but to concentrate on job seeking. Thus, when the aggregate demand falls and with it the derived demand for labour power, people do not immediately recognize the overall decline in wage levels, but rather get the impression that only their own wage has fallen. (Those who have been unemployed see only that the wage of a job available to them has fallen). The result is that some of them withdraw their labour supply, thus increasing unemployment.

It was with the aim of rescuing the neo-classical premise, with a lesser modification of the assumptions, that Lucas and Rapping (1969) developed their *intertemporal substitution hypothesis*. The notion of a reserve wage that played a central role in the search theory is now replaced by that of *permanent wage*. If we suppose that the consumption of leisure is substitutable between periods, a decline in the current wage relative to the permanent level would result in an increase in the current consumption of leisure, which is the same thing as a voluntary decrease in labour supply. Just as in the search theory, unemployment arising out of a decline in aggregate demand is a voluntary one.

The most significant difficulty common to these hypotheses is that they do not comply with the stylized facts on labour turnover. First, if we look at the composition of increases in workers, the rate of new hirings declines during recessions, but at the same time, the proportion those recalled within the total increases. This latter fact implies that previous job separations by workers has most likely been involuntary. Second, voluntary separations clearly decrease during recessions. This point is totally at variance with the hypotheses in question (Tobin 1972: 8).[5] Thus, it is difficult to accept the proposition that the above hypotheses explain the major part of actual unemployment. In order to explain why involuntary unemployment is so persistent, we must go beyond the framework which always regards the labour market as a flexible wage-adjustment mechanism.

The Need for a New Framework

Up to now we have discussed the gap between the neo-classical theory and the observed facts in the United States. Of course, there is no need to jettison the framework entirely just because there exists a gap. Individual models and concepts are still quite useful. Nevertheless the framework must be expanded substantially to cope with the following three shortcomings.

The first shortcoming is that, except for a very formalistic presentation in terms of the production function, the framework lacks all but the briefest analysis of the demand side. Recall the discussion in section 3.1. We supposed that two types of jobs, A and B, were necessary for production, and each of them was most well matched to a particular position in the distribution of ability. When the ability of an individual happened to be close to one of these most well-matched positions, it claimed a rent (a differential quasi-rent) and it became a source of income disparity. Also people were generally seen as trying to raise this rent through education and training (section 3.2). However, nothing has been said about why particular types of jobs, not to mention the number of jobs to be combined in the production process, were chosen in the first place. A moment's reflection shows us that the appearance of this rent and its distribution among individuals depend critically on the rigidity and exogeneity of the types of jobs used in the production process.

The prima facie most plausible explanation for the assumption that job types and the manner in which they are combined is given, is that the production process which uses a particular combination of job types is technically dominant. To be precise, the term technically dominant refers to the fact that, given

---

[5] We can confirm the statements in the text using figures reported in US Bureau of Statistics, *Handbook for Labour Statistics*, 1981: Table 82. As more recent criticisms of the intertemporal substitution hypothesis, Altonji (1982) and Ashenfelter and Card (1982), have shown that when people's expectation of the permanent wage level is supposed to be formed by using either time-series information or consumption information as a proxy, the actual US time-series data turn out to be not predicted by the hypothesis.

the current resources of the economy (including capital equipment, land, raw materials, and distribution of ability among individuals), and given the insatiability of commodity demand, allocating human resources to a particular combination of job types A and B results in a uniformly outward shift of the economy-wide production frontier as compared with any other combination of job types. (This definition is static. If human investment is considered, then the definition must be given in terms of an intertemporal production frontier. Although the problem becomes quite complicated, the essence of the matter remains the same.)[6] Using this terminology we can now define the set of production processes, each of which is not technically dominated by any other production process, as the set of *efficient technology*.

If we were to suppose that a particular combination of job types A and B was technically dominating, or equivalently that there existed only a single element in the set of efficient technology (a combination of job types), then it would have been a very strong assumption indeed. In general, the set of efficient technology contains multiple elements, and it may very well be infinite in number.

Let us suppose an extreme case where exactly the same efficiency (that is, for the same input of labour hours, the same amount of output is obtained for each commodity)[7] as in the case of A and B is obtained whenever any pair of abilities, located opposite each other along the diameter of a circle, are combined. In effect, by modifying the range of tasks that each job involves, one is able to move correspondingly the ability position that is most well matched to each job.

The ultimate outcome of such a case is that the rent that accrued to individuals with advantageous ability positions under the combination of job types A and B disappears completely, and individuals' incomes are perfectly equalized. The distribution of ability among individuals now changes its role completely towards that of determining the frequency of job-type combinations adopted in the production process.

---

[6] On the concepts of the efficiency of the production process and the intertemporal production frontier, see the explanation given by Malinvaud (1977: chs 3 and 10(B)).

[7] Let the two pairs of the endpoints of the arbitrarily selected diameters of the ability circle be denoted by (A, B) and (A', B'). For the sake of convenience each job type that is most well matched to each endpoint is denoted by the same symbol. Then denote the production function of the *i*-th good using job types (A, B) as $F(L_A^{(i)}, L_B^{(i)})$, and similarly denote the production function of the same good using job types (A', B') by $F'(LA'^{(i)}, LB'^{(i)})$. Here $L_A^{(i)}$, $L_B^{(i)}$, $L_{A'}^{(i)}$ and $L_{B'}^{(i)}$ represent the amount of labour services measured in common man-hour units. The assumption made in the text amounts to saying that if, for all *i*:

$$L_A^{(i)} = L_{A'}^{(i)} \quad \text{and} \quad L_B^{(i)} = L_{B'}^{(i)},$$

then:

$$F^{(i)}(L_A^{(i)}, L_B^{(i)}) = F'^{(i)}(L_{A'}^{(i)}, L_{B'}^{(i)}).$$

To understand why this is so, it suffices to start from the equilibrium where there is a single pair of jobs (A and B) and suppose that some producer comes to recognize that the same efficiency is achieved by adopting a different combination of job types. Since the ability positions that are most well matched to the new job combination are not the ones that were most well matched to the old job combination, the wages paid in the market are definitely less than the value marginal product that this ability generates under the new combination of jobs. Hence, the producer in question will obtain excess profits for some time to come. However, such excess profit opportunities are soon exhausted as other producers are certain to follow the new practice, bidding up wages. It will then be recognized that excess profits can also be realized by a third and/or fourth type of job combination, and the process just described will continue to repeat itself. In the end, each ability position will be matched with the most suitable job combination. As a result, every worker now receives the same income.

Needless to say, the foregoing is only a hypothetical situation. It clearly shows, however, that, if there are many elements in the efficient technology set, the pattern of income distribution among individuals becomes quite different, depending on which particular combination of jobs is actually adopted.

In the course of economic development, there has been a great change in working conditions. The spectrum of organization has also become broader: from small family businesses to partnerships of at most a few members, wholesale merchants' distribution system, and further division of labour and co-operation, and to modern factories and offices characterized by large-scale hierarchical organization. While in the earlier organizations the supplier of labour power determined working conditions and activity levels, as well as the content of the product, there has been a great qualitative change in the nature of organizations since the advent of modern workshops and offices in that it is now the capitalists (or managers) who decide on those matters. The capitalists, as the employer, allocate tasks to workers at their discretion within the confines of the employment relationship. The capitalists' primary concerns lie, of course, in achieving profits and capital accumulation. Hence, it is not surprising that even if there were many types of technologically efficient working conditions, what is ultimately chosen depends very much upon the capitalists' distribution objectives as well as their desire to retain managerial prerogatives.[8]

---

[8] While in the ordinary microeconomic discussion of the producer's behaviour the focus is on minimizing cost and choosing a profit-maximizing output within the confines of a given job arrangement, our focus here is on the choice of job arrangement itself.

An exception to this focus, which discusses the arrangement of production organization within the neo-classical framework is, of course, the classical discussion of the rationale of the firm by Coase (1937). Coase argues that the manager's scope for discretionary command over workers diminishes the transaction costs that would be required in an alternative production arrangement of purchasing individual services one by one in the market, and thus provides the rationale for the establishment of firms. Such a viewpoint has been further elaborated by Simon (1951) and Williamson (1975: chs 2 and 4). However, even in this line of thought the focus of the analysis is on the form of organization, and not on the choice of technology and division of labour.

History provides eloquent testimony, as in the reality of female and child labour in England during the Industrial Revolution, that when the power of capital is unchecked, it can often lead to brutal working conditions lacking in humanity. Further discussion of the basic determinants of working conditions are presented in section 5.2.

The second shortcoming of the neo-classical approach is that it tends to ignore the gap between labour power as an object of exchange in the market and the actual labour (which is what counts in production) supplied by workers.[9] Labour power exchanged in the market refers to an agreement on the part of workers to follow the directions of the employer (though within prescribed limits) for a certain number of hours. The rewards which workers receive are determined in some cases (such as fruit picking) by perfect *piece rates*, and in some other cases by the profit-sharing system, but in the majority of cases they take the form of *time rates*, that is, a rate of payment per specified period of time. Although a worker must remain for a certain number of hours at the workplace, the intensity of work required is generally a different problem.

Of course, when the outcome of an individual's work can easily be observed and the cost of hiring and discharging workers is low, market competition forces are effective in disciplining workers. The equality between the workers' value marginal product and the market time/wage rate is easily realized. In practice, however, the aforementioned conditions are not likely to be satisfied. First, when each worker's labour output is significantly intertwined with that of other workers, and therefore there is an element of teamwork, it is difficult to separate one worker's outcome from another's.[10] Also, it is hard for a person outside the team to discern and assess the extent of each worker's input. Second, in practice, new hirings and discharges both incur costs. For new hirings, it is customary for there to be interviewing and screening costs as well as initial training costs (which are usually quite firm specific) to adapt the workers to the organization, and these costs alone suffice to make labour power a fixed factor of production. Furthermore, if the discharge of workers causes friction, the additional cost of this must also be taken into account. The existence costs for new hirings and discharges therefore provides workers with a safety zone to insure continued employment.[11] Nevertheless, such a safety zone

[9] The need to distinguish between the amount of labour power and the amount of labour was emphasized by Marx (1867) in his discussion of relative surplus values. However, the central theme of his analysis was the rise of the organic composition of capital, and his argument was more akin to the neo-classical notion of the effect of capital accumulation on the marginal productivity of labour. The problem discussed here was emphasized by Ure (1835), who belonged to a generation earlier than Marx. See the discussion in section 5.2.

[10] The simplest example is that of two persons lifting a heavy item of luggage. Whereas each person knows how much effort the other person is exerting, outsiders have difficulty observing each person's input separately. This point was emphasized by Alchian and Demsetz (1972).

[11] Becker (1962) and Oi (1962) raised this point very clearly. The *insider–outsider* approach of Lindbeck and Snower (1986) and Solow (1985) applied this notion to the explanation of wage rigidity and unemployment.

is not necessarily robust, and is subject to withdrawal when there is a severe decline in demand for a product.

At any rate, within certain limits workers have scope of their volition to control their work intensity. The result is a divergence between the exchange of labour power and the exchange of amount of labour. If employers are to extract actual labour from workers (more than the level they would provide voluntarily), they must provide workers with some kind of incentive schemes, including rewards or penalty. The foregoing discussion leads to a view of the labour market as not only a market of simple or joint commodity exchange, but also a market with *incentive-dependent exchange*.

Thus far we have considered the problem of work intensity only in relation to each period, that is, in static terms. However, the problem may extend to the dynamic domain. Consider the situation where on-the-job training is jointly exchanged with labour service. There is no need to ask whether the training is general or firm specific in character. Although it is the employer who promises to offer training opportunities to workers, the persons who actually conduct the training are often existing senior workers. Whether or not these senior workers carry out their role effectively seems also to depend upon the nature of the incentive schemes that the employer offers them.[12] If they failed to carry out the expected role, there would be a breach of contract by the employer. Thus, it would be desirable for a model of incentive-dependent exchange to be extended to cover the case of joint exchange in relation to on-the-job training.

Discussion of the theory of incentive-dependent exchange is the main theme of section 5.5. This form of exchange gives rise to features such as wage rigidity, involuntary unemployment, and segmented labour markets.

Finally, the third problem with the neo-classical approach is that it ignores the possibility that workers acting in concert might exert visible or invisible forces to modify their terms of employment. Of course, there may well be an opposing argument to the effect that, even if social rules and organization exist, they are merely surface phenomena below which there are complex structures, and they have nothing to do with the way in which resource allocation and income distribution are determined. In fact, the reason why the traditional labour market theories continued to ignore such organizational factors as trade unions seems to rest upon the view that anonymous forces of market competition would in the final analysis dominate any form of organizational forces. Whether such a viewpoint is justified or is mere wishful thinking must be examined carefully. Our analysis below points out the existence of a regime in which workers' collective forces do have real effects on the allocation of resources in the system.

---

[12] This factor was pointed out by Doeringer and Piore (1971: 84). Thurow (1975) took this as the starting point of his job competition model (cf. section 5.4).

5.2. DIVISION OF LABOUR AND TECHNOLOGY

The degree of division of labour is dependent upon the size of the market, as the well-known proposition of Adam Smith states. Smith himself considered a wide spectrum of division of labour, from ordinary 'social division' where occupations are divided, to 'procedure or process division', where labour is divided by the manufacturing process. However, where to draw the line between 'social' and 'process' is vague. For example, an advanced wholesale system has the characteristics of social division, where each procedure can be geographically and operationally independent. The same situation can also be observed in the systems employed by modern component subcontractors.

But the most innovative aspect of Smith's proposition was the realization that the division of labour will increase the technical efficiency from the same amount of labour input. Moreover, there are no limits in the enhancement of efficiency, and the only limitation is the demand for output confronting the organization. In modern terminology, this describes the theory of increasing returns. Note that Adam Smith built his theory upon the manual labour economy that existed before the Industrial Revolution. The individuality of large-size power plants was not seen as the source of increasing returns. The essence of the scale economy was simply derived from the subdivision and expertise of labour.[13]

The account of manufacturing pins by the subdivision of labour is the most famous passage in the *Wealth of Nations*. If one worker carries out all the procedures, from stretching the wires to cutting and piercing, he may make only a few dozen needles in a day. If several workers specializing in each process did the work, the daily output per worker would be a hundred times more. Smith saw the merits of specialization as: (1) the improved craftsmanship of each worker; (2) the saving of time lost previously when moving from one process to the next; and (3) facilitating and shortening the labour process, and eliciting technology that will allow one worker to do the work of more (Smith 1776, 1904: vol. I: 9).

Criticism of Smith's Theory of the Division of Labour

It is unnecessary to explain that concentration on and repetition of one type of work leads to the achievement of expertise, and understanding of work leads to the development of labour-saving machines. Marglin (1974) nevertheless criticized Smith's theory in great detail, and proposed the need to

---

[13] Refer to Young (1928) and Piore (1980*b*) for a modern interpretation of Adam Smith's theory of specialization and market expansion. The factors of increasing returns are mentioned in detail in Marx's *Das Capital*, but capital is regarded as the main factor. He regards entrepreneurs' motivations to accumulate capital as triggering the ensuing survival game. See Negishi (1989: 89–95) for how Adam Smith's theory manages to harmonize increasing returns and free competition.

reconsider the factors leading to procedural division. Smith speculated that there could be unlimited division of work.[14] Therefore, the skills of the individual craftsman would contract as the subdivision proceeds. Marglin also denies the possibility of the invention of new technology by drawing on Smith's own words in his own theory. Repeating dreary work might cut short a man's creativity, he stated, but never expand it.[15] Indeed, as Young and Piore have pointed out, advancing technology does reintegrate separate procedures into different patterns (Young 1928: 530; Piore 1980*b*: 76). Therefore, skilled workers who specialized in a particular task may find it hard to understand other processes, and may not be motivated to accept reintegration.

The technical basis for specialization lies in Smith's second merit.

A man commonly saunters a little in turning his hand from one sort of employment to another. When he first begins the new work he is seldom very keen and hearty; his mind, as they say, does not go to it, and for some time he rather trifles than applies to good purpose. (Smith 1776, 1904: vol. I: 10–11)

However, as Marglin has also mentioned, it is necessary for one person to work continuously at a particular task for a certain period of time to increase efficiency. Therefore, the reason for specialization is not to prevent a person from working equally well at different operations at the same time. If the work is such that the physical and mental elements of the entire procedure are made portable, then it will be unnecessary for a worker to specialize in a single field (Marglin 1974: 66–7).

[14] Marglin recognized the distribution of production technologies, management, and skills among parties and the initiative to choose among production technologies as the essential sources of economic power. This is also a criticism for the tradition of neo-classical economics, which considers labour force just one element of production factors in general, or, at best, the one involving friction or market imperfection. At the same time Marglin criticizes Marxian economics, which developed an explanation much like that of neo-classical economics, although emphasizing 'class antagonism' between capital and labour: Marglin's studies inform the excellent historical researches of radical economists into how the labour market reached its current state of segmentation (Stone 1974; Edwards, Gordon and Reich 1982). Furthermore, in dual labour market theory (which is based on the tradition of institutional labour economics led by Piore) Marglin deepened the analysis of skills and knowledge, and played a part in making its theoretical basis stronger. (For the most important works in this tradition, see Piore 1980*b* and Sabel 1982.) These different traditions actually compliment our understanding of labour market structure, which the following sections aim to show.

[15] Smith said: 'In the progress of the division of labour, the employment of the far greater part of those who live by labour comes to be confined to a few very simple operations. But the understandings of the greater part of men are necessarily formed by their ordinary employments. The man whose whole life is spent in performing a few simple operations, of which the effects too are, perhaps, always the same, or very nearly the same, has no occasion to exert his understanding, or to exercise his invention in finding out expedients for removing difficulties which never occur. He naturally loses, therefore, the habit of such exertion, and generally becomes as stupid and ignorant as it is possible for a human creature to become.' (Smith 1776, 1937: 734)

Division and Specialization of Work, and the Theory of Labour Management

From the above discussion, it is clear that advances in technologies may be brought about by subdividing labour, but at the same time it is also clear that the unlimited diversification of operations and specialization on the part of each worker are not necessary conditions for achieving efficiency. Then why did diversification and specialization, such as that in the case of Smith's needle manufacturing, occur?

First, *household manufacturing* or small partnerships that were in a position to easily introduce specialization in stages were indeed suppliers to capitalized firms for many of their requirements. It is possible to achieve efficiency by repeating the same work every day, but the manufacturing process will be relatively long if the final output involves ten or 20 steps over several days. Huge inventory will be required to establish credibility as a stable supplier, so the stock-holding cost will be very high (expect where the output is significantly distinct that the manufacture of goods ordered ensures a profit). Future fluctuations in demand and prices will also be the source of increased risk. Also where the capital market is less developed, it will not be easy to find the capital necessary (to cover design costs and inventory-holding costs) to start this type of specialization, with its lengthy time span. Accordingly, the financiers who took sufficient precautions against fluctuating demand, achieving synchronized manufacturing procedures and specialization, acquired clear competitive advantages.

Second, why did entrepreneurs (or financiers) choose diversification and specialization as the way to manufacture? Marglin, using the theory developed by Ure (1835), an economist writing a decade before Marx, reasoned that it was inevitable that entrepreneurs would manage labour in this way. To ensure that workers obeyed directions, Marglin suggested that it was necessary to destroy the independence and pride of craftsmen (or potential craftsmen), or those who were not accustomed to the rules of ordered production. The independence of workers derived from their knowledge and skills (broadly defined as their knowledge of raw materials, their skills in production processes, even their knowledge about market distribution). Marglin reasoned that the transition from the putting-out system to factory production was not undertaken in order to increase technological efficiency, but rather from the desire on the part of the entrepreneur to control workers effectively (Marglin 1974: 81–4). His assertion theory is termed the 'Theory of Labour Management'.

On the other hand, there is no doubt that specialization was the motivation for advances in technology. As mentioned before, technology is employed to reintegrate various specialized operations. Furthermore, the Industrial Revolution gave birth to advances in technology, and it is apparent that these affected the structure of specialization and henceforth started the loop. But if this is true, is the form of specialization wholly dependent on the development of technologies once the process of automation starts? In a sense, Marx was one of the economists captivated by the rapid advances in technology. He saw a trend whereby workers would return to simple and analogous tasks as machines developed.[16] However, this perception cannot be regarded as wholly accurate. The argument can be sought conceptually in Ure's understanding of the work of Arkwright, the founder of modern factories.

The main difficulty [Arkwright faced] did not, to my apprehension, lie so much in invention of a proper self-acting mechanism for drawing out and twisting cotton into a continuous thread, as in the distribution of the different members of the apparatus into one co-operative body, in impelling each organ with its appropriate delicacy and speed, and above all, in training human beings to renounce their desultory habits of work, and to identify themselves with the unvarying regularity of the complex automation. To devise and administer a successful code of factory discipline, suited to the necessities of factory diligence, was the Herculean enterprise, the noble achievement of Arkwright. (Ure 1835: 15; Marglin 1974: 84).

Consequently, the secret of Arkwright's success was not in the spinning machine he developed, but in training the work to work at the machines in a disciplined fashion. The new knowledge of technology and the invention itself do broaden the technological possibilities, but these are purely intangible assets. How much they actually contribute to the manufacturing process depends more upon the handling of the machines, and the management of the attitudes of the workers operating in either the unautomated process or with the machines.

Historical Studies of the Labour-Control Hypothesis

The above discussion indicates that the control of workers remains an important issue in the history of automation. But it does not verify Marglin's

---

[16] As Marx himself says, 'It would be possible to write quite a history of the inventions, made since 1830, for the sole purpose of supplying capital with weapons against the revolts of the working class.' (Marx 1867, vol. 1, ch. 1: 380) It is not assumed that changes in technology are exogenous in the sense that group activities by workers will promote labour-saving technology or automation (Rosenberg 1976: 117–20). However, Marx appears to have had no doubt that automation would permit workers to return to more analogous and simpler tasks. In this connection, he refers to Adam Smith's *The Wealth of the Nations*: 'Equal quantities of labour must at all times and in all places have the same value for the labour. In his normal state of health, strength, and activity, and with the average degree of skill that he may possess, he must always give up the same portion of his rest, his freedom, and his happiness.' And he comments on this as follows: '[Adam Smith] has a presentiment, that labour power, but he treats this expenditure as the mere sacrifice of rest, freedom, and happiness, not as at the same time the normal activity of living beings. But then, he has the modern wage-labourer in his eye.' (Marx 1867, vol. 1, ch. 1: 39)

There are two relevant points in this short critique. The first point, as in Marx's famous theory, is that labour originally comprised positive and subjective work towards nature, and was one of the most positive activities in life. Second, the definition of labour does change over time. The growth of productivity under the capitalist economy—notably the growth in automation and specialization of work—meant that the original meaning of manual labour became redundant.

core proposition that the entrepreneur's desire to control workers was the source of the distinctive form of procedural specialization within the overall diversification and specialization of the manufacturing procedure. Nevertheless, later historical studies (Stone 1974; Edwards 1979; Edwards, Gordon, and Reich 1982), and the results of numerous tests of 'quality of labour' and re-engineering of work, show that the labour-control hypothesis does correspond with the reality.

Let us introduce an example from Stone's study of changes in US steel manufacturing organizations, the first of a number of historical studies.

This study is also valuable as an example of the creation of an internal labour market and the steps involved in formalizing it, as discussed later. As the reader may already be aware, the steel industry experienced a rapid increase in productivity. The technological advances in this industry did not occur until the end of the nineteenth century. However, the existing innovations in technology, such as the huge blast-furnaces, the Bessemer converter, and the Siemens–Martin open-hearth furnace for steel, common in modern plants (and complete in their technology), were not in practice easy to install. Harsh conflicts arose between the existing labour force and the proponents of restructuring to implement specialization.

According to Stone, there was a major change in the organization of production of the US steel industry during the 20 years from 1890 to 1910 (for the record, 1890 was the year when the USA became the largest steel-producing nation in both metal and steel, overtaking the UK). The largest transition took place in the roles of skilled workers and their positions. Before 1890, the dominant form of manufacturing organization was the equal partnership between the entrepreneur supplying capital and equipment, and skilled workers supplying technical knowledge, skills, and labour. The organization's structural core consisted of (1) the sliding-scale system, the system deciding the distribution of income between partners; (2) the contract system, the system deciding the employment pattern and distribution of income of skilled and unskilled workers. The sliding-scale system may also be called the fluctuating-wage system. The wage was paid based on the tonnage rate of metal output. The consequence is that when the market price of the output changed, the tonnage rate changed accordingly, so that the profits and risks in the market were divided between the partners in the same way as in the profit-distribution system. On the other hand, the contract system was a system in which skilled workers agreed to a tonnage rate and hired unskilled workers to assist them. Hence, the skilled workers managed operations, and decided on the distribution of wages between the workers. The unskilled workers hired as helpers acquired know-how and skills from the skilled workers. The form of apprenticeship formalized in this system was ruled and administered by the Amalgamated Association of Iron, Steel and Tin Workers.

This type of system collapsed rapidly as technology advanced and markets expanded. The introduction of the Bessemer converter, and the Siemens–Martin open-hearth furnace of steel, together with enlarged capacities in related furnaces, caused the links in the procedures between one stage and the next, such as the transportation, installation, etc., of raw materials, where the procedure was still heavily dependent on manual labour, to appear as obstructions.[17] These impediments were not only for purely technical reasons, but because the control of operations was in the hands of skilled workers. Furthermore, as prices decreased as the market became more competitive, wages remained at the lower level of the contractual agreement, and the entrepreneurs' share began to drop continuously (that is, the sliding-scale system existed only in name). Hence the partnerships of skilled workers and entrepreneurs came to have opposing interests. The opposition concluded with the entrepreneurs destroying the apprenticeship system. The 1892 lockout at the Homestead Steel Manufacturing plant of Carnegie Steel (part of US Steel at the time) was a dramatic example of entrepreneurs aiming to destroy the production system then in operation. The four months' 'war', killing many workers, concluded when the Federal and State governments allied with the entrepreneurs, and the workers lost, with the apprenticeship system crushed. The union quickly declined after the incident, and was annihilated by 1910. This also meant that the former specialization and the system of skill acquisition were completely destroyed. Steel manufacturers dealt with the obstructions by means of heavy industrial machines such as electrical cranes. As one entrepreneur boasted, even in open-hearth-furnace operations, the work where the greatest skills were needed before, an average worker became competent in six to eight weeks. Most of the former operations carried out by skilled workers were replaced by so-called partially skilled operations.[18]

The newly developed organization was determined to seize the knowledge and know-how previously monopolized by the skilled workers from the labourers. As a result, a pyramid-shaped system came into being, with clear

---

[17] According to Landes (1972: 255, note 2), the volume of the furnace was limited to the amount of molten steel (approximately 200 kg) a strong worker can mix manually when using the former paddle method. With the Bessemer converter, the limitation became how far the machine could be tilted, allowing molten steel to be extracted. As a result, the volume of furnaces increased from two to five tons, and by the end of the nineteenth century, furnaces with a volume of 20 or 25 tons were possible. Landes's research covered the UK and Germany, but the results can be assumed to apply to the USA also.

[18] Speech by C. Schwab, CEO, Bethlehem Steel in 1902, referred to in Stone (1974: 133). Nevertheless, as Sabel (1982: 60–1) also points out, accepting an entrepreneur's words at face value may confuse hope and facts.

The term 'partially skilled' was first used in a 1910 government report, and was discussed by Stone (1974: 124). At that time, according to the population census, workers newly classified as 'skilled' workers were mechanics or technical engineers, or managers adjusting and managing workers and machines.

The difference between partially skilled and skilled can be thought of as akin to the difference between the knowledge and skills the workers have. This is interpreted in terms of whether the knowledge or skills are sectoral, or comprehensive and higher (the knowledge possessed by former skilled workers is included here). Therefore, it may be a delusion to say, as Stone does, that partially skilled workers do not possess many techniques or much knowledge.

demarcation between tiers. The pyramid comprised: a new business administrative tier (or staff) consisting of a relatively small number of personnel (mainly college graduates) who managed the plans, designs, and adjustments to the entire production activities of the firm and themselves; numerous workers operating in specialized fields under the instruction of various managers; and their managers in charge (or line). One of the most significant outcomes of the transformation was the research and experiments in the field of 'scientific management' by Frederick Taylor, manager of Bethlehem Steel Manufacturing. His experiments treated human labour and machines as equivalent, and tried to rationalize operations by completely removing redundant moves and time. Even though Taylor's dictatorial administrative method itself did not become established, his theory of removing managerial rights and the knowledge base from workers remains as the principle of procedural management.[19]

A hierarchy of work processes and the internal promotion system were the key factors in the new pyramid. Hiring was done through a limited port of entry, and the system was to transfer the workers to higher stages of related works by a predetermined route, or the job ladder. The ladder was based on the natural development of skills and knowledge (the workers being expected to be familiar with and to be ready for the promotion, by having seen the next step while working in their current position). At the same time, the system was also intended to prevent voluntary resignations, and incorporated incentives to increase labour density. Furthermore, by differentiating workers according to their abilities, it had the significant political motive of preventing workers from uniting by means of 'order based on separation').[20]

Workers' skills were not destroyed by the new hierarchy. There were still broad areas of know-how regarding machine operations, operating skills that could not be automated, of machine maintenance, and comprehension in fields such as clerical work and sales. (The field of on-the-job training discussed in section 3.2 is related to such skills.) What differentiates these skills from the craftsmanship of the past is that these new skills are all local and not always related to each other when one considers the entire production system.[21]

The changes in steel manufacturing organizations with their specialized skills and internal promotion ladders seem sophisticated, but in practice procedural division through specialization and diversification (and also partial machine

---

[19] See Braverman (1974: 85–152) for more details.

[20] Stone traces the advice on the employment system in articles in *Iron Age*, a steel industry paper, from 1930. In *Labor and Compensation* (Broomfield), a managerial manual published in 1918 dead-end jobs had already been criticized for more than ten years, with reasons such as inability to work and to move forward made workers tense, and the tasks lacked the human touch, and work itself was not the problem, but the formation and management of work lacked motivation and attraction were given. The solutions proposed were 'more liberal promotions and transfers', and they were said to have been broadly accepted.

[21] Stone states that the job ladders and internal promotion systems were almost completely artificial, since skill had disappeared (Stone 1974: 136). However, his assertion may be too severe in light of the discussion in footnote 18.

operation) became common. It seems reasonable to state that this organizational transition was brought about by the maximization of technical efficiency through advances in technology (using the same arguments as Adam Smith), but that the speed of technological advances was too great, and caused severe frictions (impediments to production and union issues) during the transition.[22] Or, can such interpretation be accepted without any qualifications?

It is true that new technologies add more value than reintegration during automation of work procedures that were formerly separate processes using old technologies, and the momentum of technological knowledge development significantly affects inventions.[23] Hence, the separation of not only experienced workers, but also engineers with a knowledge of abstract principles and entrepreneurs who can value their economic efficiencies is unavoidable.

Nevertheless, acknowledging these points and considering the above arguments are totally different matters. Technical findings and inventions will expand production possibilities, but they do not make the decisions about where they will be used in economic activities, and how they will be adopted, if they are. Such decisions are based upon economic calculations. The main issue is who selects. Let us reconsider the example of steel manufacturing. Under the former organizational structure, skilled workers held the rights to formalize and manage operations, and to training, even though the entrepreneurs' shares were declining due to falling market prices brought about by increased competition. The new machines were introduced to enable the entrepreneurs to make greater use of the profit opportunities in the market and to recover and increase their own share in these, and at the same time to take control of management. The revolution in the organization of production was thorough because it was directly related to regaining management rights and the right to select new technologies. Hence, it is too simple to attribute the change just to friction or technological efficiency. This is one of the reasons to support the labour-control theory.

Labour unions reappeared in US steel manufacturing in the late 1930s during the Great Depression (the first labour agreement was signed by US Steel in 1937). The newly formed unions were not stratified, like the former unions, but came into being as industrial unions that approved the basic structures of the existing firms. As a result, progress was made in setting wage levels and

[22] If these historical changes were referred to in neo-classical terms, it would be said that the processes of labour adjustment were a transfer from a labour-intensive stage of production undergoing technological transformation (production frontier) to another different, capital-intensive stage. Moreover, the effects of the changes in skilled labour did not end at the marginal adjustment of employment, but affected all workers (gross employment), causing the severe friction.

[23] See Landes (1972) for more details and (Landes 1972: 249–69) for the steel industry. Rosenberg (1976) called the advances of knowledge, developing with independent momentum, 'knowledge disequilibria', and described them as one of the three key factors guiding development in technology. The other two factors, already discussed in this section, are labour management (which is depicted as playing a significant role in nineteenth-century Britain), and external factors, such as war, which cut off the supply of materials.

eliminating disparities, employment (especially in relation to the rights of existing workers), and also in limiting operational controls. Nevertheless, the skilled workers did not regain the powers they had lost half a century earlier.

Experiments in Work Expansion and Re-engineering

Next, let us examine (but not in detail) other evidence in support of the labour-control theory. We look at whether there were other ways to organize operations to achieve the same production efficiencies from a simple technological efficiency point of view, and at the same time assuring greater output from the workers. Many countries have gone through a process of re-engineering of labour, through procedures such as restructuring labour organizations, expanding the operational area per worker, abolishing assembly lines, and independent group management of operations, since the ten-year period of change in UK mining that started in 1948. In many cases, they clearly achieved reduced absenteeism, and increased productivity in terms of both quality and quantity, through greater worker involvement and savings in managerial tasks at the level of the smallest units.[24]

Then why have such processes not been more broadly adopted? In many cases, these experiments have ended after a year or two. They have done so because production efficiencies increase as more workers participate, and take on more responsibilities, but the consequence is that a redistribution of power between employers and employees becomes unavoidable.[25] In other words, employers are interested in 'productivity' that will rearrange workers into more profitable jobs, and in regaining control over decisions on team size and standard output levels, but not in productivity itself. This verifies Marglin's theory that specialization occurs not just for the reasons of technological efficiency advanced by Adam Smith, but also because of entrepreneur's desire to increase their share of distribution and to control and manage workers' operations.

Conclusion

We have now surveyed the factors that control the process of specialization of labour. Not wishing to view this process simply as technological determinism, that is, as only an advance in technological knowledge, we have examined the historical background. Neo-classical economics goes further in analysing economic trends when technologies are given, but what changes the basic structures of technologies and the production organizations

---

[24] Refer to US Department of Health, Education and Welfare (1973), a research report covering a very broad area; its groundwork, the reports in O'Toole (1974) (especially the survey by Davis and Trist (1974)); and Levitan and Werneke (1984) for more recent coverage of the outcomes of work restructuring.

[25] This point is emphasized in Levitan and Werneke (1984: 33). They also suggest that workers who join management may place more emphasis on work and a decrease in numbers, moreover destroying the employee's rights. Their attitude towards the changes is not clearly defined.

underlying them is still unknown. To understand the argument of this chapter, and characteristics such as duality and specialization in the labour market, we must examine the economic and social factors that brought about the changes in the basic structures of the market. Stone's study examined only one industry, steel, but it shows us how the internal labour market, the most systematic core of the entire labour market, began. In this study, we saw that the characteristics of this market are job-skills ladders for each type of work (and training systems for passing on such skills), internal promotions, and wage and other bonus systems incorporating incentives. The next section analyses the structures of the specialized labour market, and how these affect the individual's income distribution.

5.3. THE DUAL LABOUR MARKET HYPOTHESIS

Let us discuss the vertical side of the modern capitalistic world. What constitutes the whole labour market and why is it constructed in this way?

The analysis of the labour market known as the dual labour market hypothesis (or the segmented labour market hypothesis) asserts that the labour market is segmented. Although there are differences between countries, since their implicit growth paths differ, there are common factors. These are: (i) labour markets are segmented qualitatively into the 'internal labour market' and the 'external labour market', and similarities in the reasons for the segmentation, as well as (ii) the individual labour market is further segmented in terms of quality into an 'upper tier' and a 'lower tier'. Formally, economic duality exists between the urban and rural sectors, the modern and traditional sectors, large and smaller firms, etc., but these differences must to be clearly distinguished from the duality under discussion (the concept of duality in relation to firm size will be discussed in section 6.1).

Piore's Dual Labour Market Hypothesis

The basis of the dual labour market hypothesis was explained by Doeringer and Piore (1971). The hypothesis was expanded in Piore's later studies (1975, 1980*a,b*).[26] Piore's contribution lies in his point that the characteristics of each segmented market are prescribed by differences in workers' learning

---

[26] Piore (1975) developed the view that differences in work-related learning plays a basic role in the classifications of the labour market, and this view is repeated in Piore (1980*b*), which provides a comprehensive description of the dual labour market hypothesis. Radical economists (see note 14) see the basis of the separation as lying in the difference between the centre where output demands are stable and the periphery where they are more unstable, rather than in differences in learning characteristics. As discussed later, Piore views the difference relating to stability of output demands as a substantial characteristic distinction between the internal and external markets. However, he establishes this by viewing existing differences in labour that have significant effects (in terms of different characteristics) on output markets with separate stable demand. See the contrast with Ujihara (1954), the pioneer of the dual market hypothesis before the US researchers, in section 6.1.

opportunities or differences in their knowledge and skills. In the following paragraphs, let us review his analysis.

First, we discuss each partial market which composes the internal labour market. The staff engaged in specialized, technical, or managerial work constitute the upper tier. Their work involves much learning. This learning includes considerable work competence and structural understanding of abstract relations between one type of work and another. Therefore, cognitive ability and/or trainability are essential. Also knowledge gained in their education is so general that it can be applied in other positions, so the workers in this tier will always be seeking higher incomes and better learning opportunities, regardless of the internal and external labour markets of the firms in which they work. Hence, the potential labour mobility of such workers is very high, and it can be said that the market is competitive in terms of work provision and income distribution. It is a good example of the theory of the joint exchange of human investment discussed in section 3.2.[27] Furthermore, jobs are stable, with people being valued for their accumulated knowledge and skills in the competitive market. Incomes are generally high, and rise with experience. The performance of each individual is highly independent in this tier, and controls on work tend to be highly endogenous. Moreover, workers in this tier are enormously motivated by their interest in the work itself. Needless to say, they are in the most gifted tier.

The lower tier is described in the previous section. This is the tier comprising mainly production workers and clerical workers. Their work also involves learning opportunities, but the knowledge and skills gained tend to be more abstract. Their work is usually difficult to organize, and the operations they carry out tend to be those left behind by automation, difficult to co-ordinate with other work, and their role in the complete labour process unclear. It is difficult to motivate the workers to work, and employees need to employ control supervisors and external factors. Abstract knowledge involves the following. First, learning is highly dependent on on-the-job training by senior

---

[27] In my opinion, to depict this integral trading in terms of on-the-job training with hourly inputs (see section 3.2) will produce an unnatural result. The integral trading subject to learning opportunities discussed here seems more similar to pure operational learning (see section 3.2), because it is strongly affected by feedback of results regarding thoughts and decision making in relation to work.

In his theory of the integral trading of labour and learning opportunities Rosen (1972*b*) assumes that training costs will be greater as depth of learning increases. Therefore, given that length of life is limited, workers will tend to learn with more intensity in their younger years, and transfer to jobs requiring less intense learning as they grow older. Whilst age and rank in the internal labour market are assumed to be correlated, the higher ranks will involve less intense learning. This conclusion is not what we would expect. To think that those in the higher ranks in the internal labour market make decisions on more technical matters and hold responsibilities based on broader fields of knowledge is more natural. Therefore, it is more appropriate to conclude that more learning, accrues to higher ranks.

See Ishikawa (1984) for further details on integral trading in the market, with regard to pure operational learning opportunities and the characteristics of the wage curves they generate.

workers. Second, firm-specific knowledge increases with skill. Third, employers value schooling, not for the cognitive skills it develops, but for its development of habits such as obedience, acceptance of rules, and self-reliance. The first and second factors motivate employers to ensure stability of employment. Additionally, the costs of workers changing jobs are immense (these circumstances causing workers and employers to share training costs are as described in section 3.2). So stable employment conditions, as mentioned in section 5.1, will emerge, and patterns of labour such as limited wage competition, internal promotion, and other incentive systems will begin to develop. The development of patterns of labour can involve working with labour unions or making similar rules unconsciously without labour unions. The wages of this tier are smaller than those of the upper tier, but have an upward trend over time.

The tier that does not belong to either upper or lower tier and is characterized by skilled craftsmanship is called the 'craftsman tier'. The skilled workers in the heavy metals industry in the past (refer to the last section) are a good example of this. Some occupations such as modern construction and pipeline workers are similar. The knowledge and skills of this tier are similar to those of the lower tier in that they are general and abstract, but the fact that all work processes will gradually be covered, as experience and understanding are acquired, means that the characteristics of mature skills are consistent with the upper tier. Reflecting these learning characteristics are the tendency of being internally motivated to work and high independence, but at the same time the learning process is highly dependent on teaching by senior workers through on-the-job training, and mature workers widely make rules in relation to working conditions. Of course, the cognitive abilities developed by schooling are not so obvious. The craftsman tier is located between the lower and upper tiers.

In contrast to the internal labour market, the 'external labour market' involves almost no learning, or opportunities for progress. The term 'dead end' aptly describes this market. The work involved consists mainly of production, distribution, back office services and the operation of simple machines and the work of cashiers, or physical work such as the transportation of heavy goods, cleaning, and night watch services. The significant characteristic of the external labour market is that as it involves no learning, training costs when hiring and firing can be ignored. In other words, there is no establishment as such for the employer. Therefore, workers are not organized and there are no customary rules of labour, so that the continuation of employment depends significantly upon uncertain factors such as business cycles and employers' disposition and tempers. Wages are generally low, and in many cases remain at the legal minimum. Also, even if workers continue for a long time in one job, it is very common for there to be no increases in wages. School education is not subject to employers' appraisal. In such work, workers are not motivated internally, and (if not paid by piece rates) workers are often strictly supervised by employers. As long as they remain in the external labour market, there will be a clear distinction between their lifetime prospects and those of workers in the internal labour market.

This description of the labour market leaves unanswered such questions as: Why does labour market segmentation occur? And why do workers continue to supply labour to the external labour market if the terms are so bad?

With regard to the first question, the first point of Piore's answer brings to mind the well-known industrial organization debate as to why small and middle-sized firms do not disappear even if large-sized firms centralize production because of market expansion. In other words, labour demands for the external labour market emerge as buffers against volatility and uncertainties in the business cycle which cannot be erased. Alternatively the external labour market enables investors to shift volatility risk to (part of) the workforce.[28] Second, expansion of the internal labour market (especially the lower tier) not only does not increase the payment of fixed commissions, by firms, but also decreases the relative negotiating powers of employers by expanding the membership of labour unions. Piore states that the US external labour market expanded at the time of the liberalization of union activities in the late 1930s and as a residue of the controlled economies of the Second World War; and the rapid expansion of the external labour markets of Italy and France was caused by the 1968 employment disputes (Piore 1980*a*; Edwards, Gordon, and Reich 1982: ch. 5).

In answer to the second question, why labour is supplied to the external labor market, Piore states that workers prepared to supply labour to the external labour market, with its poor conditions, may be divided into two groups. The first group consists of people who wish to be employed in the internal labour market but have not been successful in this respect. These are obviously involuntary suppliers of labour. Various reasons account for the second group, but they are people who have decided to supply labour, despite the poor working conditions, because their commitment to work is low. The first group includes high proportions of minorities and females (Doeringer and Piore 1971). The second group involves people working in various locations, and consists of agricultural workers, students, domestic engineers, seasonal migrant workers, or younger people not yet independent of their parents. These workers are mainly intent on earning extra income. They supply labour despite poor conditions because they consider their work to be supplementary or temporary.[29]

---

[28] Other writers, such as Averitt (1968), also mention that 'central firms' transfer business cycle risks by using 'peripheral firms' as buffers.

[29] Piore (1973) discusses the possibility that many of these people may try to achieve a target income. Such workers will work longer hours for lower wages (displaying a labour supply curve with a rightwards slope). However, from related statistical studies such as for female labour supply behaviour, a better interpretation might relate to setting reserve wages and labour supplies based on them. Killingsworth (1983: chs 2 and 3), in an econometric analysis of the labour supply function, verifies that the wage elasticity of female labour supply is very high. The wage rates of part-time female workers in Japan has also been entirely unrelated to business cycles (since the 1970s). This characteristic is particularly noticeable where it does not fall during bad times (hence, the elasticity of labour supply seems unlimited). This is said to happen because workers set the reserve wage too rigidly.

Statistical Verification of the Dual Labour Market Hypothesis

How many people belong to the internal labour market and the external labour market in reality? Can stability of employment, the form of the age–income curve, the importance of schooling, authority/subordinate relations, the characteristics mentioned for each tier be verified in practice? Is it true that the external labour market includes many involuntary workers? It is obvious that these are the issues that must be verified to prove the dual labour market hypothesis. Verification requires positive analysis using quantitative data. Because the notion of the internal and external labour markets is derived from studies of individual firms or labour unions by professional researchers, and has been used in a number of surveys of individual areas of the labour market, it is itself a theory based on analytical research. But if this concept reflects reality, it must be proven by statistical analyses also.

Statistical verification of the dual labour market hypothesis has attracted some interest, but cannot be said to have accumulated sufficient results for the purpose of proof. The main reason for this is that even if the internal and external labour markets within each firm may be classified relatively easily, it is difficult to establish a basis for classification that can be uniformly applied across the entire labour market and capable of fitting quantitative data.

If one is in a position to obtain ideal data easily, collecting data for each individual on the characteristics and scope of on-the-job learning, the crux of the dual labour market hypothesis, then verification by normal methods— numerically indexing then classifying—becomes possible. But as mentioned in the last chapter, direct information on worker's learning and training is extremely difficult to obtain. Therefore, it has been necessary to develop non-evidentiary methods of classification by working backwards from collectable data on employment experience and wages.

As a result, the methods formerly used for establishing detailed classifications of industries or employment were developed as follows. First, the allocation of each industry or employment to either the internal or the external labour market was decided on the basis of specific variables such as wage level, volatility of employment, and necessary qualifications, etc. Then sectoral differences in wage formation were sought. But because of the arbitrary nature of the classification, the basis for decisions, and the selection of variables correlated with wage levels, estimation bias (in other words, the truncation bias that arises as a result of regional restrictions of the independent variables) emerged. The bias reduced the effects of educational background and age in external-market industries and employment where wages were low (Cain 1976: 1246–47). It is difficult to conclude that there were any persuasive verifications of the hypothesis.[30]

---

[30] Osterman (1975), the pioneer of these studies, classified jobs according to their stability and autonomy, then estimated the revenue function. The common effects of schooling and age were

As for verifying the involuntary nature of the external labour market, this was formerly approached by asking how much (intergenerational) sector mobility existed between the internal and external labour markets. The neo-classical approach, on the basis of empirical results that emphasized high mobility from the external sector to the internal sector (Okun 1973; Leigh 1976), held that the dual labour market hypothesis did not apply (Wachter 1974: 649; Cain 1976: 1231). But there are different points of view in relation to possible mobility (Osterman 1977: 221). Osterman (1980: chs 2 and 3) who studied job hopping among the young cohort, based on analyses of population surveys and detailed interview data on the younger generation in the eastern United States, found that the problem of possible mobility is basically an age problem. Access to the internal labour market decreased with age, and it became especially difficult to enter this market if workers were not already in it during their twenties. But it should be noted the inter-sectoral labour mobility and involuntary confinement in the external labour market are entirely different matters (see section 5.5). Internal labour market demand can be expected to expand continuously or temporarily during economic growth or in the course of the business cycle. In reality, it is not surprising that labour mobility to the upper tier was frequently observed in analyses focusing on the 1960s. Therefore, it is not correct to hold that there is a direct connection between the existence of labour mobility and the appropriateness of the dual labour market hypothesis.

An analysis that does provide statistical verification of the validity of classifying the market into internal and external sectors and the involuntary nature of the external labour market is that of Dickens and Lang (1985a,b). They assumed the existence of two sectors, compensating by different methods for each individual's attributes (age, education, experience, marital status, race, region), and for each individual computed a lifetime income, having knowledge of the correct compensation method for each sector. They assumed that individuals gained employment in the sector providing the higher income. They,

observed, and their explanatory powers were very high as compared with the external labour market where wages were unaffected by schooling and age. But there are shortcomings in this study. First, there are no objective measures of autonomy, and the classifications are arbitrary (management and technical engineers are classified in the lower tier, a classification incompatible with the descriptions in this book). Second (even in Osterman's refutation (1977: 223)), characteristics such as occupational stability and autonomy are theoretically dependent variables, as are wages, and are significantly correlated with one another, so that they cannot deflect the bias referred to above.

If we look at other studies, we find that Oster (1979) noted the existence of controlling factors reflecting the dual structure and conducted factor analyses of many of the characteristics of each sector, taking industries classified into small groups. The central sector and the peripheral sector could be classified on the basis of these variables. This classification method was also used in Edwards, Gordon, and Reich (1982: 192–227). However, it should be noted that this is a method of classifying industries and not workers. There are many external workers in the central sector, and there are many workers who can be classified as management or internal workers in the peripheral sector. The duality of larger and smaller firms exists in the traditional and popular Japanese perspective, but the same applies here, that this duality does not refer directly to the internal and external labour markets.

then conducted a full statistical test of the hypothesis by investigating the following points. (1) Whether data volatility was better explained if the data on each individual were treated as belonging to either sector rather than to one sector only. (2) If so, what is the difference in compensation methods between the two sectors? And (3) are there any other external factors that affect the decision to seek employment in one sector or the other, apart from lifetime income differences? Their data set comprised 1980s male heads of households (all over the United States, married and unmarried employed by the private sector, and having worked for more than 1,000 hours the previous year) with a sample size of more than 2,800. Based on wage functions the expected lifetime income of the two sectors and the sector choice behaviour of each individual were simultaneously estimated using the switching regression method. The main feature of this method was exclusion of arbitrariness on the part of the analysts by allowing the subjects themselves to decide the efficiency of the classifications and the sector-specific wage structure.

The results of this analysis are that, first the null hypothesis that there is only one sector can be easily rejected, and second, as the hypothesis proposes, the log of hourly wages in one sector is statistically correlated with education and experience, while in the other sector they are not affected by these variables (the wage curve is flat), and the incomes of those employed in the latter sector are lower at almost all levels of education, and third, in the choice of employment sector, racial factors as well as lifetime income are statistically significant; therefore access to the first sector for non-Caucasians is restricted. This means that if one excludes the unacceptable interpretation that non-Caucasians tend to prefer the second sector work, unlike Caucasians, there exists an involuntary trap (or racial discrimination) in the second sector. The first sector may be thought of as the internal labour market, and second sector as the external labour market.

Furthermore, the estimation results show that on average 12 per cent of all male householders belonged to the external labour market, and looking at each attribute in turn, first, in terms of education, while 18 per cent of workers with less than 12 years of education belonged to the external labour market, as many as 10 per cent of workers with more than 12 years of education also belonged to the external labour market; and second, as to race, while 11 per cent of Caucasians belonged to the external labour market, the figure for non-Caucasians was 31 per cent; and third, when examined by age, the proportion of workers employed in the external labour market was high for those aged under 25 and over 60, the former 19 per cent and latter 30 per cent, while in the other tiers the numbers were almost flat, at around 9–12 per cent (Dickens and Lang 1985*a*: 800, Table 2 (unrestricted model)).[31]

---

[31] Let us define the percentages used here. These values are averages of sample groups used to calculate the *ex post facto* probabilities of each worker belonging to the external labour market (the secondary market), using an estimation model.

The research described above is a good example of the new method of econometrics using a qualitative dependent variable model, but it is still necessary to determine whether methods such as this can always achieve a stable structural estimation with all types of data. And analyses may be expanded to segment the market into male and female and to investigate the efficiency of further segmentation of the internal labour market. In any case, the development of statistical verification is very necessary.

5.4. THE DUAL LABOUR MARKET AND THE SCHOOLING PARADOX

What does the dual labour market hypothesis imply for income distribution among individuals? From the discussion in the previous section, if we exclude the upper tier, for which the competitive market mechanism works, and the craft tier, which has similar properties to the upper tier, and regard the lower tier as the core component of the internal labour market, we find several implications. First, the logic of wage competition, that wage adjustment fills the gap between demand and supply, implies that the main determinant of employment distribution and wage levels among different jobs and the wage differentials across these jobs is the logic of organization that is the motivation to work and the bargaining power generated from the skills of workers. Second, the external labour market can be regarded as an open competitive market but it is possible that the minimum wage, which is determined institutionally, is binding in the external labour market, depending on the conditions of demand and supply. Consequently, even if education raises individuals' marginal productivity, as is expected, and selects the individuals with high marginal productivity, the situation can arise that those who have received education cannot be provided with the job opportunity their high productivity merits and they cannot be paid the income which could be gained by the competitive mechanism. These features are an important hint in explaining the phenomenon of the 'schooling paradox' referred to in section 5.1.

Thurow's job competition model theoretically formulates this point (Thurow 1975). Now we assume that: (a) the maximum labour productivity of individuals is not determined by their own ability but by the job they do; (b) their productivity can be realized through workplace training rather than school education, while an important role of education is to make the training process smoother (that is, by improving trainability); (c) job opportunities at the port of entry for the internal labour market are restricted, and wage competition does not work as that point. Consequently workers face a job queue. And those who seek jobs thereafter try to gain higher education in order to move to the top of the job queue. Thurow calls this situation 'job competition'. The most important point of this argument is that education is the necessary condition for higher income, but it is not a sufficient condition for it.

However, as Thurow's argument gives exogenously the demand for skilled workers and wage differentials across various jobs, there is no discussion there of the impact on wage differences and income distribution among individuals of equalizing schooling and an increase in the bargaining power of workers in the internal labour market. Therefore in the following discussion we reorganize Thurow's model into the simple dual labour market model and answer these questions by assuming that the jobs in the internal labour market are limited to a single type and that alternative jobs can be found only in the external labour market. This simplification will clarify whether the existence or non-existence of restriction of wage competition at the point of entry to the internal labour market generates a significant difference in long-term income distribution. The following analysis is developed in detail by Ishikawa (1981b).[32] The issue of work motivation is not discussed until the following section. Furthermore, we do not consider the factors determining the strength of the bargaining power of employees here.

The Framework of the Model

We return to the world of the production system again and proceed with the argument. We reconstruct the production model introduced in section 3.1, and suppose that there is a representative firm producing a single output with three factors of production including capital (K). The first type of labour (L_1) is the *internal labour* which organizes the firm-specific knowledge and skill, and the second type of labour (L_2) is unskilled and perfectly variable *external labour*. The production technique is as follows. (i) The three factors of production follow the constant return to scale. (ii) Capital and internal labour are strictly complementary, and the units of capital equipment must be manned by internal labour in fixed proportions. (iii) These two factors and external labour are smooth substitutes for each other. Assumption (ii) reflects the empirical outcome referred to in section 5.1, and is simple, to make the analysis easy. From now on, the workers in the internal labour market are referred to as 'internal workers' and it is assumed that a single unit of internal labour is provided per internal worker in each period. Similarly, the 'external worker' is defined as those who work in the external labour market and in each period a single unit of external labour is provided per external worker.

In order to increase production capacity, the firm needs not only to purchase capital equipment but also to adjust the existing organization. And because of assumption (ii), it must increase the number of internal workers at the same time, therefore also increasing training. In contrast, to contract production

---

[32] If we divide the dual economy into the urban sector and the rural sector, the non-competitive wage determination in the urban sector leads to job queues in the urban sector and excess labour in the rural sector. This is the model used by Harris and Todaro (1970), which is qualitatively similar to the one developed in this section. The author's argument can be regarded as further developing their model, using the general equilibrium framework.

capacity, organizational adjustment costs and the frictional cost of dismissing internal workers are necessary, even if it is possible to sell the capital equipment. These kinds of costs are termed the *growing cost*. The growing cost of existing capital items is a function of the growth rate (g) of the production equipment or the internal worker; at the same time, its marginal cost is increasing in line with the growth rate. It is for this reason that rapid expansion or contraction is a heavy burden on the organization.[33]

Thus, capital equipment and internal workers are fixed resources for the firm. As long as changes in product demand are treated as temporary, the firm adjusts employment by means of external workers, a process which can be presented as the buffer mechanism of external labour. It decides positive or negative growth only if long-term profit opportunities change.

As we assume that the external labour market is competitive, the wage for external labour, w_2, is determined according to the principle of marginal productivity.[34] On the other hand, the marginal productivity of capital and internal labour cannot be defined independently, so that it is only meaningful if measured in terms of both a unit of capital and the corresponding internal labour (hereafter, the *fixed factor mixture*). Due to assumption (ii), production factors can be regarded as of two types: external labour and the fixed factor mixture. Thanks to the characteristics of the constant return to scale, the marginal productivity of the fixed factor mixture is equivalent to the residual of the product value less the payment of the marginal productivity of external labour. We call the market value of this marginal productivity, represented per unit of capital, the *fixed factor rent* (R_c).

The remaining problem is how the fixed factor rent can be distributed between the profit rate of capital (R) and the wage for internal labour (w_1). Based on the argument presented in section 5.1, the solution is presumed to be determined as a bargaining solution within the safety area of employment for internal workers. If we define the *safety area of employment* as in the standard literature, it is the set of internal wage w_1 that guarantees continuous employment for all internal workers, assuming rational behaviour by capitalists. The lower bound of its set is clearly w_2. On the other hand, its upper bound is given as the wage level at which the profit rate is realized that causes the capitalist to be satisfied with the current stock of capital and internal labour, even if this results in a zero growth rate (R_0). Thus the determination of the level of R_0 largely depends on the expectation of the employer about the movement of future profit opportunities. Even if the profit rate remains the same R_0 will clearly be higher in the case where employers predict that the profit rate will

---

[33] The concept of the growing cost was originally developed by Uzawa (1968). For simplicity we suppose that the entire training cost for employees hired is borne by the employer.

[34] In short-term business downturns, the wage rate clearing the external labour market may be below the minimum wage level or the reservation wage, so that unemployment may occur there. However, even in this situation employers are satisfied, and the principle of marginal productivity holds true.

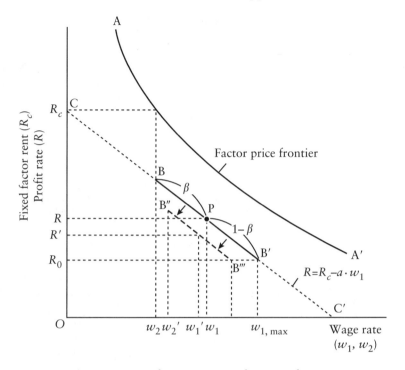

Figure 5.1. *Fixed Factor Rent and its Distribution*

decline than in the case where they predict that it will remain the same (the case of static expectation). In the following discussion, in which we focus on long-term income distribution, we assume the static expectation is appropriate.[35]

The bargaining solution (w_1, R) is the weighted average reflecting the bargaining power between the upper and lower bounds of the safety area of employment. We confine our discussion to the case where bargaining power is given exogenously and is stable in the long run. The mutual relationship between factor prices (stated above) is shown in Figure 5.1. The horizontal axis

---

[35] The theoretical framework in this section can be extended to the short-term situation where economic upturns and downturns are repeated. Additional considerations are then also required. First, this argument is based on the assumption that the safety area of employment is not an empty set. Indeed this assumption can be satisfied around the long-run equilibrium. However, in the short-run phase, R_0 will rise, largely due to the pessimistic expectation of the future and it is likely that the assumption cannot be satisfied. Then, internal workers will be forced to choose whether to keep their employment or their wage level. This choice will depend on alternative job opportunities, the power of the internal workers, etc. Thus we need to reintroduce the concept of the diversity of workers.

Second, some will be of the opinion that workers care not only about their current wage level but also about the growth rate of the firm where they are employed. Opportunities for promotion and related earnings growth is limited at higher positions in the organizational hierarchy. If the overall growth rate of the organization increases, promotion opportunities and expected lifetime

presents the wage levels of internal and external labour, and the vertical axis presents fixed factor rent and the profit rate. The downward curve AA′ represents the factor price frontier between external labour, w_2, and fixed factor rent, R_c. w_2 is determined as the competitive price, and R_c is determined in accordance with it. We next consider the pair comprising a single unit of capital and a units of internal labour, and then the following relationship between R_c, R, and w_1 can satisfy the identity of:

$$R_c = R + a \cdot w_1. \tag{5.1}$$

The line CC′ presents this relationship. Given the level of R_0, the part of this line denoted as BB′ reveals the actual bargaining frontier. The set of w_1 defining the safety area of employment can be represented as the interval $[w_2, w_{1,\max}]$ on the horizontal axis. When the bargaining power of internal labour is presented as the parameter β $(0 < \beta < 1)$, the bargaining solution (w_1, R), can be determined as the point P which cuts the bargaining frontier BB′ by interior division of $\beta : 1 - \beta$.[36]

How will the bargaining solution change when the external wage w_2 increases? We examine its effect in Figure 5.1. The increase in w_2 makes R_c fall, so that the CC′ curve shifts downward. Thus the bargaining frontier BB′ also moves downward, and the new frontier B″B‴ becomes shorter than BB′. From the figure, we can confirm that the wage difference $w_1 - w_2$ necessarily shrinks and at the same time the profit rate R necessarily falls although the direction of the effect on the wage of internal labour w_1 is undetermined. The external labour wage, w_2, is determined by the amount of capital and the number of external workers, that is, it is equal to the labour force minus the internal workers, at each date. In practice, w_2 increases monotonically with the ratio of capital to external labour $(K/L_2 = k)$.

We next turn to the structure of the labour supply. Within the labour force (N), the predetermined units are internal workers, and the remainder are external workers. Assuming a population growth rate of λ, new workers λN enter the labour market at regular intervals. The problem is how these new workers are absorbed into the internal or external labour market. Hence we next consider the following situation. At birth, each individual decides, on the basis of the expected benefit and cost, to receive education, which is the necessary

income will also increase (Marris 1964; Aoki 1982). This scenario can be useful only if an additional layer is introduced to our model. It is not necessary to further consider these additional layers as long as we focus on the determinant of long-run income distribution.

[36] As Ishikawa (1981*b*: 9 footnote 8) described in detail, this bargaining solution can be interpreted from the traditional bargaining game (Zeuthen 1930; Nash 1950; Harsanyi 1956) or its recent application (Aumann and Kurtz 1977; Aoki 1980). The value of β can be determined by looking at attitudes to the failure of bargaining, that is the strength of the relative risk aversion among the bargaining players (the less risk averse they are, the more β will increase). However, this interpretation assesses strong co-ordination between workers and the existence of a collective preference determining attitude to risk, and it generates another problem to be solved.

condition for entering the internal labour market. Time consumption is ignored here. At the end of the period when those to be hired are chosen, and in the next period, the labour force is supplied with existing workers. We assume that there are differences in the backgrounds of individuals, generating differences in the cost of education. However, we assume that the differences among individuals are exogenous, and follow the same pattern across different generations.[37]

Further, we make the following assumptions about the labour demand for new workers. First, newly hired internal workers necessitated by the growth of firms in each period are chosen from among new workers with a certain level of education. The reason why newly hired workers must have a certain level of education is that it is much easier for firms to incorporate them into the structure of the organization and to train them on the job. Second, we shall assume that the productivity of a worker once employed and trained (in the case of internal labour) is determined by the nature of the job and not by individual attributes or characteristics. These two assumptions relate to Thurow's assumptions (a) and (b).[38]

Finally, we shall assume a market interest rate r, with effects on the firm's investment and education, that is constant over time. This means that the savings supply is thus considered to be adjustable and unaffected by the investment decisions of firms. In order to construct a completely closed model of income distribution, we would have to enquire into the mechanism in which savings interact with investment and in which the market rate of interest is determined endogenously. However (as with most models of earnings distribution) these indirect linkages are beyond the scope of this section. (The determination of the market interest rate will be examined in section 7.3.)

Long-Run Determinants of Income Distribution

The important feature of the internal labour market represented in Thurow's job competition model is that the internal wage w_1 does not react to the gap between the labour demand and the supply at the point of entry to the market. In our formulation, the labour demand is gL_1, and the labour supply is $p\lambda N$, where p is the proportion of educated workers among the new entrants in the labour force. In order to examine the determinants of income distribution in the real world, it is useful to reverse the model and find out what happens if there is ideal competition.

More specifically, we term the payment to newly educated workers the education premium, hereafter denoted by x. This is the price for obtaining the commitment that the new, educated entrants will continuously work for

---

[37] It is clear that an indefinite life expectancy and instantaneous education are not crucial assumptions in this model.

[38] Thurow's assumption (a) concerns maximum productivity, and it just represents potential capacity. As noted earlier, however, we do not consider the motivation problem in this section, and it is assumed that potential productivity is always realized.

the current firm as its specific labour force. The evaluation of these workers is based on the assumption that they will not be dismissed or leave voluntarily.[39] It is noteworthy that the education premium may become negative. This means that the educated entrants will pay to secure a job opportunity in the internal labour market. In this case, its absolute value is termed the *entry fee* for the internal labour market.[40]

In the world the education premium is paid, both firms and new entrants will decide on their investment, based on the expectation of x at the end of the period, that is x^e. In the long-run equilibrium we consider, the expected value is necessarily the same as the one that is realized, so we do not distinguish them and we can proceed with the argument, only using the symbol x.

How is the level of the education premium determined? Let us first consider the firm's growth rate determining the labour demand for the newly educated. From the previous assumption about the growing cost, it can be found that the optimal growth rate is a monotonically increasing function of the net profit rate $R - rax$, that is, the difference between the profit rate R at any time and the permanent interest rate payment per unit of capital, rax.[41] This relationship can be written as $g = g(R - rax)$. Then the

---

[39] If we allow dismissals and voluntary separations to occur, as long as the employment contract continues, workers can pay the interest for the premium (rx) to firms in each period if $x > 0$, and firms can pay the interest for the entry fee $(|x|)$, that is $r|x|$, to employees in each period if $x < 0$. However, this payment rule can preclude either dismissal or voluntary separations, but cannot promote one rather than the other. If $x > 0$, dismissal is more likely to occur in an economic downturn, compared with the case where firms pay x all at once. As the following discussion points out, the consideration of the possibility of mutual default is one of the factors precluding the evaluation and actual payment of x.

[40] In order to avoid misunderstanding, we should clarify one important point. Some readers may think that the level of x is the value of the share of the training cost α in firm-specific skills. Joining the firm-specific labour force implies that workers accept the learning opportunities the firm offers, and this has the effect of reimbursing some part of the training cost (see footnote 33) if $x < 0$. However, this interpretation is misunderstood for the following reasons. First, x is the value of the stream of benefits fixed in advance, and it does not represent the sharing of investment that occurs when a share of the training cost α changes the mutual benefit streams. Second, and more crucially, α is determined in the subjective equilibrium, although it is complicated by the game-theoretic equilibrium between the firm and the worker, given the market wage rate, so that it is completely independent of the scarcity of workers participating in the investment. On the other hand, x is determined in the market equilibrium, implying that the internal organization of the firm adjusts the predetermined market wage, balancing the relative scarcity of workers and job opportunities. Thus, the determinant of α is not considered in this volume.

[41] According to Uzawa (1968), we represent the growing cost of the firm as $I = \phi(g)K$ $(\phi'(g) > 0, \phi''(g) > 0)$. The condition for the optimal growth rate g to maximize the value of the firm is:

$$\frac{R - (\phi(g) + axg)}{r - g} = \phi'(g) + ax.$$

(The terms equalized are so-called Tobin's q.) This equation can be rewritten as:

$$\frac{(R - rax) - \phi(g)}{r - g} = \phi'(g),$$

and g is a function of r and $R - rax$. As r is assumed to be constant, we can obtain the expression given here.

minimum gross profit rate R_0, which coexists with the safety of employment for internal workers, can be decided *as* $R_0 = \underline{R} + rax$, if $\underline{R}$ satisfies with $g(\underline{R}) = 0$. As $\underline{R}$ only depends on the characteristics of the growing cost and the interest rate, its level is independent of the external labour wage w_2.[42] When R_0 is determined, R and w_2 are also determined from the relationship in Figure 5.1 respectively.

$$R = \{(1 - \beta)R_c(w_2) - (1 - \beta)aw_2 + \beta\underline{R}\} + \beta rax, \tag{5.2}$$

$$w_1 = (1/a)\{\beta R_c(w_2) + (1 - \beta)aw_2 - \beta\underline{R}\} - \beta rx. \tag{5.3}$$

It is noteworthy that the right-hand side of both equations can be decomposed into the part depending on the education premium x and the other part. Focusing on the part that depends not on x but on w_2 and β, equation (5.1) with respect to the distribution of fixed factor rents can be satisfied among $R^*(w_2, \beta)$ and $w_1^*(w_2, \beta)$.[43] That is:

$$R_c(w_2) = R^*(w_2, \beta) + a \cdot w_1^*(w_2, \beta).$$

In sum, given w_2, β, and x, the firm growth rate can be determined as:

$$g = g[R^*(w_2, \beta) - (1 - \beta)rax].$$

Next we turn to the determination of the proportion of educated workers, p. They can expect to be hired in the internal labour market through the adjustment of the education premium. The present value of the expected return on education can be represented as $\{(w_1 - w_2)/r\} + x$. Individuals choose education if their present value of return on education exceeds the cost of education c. The distribution of the education cost among individuals is given exogenously, so that p can be presented as a monotonically increasing function of $\{(w_1 - w_2)/r\} + x$.

This relationship can be expressed, using (5.3), as:

$$p = p\left[\frac{w_1^*(w_2, \beta) - w_2}{r} + (1 - \beta)x\right].$$

It has already been stated that the education premium can be determined from the condition that:

$$p\lambda N = gL_1.$$

[42] Substituting $g = 0$ into the optimal growth condition in footnote 41, $\underline{R}$ is represented as:

$$\underline{R} = \phi(0) + r\phi'(0).$$

[43] Further, from equations (5.2) and (5.3), the partial derivative of $R^*(w_2, \beta)$ and $w_1^*(w_2, \beta)$ with respect to w_2 is equal to the sign of the partial derivative of R and w_1 to w_2.

Combining this condition with the steady growth condition $g = \lambda$, the long-run equilibrium conditions determining x and w_2 are finally:

$$g[R^*(w_2, \beta) - (1 - \beta)rax] = \lambda. \tag{5.4}$$

$$\rho \left[\frac{w_1^*(w_2, \beta) - w_2}{r} + (1 - \beta)x \right] = \frac{ak(w_2)}{ak(w_2) + 1}. \tag{5.5}$$

($k(w_2)$ is the capital–external labour ratio represented by the parameter w_2.) If we now turn to Figure 5.2 we see that the curve GG′ is the locus representing the relationship (5.4) that the expected firm growth rate is equal to the steady state growth rate. It is straightforward to verify that this curve is downward sloping. On the other hand, the curve PP′ represents the relationship (5.5) that satisfies the labour supply condition under the steady state. It is also easy to verify that this curve is upward sloping. We can interpret the former as *the education demand curve* and the latter as *the education supply curve*. The

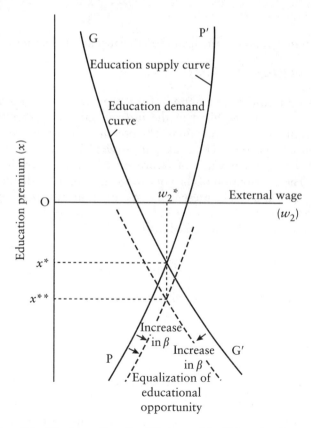

Figure 5.2. *The Long-Run Equilibrium of the Education Premium*

long-run equilibrium is presented as the intersection of these two curves.[44] The figure shows a negative education premium, which is the case when new entrants pay an entry fee to firms.

Before proceeding with the argument, we need to state the comparative static characteristics of this equilibrium. First, we show the effect of equalizing the educational opportunity. Equalizing the opportunity means in the model that the distribution of education costs shifts among individuals and for most of them the education cost is reduced. Then the education supply curve PP' moves downward while the education demand curve does not move. Therefore, in the new long-run equilibrium, the external labour wage rises and the education premium falls. Further, the proportion of educated workers p increases, and with it the permanent wage difference between internal and external labour, and $w_1^*(w_2, \beta) - w_2 + (1 - \beta)rx$. The equalization of educational opportunity clearly equalizes income distribution. This is the interpretation of the human capital theory based on the competitive labour market, discussed in section 3.1.

The second characteristic, the effect of change in the bargaining power β, is more striking. The change in the bargaining power causes the education demand and supply curves to move downwards, always by the same proportion.[45] Therefore, the external wage w_2 does not change, and only the

---

[44] The formulation of the dynamic process of x^e and k outside the long-run equilibrium is given by Ishikawa (1981*b*: 13–14).

[45] If we examine the shift of the education demand curve and the education supply curve with w_2 being fixed, the former is:

$$(1 - \beta)r \cdot \Delta x = \left(\frac{1}{a}\frac{\partial R^*}{\partial \beta} + rx\right)\Delta\beta,$$

and the latter is:

$$(1 - \beta)r \cdot \Delta x = \left(-\frac{\partial w_1^*}{\partial \beta} + rx\right)\Delta\beta.$$

For any β,

$$R_c(w_2) = R^*(w_2, \beta) + a \cdot w_1^*(w_2, \beta)$$

is satisfied, so

$$-\frac{\partial w_1^*}{\partial \beta} = \frac{1}{a}\frac{\partial R^*}{\partial \beta}.$$

Therefore, the value of $\Delta x/\Delta\beta$ should be the same in both relationships. Substituting $\partial R^*/\partial \beta$ into the above equation,

$$\frac{\Delta x}{\Delta\beta} = \frac{-1}{ra(1 - \beta)} \cdot \{R_c(w_2) - aw_2 - R_0\},$$

and the sign in { } is necessarily positive (from Figure 5.1). Thus, $\Delta x/\Delta\beta < 0$ holds. This result is essentially based on the identity with respect to the distribution of the fixed factor rent, and does not depend on the figure of the bargaining solution we presume.

Table 5.2. *Comparative Static Analysis of the Long-Run Equilibrium Involving the Payment of the Education Premium*

	External wage (w_2)	Permanent wage difference between internal and external labour	Net profit rate	Proportion of internal labour (p)
Equalizing education opportunity	+	−	0	+
Bargaining of internal labour	0	0	0	0

Note: The permanent wage difference between internal and external labour $= w_1^*(w_2, \beta) - w_2 + (1 - \beta)rx$, and the net profit rate $= R^*(w, \beta) - (1 - \beta)rax$.

education premium changes. Due to the equilibrium conditions (5.4) and (5.5), we can also confirm that there is no change in the net profit rate, the permanent wage difference, or the proportion of educated workers. That is, the adjustment of the education premium neutralizes the entire effect of changing the bargaining power.

The above conclusions are summarized in Table 5.2. The changes in the organizational and institutional factors in the internal labour market have no effect on resource allocation, especially price formulation. Therefore, it is quite plausible to maintain that equalizing the educational opportunity has the same influence as in the neo-classical competitive labour market. We must suppose that this is why most neo-classical economists are sceptical of the importance of the dual labour market hypothesis.[46]

The Constrained Long-Run Equilibrium

If the education premium or entry fee is not paid, does the situation change? In this case the quantity constraint occurs, as formalized by Clower (1965). As the so-called short-side principle is allowed, the trend of either the demand or supply side cannot be realized except when equilibrium is reached by accident, so that they are forced to behave differently because of the quantity constraint. Figure 5.2 can illustrate these arguments. First, the non-existence of the education premium means that x is fixed at zero. Then, education supply exceeds education demand in the figure; that is, there is an excess of supply among the newly educated labour force. In this case, the long-run equilibrium is given by the point of intersection of the education demand curve GG' and the horizontal axis. Next, job rationing occurs on the employee side. The newly educated

---

[46] Tobin (1980: 50) stated that the Modigliani–Miller theorem for corporate finance and Barro's neutrality theorem with respect to fiscal policy represent *the downgrading of a social institution*. The phenomenon of powerless institutions described here is quite similar to his statement.

Table 5.3. *Comparative Static Analysis of the Constrained Long-Run Equilibrium*

	External wage (w_2)	Permanent wage difference between internal and external labour ($w_1 - w_2$)	Net profit rate (R)	Proportion of internal labour ($p\,\theta$)
Situation under the demand constraint				
Equalizing education opportunity	0	0	0	0
Bargaining of internal labour	−	+	0	−
Situation under the supply constraint				
Equalizing education opportunity	+	−	−	+
Bargaining of internal labour	+	+	−	+

Note: A detailed explanation of the factors involved is given in the text. Under the supply constraint, $\theta = 1$.

workers who are not hired in the internal labour market are all absorbed into the external labour market. In contrast, in the case where the education demand curve intersects the education supply curve above the horizontal axis, job rationing occurs on the employer side. Then, the long-run equilibrium is given by point of the intersection of the education supply curve PP′ and the horizontal axis. The former can be called *the demand constraint situation*, and the latter *the supply constraint situation*.

It is only in the supply constraint situation that the equalization of educational opportunity affects the long-run equilibrium. On the other hand, change in the bargaining power has an effect on both constraint situations. These effects can be easily confirmed by examining the direction of the shifts of both curves stated above and checking which shift is influential in determining the long-run equilibrium. Table 5.3 summarizes the effects of these and other variables. (As x is zero, the permanent wage difference and the profit rate are equal to their ordinary levels.)

When educational opportunity is equalized under the demand constraint, it can be shown quite straight forwardly that the result is as shown in the top row of Table 5.3. While the proportion of educated workers p increases, a larger proportion of them suffer as a result of the rationing. Consequently, these changes net each other out, and the ratio of workers in the internal labour market does not change at all.[47] This is the detailed explanation of the education paradox in the general equilibrium framework. The equalization of

[47] In consideration of the quantity constraint generating job queues for internal labour, the current discounted value of the profit on education is $\theta^e(w_1 - w_2)/r$ while θ^e is the expected

educational opportunity does not affect income distribution and further, the correlation between education and income tends to be weakened as a result. This means that Thurow's interpretation is also plausible in relation to the point of general equilibrium.[48]

Next, the effect of the increase in the bargaining power of employees under the demand constraint can be explained as follows. If the external labour wage is constant, the fixed factor rent $R_c(w_2)$ is also constant, so that the increasing bargaining power clearly lowers the profit rate. However, the profit rate must be kept constant as long as the same rate of growth λ must continue to satisfy the firm's growth trend. This results in a reduction of the external labour wage. As the external labour market is competitive, the increase in the supply of external labour can only reduce the external wage; thus, the ratio of internal labour falls. The internal labour wage w_1 rises for the same reasons: first, from the increase in the fixed factor rent, and second, from the increase in the share of distribution. Consequently, the wage difference $w_1 - w_2$ increases. Due to the quantity constraint, the proportion of the educated labour force does not always increase, but the ratio of educated workers who are involuntarily hired in the external labour market, that is, the rationing ratio, always increases.

In contrast with the neutral result in the non-constrained model, this result implies that organizational and institutional factors play crucial roles in resource allocation and income distribution. We should point out also that the increase in the bargaining power of internal labour enlarges the inequality of the wage distribution while raising the income of internal labour relative to profit. The smaller proportion of internal labour employees can earn higher incomes, but the income of external labour falls.

Finally, in the supply constraint model, the equalization of educational opportunity equalizes income distribution. This is similar to the result observed

---

discount rate. Thus, the proportion of educated workers suffering the quantity constraint is:

$$p = p\left[\frac{\theta^e(w_1 - w_2)}{r}\right].$$

In the long-run equilibrium under the demand constraint, $\theta^e = \theta$ and

$$p\left[\frac{\theta(w_1 - w_2)}{r}\right] \cdot \theta = \frac{ak(w_2)}{ak(w_2) + 1}.$$

Therefore, the equalization of educational opportunity makes the $p(\cdot)$ function move upward. Then θ falls and p rises as long as w_2 and w_1 are constant. The formulation of the dynamic process of θ^e and k outside the long-run equilibrium is given by Ishikawa (1981*b*: 18).

[48] This explanation of the education paradox can be extended to the case of variable education. See Ishikawa (1981*b*: 28, footnote 19). Then, the education premium market would adjust the demand–supply gap by two variables: the education level generating the premium and the reward (price) rate for an additional unit of education. Without the premium market, the quantity adjustment of the minimum education level required for hiring in the internal labour market would substitute for the simple job queue. The equalization of educational opportunity only raises the minimum requirement of education for the internal labour market, that is, it causes educational inflation, resulting in the educational paradox.

in the non-constrained competitive model. However, it is also similar to the results in the demand constraint model, that organizational and institutional factors are important for income distribution. Therefore, it is not clear whether the wage difference between internal and external labour is widened under the supply constraint as these two effects work in different directions. This is because an increase in the internal labour wage will encourage more workers to take up education, and the pressure for external labour is weakened.

Conclusion

This section has examined factor price formulation and income distribution in the dual labour market under conditions of long-run equilibrium. It depends on the education premium or entry fee, which adjusts labour demand and supply through a price, whether or not the factors characterizing the internal labour market, such as the institution itself, practices, and bargaining power, act as determinants of income distribution. If the education premium is actually paid, the theory of the dual labour market hardly explains the formulation of the distribution mechanism. (Of course, section 5.2 provides a broader consideration of the theory of the division of labour in general.) We conclude by considering the plausibility of the education premium or entry fee in practice.

First, is it possible to find the solution by observing whether a premium is paid at the time of hiring? Indeed, a premium is paid for some professional workers such as sports players in the form of a financial contract. It is clear that such payment reflects the scarcity of trainable individuals, as evaluated by the employer. However, at the time of hiring, it is quite rare for a premium to be offered as a temporary payment from one side to the other. Nevertheless, we should not rely just on appearances. It is possible that the premium may be implicitly paid through continuous interest payments during the employment period and by controlling the age–income profile (see section 6.2 for details).

On the other hand, even if the premium is actually paid, the payments will have to completed in a relatively short period. This is because the possibility of default on payment after hiring cannot be ruled out. This problem will be especially serious in the actual economy where there is imperfect information on fluctuations in transfers and on employment opportunities. Thus, the premium would be time limited.

The potential payment of the education premium may be asymmetric, depending on whether it is positive or negative. In the case of negative payment, when there are shortages of employment opportunities in the internal labour market, and the competition requires payment of an entry fee, there are some reasons for not paying the fee. First, the capital market is imperfect; the liquidity constraint is quite substantial, especially for newly graduated workers. Second, an entry fee means that job opportunities have to be purchased for money. However, from the viewpoint of social fairness there will be strong resistance among individuals with the same ability to paying money for job opportunities.[49] On the other hand, if the potential education premium is positive, the liquidity constraint is less serious as the payment is offered by firms rather than by workers. And then the social constraint with additional payments for the protection of workers will not be so serious in the long-run equilibrium. (In the phase of short-run fluctuations, these is another constraint, adjustment of payment to existing workers; this point is considered in section 6.2.)

In sum, it can be suggested that the potential education premium may be actually paid, depending on whether it is positive or negative. This kind of asymmetry has a similar structure to the downward wage rigidity hypothesis of Keynes, that the nominal wage rate can be adjusted upwards, but not downwards. Whether this proposition is true or not can only be verified by empirical research. Detailed empirical work on this point should be conducted in the future. However, the author attempted a tentative study of the labour market for newly educated workers in Japan, and its conclusions are mostly consistent with this asymmetry hypothesis. Section 6.2 provides details of this.

Returning to the world of the long-run equilibrium theory, the situation that is likely to generate the positive education premium can be summarized as follows: (1) relatively high education costs, or inequality of opportunity for education; (2) the weak bargaining power of internal labour; and (3) optimism on the part of employers, that is, optimistic evaluation of future benefit opportunities. It is interesting to compare the different experiences of different countries and at different periods, on the basis of these factors.

5.5. THE PRODUCTIVITY INCENTIVE AND THE WORKER'S BARGAINING POWER

In the previous section we set out a model of the dual labour market economy with institutional wage setting in the internal labour market sector, and examined the interaction between firms' investment behaviour and individuals' educational investment behaviour. By so doing we have arrived at various determinants of long-run income distribution. However, this analysis focuses on the relationship between the internal and external sectors of the market, and not on the nature of the internal labour market itself. What we learned from the analysis is that if the firms' desire for growth exceeds the willingness of individuals to invest in education, then firms may opt to pay a premium for

---

[49] In the upper tier of the internal labour market (professionals, technicians, and managers), which is not considered in this section, there may be cases where jobs can actually be purchased, and such an action is allowable in society. The typical case is the acquisition of administration rights, that is, purchasing jobs for administrators by purchasing company stock. Another case is that of the children of doctors enrolling in medical college simply by the payment of substantial fees. That implies the purchasing of jobs as doctors because enrolment mostly guarantees that they will become doctors. While there is criticism of this custom within society, it has no power to prohibit such practices yet.

education when trying to hire new workers, while workers would wish to pay a premium (that is, an entry fee) to employers in order to get employment when there are fewer jobs than there are applicants. In such a case institutional wage determination is nullified and the situation that arises in the long run is exactly the same as if free competition prevailed in the market.

The principal point that will be made in this section is that, even when the nullifying forces against the institution of internal labour markets operate in relation to the external labour market, the story does not end there. Even when we admit the existence of competition with the external market, there is another factor inside the (lower tier of the) internal labour market that obstructs market clearing. This is the problem of work motivation, which we called *incentive-dependent exchange* in section 5.1. In order to understand this aspect, there is no need for a complicated model involving education as a prerequisite for entering the internal labour market. We only need the circumstance such that the internal labour market is always subject to the forces of potential competition from the external sector. Therefore, in the following discussion, we suppose a world of homogeneous workers wherein any worker can become an internal sector worker so long as he or she receives initial training.

The Efficiency Wage Hypothesis

The most primitive formulation of incentive-dependent exchange is the hypothesis of the *efficiency wage* or the *productivity wage*. As the wage rate rises the workers' feelings of loyalty toward the firm or their consciousness of fair exchange are aroused, and the work intensity they voluntarily supply rises. Although this proposition has a weak point in that it depends critically on the particular preferences and the psychology of workers, it is worth considering, to see what the argument leads to.[50]

Consider a representative firm with given capital equipment. Labour power is the only physical and variable factor of production. The working hours per worker are institutionally fixed. The amount of output depends on the product of the number of workers and the average work intensity per worker. There exists a fixed number of homogeneous firms in the economy, and the product market is purely competitive. (We shall set the product to be the numeraire.)

---

[50] Adam Smith pointed out that, in the case of jobs dealing with precious materials and large amounts of money and hence requiring a significant degree of trust, paying a lucrative wage to the workers would secure reliable execution of tasks. He adduced such a circumstance to be a source of wage disparity among workers (Smith 1776, 1904: vol. I: 116–17)). Such an idea goes back to Cantillon. We can recognize here a primitive formulation of the idea that productivity changes in line with wages. Akerlof (1982) attempted a sociological explanation, examining people's notion of fair exchange. Solow (1979) gave much momentum to subsequent research efforts to apply this idea in explanation of involuntary unemployment. Yellen (1984) gives a succinct survey of the development of the efficiency wage hypothesis.

Wages are paid on the time-rate basis. It is well known that prior to the establishment of such an institutional practice there was a long historical battle between the employers and workers about piece-rates.[51] The labour supply N is fixed, and the supply of labour power is inelastic. The foregoing assumptions are common throughout this section.

Assume that the work intensity voluntarily supplied by each worker is expressed as an upward-sloping curve with respect to the wage rate. The curve is further assumed to be strongly convex upwards. Its shape is similar to the curve EE' in Figure 5.4 (reproduced later in this section). If the firm learns about this relationship through its experience, it will obtain monopsony power in the sense that it would now be able to control the intensity of work supplied by workers by offering different wage rates. The firm now makes optimization with respect to both the number of workers and the wage rate. First, for any given wage rate, the demand for labour power (measured in terms of the number of workers) follows the marginal productivity principle. Namely, the increment in the value of output contributed by the last worker hired equals the wage rate per efficiency unit (work intensity) supplied. Second, for any given number of workers, the optimum wage rate is determined at the level whereby the increment in the value of product coming from the increased work intensity that a dollar increase in the wage rate brings about just equals its cost,

---

[51] Stone (1974: 129) states that shortly after the destruction of the craft union in the United States steel industry (cf. section 5.2) employers first introduced the piece-rate wage system as an incentive scheme to raise the productivity of newly created semi-skilled workers, but that it soon failed completely.

> However, the employers soon found that straight piece work gave the workers too much control over their wages. That is, when it succeeded in stimulating workers to increase their output, their wages soared above the going rate.
>   Employers would then cut the piece rates to keep the wages in line. Once they did that, however, they had reduced the piece rate system to simple speed-up—a way of getting more work for the same pay. Workers responded to the rate cuts by collectively slowing down their output, so that the system defeated itself, leaving employers back where they had started.

In other words, the reason for the failure was that while it might have solved the productivity incentive problem for the employer, it at the same time effectively gave workers the right to control and decide how much income they would earn.

In one sense, there is perhaps no question that provides a greater contrast between the neo-classical and political economy approaches than that of the piece-rate system. In the neo-classical theory, the question is posed by asking what kind of incentive reward system is socially (i.e., for the employers as well as workers) optimum. The studies of Lazear and Rosen (1981) and Green and Stokey (1983) considered the problem in relation to the situation where, in evaluating the outcome of each worker's productive efforts it is not possible to discern the productivity shocks that are common to all workers and those that are specific to variations in individual effort. According to Lazear and Rosen, if workers are risk neutral, then it would be socially optimal to adopt the piece-rate system; that is, pay on the basis of observed work intensity. (For discussion under more general assumptions, see Green and Stokey.) However, the supposition that the payment system can be freely chosen implies that the workplace is a political vacuum, a circumstance that does not hold in reality.

namely a dollar. Because of the strong convexity assumption of the work intensity curve this level is uniquely determined.

When these conditions are compared, we observe that the wage rate is determined independent of the number of workers who are hired. The criterion for the optimum then reduces to stating that the elasticity of work intensity (productive efficiency) with respect to the wage rate is unity. Furthermore, this condition is equivalent to the condition for minimizing the labour cost per efficiency unit, which explains the origin of the name of the hypothesis.

What we have just discussed is the manner by which the wage rate offered and the number of workers hired by the representative firm are determined. If the total number of workers thus demanded by all firms in the economy falls short of the population N, then each firm can realize its wish, whereas if it exceeds N, ultimately the wage rate is determined by the level that clears the market. In the latter case, the status of the firm as a monopsonistic agent ceases to hold.

The foregoing result can easily be confirmed with the aid of Figure 5.3. The optimality condition for the representative firm can be expressed as two downward-sloping curves WW' and LL' in the (L, w) plane. The WW' curve represents the optimum wage rate given the level of employment, while the LL' curve represents the optimum size of employment given the level of wage rafe. The WW' curve is seen to have a smaller slope than the LL' curve, at least in the neighbourhood of the intersection. Naturally, the intersection point EA gives the optimum wage rate w^* (hereafter called the *efficiency wage*) and the

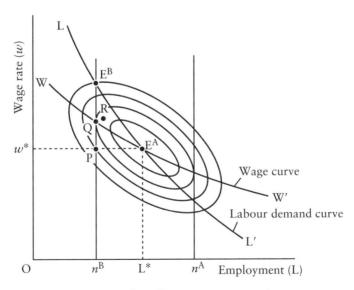

Figure 5.3. *The Efficiency Wage Hypothesis*

optimum number of workers L*. The contour maps centring around EA are the iso-profit curves, with naturally higher levels of profit as we move toward the centre.

Now, the fact that the optimum combination (w^*, L*) is realized when the number of workers available (N/number of firms) is given at the level n^A should be obvious, for the profit becomes maximum at that point.

In contrast, when the number of workers available for the representative firm is only n^B, then its desire is restrained. If the firm recognizes n^B as a quantity constraint, then it would raise the wage rate to Q along the WW' curve. However, this is not the final destination, for each firm may also recognize an opportunity for further improvement in profits. Suppose one firm tries to steal some workers from other firms by slightly raising the wage rate, so that R in the figure is achieved. Firms that recognize the advantage of such an action prior to other firms will obtain extra profits. Sooner or later, however, other firms are certain to follow, and the wage rate is successively bid up until, at E^B, there is no further opportunity for stealing workers. This point is simply the full-employment competitive equilibrium.

It goes without saying that the really new proposition advanced by the efficiency wage hypothesis lies in the case, such as n^A, where the level of the efficiency wage is higher than the potential competitive wage, and the market comes to an equilibrium leaving excess supply in place. The workers without a job may try to bid down the wage rate, but the firms are not willing to accept them. Those workers thus remain involuntarily unemployed, or else work in the external labour market. This illustrates in a very simple way that firms' policies generate a tendency to obstruct market clearance.

Two limitations to the foregoing discussion must be pointed out. First, what is crucial in defining the efficiency wage is the voluntary attitudes of workers towards work intensity. Although the existence of preferences and psychological attitudes on the part of workers seems realistic to the author, the correct perception of the productivity incentive seems to lie in the fact that not only do firms utilize workers' attitudes towards work intensity supply, but they also actively create work intensity itself. In this sense, the efficiency wage hypothesis is not an adequate theory.

Second, the hypothesis presumes that workers are entirely passive subjects. Such a formulation is far removed from the recognition (see section 5.2) that the workplace is rather an eternal battleground between employers and workers in relation to workers' discipline and managerial prerogatives for control. By explaining the expanded model which takes account of the above criticisms we discuss below the determinants of employment and income distribution within the internal labour market.[52]

---

[52] The following analysis is based upon Gintis and Ishikawa (1987) which extended the studies of Calvo (1979) and Shapiro and Stiglitz (1984). Calvo and Shapiro and Stiglitz made theoretical improvements to the first issue pointed out in the text, but they omitted the second point

A Generalized Incentive-Dependent Exchange Hypothesis

We continue to suppose the institutional arrangement of wages paid by time-rates. Workers agree to work for a prescribed number of hours as directed by the employer, but how hard they work is ultimately decided by workers themselves. As already stated in section 5.1, this situation reflects the fundamental incompleteness of the contract (*à la* Coase) in that it is not possible to write a contract for every detailed aspect of the work beforehand. Of course, if the employer could easily assess the outcome of labour for each worker, then he or she would try to dismiss unproductive workers. However, the dismissal would certainly incur a replacement cost in the form of hiring and training a new worker. Moreover, the dismissal might incur the opposition of the entire workforce, resulting in obstruction of production. Therefore, in practice, a firm cannot dismiss workers immediately even if they do not work diligently. Thus there arises a three-way contest in relation to work intensity among the employer, the worker as an individual, and the workers as a group. By analysing the nature of this contest in detail, we are able to obtain a perspective on the nature of the bargaining power of workers, and the role it plays in determining the volume of employment and income distribution.

Suppose that a representative firm offers a fixed sum of wages per period to workers and at the same time offers them an option to renew their contracts should the firm observe at the end of the current period that their work attitude (that is, work intensity, to be denoted hereafter by i) is acceptable. Suppose that the firm sets a criterion for employment renewal. It ranks workers in terms of individual work intensity, and states that it will keep the workers above a certain pre-announced rank and dismiss the rest. Call the proportion of the latter the *dismissal rate* and denote it by f.

Suppose also that the firm decides on the intensity with which to monitor the activities of workers, or equivalently, the degree of accuracy with which it evaluates the work intensity of each worker. The intensity of monitoring is denoted by s.

The firm makes its intention about (f, s) clear to workers. In other words, the firm places the demand for workers in the market by offering a contract package (w, f, s). We would like to know what particular package of (w, f, s) is realized as an equilibrium in the market, and how the distributions of employment and income are determined.

altogether. Also, as to how the level of work intensity is determined, Calvo left its microeconomic foundation as a black box, while Shapiro and Stiglitz avoided the problem to begin with by assuming the existence of an exogenously fixed norm. Gintis and Ishikawa (1987) considered the second issue raised in the text, determined the level of work intensity endogenously and derived comparative static properties rigorously, and finally discussed and classified the possible types of equilibrium in the labour market as a whole, looking at the worker's generalized current utility function in relation to income and work intensity. For a detailed mathematical analysis of the results summarized in the text and discussion of their relationship with existing literature, the reader is referred to the original article.

What sort of contract the representative firm offers depends generally on factors such as technology levels and monitoring costs, workers' attitudes both as individuals and as members of a group, and finally, the overall state of demand and supply in the labour market. Among these factors, the effects of production technology and monitoring costs are fairly obvious, and they do not require detailed analysis. In particular, if (as will be supposed below) the unit labour cost (that is, the cost per employee) is independent of the size of employment, (w, f, s) becomes completely independent of production technology, just as w became independent of technology under the efficiency wage hypothesis.

On the other hand, if there arises excess demand for workers, reflecting the overall condition of demand and supply in the labour market, then the dismissal rate f should become zero. The reason is that the worker, even if he or she is dismissed, can immediately find a job in another firm, and therefore the threat of dismissal (while it may be costly for the employer) has no additional deterrent effect on workers. In other words, the dismissal rate f is effective as an incentive measure only when workers incur a real economic loss by becoming unemployed.

The question of the attitude of workers, both as individuals and as members of a group remains. The dismissal policy aims to induce emulation and competition among individual workers, thereby raising their work motivation[53] and simultaneously it aims to obstruct co-operation between workers. Certainly each worker has good reason to respond positively to an individual incentive scheme. It was the individualistic economic motive that made him or her seek employment in the first place. But at the same time, working together with others may possibly ferment social consciousness among workers, calling for mutual help and solidarity, which would curb the dominance of individualistic motives.

There is no general theory to explain how the relative weights of individualistic and social motives are determined. Hence, as a second-best measure we adopt the following crude dichotomy. When each worker chooses his or her work intensity level, he or she does so on the basis of individual motives. However, when dismissal occurs *ex post*, workers will resist in concert, imposing a friction cost on the employer.

It is supposed that this friction cost is proportional to the number of workers dismissed, and is also the greater, the higher the level of work intensity of the dismissed workers. (The implicit assumption is that workers themselves can mutually observe the true work intensity, at no cost to themselves.) The rationale for this assumption is, of course, that, the greater the friction cost, the greater the degree to which dismissal is regarded as an unfair penalty.

The employer chooses (w, f, s) by taking into account these two types of behaviour on the part of workers. Among the three variables, a rise in the

---

[53] The main idea involved here is based on the notion of the emulation effect among workers, discussed in Ishikawa (1981a).

monitoring intensity, s, affects the worker's behaviour by raising the effectiveness of a given dismissal rate, f. Hence it can be substituted for the dismissal policy. Because it plays little independent role in the following development of the theory, it will be assumed below that s is exogenously given and the discussion will focus on the determinants of (w, f).

Suppose the number of firms is given, and, without loss of generality, it is normalized to unity. The economy is assumed to be in a stationary state.[54] By stationary we mean that the content of the contract and the size of employment do not change over time, and that new hirings occur only to replace dismissed workers.

In each period immediately before the market opens each worker is in a state of being either employed in some firm as a member of its internal labour force, or without a job. In the latter case, as soon as the labour market opens, the worker either is hired in the internal labour market (called *re-employment*) or stays *unemployed* for the current period.

Unemployment is to be construed here also as including employment in the external labour market. (In reality, external labour and unemployment are likely to form another layered structure, but it should be easy to extend the following analysis to such a case.) The unemployed workers are assumed to receive an income of $\underline{u}$ (in utility terms). This income can be interpreted flexibly to consist of the value of home work, social security benefits, or external labour income at the level of the minimum wage. Alternatively, with a slight extension of the model (which we do not discuss further here), it can be regarded as an endogenously determined wage level of the external labour market (as in section 5.4). We call u *external utility income*.

Definition and Typology of the Labour Market Equilibrium

It may be expected that competition in the labour market operates in terms of the utility level that the contract (w, f) gives to each worker. The utility referred to here includes not only the current utility flow but also the stream of expected utility flows arising in the next period and thereafter. By recalling that there are two types of workers at the beginning of each period (just prior to the opening of the market), one employed and the other unemployed, let us see how the utility levels of each type are determined.

On the one hand, the employed worker receives the current utility flow which depends on income and work intensity $u(w, i)$, and faces the probabilistic events of either continuing to be employed (that is, his or her contract is renewed) or becoming unemployed (he or she is dismissed). Denoting the probability of becoming unemployed by d, the present value of the expected utility stream of the employed by V_e, and that of the unemployed by V_u, V_e is

---

[54] The conclusion here will not undergo any change even if free entry of firms is allowed and the profits (or, alternatively, the competitive rate of return on capital outlaid) are destined to become zero.

defined under the stationary circumstance by:

$$V_e = \frac{1}{1+r}\{u(w,i) + dV_u + (1-d)V_e\},$$

where r is the market rate of discount assumed to be constant over time. By solving V_e from this relationship, it is expressed as:

$$V_e = \frac{u(w,i) + dV_u}{r+d}. \tag{5.6}$$

On the other hand, whether unemployed workers are re-employed or stay unemployed after the market opens is determined probabilistically. If they stay unemployed they will receive the external utility income $\underline{u}$, and retain the status of unemployed at the beginning of the next period. Denoting the probability of re-employment by a, the present value of the utility for the unemployed worker V_u is defined, again under the stationary circumstance, as:

$$V_u = aV_e + \frac{1-a}{1+r}(\underline{u} + V_u).$$

From this, V_u is solved as:

$$V_u = \frac{1-a}{r+a}\underline{u} + \frac{a(1+r)}{r+a}V_e. \tag{5.7}$$

Among the two probabilistic quantities appearing in the expressions of V_e and V_u, d depends on the dismissal policy of the firm as well as indiviudals' response to such an incentive scheme, and hence it is variable through individual worker's choice, while a is the ratio of the replacement demand for workers fL over the size of the pool of workers without job $(N - (1-f)L)$, and therefore, it is not under the direct control of unemployed workers.

Each of the employed workers will try to maximize V_e, taking as given the contract (w, f) offered by the firm and the level of the present value of utility for the job-losers, V_u. The reason for taking V_u as given is that each worker cannot modify its level directly, which is analogous to the participant in a competitive market who takes the price as given. When the level of V_u that is derived from the maximized V_e and the level of a generated by the firms as a whole does not equal the original level of V_u that was initially taken as given, then workers as well as firms change their behaviour. And when the two become equal, expectations of both workers and firms are satisfied, and the labour market realizes equilibrium in the sense that no one is led to change their behaviour.

The maximized V_e must at least be equal to or greater than V_u. In that sense V_u expresses the level of the reservation utility (in present value terms) for the employed workers. In order to consider what types of equilibrium are possible in the labour market, we first modify (5.7) to observe that:

$$V_e - V_u = \frac{1-a}{r+a}(rV_e - \underline{u}). \tag{5.8}$$

This relationship implies that V_e and V_u become equal only if $a = 1$, namely the case of full employment, or else $rV_e = \underline{u}$. The latter relationship can be rewritten, using (5.6), as $u(w, i) = \underline{u}$. In other words, it is a state in which the same minimum utility is obtained no matter whether the worker works in the firm or not. It is the circumstance of voluntary unemployment. It may alternatively be interpreted as a state in which internal jobs and external jobs are indifferent.

In contrast, the case $V_e > V_u$ corresponds to $a < 1$, implying the existence of unemployment. The unemployment occurring here is, of course, involuntary. This case can further be divided into one where $a = 0$, where there is no dismissal of workers (just as in the original efficiency wage model), and the other with $0 < a < 1$, where there is dismissal of workers.

Determination of the Labour Contract and the Level of Employment and their Comparative Static Properties

The foregoing shows the types of alternative patterns of long-run stationary equilibrium that is possible in the labour market. Consider next how (w, f) and the size of employment L are determined. First, let us discuss the nature of the isoquants of work intensity over the (w, f) space on the basis of individual workers' behaviour and for a given market parameter V_u. Figure 5.4 depicts the worker's indifference curves in the upper part—the (w, i) plane, and the isoquants of work intensity in the lower part—the (w, f) plane, with the wage rate w being the common horizontal axis and with the work intensity i being the upper and the rate of dismissal f being the lower vertical axis.

There are many possible varieties to the shape of the workers' indifference curves. We take up the case where, as depicted in Figure 5.4, they are (strictly) convex leftward and the locus of tangency points with the vertical lines (the curve EE′) becomes upward sloping and, moreover, strongly convex upward. Such a supposition, in turn, implies that (i) the higher the income, the higher the level of worker satisfaction (ii) the worker has a notion of the fair intensity level of work for each given wage, and that it rises as the wage increases. It is the curve EE′ that corresponds exactly to the fair work intensity level envisaged by the worker. Also, such a notion seems to underlie the positive relationship between work intensity and wage, as assumed in the original efficiency wage hypothesis. The level of the efficiency wage, w^*, obtained earlier corresponds to a point in the figure where a straight line emanating from the origin O becomes tangential to the curve EE′. It is hereafter assumed that $u(w^*, i^*)$ is greater than the external utility income $\underline{u}$.[55]

---

[55] When $u(w^*, i^*) < \underline{u}$ holds, the state of voluntary unemployment whereby every worker receives utility equalling $\underline{u}$ would emerge as a conceivable type of labour market equilibrium, replacing the possibility of the involuntary unemployment equilibrium with the wage set at the efficiency wage level. It cannot be determined a priori which of the two, $u(w^*, i^*)$ and $\underline{u}$, is greater.

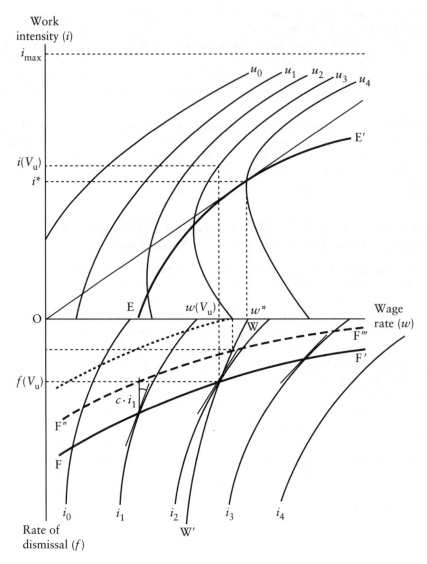

Figure 5.4. *A Generalized Incentive-Dependent Exchange Hypothesis*

Note: V_u is given.

The fact that the firm uses the dismissal policy as an additional incentive measure means that the workers are induced to work above the curve EE′. Each worker tries to ensure that his or her work intensity cannot be assessed by the employer as not matching that of other workers, and therefore works harder than his or her voluntary supply level as represented by the curve EE′.

A little more formal explanation might be useful. The first point to note is that, even though the dismissal rate f is given, the probability of dismissal for an individual worker is variable, depending on the degree by which the worker's own work intensity deviates from that of the average worker. A more concrete form of this dependency can be derived objectively by specifying a particular monitoring technology for the firm.[56] The subjective equilibrium of a worker is then realized by the condition that the marginal current utility loss incurred by a small increase in the work intensity just equals the marginal utility gain, defined by the marginal increase in the probability $(1-d)$ of contract renewal times the advantage in utility thereby obtained $(V_e - V_u)$. This condition implies that the effectiveness of the dismissal policy presupposes a positive gap between V_e and V_u. When every worker behaves in the same way they all end up working at the average intensity level (to be called the workers' *group equilibrium*). However, even in such a situation the mutual emulation effect continues to operate.[57]

On the other hand, when the market achieves full employment or voluntary unemployment with $V_e = V_u$, the supply of work intensity is determined at a level where the marginal current utility loss is zero. That is, however, simply a point along the EE' curve. Of course, in such a situation there is no reason for the firm to incur the costs of dismissing workers. The mutual emulation effect of workers ceases to operate here. The group equilibrium will then be a mere collection of independently realized individual equilibria.

---

[56] For instance, if the employer's evaluation of each worker's work intensity is independent of other evaluations, and the observed value follows a triangular distribution with range m on each side of the true value and with the maximum probability density m at the mode of the distribution, then the function d has the expression

$$d = \frac{1}{2m^2}(i - i_g - m\sqrt{2f})^2$$

in the region of the group equilibrium where every worker behaves in a similar manner, and with the region satisfying $(1/2) > f > 0$. The term i_g in this expression refers to the average work intensity of workers. The qualification $(1/2) > f$ is easily satisfied if the friction cost due to worker dismissal is sufficiently large. (See Gintis and Ishikawa 1987: 113–18.)

[57] Under the supposition made in footnote 56 it can be shown that there exists a symmetric Nash equilibrium whereby each worker works with intensity $i = i_g$, which is determined by the relationship:

$$V_e - V_u = \frac{m}{\sqrt{2f}}\{-u_i(w, i_g)\}$$

(Gintis and Ishikawa 1987: Appendix). It is this Nash equilibrium that we call the group equilibrium. It may occur to the reader to ask why, if every worker is ultimately to work with the same intensity and the observed disparity in work intensity among workers is to be reduced only to observational errors, rational employers would bother to spend resources on monitoring. This argument is, however, a conclusion turned upside down and, therefore, is not a correct one. It is only because the employer spends resources on monitoring that workers behave as described.

The lower half of Figure 5.4 depicts the isoquants of work intensity in the situation of group equilibrium. The isoquants are drawn on the basis of a specific parameter value V_u, and therefore, except for the horizontal intercept points (which remain unchanged despite changes in V_u) they shift rightwards as V_u increases. The horizontal intercepts correspond to the points along the curve EE', and they express the wage levels at which each work intensity level is supplied voluntarily. Because the emulation effect does not operate along the curve EE', the work intensity does not change in the face of changes in V_u. The shape of the isoquants is not definitively characterized, as it depends, in general, on the nature of the worker's current utility function as well as the strength of the emulation effect, but the shape given in the figure seems to be the normal case.

We turn now to the firm's choices. The constraints on the firm are the isoquants of work intensity just discussed and the friction cost per dismissed worker, which we suppose to be a strictly increasing function of work intensity, $c(i)$. By minimizing the total labour cost per work intensity with respect to w and f, which in itself constitutes a part of the conditions for profit maximization, we can obtain the optimum level of w, given f and V_u, and similarly the optimum level of f given w and V_u. In the figure, the former is represented by the curve WW' (called the *wage curve*), while the latter is represented by the curve FF' (called the *dismissal rate curve*).

The curve WW' expresses the condition that a marginal increase in wages (seen as a cost) is equal to the net value marginal product (the gross marginal product, from which is subtracted an increase in the friction cost) that it induces, which is a condition quite similar to that of the efficiency wage hypothesis. This curve necessarily originates from w^* (the efficiency wage) on the horizontal axis, but other than that it can generally become upward sloping or downward sloping. The normal case, however, seems to be an upward-sloping curve, with an increase in the dismissal rate bringing about some economizing effect on wage payments. (In fact, to be more rigorous, when the utility function $u(w, i)$ is approximated by a linear function it is definitely upward sloping.)

On the other hand, the curve FF' expresses the condition that the marginal rate of substitution between the two factors w and f in generating work intensity is equal to the ratio of the marginal cost of each factors $(1/c(i))$. Geometrically speaking, it is the locus of the tangency points between each isoquant and a straight line with the slope $1/c(i)$ evaluated at the corresponding work intensity level. (In the figure, the tangency point between the isoquant $i = i_1$ and a line with the slope $1/c(i_1)$, specified further to be $1/ci_1$ below, is highlighted.) Since the slope of the tangent $(1/c(i))$ declines as i increases, the curve FF' is necessarily upward sloping, and moreover, its slope is always less steep than that of the corresponding isoquants. The employer achieves cost minimization at the intersection of the curves WW' and FF' (subject to an additional constraint that, when the curve WW' is upward sloping, it cannot be steeper than the curve FF$'$ at the intersection points.) Figure 5.4 depicts the case where a positive dismissal rate is actually chosen.

What effects does an increase in the workers' collective power have on the behaviour of firms? We have already stated that such a change is expressed by an increase in the frictional cost for the employer. For the sake of simplicity, consider the case where the unit dismissal cost $c(i)$ is expressed by ci, with the parameter c measuring the strength of workers' collective power.

Under this simplified assumption, we can easily verify that the curve WW$'$ stands still, while the curve FF$'$ shifts upward in the face of a rise in c. In fact, the curve WW$'$ then reduces itself to represent the unitary elasticity condition $i_w w/i = 1$ discussed earlier, and becomes independent of c. The new dismissal rate curve is depicted as the broken curve F$''$F$'''$. The intersection point now moves towards the upper right, and the firm's choice is now shifted towards less dismissal and a higher wage rate, that is, relying more heavily on the wage incentive. (However, if the curve WW$'$ were downward sloping to start with, then both the dismissal rate and the wage rate would have declined.) If c increases further, then the dismissal rate curve shifts even further upward, depicted by the dotted curve in the figure, so that it would no longer have an intersection point with the curve WW$'$ in the region with $f > 0$. The result is that the employer chooses $(w, f) = (w^*, 0)$, which is exactly the same as the original efficiency wage hypothesis.

The foregoing analysis of the behaviour of workers and firms pertains to the circumstance where the level of the reservation utility V_u is given and fixed. There is no guarantee that the chosen V_u equilibrates the entire labour market. As we have already stated, market equilibrium requires equality of the level of V_u generated objectively (via equation (5.7)) by the behaviour of workers and firms, on the one hand, and that originally given as datum, on the other. However, with the addition of some further regularity assumptions we can show that there does indeed exist an equilibrium for the labour market characterized here. Furthermore, we can verify that the comparative static properties of the collective power of workers stated above hold even as a market experiment (that is, after adjustment of V_u by the market is taken into account).

Another important comparative static property concerns the effect of a change in the external utility income u. It can be demonstrated within a regime having a positive dismissal rate that an increase in u brings about a rise in the wage rate w, a decline in the dismissal rate f, a rise in the work intensity i, a fall in the size of employment L, each evaluated as a first-order effect. The underlying reason is that an increase in the reservation utility brought about by a rise in u makes it more advantageous for the firm to secure effective labour services by an increase in work intensity rather than by an increase in the number of workers.[58]

---

[58] The proofs of the proposition set out here are given in Gintis and Ishikawa (1987: Propositions 4–6). By 'first-order effect' is meant the comparative static properties evaluated with

Alternative Regimes of Labour Market Equilibrium and the Conditions Governing the Occurrence of Regimes

Which type of equilibrium the labour market falls into depends on the strength of workers' collective power, in addition to the size of the working population (N) and the nature of the workers' voluntary work intensity supply (the curve EE' in Figure 5.4).

The resulting typology is given in terms of Table 5.4. The entry 'Voluntary supply present' designates the case where, just as in Figure 5.4, the curve EE' is upward sloping, while the entry 'Voluntary supply not present' designates the case where the curve EE' coincides with the horizontal axis, implying that work intensity is always a disutility in the worker's preference. In the latter case the isoquants of work intensity in Figure 5.4 will never have intercepts along the horizontal axis, implying that the curve WW' and the curve FF' necessarily meet in the region with a positive dismissal rate. Intuitively, wages alone in such a case have no incentive effects at all, so that, no matter how high c is, firms must simultaneously employ the incentive generated by the threat of economic loss which unemployment brings about. Consequently labour market equilibrium involves involuntarily unemployed workers.

The foregoing analysis shows that, even if workers are perfectly homogeneous, there still is scope for inequality in employment and distribution of income. In reality, the productivity incentive system discussed here is reinforced by the pyramid-like hierarchical structure and the internal promotion scheme constructed in the internal labour market, and accordingly there is an added degree of income disparity among workers.[59]

Our analysis also shows that the collective power of internal sector workers does exhibit an influence on income distribution. An increase in the collective power (in the regime where the dismissal rate is positive, and a first-order effect) lowers the risk of job loss and in this way increases job stability, while at the same time it increases the disparity between the utility level and the external utility income and lowers the profit as well as the employment size of the internal sector itself. Note that the latter effect is qualitatively the same as the

---

the use of a linearly approximated utility function of $u(w, i)$ around the original equilibrium. Such an approximation is used because it is next to impossible to obtain any explicable signs by the non-linear utility function in comparative static analysis, whereas it is possible to find solutions using a quadratic or cubic equation.

[59] We should note here that work motivation can also be raised purely by means of an internal promotion system. In such a case the involuntary unemployment in the labour market discussed in the text is now transferred into involuntary employment within the firm, and no unemployed workers are created outside the firm. In reality, the internal promotion system and the incentive wage system are working simultaneously. For attempts to investigate the disparity of wages corresponding to the hierarchical structure of the firm from the perspective of work motivation, see Calvo and Wellisz (1978, 1979). However, they leave many important aspects of the problem untouched.

Table 5.4. *Alternative Regimes of Labour Market Equilibrium and Factors Affecting the Determination of the Regime*

Work intensity	Size of population/ Strength of workers' collective power		Characteristics of wages and employment
Voluntary supply present	N: small		• Competitive equilibrium wage and full employment
	N: large	c: large	• If $u(w^*, i^*) > \underline{u}$, efficiency wage, involuntary unemployment equilibrium • If $u(w^*, i^*) > \underline{u}$, voluntary unemployment equilibrium with $u(w, i) = \underline{u}$
		c: small	• Involuntary unemployment equilibrium with incentive wage and dismissal
Voluntary supply not present	Independent of N and c		• Involuntary unemployment equilibrium with incentive wage and dismissal

increase in the internal workers' bargaining power β under the demand constraint regime discussed in section 5.4. Thus, viewed on the macro scale, the solidarity of workers in the internal sector raises the workers' income on average, yet, at the same time, incurs a dilemma that the increased income is not necessarily distributed equally among all workers, both within the internal sector and in relation to the external sector.

The Possibility of Achieving Full Employment through Competition in the Level of Bonding

There is an opposing view to the theory just explained. It states that the productivity incentive problem can easily be resolved even within the Walrasian framework of the competitive market, and such an organizational factor as workers' collective power amounts to nothing in determining the final outcome.[60]

Let us defer for a moment the question of whether or not the argument is realistic, and suppose that the worker who seek employment in the internal sector lodges a bond, b (measured in terms of utility), with the employer prior to the actual labour service. Simultaneously a stipulation is included in the

---

[60] This point has been raised frequently. See Yellen (1984) and Carmichael (1985). The bonding mechanism and its applicability to the real world was first discussed by Becker and Stigler (1974). Eaton and White (1982) discuss in detail the limitations imposed by imperfect capital markets. On the other hand, Lazear (1979) has shown that a pure seniority wage system has an effect similar to the bonding mechanism.

(w, f, s) contract to the effect that should the worker's performance be poor and the contract not renewed, the worker forfeits the bond; on the other hand, if the contract is renewed then it will be returned to the worker.

Under such terms of employment, V_e is expressed by:

$$V_e = -b + \frac{1}{1+r}\{u(w,i) + dV_u + (1-d)(V_e + b)\},$$

and, from this, (5.6) is modified to read:

$$V_e = \frac{u(w,i) + dV_u}{r+d} - b. \tag{5.6'}$$

Observe that the value of V_e is reduced by exactly the amount of bond, and that the latter has no effect at all on the worker's decision about work intensity.[61] On the other hand, the introduction of a bond has, for the employer, the effect of decreasing the unit friction cost $c(i)$ by exactly the (pecuniarily equivalent) amount of the bond. Hence, it has just the same effect as a decline in the workers' collective power.

Suppose that, prior to the introduction of a bond, involuntary unemployment existed. (It does not matter whether the dismissal rate was positive or zero; hereafter we consider the case of a positive dismissal rate.) If the workers without a job offered to lodge a bond with the employer, employers would be pleased to accept such an offer. Hence, all workers (including those whose contracts have been renewed) must start doing the same, and there will be a competition with respect to the level of the bond. The situation is quite analogous to the competition over the amount of the entry fee discussed in section 5.4. We already know that an increase in the amount of bond decreases the wage and increases the size of employment. Hence, so long as involuntary unemployment continues to exist, the level of the bond must rise, and ultimately equilibrium with full employment or equilibrium with voluntary unemployment (with wages equalling the external utility income) is reached. Any organizational elements within the internal labour market are completely nullified by the operation of wage competition through the back door.

---

[61] If the employer is to return the bond with interest, then the level of bond affects the decision of the workers. In fact, in such a case, V_e is no longer (5.6'), but is expressed as

$$V_e = \frac{u(w,i) + d\{V_u - (1+r)b\}}{r+d}. \tag{5.6''}$$

Thus, for workers the situation is as if the reservation utility V_u has decreased by the amount of $(1+r)b$. In a regime with $f > 0$, an increase in b raises the work intensity chosen by workers (Gintis and Ishikawa (1987: Proposition 1) for a given (w, f, s). However, the essential point that a rise in b increases the size of employment, and thus decreases unemployment, is unchanged.

The bond contract originated from the idea of placing a collateral in a financial loan contract. However, whereas the collateral of a loan is legally buttressed in the form of collateral rights and its use is widespread, a literal bond contract is not seen in practice within a labour contract. Why is this so? Three reasons may be adduced in that regard.

First, although the bond itself takes a pure pecuniary form, conceptually it has a similar effect to taking a human being as collateral. Human reason has developed various social regulations (including a ban on slavery) and social welfare programmes, even within an otherwise market economy, to defend the human dignity of people who are in desperate economic need, and no doubt the same human reason imposes a moral regulation to prevent this kind of contract.

Second, a labour contract has a distinctively different character from a financial loan contract in that, whereas in the latter the disappearance of debt becomes apparent to everyone once the borrower pays back the debt, in the former case the question remains unresolved of who, and by what measure, judges the appropriateness of the work intensity supplied. In the formulation centring on equation (5.6′), it has been implicitly assumed that the workers unconditionally trust the good will of the employer. Such trust, however, does not exist a priori. On the contrary, it is quite likely that persistent conflicts might develop with respect to the justifiability of the employer's judgement. In such a case, the existence of a bond contract could easily become an additional source of friction.

Third, whenever bonds actually require to be posted in full at the beginning of a period of employment, the problem of imperfection in the capital market, already discussed in the context of entry fees, again raises its head. Because of the existence of the borrowing constraint, this mechanism may cease to operate whenever the amount of a bond becomes sufficiently large.

Of course, we can conceive of a contract that is different from the literal rendering of the concept. One such mechanism is the seniority wage system. This system has an advantage in that it can expect to have the same effect as a bond contract and yet it can ameliorate people's moral repugnance to the notion of a bond, and also ease considerably the problem of borrowing constraints.

A difficulty remains, however, as it must still face the second constraint noted above. And indeed to the author this second barrier seems a serious one. We may, of course, admit the possibility that in a particular social, cultural, and historical environment a relationship of trust between employer and workers might be developed. Yet, it must be worked out and is not simply in place. (For an empirical study of the operation of a bond contract in the form of a seniority wage in Japan, see section 6.2.) At any rate, the argument that the bond contract makes the discussion in this section completely meaningless is too extreme.

Incentive-Dependent Exchange and the Distribution of Employment and Income

We turn next to other implications of the model, in particular, to the structure of the labour market and the distribution of income. First, the internal labour market as a field of incentive-dependent exchange formulated here is definitely a competitive market. Thus, for example, when there is an increase in the number of the working population, the equilibrium wage rate declines through competition, which is quite analogous to the properties of the Walrasian market. (The exception is unemployment regimes where the wage rate equals either the efficiency wage or the external utility income; in such regimes it remains the same.) The essential difference from the Walrasian market is, however, that equilibrium might accompany excess supply.

Second, in the case of an involuntary unemployment equilibrium with positive dismissal, there actually occurs an inward and outward flow of workers between the internal labour market and the pool of unemployed (or external) workers. In fact, a frequent criticism of the dual labour market hypothesis has been that there is a significant degree of labour mobility between the internal and external sectors so that the workers in these two sectors cannot be said to form non-competing groups (section 5.3). A theoretical case can be made from our model such that rationing of workers can coexist with labour mobility. In this sense we can mitigate the force of such a criticism.

In practice, however, the frequency of disciplinary job separation, to the extent that it appears in the statistics, is fairly small, especially in comparison with that of voluntary separations and dismissals due to business downturns.[62] Therefore, in order to explain the observed magnitude of labour mobility between the two sectors, consideration of the latter two circumstances seems necessary.

If it is a matter of exogenous separations, then it can easily be incorporated into the model. Also if the separation rate depends (negatively) on the difference between the employer's own and other employers' wage levels, then involuntary unemployment becomes more likely to occur as the wage rate is pushed up further by emulation on the part of different employers (so as to keep their present workforce and avoid the costly replacement of workers, see Stiglitz 1974; Calvo 1979).

---

[62] This point can be verified from the statistics on separation rates in both Japan and the USA. Under the supposition made in footnote 56, however, it can be shown that the dismissal rate chosen by the firm must necessarily be less than the market rate of interest, r. (If the voluntary separation rate is positive, then the dismissal rate must be less than the sum of the separation rate and the market rate of interest.) Therefore, even theoretically f is not expected to have a large value.

As to the effect of short-run demand fluctuations, there are some fragmentary discussions which show that firms tend to resort to Keynesian employment adjustment in response to unanticipated demand shocks (Akerlof and Yellen 1985), and yet that firms tend at least partially to hoard internal workers in response to anticipated and recurrent stochastic shocks (Gintis and Ishikawa 1986), and the research agenda still seem to be open. Such investigations will answer the important question of what effect short-run macroeconomic fluctuations have on the distribution of income.

Third, the fact that rationing exists even in equilibrium leads prima facie to an expectation that the model developed here might be applied to explain the so-called discrimination phenomenon over wages as well as employment. However, we must take care in making such an interpretation.

In the first place, as long as workers are homogeneous with respect to preference and ability, there will never be discrimination (on a general scale) in the allocation of opportunities according to such ascriptive traits as race and sex. The reason is as follows. Suppose that men and women have different re-employment ratios. Imagine that men have a higher ratio. In such a case, the utility loss due to non-renewal of contracts is higher for women than for men. This implies that, under the same contract (w, f, s), women's work intensity becomes higher than that of men. Therefore, profit-maximizing firms will start to hire women, contradicting the initial supposition that the re-employment ratio of men is higher. Needless to say, this does not rule out the possibility that employers may discriminate in petty or secret ways. So long as they do not affect the macroscopic re-employment ratio they can realize their wish at no cost.

In the second place, if there exists a significant correlation between some ascriptive trait (such as sex) and the voluntary separation propensity (as a matter of preference) then the story becomes different. In fact, the separation rate of young women is known to be higher than that of men of the same age group. Because of a higher likelihood of voluntary separation women tend to discount, more highly than men, the advantage in the future utility flow obtainable by continuation of employment. Therefore, other things being equal, employers are led to offer more expensive incentive schemes in order to secure the same work intensity from women as from men. This provides a rationale for restricting the employment of women (Bulow and Summers 1986).

Care must be taken, however, when we associate a particular type of preference with persons possessing a particular ascriptive trait. For instance, even if it is true that women's separation rate is high, it may just as well be true—due possibly to intertemporal substitution—that women's current work motivation (their voluntary work intensity supply) is also high. It is conceivable that the latter may end up offsetting the disadvantage caused by the high separation ratio. Hence, although it is logically correct that a greater separation rate *ceteris paribus* generates what is known as discrimination as an equilibrium phenomenon, it nevertheless falls short of explaining the actual disparity in employment opportunities between men and women.[63]

5.6. THE LABOUR MARKET AND THE DISTRIBUTION OF INCOME: CONCLUSION

An understanding of the formation of personal earnings distribution seems to require as its basis consideration of: (i) how people learn through education and training and how the result of this learning is reflected in the placement of employment; (ii) how strong individual workers' spontaneous work motivations and their collective motives for co-operation are, respectively; (iii) and what kind of incentive schemes employers adopt, and what kind of market regime (cf. Table 5.4) appears as a result, both within a framework of the labour market that would allow quantitative rationing to emerge in equilibrium. Our analyses in sections 5.4 and 5.5 complement each other in providing a theoretical framework with which to interpret the experiences of various countries in different periods and to examine the effectiveness of social policies designed to promote equality in income distribution.

The neo-classical approach has greatly enriched our analytical tools concerning distributional phenomena, clarifying the nature of the individual's rational choice, in particular, in relation to investment in economic ability and informational learning under conditions of uncertainty. However, because it sought the world to which such tools were applied in the Walrasian competitive market (with the possibility of joint exchange), both as a perception of reality and as a normative ideal, it always remained content with a theoretical prediction and a social policy guideline stating that equalization of education and training was the primary means of bringing about equality in the distribution of earnings.

In fact, however, the massive social expenditure on education and training in the United States during the 1960s (under the *Great Society* programme) did not generate the outcome that it was expected to achieve. It is from review of

---

[63] In trying to understand the difference in employment opportunities and the accompanying difference between men and women it is quite natural to pay attention to the difference in the average separation rates between the two sexes. Indeed, the point that employers, who are not themselves in a position to know each worker's separation probability, use information on the average rate of separation by each ascriptive group and thus bring about disparity in employment opportunities, is widely accepted as the theory of statistical discrimination (Arrow 1972; Phelps 1972).

However, it may not be correct to attribute the various reasons for differential separation rates to the single item of differential preferences. It is possible that a vicious circle is operating here. The effect of this is that the barriers in on-the-job learning opportunities, once they are somehow formed (and even if these barriers themselves have tendency to disappear in the long run, reflecting competition among employers), may perpetuate themselves by raising the separation rates of women who are otherwise not different at all from men. That, in turn, further restricts the learning opportunities of women, and so forth. Much empirical work remains to be done, to delineate exactly what is explained by these circular effects from the pure element of preference.

this failure that the dual labour market hypothesis gained its momentum. The dual labour market has close affinity with Keynesian macro theory in that it supposes the existence of a persistent demand constraint in the economy. In fact, it emphasizes the need to maintain high aggregate demand for internal workers as a means towards equalization of income.[64]

Our analysis in this chapter has shown, however, that we should not sub-jugate the neo-classical competitive market hypothesis and the dual labour market hypothesis to a dogmatic choice among alternatives (sections 5.4 and 5.5). Indeed, if the following conditions are met, namely that: (i) the voluntary supply of work intensity is high; (ii) the collective power of workers is strong; and (iii) the rate of economic growth is high, then there is a good opportunity for the neo-classical competitive market to emerge. The reasons for this are that, first, there is a force tending to the production of full employ-ment, in the form of productive incentives, and second, competitive bidding in the form of the educational premium (or negative entry fee) is expected to occur in the circumstance in question. On the other hand, whenever one of these conditions is not met, it is possible for involuntary unemployment (or a seg-mented external labour market), as well as the schooling paradox, to occur. These circumstances, of course, tend to vary according to place and time period, and there seems to be scope to undertake valuable comparative studies across nations and across time.

Although the foregoing analysis supposed that workers' spontaneous work intensity supply attitude was exogenous, in reality, it is believed to be an inherently endogenous variable of the economic system.

In the first place, it is hard to imagine that people's work motivation is totally unrelated to the content of the job. For those types of job with much scope for learning and/or for holding high-level responsibilities, work motivation will naturally be higher (sections 5.2 and 5.3). On the other hand, it is hard to expect much spontaneous work motivation to arise from dead-end jobs that lack any learning content or responsibility. There is even a possibility of a vicious circle: taking a dead-end job enhances the workers' aversion to work itself, and that would further perpetuate the taking of such a job. Moreover, there is even a danger that such an effect might be transmitted across genera-tions in a household, that is, from parents to children.

In the second place, the spectrum of jobs that an economic system has seems largely to be an outcome of employers' economic decision making, and it may very well reflect the social conflict between employers and workers over control of the workplace. The analysis in section 5.5 modifies the neo-classical tradi-tion of treating the production process solely in terms of the technical input–output relationship by endogenizing a part of the social relationship between

---

[64] The works of Sabel (1982: ch. 5) and Piore and Sabel (1986) go beyond the traditional policy guidelines of the dual labour market hypothesis in arguing for the need to modify the technology and organization of production, and in discussing concrete alternatives.

employer and workers, and incorporating it into the description of the production process. However, determination of the scope and content of each job remains exogenous.

These two points seem to suggest the possibility of a different policy alternative to enhance equality, apart from the ones discussed so far. This is the policy of improving the quality of the work process. Such a policy seems to have gained in relevance, especially for countries with limited scope for economic growth and (for reasons such as the mounting pressure of fiscal debts or the need for international co-ordination) with limited flexibility in activating short-run demand stabilization measures. Detailed enquiries on these points, accompanied by empirical studies, seem to be the most urgent directions for future research.[65]

[65] An alternative proposal to that given in the text is to replace the time-rate payment system by a profit- (or revenue-) sharing system, and thereby create a contrived distortion of excess demand for labour power in the market (Weitzman 1983). From a purely private point of view, it is difficult to implement the revenue-sharing system, as the more employment expands, the less income is distributed to existing workers. The proposal thus argues for government policies of tax credits and other subsidies to make the system acceptable to incumbent workers. However, it seems that this proposal is realizable only after a significant improvement has been made to the social relations between employers and workers with respect to production technology and the arrangement of work processes, resulting in the creation of a relationship of trust between them.

6

The Dual Labour Market Hypothesis and the Japanese Labour Market

What kind of contribution will the theories developed so far make to an understanding of the working of the labour market? From among the various important topics concerning the Japanese labour market we choose to focus on its dualistic structure, which has for years caught the attention of many researchers. Application of the theories to other topics is left to future researchers.

This chapter consists of two sections. Section 6.1 reviews the meaning of the dualistic wage structure in Japan, and discusses the theoretical rationale for its emergence.[1] It argues that the dualistic structure of the labour market should not simply be equated with disparity in wages and other terms of employment among firms of different size (as has been customary in the literature), but rather it should be construed as a segmentation into an internal sector and an external sector, as described by the dual labour market hypothesis. Disparity of rewards among firms of different size should then be treated as a consequence of the fact that large firms have developed the internal sector on a much wider and deeper scale than small firms. Furthermore, having noted that whether or not there is genuine wage disparity among workers depends on the existence of an involuntary barrier obstructing movement from the external to the internal sector, it points out that the existing empirical studies tend to underestimate the presence of a dual structure in the labour market.

Section 6.2 is devoted to an empirical test of whether the entry fee/bond mechanism believed to have the role of removing the entry barrier to the internal labour market actually operated in Japan. It does so by examining the cohort wage profiles of male new school graduates and their movement over time, the supposition being that, if such mechanism were ever to operate, it would do so by way of generating a seniority wage element that would necessarily be anti-cyclical in nature. The focus is placed on the new school graduates market because it is the principal port of entry into the internal labour market in Japan. Previously this portion of the market has been regarded as a very competitive one.

---

[1] Section 6.1 is a revised version of Ishikawa (1989). The main point has not changed. The author wishes to thank Konosuke Odaka and Michio Morishima for their valuable comments on the revision.

The conclusion of section 6.2 may be stated in advance. Quite strong evidence in favour of the operation of the entry-fee mechanism was found for production (blue-collar) workers who had graduated from high school and were employed in large manufacturing firms during the period of the early 1960s to the early 1970s, the so-called rapid growth era. Cross-sectionally this is the portion of the market that is believed to have developed the internal labour market features in the most exemplary fashion. However, this was the period during which there was a very strong demand pressure for new workers, and employers had very good reason to pay premiums, or equivalently, negative entry fees to workers.

In contrast, after the Japanese economy moved into the slow growth era and started to show relatively distinct business fluctuations, in the mid-1970s to the early 1980s, the relationship indicating the operation of the entry fee/bond mechanism disappeared. In practice, the slope of the cohort wage profile showed little change during this period.

Thus a feature quite analogous to the Keynesian downward wage rigidity operated around the port of entry into the internal labour market.

For high school graduates who are office workers in manufacturing industry or who work in other industries, the conclusion was broadly similar, if not so clear-cut. For college graduates, the result was even more negative. There was little sign that the entry fee/bond mechanism operated, and even if it did, the effect was quantitatively much weaker than in the case of their high school counterparts. More strikingly, there was no evidence of any premium having been paid to college graduates in the rapid growth era, a plausible interpretation being that any potentially strong pressure for the existence of a premium on the demand side was nullified by a mounting increase in the supply of college graduates, which occurred at the same time.

From these observations we generally conclude that the operation of the positive entry fee/bond mechanism at the ports of entry into the internal labour market remains questionable, and that rationing of employment opportunities is likely to occur during cyclical downturns or at times of slow economic growth. Such an empirical result is consistent with and at least partially supportive of our suggestion for synthesizing the neo-classical and dual labour market approaches (section 5.6); in particular, the proposition that the labour market is characterized, *ceteris paribus*, by neo-classical competition during high-demand phases, and by equilibrium involuntary rationing of employment during low-demand phases.

6.1. THE DUALISTIC WAGE STRUCTURE AMONG FIRMS OF DIFFERENT SIZE

It is some time since the dualistic structure between large firms and small firms in Japan first attracted our attention. In the labour market, it has been repeatedly pointed out that even now there remain various disparities associated with firm size: wages, bonuses, fringe benefits, job security, work-place environment and safety, methods of resolving labour disputes, etc. As we observed in Table 1.4, the majority of Japanese workers belong to small firms. Thus, the existence of these disparities is thought to have played an important role in shaping the distribution of earnings.

Many efforts, both theoretical and empirical, have been made to explain the emergence of these disparities (Shinohara 1970: ch. 8; Koike 1981*a*: s. 6.1; Odaka 1984: ss. 1 and 8; Hashimoto and Raisian 1985). However, it is difficult to conclude that the researchers have reached firm agreement about the reasons. One of the difficulties stems from the lack of a common framework for evaluating disparities. The section, which applies the theory of the labour market developed so far, examines in what sense the dualistic structure is associated with firm size.

First, let us examine the current state of the wage disparity between workers in large and small firms. Based on the 1985 Wage Census (*Basic Survey on Wage Structure 1985*), Figure 6.1 depicts the wage distributions of workers in two different age groups in firms with more than 1,000 employees and in firms with 10 to 99 employees. The wage data are derived from the monthly scheduled cash earnings of the workers in manufacturing, whom we divide into production workers and clerical/supervisory workers. We take the average of all educational levels and express the data in logarithmic form. The reason we select 30 to 34 and 45 to 49 as the two age groups is that those in the former group are in transition from the initial investment period in the workplace to the harvesting period; and those in the latter group on average reach their peak wage at this age. From Figure 6.1, we can observe that for those in their early thirties, the distributions for the two firm sizes overlap, both for production workers and for clerical/supervisory workers. Moreover, the mode of the two distributions is almost identical in the case of the clerical/supervisory workers. However, if we look more closely, we can find such characteristics as: (a) the firms with more than 1,000 employees (hereafter called large firms) have a smaller dispersion in distribution than those with 10 to 99 employees (hereafter called small firms); and (b) the distributions for small firms have a thicker tail at the lower earnings levels.

For workers in their late forties, the distributions still overlap but, both for production workers and for clerical/supervisory workers, the distributions are no longer similar among firms of different size; (c) for production workers, the distribution is still concentrated in large firms as for the workers in their early thirties, but it is dispersed and is skewed downward in small firms; and (d) for clerical/supervisory workers, the dispersion and the mode of the distributions are similar among firms of different size but the distribution is skewed downward in small firms while it is skewed upward in large firms.

Features (b), (c), and (d) above characterize the (gross) wage disparity among firms of different size. (Though we do not include figures for the wholesale or retail industries their distributions exhibit similar characteristics to those for

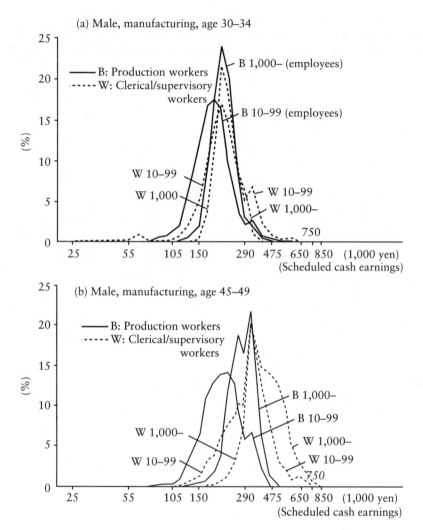

Figure 6.1. *Wage Distribution between Large and Small Firms*

Source: Ministry of Labour, The Basic Survey on Wage Structure (1985: vol. I, Table 3).

manufacturing.) They show not only that the age–wage profile is steeper in large firms than in small firms, which is frequently mentioned, but also that the degree of the wage disparity among firms of different size increases as the age increases. The disparity increases further when we take into account bonuses and the fringe benefits. Moreover, it is known that the disparity is even bigger for female workers than for male workers.[2] The overlap of distributions means

---

[2] Morishima (1988), based on data from Tachibanaki (1982) plus some additional more recent data), shows that there exists a wage disparity in the sense summarized below. (This paper is

that there are other factors that influence wages, independent of the size of firms. As a matter of fact, many studies of the earnings function, as I will explain later, have regarded schooling and tenure as the factors influencing wages and have tried to estimate the genuine effect of firm sizes on wages by removing the effects of these factors.

Why do such wage distributions emerge? The simplest interpretation is that, as a result of perfect competition in the labour market, they reflect the abilities of individual workers, both inborn and acquired through education and/or job training. The difference in wage distributions among firms of different size, according to this interpretation, occurs because large firms are more likely to be successful in selecting and hiring workers who have high trainability at the end of their school education. Actually, support for this hypothesis based on ability difference is high among Japanese labour economists (Odaka 1984: s. 1; Koike 1981*a*: s. 6).

The difficulty of this interpretation is that it fails to explain convincingly why large firms can succeed in hiring more able workers. If the size itself is some-thing a worker prefers, large firms will be able to collect a rent from this preference and, as a result, will offer proportionately lower wages. In the same way, when large firms relatively often provide scarce and superior learning opportunities, which I think is the case, they can also collect a rent from the workers. (Please recall the concept of the entry fee discussed in section 5.4.) Hence, even if these advantages at large firms attract able workers, they do not necessarily explain high wages there if we subtract the workers' payment to the firms for the provision of these advantages. Namely, the workers enter large firms by sacrificing some income (the principle of equalizing difference). However, it undermines the explanation to say that the average wage in large firms is higher because they have larger numbers of able workers.[3]

---

unpublished. I quote the results with the author's permission.) First, for white collar workers, both male and female aged 30 to 34, the wage disparity among firms of different size does not change, in the sense that it shows no trend in quantity during the period 1958 to 1985. (Tenure as well as age is also controlled. The same applies to the following estimation.) However, for the older workers, the wage disparity is less. This is because the age–wage profile becomes less steep. Second, for blue collar workers, there is still a large wage disparity for both male and female workers. Compared to the workers in large firms, male workers aged 30 to 34 in small firms earn about 70 per cent of what workers in large firms earn, while the figure for older workers is 60 to 70 per cent though the figure has improved a bit. The older, female employees in small firms earn less than 60 per cent [of what their counterparts in large firms earn] even now. Moreover, for this section of female workers, [level of] schooling does not have any effect.

[3] As will be discussed in section 6.2, if there is asymmetry of information with respect to the ability of workers at hiring and if more able workers have higher reservation wages, there is an incentive for firms to offer wage rates above the competitive equilibrium level. If large firms do so more frequently because they have the financial capacity, this can be one explanation of the wage disparity. Though this element is significant to the wage contract at the time of hiring, it does not necessarily explain wage disparities between those with some tenure, when we take into account the workers' informational learning ability after hiring.

Another hypothesis about the labour market is that it is not either homogeneous or competitive but is segmented into partial markets, and that the competition between partial markets as well as within some partial markets is incomplete. This is the view of the dual labour market hypothesis that we examined in the previous chapter. This hypothesis has developed through independent empirical observations, both in Japan and in the USA. In this view, differences in workers' abilities prior to employment are given a minor role and rationing in the market is regarded as the principal cause of wage disparities. This hypothesis does not directly explain the difference in wage distributions among firms of different size. The criterion of market segmentation is not the size of firms. Instead, according to this line of thought, higher proportions of large firms than small firms are thought to have partial markets that exhibit rationing and, as a consequence, the wage disparity among firms of different size emerges.

In this section, I explain wage disparity among firms of different size mainly from the latter approach. However, in supposing that the learning opportunities at the workplace play a major role in forming earning ability, it has a common element with the first approach. The point that the nature of learning opportunities in each segmented market and the labour management necessitated by it are strongly related to the emergence of the rationing phenomenon is a characteristic claim in the latter approach.

The discussion proceeds as follows. I first examine how to define the wage disparity and, recalling the dual labour market hypothesis, analyse the factors that persistently produce such wage disparity. Next, I discuss how the dual labour market hypothesis explains the disparity among firms of different size though its basic way of understanding structures is unrelated to the size of firms. Finally, I critically evaluate the hypothesis based on ability difference.

Definition of a Genuine Wage Disparity

Not all of the wage disparity consequent upon market evaluation refers to the 'disparity' that causes a problem in distribution. Both the disparity caused by the effect of education and training in which individuals invested in the past and that which reflects the preference of individuals about the quality of job, which is called the equalizing difference, are typical examples of innocuous disparities. Moreover, the disparity caused by inborn talents (such as artistic talent, athletic ability, ability to think logically, management ability, etc.) should be considered as redistribution, which goes beyond the issue of how the market should evaluate, even though it certainly has distributional implications. In the market evaluation, we say that the 'genuine wage disparity' that is problematic exists when there are workers who have the same ability and the same preference and yet do not obtain the same job opportunity. The dualistic structure of the labour market has clear meaning only when the disparity defined above exists.

The size of firms itself does not cause the genuine disparity. First, let us remind ourselves of two fundamental theorems that hold in the competitive labour market. First, when the quality of workers is the same, their wage should be identical, independent of the capital equipment and size of organization of the employers. Even if large firms have higher proportions of capital equipment and higher average productivity per worker than small firms, the wages should be identical. In this way, the marginal productivity principle shields the phenomena in the labour market from the variation in the product markets. Second, if the quality of workers is the same, the differences in skill (learning) that emerge among workers do not cause differences in their lifetime income as long as the skill (learning) is generally useable in labour market. As explained later, even when the benefit of the skill is confined to the current firm, the *ex ante* lifetime income is equalized to that from other job opportunities as long as the evaluation is discounted by the risk of the loss from unintended turnover. When individuals are faced with various learning opportunities on an equal footing, the high cost of learning at earlier periods has to be compensated by a higher income at later periods. Hence, even when large firms have some advantage in the breadth and depth of job opportunities over small firms and thus provide more training, which causes the wage difference (theoretically speaking, a negative one for junior workers and a positive one for senior workers), it does not constitute a genuine wage disparity.

Even when the real labour market is comprised of workers with various qualities, the criterion for the genuine disparity remains the same as above: whether there is a disparity among a group of workers of the same quality.

The Dual Structure View and the Dual Labour Market Hypothesis

The view that the labour market is comprised of segmented markets that are qualitatively different (and have different wage structures) emerged from independent observations of reality, in the form of Shojiro Ujihara's 'dualistic structure' model (Ujihara 1954, 1966) in Japan and Doeringer and Piore's 'dual labour market hypothesis' in the USA. Both are quite similar in regarding the internal labour market, whose main characteristics is the existence of firm-specific skills, and a peripheral (external) labour market that serves as a pool of excess labour supply as the core concept of the dual structure. Ujihara's hypothesis was proposed in the early 1950s. Even though its originality is outstanding, its scope is severely limited by the conditions of that era. That is, Ujihara regarded the existence of firm-specific skills and the lifetime association of workers with a company as symptoms of the pre-modern nature of the Japanese economy. (He explains this as follows. Since there was an excess supply of unskilled workers in villages and in small urban manufacturing industries, and since manual skills were prevalent due to the backwardness of technological development, and since there existed a technological gap among firms of different size due to the co-existence of large firms and small firms as a result of the peculiar method of capital accumulation in Japan, the acquired skills could not be applied generally.) He thus did not see that the dual structure can be a consequence of a universal, rational logic. In this respect, though this point is developed later, I think that we ought to give higher credit to the dual labour market hypothesis, which has been shaped by critical interaction with the human capital theory and its empirical research.[4]

I have explained the dual labour market hypothesis in detail in section 5.3. There, I made the following observations. The market is divided into the internal labour market and the external labour market, and the former is subdivided into the upper tier and the lower tier, with the craft jobs in the middle. As the basis of market division, the characteristic differences in learning opportunities, knowledge, and skills of workers exist. Moreover, these differences cause corresponding differences in labour management practices. In some markets it was pointed out, a practice that restricts competition emerges to maintain the structure of learning and skill in the workplace. Employers like to divide the labour market into the internal and external markets, since they want a buffer against the fluctuation and uncertainty of product demand and since they need to restrict the number and power of internal workers in order to suppress wage costs and need to maintain the flexibility of labour management.

How is this view of the labour market as a dualistic structure related to the differences between large and small firms? Since the former is a categorization of learning and skills on the part of workers and the latter is derived from the size of organization (the employers' side), they differ fundamentally in nature. Moreover, small firms are a group of firms that are qualitatively quite different. Among the workers in small firms, some, like doctors and lawyers, have the characteristics of the upper tier while some employees in such sectors as wholesale, retail, construction, and transportation have the characteristics of either craft jobs or external unskilled labour. In addition, manufacturing firms that undertake subcontracting serve as an external labour market in relation to the parent company and, at the same time, within the firms, there is a two-tier structure with the management in the upper tier and the core workers in the lower tier. As the subcontracting is repeated, there will be more layers and structures. In this way, it is not correct to view small firms as a group of uniform and homogeneous organization.

Roughly speaking, we can say that the large firms, by means of mass production, provide the goods and services for which demand is stable while small firms undertake subcontracting from large firms, or produce specialized goods in small quantities, or engage in traditional business on a small scale. Mass production naturally develops a uniform system of production and training.

---

[4] In his early works Koike (1971, 1999) refuted Ujihara's hypothesis that the Japanese system is pre-modern and pointed out the commonality between the Japanese and American internal labour markets. His recent tendency is, however, to illustrate the differences between the Japanese and American labour markets by emphasizing the breadth of Japanese on-the-job training.

Therefore, large firms tend to have a larger internal labour market, especially the lower tier that is its core part, than small firms.

Rationales for the Occurrence of Genuine Wage Disparity

One of the main claims in the dual labour market hypothesis is that there is involuntary labour supply in the external market. This can be rephrased as the situation where access to learning opportunities is rationed. If the lower tier in the internal labour market satisfies the condition of the competitive market fully, involuntary labour supply will disappear through the adjustment of internal wage rates. However, as we saw in section 5.3, reflecting the nature of its learning and skills, the lower tier of the internal labour market is likely to have rationing even in equilibrium. First, since the learning has elements specific to a firm, the investment in learning is shared by an employer and a worker to reduce the separation rate of workers. (In Ujihara's theory, there is no counterpart to this concept of joint investment.) Second, the continuation of a stable employment relationship gives power to workers as a group and necessitates the creation of rules and practices to deal with conflicts between an employer and employees. In this respect, the implementation of on-the-job training has a special importance. The stable implementation of on-the-job training needs trust and co-operation among workers. Hence, the employer needs to remove the factors that may cause the workers to compete and to fight against each other, even if they are norms in the external market. As a result, there is rationing between the lower tier of the internal labour market and the external labour market. These two reasons were originally pointed out by Doeringer and Piore. The wage disparity here satisfies the criterion of the genuine disparity.

As we saw in section 3.2 (please recall Figure 3.10), a firm-specific skill necessitates joint investment by an employer and a worker, that is, the sharing of the costs of investment and its returns. Now suppose that firm A offers the opportunity of firm-specific skills while firm B does not. We assume that firm A and firm B are otherwise identical and that the marginal value product without training in both firms is identical (B(0) in Figure 3.10). To simplify the analysis, we assume that the marginal value product is constant independent of employment level. (The conclusion is unchanged even without this assumption.) As a result of skill acquisition, a worker in firm A obtains a higher lifetime income than a worker in firm B. In this sense, the wage in firm A is more than the competitive wage.[5] On the other hand, firm A also obtains excess rent.

[5] Moreover, if the capital equipment is complementary to the learning opportunities, the wage disparity will depend on the average productivity. The paying ability hypothesis, which receives some support as explaining the wage disparity between large firms and small firms, is justifiable in this circumstance. A concrete model in which the wage level depends on the average productivity reflecting the firm-specific skills is presented in section 5.4. In such a case, the duality in the capital market that Shinohara (1970) emphasized also becomes influential in causing the wage disparity. See also footnote 9.

However, for the genuine wage disparity generated in this way to survive in the long run, two conditions have to be satisfied. The first is that competition with respect to the entry fee at the port of entry is restricted in some way. The second is that the learning opportunity is monopolized practically by a small group of firms. We examine these conditions in turn.

Workers naturally prefer working at firm A to working at firm B. The competitive pressure from the workers can be absorbed if firm A collects an entry fee from the workers. Eventually, the entry fee increases to the point where the workers feel indifferent between working at firm A and working at firm B. In that case, however, the present value of the excess rent (QR in Figure 3.10) that the workers were supposed to obtain from working at firm A is entirely taken by the firm. That is, the joint investment does not benefit the workers. Doeringer and Piore argued that competition among workers undermines the foundation of on-the-job training. Their argument is certainly able to explain the suspension of hiring at the mid-career period or restriction of wage competition within a firm but is not applicable to competition at the point of entry of new employees. Hence, we need to examine the validity of the concept of the entry fee that was introduced in section 5.4.

Now, I turn to the second condition. Firm A can obtain the entire excess rent and thus can grow at a far higher rate than firm B. However, for that situation to continue, firm A has to monopolize a learning opportunity in the market, as we have seen in section 3.2. This is feasible when one or more of the following conditions is satisfied: (i) the learning opportunity is rooted in a truly scarce management resource at firm A, (ii) the product market has an oligopolistic structure and does not allow the entry of other firms even when the learning opportunity itself is easy to mimic, and/or (iii) other firms cannot utilize the learning opportunity due to constraints in obtaining the funds for human capital investment even when the learning opportunity itself is easy to mimic.

On the other hand, if the learning opportunity is easy to mimic and there are no constraints, not only firm B but also other firms will charge an entry fee to obtain the excess rent. In this way, there will be competition among firms for workers and eventually the excess rent that the firms expected will go to workers. In the process, α (the ratio of the firm's share of training costs) will decline and will eventually become close to zero.[6] In the end, the lifetime income of all the workers increases by B(0)U in Figure 3.10 in terms of the present value and the long-run equilibrium is reached. That is, it is the same

---

[6] The reason that α declines is that the firms that offer a contract in $\triangle$RQT of Figure 3.10 can hire workers even if the market competition becomes tight. Eventually, the entry fee causes competition among employers and drives the contract to the upper-left side in the figure. Of course, strictly speaking, the final α should be a little bit bigger than 0. This is because the workers do not invest alone.

situation as applies in the case of the general skill and the genuine wage disparity disappears. This equilibrium is stable in the sense that, if a firm is disappointed at the loss of excess rent and stops offering the learning opportunity, the excess surplus reappears with the remaining firms and, after some adjustment, the long-term equilibrium is restored.

Another important factor that causes rationing in labour market and the genuine wage disparity is the issue of labour management. By modifying the simple efficiency wage hypothesis (see section 5.5), I demonstrate this point.

Let us suppose again that there are firm A and firm B in the economy. At firm B, we assume that workers are directly monitored and that their work intensity is always 1. At firm A, the work intensity i determined by the difference between the wage offer of firm A and that of firm B. This is depicted as the labour intensity curve at the left side of Figure 6.2. In the figure, the vertical axis measures the wage rate of each firm in the goods unit, w_A and w_B respectively, and the wage rate of firm B, w_B, is assumed to be given. Since the labour intensity curve is drawn given w_B, it shifts upward when w_B increases. It is naturally assumed that the labour intensity in firm A is low when w_A is equal to w_B, that is:

$$i(0) = \underline{i} < 1.$$

On the right side of the figure, the marginal productivity curve $L_B L_B'$ of firm B that corresponds to the labour demand curve LL' in Figure 5.3 and

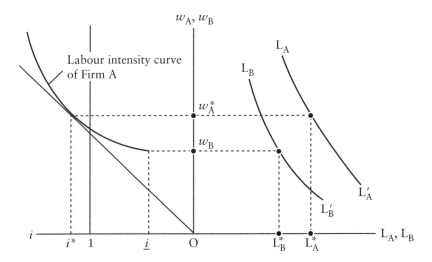

Figure 6.2. *The Efficiency Wage Hypothesis and Wage Disparity among Firms of Different Size*

the marginal productivity curve $L_A L'_A$ of firm A are drawn. The latter[7] takes into account the change of labour intensity corresponding to the change of w_A. Each curve describes the optimal employment level L_B and L_A respectively given the wage level w_A and w_B. The optimal incentive wage level w^*_A for firm A is given by the tangent point of the line originating from the origin and the labour intensity curve in the left side of the figure, (in the same way as in the upper side of Figure 5.4). There is certainly a positive difference between w^*_A and w_B.

What is the equilibrium in a labour market with this structure? The total labour supply is considered to be given. In the short run, the number of firms for each firm type (firms A and B) is considered to be fixed. The wage of firm B serves the role of adjusting the demand and supply in the labour market as a whole. w_A keeps a positive difference to w_B when w_B changes. When the total supply of labour is equal to the total demand, market equilibrium is attained. In the long run, whether the profit of a certain type of firm exceeds the normal profit or not affects the number of firms of that type, and equilibrium is achieved when there is neither entry nor exit. In this way, both in the short run and in the long run, a genuine wage disparity emerges, which is used to maintain the incentive at firm A. Hence, the different patterns of labour management among firms of a different size cause the dualistic structure of wages. As explained in section 5.5, this kind of disparity can be sustained in the long run only when competition in relation to bonding works imperfectly.

Wage Disparity among Firms of Different Size

We have discussed above the condition under which the existence of firm-specific skills and the necessity for incentives from the point of view of labour management, which are characteristics of the lower tier in the internal labour market, cause a genuine wage disparity with the external labour market. It is apparent that firm A represents the employer of lower-tier workers and firm B represents the employer of the external labour force in the purest way. Next, we see how the above discussion is related to the wage disparity between large and small firms, which is the subject of our original question. By doing so, we can judge whether the wage disparity that we still observe is a structural disparity or not.

---

[7] When the production function is given by $X_A = f_A(i \cdot L_A)$, the condition for the optimal employment is $f'_A \cdot i = w_A$. Hence, the slope of the curve that represents this condition (given w_B) is given by:

$$\frac{dL^A}{dw^A} = \frac{1 - i'f'_A}{i^2 f''_A} - \frac{i'L_A}{i}.$$

Here, it is assumed that $i = i(w_A - w_B)$, $i' > 0$, and $i'' < 0$. Though the sign of the right-hand side is not generally determined, the second term is always negative and the first term has the same sign as $(i'w_A/i) - 1$. Thus, when $(i'w_A/i) \geq 1$, the right-hand side is necessarily negative.

As I have explained above, the established lower tier in the internal labour market exists more frequently and extends to a larger proportion of the employees in large firms than in small firms. Hence, as long as the qualification including the restriction of competition by means of an entry fee is satisfied, the wage difference between large firms and small firms is a genuine wage disparity.

Moreover, the difference in firm size itself has additional consequences. First, let us look at labour management. It is not so difficult to imagine that the difference in firm size gives rise to different forms of labour management. In large firms, responding to the extensive division of labour, a hierarchical bureaucracy is set up and this serves as the fundamental mechanism of labour management. In such an organization, external work incentives play an important role. It is likely that the incentive wage system described in the previous subsection is employed, together with an internal promotion system and seniority wage system. On the other hand, in small firms, the distance between an employer and an employee is small and thus direct monitoring is easy. Moreover, the feeling of a family may be generated to internalize the work incentive there. In this way, large firms become more like type A and small firms become more like type B.

Some, however, question the validity of the concept of firm-specific skills. Doeringer and Piore describe 'the idiosyncrasies of the particular pieces of equipment and the smell of equipment' as their example of this concept but it is not really convincing. Since the human being is not a primitive animal that has only reflexes, even concrete and repetitive skills can enhance adaptability to different jobs and different environments and thus entail the element of general learning. Hence, it is difficult to find purely firm-specific skills. It is a matter of degree.

Koike, in a series of works (Koike 1977, 1981*a*, *b*) has taken another line of criticism. In Japanese firms, workers obtain a wide range of knowledge through job rotation and thus, even though each operation is narrow and specialized, they gradually acquire the skill to overview the entire production process, which has high general applicability. Yet, the author judges that the concept of the firm-specific skill can fully withstand these criticisms. One reason is that, though a wide range of skills enhances workers' adaptability to changes of situations and contributes to increasing workers' internal desire to work, a higher degree of coherent integration of the knowledge is difficult since the knowledge is based on concrete experiences that were originally unrelated to one another. Another reason is that the learning process of each worker's information (see section 3.4) itself has an element specific to a firm since workers have varied abilities and since it is not known beforehand what ability each worker has.[8] Of course, a part of the accumulated knowledge (the strong

---

[8] The following description of informational learning is inspired by the interesting analysis of Ohashi (1978). However, Ohashi's intention (p. 98) to formulate a model of the mechanism that

and weak points of each worker) can be transferred to other firms and, in that sense, it becomes general knowledge. However, we can give two kinds of defence to this argument: (i) the more particular and concrete the job that is used to learn about the worker, the less useful the information is, and (ii) firms tend to conceal information about personnel as much as possible and specialized knowledge is deliberately pursued. In this interpretation, the formation of broad-based skills through job rotation can be regarded as an effect of broad-based informational learning. In other words, Japanese firms (compared to European or American firms) accumulate more knowledge specific to the firm.

By the way, Koike pointed out another interesting fact (Koike 1981a: ss. 1, 2): in Japanese small firms, (a) there is internal human training based on job rotation, (ii) the degree to which this is implemented, however, varies greatly among firms, and (iii) the domain in which rotation is practised, as well as the range of workers who participate in it, is narrower even when the job rotation is implemented. In this way, the formation of knowledge specific to a firm as the result of informational learning varies, depending on the size of firms. This provides the source of the wage disparity between large firms and small firms.

In the last subsection, I stated that, even when training entails firm-specific skills, the conditions for the long-term persistence of the wage disparity are undermined if the learning opportunities are freely transplantable among firms. Even though know-how is necessary to implement informational learning about workers' skills, there is not much difficulty in teaching this know-how to other firms. However, broad job rotation entails high opportunity costs and thus some firms may not be able to finance it. Moreover, for the same reason as applies in the case of human investment, there is a large constraint on borrowing for human investment. Hence, it is possible that the lack of financial ability causes the restriction of the investment. This corresponds to the situation where the optimal investment rate λ^* is not attained due to the borrowing constraint in Figure 3.10. Comparing the financial background of large firms with that of small firms, it becomes obvious that there is a difference between them both as regards the accumulation of workers' firm-specific skills and knowledge and concerning the amount of informational learning about workers' characteristics. Given these differences, if the mechanism for the entry

brings about firm-specificity by a means different from firm-specific training is not necessarily successful. That is, Ohashi assumes that the income of each worker does not directly depend on the expected productivity of each worker that is revealed gradually through doing a job, and that it is determined by the average productivity of all the workers who do the same job, However, a system that has this kind of informational slackness can be sustained only when the information obtained about the workers becomes knowledge specific to the firm. If other firms can obtain the information easily, the wage is determined at the level equal to the expected productivity. This point is explained in Harris and Holmstrom (1982) (see section 3.4). However, as the discussion that follows in the main text shows, Ohashi's implicit assumption is not entirely unrealistic.

Table 6.1. *The Effect of External Experience and Internal Experience on Wage Rate or Turnover Rate*

	(1) Wage rate (1979)		(1) Turnover rate (1982)	
	Ages 15–30 (%)	Ages 31–55 (%)	Ages 15–30 (%)	Ages 31–55 (%)
External experience	+2.1	+0.5	+0.3	0.0
Internal experience	+5.5	+4.3	−3.2	−0.3

Accompanying table

Sample average	Ages 15–30	Ages 31–55
Wage rate (natural logarithm)	8.70	9.19
Turnover rate 1981–2 (%)	8.6	3.5
Schooling (years)	12.5	11.7
Outside experience (years)	2.2	9.7
Internal experience tenure (years)	4.7	14.4

Notes: Each value in the table evaluates by how much an additional year of external experience or internal experience increases the wage rate or turnover rate respectively. For the second-order terms of explanatory variables, the evaluation is taken as the average of those variables. External experience is defined as:

External experience (years) = Age − Schooling − Tenure − 6.

The sample average of the variables is given in the accompanying table. The wage rate is given by the natural logarithm of the hourly wage (with 0.1 yen as the unit) that is derived by dividing the total yearly main earnings by the yearly working hours at the time of the survey (October).

In all cases, the data include only male employees and exclude both temporary and daily workers.

Source: Estimations are based on Mincer and Higuchi (1988: Sample attributes in Table A.1; Estimated values in Column (C) of Table A.2 and Column (B) of Table A.3). The estimation of the wage rate is based on samples from the panel data of the *1979 Employment Status Survey Results for Japan* and that of the turnover rate is based on the results of the same survey in 1982.

fee is incomplete, then wage disparity emerges in the long run between large firms and small firms.[9]

The statistical data that are consistent with the importance of firm-specific skills have been shown repeatedly in studies of the Japanese earnings function (Shimada (1974) initiated this line of research). Column (1) of Table 6.1, based on the estimation of the earnings function by Mincer and Higuchi (1988), compares the effect on wage rates of an additional year of working within the

---

[9] Shinohara (1970) emphasizes that the incompleteness of the capital market depends on firm size. This factor is highly applicable to the issue of financing firm-specific skills. Also, the oligopolistic structure of the product markets, which Ito (1962) emphasizes, is certainly an additional factor.

company with that of a year's work outside the company. The effect of internal experience is far greater than that of external experience and moreover the effect of internal experience does not diminish even at higher ages.[10] In addition, as column (2) in the same table shows, the accumulation of internal experience increases the probability of further continuation of tenure.

Figure 6.3 is based on the same data source as Table 6.1 (covering male employees, either production or clerical/supervisory workers, in manufacturing, and taking an average over all educational levels) and depicts the distribution of tenure for each 10-year age group age step for each firm size (10 to 99, 100 to 999, and over 1,000 employees). Overall, except that clerical/supervisory workers have a higher tendency to have long tenure than production workers, the patterns for both production workers and clerical/supervisory workers are similar. Between large firms (over 1,000 employees) and small firms (10 to 99 employees), there is not much difference in the age group of those aged 60 and over, but there is a large difference in the age group between 30 to 59. The medium-sized firm (100 to 999 employees) is located in the middle in terms of its pattern. The differences between large firms and small firms are symbolized by the following findings. (i) In the age group 30–39, in small firms the turnover rate of clerical/supervisory workers is 30 per cent and that of production workers is 36 per cent. On the other hand, the turnover rate in large firms is about 4 per cent. (ii) In small firms, 20 to 26 per cent of workers between the ages of 40 and 59 have tenure of 0 to 4 years and the distribution of tenure is flat. On the other hand, in large firms, the

---

[10] Hashimoto and Raisian (1985: 730, Table 5) estimate the earnings function that has similar properties, based on the cross-tabulation of male workers in the 1980 Wage Census. The estimate includes three different firm sizes: large, medium, and small. The strong effect of tenure characteristically appears in large firms. Moreover, they make a comparison with the US earnings function.

On the other hand, by using a vast array of panel data of male (non-managerial) workers who are members of a specific job class from the same 1980 Wage Census, Ono (1989: s. 2) shows that age has greater effect than tenure and claims that the hypothesis based on the idea that the wage level is set to guarantee minimum subsistence is more valid than the hypothesis based on firm-specific skills. The minimal effect of tenure is contrasted with almost all of the previous estimations including the result in Table 6.1. This author does not deny that there is some element of subsistence pay in the wage system of the internal labour market, which contributes to the stable labour–management relationship and makes the adaptation to new technology easier. However, the finding that the effect of tenure is small seems to be influenced by biases such as that from domain restriction (the truncation bias). First, the majority of the 'job classes' in the survey were originally single-skill jobs that represented each manufacturing industry in the mid-level industry classification and then the jobs in other industries that require specific qualifications were gradually added. Thus, only 30 per cent (in 1989) of male workers belonged to a classified job class (this interpretation is based on information from the creator of the statistical method at the Ministry of Labour). Ono chose only entries for which the heading 'job class' was completed and, in that sense, does not have a representative sample. Especially, since it only includes jobs for which there is a clear job qualification, a bias toward the lower evaluation of tenure is likely. Second, since the job hierarchy above foremen and sub-managers is excluded from the samples, the dependent variables do not have those above a certain level since promotion is strongly linked to tenure. Hence, it is no wonder that truncation bias, which underestimates the coefficient of tenure, occurs.

(a) Production workers, male, manufacturing

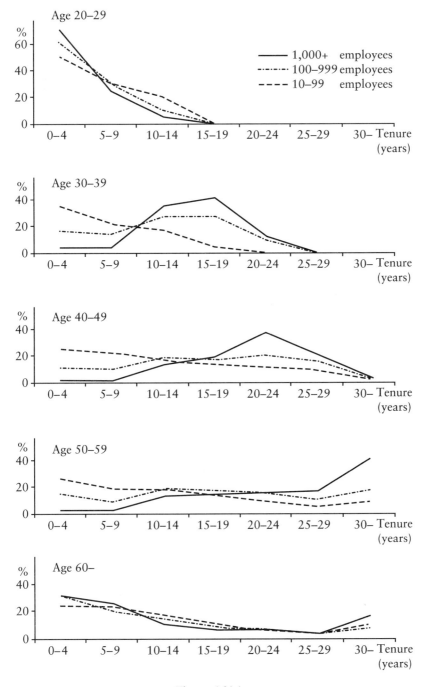

Figure 6.3(a)

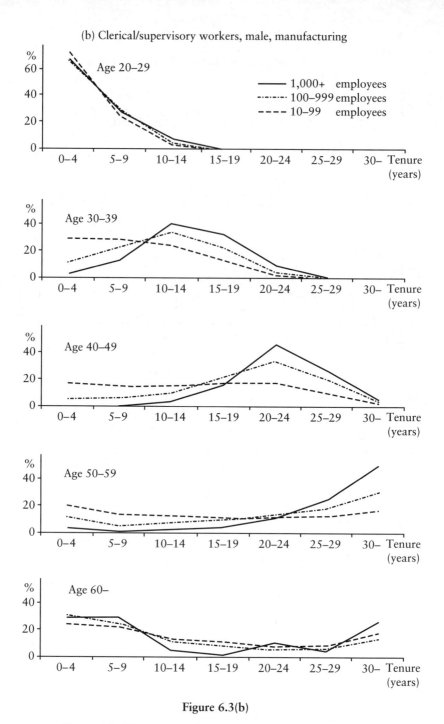

Figure 6.3(b)

Figure 6.3. *Tenure Distribution among Large, Medium, and Small Firms by Age Group*

Source: Ministry of Labour (1985: vol. I, Table 2).

distribution has a large peak at a point of long tenure.[11] These facts clearly reflect (a) the low degree of joint investment in skills by workers and employers in small firms and (b) their high degree of dependence on the external labour market as a buffer.

Qualifications to the Ability Difference Hypothesis

As stated at the beginning of this subsection, the majority view among Japanese labour economists is that most of the wage difference among firms of different size reflects the differences in quality and ability of workers in large firms and small firms. Large firms not only employ workers with high general ability through selection at hiring but also increase their productivity through extensive job training. In fact, many of the empirical research studies of the wage disparity among firms of different size, based on the cross-tabulations of the Wage Census, have estimated the disparity attributed to the effect of firm size by controlling the factors that influence the ability of workers such as schooling, age, and tenure together with gender and job, and have concluded that the disparity thus estimated (called the 'pure disparity') is much smaller than the effect of experience (or ability), represented by factors such as age and tenure.[12]

If we were to accept the results of these estimations and their interpretation, we would attribute the remaining pure disparity among firms of different size to the differences in workers' ability due to either inborn characteristics or the quality of their education and we would explain all of the average wage difference among firm of different size in terms of the differences in workers' ability. Is this really so?

I have two kinds of reservation about this argument. First, the claim that the pure size factor estimated above is explained away by the unobserved inborn

---

[11] This characteristic has been consistently observed since Ujihara (1954: 418) originally pointed it out. In Hashimoto and Raisian (1985: 726, Table 3), the distributions of tenure for male employees among firms of different size in Japan are compared with those in the USA for the year 1979.

[12] Strong support for the ability difference hypothesis can be found in Koike (1981*b*: 195–9) and Odaka (1984: 38–9, 273). For the empirical studies that form the basis of these claims, see Blumenthal (1968), Stoikov (1973), Ono (1973: s. 8), Tachibanaki (1975), (1982), and Koike (1981*a*: s. 6.1). Odaka (1984: 31–9) provides an excellent survey of the first four of these, comparing and interpreting their results. He points out that the pure disparity among firms of different size that is estimated after standardizing the attributes and using variance analysis moves in parallel with the original (gross) average wage disparity among firms of different size.

As a typical example of variance analysis, Tachibanaki (1975: 576, Table 9), (1982: 451, Table 1) has shown that, after decomposing the earned incomes including bonus (based on the data in the Wage Census) into six factors such as gender, job, age, schooling, tenure (experience) and firm size, the extent to which firm size explains the variation in earned incomes, given as a ratio, was between 10 and 20 per cent in late 1950s, but it declined after that and was smallest, at 5.1 per cent, in 1966. Then, it reversed course and increased to 15 per cent in the late 1970s (refer to Tachibanaki (1975: 576, fn. 7) for the method of computation).

abilities of workers or differences in the quality of education is hardly supportable given the fact that the explanatory power of IQ tests is extremely low,
as we observed (except for the upper tier of specialized or managerial jobs) in
section 4.3.

Second and more importantly, the above method, which defines the disparity
among firms of different size by the residuals after taking out the effects of
experience (age and tenure), clearly underestimates the disparity. As Figure 6.3
shows, large firms have a distribution of tenure (within the same age group)
that is skewed more upward than that of small firms and this face reflects the
intense and continual learning and accumulation of ability that occurs after
hiring at large firms. Hence, we need to include the factor that causes the
differences in tenure distributions in the disparity among firms of different
size.[13] Of course, it is obvious that the intensity and length of learning does not
cause the genuine wage disparity by itself. (i) The variation in learning intensity
among firms may simply bring about the phenomenon of equalizing difference
and (ii) it is generally rational to give more intense training when large firms
succeed in selecting workers who have high trainability as an inborn characteristic. However, except during a very short period in the high-growth era,
there has never been a reverse disparity among firms of different size (after
controlling for gender, job, and schooling) with respect to the average wage of
young workers (including their initial wage). This fact implies that there are
reasons other than the two given above; there has to be a genuine wage disparity through the rationing of learning opportunities.

From the above discussion, I can conclude that the genuine wage disparity
that exists between large and small firms includes most aspects of what previous researchers have estimated as the pure wage disparity and some part of
what they have estimated as the effect of different tenure. It is for future
research to provide a more precise quantitative expression to these findings.

Concluding Remarks

In Japan, the wages and the working conditions in large firms and small firms
are still quite different. This subsection has focused on the aspect of wage
differentials and analysed why wage disparities persist in the long term among
firms of different size. This subsection has critically examined the prevailing
interpretation in empirical studies, that the wage disparity among firms of
different size reflects differences in workers' average quality at hiring; in
addition, this subsection has provided an alternative explanation based on the
dual labour market hypothesis. I have argued (i) that the genuine wage disparity should be defined as the consequence of involuntary rationing in the

---

[13] This is correctly pointed out by Stoikov (1973: 1103). Mincer and Higuchi (1988: 103,
footnote 15) also state the same implication. However, none of these authors considers that
rationing of learning opportunities by firms occurs.

market for the supply of labour by homogeneous workers; (ii) that differences in the nature of learning in the labour process, together with the corresponding system of labour management, which is the fundamental concept in the dual labour market hypothesis to classify and understand the market structure, cause the genuine wage disparity; and (iii) that these factors in fact are significant in explaining the wage disparity between large and small firms. The discussion can be summarized as follows.

The core concept of the dual labour market hypothesis is that internal labour (lower tier) and external labour are contrasted and that the source of the wage disparity is rationing to internal labour (lower tier). Since both large firms and small firms have both types of workers, size itself is not the cause of the disparity. However, (a) large firms have a larger proportion of internal labour than small firms, and (b) among internal workers, the learning intensity of firm-specific skills (including informational learning about the characteristics of workers) is higher at large firms. Thus, on average, the wage disparity emerges among firms of different size. Factor (a) is a strong reflection of the fact that the subcontractors that make up a large proportion of small firms play the role of external labour to large firms. It is too great a risk for the subcontracting firms to have an internal labour force as large as that in large firms. As for factor (b), even if it is optimal for small firms to provide as many learning opportunities (including job rotation) to the hired workers as are provided in large firms, there is a high possibility that the borrowing constraint will limit their ability to do so.

In terms of labour management, the external incentive to work is important for the (lower-tier) workers in the internal labour market. Due to factor (a) above, large firms have a higher proportion of those who are paid an incentive payment. On the other hand, in small firms, the need for an incentive payment is reduced since the small size of such firms makes direct monitoring by the employer and the internalization of workers' motivation relatively easy. This also explains the emergence of the wage disparity.

6.2. EMPIRICAL ANALYSIS OF THE ENTRY FEE/BOND MECHANISM

The dual labour market hypothesis views the labour market as having a dual structure comprising internal labour markets formed within individual firms, on the one hand, and an external labour market, on the other. Internal labour markets are characterized by institutional wage setting, which often causes rigidity in the wage rate and leads to quantitative rationing of employment. If we take note of the fact that internal markets are more often and extensively developed among big firms than among small firms, such rationing implies the existence of genuine wage differentials due to firm size—the so-called dualistic wage structure between large and small firms. (For a review of this concept, see section 6.1.)

While once inside the firm wages may be inflexible, wage competition may still operate at the port of entry into the firm. In section 5.4, we discussed the role of the entry fee as a medium to clear imbalances at the port of entry, and saw that, where there is free competition in the amount of the entry fee, the entire labour market realizes exactly the same resource allocation and income distribution in the long run as in cases where the overall wage levels can move freely. (see Table 5.2.) A similar proposition can also be made for the theory of rationing based upon productivity incentives. As we confirm in section 5.5, if workers have to lodge a bond at the time of entry, to be confiscated by the employer if he is dissatisfied with the workers' performance, then involuntary employment rationing due to the problem of productivity incentives actually disappears. If the level of the bond that is lodged can be adjusted competitively, then even if the main body of the wage is not flexible, the bond can satisfactorily play the role of a substitute. In sum, the entry fee/bond mechanism constitutes a back door through which imperfection in the labour market can be jettisoned. Whether or not the entry fee/bond mechanism works in reality is rightly an empirical matter. In testing this point, we must address the following issues.

As we have already discussed in sections 5.4 and 5.5, there is a possible asymmetry in the workings of the entry fee/bond mechanism depending on whether excess demand or excess supply rules the market. First, even in the world of the efficiency wage hypothesis, a market under excess demand makes a competitive wage increase, and rationing does not appear. Therefore, the bonding cannot become negative. Second, when firms have so large a demand for new workers to be met, they would be prepared to pay a premium (that is, negative entry fees) to the new workers even if this should require additional compensation to existing workers.[14] Under conditions of excess supply in the labour market, however, some factors causing market imperfection may restrict the payment of a positive entry fee/bond and rationing of employment opportunities occurs as a result. Consequently, asymmetry is here defined such that the negative fees are paid, but positive fees or bonds are not paid. This feature is quite analogous to the Keynesian upward flexibility and downward rigidity of nominal wages.

---

[14] The *Asahi* newspaper report (morning edition, 6 August 1989) of the result of a survey conducted by the Institute of Labour Policy (*Romu Gyosei Kenkyusho*) suggests that such a policy is actually realized. The report states:

> This year's initial salary of college graduates in large and medium sized firms, as surveyed by the Institute of Labor Policy, is 164,500 yen; 7,500 yen or 4.7% up from the last year. It far exceeds the increase in the base wage of the existing job holders. Asked how to fill this gap, 44% (103 companies) of the companies who responded (totaling 236) answered that they have 'adjusted' the latter's salary in the spring. . . . Those who receive such a 'special increase' are limited to young employees. The most frequent are workers who enter the second or the third year of employment, and the maximum age limit rests somewhere around 30. The oldest worker was a college graduate, aged 38, and with 16 years of continuous service.

Next, even if new workers pay a positive entry fee or bond, it is more realistic to suppose that the entry fee/bond is paid in continuous instalments rather than as an outright lump sum. For workers just beginning their careers, the borrowing constraint must be severe. On the other hand, it is difficult to suppose that the instalment payments would go on for ever, since workers are free to leave, and the employers in a buyer's market have a superior bargaining position to that of workers. The entry fee/bond thus reveals itself in the form of lower initial net earnings of workers.

Figure 6.4(a) shows an example of the net wage profile where the instalment payment of the fee or bond is a fixed amount. As a result of the payment being concentrated in several periods at the beginning, the net wage profile is step-wise. Of course, the payment need not be actually fixed in every period. If the amount of instalments decreases gradually over time, the net wage profile will be smoothly upward sloping. It does not matter whether the wage profile is step-wise or increases smoothly. Our supposition is that the slope of the wage profile is able to move proportionately, reflecting changes in the total amount of fees or bonds. When excess supply in the labour market makes it more difficult to find a job, new workers are prepared to pay a larger amount of positive fees or bonds in the initial period. As a result, their wage profile will become steeper than the profile of workers who enter through the less restrictive port of entry and pay a smaller amount of fees or bonds. On the other hand, Figure 6.4(b) shows the case of negative entrance fees paid in a fixed amount at each initial period. The new workers in a seller's market have a superior bargaining position to that of employers and require the payment by employers to be made in a short period of time. As the labour shortage of new workers is more severe for firms, employers are ready to pay a larger amount of negative fees. Thus, the slope of the wage profile will become flatter for the workers who have entered, because of the more excessive demand of the labour market.

The slope of such a wage profile can be defined by comparing the net wage at the date of entry (t_0) and the net wage paid at the date ($t_0 + h$), h years after

(a) The case of a positive fee or bond   (b) The case of a negative entry fee

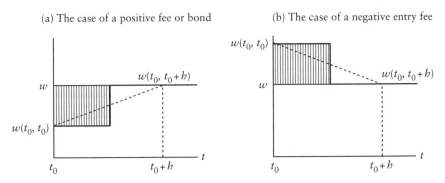

Figure 6.4. *The Effect of the Entry Fee/Bond in Seniority Wage Payments*

entry. Its definition is commonly available for both the positive entrance fee/ bond and the negative entrance fee. The profile defined above is plotted in both parts of Figure 6.4. In the case of the negative entry fee, the wage profile is shown as being negative sloped. However, as is shown later, another pressure raising wages over time would work at the same time, so the observed age–earnings profile need not be downward sloping.

If the account story is true and the entry fee/bond mechanism does operate in the form of seniority wages, then the slope of cohort wage profiles must move in an opposite direction to the cyclical condition of the date of entry. This subsection investigates whether or not such an entry fee/bond mechanism has actually operated in the Japanese labour market. It is based upon time series data on the slope of cohort wage profiles prepared separately for several industries and school attainments based on the Wage Census.[15]

The Relationship between the Age–Earnings Profile and the Net Seniority Wage Slope

If the existence of an entry fee/bond were to generate an increase in wages with seniority, then its effect should be felt by changes over time in the wage level, that is, the slope of the age–wage profile, of worker cohorts sharing the same entry date. However, changes in the nominal wage level reflect other factors as well: (a) overall productivity changes through technical progress, (b) overall wage changes (for all workers) that reflect changes in consumer prices, business fluctuations, and changes in workers' bargaining power, and (c) human capital formation through on-the-job training (OJT) and revelation of worker ability through on-the-job learning (OJL).

The effects of factors (a) and (b) can be eliminated by discounting the original cohort wage slope by changes in the average nominal wage of all workers in the group (with common industry, firm size, school attainment, and job type) to which the cohort belongs. This discounting, however, does require care in adjusting for compositional changes, that is, changes in the average age and/or duration of service, in the workforce between the two comparison dates. If another kind of wage redistribution among workers occurs, depending on cyclical conditions, more careful adjustment will be further required in addition to discounting by the average wage changes of the group.[16]

Evaluation of factor (c) is difficult. We shall suppose that the quality, intensity, and time patterns of OJT and OJL are stable over time, and that the only change that is allowed to take place appears in the form of a long-run trend. This is because the system of OJT and OJL established in each firm is

---

[15] Yuji Genda Collaborated in the empirical analysis in this section. The detailed results of our analysis are reported in Ishikawa and Genda (1989).

[16] This is the point of divergence from the previous studies of the change in the slope of the age–income profile using cross-sectional data at the same date. At the end of this section, we consider these by comparing the 'intra-organization redistribution effect' and the 'sunk cost effect'.

considered to be fairly stable. Although the number of trainees may vary over business cycles, the content of training for each trainee should not vary greatly. (This supposition is re-examined later.)

The slope of the wage profile after adjustment is made for (a), (b), and (c) (trend components only) is called the *net seniority wage slope*, and this becomes the main focus of our study.

The Wage Slope Equation

Let us formulate the model algebraically. For a worker cohort in one industry and with the same level of schooling who entered the firm at the same date t_0, the average nominal wage at date of entry is denoted by $w(t_0, t_0)$, and the average nominal wage at the date of h years after entry by $w(t_0, t_0 + h)$. The average nominal wage of all the workers in the same industry/schooling group at time t_0 is defined as $\underline{w}(t_0)$ and at time $t_0 + h$ as $\underline{w}(t_0 + h)$. (In the following, the data are distinguished by industry and schooling level, but the notation for these variables is ruled out for simplicity.) The seniority wage slope after adjustment of (a) and (b) but prior to adjustment for changes in the composition of age/duration of service between the two dates $(t_0, t_0 + h)$, denoted by $S(t_0, t_0 + h)$, is defined by:

$$S(t_0, t_0 + h) = \frac{w(t_0, t_0 + h)}{w(t_0, t_0)} \bigg/ \frac{\underline{w}(t_0 + h)}{\underline{w}(t_0)}. \tag{6.1}$$

The expression $\underline{w}(t_0 + h)/\underline{w}(t_0)$ in the denominator is the discount factor for (a) and (b). Note that S is now a real quantity. We have direct observations for each term in (6.1).

We next define an imaginary variable $\underline{w}^*(t_0 + h)$ to be the average nominal wage for an industry/schooling group at date $t_0 + h$ such that the age/duration of service composition of the workforce is matched to that of date t_0. Then the 'true' seniority wage slope after adjustment for (a) and (b), denoted by $\underline{w}^*(t_0 + h)$ becomes:

$$N(t_0, t_0 + h) = \frac{w(t_0, t_0 + h)}{w(t_0, t_0)} \bigg/ \frac{\underline{w}^*(t_0 + h)}{\underline{w}(t_0)}. \tag{6.2}$$

By comparing (6.1) and (6.2), we obtain:

$$N(t_0, t_0 + h) = S(t_0, t_0 + h) \cdot \frac{\underline{w}(t_0 + h)}{\underline{w}^*(t_0 + h)}. \tag{6.3}$$

Since $\underline{w}^*(t_0 + h)$ is not directly observable, we shall estimate it by specifying a familiar long-linear earnings function. If we represent the compositional variable by the average duration of service (in number of years) of the workers in a group to be denoted by D, then we can express the earnings function as:

$$\ln \underline{w}(t_0 + h) = b_0(t_0 + h) + b_1 \cdot D(t_0 + h), \tag{6.4}$$

where $b_0(t_0 + h)$ is a linear combination of explanatory variables other than $D(t_0 + h)$. We can then estimate $\underline{w}^*(t_0 + h)$ by:

$$\ln \underline{w}^*(t_0 + h) = b_0(t_0 + h) + b_1 \cdot D(t_0). \tag{6.5}$$

By taking the difference of (6.4) and (6.5), we obtain the relationship:

$$\ln \frac{\underline{w}(t_0 + h)}{\underline{w}^*(t_0 + h)} = b_1(D(t_0 + h) - D(t_0)). \tag{6.6}$$

Since $D(t_0 + h)$ and $D(t_0)$ are directly observable, the only remaining task required to estimate $\underline{w}^*(t_0 + h)$ is to estimate the unknown parameter b_1. It can be indirectly estimated in the equation and then finally estimated, as will be explained later.

To examine the influence of (c), let us decompose $N(t_0, t_0 + h)$ into the product of two elements. The first part, $\alpha(t_0, t_0 + h)$ expresses the increase in individual worker productivity due to OJT and OJL. The second part $\beta(t_0, t_0 + h)$ expresses the pure seniority wage components, which, in turn, are due to the entry fee/bond effect. We thus have:

$$N(t_0, t_0 + h) = \alpha(t_0, t_0 + h) \cdot \beta(t_0, t_0 + h). \tag{6.7}$$

$\beta(t_0, t_0 + h)$ must be the pure slope of the seniority wage that is defined in Figure 6.4. We have already noted that $\alpha(t_0, t_0 + h)$ is not directly observable. Instead we suppose that it varies gradually over time. More concretely, we suppose an exponential trend:

$$\alpha(t_0, t_0 + h) = a_0 \cdot \exp\{a_1 \cdot t_0\}, \tag{6.8}$$

where a_0 and a_1 are constants which depend on industry, education, and the duration of service h.

By taking the natural logarithm of both sides of (6.7) and (6.8), we obtain:

$$\ln \beta(t_0, t_0 + h) = \ln N(t_0, t_0 + h) - \ln a_0 - a_1 \cdot t_0. \tag{6.9}$$

Our testing hypothesis is that the pure seniority wage component $\beta(t_0, t_0 + h)$ is negatively related to $X(t_0 - 1)$, the index of business activity (or the tightness of the labour market at the point of entry) at the date $(t_0 - 1)$ at which the contract is signed. We thus investigate if the parameter c_1 in the regression equation

$$\ln \beta(t_0, t_0 + h) = c_0 + c_1 X(t_0 - 1) \tag{6.10}$$

takes a negative value.

Because $\beta(t_0, t_0 + h)$ is not directly observable, we shall substitute (6.6) and (6.9) for the logarithmic expression of (6.3), and then derive:

$$\ln S(t_0, t_0 + h) = (c_0 + \ln a_0) + a_1 t_0 - b_1 \{D(t_0 + h) - D(t_0)\} + c_1 X(t_0 - 1) + u(t_0). \tag{6.11}$$

We have here added an error term $u(t_0)$ which is supposed to be uncorrelated with all the variables in the right-hand side of (6.11). The error term $u(t_0)$ is assumed to take 0 as its mean and a constant variance. Theoretically b_1 must be non-negative and is expected to be around the order of the normal nominal return of investment. Using the above modification, our present apparatus does not require the earnings function (6.4) to be estimated separately. a_1 can take either a positive or a negative sign. It is actually possible that the estimated result of a_1 may involve all the other trend factors apart from the change in human capital formation through OJT and OJL.

The Object of Study and the Data

The industries we have chosen for study are manufacturing, finance and insurance, wholesale and retail, and transportation and communication, using the Wage Census (Ministry of Labour, the formal title being *The Basic Wage Structure Survey*). In manufacturing, we further differentiate between production and non-production. The levels of schooling we distinguish are high school and college graduates. We have further restricted the analysis to male regular employees in firms with 1,000 and more employees. Such a group of firms is believed to have developed internal labour markets most extensively. The dependent variable $\ln S(t_0, t_0 + h)$ is calculated on the basis of comparison of monthly scheduled wages at the date of entry (t_0) and five years after entry $(t_0 + 5)$, and at the date of entry and 10 years after entry $(t_0 + 10)$. This is based on the assumption that it is sufficient to focus on the seniority wage effect of entry fees/bonds in such a short period as five or 10 years: since the agents on the short side of the market (that is, those that can demand payment) normally have relatively strong bargaining power, contracts will be made so that the payment is complete within a fairly short period of time. We have constructed quasi-cohorts, based on cross-matrix data for the years 1964–87. Therefore, for the five-year slope we can take t_0 as ranging from 1964 to 1982, with 19 observations altogether, and for the 10-year slope we can take it as ranging from 1964 to 1977, with 14 observations.[17]

[17] The Wage Census gives us the average monthly base wage figures (i.e., excluding overtime pay and bonuses) and the estimated number of regularly employed workers (see Appendix 1 to the Wage Census for a detailed definition) for each grouping—by industry, firm size, sex, level of schooling, age (18–19, and thereafter 20–24, 25–29, and so on), and duration of service (0, 1, 2, 3–4 years, and thereafter 5–9, 10–14, and so on). Although we would like to construct a cohort rigorously, the available data are limited in such a way that: (i) the duration of service variable is

Next, we explain another important variable, the business activity indicator. Although we would like to have direct indicators of the tightness of the entry labour market, we have not been able to secure them; the 'job opening/job applicant ratio for new entrants to the labour force' on an industry-wide basis customarily used for this purpose is not available for the entire span of our study (the index is prepared by the Bureau of Occupational Stability, Ministry of Labour). Therefore we have used two kinds of industry-wide macro indicators as proxy variables.

The first variable is the real growth rate of the industry-wide gross domestic product one year ahead of new entry, $t_0 - 1$. Hereafter we call this simply the 'GDP growth rate'. The second variable is the ratio of the industry-wide real rate of investment in plant and equipment (on an in-progress basis) over the previous year's real capital stock. Hereafter this is simply abbreviated as the 'investment

very finely classified for the early phase of employment, but after five years the bands are very broad (i.e., five-year bands); (ii) although for college graduates the age band 20–24 corresponds well with entry to the workforce, for high school graduates (whose initial entry occurs in the age band 18–19) the age bands do not match the duration of service bands very well. Consequently, as a second-best solution, we have constructed quasi-cohorts in the manner shown in the following table. For both high school and college graduates, the starting age band of the cohort (corresponding to t_0) is taken at 18–19 and 20–24, respectively.

The Composition of Cohorts by Schooling

Entry date	Age	Years since entry	Responding variable
High-school graduates			
t_0	18–19	0	$w(t_0, t_0)$
$t_0 + 5$	20–24	5–9	$w(t_0, t_0 + 5)$
$t_0 + 10$	25–29	10–14	$w(t_0, t_0 + 10)$
College graduates			
t_0	20–24	0	$w(t_0, t_0)$
$t_0 + 5$	25–29	5–9	$w(t_0, t_0 + 5)$
$t_0 + 10$	30–34	10–14	$w(t_0, t_0 + 10)$

In this table, the $w(t_0, t_0 + 5)$ cell of high school graduates essentially consists of workers aged 23–24 and with 5–6 years of service, the $w(t_0, t_0 + 10)$ cell consists of workers aged 28–29 and with 10–11 years of service. Since the new college graduates are limited to age 22 and above, the $w(t_0 + 5)$ cell essentially consists of workers aged 27 and above and with 5–7 years of service, while the $(t_0 + 10)$ cell consists of workers aged 32 and above and with 10–12 years of service. The problems with such a cohort construction are that: (i) the high school cohort includes those workers who, five or 10 years ago, were aged 19 and already had one year of service; and that (ii) the college cohort includes those workers who, five or 10 years age, were aged 24 and already had one or two years of service. Since we calculate the seniority wage slope on the basis of comparison between workers just hired (i.e., zero years of service) and workers including these additional members, we are almost certainly overestimating the slope. Our study, however, deals with time series data, and furthermore, we do not expect such a distortion in the data to lead to underestimation of the effect that we are trying to detect. On these grounds we find it adequate to use such quasi-cohort data.

rate'. The former variable is readily obtained from the *National Income Account Tables*, and the latter comes from *Private Firm Capital Stock*. Both are prepared by the Economic Planning Agency. We specifically use the current investment rate (at the entry date), for the underlying variable that determines investment today is the employers' long-term expectation the previous year, but the latter also determines the demand for new employees this year.[18]

---

[18] The variable $X(i, t_0 - 1)$ we use in this regression estimate is defined by:

$$\text{CHGDP}(t_0 - 1) = \ln\left\{1 + \frac{\text{RGDP}(t_0 - 1) - \text{RGDP}(t_0 - 2)}{\text{RGDP}(t_0 - 2)}\right\},$$

or:

$$\text{INV}(t_0) = \ln\left\{\frac{\text{RK}(t_0) - \text{RK}(t_0 - 1)}{\text{RK}(t_0 - 1)}\right\},$$

where RGDP refers to the industry-wide gross real domestic product, and RK refers to the industry-wide real private firm reproducible capital (with 1980 as the base year of the deflator). The reason for inserting one into the parenthesis of the definition of the GDP growth rate is that there are several years where the growth rate was recorded as negative.

When we take $X(t_0 - 1)$ to be $\text{CHGDP}(t_0 - 1)$, we can safely assume it to be independent of the error term. Therefore OLS becomes appropriate for estimation. On the other hand, when we take $X(t_0 - 1)$ to be $\text{INV}(t_0)$, a negative correlation arises between $X(t_0 - 1)$ and the error term.

This is seen as follows. As we have already explained, the idea behind using $\text{INV}(t_0)$ lies in the fact that the investment rate and the demand for new regular employees are jointly determined by the same long-term expectation of employers. Since the employers' expectation is not directly observed, we can use the investment rate as an observable proxy for the demand pressure to hire new workers. In fact, it has been already noted in section 5.1 that real capital stock and the skilled labour force are complementary factors of production. Let us denote the unobservable entrepreneurial long-term expectation as $Z(t_0 - 1)$, and denote the demand pressure for new employees as $X(t_0 - 1)$. Then we have a model,

$$X(t_0 - 1) = f \cdot Z(t_0 - 1) + v_X(t_0 - 1) \quad f > 0$$
$$\text{INV}(t_0) = g \cdot Z(t_0 - 1) + v_I(t_0) \quad g > 0,$$

where v_X and v_I are the error terms that are independent of $Z(t_0 - 1)$. By substituting them into (6.11) to eliminate $Z(t_0 - 1)$, (6.11) is rewritten as:

$$\ln S(t_0, t_0 + h) = (c_0 + \ln a_0) + a_1 t_0 - b_1\{D(t_0 + h) - D(t_0)\} + (c_1 f/g)\text{INV}(t_0)$$
$$+ \{u(t_0) + c_1 v_X(t_0 - 1) - (c_1 f/g)v_I(t_0)\}.$$

It is clear that the new error term in the second line is correlated negatively with $\text{INV}(t_0)$. Because of this simultaneity OLS will normally underestimate (or overestimate the absolute value of) the coefficient of INV. In order to eliminate such a bias in the estimator, we shall estimate equation (6.11) by the instrumental variables (IV) method, using the variables shown in Table 6.2 as the instruments.

The correlation coefficient between the business indicators (CHGDP(-1), INV) in the overall testing period (1964–82) is high for manufacturing (0.70) and transportation and communication (0.82), as we can predict, but it is low for finance and insurance (0.28) and wholesale and retail trade (0.25). It is known that how to estimate the productivity of these two industries is quite a serious issue, and it is more likely that INV is a more appropriate indicator.

Characteristics of the Data

The actual relationship between the seniority wage slope (S) and the business activity indicator (X) for high-school-graduate production workers and college-graduate non-production workers in manufacturing are shown in Figure 6.5. The GDP growth rate is used as the business indicator on the left side of the figure, and the investment rate is on the right. The solid line connecting the scattered points shows the movement of the five-year slope over time, whereas the dotted line shows the movement of 10-year slope over time (point 64 shows the year 1964, which is the start of the observation period). The dotted line rather than the solid line occurs in the top part, reflecting the accumulation of experience through an additional five years of service (or,

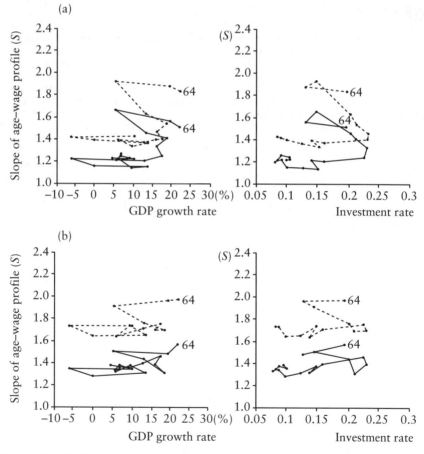

Figure 6.5. *The Seniority Wage Slope and the Index of Business Activity. (a) High-School-Graduate and (b) College-Graduate Production Workers in Manufacturing*

internal promotion based on it). Overall productivity growth during the whole period has been already discounted in calculating the S variable. We observe that the two lines are almost parallel with each other over the common time period.

Our first observation from the figure is that between 1964 and the early 1970s an anti-cyclical movement of the slope is noted for high school graduates. Such an observation is consistent with the hypothesis in question. Since the later 1970s, however, the anti-cyclical movement seems to have disappeared. On the other hand, for college graduates no anti-cyclical relationship seems discernible for any period.

We must be careful, however, not to read too much from these graphs. As the mean duration of service for high school graduates increased markedly from 1964 to the early 1970s ($D(t_0 + 5) - D(t_0)$ actually increased from the 1964–8 average of 0.22 to the 1969–73 average of 2.06), (6.11) indicates that this change in the mean duration might have the effect of lowering the level of S. Thus there is good reason to suspect that the movement of S is a spurious one which is caused by this effect, and it is independent of the entry fee/ bond mechanism. Therefore, it should not be stated before estimating equation (6.11) if there is a true relationship between the pure seniority wage slope and the business activity indicator.

We estimated equation (6.11) using the five-year wage slope $\ln S(t_0, t_0 + 5)$ as the dependent variable, and the estimated results of the coefficient c_1 are shown in Table 6.2. The results differentiate the two business indicators, GDP growth rate and the investment rate. In addition to estimating the equation for the overall period 1964–82, we also consider the possibility of structural change in the entry fee/bond mechanism, dividing the overall period into the

Table 6.2. *Estimated Coefficient of the Index of Business Activity in the Regression of the Slope of the Age–Wage Profile (Manufacturing, Log Five-Year Slope)*

Cohort	Period	GDP growth rate	Investment rate
High-school-graduate production workers	1964–82	$-0.202(-1.54)$	$-0.069(-2.07)$
	1964–73	$-0.553(-3.37^*)$	$-0.135(-2.71^*)$
	1974–82	$-0.111(-1.12)$	$-0.048(-0.96)$
College-graduate workers	1964–82	$0.048(0.27)$	$0.002(0.31)$
	1964–73	$-0.021(-0.07)$	$0.002(0.03)$
	1974–82	$-0.056(-0.63)$	$-0.024(-0.62)$

Notes: Figures are the estimated coefficient c_1 in (6.11), and values of t are in parentheses. The OLS is employed in the case of the GDP growth rate as the index of business activity, and the instrumental variable method in the case of the investment rate. In the latter case, the instrumental variables are the investment and GDP growth rates in the previous year and the average growth rate of the real wage for the group. *represents statistical significance at the 5% level.

period of rapid growth, 1964–73, and the low-growth period after the first oil shock, 1974–82. The estimated marginal return of duration of service b_1 is almost equal to 8 per cent for high school graduates and 3.5 per cent for college graduates (independent of business indicators), and they are consistent with the theoretical prediction. The coefficient a_1 represents the weak negative trend during the overall period while the trend disappears after the first oil shocks among high school graduates.

The estimated coefficient c_1 of high school graduates, shown in the table, is negative but statistically insignificant during the overall period. When we estimate it by dividing the overall period into two, however, the coefficient becomes negative and statistically significant during the period of rapid growth. On the other hand, the absolute value of the coefficient of the low-growth period declines by one-third or one-quarter compared with that of the rapid-growth period and the significant effect disappears again. Looking at the results of college graduates, we cannot find any significant direction for the overall period and the sub-sample period. Following on from the points made above, nevertheless the impression obtained from Figure 6.5 can be mostly confirmed through regression analysis.

Implications of the Estimated Results

Similar equations are also estimated for the 10-year seniority wage slope of other industry and education groups. Then, considering the possibility of partial adjustment of wage slopes and of time-series correlation of the error term, we attempt to estimate several modifications of equation (6.11). The detailed results of these examinations provide the following conclusions.

1. For production workers in manufacturing industry, for whom historically the internal labour market had most typically developed, there exists a clear negative correlation between the net slope variable and the business indicators until the early 1970s (that is, during the so-called rapid-growth era). With the advent of the slow-growth era this negative correlation almost completely disappears. Noting that the cyclical indicators are mostly rising in the rapid-growth era whereas they are largely diminishing in the slow-growth era (see Figure 6.5), we find that in the former period the entry fee/bond effect actually operated in the form of employers' payment of premium to workers, and that in the latter period the hypothesized effect played no role.

2. For cohorts other than production workers in manufacturing industry, we have discovered a rather distinctive difference in the nature of correlation between the slope variable and the cyclical indicators. With a few exceptions, broadly similar tendencies are observed for high school graduates. Thus a premium (or a negative entry fee) was paid during the rapid-growth era, while the entry fee/bond was not paid during the slow-growth era. Also the negative correlation for the earlier period is confirmed

more often when the investment rate, rather than GDP growth rate, is taken as the cyclical indicator. This suggests that the demand for new regular workers indeed responds more to long-term entrepreneurial expectations than to short-run business conditions.

3. For college graduates, there is no clear relationship between the slope variable and the business cycle. This finding holds for both the rapid-growth era and the slow-growth era. In other words, rationing seems to have operated for these workers throughout the period of our study. Some caveats, however, are in order. For a few industries (finance and insurance, transportation and communication) there was some indication of a negative correlation during the slow-growth era, which might be interpreted as evidence of the working of the entry fee/bond effect, or as evidence of competitiveness in the new entry labour market for college graduates. Yet, as the evidence is still very spotty, it is difficult at this stage to make a firm judgement on the significance of the 'reverse asymmetry' result.

4. Disregarding the ambiguity of conclusion 3, conclusions 1 and 2 together show that the Japanese labour market in the low-growth era had a propensity to generate rationing of new employment under the demand constraint regime proposed by the dual labour market economists, and this seems to have occurred; while it also played a role in the neo-classical competitive market in the rapid-growth era. This implication is quite consistent with the co-ordinated theoretical framework the author presents in section 5.6.

It is well known that income distribution among individuals was equalized during the rapid-growth period. If we seek the reason for this phenomenon, we reach the conclusion that the Japanese labour market behaved structurally like the neo-classical competitive market in the period. As is shown in sections 3.1 and 3.2, the neo-classical labour market is the world where both demand and supply factors have an effect on the allocation of labour services, and it has the following characteristics: (i) an increase in labour demand combined with capital accumulation will raise labour income relative to other resource services; and (ii) the increase in opportunities for high income through education and skill formation will promote human capital investment and equalize labour income distribution. However, this equalizing force appears no longer to have been operating from the mid-1970s until at least the early 1980s. This seems to correspond well with the fact that the tendency towards quality in the size distribution of income reversed after the mid-1970s.[19]

[19] By virtue of significant business upturns since 1987 the new entry labour market of 1988 and 1989 turned out to be a strong seller's market. It is quite intriguing to see how such a change in circumstances affects our tests of the entry fee/bond effect. In fact, the rise in the entry wage rate is reported to be significant. (Cf. footnote 14.) The as yet unknown data points we will get several years from now will tell us the validity of our proposed interpretation to the effect that the structural change that occurred in the early 1970s is not a permanent change in the labour market structure but an alternation of regimes within the same dual labour market framework.

Structural Differences between High School and College Graduates' Labour Markets

How should we interpret the difference in the conclusions for high school and college graduates? There seem to be two aspects worthy of consideration. The first is the structural difference between the high school graduates' labour market and the college graduates' labour market, and the second, the increase in the average level of schooling that resulted from an enormous rise in the college attendance rate.

A large proportion of college graduates take up professional, managerial, and technical occupations. Such occupations are construed as an upper tier within the internal market sector (Piore 1980a). Piore argued that this stratum enables the labour market to work as a competitive market. Thus, it is a world in which payment is made on the basis of informationally revealed ability (or marginal productivity), and where opportunities for general learning and actual labour services are jointly exchanged.

However, two reservations seem necessary. First, not all college graduates assume upper-tier jobs. Many of them, in fact, occupy middle-level management jobs that are more lower tier than upper tier in nature. An increase in the supply of college graduates naturally raises the proportion of those employed in such jobs. Wage formation there follows the institutional rules that are characteristic of lower-tier jobs. Also in a country like Japan where workers' careers are normally developed through internal promotion, all college graduates are assigned predominantly lower-tier jobs in the initial phase of employment, and then they are gradually selected to move on to upper-tier jobs. Therefore, it is difficult to conceive of a situation where wage competition becomes effective immediately, during the process of entry to the firm.

Second, under the lifetime employment and internal promotion system, employers, in hiring potential future upper-tier workers, have strong incentives to screen and sort out workers with high trainability. However, in the process of hiring information about a (would-be) worker's trainability is most likely to be asymmetrically distributed between the employer and potential employees. Consequently, it becomes likely that employers will offer higher prospective lifetime wages (which embody general prospects about the future course of jobs and income, uncertainties apart) than the market clearing level in order to attract highly trainable workers with a high reservation wage. Under such circumstances, the expected lifetime wage that is implicitly contracted by the employer and workers becomes flexible upwards but rigid downwards.[20] This point is strictly formalized in a one-period model by Weiss

---

[20] The employees avoid adjustment of wages and prefer to accept fluctuations in the quality of new workers (e.g., a decline in quality during a boom) is well known as Reder's hypothesis. Reder (1955) himself does not specify clearly how the choice is made between the alternative of accepting a wage change and maintaining quality, on the one hand, and maintaining wages and accepting a quality change, on the other.

(1980). Consequently, the firm's behaviour to minimize the wage cost per average productivity expected to employees is induced, which is the same as the efficiency wage hypothesis.[21]

We have just argued that the Japanese college graduates' new entry labour market may more appropriately be interpreted as a market where efficiency wages, as employers' instrument for informational sorting of workers, prevail than as an ordinary competitive market. Such an efficiency wage concept is different from the widely discussed concept of an efficiency wage as a medium for raising work motivation. As Piore notes, workers in the upper tier (or who are due to enter the upper tier) are expected to have an intrinsic work motivation and self-discipline by virtue of the general applicability of the knowledge they have obtained and the responsibility associated with the job, and further derive strong work motivation from the prospect of internal promotion. On these grounds the labour markets for college graduates and high school graduates differ structurally.[22]

Needless to say, the efficiency wage hypothesis on informational grounds must also face the possibility of being nullified by competition from entry bonds. By entry bonds we mean the sum of money lodged by a worker at entry such that if, as a result of on-the-job learning, the worker's qualifications turn out not to be sufficient, then the employer is free to expropriate the money. Our empirical results, stated above, show that such a bonding mechanism did not operate, at least not on a major scale.

Changes in the Structure of Labour Supply

We have argued that college graduates' new entry market might be structurally different from that of high school graduates. Yet the possibility remains that, leaving aside for the moment the reasons for this, the two entry markets exhibit the common phenomena of negative entry fees (or the payment of a premium by employers) in the face of cyclical upturns and rationing in the face of cyclical downturns. Why is it then that for college graduates we have not found any

---

[21] Weiss's original model is a one-period model, and furthermore, high-ability workers there are supposed to initiate self-employment when satisfactory earnings are not obtained from outside employment. It is this assumption that brings about the monotonically increasing relation between the reservation wage and the unobservable ability of workers, which provides the crucial rationale for the efficiency wage result. Our proposal here is to replace the one-period contract by a long-term contract, and to suppose that workers anticipate employers' future on-the-job learning of their ability in forming a positive relationship between their general trainability (as yet unobserved by employers) and the (lifetime) reservation wage. Except in a few occupations it is not realistic to suppose that high-ability individuals can realize their individual productivity easily by self-employment, for self-employment usually requires a large set-up cost (Weitzman 1982).

[22] We may suppose that information about worker quality at the time of entry is much more precise for college graduates than for high school graduates (e.g., through differences in the difficulty of the entrance examination). However, the existence of multiple index groups does not change the essence of the argument here. It merely implies that employers begin to hire workers from the highest index group and then progressively hire from successively lower index groups, and the fact that rationing occurs in the marginal group does not change.

evidence of premiums actually having been paid in the seller's market stage of the rapid-growth era? The answer to this question seems to lie in the changes in the structure of labour supply.

Recall that our cyclical indicators represent mainly the pressure of labour demand, and they do not necessarily represent accurately the tightness of the new entry market. In particular, during the period of enormously rising labour demand, starting in the latter half of the 1960s and continuing to the early 1970s, there is a good reason to believe that the balance of new labour supply between high school graduates and college graduates shifted greatly as a result of the increasing rate of college attendance. In fact, using the Basic Survey of Schools (published annually by the Ministry of Education), several corresponding results can be found, as follows:

(a) Changes in supply, in terms of the number of school graduates, were relatively modest after 1975. There are, however, significant fluctuations in the preceding period.
(b) From 1964 to 1973, the rate of increase in the numbers of college graduates and of job takers among them almost uniformly exceeded those of high school graduates. The only exceptions were the years 1965 and 1966, the years of the well-known baby boom generation. Such a tendency has not been found since 1974.
(c) From 1968 to 1976, the number of job takers straight out of high school tended to decrease each year, the magnitude of the decrease exceeding −9 per cent for some consecutive years. During the same period the gap between the rate of increase in the number of high school graduates and that of job takers among them widened significantly. This gap naturally corresponds to the rise in the college attendance rate.
(d) The number of job takers straight out of college continually increased until 1974, and, in particular, from 1964 to 1971 the rate of increase was so high as to lie between 5 and 15 per cent every year.

It should be clear by now that the demand pressure for new high school graduates has been reinforced by the relative and sometimes absolute decline in their supply. In contrast, the demand pressure for college graduates has been significantly offset by a marked increase in their supply during the same period. It is quite likely then that our cyclical indicators have overestimated the true extent of market tightness in the college graduates' entry labour market. We feel quite certain that the main reason for the non-payment of negative entry fees lay in the increased supply of college graduates.

The Possibility of Alternative Interpretations

The above conclusion in relation to the entry fee/bond effect may not be the only possible interpretation of the empirical results. Our interpretation is based on two important presumptions: (a) that the training intensity for new employees varies over time only in the form of a trend, and, specifically, it is not affected by the cyclical phase of the entry date, and (b) that the *ex post* cyclical fluctuations five or 10 years later should affect the wage rate of all workers in the same industry and schooling pair alike. If these presumptions are not satisfied, it is possible to interpret the results differently. We will clarify the reservations to our empirical results by re-examining these points, and explain the relationship with the previous empirical studies of the wage profile.

With regard to presumption (a): If the cyclical condition of the hiring date were to alter the distribution of trainability among entering workers (as perceived by employers), then the mean level of investment in new employees would also change. For instance, if a business upturn lowers the average trainability of workers being hired (as supposed by Reder 1955), the average training intensity is expected to become lower. Then the slope of the cohort wage profile becomes flatter for a reason that is quite different from the effect of negative entry fees. That is, the negative correlation between the wage profile and the business indicators may have occurred from this change in human capital investment for newly hired workers, which is independent of the entry fee/bond effect.

On the other hand, however, it may also be rational to increase the training intensity of those who are hired during business upturns. In order to maintain the existing productions process, it is necessary for employers to keep up the training of employees already hired, and, therefore, to increase the training intensity for less trainable workers. As a result, the cohort wage profile of these workers would become steeper, and it generates a positive correlation between the wage profile and business indicators.

It is impossible to tell in advance which of the above two effects will be more plausible. In order to ascertain this point, we must have data that directly inform us of the amount of training that workers get. And there remains the problem of how we interpret the observed asymmetric phenomena from the viewpoint of human capital investment theory. Our interpretation is appropriate if the above two effects, having different effects on the correlation, could offset each other. This is the first reservation in relation to our empirical study.

With regard to presumption (b): Existing studies of the slope of age–earnings profiles have customarily investigated the presence of a contemporaneous correlation between wage differentials due to age and cyclical conditions. The presumption of such works is that (b) does not hold. One of the representative works following this line of research is that of Ono (1973, ch. 7). He studied the manufacturing wage data of the 1950s and 1960s and found a tendency for a negative correlation between age–wage differentials and cyclical conditions, and also found that, after around 1960, the age differentials stopped increasing and started to decrease, and continued to decrease throughout the 1960s. Ono adduces the competitiveness of the entry labour market and the strengthening of young workers' voice inside the labour union as reasons for his findings:

Labour shortage made its strongest impact on the newly graduated labour force, and raised their initial salaries. If trade unions had stuck to the existing life-cycle wage profile patterns, then the decrease of wage differentials might have been either hindered or made much smaller.... The circumstance [that prevented it from actually occurring] was the strengthening of the voice of young union members as a result of the labour shortage. Consequently, unions had to allocate a larger share of the increment in total wage bills to young members. (Ono 1973: 135–6).

The fact that the young workers' wage rate (including the initial entry wage) rose relative to that of old workers can be explained equally well in terms of the negative entry fee effect. While we do not deny the possibility that the tight entry labour market induced restructuring of the balance of power within members of the labour union and changed the distribution of the pie in favour of young workers (for short, we call this the 'intra-organization redistribution effect'), there is no quantitative measurement of how independently important this hypothesis has been. Hence Ono's findings need not be construed as evidence against supposition (b).

On the other hand, there is an argument (made by Hashimoto 1975 and Raisian 1979) which calls for a positive association between the slope of the contemporaneous age–wage profile and the cyclical indicators. This is quite the opposite of Ono's argument. The basic idea is as follows. When investment in firm-specific skills proceeds continually with its costs being shared by employers and employees, the higher the worker's age (or duration of service), the higher is the cost already sunk and the higher is the value of continued employment. Hence, in a cyclical downturn, older workers are more willing to accept wage cuts than young workers, while in a cyclical upturn, older workers' bargaining position *vis-à-vis* the employer is reversed and they receive more wage gains than their younger colleagues. Hence the slope of the wage profile moves pro-cyclically. Let us call this the 'sunk cost effect'.

If the sunk cost effect actually exists, then the coefficient of the cyclical variable in our model becomes subject to an over-estimation bias. In such a case, the sign of no correlation as reported can no longer be interpreted as evidence countering the entry fee/bond effect. In this case, it is necessary to change our current interpretation.

We do not yet have strong empirical support for the sunk cost effect. Raisian (1979: 492) reports a study of Panel Study on Income Dynamics (PSID) data in which he finds a tendency in favour of the sunk cost effect for the non-union sector, but at the same time finds a tendency opposite to the sunk cost effect for the union sector. It is not clear, however, why there arises such a difference in behaviour between the union and non-union sectors. At the time of writing it is premature to interpret it as evidence of the sunk cost effect. As for Japan, we have already noted an opposite tendency to the sunk cost effect throughout the 1960s, and also for the period after the 1970s we know that wage differentials due to age or experience are very stable (Tachibanaki 1982: 449–50; 1984: 20, Table 11).

On the other hand, using the same data set, Higuchi (1989: 484–6) estimates the equation of the growth rate of annual earnings for manufacturing workers during 1970 and 1986. Higuchi finds a statistically significant negative coefficient on the cross term between duration of service within firms and job entry application rate. (This result is obtained for each different category of firm size.) This result indicates that the wage growth rate in economic upturns is higher for short-tenure workers than for long-tenure workers. This is in complete contrast with the sunk cost effect. At the same time, however, Higuchi further classifies industries, and examines the relative wages of different industries in the same age group. Then, he concludes that the rapid appreciation of the yen significantly reduces the wage of senior workers in the traded goods industries (in comparison with the non-traded goods industries) (Higuchi 1982: 494–5, Table IV). This result is in turn consistent with the sunk cost effect.[23] Therefore, we have not yet found any definitive conclusion about the empirical results of the sunk cost effect.

Decomposition into the Entry Fee/Bonding Effect and the Cross-Section Effect

These results indicate that our interpretation is not subject to any serious bias nullifying the entry fee/bonding effect. Is it possible, however, to confirm in our data themselves where such a bias exists or not? Fortunately, our cohort data contain plentiful information to decompose the wage redistribution effect within the same time. Next, we attempt to modify our model, inducing it.

We stay with presumption (b), and assume that the slope of the age–wage profile computed from cross-section data instead of cohort data depends on the business indicator at the time. We reorganize the two ratios in the right-hand side of (6.2), and we presume that:

$$\ln \frac{w(t_0, t_0)}{\underline{w}(t_0)} = \ln r(t_0) - (s_1' + s_1 X(t_0 - 1)) \tag{6.12}$$

$$\ln \frac{w(t_0, t_0 + h)}{\underline{w}^*(t_0 + h)} = \ln r(t_0 + h) - (s_2' + s_2 X(t_0 + h - 1)). \tag{6.13}$$

---

[23] The result in the first half of Higuchi (1989) is not directly comparable with our result because the former does not distinguish production and non-production workers and the observation periods are different. However, the estimated coefficients in Table 6.3 are consistent with it. The result in the second half of his paper does not necessarily appear to be a strict test of the sunk cost effect because it examines wages by age group instead of years of continuous service due to raw data constraints. Also it does not decompose the fluctuations in the exchange rate into persistent changes and transitory changes when using the exchange rate as an explanatory variable in the regression. The reason for the inconsistency between the results in the first and second halves of the paper require explanation.

If s_1 and s_2 are positive, it would mean the operation of the sunk cost effect, whereas if they are negative it would mean the intra-organization redistribution effect. We call the overall effect reflected in these coefficients the cross-section effect. We expect s_1 and s_2, and the constant terms s_1' and s_2' to be of roughly the same magnitude, respectively. On the other hand, $r(t_0)$ and $r(t_0 + h)$ are the wage-slope generating factors after the cross-section effect has been adjusted, and then, $r(t_0 + h)/r(t_0)$ substitutes for $N(t_0, t_0 + h)$ to represent the pure slope of the wage profile $\beta(t_0, t_0 + h)$. Therefore, (6.9) is now transformed into:

$$\ln \beta(t_0, t_0 + h) = \ln r(t_0 + h) - \ln r(t_0) - \ln a_0 - a_1 \cdot t_0. \qquad (6.14)$$

Of course, (6.10) does not change at all. Using (6.3), (6.6), (6.12), and (6.13), we can represent the relationship between $r(t_0 + h)/r(t_0)$ and the observed wage profile $S(t_0, t_0 + h)$ as follows:

$$\ln r(t_0 + h) - \ln r(t_0) = \ln S(t_0, t_0 + h) + (s_2' - s_1') + s_2 X(t_0 + h - 1)$$
$$- s_1 X(t_0 - 1) + b_1(D(t_0 + h) - D(t_0)). \qquad (6.15)$$

We introduce (6.15) into the right-hand side of (6.14), and (6.10) left-hand side of (6.14). Then the regression equation instead of (6.11) is:

$$\ln S(t_0, t_0 + h) = \{c_0 + \ln a_0 - (s_2' - s_1')\} + a_1 \cdot t_0$$
$$- b_1(D(t_0 + h) - D(t_0)) + (c_1 + s_1)X(t_0 - 1)$$
$$- s_2 X(t_0 + h - 1) + u(t_0). \qquad (6.16)$$

Therefore, if the above supposition is a correct one, then c_1 in (6.11) is over-estimated when s_1 and s_2 are positive, whereas it is underestimated when s_1 and s_2 are negative. Although s_1 and c_1 are not identifiable in the new equation, we are able to check the existence of a bias in the estimation of c_1 by estimating s_2 simultaneously.

We have tentatively re-estimated the equation of the five-year slope $S(t_0, t_0 + 5)$ of production workers in the manufacturing industry (for which the entry fee/bond effect was most clearly seen) by adding CHGDP(-1) and at the same time CHGDP($+4$), that is, the GDP growth rate at four years after entry, as business indicators. The estimated coefficients for each business indicator are shown in Table 6.3. The equations are estimated both for the entire period (1964–82) and for the sub-periods 1964–73 and 1974–1982. In order to compare them with the original estimated results easily, the estimated coefficients of CHGDP(-1) using (6.11) are also shown in the upper half of the left column in each period.

Table 6.3 shows that for all three periods, the coefficient of the new variable did not affect the coefficients (as well as the t-values) of the original variables. The estimated coefficient of CHGDP($+4$) was positive for 1964–73 and

Table 6.3. *A Comparison between the Entry Fee/Bond Effect and the Cross-Section Effect (Manufacturing, High-School-Graduate Production Workers, Log Five-Year Slope)*

Period	GDP growth rate (in previous year) CHGDP(−1)	GDP growth rate (after four years) CHGDP(+4)
1964–82	−0.202(−1.54)	—
	−0.175(−1.34)	0.179(1.21)
1964–73	−0.553(−3.37*)	—
	−0.526(−3.04*)	0.094(0.79)
1974–82	−0.111(−1.12)	—
	−0.130(−1.20)	−0.217(−0.69)

Notes: The figures in the left-hand column are the estimated coefficient $s_1 + c_1$ and those in the right-hand column are the estimated coefficient $-s_2$ in the regression equation (6.16). The t-values are in parentheses. The OLS is employed. It is theoretically expected that s_1 and s_2 are almost the same. *represents statistical significance at the 5% level.

negative for 1974–82. Therefore, so far as the direction is concerned, the earlier period is consistent with the intra-organization redistribution effect while the latter period is consistent with the sunk cost effect. However, neither of these two effects is statistically significant.

From the above results, we can derive two main conclusions, First, presumption (b), assuming that the cross-section effect can be ruled out, is supportable at least for this industry/education group. Second, the negative correlation between the slope of the wage profile and the business indicator, which was observed in the rapid-growth era, can be explained more appropriately by our negative entrance fee effect than by the intra-organization redistribution effect that Ono has stressed. Using the characteristics that s_1 and s_2 are approximately equivalent, we actually decompose the estimated result on CHGDP(−1) in the period 1964–73 into s_1 and c_1. Then, they are:

$$s_1 \doteq -0.094, \quad c_1 \doteq -0.432.$$

That is, of the statistically significant negative coefficients, the intra-organization distribution effect can explain 18 per cent of them. On the other hand, the entrance fee effect is dominant, explaining 82 per cent of them. This result suggests that in order to examine the slope of a wage profile, it is important to consider the possibility of a long-term contract at entry and analyse the cohort data for it.

Conclusion

Consequently, our interpretation in points (1) to (4) (see subsection, 'Implications of the Estimated Results') appears to be quite robust, while alternative interpretations are allowable. Of course, however, there are many points that must be examined in more detail: the increasing number of observations, improvements in business indicators, understanding the meaning of time-series movement for wage profiles, the examination of different-sized firms and female workers, etc. It will also be interesting to compare the movement of wage profiles between countries. More detailed and comprehensive studies will be conducted in future.

7

The Generation and Distribution of Wealth

Wealth is the source of annual income for each household and for the whole national economy. Wealth can be divided into human wealth (an asset) and physical wealth (an asset). With regard to the former, we have already considered how the work ability of each individual is accumulated and how information on each individual's ability is collected. We have also seen that human wealth cannot be simply attributed to individual ability. This is because whether individual ability is fully utilized, and whether utilization is always accompanied by new learning opportunities depends in large part on social and institutional factors such as the form of division of labour, how wages and employment are determined, and the incentive scheme that encourages voluntary work effort.

In the real world, wealth as a physical asset takes a variety of forms. It includes real assets and financial assets. Housing, durable consumer goods, gold, jewellery, and artistic objects (which we usually hold in order to obtain direct utility) can be regarded as part of wealth since they serve to store purchasing power or as potential sources of income. Money as a medium of exchange and cash as a means of storage of purchasing power also constitute part of wealth in the sense that they are potential sources of income. However, the core physical asset is evidently that which is directly or indirectly invested as a means of production and from which we expect returns to production activities. Whether it takes the form of a real asset from which we directly seek profits or the form of a financial asset from which we indirectly seek returns depends on the distribution of information associated with investment opportunities, the necessary scale of investment funds, and the financial system reflecting the form of risk bearing.

How, then, is wealth as a physical asset generated and how is its distribution across households determined? Why is it that the distribution of wealth is far more skewed than that of income? What factors determine the rate of return on physical assets? Why is it that the value of an asset, and hence the distribution of wealth, often displays huge fluctuations even over short periods?

This chapter discusses the basic determinants of the generation of wealth and its distribution across households. It consists of four sections.

Section 7.1 considers the life cycle motive as a basis of household saving behaviour, paying particular attention to the role played by the pension annuity system. We further discuss the theoretical rationales for the occurrence of the precautionary motive and the bequest motive in relation to saving, and examine their impact on the accumulation of wealth within one generation of a household and on the patterns of transmission of wealth over generations. Transmission of wealth from parents to children has traditionally been regarded as an important determinant of the distribution of wealth and social class mobility in the long term. Two classes are shown to exist: one which involves regression towards the mean in wealth holding, and another involving cumulative expansion in the dispersal of wealth. Some important empirical results are also discussed.

Section 7.2 discusses the role of education in transmitting wealth between parents and children. The basic idea is that education and material wealth naturally become substitutable assets in transmitting wealth over generations. We examine the impact of education on the dynamics of wealth holding, paying particular attention to how the paucity of parental wealth constrains the educational opportunities of children.

Section 7.3 turns to of topic of macroeconomics and looks at how the rate of return is determined in the long term. It thereby shows how the theoretical discussions in this book form a general equilibrium framework. Furthermore, we continue the discussion of section 7.1 in supposing the possible existence of two classes of households differing in levels of wealth and propensity to save, and examine whether the two classes persist or whether they are reduced to a single class in the course of economic growth. The conditions that separate the two regimes are also discussed.

Section 7.4 takes up the question of asset price fluctuations and related expectations. Asset price fluctuation is considered to be one of the major causes of generation of huge wealth in the short term. However, there is an added dimension to the problem. How is fluctuation anticipated by market participants? In the world where assets themselves are traded in the market, the value of assets comes to depend much on the market's expectation of what the future price of assets will be. If people differ in the accuracy of their expectations (called informational power) there is scope for quasi-rents to be harvested by informationally superior groups. On the other hand, there is an argument stating that quasi-rents are not possible, as people can read others' superior information from the current market price of assets. This section considers the conditions in which the latter argument holds in an environment where people have different informational power, and then argues that those conditions are rarely met in practice. The asset market seems to be a world which has considerable scope for money games.

7.1. HOUSEHOLD SAVING AND INTERGENERATIONAL TRANSMISSION OF WEALTH

This section examines how household saving is determined and thereby derives its implications for the long-term distribution of wealth. This theme has been traditionally discussed as involving the problems of the accumulation of wealth within a generation and the transmission of wealth to succeeding generations. The theoretical analyses of the problems are sufficiently well developed, and recent analyses have focused on the extent to which empirical research can validate the theoretical models. Since it is rather difficult to obtain data on household wealth, researchers conducting empirical studies devote considerable efforts to gathering the data, or by designing empirical methods which do not require direct data. In the following pages, we first survey the theoretical analyses and then discuss some important empirical results.

The organization of this section is as follows. First, we discuss the life-cycle hypothesis that is most commonly used in analysing household saving. After summarizing the characteristics of pure life-cycle saving, we consider how these characteristics are affected by the introduction of uncertainty in length of life. We compare the case where an annuity market exists with the case where it does not, thereby shedding light on the characteristics of so-called precautionary saving. Second, we consider the bequest motive [in transmission of wealth] from the parents' generation to the children's generation. In addition to the bequest as unidirectional altruism from parents to children, we consider the possibility of the bequest as a form of implicit insurance between parents and children. Third, we discuss the long-run dynamics of household wealth holding, taking into account the intergenerational transmission of physical wealth in the form of a bequest. Fourth, we examine the empirical debates on the relative importance of wealth created by life-cycle saving and wealth created by the bequest motive. We also discuss the empirical results on the long-term patterns of transmission of wealth over generations. Throughout this section, we take macroeconomic price variables such as wages and the rate of return as given.

Life-cycle Saving

The household determines the time path of its consumption, anticipating major events in the course of a lifetime. The transfer of consumption from the present to the future is (*ex ante*) life-cycle saving. Examples of major economic events occurring over a lifetime include the purchase of housing, expenditure on education, and support in old age (after retirement). Due to the recent development of consumer finance, we may also make saving by consuming first and repaying the loan later. This is *ex-post* life-cycle saving with the transfer of consumption from the future to the present. This type of saving is observed in some expenditures, such as housing purchases and education.[1]

---

[1] However, in the present national economic accounting system, the purchase of housing (which is a durable consumer good) is classified as an investment, while expenditure on education is classified as consumption. Hence, if the household borrows money and buys a house, the net asset position is unchanged since the negative financial asset and the positive real asset cancel each other. On the other hand, in the case of educational expenditure, only the negative financial asset is registered and the asset position becomes negative. However, in either case, their is no difference, in that *ex-post* saving is generated.

The first characteristic of life-cycle saving is that the wealth of each household becomes zero at the end of its lifetime. Of course, real assets such as land and housing have been converted into money and dissaved until that time. In a stationary economy where households that end their lives are gradually replaced by those who are newly born at each period, positive saving and negative saving cancel each other. Hence in such an economy, gross national saving is zero and the total amount of the national wealth is constant. Positive saving, that is, the accumulation of wealth, occurs in a national economy only if the positive saving of households who accumulate wealth exceeds the negative saving of those who dissave wealth due to population growth or productivity (income) growth.

The second characteristic is that the stock of wealth is positive even if the flow of saving in the national economy is zero. Wealth is preserved although those who hold it gradually change. To expand upon this point, we can define the wealth of the national economy as the sum of the wealth held by the households living at a point of time.

The third characteristic is that age is the most important determinant of the level of wealth held by each household. Time is the resource which is equally given to all households. Hence, as long as preferences and annual income do not differ very much, the divergence in the wealth level across households can be explained by differences in age. If there is a permanent difference in income across households, this will be an additional explanatory factor. However, the difference in wealth level cannot exceed the difference in income if the households are of the same age.[2]

There is no doubt that life-cycle saving is an important ingredient in household saving. However, we have much evidence which suggests that the life-cycle hypothesis cannot fully explain saving and wealth in the real world. First, dissaving in old age is very slow. This phenomenon is commonly observed in the USA, the UK, Canada, and Japan, and has been confirmed by the results of empirical studies which carefully control for a variety of factors (Shorrocks 1975; Mirer 1979; King and Dicks-Mireaux 1982; Menchik and David 1983; Diamond and Hausman 1984; Ishikawa 1987; and Hayashi, Ando, and Ferris 1988). Second, research on probate in the USA and the UK gives us direct evidence that huge wealth is transmitted over generations (Harbury 1962;

---

[2] This property is strictly established when the intertemporal utility function is homothetic, i.e., when Friedman's hypothesis that permanent consumption is proportional to permanent income holds true. Although the empirical evidence on this proportionality hypothesis has been mixed (see Mayer (1972) for a summary of early empirical studies), King and Dicks-Mireaux (1982: 265) obtained a result consistent with the hypothesis using data on household wealth (including the estimated value of the public pension) in Canada. However, it seems that the empirical result crucially depends on the extent to which data on the high-income and high-wealth class, which is difficult to capture precisely, can be included in the empirical analysis. In fact, Menchik and David (1983), to whose work we refer below, demonstrate that the elasticity of bequests is much larger than unity in the high-wealth class, indicating the apparent existence of non-linearity (non-proportionality) (see Table 7.1).

Harbury and McMahon 1973; Harbury and Hitchens 1976; and Menchik 1979). Third, the difference in the wealth level within a generation of the same age is almost the same as the difference in the wealth level over the whole economy. In other words, the life-cycle hypothesis can hardly explain the actual difference in the level of wealth (Atkinson 1971*b* and Brittain 1978: 66–72; see Table 1.6 for the case of Japan). Even if we take into consideration the differences in income and in rate of return on assets within a generation of the same age, this point remains unaltered (Oulton 1976).

The Precautionary Motive and the Bequest Motive

How, then, can we explain these facts? If saving is a preparation for old age, one must bear in mind the problem of the uncertainty of length of life. However, as long as the annuity market is perfect, the existence of such uncertainty will not affect the situation. In fact, the three characteristics mentioned above hold true without any modification since households can perfectly hedge against the risk of uncertain length of life by an appropriate purchase of annuity. However, the annuity market suffers from well-known imperfections, which may not be completely removed even by the introduction of a public pension system. When the annuity market suffers from imperfections such as supply constraints or a disadvantageous rate of return, households save more by using the ordinary measure of saving. This is called saving on the basis of the 'precautionary motive'. In the presence of precautionary saving, wealth is not perfectly dissaved at the end of a lifetime and, as a consequence of this, wealth is transmitted to the next generation.

The existence of precautionary saving is consistent with the observation in many countries that households dissave wealth very slowly after retirement. Also, the occurrence of a bequest, although it is accidental and involuntary, is consistent with the observation which contradicts the second and third characteristics that the life-cycle hypothesis predicts.

However, we need not consider all bequests to be accidental or involuntary. We may think of an implicit insurance contract on the basis of family ties, which virtually pools the consumption plan and wealth holding between parents and children and substitutes for an annuity. In this case, the generation that dies earlier transfers the bequest to the generation that remains alive. Thus, the bequest occurs accidentally but not involuntarily. Further, we may think of the bequest as altruism on the part of the parents.[3]

The precautionary motive and the bequest motive are important in understanding household saving behaviour. In the following, using simple models,

---

[3] When we discuss the behaviour of families, we should keep in mind the following aphorism of a sociologist: 'We know too much about the family to be able to study it both objectively and easily. Our emotions are aroused quickly by the behavior of families, and we are likely to feel that family patterns other than our own are queer or improper. We are too prone to argue about what is *right*, rather than coolly to demonstrate what *is*' (Goode 1964: 3).

we will explain the characteristics of household saving behaviours created by these motives.

Uncertainty in Length of Life and the Case of Perfect Annuity Insurance

Consider a household that lives for a maximum of two periods. The household works during the first period and retires at the end of the first period. The probability that the household will live for the second period is p $(0 < p < 1)$, the value of which is known to everybody. The household consumes part of its income (y) in the first period and invests the rest of the income in two types of assets. One is a safe bond (s) yielding a certain return; the other is an annuity (a) that pays returns only if the household lives for the second period. In general, an annuity is an asset such that its supplier continues to make the payments contracted in advance as long as the household who purchased it lives and when the household dies, the obligation to make the payments (including the repayment of the principal) expires. We denote the rate of return (the interest rate) of the safe bond by r (and denote the gross rate of return including the principal by $\rho = 1 + r$). We assume that r and y are exogenously given. (The endogenous determination of these variables is the topic of section 7.3.)

The annuity is assumed to be perfect in the sense that it is actuarially fair (which means that the annuity guarantees the same expected rate of return as the safe bond) and the household freely chooses the amount of the annuity purchase. Since the annuity supplier, who has a huge number of customers, can perfectly pool the risk through the law of large numbers, actuarial fairness means zero profit for the supplier. The payment to the household that dies at the end of the first period is zero, whereas the payment to the household that lives for the second period (ρ_a) is:

$$\rho_a = \rho/p. \tag{7.1}$$

We assume that the household maximizes the expected lifetime utility, defined as the sum of the utility derived from the first period consumption $u(c_1)$ and the expected value of the utility derived from the second period consumption, $p \cdot u(c_2)$.[4]

From these assumptions, it is evident that the household purchases only the annuity as a means of saving. This is because the bond yields returns lower than the annuity and if the household dies at the end of the first period, the bond turns out to be valueless. The amount of saving in the form of the annuity is indicated by a^* in Figure 7.1. The first period consumption is c_1^* and the second period consumption is c_2^*.

----

[4] The following is a simplified two-period version of the models developed by Yaari (1965), Barro and Friedman (1977), and Sheshinski and Weiss (1981). The results obtained in this simplified model hold true in more general models in which length of life is a continuous variable.

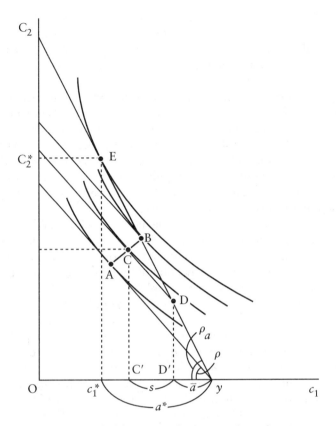

Figure 7.1. *Household Saving Behaviour with Perfect Annuity Insurance and Quantity Constraint*

Imperfection in the Annuity Market and Precautionary Household Saving

It has been traditionally pointed out that the insurance market does not work perfectly because of the existence of the problems of moral hazard and adverse selection (Arrow 1963*b*, Akerlof 1970). Rothschild and Stiglitz (1976) and Wilson (1977) considered the situation where the risks between individuals are different and information asymmetry exists in the sense that insurance suppliers do not know well the risk of each customer. They showed that in such a situation, the insurance suppliers do not elastically supply insurance given the insurance premium but supply insurance contracts which specify the price and quantity of insurance supply based on the knowledge on customers' indifference curves. They also showed that with this type of contract offer, some customers are rationed and only obtain insurance at a level lower than the optimum. The information asymmetry associated with risk does, of course, exist in the annuity market. In fact, Eichenbaum and Peled (1987) constructed a two-period economy which consists of two types of household with a high survival probability and a low survival probability and showed that an informational separating equilibrium exhibiting rationing is established as one of the market equilibrium patterns.

We may also point out other reasons why the private annuity market does not fully prevail. Annuities lack liquidity since their contracts are long term and vulnerable to future, unexpected inflation risk (as long as it does not have an escalator clause). Also, people have an inborn tendency not to want to admit the inevitability of their death. These reasons provide a rationale for the introduction of the annuity as a compulsory public pension. However, it is important to note that the introduction of a public pension may not completely remove the imperfections mentioned above.[5]

In the following discussion, we examine how household saving behaviour is changed if an annuity is imperfect, in the sense that its supply is quantity constrained although it satisfies the condition of the actuarial fairness. The point C in Figure 7.1 indicates the location of the second-best equilibrium in the case where the amount of the annuity supply is $\bar{a}$. The point C is the tangency of the budget line with the slope ρ starting from the point D and the household's indifference curve. Let us denote the intersections of the vertical lines drawn from C and D and the horizontal axis by C' and D' respectively. The length of the line $C'D'$ is the amount of saving in the form of the safe bond and the length of the line $C'y$ is the total amount of saving, that is, $s + \bar{a}$. The curve ABE kinked at the point B represents the locus of the second-best equilibrium when the quantity constraint for the annuity $\bar{a}$ as a parameter moves from zero to the optimal level a^*. The line AB is the locus of the tangency of the budget line with the slope ρ and the household's indifference curve, while the line BE is the locus along the original budget line (that is, the budget line in the absence of the quantity constraint for the annuity) In the former phase, consumption in both periods expands. This is because relaxing the constraint raises the return to the annuity in the second period and creates a pure income effect. (Here, we assume that both c_1 and c_2 are normal goods.) Therefore, the increase in the amount of the annuity supply reduces the total amount of saving. Meanwhile, in the latter phase, the household accepts the given constraint for the annuity supply and does not make an additional saving using the safe bond. B corresponds to the point where the additional saving s becomes zero. Consider the case where the constraint for the annuity supply is further relaxed. In this case, if the household can obtain a loan at an interest cost per unit of ρ, it is rational for the household to borrow, increase the annuity saving, and expand consumption in

---

[5] In practice, the public pension systems in many countries are conducted under the pay-as-you-go system instead of the reserve system assumed in the text. However, such a difference in the financing method does not affect the essence of the discussion here. In fact, Sheshinski and Weiss (1981) demonstrate that the two systems can be designed to achieve the same saving and the same income redistribution.

the first period. However, since the household's survival in the second period is uncertain, the borrowing should be the one with life insurance. As a result, the interest cost per unit is not ρ but ρ_a, which includes the insurance premium.[6] Thus, the household never borrows. Therefore, in this phase, the increase in the annuity supply only leads to an increase in total savings.

From the above discussion, we can confirm that when the optimal purchase of an annuity is constrained, bond saving, which compensates for the constrained annuity saving, is generated. This is the form of saving based on the precautionary motive. Also, we may point out some other factors, in addition to the direct supply constraint for the annuity, which have the same effects as the quantity constraint, namely, that the household may not obtain a sufficiently high rate of return on the annuity due to the lack of liquidity or the pooling of the survival probability over households with different risks. In such a case, the situation will be the same as at point A in Figure 7.1 as long as public enforcement is not introduced. Davies (1981) constructed a more realistic multi-period simulation model and demonstrated that saving based on the precautionary motive can fully explain the slow dissaving behaviour of households after retirement.

Precautionary bond saving generates an asset which is not received by anyone if the household dies at the end of the first period. This can be regarded as an involuntary bequest. However, we do not need to regard all bequests in the real world as involuntary.

The Altruistic Bequest Motive

When the parents' generation is concerned with the welfare of their children or of subsequent generations, the altruistic bequest motive is generated. Now suppose that each generation gives birth to $N = (1 + n)$ children at the end of the first period. Consider an economy where such an alternation in generations repeatedly occurs. We assume that the bequest is allocated equally to each child and that the amount of bequest per child is b_D if the parent dies at the end of the first period and b_S if the parent lives for the second period. (Both b_D and b_S are measured in terms of the value at the beginning of the second period.)[7] The

---

[6] Borrowing with life insurance is the exact opposite of an annuity. It is thought of as a composite of the sale of a safe bond and the purchase of life insurance.

[7] Let us explain why b_S can be measured in terms of the value at the beginning of the second period. The parents' generation who live for the second period actually obtain ρb_S by reinvesting b_S per child until the end of the second period, and leave ρb_S as a bequest at the time of death (i.e., at the beginning of the third period). However, if the financial market is perfect, the generation of children borrow b_S at the time of birth (i.e., at the beginning of the second period for the parents' generation) and obtain that in advance. Therefore, if the financial market is perfect, the determination of the amount of the bequest is irrelevant to the timing of the inheritance. However, if the financial market is imperfect and the borrowing constraint is binding, this is not the case. Ishikawa (1974) examines the determination of the amount of the bequest and of the timing of the inheritance in the presence of the borrowing constraint.

parental generation is assumed to maximize the sum of the utility derived from their own consumption, $u(c_1) + p \cdot u(c_2)$ and the utility derived from the bequest left to the children, $(N\{(1 - p) \cdot v(b_D) + p \cdot v(b_S)\})$. Denote the bequest which the parental generation receives from the previous generation by b_0. The sum of this bequest and the income, $b_0 + y$, is the consumable resource for the parents' generation in the first period.

Figure 7.2 depicts household saving behaviour in the presence of a perfect annuity market. The first quadrant of the figure is the consumption space (c_1, c_2), which is the same as Figure 7.1, and the third quadrant is the bequest space (b_S, b_D). In the consumption space, the budget line with the slope ρ_a, which represents the maximum possible consumption opportunity, is drawn from $b_0 + y$, and several further budget lines with the same slope are drawn to the left of it. The locus of the tangency of those budget lines and the household's indifference curves (that is, the expansion curve) is depicted as the curve OC. In the fourth quadrant, a straight line with the slope ρ/N is drawn from $b_0 + y$ to the

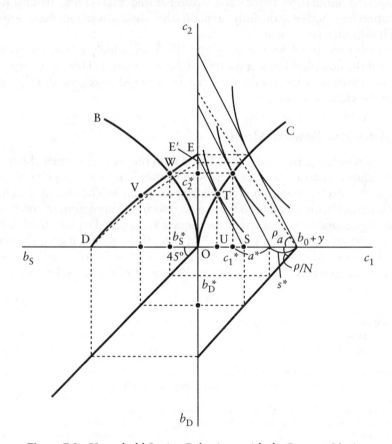

Figure 7.2. *Household Saving Behaviour with the Bequest Motive*

vertical axis. We refer to the line as 'the return curve of bond saving'. We divide the original return ρ by N to obtain the return per child. In the third quadrant, the 45° line is drawn. Finally, in the second quadrant, the locus of the point where the marginal utility of the second period consumption is equal to that of the bequest per child is depicted as the curve OB. This curve represents the household's optimal use of resources in the second period. We will explain another curve, DE, drawn in the second quadrant, later.

The most important feature of saving behaviour based on the bequest motive is the perfect specialization of saving measures: that is, the household purchases an annuity to finance second-period consumption, but an ordinary bond to finance the bequest. This is because, when the annuity market is perfect, the risk-averse household chooses the [appropriate] saving in order to leave the same amount of bequest to the children, whether the household lives for the second period or not. (This is called the situation of perfect insurance—see Appendix 7.1, mathematical note 1.) This implies that the 45 degree line in the bequest plane represents the optimal combination of bequests.

Now suppose that the household chooses an arbitrary amount of bond saving s. We denote the point corresponding to $b_0 + y - s$ on the horizontal axis by S and consider the point on the return curve of the bond saving corresponding to S. The value of the vertical axis of this point and the value of the horizontal axis of the corresponding point on the 45-degree line in the third quadrant give the amount of bequests, $b_D = b_S$, when the bond saving is s. Meanwhile, in the consumption plane, we denote the intersection of the budget line with the slope ρ_a starting from S and the curve OC by T. T represents the consumption point when the bond saving is s. The distance between the points U (the intersection of the vertical line drawn from T and the horizontal axis) and $b_0 + y$ is the total amount of saving, while the length of the line US is the amount of the annuity purchase a. The combination of the second-period consumption c_2 corresponding to T and the bequest b_S obtained above is plotted as the point V in the second quadrant.

In Figure 7.2, the point V is located below the curve OB. From the definition of the curve OB, it is known that at such a point, the bequest is excessive, that is, the marginal utility of the second-period consumption is greater than that of the second-period bequest. Therefore, at such a point, there is a downward pressure on s.

The curve DE is the locus of the point V when the amount of bond saving s as a parameter moves from 0 to $b_0 + y$. The point E corresponds to $s = 0$, and the point D corresponds to $s = b_0 + y$. The curve OB represents the optimal pattern of demand for future consumption and the future bequest, whereas the curve DE represents the feasible pattern of supply for the same variables. Therefore, the intersection of both curves, W, indicates the optimal saving behaviour of the household.

When the survival probability p increases, the household increases its annuity saving and substitutes it for bond saving. This is because the household reduces consumption and the bequest each period via the income effect created by the reduction of the rate of return on the annuity. In this case, the amount of saving, in total, also increases. This point can be explained by Figure 7.2. In the consumption plane, an increase in p reduces not only the slope of the budget line for the annuity but also the slope of the indifference curve at the same rate. Therefore, the expansion curve OC remains unchanged. As a result, the curve DE shifts downward to become the curve DE'. (The point D is fixed.) Since the curve OB is unchanged, the new subjective equilibrium moves downward along the curve OB.

How is the situation changed when the annuity saving is quantity constrained? In this case, as we have already mentioned, bond saving based on the precautionary motive is generated. If the household lives for the second period, consumption is financed by part of the gross return to the bond saving. Therefore, it necessarily holds that $b_D > b_S$. At the second-best equilibrium, the curve OB is unchanged, but the marginal rate of substitution between the consumption of both periods takes an intermediate value of ρ and ρ_a, reflecting the fact that the household cannot achieve perfect insurance; thus, the quantity constraint for the annuity essentially has the same effects as the reduction of the rate of return on the annuity (see Appendix 7.1, mathematical note 2). In the neighbourhood of the optimal combination of saving (a^*, s^*), it can be shown that the increase in the bond saving does not perfectly compensate the reduction of the annuity saving created by the quantity constraint $\bar{a}$. Put differently, in the phase where the annuity supply is constrained (although it is assumed to stay in the neighbourhood of the optimal level), the increase in the annuity supply reduces the other saving, but raises the total saving (see Appendix 7.1, mathematical note 3). This result bears some resemblance to that obtained in the phase of the line BE in Figure 7.1. However, the result may not be true when the annuity supply largely diverges from the optimal level. As in the phase of the line AB in Figure 7.1, the income effect created by the annuity supply constraint may give rise to more than one-to-one substitution of annuity saving for ordinary saving and lead to a decrease in total savings. Substitution between annuity saving and ordinary saving under an imperfect annuity market is, in this way, fairly complex.

Bequest by an Implicit Contract within a Family

There is another type of bequest in addition to purely accidental and altruistic bequests. Shoup (1966) makes the following point (applicable in the USA). Since the tax system favours a gift *inter vivos* rather than posthumous inheritance, people should bequeath in the efficient form of gift *inter vivos* if the principal object of the bequest is to leave consumable resources to children. However, a gift *inter vivos* is in practice rare. He explains that this is because people are concerned with the social power derived from wealth holding. This social power has two aspects: one promotes prestige and authority in politics and society; the other conveys controlling power over children within a family.[8]

There is a possibility that parents and children may make an implicit contract to pool their assets (conceptually) and form a joint consumption plan, with one side getting the remaining assets if the other side dies. Kotlikoff and Spivak (1981) suggest interpreting the bequest as a consequence of such a contract. Since the survival probability of parents is lower than that of children, children acquire a bequest from parents more frequently than parents acquire a bequest from children. The joint consumption plan means that children secure the (previously agreed) consumption for parents if they live for a long time. It is shown by means of a simulation analysis that such an implicit contract relationship plays a considerable role as a substitute for an annuity (Kotlikoff and Spivak, 1981: Table 3).

This idea is very interesting. Even if, in principle, such an arrangement can be made not only between family members but also within a small close group, such as a circle of acquaintances, it is limited to family members in practice. This is because a biological relationship, namely, that of parents and children, is favourable for the cultivation of a relationship of mutual trust among the members, as a premise of such a long-term implicit contract. Of course, an unconditional relationship of mutual trust is not always established between individuals just because they are family members. To the extent that each family member is an independent consumer, a device is necessary in order to monitor mutually and continuously the execution of the engagement that members should consume under the co-operative plan. Moreover, it is through such confirmation that the relationship of mutual trust is strengthened. The necessity of continuous confirmation of execution means that monetary transfer from one side to the other mainly takes the form of current income transfer (allowance) and rarely takes the form of a gift *inter vivos* by which one side dissaves its asset drastically. It is consistent with Shoup's concept of 'a motive of power within family' that each member continues to hold his/her wealth until the end of his/her life in order to fulfil the execution of the implicit contract between them.

The extended family consisting of aged persons and their children in Japan has two aspects: on the one hand it is a monitoring system for continuous and mutual confirmation of the execution of the insurance contract; and on the other it is a contrivance for strengthening the mutual trust relationship through living together and exchanging service roles. The extended family is often formed with land and housing supplied by the parents, which is an observable form of the established pooling of assets and consumption.[9]

---

[8] Bernheim, Shleifer, and Summers (1985) extended the latter aspect, and, using preliminary data analysis, argued that parents use the bequest strategically to attract children's interest. In this case, it is assumed that the bequest is held until the end of one's life.

[9] Kotlikoff and Spivak further argued that (i) the function of the family to as a substitute for the perfect insurance market gives a stronger incentive to form a family, and (ii) the largest factor

Income and Wealth

However, in a society which has seen rapid changes in politics, the economy, and culture, there are large differences in consciousness and in attitudes such as values and lifestyles even among people just one generation apart. This gap has gradually made it difficult for aged persons and their children to share their lives in the form of the extended family.[10] In such cases, a difficulty emerges, namely, how to develop the above-mentioned confirmation and mutual trust.

It is possible that the implicit contract may be changed into a clearly stated contract which can be executed by a third party. That is, the family may found a family trust fund to which each generation's annual income as well as their assets belong; each member is supplied with previously agreed annual consumption resources from the fund. Designing such a trust contract and exercising an executive function must be profitable for a trust company, since there is neither the problem of adverse selection nor the problem of moral hazard. However, in spite of there being enough incentives on the suppliers' side, execution by a third party is rarely seen in practice. This may be because of reluctance to discuss family affairs with a third party, uneasiness at the thought of a costly change to a contract due to the occurrence of an unexpected situation among family members, and the development of a public pension insurance system. In addition, the major reason seems to be that the third party solution cannot further mutual trust among family members, which is an indispensable condition for such an arrangement. In other words, because it is an implicit contract, mutual effort to improve that trust is induced.

The above argument does not eliminate the making of an altruistic bequest by parents. Rather, an altruistic bequest is thought to be parallel to the substitutability of the function of the implicit contract between parents and children for an annuity. This is because mutual trust between parents and children is a precondition for altruism.

Transmission of Wealth between Generations

In an overlapping generations model where the bequest motive functions, the amount of the bequest made by the parents' generation becomes the initial asset

causing family collapses in the USA is the popularization of public and private pensions. As argued in the text, however, there is mutual trust as a back-up point, which is not automatically set up, between what function the family can perform and what function the family actually does perform. The argument that a family itself is formed by the [substitute function] seems to have shortcomings.

[10] According to National Population Survey (Kokusei Chosa) in 1985, the number of households with people aged 65 years or over amounted to 9.03 million, which is 25 per cent of total households, and 53.2 per cent of those households were extended families of parents living with their children. On the other hand, in 1970, the number of households with aged people was 5.09 million, which is 22 per cent of total households, and 65.5 per cent of those were extended families. Although the ratio of extended families shows a diminishing trend over those 15 years, it is much higher than that in Western countries. With regard to the current situation of support for aged people, see Ishikawa (1988*b*). For the above figures, see also Ishikawa (1988*b*: 420, Table 1).

per household of the children's generation, which in turn affects the amount of the bequest made by the children's generation. This describes the process of transmission of wealth between generations. Let us consider a benchmark case where the perfect annuity market and the altruistic bequest motive exist, and examine what kind of dynamics of wealth holding will arise in the long run, on the assumption that household taste, the rate of return, and income are stationary throughout generations. With regard to household taste, the analysis will be limited to the case where both the elasticity of the marginal utility of consumption and that of the bequest are constant. Let us denote the elasticity of consumption by ε and the elasticity of the bequest by μ. The relative sizes of ε and μ decide whether a generation's own consumption or that of the next generation is a necessity (or a luxury). When $\varepsilon > \mu$, the next generation's consumption is relatively more of a luxury, and the household increases the amount of resources devoted to the bequest with an increase in lifetime resources $b_D + y$.

The relative sizes of ε and μ cannot be determined a priori (the concluding remarks of this section discuss this point). Figure 7.3(A) shows the pattern of dynamics in the case of $\varepsilon < \mu$, while Figure 7.3(B) shows the three possible patterns of dynamics in the case of $\varepsilon > \mu$ (see Appendix 7.1, mathematical note 4 for analysis). A curve we call the 'wealth transmission curve' is one that shows the corresponding relation between wealth received by the parents' generation (b_0) and the wealth per child left by the parents' generation ($b_D = b_S$), which is drawn on the basis of Figure 7.2. (The shape of curve OB in Figure 7.2 corresponds to the case $\varepsilon > \mu$.) The 45-degree line shows the situation where the level of wealth holding becomes constant from generation to generation. Cases (a) and (b) in Figure 7.3(B) occur when $\rho > N$, that is, $r > n$, while Case (c) occurs when $r \leq n$. The reason is that the slope of the wealth transmission curve converges to ρ/N asymptotically with an increase in b_0. Wealth diverges upward in Case (a), while two long-run equilibria emerge in Case (b). As the figure shows, a point near the origin, that is, a point where the wealth transmission curve crosses the 45-degree line from above, is the stable long-run equilibrium.

Therefore, as long as the amount of wealth held by the initial generation is smaller than a certain threshold value, wealth passed from parents to children has a regressive tendency towards the long-run equilibrium level. If the bequest motive is strong enough, wealth is accumulated unlimitedly irrespective of the amount of wealth held by the initial generation. In Case (c), a unique stable long-run equilibrium arises. The difference between Case (b) and Case (c) corresponds to the intuitively evident property that a household with more children can leave less wealth per child.[11]

---

[11] In reality, sociological factors not covered in the text, e.g., customs of inheritance or marriage, play an important role in wealth transmission over generations. It is evident that equal inheritance among children contributes to equalization more than inheritance by a single child

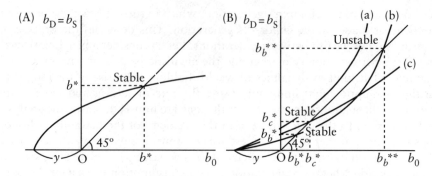

Figure 7.3. *Dynamics of Intergenerational Wealth Transmission. (A) Bequests are Necessary Goods ($\varepsilon < \mu$) and (B) Bequests are Luxury Goods ($\varepsilon > \mu$)*

When a perfect annuity market does not exist, the transmission of wealth between generations can be described as a stochastic (Markov) process, since the amount of a bequest becomes smaller with the longer life than otherwise. Therefore, another factor affecting the dispersal of wealth arises in addition to the dispersal of wealth among the initial generation. However, it is difficult to think that such stochastic variations dominate the above-mentioned fundamental pattern of dynamics and result in reversing the regression towards the mean of wealth and in increasing the possibility of upward divergence. This is because the imperfection of the annuity market has an effect which shrinks the possible opportunities open to households for consumption and bequests, and thus causes the wealth transmission curve, on average, to move downwards.[12]

Although the above argument has rested on the premise of the altruistic bequest motive, the argument is not restricted to that case. When a bequest by

under a custom such as primogeniture or ultimogeniture. The pattern of marriage also affects wealth distribution except in the case of single-child inheritance. This is clearly shown by comparing the case where marriages occur randomly and that where marriages are classified according to the level of wealth. In the former case, rich people have higher probability of marrying people who are less rich than of marrying richer people. On the other hand, poor people have a higher probability of marrying richer people. In this case, marriage is a factor that enhances equal distribution. In the latter case, marriage becomes neutral to wealth distribution since the situation is the same as if a brother and a sister married. The analysis in the text assumes the latter neutral case. In fact, as Blau and Duncan (1967: 346–60) show, classification of marriage by educational level (as the first factor) is developing, which means that classification of marriage by level of wealth is also possible because education and wealth are correlated. (Although the analysis is based on a large sample survey in the USA, the situation seems to be the same in Japan.) For theoretical analyses of these factors, see Meade (1964: 47), Blinder (1973). As for empirical analyses of the pattern of division of inheritance, there are differences among the results of observations and thus we cannot deal with this issue conclusively. That is, Menchik (1980) argues that equal division is supported by the data, while Becker and Tomes (1979) argue that there exists a tendency for the division to favour weaker children and this works as an equalization factor.

[12] See Abel (1985) and Eckstein, Eichenbaum, and Peled (1985) for rigorous analyses of wealth distribution in this case.

implicit contract among a family exists (either exists singularly or coexists with the altruistic bequest motive), the pattern of transmission of wealth between generations is almost the same as the one shown in Figure 7.3. This can be explained by the following two points: (i) a joint consumption plan under an implicit contract can play the role of an annuity, although not perfectly; (ii) the plan requires maximization of the sum of the utilities of the parents' and the children's generation, which is formally the same as the objective of the altruistic bequest motive shown in Figure 7.3 (if we regard the parental generation's utility from the bequest as the utility from consumption by the children's generation in advance).

We have examined above the theory relating to the fundamental factors that determine households' saving behaviour, and the meaning of this for the transmission of wealth between generations. Next, we examine the empirical meanings of these theoretical hypotheses.

Empirical Studies on the Amount of Life-cycle Saving

What weight does life-cycle saving occupy in the total wealth of a country? If its weight is large, differences in wealth holding among households are mainly attributed to differences of age, and there is no inequality when the whole life cycle is considered. Moreover, even if differences in income exist among people, the skewness of wealth distribution does not exceed by very much that of permanent income. In such a case, if some reason remains for concern about wealth distribution, the concern results in the problem of income distribution and thus the problem relating to wealth distribution itself has been dissolved. On the other hand, if its weight is small, the pattern of long-run wealth distribution largely depends on which pattern shown in Figure 7.3 can be applied to the transmission of wealth between generations.

With regard to the answer to this question, a keen controversy developed between Kotlikoff and Summers and Modigliani who is the originator of the life-cycle hypothesis (Kotlikoff and Summers 1981; Modigliani 1988; Kotlikoff and Summers 1988 and Blinder 1988). Kotlikoff and Summers conclude, based on their measurements, that wealth arising purely from the life cycle occupies only 20 per cent of the total wealth of the household sector in the USA, with life-cycle wealth defined as the accumulated value of the difference between income and consumption (including interest and returns). Their conclusion is consistent with the results of simulation analyses by Atkinson (1971b); Oulton (1976), and White (1978).

Modigliani refutes their conclusion in relation to the flow points. First, he estimates the stock of inherited wealth by capitalizing the flow of annual bequeathed transfers between generations, data on which are directly available, on the assumption of steady-state growth. Then, he concludes that inherited wealth is only 15–20 per cent of the total wealth of the household sector and consequently that life-cycle wealth, defined as the remainder, is 80–85 per cent of the total wealth. Second, he re-estimates life-cycle wealth, using the Kotlikoff–Summers' original model with some conceptual adjustments, and obtains the result that life-cycle wealth occupies 80 per cent. Percentages 20 per cent and 80 per cent are complete opposites, and their implications for understanding the nature of wealth distribution are also completely different. Even if some adjustments (pointed out by Modigliani), for example, a modification that support and educational expenses for children before they are independent, are included in the consumption of parents' generation, the major part of the gap remains.[13]

The most important explanatory factor for the gap between the results of the two sides is a difference in the accounting definition of life-cycle wealth. The definition is not self-evident, once we move away from the world of pure life-cycle saving. We will explain this by using a two-period model.

Consider the case where both the altruistic bequest motive and the perfect annuity exist. Our economy's representative household is the one already mentioned above. The number of households of the parents' generation is normalized by 1 and therefore that of the children's generation is N. The timing of the transmission of the bequest to the children is assumed to be at the end of the parents' life. On these assumptions, let us examine the wealth of the whole economy and its distribution across households at the beginning of the second period of the parents' generation.[14]

[13] Another factor is the treatment of durable goods. In the Kotlikoff–Summers model, all purchases of durable goods are regarded as consumption. Modigliani argues that the share of life-cycle wealth increases by 26 per cent if this treatment of durable-goods consumption is altered to one that individuals consume services from durable goods. Regarding this assertion by Modigliani, Blinder (1988) states that such a large figure of change is incomprehensible. It is true that life-cycle wealth increases if the purchase of durable goods is treated as saving since younger generations consume durable goods more extensively. However, Modigliani does not show how he obtains the figure, 26 per cent and thus we cannot say that his argument is persuasive, as Blinder indicates. Kotlikoff and Summers themselves contrast the two treatments of durable goods, while asserting that the quantitative impact is at most a few per cent. In this respect, the controversy has not been concluded.

[14] As is explained in footnote 7, each child whose parents live for a long time makes his/her lifetime consumption plan as if he/she possessed the initial resources amounting to $(\rho/N) \cdot s$ as lifetime resources, which are b_0 for his/her household. However, he/she does not actually receive that amount at the time of his/her birth. Accordingly, wealth distribution among households can be summarized as shown in the following table, where $p + N$ is the total number of families.

Frequency of households	Share of wealth holding
$\dfrac{p}{p+N}$	$\dfrac{\rho_a \cdot a + \rho \cdot s}{\rho(a+s)}$
$\dfrac{(1-p)N}{p+N}$	$\dfrac{\rho \cdot s}{\rho(a+s)}$
$\dfrac{p \cdot N}{p+N}$	0

At this point, wealth is possessed by both households of the parents' generation who have lived a long time and those of the children's generation who have inherited a bequest from parents who died at the end of their first period. Wealth held by the former is $p(\rho_a \cdot a + \rho \cdot s)$, while that held by the latter is $(1 - p)\rho \cdot s$. Remember that $p \cdot \rho_a = \rho$, then the wealth of the whole economy (the whole household sector), denoted by W, is:

$$p(\rho_a \cdot a + \rho \cdot s) + (1 - p)\rho \cdot s = \rho(a + s) \equiv W. \tag{7.2}$$

That is, W equals the value of the financial assets, including interest, that the parents' generation purchased, irrespective of the current owner. The budget constraint of the parents' generation in the first period is:

$$c_1 = b_0 + y - (a + s). \tag{7.3}$$

Using this constraint, we can decompose W in two ways.

Modigliani decomposes W into

$$W = b_0 + \rho\left(\frac{rb_0}{\rho} + y - c_1\right), \tag{7.4}$$

and defines the first term as the contribution of bequests, and the second term as life-cycle wealth. The expression in the parenthesis of the second term of the right-hand side is first-period saving, on the basis of the standard definition of income. Income is the sum of the present value, at the beginning of the period, of interest revenues generated at the end of the period plus income from labour, y. Therefore, life-cycle wealth is the accumulated value of saving including interest in the first period (each period in the multi-period case). Modigliani asserts that it amounts to 80–85 per cent of total wealth W, or 80 per cent in the adjusted Kotlikoff–Summers framework.

On the other hand, Kotlikoff and Summers decompose the same W into

$$W = \rho b_0 + \rho(y - c_1) \tag{7.5}$$

and propose to regard the second term, that is, saving from income including interest, as life-cycle wealth and the remainder as the contribution of bequests. Their interpretation is based on the understanding that the original meaning of life-cycle saving is to save a part of the income from labour during youth for retirement. If we follow Modigliani's definition, even a very wealthy millionaire living only on the current income from a bequest, not working at all ($y = 0$), and being able to save has large life-cycle wealth. There is a sense of incongruity in this alternative definition. In the alternative definition, the weight of life-cycle wealth is clearly smaller than in Modigliani's definition.

Consequently, Modigliani's definition stresses the point that wealth depending on income from a bequest means a part which can be consumed but is not consumed by a household, while the Kotlikoff–Summers' definition stresses the point that larger saving is possible in the presence of income from a bequest. However, neither argument gives sufficient consideration to the point that consumption and saving are endogenous variables. Therefore, it cannot be said that either is a logically correct evaluation method.

How, then, can we answer the original question? Following the suggestion of Blinder (1988), let us consider its similarity to the problem of how output is distributed to each production factor when production is carried out by different factors of production. When we regard wealth as output generated by initial wealth (that is, a bequest) and income (originally, the available working time of a household) as production factors through a household's preferences as a production function, the problem resembles the issue of distributing output to production factors according to the contribution by each. This is the classical problem known as the 'adding up problem' after Wicksell. For the production problem, it is settled by the marginal productivity hypothesis under either global homogeneity through production technology or local homogeneity by zero-profit condition through the entry and exit process. However, as for household consumption and saving, there is no guarantee of satisfaction of such a nature. Therefore, if we try to evaluate the contribution in the same way as the marginal productivity hypothesis, a positive or negative surplus generally occurs. A theoretical solution to this problem remains to be dealt with in the future.

Since we cannot ascertain which decomposition method should be adopted, it might be meaningful as a rule of thumb to take a medium number between the numbers derived from the above two definitions. With regard to Modigliani's approach to estimating the stock of bequests (b_0), it is also pointed out that there is a considerable possibility of under-evaluation of the stock of bequests. That is, the flow data on wealth transmission between generations, which are the basis of estimation, are fragmented and incomplete; there is a high possibility of under-declaration especially among the wealthier classes holding large assets; and it is doubtful that the data can accurately capture the actual amount of gifts *inter vivos*. Putting these accounts together, we may conclude that it is clearly hard to subscribe to Modigliani's assertion that life-cycle wealth occupies 80 per cent. There seem to be grounds to rely on the assertion that wealth transmitted through bequests occupies considerable weight in the total amount of wealth. Studies to establish the quantitative size and to distinguish the part due to the precautionary motive and the other part, as well as the development of a theoretically-correct measurement method, are left to future researchers.

Empirical Studies on the Elasticity of Bequests

The empirical importance of bequests suggests that the inequality of wealth distribution is largely derived from the transmission of wealth between generations. What pattern does the transmission of wealth between generations follow? The size of the elasticity of bequests, ε/μ, determines the pattern.

A series of studies for the UK by Harbury (Harbury 1962; Harbury and McMahon 1973; Harbury and Hitchens 1976) show, by collecting data on b_S's and b_0's with respect to the same households, that there certainly exists a class which has succeeded to a huge amount of wealth over generations. This fact supports the existence of households whose wealth holding does not tend to regress towards the mean (that is, $\varepsilon/\mu > 1$).

The most careful study for estimating the value of ε/μ directly is that by Menchik and David (1983). By gathering data on individual tax returns for 20 years in the State of Wisconsin in the USA and, in addition, by collecting probate records and the accompanying inheritance tax reports at the individual's death, they estimated the value of the elasticity of bequests to permanent income during one's life. Permanent income corresponds to y in our model. Although their data set is not complete, in the sense that it does not include data on the initial asset b_0, their research is epoch-making in comparison with what preceded it since they use data on actual long-run series of individual incomes.

Their conclusion may be summarized as follows. Bequests are luxury goods for all individuals within each cohort classified by year of birth. That is, bequests increase more than proportionally with permanent income. However, this does not mean that $\varepsilon/\mu > 1$, as a property of preferences, is equally possessed by all individuals. It should rather be understood that the propensity for bequests is higher in the classes with higher permanent incomes. In fact, as Table 7.1 shows, although the elasticity of bequests is positive, it is far less than unity and statistically insignificant for the individuals whose permanent income falls within the 80th percentile (from the bottom) within each cohort. On the other hand, as for households whose permanent income belongs to the highest 20 per cent, the propensity takes the higher value, that is more than 2 or 3 (although the value falls if we control for time of death and occupation, it is still larger than unity). Furthermore, by comparing cohorts classified by year of birth, whose absolute levels of permanent income differ owing to income growth (see rows (4) and (5) in the table), we can confirm that the propensity for bequests does not depend on absolute level of permanent income, but on relative position within the same cohort.

The above conclusion is consistent with previous empirical results that the elasticity of bequests to income of the parents' generation is larger than unity, obtained by using other cross-sectional data sets (Adams 1980: Table II and Tomes 1981: Table 2, equation 6). In particular, the point that the propensity for bequests does not depend on absolute level of lifetime resources but on relative position within their distribution is also consistent with the following fact: the elasticity of bequests to the absolute income level of the highest 21 per cent of the wealth holding classes is less than unity and lies between 0.8 and 0.9, which is estimated from an analysis of the time series of aggregate-level inheritance tax statistics (Adams 1980: Table III).

Table 7.1. *Estimated Result of Bequest Elasticity: Using Matched Data of Probate Records and Long-Term Tax Reports in the State of Wisconsin*

		1910–24	1900–9	1890–99	1880–89
(1)	Number in sample	238	464	699	528
Bequest					
(2)	Median	8,142	9,270	8,786	7,389
(3)	80th percentile	27,740	28,430	24,970	23,490
Permanent disposable income					
(4)	Median	5,740	5,056	3,540	2,416
(5)	80th percentile	7,520	7,115	5,346	4,013
Estimated value of the elasticity					
(6)	Permanent income percentile 0–50	0.29^{ss}	0.59^{ns}	0.42^{ns}	0.35^{ns}
(7)	Permanent income percentile 51–79	0.37^{ns}	0.28^{ns}	0.71^{ns}	-9.70^{ns}
(8)	Permanent income percentile 80–100	3.92^{s1}	2.39^{s1}	2.06^{s1}	3.27^{s1}
(9)	Permanent income percentile 80–100: death assumed at age 72	2.70	2.0	2.03	4.75
(10)	Permanent income percentile 80–100: death at age 72 and self-employment assumed	1.88	1.42	1.33	1.97

Notes

1. The population of samples consists of males who filed tax returns in Wisconsin in the years 1946–64. The data used here were found by identifying dead individuals and tracing their probate records. 'Bequest' means the sum of net inherited estate, life insurance proceeds, and *inter vivos* transfers which appeared in the probate records, discounted forward to the subject's death (at a real after-tax interest rate of 1%).
2. All the absolute amounts are represented by real dollar values measured by the consumer price index (1967 = 1).
3. Permanent (annual) disposable income is calculated as follows. Real disposable income in each year is discounted by a real after-tax interest rate to the value at age 65 and summed up. Then, the sum is divided by the number in the sample. The average observation period for each household is 10 years.
4. The elasticity in each category is evaluated at the income percentile points 25%, 65%, or 90%.
5. The superscripts in rows (6), (7), and (8) are derived from Menchik and David (1983: Table 4). Superscripts s_1 or s_5 denote that the estimated value, which is the basis of each figure (Table 4 in the original paper), is statistically significant at the significance level at 1% or 5%, respectively, and *ns* denotes that it is insignificant at the 5% level.

Source: Menchik and David (1983: Table 3 for rows (1)–(3), Table 2 for rows (4)–(5), Table 6 for rows (6)–(10)).

Concluding Remarks

Although the evidence is fragmentary, the empirical studies discussed above show that wealth transmission on a large scale is restricted to the large-wealth-holding class and that the elasticity of bequests to lifetime income is large in that class. This fact suggests another image, different from an aggregate economy consisting of identical households motivated by almost identical tastes. It rather implies that there is support for the view that a whole economy is divided into households leaving relatively small amounts of bequests as insurance for the next generation and fewer households pursuing wealth accumulation itself as their main purpose (in other words, finding utility in the economic and social power brought by wealth) and the latter's wealth is passed on to the next generation as a bequest voluntarily or involuntarily. Therefore, while regression towards the mean of wealth over generations arises for most households, there is a high possibility that cumulative wealth accumulation occurs for some households.

7.2. EDUCATION AS A MEANS OF TRANSMISSION OF WEALTH

The wealth transmitted between generations is not restricted to physical assets. The education of children financed by parents is also a bequest in the form of a gift *inter vivos* because of its effect on human capital investment. The dynamics of wealth transmission should be considered for total assets, defined as the sum of the present values of income from labour, including the return on educational investment (= human capital), and physical assets. This is because what the parents' generation safeguard are life resources as a whole including the earning ability of each child after independence. We call the total assets transmitted from parents to children the 'gross bequest' in order to distinguish it from the bequest discussed in the previous section.[15]

Let us modify the two-period model used in the previous section and assume that N children are born in an economy (that is, are capable of work) at time $1 - \delta$ $(0 < \delta < 1)$ in the first period of the parents' generation and they continue to remain in their parental households during the period of length δ until the beginning of the second period when they become independent. The parents give each child an education for the length of e. The cost of education is an opportunity cost of wage income during the interval and other direct costs are assumed away. As a consequence of education, the child's earning ability becomes $y(e)$ per unit of time, where one period corresponds to the length of 1. As in section 3.2, a graph of $y(e)$ is called the 'educational effect curve' and it is assumed to be strongly upwardly convex and smooth. For simplicity, the degree of diminishing returns is strong enough and the chosen e always lies in the interval $0 < e \leq \delta$.

From the above assumptions, each child brings income of $(\delta - e) \cdot y(e)$ to his/her parental household after finishing education and possesses human

---

[15] Let us explain the difference between the concepts of net and gross bequest. The gross bequest is a total asset as defined in the text, i.e., the sum of human and physical assets evaluated at the time of the economic independence of children, as in footnote 7. However, human assets include the value of earning ability with no educational investment (denoted later by $y(0)$). Therefore, we subtract that value from the gross bequest to obtain a net contribution from parents to children, i.e., the net bequest.

capital $y(e)$ at the time of independence. Following the previous section, let us denote the physical assets acquired at that time by b_D or b_S. Then, the total assets (the gross bequest) of parents who die at the end of the first period and of those who survive into the second period are, respectively:

$$\omega_D = b_D + y(e) \qquad (7.6)$$

$$\omega_S = b_S + y(e). \qquad (7.7)$$

Similarly, by using the notation of the previous section, let us denote the initial resources of the parents' generation by:

$$\omega_0 = b_0 + y. \qquad (7.8)$$

As the target of the bequest motive has moved into the initial total assets of the children, b_D or b_S in the utility function of the parents' generation is replaced by ω_D or ω_S, respectively. Throughout the remainder of this section, a perfect annuity market is assumed to exist. As a result, the parents' generation behave in such a way as to achieve the perfect insurance condition $\omega_D = \omega_S$, which is the same as in the previous section.

What educational level does the parents' generation choose? Parents with an altruistic bequest motive choose the same educational investment level as if the children themselves had chosen it at birth. The reason is that the parents' generation determine the allocation between their own consumption and the gross bequest by introducing the next generation's lifetime resources (at the time of independence) into their own budget constraint. Without other constraints, described later, the aim of utility maximization for the parents' generation is to maximize a joint pool of resources for both parents and children. For this purpose, the present value of the net returns of the educational investment to the children, evaluated at the beginning of the first period or the time of the economic birth of children,

$$V(e; 1 + \delta) = \left(\delta - e + \frac{1}{\rho} \right) y(e) \qquad (7.9)$$

should be maximized. (Here, $1 + \delta$ in $V(\ )$ means the length of the planning period.)

The maximization must satisfy a condition (see Appendix 7.1, mathematical note 5):

$$\frac{y'(e)}{y(e)} = \frac{1}{\delta - e + (1/\rho)}. \qquad (7.10)$$

Thus, it is possible to apply the theory of the optimal educational investment for an individual, discussed in section 3.2 (Becker 1974: 1077, Ishikawa

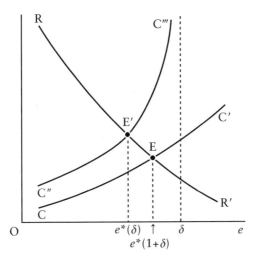

Figure 7.4. *Parental Choice of Children's Educational Level*

1975: 995) without any changes. Figure 7.4 illustrates condition (7.10). A downward-sloping curve, RR′, represents the marginal profit of investment indicated by the left-hand side while an upward-sloping curve, CC′, represents the investment cost discounted by the length of the payout period denoted by the right-hand side. The optimal educational level e^* is given at the intersection point E of the two curves.[16] The size of e^* clearly depends on the length of the planning period. Therefore, remembering that the length of the planning period is $1 + \delta$, we employ the expression $e^* = e^*(1 + \delta)$.

If the educational effect curve is exogenously given, and moreover the financial market is perfect, the chosen educational level is independent of the level of wealth of the parents' generation. The amount of the chosen gross bequest from which the maximized human asset is subtracted is the physical asset left as a bequest by the parents' generation.

On the other hand, when there is no altruistic bequest motive, as for example when parents pursue pure life-cycle behaviour, the idea of a joint resource pool for parents and children loses its meaning. In that case, the optimal educational level for parents is the level at which they can maximize the revenues contributed to the parental household by the children:

$$V(e; \delta) = (\delta - e) \cdot y(e). \tag{7.11}$$

Assuming the case of the interior solution, we find that the cost curve shifts upward by reflecting the shortening of the payout period and the optimal point

[16] This point is unaltered even if the efficiency of education is higher, $e > \delta$, i.e., even if it is rational to continue the educational process beyond the time of economic independence. Thus, it is not essential to assume $e < \delta$ in the text. See the analysis using a continuous-time model in Ishikawa (1975: 991–5).

moves to E' where $e^* = e^*(\delta)$, as shown in Figure 7.4.[17] The children are regarded as a *de facto* pure supplementary labour force by the parents. Naturally, the children come to view their education as inadequate. Even though the children try to make up for their inadequate education after they achieve economic independence, they can never attain the original optimum level, since the payout period of the investment is too short. In this situation, the children have an incentive to hold a mutual support contract similar to the above-mentioned implicit insurance contract within a family as a substitute for an annuity: that is, a contract to exchange the grant of optimal education for the children for the support of parents in their old age by the children. However, the realization of such an exchange is premised on the building of a relationship of mutual trust within the family that guarantees the execution of the contract.[18] Therefore, the same optimal educational investment as in the case of altruism can be achieved only when such mutual trust is present.

The Non-negative Physical Bequest Constraint

There is an institutional factor which requires a revision of our result with regard to the choice of the optimal level of education under the bequest motive. That is the commonly accepted idea that parents cannot leave negative physical assets to their children. Although $\omega_D = \omega_S$ clearly decreases with the reduction of ω_0, the optimized level of the human asset $y(e^*)$ remains the same. Therefore, when ω_0 decreases continuously, the bequest left as physical asset $b_D = b_S$ reaches zero at a certain level of $\underline{\omega}(\underline{\omega})$ and becomes negative below the level.

In a phase where the physical bequest cannot be negative, that is, the additional constraints

$$y(e) \leq \omega_D \tag{7.12}$$

$$y(e) \leq \omega_S \tag{7.13}$$

are effective, the optimal investment behaviour maintains the characteristics of both complete insurance ($\omega_D = \omega_S$) and second-period consumption financed by a pension annuity. In addition, the optimal investment behaviour is characterized by the following three conditions (see Appendix 7.1, mathematical note 6: (i) no physical bequest ($s = 0$); (ii) the condition which determines the

---

[17] The interior solution exists when the local maximum value of $V(e; \delta)$ is larger than $V(0; \delta) = \delta \cdot y(0)$. The marginal return of education is assumed to be large enough initially.

[18] Ishikawa (1975: footnotes 18, 19) clarifies the conditions in which the contract of mutual support between parents and children is Pareto-improving, i.e., it recovers the optimal educational investment level and improves the welfare of the parents' generation simultaneously. At the same time, he also indicates that it is difficult to ensure the enforcement of such a contract.

second-best level of education,

$$\frac{y'(e)}{y(e)} = \frac{1}{\delta - e + (1/\rho) \cdot (v'(y(e))/u'(c_2))}; \qquad (7.14)$$

and (iii) the gift of physical assets to the children made by the relative reduction of their parents' consumption *per se* c_1, c_2:

$$v'(y(e)) < u'(c_2) = \left(\frac{1}{p\rho_a}\right) u'(c_1). \qquad (7.15)$$

By comparing (7.14) and (7.15), we can find that the planned period of education is effectively shortened (and thus the curve CC' in Figure 7.4 also shifts upward in this case). That is, in the phase where the non-negative physical bequest constraint is effective, both the children's human assets and their total wealth have a monotonically increasing relationship with their parents' wealth (ω_0).

However, it may not be plausible to preclude the possibility of a negative physical bequest a priori. Specifically, deviation of the educational level from its optimal level, as in the case of the non-existence of the bequest motive, will give the children an incentive to demand optimal education from their parents. In that case, there remains room for an agreement similar to the previously mentioned mutual support agreement such that the extension of the period of education is achieved in exchange for the acceptance of a certain amount of debt by the children.[19]

The Minimum Consumption Constraint

When consumption is restricted to the minimum livelihood level of the poorest class, a more serious constraint on children's education will appear. If parents' wealth ω_0 decreases sufficiently below $\underline{w}$, there is a possibility that

$$c_1 = \omega_0 + N(\delta - e) \cdot y(e) - a = \underline{c}_1 \qquad (7.16)$$

$$c_2 = \rho_a \cdot a = \underline{c}_2, \qquad (7.17)$$

where $\underline{c}_1$ and $\underline{c}_2$ denote the minimum consumption level in each period. That is, the minimum level of livelihood is barely attained in both period 1 and period 2 (in this case, $s = 0$). In such a case, by (7.16) and (7.17), the level of education is passively determined so as to satisfy

$$(\delta - e) \cdot y(e) = \frac{1}{N}\underline{c}_1 + \frac{1}{N\rho_a}\underline{c}_2 - \omega_0. \qquad (7.18)$$

---

[19] The characteristics of the comparative static for optimal behaviour with the effective non-negativity constraint are shown by Tomes (1981).

That is, the level of education is restricted to the level at which children can earn income which exactly compensates for the insufficiency of their parents' resources. However, the highest feasible level of education is given to children, reflecting the parents' bequest motive. Therefore, to the extent that there is even a slight surplus of parents' wealth, children are given a level of education greater than the level at which the children's income $V(e; \delta)$ is maximized. Of course, the level of education decreases with the reduction of the surplus and eventually reaches $e^*(\delta)$, which is the level where the bequest motive is not present.[20] This argument describes the situation that arises in conditions of severe poverty, where children cannot receive adequate education.

The significance in practice of the minimum consumption constraint depends on the aggregate conditions of the economy such as the time and the place, and the conditions of the labour market. There are many countries, even among the developed capitalist countries, which have deep-rooted problems of poverty. One of the biggest problems generated by poverty is the fact that restricted educational opportunities for children cause the reproduction of poverty from generation to generation.[21]

The Dynamics of Transmission of Wealth Including Human Assets

Let us consider the case of the altruistic bequest motive. The intergenerational wealth transmission curve is very similar to the one in Figure 7.3 except for the following two points. First, the axes indicate total assets (ω) instead of physical assets (b). Second, there are some kinked points in the curve owing to both of the constraints, non-negative physical bequests and minimum consumption.

---

[20] The above argument is meaningful when the parents' wealth ω_0 satisfies

$$\omega_0 \geq \frac{1}{N}\underline{c}_1 + \frac{1}{N\rho_a}\underline{c}_2 + \{\delta - e^*(\delta)\} \cdot y(e^*(\delta)) \equiv \omega_m.$$

With wealth at less than this level, the consumption amounts $\underline{c}_1$ and $\underline{c}_2$ are not possible. On the other hand, we have still to consider the case where $\omega_{\mathrm{crit}} < \omega_0 < \underline{\omega}$, where ω_{crit} denotes the critical value of ω_0 at which the minimum consumption constraint conditions (7.16) and (7.17) are both effective, and furthermore the consumption constraint is effective in only one of the periods. However, in that case, since the optimal interior allocation between consumption and education is pursued in the period when the constraint is ineffective, its qualitative characteristic is close to that of the case where there is no material bequest, which we have already seen. Thus, the detailed analysis is omitted here.

[21] For example, Banfield (1968) deals with the poverty problem in US cities and, among the factors obstructing the removal of poverty, he emphasized the existence of a disposition not to be willing to make current sacrifices for future prospects, i.e., a myopic or short-term perspective, among a sub-culture of people, and the reproduction of such a disposition from generation to generation. This argument, like the argument on a culture of poverty, caused a controversy. However, Banfield himself recognizes that such a disposition among people is strongly prescribed by the constraint of economic resources and points out that a large-scale transfer of resources is necessary in order to break out of the vicious circle (*op. cit.*: 219–20).

The property that the long-run dynamics depends on the values of both ε/μ and r/n can apply as before. There is thus no need to repeat the discussion in the previous section.

New properties to which we should pay attention are as follows. First, if stable long-run equilibrium exists, depending on the location of the equilibrium point in relation to the several kinked points, there is a tendency to revert to one of three situations: (i) positive physical assets and the optimal level of education; (ii) no physical assets and the second-best level of education; or (iii) no physical assets and a low level of education due to minimum consumption. Second, in the case where, in addition to stable equilibrium, unstable equilibrium exists above the stable one, there arises a process where physical assets increase cumulatively with a constant level of education, once a generation's wealth exceeds the level corresponding to the unstable equilibrium. (Note that the level of education is constant if the educational effect curve is unaffected. There is a qualification with respect to this point which will be referred to in the next section.) Third, there is a possibility that, besides the stable equilibrium, an unstable equilibrium may exist to the left of the stable one. That is the case where the two constraints previously mentioned create a sharp kink in the wealth transmission curve at a low level of wealth. In this case, households that started with wealth below a certain critical level cannot get out of the vicious circle of poverty.

The above discussion tells us that, roughly speaking, if the parents' generation has the bequest motive in relation to the lifetime resources of the children's generation, including their earning ability, a gift *inter vivos* accounts for a large part of the wealth transmitted from parents to children in wealth classes below the middle level. In practice, many household sample surveys concerning the amount of inherited bequests in the USA indicate that the amount of bequests in the form of physical assets is almost zero for a majority of households. Conversely, it should be noted that just because no physical bequest is observed does not necessarily mean that the bequest motive is non-existent.

Correlation between Parents' Wealth and Children's Education: Reconsideration

As reasons for the dependence of the education received by children on the wealth of their parents' generation, besides both the non-negative physical bequest constraint and the minimum consumption constraint, already mentioned, we can cite also: (i) the effective borrowing constraint on the parents' generation due to the imperfection of capital markets; (ii) the demand for education as a consumption good as well as an investment good; and (iii) the relation of the shape of the educational effect curve to the wealth of the parents' generation. The first reason, the imperfection of capital markets, has already been discussed, in section 3.2. Human assets do not function as collateral for financial loans in the same way as tangible wealth. Therefore, when borrowing for the costs of children's education is necessary, the amount of borrowing is restricted by the value of the parents' tangible wealth as collateral. Of course, the borrowing restriction is relaxed by scholarships and educational loan systems run by educational and public financial institutions, the latter of which have been developed recently.

The second reason, the case in which education has the character of consumption goods, relates to the case in which education aims at the acquisition of non-economic abilities and the enrichment of the individual's value orientations and attitudes to life. The level of education chosen in this case may be excessive from the viewpoint purely of investment. That is, education is extended to the level at which the marginal utility of education itself just offsets the disutility from the reduction in the investment value (human assets).[22] Although the wealth transmission curve shifts downward due to the decrease in human assets, a large part of the downward shift is cancelled by a substitutional increase in physical assets bequeathed by parents (the substitution, of course, is not perfect). However, the weakened degree of wealth transmission does not mean the same situation in the lifetime utility term.

The third reason, which probably attracts empirical interest most frequently, is a relationship between parents' wealth and the educational effect curve. An important factor which makes the levels of education different among people is the differences in the efficiency with which much the same volume of inputs can be transformed into an increase in earning ability. As we have already discussed in sections 4.3 and 4.4, there are two different empirical views of the determinants of that efficiency: one emphasizes the role of the innate abilities of each individual (for example, cognitive ability measured by IQ tests); the other emphasizes the role of social and economic environments of the family bringing up each individual.

From the former standpoint, there is no direct causality in the observed positive correlation between parents' wealth (their income and occupations being proxy variables) and children's education, or in the positive correlation between parents' wealth and the elasticity (efficiency) of the educational effect behind the observed correlation; rather an apparent correlation is observed, which is produced by a hereditary process. The extreme form of the argument is as follows. Suppose that the elasticity of the educational effect curve (hereafter, the elasticity) is determined completely by heredity and that genotypes determining the elasticity are exactly inherited over generations. In addition, suppose that members of the initial generation possess the same value of physical assets (b_0). In that case, the wealth transmission curve in Figure 7.3 moves upwards for those with superior genotypes which make the elasticity greater. Therefore, after several generations, households with large amounts of physical

---

[22] The reason why human assets decrease while earnings in each period increase with the level of schooling is that the effect of the reduction in the working period by the extension of the period of education dominates the effect of the revenue increase which decelerates with the period of education.

assets necessarily have large elasticity (this argument can apply to patterns (A) or (B) in Figure 7.3). This means that the correlation between a household's wealth and its children's level of education is an apparent correlation made by genes through their history.

As we have already mentioned, it is confirmed that, to some extent, generic factors lie in the inheritance of IQ between generations. However, in the field of empirical research on the earning function, there is near-consensus that IQ factors themselves affect income or human asset values insignificantly except in the case of some special occupations such as managerial occupations. In other words, the influence of IQ factors on the elasticity of the educational effect remains possible only in very limited sorts of occupations. Therefore, the explanation that the correlation between children's education and their parental generation's wealth is largely an apparent correlation due to hereditary sources is not persuasive. It is quite possible that behind the correlation there are some direct causal relationships, discussed in sections 4.3 and 4.4.

When the elasticity of the educational effect directly relates to the parental generation's wealth (the sum of lifetime resources), the earning ability of the children's generation is an increasing function of the parental generation's wealth. Therefore, the wealth transmission curve in Figure 7.3 shifts upward with an increase in the parental generation's wealth. Eventually, a new wealth transmission curve is drawn by connecting points on the curves, which shift continuously. Figure 7.5 shows this relation (here, γ indicates the elasticity of the educational effect curve). For simplicity, in this figure we ignore all the effects of both the non-negative physical bequest constraint and the minimum consumption constraint (there cause kinks in the curves). The curve shown by

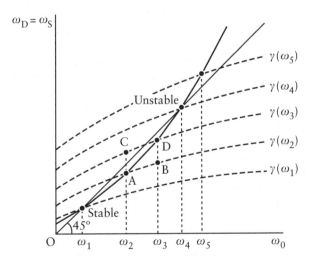

Figure 7.5. *The Wealth Transmission Curve When the Parental Generation's Wealth Affects the Elasticity of the Education Effect*

a bold solid line is the new wealth transmission curve. Specifically, as shown in the figure, when the correlation between the elasticity and the parental generation's wealth is sufficiently strong, even though there was originally a strong tendency to regress towards equilibrium with $\varepsilon < \mu$, it is possible that the slope of the wealth transmission curve may become steeper and there may be an unstable equilibrium which causes an expansion of wealth accumulation. On the other hand, even in the case of both $\varepsilon > \mu$ and $r > n$ where unstable equilibrium existed originally, the strong correlation between the elasticity and the parental generation's wealth causes the boundary of the unstable domain to shift downward. As a result, the correlation causes a greater possibility of division into two classes, depending on the initial generation's wealth holding: in one class both human and physical assets tend to regress towards the long-run equilibrium levels over generations; the other class accumulates both types of asset.

Concluding Remarks

The existence of a bequest does not itself necessarily explain large disparities in households' wealth which are larger than the size distribution of income. This is because when bequests exist we can still expect considerable regression of wealth towards its average in the passage of generations.

However, there is a situation in which large disparities in wealth holding arise through the intergenerational transmission of wealth. Where the bequest is a luxury, a household that acquires more than a certain critical amount of wealth tends to continue to accumulate wealth over generations. Even in cases where a bequest is not a luxury, if the correlation the between parents' wealth and the educational effect curve is strong, a household possessing more than a certain amount of wealth starts to accumulate wealth, since an increase in wealth itself improves the circumstance of wealth accumulation. As for the classes possessing less than a certain amount of wealth, on the other hand, there is the possibility of the vicious circle of poverty in which the insufficiency of the parents' wealth induces insufficient human assets for their children and this is transmitted further to future generations. One of these extremes or both are thought to give rise to large disparities in wealth holding which are not induced by differences in age or permanent income.

A statistical test of such hypotheses is not easy because of data limitations. In fact, there have been only few data analysed statistically, including those studied by Menchik and David (1983) mentioned earlier. As was explained in the previous discussion, Menchik and David showed that households can be divided into two classes: a majority belong to a class having small physical bequests and small elasticity to lifetime income; and a small number belong to the wealthy class characterized by large physical bequests and large elasticity.

Tomes (1981) aimed to examine the possibility of substitution between human and physical assets, in a study based on a sample survey in Cleveland

City in 1964–5, with data collected by interviewing households which inherited estates. Tomes shows that there is a statistically significant negative correlation between the amount of a physical bequest and children's income after controlling the estimated amount of the permanent income (a proxy variable for wealth) of their parents. That is, physical assets as a bequest have the role of compensating for differences in children's earning abilities. Based on the estimated result that the elasticity of the physical bequest to the estimated parents' permanent income is 1.7 when children's income is not controlled (that is, not included in the dependent variables) and is 0.8 when children's income is controlled, Tomes also argues that the existence of substitution between human and physical assets causes the strong tendency of regression towards the mean over generations in wealth holding (Tomes 1981: 947).[23] However, there are some qualifications to Tomes' result. First, the factor prescribing the degree of regression towards the mean in wealth holding should be the elasticity of bequests measured without controlling the children's income, which is different from Tomes' procedure. Comparing the four points A, B, C, and D in Figure 7.5 helps us understand this (let us assume that each transmission curve in the figure represents the average tendency among households and that many households with the same wealth level ω_0 are, in effect, distributed vertically around the curve). It should be noted that both children's levels of education and their income are the same between each pair of points, A and B, or C and D. As previously explained, the effect of parent's wealth is correctly estimated by comparing A and D. On the other hand, measurement when children's income is controlled corresponds to a comparison between A and B (or C and D). Therefore, if one says that the elasticity of the latter is less than unity, this means the original elasticity is under-valued. Thus, the above-mentioned value of elasticity, 1.7, is quite meaningful. This point makes the result consistent with those of Menchik and David (1983) and Adams (1980). Therefore, even though substitution between physical and human assets is observed, this is not the direct source of the strong tendency of regression towards the mean.

Second, from the same data set, Tomes simultaneously deduces the following two results: (i) if the estimated parents' permanent income is kept constant, the elasticity of physical bequests to children's income is negative (−1.92 or −0.74); (ii) an increase in the estimated parents' permanent income improves the children's income. The second fact corresponds exactly to a movement

---

[23] The estimation is done using Tobit or Heckman's two-step procedure, since the amount of the bequest is zero (strictly speaking, less than $500) for a little more than 40 per cent of the sample. The elasticity of the bequest to children's annual income and the elasticity to the estimated parents' income with children's income controlled are calculated from Table 2, equation 1 and Table 3, equation 5, and the elasticity without controlling of children's income is calculated from Table 2, equation 6 in the paper (all the values of elasticity are measured at the mean point of bequests in the sample). Parents' permanent income is estimated by matching corresponding data on the parents' attributes to the earning function estimated on the basis of the children's income. This is clearly a first approximation.

from A to D in Figure 7.5. With respect to this point, by analysing the same data, Adams shows a similar result, that the elasticity of the number of years of children's schooling to parents' income is 0.3–0.4 (Adams 1980: Table IV). Result (i) suggests a very strong substitution between human and physical assets as bequests. However, this is not necessarily consistent with other estimation results. If feature (i) is correct, it means that a household at point B in Figure 7.5 has human assets that are less than the average among those whose parents' permanent income is the same. Thus, from (i) we can say that a household at B must acquire more physical assets than households at D. However, this contradicts the above-mentioned result that the estimated elasticity of physical assets to parents' permanent income is greater when children's income is controlled than when it is not.[24]

Third, the evidence, found by Menchik and David (1983), that the elasticity of the bequest depends on the relative position of the household in wealth distribution and moreover the elasticity shows strong non-linearity, that is, it increases rapidly for the upper classes, suggests a possibility that the degree of substitution between human and physical assets may change largely in accordance with movements in the relative position of parents' wealth. However, Tomes' estimation equation is not formulated to detect such a non-linear effect.

Regardless of the qualifications mentioned above, Tomes' contribution should be valued from the viewpoint that he found that human assets make up a large share of transmitted wealth and, to some extent, have a substitutional relation to physical assets and thus that we should think about the intergenerational mobility of wealth as including human assets. Empirical research on intergenerational wealth transmission is a field where there are still many problems for future research to consider.

7.3. DETERMINATION OF THE RATE OF RETURN AND WEALTH DISTRIBUTION IN THE LONG RUN

The argument thus far has investigated the meaning of differences in households' behaviour to the generation of wealth and its distribution, with a macroeconomic factor price system as given. However, the prices of the labour force and capital and the rates of return on financial assets are also strongly related to wealth distribution. For this reason, in this section we broaden the object of our study to include macroeconomic market relations and investigate the determinants of long-run wealth distribution by considering how income distribution and the rate of return on assets are determined.

---

[24] The possible reasons for this inconsistency are the effect of measuring children's earnings abilities by their annual income, which fluctuates from time to time, and the effect of complicated interactions between the variable and other variables controlled simultaneously in the estimations. In addition, as Menchik and David point out, there remains the problem of the procedure for estimating the parents' permanent income.

The object of our analysis is a simplified aggregate economy which consists of three sectors: households, firms, and a bank-cum-monetary authority. We have already examined the behaviour of firms as investors in section 5.4, and thus we will focus this chapter's analysis on the point that the financial cost for firms or the rate of return for investors are determined through an interaction between financial devices for investment and households' preferences with regard to the composition of wealth. The determination of the rate of return means the determination of a variable dealt with in the same way as throughout this book so far and concludes the framework of this book's analysis in a macroeconomic sense.

The macroeconomic model constructed below depends on Metzler's classical framework of analysis (Metzler 1951) with respect to the effect of the differences in money supply rules on interest rates. The bank-cum-monetary authority is an agent that supplies credit corresponding to the demand for investment finance and intended to stabilize prices. Credit is provided in the form of money supply by banks in exchange for securities (shares) newly issued by firms. Price control is assumed to be achieved by adjusting the quantity of money through the market operations for securities. Household wealth is defined as the sum of the value of money supplied in that way and the value of securities held by households. How the determinants of the rate of return and of the distribution of wealth holding are mutually related is another focus of the analysis. Before discussing wealth distribution, we must first define the structural differences that exist among households. Two possible types of household are allowed in advance. The first type is the 'working class', the members of which intend to acquire wealth for the security of themselves or their families. The second type is the 'wealth holder (capitalist) class', the members of which have property income as the main part of their wealth and pursue wealth accumulation itself. Although it is possible for these two classes to exist, they need not, of course, do so. Investigating what conditions determine whether the two classes are maintained or are reduced to a single class is also an important object of our analysis.

The Framework of an Aggregate Economy[25]

Let us consider an economy consisting of a firm sector, a household sector, and a banking sector. There are two types of financial wealth: money and shares,

---

[25] The model used in this section is based on Ishikawa (1980). The paper extends studies by Kaldor (1966), Moore (1975), and others, which deal with the financial aspect of capital accumulation, to the analysis of a macroeconomic general equilibrium system including stock variables, namely, money and shares. The model used in the paper is modified in this section in two respects. First, we assume that a household does not differentiate between the components of its income, real revenues and expected capital gains in each period, and saves both at the same rate. Second, the case of constant real wages is also considered, as an alternative assumption about the completion of the system. With regard to the first point, although our assumption in this section is logically more consistent with the hypothesis of rationality, many suspicions about this assumption have been presented, from the empirical viewpoint.

which are demanded by households. We ignore firms' demand for financial assets. We assume the same investment behaviour of firms as in section 5.4. As for labour supply, however, we assume for simplicity that all workers are homogeneous and do not need training.

The investment cost (measured in terms of products) needed in order to realize the growth rate g of a firm's capital equipment (K) is $\phi(g)K$. This cost includes the depreciation cost of capital. A firm finances part of the investment cost with retained earnings from current benefits (RK, where R represents the rate of profits), and the remaining part with newly issued shares. The corporate saving rate (s_f) is assumed to be constant. Thus, the amount of corporate retained earnings is $s_f RK$ and the amount of newly issued shares in real terms is $(\phi(g) - s_f R)K$.

The banking sector is an institution for the creation of credit and also carries out monetary policy. We assume that all the new shares issued by firms are first held by banks and then new money is supplied based on the shares. The bank-cum-monetary authority is assumed to adjust the amount of credit (money supply) so as to keep the price level constant through the selling and buying of shares in the asset market which opens at the beginning of each period.[26]

Next, we will explain the share market. Under the assumption that individuals have static expectations about the future movements of the rate of profits per unit of capital R and the rate of return on shares (r), the investment plan which maximizes the value of the representative firm is one which maintains a constant growth rate g ($g < r$) satisfying

$$\frac{R - \phi(g)}{r - g} = \phi'(g) \qquad (7.19)$$

after the current period (Uzawa 1969). The maximized (real) value of the firm (V) is represented by:

$$V = \phi'(g) \cdot K \qquad (7.20)$$

---

[26] Since this section is not concerned with inflation, the analysis is simplified by regarding the rate of the price increase as zero. In addition, the formulation of the financial market here follows the so-called beginning-of-the-period approach. That is, it is assumed that the balance-sheet constraint of stock variables, which is independent of the budget constraint of each period's flows of revenues and expenditures, is effective at the beginning of each period and that assets are exchanged at the beginning of the period. Therefore, money supply is not controlled through the adjustment of the amount of flows, or the acceptance of newly issued shares (i.e., ΔM), but through the open-market operations in the share market which opens at the beginning of the next period. The additional money supplied during the period is used for investment funds, then is distributed to households through the production process, and finally ends as the same amount of household saving. Therefore, there is no decision making by households with regard to the allocation of saving as that of the current period flows to money and shares and, if anything, the allocation is determined *ex post* when the asset composition is adjusted at the beginning of the next period. Such artificiality is a disadvantage of the approach. For a comparison of the beginning-of-the-period and the end-of-the-period approach, see Foley (1975).

with g which satisfies (7.19). Since investment is financed without borrowing, V equals the total value of shares in the firm. Furthermore, reflecting the increase in capital, 'the total value of the firm = the total value of shares' at the beginning of the next period is expected to increase at the same rate. Therefore

$$\Delta V^e = gV \tag{7.21}$$

is the expected increase in the total value of shares. This value is the sum of the value of newly issued shares and the expected capital gains of existing shares. Since the former is $(\phi(g) - s_f R)K$, the part made up of expected capital gains (denoted by G^e) is evaluated at:

$$G^e = \{\phi'(g) \cdot g - (\phi(g) - s_f R)\}K \equiv \{s_f R + \psi(g)\}K. \tag{7.22}$$

Let us call $\psi(g)K$ a 'growth premium', which reflects the growth of the firm. The growth premium generally takes a positive or a negative value and increases with the rate of capital growth g.

The rate of return on shares r is defined as the sum of the rate of return on dividends and that on expected capital gains. The fact that V equals the total value of shares and that $(1 - s_f)RK$ equals dividends, from (7.20) and (7.22) induce a relation:

$$r = \frac{(1 - s_f)R}{\phi'(g)} + \frac{\{s_f R + \psi(g)\}}{\phi'(g)}. \tag{7.23}$$

The fact that the expected capital gains equal the sum of retained earnings and the growth premium means that whether to receive the current period's profit as dividends or not is irrelevant from the viewpoint of an investor's returns. If we regard the left-hand side r as the rate of return required by investors in the market and the right-hand side as the rate of return in fact achieved by the firm, this equation indicates the arbitrage condition of the market investors. However, (7.23) is equivalent to (7.19). Thus, the optimal investment condition (7.19) is also satisfactory in its effect for share investors.

As for households, we suppose the possible existence of two classes, as mentioned before. One is the class which supplies labour and saves a constant fraction s_w of total income including wage revenues. We can regard it as the standard working class. Another is the wealth holder (capitalist) class which makes profits from assets for the majority of its revenues and has a much higher propensity to save than a working household. We suppose that this class does not work (much) at all.

Wealth is defined as the sum of the real value of money and shares held by households at the beginning of each period. How wealth is allocated between money and shares, that is, choice of portfolio, depends on the rate of return on shares r. The demand for the real money balance (M/p) is assumed to be formed as a constant ratio to wealth holding $l(r)$ $(l'(r) < 0)$. Furthermore, let us suppose that the portfolio choice behaviour of the two classes is identical. Hereafter, we denote the ratio of existing shares held by households to the total by λ and the ratio of those held by banks by $1 - \lambda$. In addition, we also denote the ratio of the existing shares held by the working class to those held by all households by λ_w and the ratio of those held by the wealth holder class by λ_c (thus, $\lambda = \lambda_w + \lambda_c$). Because of the identical portfolio choice behaviour of the two classes, a fraction (λ_w/λ) of the total amount of money is held by workers and a fraction (λ_c/λ) is held by wealth holders. Hence, working households' wealth (W_w) and wealth-holder households' wealth (W_c) are:

$$W_w = (\lambda_w/\lambda)\{m + \lambda\phi'(g)\}K \tag{7.24}$$

and

$$W_c = (\lambda_c/\lambda)\{m + \lambda\phi'(g)\}K \tag{7.25}$$

respectively, where m represents the real money balance per unit of capital (M/pK). The income of a household is defined as the sum of wages, dividends, and expected capital gains. In the banking sector, capital gains also appear corresponding to the amount of shares held in the sector. Since the bank-cum-monetary authority is a pure financial institution in character, it does not spend its income and all of its dividend income is assumed to be transferred to workers and wealth holders in proportion to their income. The ratio is $(1 - \pi + \lambda_w\pi): \lambda_c\pi$, where π represents the ratio of profits to products. The expected capital gains of shares held by banks is assumed to be transferred to each class in the same proportion as dividends. Then, income per unit of capital of working households and that of wealth-holder households are:

$$
\begin{aligned}
y_w = {} & \frac{1 - \pi}{\pi}R + \lambda_w\{(1 - s_f)R + (s_fR + \psi(g))\} \\
& + \frac{(1 - \pi(1 - \lambda_w))(1 - \lambda)}{1 - \pi + \lambda\pi}\{(1 - s_f)R + (s_fR + \psi(g))\}
\end{aligned}
\tag{7.26}
$$

and

$$
\begin{aligned}
y_c = {} & \lambda_c\{(1 - s_f)R + (s_fR + \psi(g))\} \\
& + \frac{\lambda_c\pi(1 - \lambda)}{1 - \pi + \lambda\pi}\{(1 - s_f)R + (s_fR + \psi(g))\}
\end{aligned}
\tag{7.27}
$$

respectively. The first, second, and third terms of workers' income (y_w) mean, respectively, wage income, dividends and expected capital gains, and the transfer of dividends and expected capital gains from the banking sector. Similarly, the first and second terms of wealth holders' income (y_c) mean, respectively, dividends and expected capital gains, and the transfer of these from the banking sector.

Steady-State Growth Equilibrium in the Aggregate Economy

In the aggregate economy characterized by the behaviours of firms, banks, and households as described above, equilibrium will obtain for each period of time in four markets: the product market, the money market, the share market, and the labour market. Those states are illustrated within the framework of the standard IS-LM analysis. As for the labour market, however, full-employment is not always attained. Real wages can be rigid for various reasons and there can be involuntary unemployment. The economy is growing continuously, owing to growth in the labour force (ΔN) and capital accumulation (ΔK).

In the following discussion, we focus on the long-run characteristics of this system, and we confine ourselves to the case where both capital and the employed labour force grow at a speed of g. When full employment is maintained, g equals the growth rate of the labour force (that is, the natural rate of growth), while the profit rate R and the share of profits π are determined in the same way as the marginal productivity hypothesis describes. On the other hand, when the real wage rate is exogenously given, R and π are determined first, and thereafter g is determined endogenously. Therefore, depending on which phase obtains, either R or g is exogenously given.

Steady-state equilibrium requires five conditions: (i) an equilibrium of the product market for each period; (ii) an equilibrium of the money market for each period; (iii) a condition of equality between the optimal investment rate of firms and the steady-state growth rate; (iv) a condition of equality between the supplemental demand for money due to growth and the supply of newly issued money; and (v) stability of distribution of wealth between workers and wealth holders.

Since our definition of income includes expected capital gains, we can replace condition (i) by a condition: Saving = Investment + Expected Capital Gains.[27] In steady-state growth, actual capital gains are equal to expected capital gains.

---

[27] This question is derived as follows.
Using the definition of saving:

Saving $\equiv$ Income – Consumption,

we get:

Demand for products = Consumption + Investment = (Income – Saving) + Investment.

On the other hand, since

Income $\equiv$ Production (Supply of Products) + Expected Capital Gains,

a condition, Demand for Products = Production (Supply of Products), is equivalent to:

Saving = Investment + Expected Capital Gains.

Thus, by using (7.26) and (7.27), the condition is again represented by:

$$s_w \left\{ \frac{1-\pi}{\pi} R + \frac{\lambda_w + (1-\lambda)(1-\pi)}{1-\pi+\lambda\pi} \{R+\psi(g)\} \right\} + s_c \frac{\lambda_c}{1-\pi+\lambda\pi} \{R+\psi(g)\}$$
$$= \phi(g) + \psi(g). \tag{7.28}$$

(The expression is per unit of capital and this is applied to the remaining part.) Note that corporate savings ($s_f R$) on both sides offset each other.

The equilibrium condition of the money market (ii) is, by using the definition of the wealth of each class, represented by:

$$l(r)\{m + \lambda\phi'(g)\} = m. \tag{7.29}$$

This simple expression depends on the assumption that the portfolio behaviour of each class is identical. By rewriting the investment decision criterion of firms (7.19) or (7.23), condition (iii) is given as:

$$r\phi'(g) = R + \psi(g). \tag{7.30}$$

By considering the condition that the creation of credit equals the newly issued corporate shares each period, condition (iv) can be expressed by:

$$\phi(g) - s_f R = g \cdot m. \tag{7.31}$$

The right-hand side is the supplemental demand for money, which makes up for the depreciation of money due to economic growth.

Condition (v) requires that the wealth accumulation rate of workers and that of wealth holders ($\Delta W_w/W_w$ and $\Delta W_c/W_c$, respectively) are the same. The newly accumulated values of the wealth of each class are the first and second terms of the left-hand side of (7.28). By calculating the ratios of these values to (7.24) or (7.25), condition (v) is rewritten as:

$$\frac{s_w}{\lambda_w} \left\{ \frac{1-\pi}{\pi} R + \frac{\lambda_w + (1-\lambda)(1-\pi)}{1-\pi+\lambda\pi} \{R+\psi(g)\} \right\}$$
$$= \frac{s_c}{1-\pi+\lambda\pi} \{R+\psi(g)\}. \tag{7.32}$$

By these five equations, the unknown five variables, r, m, λ, and λ_w, as well as either R or g, are determined. What we are interested in are the determinants of the rate of return on corporate shares r, the state of wealth distribution between workers and wealth holders shown by the ratio λ_w/λ, and the determinants of g when g is endogenous.

The Pasinetti Theorem

Condition (v), that the distribution of wealth between the two classes is stationary when the income of one class comes only from assets, gives rise to an interesting property called the Pasinetti Theorem (Pasinetti (1962)). That is, the rate of return, factor prices, and factor shares (r, w, R, π) under conditions of full employment; or the rate of return and the rate of growth of the system under conditions of unemployment, are independent of the saving rate of workers (s_w) and their share of wealth holding (λ_w).

An important logical step in order for this theorem to hold is the property that the rate of household saving in a whole economy is independent of both the rate of saving of workers and their share of wealth holding. It is not so difficult to understand why such a property holds. That is, since assets are the only income source for wealth holders, the growth rate of wealth is independent of their current share of wealth λ_c; and thus, in an economy where workers and wealth holders accumulate wealth at the same rate, workers' saving (= workers' accumulation of wealth) is equal to the amount of saving which wealth holders would generate if workers gave up their entire wealth to wealth holders. Therefore, the sum of the savings of the two classes, which is aggregate household saving, equals the saving which wealth holders would generate if they possessed all the wealth. After all, household saving is determined as the income from assets (direct and indirect dividends and capital gains) multiplied by the rate of saving of wealth holders.

In fact, multiplying each side of equation (7.32) by λ_w and then substituting its right-hand side for the first term of the left-hand side of (7.28), we rewrite the equilibrium condition of the product market as:

$$\frac{s_c \lambda}{1 - \pi + \lambda \pi}\{R + \psi(g)\} = \phi(g) + \psi(g), \tag{7.33}$$

which does not include s_w or λ_w at all. Other equilibrium conditions of the macroeconomic system, (7.29), (7.30), and (7.31), have neither s_w nor λ_w, reflecting the assumption of common portfolio behaviour on the part of workers and wealth holders. Thus, we can verify that neither s_w nor λ_w influences the determination of the rate of return, the rate of profit, or the share of profit in a system where the natural rate of growth is given. In the same way, when the rate of return and the rate of growth of the system are determined, and the share of profit is given, both s_w and λ_w are independent of the determination of these endogenous variables.

After all, the rate of saving of workers only influences the determination of the share of wealth of workers and wealth holders. In fact, the ratio of workers' wealth to total wealth held by private (non-banking) sectors is given by:[28]

$$\frac{\lambda_w}{\lambda} = \frac{s_w}{s_c - s_w} \frac{s_c\{R + \pi \cdot \psi(g)\} - \pi\{\phi(g) + \psi(g)\}}{\pi\{\phi(g) + \psi(g)\}}. \tag{7.34}$$

---

[28] Solving (7.33) with respect to λ, we get:

$$\lambda = \frac{(1 - \pi)(\phi(g) + \psi(g))}{s_c(R + \psi(g)) - \pi(\phi(g) + \psi(g))}. \tag{7.33'}$$

It is clear that this ratio becomes larger as the workers' rate of saving grows larger.

However, this theorem is obviously limited in its application. Workers cannot have more wealth than the wealth of the whole private sector. Naturally, when the workers' rate of saving is larger by a certain amount than that of wealth holders, workers possess the entire private wealth ($\lambda_w/\lambda = 1$) and wealth holders are virtually banished from the economy. That means the economy ends up with only a single class (see Appendix 7.1, mathematical note 7).

Full-Employment Steady-State Growth Equilibrium with Two Classes

Let us call an economy to which the Pasinetti Theorem is applied a two-class economy. Next, we will investigate the property of the growth equilibrium of an economy where two classes exist and full employment is attained. The natural rate of growth g is given.

Figure 7.6 illustrates how the rate of return r is determined in such an economy. The horizontal axis indicates the ratio of the real money balance to the stock of private share holding ($m/\lambda\phi'(g)$) and the vertical axis indicates the rate of return (r). The curve Z^D corresponds to (7.29) and shows the values of ($m/\lambda\phi'$) which equilibrate the money market for any given r. It also implies the relative size of demand for money to that for shares. It is downward sloping and its shape depends on households' liquidity preference function l. On the other hand, Z^S is the relationship between $m/\lambda\phi'$ and r derived from the combination of (7.30), (7.31), and (7.33). It implies the relative size of supply of money to that of shares in the long run. Its slope is indeterminate.[29] However, for the stability of the rate of return in the long run, r has to increase whenever Z^D is

Putting (7.33') into (7.32), workers' share of equity is:

$$\lambda_w = \frac{s_w}{s_c - s_w} \frac{1 - \pi}{R + \psi(g)} \left\{ \frac{R}{\pi} + \frac{s_c\{R + \psi(g)\} - \{\phi(g) + \psi(g)\}}{s_c\{R + \psi(g)\} - \pi\{\phi(g) + \psi(g)\}} \psi(g) \right\}. \tag{F.1}$$

The ratio of this (7.33') leads to (7.34) in the text.

Incidentally, as is clear from the text, an important assumption for the Pasinetti Theorem is the existence of a single wealth-holder class. It does not matter if the working class has multiple subgroups with different wage incomes and saving rates, in which case s_w in the text is to be interpreted as a (weighted) average within the working class. Also it may be added that explanation of the Pasinetti Theorem in the text modifies both the confusing discussion of Kaldor (1966) (especially in his appendix) and the negative view of Davidson (1972), in a system that includes financial assets like money and shares.

[29] The curve Z^D is drawn as:

$$\frac{m}{\lambda\phi'(g)} = \frac{l(r)}{1 - l(r)}.$$

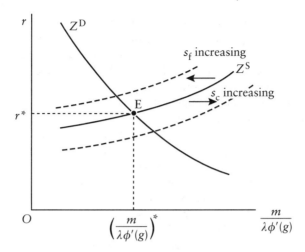

Figure 7.6. *Determination of Two-Sector Steady-State Growth Equilibrium and Rate of Return*

larger than Z^S and decrease whenever Z^D is smaller than Z^S. Therefore, the Z^S curve should intersect Z^D from below.

In the following discussion, we assume that the long-run stability condition of the rate of return holds. An increase in the corporate retained earnings ratio, s_f, shifts the Z^S curve to the left and an increase in wealth holders' rate of saving, s_c, shifts the curve to the right. The rate of return in the steady-state growth equilibrium is determined by the intersection E of the two curves.

The steady-state growth equilibrium of the two-class economy has the following comparative statistic properties. First, the rate of return is actually what Metzler called the money rate of interest, and all the factors altering the money supply relate to the determination of the rate of return, r. On the other hand, since there is a one-to-one correspondence by arbitrage (7.30) between the rate of return on shares, r, and the rate of profits, R, monetary factors also affect the factor shares. The main factor affecting the money supply is firms' retained

On the other hand, from (7.31) and (7.33′),

$$\frac{m}{\lambda\phi'(g)} = \frac{(\phi(g) - s_f R)\{s_c(R + \psi(g)) - \pi(\phi(g)) + \psi(g))\}}{(1 - \pi)(\phi(g) + \psi(g))^2} \tag{F.2}$$

is derived. Noting that π in the right-hand side is a function R and that R is again a function of r through (7.30), another curve regarding r comes up. This the curve Z^S. It is obvious that the Z^S curve shifts leftward when s_f goes up and rightward when s_c goes up, while it is not determinate in which direction the Z^S curve shifts with the change in the given natural rate of growth g, since the relationship between R, π, and r does not stay as it was.

Also in the case of unemployment, which is dealt with later in the text, a similar Z^S curve is drawn, by starting from (F.2) and keeping R and π unchanged, and noting that g is a function of r through (7.30). Shifts of the curve due to s_f and s_c are also similar.

earning ratio, s_f. An increase in the retained earnings ratio, s_f, suppresses banks' credit supply and thus makes the household sector's demand for money excessive relatively to money supply. Therefore the rate of return on shares, r, rises and so does the rate of profits, R. A rise in R has the effect of raising the share of the wealth of the working class relative to that of the wealth-holder class. (See Appendix 7.1, mathematical note 7.) Thus, corporate saving participates in the determination of factor prices and the shares of wealth in the long run, even when it has no macroeconomic effect within each period.

Second, real forces also, of course, participate in the determination of the rate of return. A rise in the rate of saving of wealth holders, s_c, as long as the rate of profits, R, does not change, should be compensated by a drop in the ratio of shares held by the private sector (λ) to maintain the same amount of savings (see (7.34)). Then a larger portion of shares is absorbed by the banking sector and money supply becomes excessive, relative to demand. Therefore, a downward pressure works on the rate of return on shares and eventually both the rate of return, r, and the rate of profit, R, go down. As for the distribution of wealth between the working class and the wealth-holder class, a rise in the rate of saving of wealth holders raises the share of wealth holding of wealth holders, directly and indirectly (through a drop in R). A rise in the natural rate of growth, g, is usually expected to raise both the rate of return, r, and the rate of profit, R, but the direction of the effect is not necessarily shown unambiguously because of the intervention of monetary factors.[30]

Third, as we have already seen, a rise in workers' rate of saving has no effect on the rate of return and factor prices. It only raises the workers' share of wealth holding relative to that of wealth holders.

Full-Employment Steady-State Growth Equilibrium with Single Class

Workers' share of wealth holding, λ_w/λ, will equal unity when the amount of saving which workers would generate if they possessed the whole private wealth sector just equals the amount of saving which wealth holders would

---

[30] In the original Pasinetti Theorem, the rate of profit, R (the rate of return, r), is determined from:

$$R = \frac{g}{s_c},$$

which means that they do not depend on anything but the rate of growth and the saving rate of wealth holders. It is rewritten for the world described in this section from (7.33) as:

$$r = \left(\frac{g}{s_c}\right) \Big/ \left(\lambda + \frac{\lambda\pi(1-\lambda)}{1-\pi+\lambda\pi}\right).$$

Since monetary factors as well as real factors participate in determining λ and π, the original Pasinetti Theorem's strong proposition about the rate of return does not hold.

generate if they possessed the same wealth. That is, when:

$$s_c(R + \psi(g))\lambda K = s_w^*(1 - \pi + \lambda\pi)(Q + \psi(g)K) \quad (7.35)$$

holds; where s_w^* denotes the value of workers' rate of saving which realizes $\lambda_w/\lambda = 1$, and Q denotes output.[31] When workers' rate of saving, s_w exceeds s_w^*, there are virtually only workers in the economy. In that case, the equilibrium condition of the product market (7.28) comes to be represented by:

$$s_w \left\{ \frac{R}{\pi} + \psi(g) \right\} = \phi(g) + \psi(g). \quad (7.36)$$

This is exactly the same as the neo-classical steady-state growth equilibrium condition except that it includes the term about capital gains.[32]

The single-class economy has very different properties from the two-class one. First, the rate of return is the real rate of return. This is clear because (7.36) by itself determines the rate of profit, R. A rise in the natural rate of growth, g, brings about a rise in R, and a rise in s_w, a drop in R. The rate of return on shares, r, varies in the same direction with R, owing to the arbitrage

---

[31] When the workers' saving rate equals s_w^*, which is the critical saving rate defined in the text, (7.33) and (7.34) still hold. Assuming the left-hand side of (7.34) to be unity and solving as to s_w^*, we obtain:

$$s_w^* = \frac{\phi(g) + \psi(g)}{((R/\pi) + \psi)}. \quad (F.3)$$

This expression is equivalent to:

$$(\phi(g) + \psi(g))K = s_w^*(Q + \psi(g)K).$$

This is the case where workers can finance, directly or indirectly, the exact amount of investment that the system needs. Also putting (F.3) into (7.33), we obtain:

$$s_w^* = s_c \frac{R + \psi}{R + \pi\psi} \frac{\lambda\pi}{1 - \pi + \lambda\pi} \quad (F.4)$$

It is easy to see that (F.4) is equivalent to (7.35) in the text. (F.3) and (F.4), two expressions of the critical value s_w^* which is the boundary between the one-class and the two-class world, is an extension of the Samuelson and Modigliani (1966) critical value of the saving rate in an economy with only real capital:

$$s_w^* = g \cdot \frac{\pi}{R} = s_c \cdot \pi. \quad (F.5)$$

[32] The economy whose interest rate is determined by the equality between investment and saving is what the loanable fund theory assumes. However, our model in this section has a market of stock variables, but not a loanable fund market. The rate of return is adjusted nowhere else than in the market of asset stocks. This equation simply means that the adjustment of the rate of return each period is finished only when the rate of return called at the asset market equals the value of the rate of return guaranteeing the equilibrium of the product market.

relationship (7.30). (At the level of r thus determined, the Z^S curve is horizontal.) Second, the corporate saving rate just participates in the determination of the relative supply of the real money balance to real capital stock (m) and plays only a minimal macroeconomic role. The money market does nothing but determine the ratio of private share holding consistent with both r and m, which have been already determined.

Steady-State Growth Equilibrium with Involuntary Unemployment

In section 5.5, we discussed the possibility of two long-run equilibria; one is an equilibrium where efficient wages are obtained and involuntary unemployment persists, the other is one where competitive wages obtain and full employment is achieved. The discussion can be extended to a growth economy where the population grows at the natural rate and capital is accumulated.[33] In the following discussion, we adopt the efficiency wage hypothesis as the prototype and look into the determination of the rate of return and the distribution of wealth when real wages are determined at the level of optimum incentive wages.

Once real wages are determined, the determination of the rate of profit, R, and the share of profit, π, follows. Therefore, the macroeconomic system of (7.29)–(7.31) and (7.33) is to determine r, m, and λ, and the rate of growth of the system, g. From (7.30), we know that an increase in either the rate of return, r, or the rate of growth, g, decreases the other. Since the rate of profit, R, is given, investment is suppressed when the rate of return which the market requires (r) goes up.

In a phase where two classes exist, all four variables are simultaneously determined. Just as in the case of full employment examined before, the rate of profit has the properties of the money rate of interest, the level of which is determined by the intersection of the Z^D and Z^S curves drawn as in Figure 7.6. The comparative-static properties of the steady-state growth equilibrium, with the assumption of the long-run stability of the money market, are very similar to those in the full-employment case. The only difference is that the effects that came via a change in the rate of profit, R, now come via that of the growth rate, g. For example, a rise in the corporate retained earnings ratio (s_f) pushes the rate of return, r, up and pushes g down, for the same reason as in the

---

[33] Suppose the production per unit of capital is expressed as the product of the labour–capital ratio ($n = N/K$) and the efficiency of labour, i. Corporate profits for each period are:

$$\Pi = K\{f(i(w)n) - wn\}.$$

For each period, since K is given, the firm's choice of wage rate and the volume of employment are independent of capital, K, already accumulated. Thus it is easy to extend the efficiency wage hypothesis to the world of steady-state growth.

full-employment case. A drop in g raises the workers' share of wealth (λ_w/λ). A rise in the wealth holders' saving rate (s_c) also lowers the rate of return for the same reason as in the full-employment case, and thus the growth rate, g, increases. The increase in the growth rate, by magnifying the expansive effect on differences in the saving rates, raises the workers' share of wealth. (See Appendix 7.1, mathematical note 7.)

Also for the steady-state growth equilibrium with a single working class, by exchanging the roles of g and R, we find that its comparative-static properties are almost the same as those of the full-employment case. The equilibrium condition of the product market (7.36) by itself determines the rate of growth. It has a classical aspect, in that the rate of growth goes up as the rate of saving becomes higher. The rate of return, r, is settled so that it is compatible with the rate of growth, g, determined as above and the given profit rate, R. It is a totally real rate of return. The real supply of money, m, and the ratio of private share holding, λ, are entirely passively determined. The corporate saving rate plays no macroeconomic role except to determine the real supply of money.

What should be considered is the gap between the endogenously determined growth rate and the natural rate of growth. First, when the former exceeds the latter, the economy is certain to hit the ceiling of full employment sooner or later. It is true that there are cases where the natural rate of growth itself is virtually raised so that the gap is filled; this may occur through such factors as labour-saving technological innovations, reorganization of the female and senior members of the labour force and the introduction of an immigrant labour force. Second, when the latter exceeds the former, the unemployment rate increases without limit. In that case, it is inevitable that some drastic adjustments of economic structure should be carried out.

Wealth Distribution Within a Class

So far we have looked into the determinants of the macroeconomic distribution of wealth. We can also refer to some general properties regarding the distribution of wealth within each class. Those properties are unrelated to and independent of all of the phases, that is, either full employment or involuntary unemployment, is attained.

First, within the working class, as long as the saving rate and wage incomes are identical among households, the differences in initial wealth holding are dissolved as time passes and wealth holding moves towards perfect equalization. In order to confirm this point, suppose that there are two types of household, namely, those with large wealth holdings and those with small wealth holdings, at the initial point of time. Although each household's asset income is proportionate to its level of wealth, these households' wage incomes (strictly speaking, income consists of wage income and transfer income which is allocated as wages from the dividends and capital gains of the bank-cum-monetary authority) are the same. Thus, the ratio of current saving to the existing wealth holdings, that is, the rate of growth of wealth, is always higher for the households with small wealth holdings than for those with large wealth holdings. Thus, a force to equalize the size of wealth holdings works all the time. This is the point that Stiglitz (1969) made. The cause of persisting inequalities of wealth among workers is either differences in rates of return or rates of saving, or differences in wage incomes. On the other hand, if there is not a sharp difference in the rates of return or rates of saving, the level of wealth of each working household is proportionate to its (permanent) wage income, which differs among households. Therefore, equalization of permanent wage incomes naturally brings about equalization of the distribution of wealth.

Second, when the wealth holder class exists, there is no wealth-equalization tendency, such as that which exists among workers. This is because, as long as the rate of return and the rate of saving are the same among households, the rate of growth of wealth is independent of its level and thus the initial differences in wealth holdings remains, permanently.

The Long-Run Distribution of Wealth in a Whole Economy

As we saw above, there is a large difference between the working class and the wealth-holder class in that regression towards the mean in relation to wealth works within the former, but not within the latter. Therefore, wealth distribution among households is very much affected by whether the aggregate economy generates a single-class equilibrium or a two-class one. In the former case, there is regression towards the mean in relation to the distribution of wealth, except as regards the part of wealth that is due to differences in permanent incomes. After all, a problem about equalization of wealth results in a problem about equalization of incomes. In the latter case, in contrast, since there is no tendency of regression towards the mean within the wealth-holder class originally characterized by large wealth holdings, the long-run distribution of wealth as a whole has a thick tail for the lower ranks and is spread thinly over the upper ranks (that is, it is positively skewed). In particular, it is more skewed than the distribution of earned income. This corresponds to the characteristics of wealth distribution observed in reality.

The discussion so far has limited application to the real economy, since we have assumed that households last indefinitely. If we take into account the fact that the life of a household is finite, the process of wealth growth can stop well before sufficient equalization is achieved, even if the level of wealth and its rate of growth are conversely correlated.[34] In that case, what is important is how and to what extent earning ability and parental wealth can be

---

[34] The fact that life is finite is an equalizing force, in the sense that it restricts the range of wealth distribution, in the phase of stochastic dispersions in wealth holding caused by uncertainty is the rate of return (see section 7.4). Therefore it is not accurate to emphasize its function of limiting the equalizing force.

transmitted to children. If sufficient redistribution of earning ability and wealth occurs, another tendency of equalization, independent of the above intra-generation equalization, is generated. These topics were discussed in section 7.2.

Summary and Concluding Remarks

In this section, we have discussed how the rate of return on assets and the factor prices of labour and capital are determined, by constructing an aggregate equilibrium growth model which incorporates household saving, corporate investment/saving, and the banking sector's money supply behaviour. If we consider the dual labour market hypothesis, we find that there can be two kinds of steady-state growth equilibrium: an equilibrium with full employment and one with involuntary unemployment. In the former, the rate of return of the system and the rate of growth are simultaneously determined so as to be consistent with the real wage rate socially determined; in the latter case, the rate of return of the system and the rate of profit are simultaneously determined so as to generate the rate of investment that attains the natural rate of growth.

Our model deviated from the standard macroeconomic model in that we incorporated the existence of households with different saving motives. That is, in addition to ordinary working households, we introduced wealth-holder households which accumulate wealth for its own sake, and in whose wealth income from assets accounts for a dominant part. However, it is not self-evident that such a class may infact be observed in an economy. Since workers save also from wave income which makes up a large share of total output, it is possible that the rate of accumulation of workers' saving is greater than that of wealth holders, even though the workers' saving rate is small. In this case, the whole economy consists, in the long run, only of workers. The neo-classical world which consists of homogeneous households which work and save is exactly that case. In the steady-state growth equilibrium with a single working class, the rate of return is what Metzler called the real rate of return. This conclusion does not depend on whether full employment is realized or not in the labour market.

On the other hand, there is a growth equilibrium where the wealth-holder class is visible. Moreover, as is known from the Pasinetti Theorem, the rate of return of the system is independent of the workers' saving rate. There is still more. As we showed as an extension of the Pasinetti Theorem, the rate of return is what Metzler called the money rate of return in the steady-state growth equilibrium with two classes: both wealth holders and workers. Therefore, the pattern of households' preferences for assets and the way in which investment finance functions as the base of the money supply help to determine the rate of return and factor prices. In particular, a rise in the corporate retained earnings ratio, by weakening the need for bank credit, brings about a relative decrease in money supply and raises the rate of return on assets. It also changes the share of wealth of workers and wealth holders in a favourable direction for workers. Therefore, even if corporate saving has a one-to-one substitutional relationship to household saving in each period, it has a significant influence on the aggregate economy in the long run.

Therefore, it makes a great difference to the system, in macroeconomic terms, whether the economy has two classes, including wealth holders, or just one class. On the other hand, whether full employment is realized or not, may generate a difference in endogenous variables of the system; that is, the rate of profit is endogenous in the former and the rate of growth in the latter. However, it is irrelevant whether the rate of return is monetary or real. Whether the system has one or two classes depends, to begin with, on the factors which would determine the rate of return in a two-class world, together with the difference between the saving rate of workers and that of wealth holders. This is because a rise in the corporate saving rate, which has an increasing effect on the rate of return, raises workers' share of wealth holding.

The distinction between the economy with a single class and that with two classes also brings about a peculiar difference in the transition of wealth distribution among (individual) households. In an economy consisting only of workers, wealth distribution shows an equalizing trend over time, as long as there is little difference among individual households' saving rates. Eventually, wealth distribution where the wealth of each household is proportionate to its (permanent) wage income will be brought about. In a two-class economy, a similar equalizing trend works within the working class, but not within the wealth-holder class. Partly because of this lack of regression towards the mean in the upper class, wealth distribution is far more skewed than income.

Whether the economy has one class or two is an entirely empirical question. It is true that there are actual problems such as how to draw a clear dividing line between the two classes or what kind of argument should be applied to the phases of steady-state growth equilibrium. However, it gives us a useful standpoint for comparing different times in an economy and for comparing national economies.

When we look at post-war Japanese financial wealth distribution among households, for which data are available for a long period, we find that equalization took place in the rapid growth era of the 1960s and that unequalization seems to have taken over from the late 1970s to the late 1980s. (See footnote 7 in section 1.2.) It is as if the Japanese economy was wandering from a two-class world to a one-class one and back to a two-class world. Such a change is thought to be mainly due to a sharp rise in workers' saving rate during the rapid growth era and its moderate decline since the 1970s. (Remember (7.34).) In these days when we are moving towards a rapid ageing of the population, whether the workers' saving rate will continue to go down or not is unclear since it depends on changes in such matters as the public pension system, job opportunities for senior people, and the care of older people. However, we can still say that it is hard to expect the saving rate to go back to the high level of the first half of the 1970s.[35] Therefore, it seems that, unless other conditions change significantly, we can never exclude the possibility that the Japanese economy may revert to a two-class economy.

On the other hand, we have already seen (in section 1.2) that there are serious inequalities of wealth among households in the USA and the UK. This, together with the low saving rate of workers in these countries, seems to illustrate the typical two-class world discussed in this section. Future research will be needed to provide quantitative results to substantiate the argument derived from this impression.

7.4. THE FLUCTUATION OF ASSET PRICES AND THE DISTRIBUTION OF INFORMATIONAL POWER

That distribution of wealth changes greatly in quite a short period of time has been demonstrated eloquently by a contemporary (1985–7) episode of soaring land prices in the Japanese economy. Such a rapid change in wealth ownership far exceeds the normal annual flow of savings out of disposable income. In order to understand the change in household wealth ownership, it is clearly not sufficient to understand just the behaviour on savings.[36]

Investigation of the effects of changes in asset prices on the distribution of wealth requires consideration of not only why prices change, but also how much of the price change is foreseen by individuals. In fact, both the magnitude and the timing of price change and the distribution among individuals of capital gains thereby accrued differ greatly depending on whether all individuals foresee the price rise or such foresight is either entirely non-existent or limited to a tiny group of individuals.

In the former case, the current price rises immediately, and the value of the initial endowment rises fully and uniformly. There will be no above-market average rate of return to the *ex-post* owner. In the latter case, the current price is not much affected, and the prospective capital gains will accrue to *ex-post* holders, in particular, with a greater weight to wealth holders having superior foresight. Such arguments are not without their opponents, however. Those

---

[35] See Horioka (1990) for a comprehensive review of empirical research on the time-series transition of the Japanese household saving rate and reasons why the saving rate is higher than those of other countries.

[36] Thurow (1975: ch. 6) stresses the importance of the short-run formation of large wealth due to capital gains. His argument is an attempt to explain the largely skewed wealth distribution by the existence of both the positively skewed stochastic distribution of price changes and the wealth-preserving behaviour of individuals who acquire large wealth at a single time. For this he relies on the random walk hypothesis on the basis of the efficient capital market hypothesis (mentioned later). Our theme in this section is to critically scrutinize such an assertion. We introduce the concept of informational power and describe its role. Figlewski (1978) is an earlier study along similar lines. However, there are inconsistencies in the assumptions behind the argument of that study (explained later in footnote 44) and there is no accurate definition of the expectational equilibrium where a market exerts the largest function of information aggregation. The following description also aims to correct that analysis.

who disagree pose the efficient capital market hypothesis, which argues that, because people learn other people's information rapidly through the level of current price, the current price will itself reflect whatever superior information is available in the market, leaving no rent left for people who originally had the superior information.

This section uses the corporate stock market as representative of the asset market and formulates an extended version of the efficient capital market model, with allowance for disparity in informational quality among individuals. On the basis of such a framework it discusses the circumstances under which disparity in informational quality becomes an effective actor in determining wealth distribution.

The Stock Market and the Causes of Large Fluctuations in Stock Prices

There is little question that the modern market economy achieved enormous expansion of production by succeeding in separating the managerial effort of searching for and realizing good productive opportunities from the effort to suitably finance the projects. Prerequisites for success in the former certainly include originality, capacity for innovation, and incessant effort towards improvement on the part of managers, while success in the latter rests on the capacity for appropriately judging the risk as well as agility and resoluteness on the part of investors. Needless to say, in both cases actual success depends much on good luck.

It is the stock market which has been most instrumental in separating these two types of effort. It is at the same time recognized that the very conditions that enable the separation to take place allow room for abrupt and large fluctuations in stock prices. An important characteristic of the productive investment opportunity is that the economic benefits of new knowledge brought about by innovative and managerial effort do not dissipate quickly, as it requires a fair amount of time for others to assimilate the new knowledge and put it into imitative operation.

In contrast, the new information about the productive opportunity of a firm immediately affects the stock price of that firm as forces to equalize the rate of return on investment operate powerfully in the financial market. Furthermore, since new opportunities for innovation arise as stochastic events, stock price fluctuations naturally become stochastic events. Borrowing Thurow's (1975: 149) expression, people who happen to buy stocks immediately before the new knowledge is capitalized in the market become successful.

The foregoing discussion suggests the first and most important source of a stock price change; namely, a foreseen change in the future stream of dividends as fruits of firm activity.

Second, recalling that stocks can be bought and sold freely in the futures market, the stock price can alternatively be looked upon as reflecting the expected price that will prevail in the market tomorrow. A possibility then arises that an expected future stock price once somehow diverted from the present value of predicted dividend streams cumulatively and yet self-fulfillingly keeps rising. Such a movement in expected and current prices, because it satisfies investors' period-by-period arbitrage condition, is called a 'rational bubble'.[37] The most significant characteristics of the movement of the bubble are that it is a social-psychological matter encompassing all investors, and it is not possible to predict when it starts, nor when it terminates.

There is also another type of bandwagon phenomenon called an 'irrational bubble' (Shiller 1984), which brings about a cumulative movement in the stock price (irrespective of how illogical this is). Like a rational bubble, when it arises and when it ends is entirely unpredictable. In any case, these social-psychological elements certainly operate as the second major source of stock price fluctuations.

Third, acute fluctuations in stock prices can occur purely as a monetary phenomenon. Such is the case when the market interest rate as the rate of discount of future dividends varies without much accompanying change in the general price level.[38] Thus, for instance, if money supply is increased in a closed

---

[37] Let us denote the stock price in the current period (period t) by p; dividends paid at the end of the current period by $E(d_t \mid I_t)$ and the expected stock price on the next period by $E(p_{t+1} \mid I_t)$, both of which are based on given information; and the rate of discount (including a risk premium) by r. Then the arbitrage condition among assets realized the relation:

$$p_t = \frac{E(d_t \mid I_t)}{1+r} + \frac{E(p_{t+1} \mid I_t)}{1+r}. \tag{F.6}$$

Since this arbitrage condition is expected to be realized in each future period, we can generate a first-order difference equation with respect to expectation by using the law of the iterated expectation. The problem is how to establish the initial condition. If

$$\left(\frac{1}{1+r}\right)^n E(p_{t+n} \mid I_t) \to 0 \tag{F.7}$$

is satisfied with $t \to \infty$, the current stock price can be acquired as the sum of the present value of predicted dividend streams. This corresponds to the so-called fundamental solution. However, there is no a priori guarantee of (F.7). Generally, the sum of the fundamental solution and, e.g., any c_t satisfying

$$c_t = \frac{1}{1+r} E(c_{t+1} \mid I_t) \tag{F.8}$$

is also a solution of (F.6). The above term is called a rational bubble. (The term 'rational' is used because the equation satisfies the each-period arbitrage condition.) From (F.8), we find that the bubble is explosive. In fact, when a price progresses along the path satisfying (F.8), the bubble expands self-fulfillingly and cumulatively. We can obtain a possibility of sudden collapse of the bubble at any time, by modifying (F.8) and introducing a pure stochastic death process (in this case, the rate of discount increases, reflecting the death probability).

[38] And more generally, when the real interest rate varies. In addition, when investors have risk-averse preferences, the risk premium may vary due to variation of the preferences. See an empirical

economy with surplus production capacity, the interest rate will fall, the demand for stocks that are imperfect substitutes for bonds will increase, and the stock prices are expected to rise instantaneously. Under such a circumstance, the value of the initial endowment in stocks *ceteris paribus* rises uniformly, and a large disparity in wealth holding is created between those who own stocks and those who do not.[39]

The Distribution of Informational Power

One of the key elements to success or failure in stock investment is the ability to evaluate precisely how much return each asset generates and the quality of information used in making the evaluation. (The two are believed to be positively correlated.) In the following discussion, the combination of the quality of information and the ability to evaluate the information is called informational power. Informational power is considered to be a major factor in generating various fund management institutions, for example, trust and mutual funds. Individuals with superior informational power can achieve higher rates of return than ordinary individuals and at the same time succeed in reducing uncertainty. Therefore, differences in informational power are likely to affect greatly the distribution of wealth.

In the field of corporate finance, there exists a persistent opposition to the aforementioned view. According to Fama's (1970) assessment, the market is capable of getting all the information of individual investors reflected in current stock prices, and hence, the rate of returns individual investors obtain (on average) does not depend on the amount of informational power. Such a view is termed the efficient capital market hypothesis. This hypothesis implies, after all, that differences in informational power are unrelated to the distribution of wealth. Financial institutions that specialize in fund management are, according to this view, no more than mere fiduciaries making transactions on behalf of individual investors. Which viewpoint is the correct one?

---

study by Grossman and Shiller (1981) for the former factor and one by Poterba and Summers (1986) for the latter factor. Ueda (1990) tests the latter factor in Japan.

[39] Takayama *et al.* (1989) and Tachibanaki (1989) describe in detail how the huge capital gains that accrued to households who happened to hold stocks or land in the capital and metropolitan area have caused large inequalities in wealth distribution from 1985 to 1987 in Japan. Why were such phenomena as well as huge capital gains in aggregate levels generated at that time? A possible explanation is that increases in the money supply due to macroeconomic factors in that period brought about surpluses of domestic funds and induced the speculative demand for land and stocks. In the same period, the UK experienced the same changes in the asset prices of lands and stocks, though the size of the changes was smaller than of those in Japan. This fact suggests a high possibility that correlations between international macroeconomic and financial policies had been working. A result of a study by Asako, Kanoh, and Sano (1990) strongly indicates the possibility of the bubble phenomenon. In addition, other non-macroeconomic factors such as distortions of tax system were possibly also operating.

An Extended Grossman Model

Grossman (1976) has contributed to formulating rigorously the idea of an efficient capital market, whose theoretical structure had not been necessarily clear. While Grossman himself formulated the model under the assumption that each investor's information is of homogeneous quality (that is, only the content of information differs), his formulation will be extended here to cope with the circumstance that the quality of individuals' information is different; some have superior informational power, while others have poorer informational power. At the same time, Grossman's assumption that investors have a constant absolute degree of risk aversion will be replaced by what is sometimes argued is a more realistic assumption, that of a constant relative degree of risk aversion (Friend and Blume 1975). This last assumption allows individuals' demand for risky assets to depend on the amount of their wealth.

Consider a stock market with two periods. Investors are assumed to choose between a safe asset with a fixed rate of interest r and a corporate stock whose rate of return is uncertain. The demand for corporate stocks occurs as a result of individual choice. Rate r is supposed to be given exogenously. The return on corporate stocks is assumed to be generated purely in terms of capital gains or losses. Thus by denoting the stock price of period 1 (the current period) by P_0, and the stock price of period 2 (the future period) by P_1, the rate of return, denoted by r_s, is defined as:

$$r_s = \frac{P_1 - P_0}{P_0}. \tag{7.37}$$

Since the current price (P_0) is observable in the market, uncertainty in the rate of return (r_s) is equivalent to uncertainty in the future price (P_1). In what follows the model is worked out primarily in terms of the variable P_1, yet it is worth remembering that the model can be switched at any time to one with the rate of return as the primary variable. The following assumptions will be made concerning the movement of P_1. There exists an objective probability distribution defined over P_1 with density $g(P_1)$, which follows a normal distribution with mean $\underline{P}_1$ and variance σ^2. All market participants know such to be the case. Nature is supposed to select the true value out of this distribution.[40] In the current period individuals cannot know the true value, but can obtain some relevant information (a prediction) which centres around the true value.

The quality of information is defined by the average size of the error from a true value. Suppose that there are n investors, and that each investor gets information of different quality. The indicator of information y_i $(i = 1, 2, \ldots, n)$

---

[40] An alternative assumption is that $g(P_1)$ is a posterior distribution from the Bayesian viewpoint and each agent has the same posterior distribution. The following argument would not be changed by the alternative assumption.

is assumed to take the form:

$$y_i = P_1 + \varepsilon_i, \tag{7.38}$$

where ε_i follows a normal distribution with mean 0 and variance σ_i^2. The expectational errors of each individual, $\varepsilon_i, \varepsilon_j$, are assumed to be mutually independent.

The specification made here amounts to saying that every piece of information satisfies the criterion of lack of bias, and yet disparity in individuals' informational power exists and is expressed by the difference in the size of variance of the expectational error. The extent of disparity in informational power among individuals is normalized to satisfy:

$$\frac{1}{n}\sum_{i=1}^{n}\frac{1}{\sigma_i^2} = 1, \tag{7.39}$$

that is, the harmonic mean of the variance of expectational error over n individuals is unity. As long as n is finite this means that differences in informational power are also finite, which, in turn, implies that no one is able to know the true future price beforehand. (The case when this supposition does not hold is discussed at the end of this chapter.) Each individual has his or her own initial endowment of wealth.[41] Denote the sum of wealth owned by all individuals by W_0 and each individual's share by w_i ($\sum w_i = 1$). Also denote the amount of investment in safe assets by B and the amount of investment in stocks by X. Then each individual's budget constraint becomes:

$$P_0 X_i + B_i = w_i W_0. \tag{7.40}$$

On the other hand, the level of wealth in the next period, denoted by W_{1i}, becomes:

$$W_{1i} = (1 + r)B_i + P_1 X_i. \tag{7.41}$$

Since P_1 is stochastic, W_{1i} also becomes a stochastic variable. Each investor is supposed to maximize the expected utility of W_{1i}.

Assuming that the degree of relative risk aversion is constant, which is denoted by c_i (> 0), the demand for stocks is determined as:

$$X_i = \frac{E(P_1 \mid I_i) - (1 + r)P_0}{c_i \text{Var}(P_1 \mid I_i)} \cdot \{w_i W_0\}, \tag{7.42}$$

where I_i represents the individual i's information set in forming the expectation of P_1. Thus, the demand for stocks is proportional to the expected return

---

[41] Although it is naturally desirable to consider each initial amount of safe asset holding and stock holding, here we consider the initial holding as the amount of money, for simplicity.

premium obtainable per unit holding of a risky asset over that of a riskless asset. It is also proportional to the reciprocal of the degree of relative risk aversion as well as to the magnitude of risk itself.[42] The content of I_i is specified subsequently.

Finally, let the total supply of stocks be given and be denoted by $\underline{X}_0$. Then the market determines the current stock price P_0 such that

$$\sum_{i=1}^{n} \frac{E(P_1 \mid I_i) - (1+r)P_0}{c_i \text{Var}(P_1 \mid I_i)} \cdot w_i = \frac{X_0}{W_0} \tag{7.43}$$

is satisfied.[43]

The foregoing is the general framework of the stock market whose properties we consider subsequently. The future stock price P_1 represents the value of an equity over the final return (both the dividend and the principal) to investment to be paid at the end of period 1, and P_0 represents the current evaluation of such an equity. This model is still unrealistic in that it does not deal with the stock of the firm as a going concern, but it does illuminate sharply how the stock market aggregates individual investors' information, which is our concern here.

Market Equilibrium with Individual Information

When each individual's expectation of P_1 is based totally on his or her own information, that is, when $I_i = \{y_i\}$, the outcome of investment depends on the difference in the quality of information that each individual has. In fact, using Bayes's Theorem, the posterior probability distribution of P_1 upon observing y_i becomes a normal distribution with:

$$E(P_1 \mid y_i) = \frac{1}{1 + \theta_i \sigma^2} \underline{P}_1 + \frac{\theta_i \sigma^2}{1 + \theta_i \sigma^2} y_i, \tag{7.44}$$

$$\text{Var}(P_1 \mid y_i) = \frac{1}{1 + \theta_i \sigma^2} \sigma^2, \tag{7.45}$$

---

[42] (7.42) is derived in a standard manner. This can be done by representing W_{1i} in terms of $w_i W_0$ by using (7.40) and (7.41); by taking Taylor expansion of $U(W_{1i})$ around $w_i W_0$ to get the second-order approximation; and taking the limit value of its expectation. The first-order condition is (7.42). Note that the probability distribution about P_1 depends on the corresponding individual's information.

[43] An equivalent representation in terms of the rate of return is:

$$\sum_{i=1}^{n} \frac{E(r_S \mid I_i) - r}{c_i \text{Var}(r_S \mid I_i)} \cdot w_i = \frac{P_0 X_0}{W_0}.$$

where $\theta_i = 1/\sigma_i^2$ expresses the level of the quality of information or the level of informational power. Quite naturally, the higher the quality of information, the more weight an individual places upon his or her own information in forming an expectation of P_1, and the smaller will be the degree of uncertainty as expressed by the posterior variance. By substituting (7.44) and (7.45) into the market equilibrium condition (7.43) and after rearrangement, the current market price P_0 is determined as:

$$P_0 = \frac{P_1 \sum_{i=1}^{n} (w_i/c_i) - \sigma^2 \underline{X}_0/W_0}{(1+r)\sum_{i=1}^{n}(w_i/c_i)(1+\theta_i\sigma^2)} + \frac{\sigma^2 \sum_{i=1}^{n}(w_i/c_i)\theta_i y_i}{(1+r)\sum_{i=1}^{n}(w_i/c_i)(1+\theta_i\sigma^2)},$$

(7.46)

which is seen to aggregate each individual's information with weights that are proportional to the individual's level of informational power and to the individual's share as well as to the reciprocal of the degree of risk aversion.

What advantages, then, do individuals with large informational power have relative to those with small informational power?

First, note that the expected future price as formed by (7.44) on average understates the true price P_1 when P_1 is greater than $\underline{P}_1$ (that is, its distributional mean), while, on average, it overestimates P_1 when P_1 is less than $\underline{P}_1$. Now the extent of understatement or overstatement is, again on average, the smaller, the larger the informational power (see Appendix 7.1, mathematical note 8). Hence, individuals with larger informational power duly invest more when the future price is expected to be on the high side, and invest less when it is expected to be on the low side, as compared with individuals with smaller informational power. In this way informationally powerful individuals get more returns over time from stock market investment.

Second, the posterior risk of investment as expressed by (7.45) is the smaller, the larger is the informational power. Hence informationally powerful individuals *ceteris paribus* invest more heavily in stocks.

Informationally powerful individuals thus on average outperform the market. Quite naturally, therefore, these individuals' share in the total stock holding and, in turn, their share in the total wealth holding become larger than those of the less informationally powerful individuals.

Needless to say, however, because the market price of stock is stochastically determined, movement in the distribution of wealth is not expected to be monotonic. In so far as the stock market is opened repeatedly, informationally powerful individuals will put more and more wealth into the stock market, resulting in larger absolute amounts of fluctuation in their wealth. Hence, there is no necessity that the highest θ_i individuals will eventually hold all the wealth in the economy (that is, that $w_i \to 1$). It would be an interesting task to work out the full outcome of the dynamic process, but such a task will not be taken here.[44] Instead, we next examine the criticism that the expectation forming mechanism discussed above is overly naïve.

Informational Learning through Prices and the Efficient Capital Market Hypothesis

If individuals come to understand the structure of the stock market such that the current market price aggregates the information of all individuals in the manner described by (7.46), then they can each start learning other individuals' information through the ongoing market price. In particular, individuals with relatively small informational power realize that they had better learn as much as possible from other individuals' information that is reflected in the market price. Not only that. Even individuals with large informational power should find it beneficial to incorporate some of other individuals' information since other individuals are getting independent information on their own. In this way, all individuals, though differing in terms of the weight they accord to their own information, are ready to learn from other individuals' expectations through the market price.

Such behaviour on the part of individuals is certain to destroy the initial equilibrium (7.46) before actual transactions take place, and a new *tâtonnement* process should begin. The events that follow are characterized by three points.

First, in the initial stage of the reopened *tâtonnement* process, the extent of other individuals' information (as revealed through the current price) that is taken into account is proportional to the reciprocal of his or her quality of information. Hence, the new market clearing price will be based on each individual's demand that more appropriately incorporates other individuals' information. In other words, there is a definite improvement in the manner with which the market price aggregates individuals' information. On the other hand, the intrinsic informational advantage that informationally more powerful individuals have enjoyed is weakened and the degree to which they learn from the newly announced price increases. Similarly, informationally less powerful individuals will take the newly announced price even more seriously as the new price is richer in informational content than the previous one. In this way, each individual's demand is revised again, and the new market clearing price is sought.

In sum, the new *tâtonnement* process is nothing but a process, for any one, of diluting the intake of one's own information. It continues until eventually the

---

[44] Figlewski (1978) approximates such a dynamic process by a Markov process and indicates there is a solution where the expectation takes a stationary value between zero and unity as well as a case where the share of wealth of individuals with superior informational power comes to unity. However, his analysis has a fault. That is, both individuals with superior informational power and those with inferior informational power are assumed to use the same historical risk as the value of the risk of stocks ($\mathrm{Var}(P_1 \mid I_i)$ in the denominator of (7.42)) and this means the assumption of the differences in informational power, which is settled first, is not effectively used.

weight of relying on one's own information vanishes completely. Consequently, differences in the informational power of individuals have no effect whatsoever on the outcome of the ultimate equilibrium. The effective disappearance of disparity in informational power among individuals is a property that could not have arisen in the original Grossman model where individuals' information is of the same quality.

Second, the initial market price (7.46) aggregates each individual's information by according weight not only in terms of the individual's quality of information, but also in terms of the individual's share of wealth holding as well as the reciprocal of the degree of risk aversion. Thus, for instance, if an individual has a negligible share of the total wealth, his or her information, no matter how superior its quality might be, has at most a negligible effect on the market price. In other words, for any given distribution of informational power and risk attitudes there is a clear dollar voting feature.

We must note, however, that the size of wealth holding and the preference about risk in themselves have nothing to do with the quality of an individual's information. And, in fact, our *tâtonnement* process (after the initial equilibrium is established) can also be regarded as a process that dilutes the effect of those factors that are not related to the quality of information *per se*, and that separates them out from the function of aggregating information. Such a feature does not occur in the original Grossman model where the constancy of absolute risk aversion is assumed and, therefore, an individual's demand for stocks is always independent of his or her wealth level.

Can we then eschew the dollar voting feature in the final equilibrium? The answer is a refined yes. Recall the first point discussed above. It has already been pointed out that in the final stage of the *tâtonnement* process each individual's intrinsic information has no role to play in determining the level of demand for stocks, so that differences in the quality of information among individuals are effectively dissolved. The outcome of this is that the ratio of the expected return premium over risk (as expressed by the numerator and denominator of (7.42)) becomes common over all individuals. Hence, in the market equilibrium condition (7.43) (stating that the total market demand for stocks defined by the sum of the ratio in question multiplied by the reciprocal of the degree of risk aversion and by the share of wealth holding equals the supply) the distribution of wealth among individuals has a role only to determine the average degree (to be precise, the weighted harmonic mean) of risk aversion in the market. Consequently, whatever effect remains of the distribution of wealth on the current market price is completely separated from the information-aggregating role of the market price. In the special case where everyone's degree of risk aversion is the same, the distribution of wealth has literally no effect whatsoever on the market equilibrium.

Third, as a corollary to the above two points, the economic advantage that informationally powerful individuals have had in the initial equilibrium vanishes completely. No one can permanently outperform the market. The same applies to the fund management institutions that are supposed to possess specially accumulated knowledge.

The feature of the ultimate market equilibrium under the new expectational assumption is now specified rigorously. The statement that individuals' multifarious information can be aggregated efficiently is equivalent to a property in statistical theory to the effect that there exists a sufficient statistic for any sample vector $\{y_1, \ldots, y_n\}$ over the unknown parameter, the true price level P_1. In addition, the market efficiency means that the current market clearing price P_0 reveals the sufficient statistic of P_1 thereby defined. From a one-dimensional index such as price individuals can only secure one-dimensional information. However, if the latter is a sufficient statistic, each individual's own information, y_i, contains no further information. The price then reflects literally all information owned by individuals. The market equilibrium referred to here involves a certain price level such that it not only clears the market, but also reveals the sufficient statistic on the basis of which individuals decide their behaviour, and still more, such a price level is supported by the individuals' own behaviour. In other words, the market equilibrium is not simply an equilibrium, but also a self-fulfilling expectational equilibrium (hereafter simply referred to as an expectational equilibrium).

It is possible to show that there indeed exists a sufficient statistic for P_1 with the aforementioned property. In fact, it is a weighted average of each individual's information with the level of each individual's informational power used as a weight. Thus, denoting the sufficient statistic for the unknown parameter P_1 by $\bar{x}$ and taking note of the fact that $\sum \theta_i = n$, the variable is defined as (see Appendix 7.1, mathematical note 9):

$$\bar{x} = \frac{1}{n} \sum_{i=1}^{n} \theta_i y_i. \tag{7.47}$$

This statistic agrees exactly with the predictor that would have been chosen by a universal planner had he or she observed the entire vector of individual information $(y_1, \ldots, y_n)$ and chosen the predictor by the criterion of minimizing the sum of expected squared errors.[45] One of the extraordinary properties that

---

[45] Let us represent the individual's predictor by:

$$t = \sum_{i=1}^{n} \alpha_i y_i.$$

Individuals are assumed to choose $\{\alpha_i\}$ to minimize the sum of expected squared errors, $E\{(t - P_1)^2 \mid (y_1, y_2, \ldots, y_n)\}$. That is, the optimization problem is represented by:

$$\text{Min } E\left\{ \left(\sum_{i=1}^{n} \alpha_i y_i - P_1 \right)^2 \,\middle|\, (y_1, y_2, \ldots, y_n) \right\} \quad \text{s.t.} \quad \sum_{i=1}^{n} \alpha_i = 1.$$

the expectational equilibrium of the market has is that it aggregates each individual's information in a socially optimum manner. The term 'efficient aggregation' of information therefore has the connotation of not only summarizing different information comprehensively in a single index, but also aggregating information with socially optimum weights.

We have just asserted that as a result of the *tâtonnement* process individuals' diverse information is aggregated with the quality of information as a weight, and that ultimately an expectational equilibrium is reached whereby everyone comes to know the value of the sufficient statistic. In order for such an equilibrium to be realized, however, there must be a one-to-one correspondence, mathematically a monotonic functional relationship, between the current market price P_0 and the sufficient statistic $\bar{x}$, and furthermore, that every individual knows the precise structure of the correspondence. Needless to say, it is only through the current price that individuals acquire knowledge of $\bar{x}$. A different economic meaning is attached to each direction of this correspondence, from P_0 to $\bar{x}$, and from $\bar{x}$ to P_0. The former signifies the relationship that individuals can infer $\bar{x}$ on the basis of the observed price, while the latter signifies the relationship that the price obtained is a market equilibrium price based on the knowledge of $\bar{x}$. The expectational equilibrium of the market is achieved if and only if the process starting from a particular price P_0 reveals the sufficient statistic $\bar{x}$ of P_1 for the observed information $(y_1, \ldots, y_n)$, and furthermore, this $\bar{x}$ returns the original P_0 as the market clearing price. Note that when the market is said to establish an expectational equilibrium it does not mean that such P_0 exists for some particular $\bar{x}$, but rather it means that such P_0 exists for an arbitrary level of $\bar{x}$. This is the reason why an expectational equilibrium is associated with a functional relation between $\bar{x}$ and P_0. Call this relationship the equilibrium price schedule.

Suppose that such an equilibrium price schedule exists and that individuals are aware of the form of that schedule. Individuals thus perceive $\bar{x}$ by observing the current price P_0. Then the mean and variance of the distribution of P_1 after $\bar{x}$ is observed become respectively (using the fact that $\bar{x}$ is a sufficient statistic—see Appendix 7.1, mathematical note 10):

$$E(P_1 \mid \bar{x}) = \frac{P_1 + n\sigma^2 \bar{x}}{1 + n\sigma^2} \qquad (7.48)$$

By (7.38) and the independence of each individual's informational errors, the objective function results in:

$$E\left\{\left(\sum_{i=1}^{n} \alpha_i \varepsilon_i\right)^2\right\} = \sum_{i=1}^{n} \alpha_i^2 \sigma_i^2.$$

It is evident that the optimal weight is:

$$\alpha_i = \frac{1}{n\sigma_i^2} = \frac{\theta_i}{n}.$$

and

$$\text{Var}(P_1 \,|\, \bar{x}) = \frac{\sigma^2}{1 + n\sigma^2}. \tag{7.49}$$

Because of the assumed existence of the equilibrium price schedule the enlarged information set of each individual, $I_i = \{y_i, P_0\}$, is reduced to a set containing a single element, $\bar{x}$, only. Therefore, by substituting (7.48) and (7.49) into (7.43) with I_i replaced by $\bar{x}$, the market equilibrium price P_0 for any given $\bar{x}$ is determined by:

$$\sum_{i=1}^{n} \left(\frac{w_i}{c_i} \right) \frac{((\underline{P}_1 + n\sigma^2 \bar{x})/(1 + n\sigma^2)) - (1 + r)P_0}{\sigma^2/(1 + n\sigma^2)} = \frac{X_0}{W_0}. \tag{7.50}$$

By solving this equation with respect to P_0,

$$P_0 = \frac{\underline{P}_1 \cdot \sum_{i=1}^{n} (w_i/c_i) - \sigma^2 (X_0/W_0)}{(1 + r)(1 + n\sigma^2) \sum_{i=1}^{n} (w_i/c_i)} + \frac{n\sigma^2}{(1 + r)(1 + n\sigma^2)} \bar{x}. \tag{7.51}$$

Thus the market equilibrium price, P_0, is expressed as a linear and increasing function of $\bar{x}$. Conversely, so long as individuals infer $\bar{x}$ from P_0 on the basis of (7.51) using the assumed knowledge of the structural parameters,

$$I_s = \{n, \underline{P}_1, \sigma^2, W_0, \underline{X}_0, Z(w_i/c_i)\},$$

an expectational equilibrium is established for any given $\bar{x}$. Hence, (7.51) is simply the equilibrium price schedule of our stock market. Thus, by showing that such a schedule can indeed by constructed we have logically established the existence of an equilibrium price schedule which had initially been introduced as an assumption.

The main proposition of the efficient capital market hypothesis is that the process of market adjustment is so swift that the expectational equilibrium discussed here is established within each market day. If the market equilibrium (7.46) based purely on individual information and the expectational equilibrium (7.51) are regarded as two polar cases, then the reality must lie somewhere in between. Yet, as we have indicated earlier, the type of knowledge required for investors in the stock market is normally quite different from the type of knowledge required for managers. Since it is more stylized and more limited in structure (as the term 'risk class' might suggest), it can reasonably be expected that speedy learning might actually take place. Hence, the case can be made that the reality is much closer to the expectational equilibrium. It is to be noted, however, that the extraordinary properties characteristic of the expectational equilibrium hold only in the strict circumstance of the expectational equilibrium. In fact, if the process of informational learning is not completed within a single market day, then the proposition of the irrelevance of informational power in determining the rate of return no longer holds.

The Random Walk Hypothesis for Stock Prices

The above model is limited in that it is a two-period model, and therefore, it is not possible to use it to discuss how wealth distribution changes over time. However, by supposing that the gross return earned at the end of period 1 is ploughed back repeatedly into the stock market we can make a fair approximation to the real-world situation. In fact, we have already used the term 'on average' several times in the foregoing discussion, implicitly referring to a situation where investments are made repeatedly within the same framework.

In the following discussion, the efficient capital market hypothesis is assumed to hold strictly. By substituting (7.48) into (7.51) and using the facts that $E(P_1 | \bar{x}) = E(P_1 | P_0)$ and $\text{Var}(P_1 | \bar{x}) = \text{Var}(P_1 | P_0)$, we can derive a relationship between the expectational equilibrium price, P_0, and the future price, P_1, such that:

$$E(P_1 \mid P_0) = (1 + r)P_0 + \frac{\sigma^2 \underline{X}_0 / W_0}{(1 + r)(1 + n\sigma^2) \sum_{i=1}^{n} (w_i/c_i)} \qquad (7.52)$$

and

$$\text{Var}(P_1 \mid P_0) = \frac{\sigma^2}{1 + n\sigma^2}. \qquad (7.53)$$

That is, the expected value of P_1 equals P_0 multiplied by the gross rate of return on a riskless asset plus a certain risk premium. Needless to say, this expected value is common to all investors in the market. The distribution of individual wealth share (w_i) affects the risk premium component by determining the average degree of risk aversion in the market. Yet, in the special case where the degree of risk aversion is the same among all investors there will be no effect whatsoever. Furthermore, the larger the initial endowment of total wealth, W_0, and the smaller $\underline{X}_0$ is, the less (*ceteris paribus*) will be the risk premium component. The variance of P_1 is seen to be independent of the level of P_0.

We note that (7.52) corresponds to the proposition that in a fully anticipated market the movement of a stock price (to be precise, price/$(1 + r)$) follows a random walk. That the stock price moves randomly had been noted widely (Cootner 1964), but it was Samuelson (1965, 1973) who proved it to be the logical outcome to rational expectations. When investors are risk averse, the movement is no longer a strict random walk, yet nonetheless it can be approximately regarded as such (LeRoy 1973).

The above formulae verify this point within a two-period setting. Indeed, whereas there is a tendency for the risk premium component to decline over time, the first terms on the right-hand side of (7.52) and (7.53), which are in common with the expressions of the strict random walk hypothesis, never disappear. Translating this point to the real-world situation where many different stocks of a similar nature (that is, of the same risk class as represented by σ) exist, there is no regression towards the mean in the movement of wealth holding among investors, and the dispersion in wealth distribution increases over time.

Reservations with Regard to the Efficient Capital Market Hypothesis

We have several reservations with respect to the efficient capital market hypothesis explained above.

First, the assumption that there exists only a finite quantity (n) of information in the market is an important constraint of the model. If n increases without limit, it is clear from (7.49) that uncertainty of return is dissolved (by the law of large numbers), and the stock is reduced to a safe asset. However, this should not invite so much distrust of the model as it might at first appear to do, for some individuals might be looking at exactly the same indicator as others. In such a case, individuals with a common source of information can be regarded as a single group. Of course, each group can further be divided into sub-groups depending on differences in the individuals' capacity to evaluate the same information. In any case, the market can realistically be viewed as consisting of a certain number of different informational groups.

Second, what happens if the assumption, that disparity of informational power among investors is finite as implied by the normalization formula (7.39), does not hold, and if a particular investor can foresee the future price perfectly (that is, for a certain k, $\theta_k \to \infty$)? In such a case, the privileged individual would seek to obtain unlimited rent through either the buying (borrowing the funds if necessary) or the short-selling of stocks. In the end, the market price will come to an equilibrium at the level just sufficient to obtain the rate of return equalling that of a safe asset. This result holds no matter whether other investors read or do not read information from the current price (cf. (7.46)). Ultimately, in so far as actual transactions are conducted after full arbitraging activity takes place, there will be no excess return for investors with perfect information. If these investors could ever obtain excess profits, such a circumstance would occur only when there are certain imperfections in the market. For instance, (i) because of limitations in the amount of borrowing or short-selling, these investors' demands do not occupy any visible share in the entire stock market; (ii) when these investors deliberately conceal their information and restrict their demands in the market, and (iii) the actual transaction takes place simultaneously with adjustment of the market, that is, the stock market is a non-*tâtonnement* process.

Third, if there is uncertainty about the supply of stock so that the volume of total supply, $\underline{X}_0$, is not directly observable in the current market, then the current price becomes at most an aggregator of information about the future price and volume of supply, but generally not a sufficient statistic for the future price. Therefore, the expectational equilibrium discussed above never occurs (Grossman 1976: 583, Bray 1981: 591). However, in reality we may not have to worry very much about the circumstances in which the value of stock is unobservable.

Fourth, and more fundamentally, there is an element of public good involved in each individual's information. If the collection of information is costly, then there arises an incentive on the part of each investor to freeride on others' information, resulting in a dissolution of the expectational equilibrium. This, however, does not mean that a new equilibrium is arrived at with no one collecting any information at all, for it is always possible for anyone to profit by collecting information, even at cost, when no one else does so. However, as the number of individuals behaving similarly increases, those who have not collected their own information learn through the observed price, resulting in a decrease in the profits of those who collected the information. The final expectational equilibrium where there is an information cost would be such that each individual becomes indifferent as to whether he or she collects or does not collect his or her own information. This is the point discussed by Grossman and Stiglitz (1980). There arises a disparity in the *ex-post* rate of return (on average) on stocks, but such disparity is entirely explicable by means of the principle of equalizing difference.

Fifth, even if it is possible to ignore the cost of collecting information itself, we may still imagine, in a world with heterogeneous informational power, that individuals can incur investment costs in order to improve the quality of information (which is similar to human investment). Recall that we have assumed all along that informational power is exogenously given. Then a point exactly analogous to the previous one holds. That is, even if it is possible to improve one's informational power, each individual would seek to freeride on other individuals' superior informational power. In the efficient capital market not only individual information but also the quality as well as the evaluation capacity of information become a public good. However, if indeed this were the case, then it would seem hard to justify the flourishing of news media discussing the market or heavy investment in information collection on the part of institutional investors. This point is at least evidence that the efficient capital market does not hold perfectly.

Sixth, and finally, the knowledge of I_S, the set of structural parameters, which individuals must have, seems to be rather a heavy requirement to impose on individuals. In particular, it is not obvious how in a decentralized market economy other individuals' attributes, such as the number of groups (n) having different informational power and the average degree of risk aversion (weighted by the share of wealth) ($\sum(w_i/c_i)$), would be known to individuals.

Furthermore, the required knowledge does not stop there. As we have already seen, in the course of the *tâtonnement* process towards the expectational equilibrium each individual must know how his or her informational power fares in comparison with that of the average investor in the market.

Summary and Conclusion

We summarize the points made so far and contrast them with related empirical works. In an economy where ownership and control are separated via a stock market, changes in the opportunity for profit and production-related innovation in knowledge often induce a large change in the equity value of the firm. Huge capital gains then accrue to investors who happen to own such stocks. Such capital gains and entrepreneurial innovation are the two principal means by which large wealth is created in quite a short period of time. Speculative activities in land, real estate, and commodity stocks have analogous features to investment activity in the stock market. It is the capital gains of corporate stocks that we have focused on in this section.

The major cause of the occurrence of huge capital gains in a short period of time, apart from macroscopic real interest rate changes or the social-psychological reason of speculative bubbles, is that whereas the facilities and organization of production lack malleability so that it takes time for them to adapt to new knowledge, in the stock market the force of arbitrage operates immediately to equalize the rate of return over alternative assets.

Furthermore, it has been noted via experience that fluctuations in the stock price or the rate of return tend to deviate from the normal distribution in the sense that the distribution is positively skewed, has a large kurtosis (having wide tails at both ends), and large positive shocks occur relatively more frequently than negative ones (Mandelbrot 1963, and Fama 1976: ch. 1). In other words, relatively large increases in price, which ought not to happen so often, occur fairly frequently.[46]

In sum, a primary source of fluctuation in stock returns is the uncertainty of the movement of the environment for the firm. This does not mean, however, that there is no information that suggests how the firm would look in the future.

---

[46] For the fact that daily stock prices (or the rates of return) have the property mentioned in the text, see Fama (1976: ch. 1):

> if daily returns are drawn from normal distributions, for any stock a daily return greater than four standard deviations from the mean is expected about once every 50 days. Daily (stock) returns this extreme are observed about four times every five years. Similarly, under the hypothesis of normality, for any given stock a daily return more than five standard deviations from the mean daily returns should be observed about once every 7,000 years. Such observations seem to occur about every three to four years. (Fama 1976: 21.)

Almost the same property can be applied to monthly rates of return. Mandelbrot (1963) asserts that a family of stationery Pareto distributions can explain such properties as kurtosis and skewed distribution and that the family satisfies conditions of additivity such that both daily returns and

On the contrary, such information exists and is, to a certain degree, incorporated in the current market price of the stock.

This feature raises an interesting issue in the explanation of wealth distribution. If people differ in their quality of information about the future environment of the firm and also differ in their capacity to evaluate the given information (we have called the combination of these two factors informational power), then do people with superior informational power have an advantage in obtaining higher investment returns over people with poorer informational power? We have investigated this query by extending Grossman's (1976) model of the stock market to the case where individuals' informational power differs. The following conclusions resulted from the analysis.

So long as each individual's investment behaviour depends on individually obtained information, higher returns result on average to individuals with superior informational power. An exception to such a result is the case where some individuals have perfect information, that is, know the true future price, and where the market permits indefinite arbitrage to take place. Such individuals, if they wish to obtain higher returns, should, however, be content with secretive rent seeking.

It is, however, conceivable that individuals learn other individuals' information through the current market price. As the demand for stocks is revised each time new information is read from the current price, the process of market clearing is revived until finally the market incorporates into its current price every individual's information according to the weights determined by each individual's informational power. We have called such an equilibrium an expectational equilibrium. The efficient capital market hypothesis argues that in reality such an expectational equilibrium is established within each market day. Under such a circumstance, disparity in individual informational power is made completely irrelevant.

If the investment behaviour based on individual information is regarded as one extreme and that premised on the efficient capital market hypothesis as another, the way in which the dynamics of wealth accumulation evolve among individuals becomes naturally different. In the former case, investors with superior informational power achieve relatively high yields on investment, and hence may come to swamp the market in the long run. Shiller (1984: 463–4) once argued that even if there is on average a difference of 2 or 3 per cent annually between smart investors and ordinary investors, such a difference should not create enormous differences in accumulated wealth over a single

monthly returns belong to the same family of distributions. Fama himself takes the view that it is reasonable to assume normal distributions because of their analytical simplicity. (Our analysis in this section takes the same standpoint.) However, Friedman and Laibson (1989) point out the necessity for direct recognition of the factors that cause extremely large changes, which differ from ordinal accidental variations. They also propose a model which recognizes the changes in the rate of return as the sum of ordinal variations and other normally distributed variations generated by a Poisson process. This succeeds empirically to some extent.

household's lifetime, say 30 years. This argument may be correct, if we think only in terms of the expected values. Remember that the smart investors (with superior informational power) can also achieve smaller variance in stock returns in each period. Therefore, the probability of accumulating a certain amount of wealth within a specified length of time is much larger for a smart investor than for an ordinary investor. In this sense, Shiller's argument understates the impact of informational power on wealth distribution. On the other hand, in the case of the efficient capital market, accumulation of wealth has nothing to do with the difference in informational power among individuals.

What is often described as a factor reinforcing the generation of huge wealth is the wealth-preservation behaviour of successful investors (Thurow 1975: 151–2). Even if an individual obtains large wealth gains by chance, there is no guarantee that he or she will maintain that wealth position as long as the increased wealth is reinvested in the same object. Hence such an investor diversifies the composition of his or her assets much further and spreads the risk involved. In terms of our model, such behaviour can be interpreted as the case whereby investors' degree of relative risk aversion (c_i) effectively increases as the level of wealth ($w_i W_0$) increases.[47] Such behaviour certainly reinforces the positive skewness of wealth distribution. There is a long and still ongoing sequence of empirical research which investigates whether or not the efficient capital market hypothesis holds in the actual stock market. Earlier studies, as represented by Fama (1970), concluded that the market was efficient in the sense that fluctuations in the stock price tended to incorporate at least all the information that could be extracted from its past time-series data. It was because of this that the stock price data showed the feature of a random walk. However, more recent studies are sceptical of the conclusion reached in earlier studies.

First, fluctuations in the rate of returns data leave a trace of serial correlation, which is not consistent with the earlier results as it can be interpreted as evidence that the market is not using all the available information (Summers 1986, Friedman and Laibson 1989). Furthermore, there is a recognition that the discriminatory power of the earlier testing procedures was low (Shiller 1984, Summers 1986).

Second, fluctuations in stock prices tend to be excessively large in comparison with those of *ex-post* dividend flows. In so far as stock prices express the present value of the expected future dividend flows, the ratio of the variance of

---

[47] Wealth-preservation behaviour is not always a result of an increase in the degree of risk aversion. For example, a model used by Shorrocks (1988), which is explained in footnote 42 in Chapter 3, shows that investors will exhibit risk-averse behaviour in order to maintain access to a market once acquired, with a barrier, e.g., a required minimum wealth level, to obtain access to assets generating high returns; that is, there is market incompleteness, even if a household's preference is risk-neutral.

Wealth-preservation behaviour is often discussed in relation to elements of the tax system, such as inheritance tax saving. We do not discuss this argument here.

the stock price time-series over that of the time series of realized dividend flows must lie within a certain theoretical bound, and yet the ratio observed in the actual stock market lies beyond such limits (Shiller 1981, 1984, LeRoy and Porter 1981).

Third, even if fluctuation in stock prices cannot be predicted, that does not necessarily mean that the efficient capital market hypothesis holds. When the demand for stocks depends on such unpredictable forces as matters within the realm of social psychology, the stock prices can fluctuate randomly (Shiller 1984).

Fourth, if disparity in informational power does not increase stock market yields, then it would be hard to justify the significant expansion in capacity (especially in the field of processing information) undertaken recently on the part of institutional investors. The presumptions of the efficient capital market hypothesis that seem doubtful in their applicability to the real world are as follows. First, each investor must possess a fairly detailed amount of knowledge about the attributes of other market participants. It is not obvious how such knowledge can be acquired. Second, the assumption of *tâtonnement*, whereby actual transactions occur only after the expectational equilibrium is reached, seems difficult to maintain in reality. Even though it is plausible to suppose that investors' expectations are rapidly revised as they watch the market, it is more realistic to assume that revision of the expectation proceeds simultaneously with the actual transaction. When these assumptions do not hold, there is room for extra profits to accrue to individuals with superior informational power.[48]

We must leave to future investigation the task of specifying how to measure differences of informational power among individuals, and empirically to verify its impact on differences in stock market returns.

Appendix 7.1. **Mathematical Appendix**

1. The saving behaviour of the household is expressed formally as follows:

$$\text{Maximize } u(c_1) + (1 - p)N \cdot v(b_D) + p\{u(c_2) + N \cdot v(b_S)\} \tag{A.1}$$

s.t.

$$c_1 = b_0 + y - a - s. \tag{A.2}$$

$$N \cdot b_D = \rho \cdot s. \tag{A.3}$$

$$N \cdot b_S = \rho \cdot s + \rho_a \cdot a - c_2. \tag{A.4}$$

---

[48] Recently, there have been extensive developments in the regulation of insider trading and improvements in the disclosure system. These developments can be said to be aimed at realizing fair access to information among investors and thereby to raise incentives to invest in risky assets.

After obtaining b_D and b_s from dividing both sides of (A.3) and (A.4) by N and substituting them into (A.1), we maximize (A.1) subject to (A.2). The first-order conditions with respect to $c_1, c_2, a,$ and s are respectively:

$$u'(c_1) = \lambda, \tag{A.5}$$

$$p \cdot u'(c_2) = p \cdot v'(b_S), \tag{A.6}$$

$$p \cdot \rho_a \cdot v'(b_S) = \lambda, \tag{A.7}$$

$$\rho\{(1 - p) \cdot v'(b_D) + p \cdot v'(b_S)\} = \lambda, \tag{A.8}$$

where λ is the Lagrange multiplier. Notice that N does not directly appear in these expressions. (A.6) corresponds to the curve OB in the second quadrant of Figure 7.2. Erasing λ from (A.7) and (A.8) and using the relation of $p \cdot \rho_a = \rho$, we obtain:

$$v'(b_D) = v'(b_S). \tag{A.9}$$

If the household is risk averse, (A.9) implies perfect insurance, i.e., $b_D = b_S$. From the original constraints (A.3) and (A.4), this further implies:

$$c_2 = \rho_a \cdot a, \tag{A.10}$$

$$b_D = b_S = \frac{\rho}{N}s. \tag{A.11}$$

These are the conditions of the perfect specialization of saving measures stated in the text.

From (A.5), (A.6), and (A.8), as regards the marginal rate of substitution between the first-period consumption and the second-period consumption (hereafter denoted by $\mathrm{MRS_c}$), we obtain the following property:

$$\mathrm{MRS_c} \equiv \frac{u'(c_1)}{p \cdot u'(c_2)} = \rho_a. \tag{A.12}$$

2. When there is a quantity constraint, $a \le \bar{a}$ for the annuity, the constraint can be ignored if $\bar{a} \ge a^*$. Hence, in the following discussion, we restrict attention to the situation where the constraint is binding, i.e., $\bar{a} < a^*$. In this case, the first-order conditions (A.5), (A.6), and (A.8) derived in mathematical note 1 are unchanged, while (A.7) is replaced by:

$$a = \bar{a} \quad \text{and} \quad p \cdot \rho_a \cdot v'(b_S) - \lambda > 0.$$

From this inequality and (A.8), it is known that:

$$v'(b_D) < v'(b_S),$$

which implies that $b_D > b_S$ and $c_2 > \rho_a \cdot \bar{a}$. That is, the consumption at the second period is partly financed by the ordinary saving s. Further, from (A.5), (A.6), and (A.8), we obtain:

$$\text{MRS}_c \equiv \frac{u'(c_1)}{p \cdot u'(c_2)} = \rho \left\{ 1 + \frac{1-p}{p} \cdot \frac{v'(b_D)}{v'(b_S)} \right\} \equiv \rho \{ 1 + \text{MRS}_b \},$$

where MRS_b is the marginal rate of substitution between b_D and b_S. From this expression, it is evident that MRS_c takes a value between ρ and ρ_a.

3. This result is first derived by Sheshinski and Weiss (1981) and is pointed out as a case where the neo-Ricardian equivalence theorem of Barro (1974) does not hold.

The proof in the case of the two-period model in the text is given as follows.

(Proof) Denote the optimal solution in the absence of the quantity constraint by $(c_1^*, c_2^*, a^*, s^*, b_D^*, b_S^*)$ and denote also the second-best solution in the presence of the quantity constraint by $(c_1, c_2, \bar{a}, s, b_D, b_S)$. Of course, it holds that $\bar{a} < a^*$.

First, we will show that $s = s^*$, i.e., no substitution by ordinary saving, cannot be the second-best equilibrium. In fact, if $s = s^*$, (i) c_1 increases due to the decrease in the annuity saving, (ii) b_D remains $(\rho/N)s^*$, and (iii) b_S decreases due to the decrease in the consumable resource in the second period.

Properties (i) and (ii) are evident. Property (iii) is established as follows: Substituting b_S obtained from (A.2) into (A.6) yields:

$$u'(c_2) = v'\left(\frac{\rho}{N} s^* + \frac{\rho_a}{N} \bar{a} - \frac{1}{N} c_2 \right). \tag{A.13}$$

It is apparent that c_2 which satisfies this condition should be smaller than the optimal level c_2^*. (Otherwise, the left-hand side would be necessarily smaller than the right-hand side.) Therefore:

$$v'(b_S^*) = u'(c_2^*) < u'(c_2) = v'(b_S). \tag{A.14}$$

This implies that $b_S < b_S^*$. Thus, property (iii) is obtained.

Meanwhile, from (A.5) and (A.8), it is known that a condition associated with the second-best equilibrium is:

$$(1-p) \cdot v'(b_D) + p \cdot v'(b_S) = \frac{1}{\rho} u'(c_1). \tag{A.15}$$

From (ii) and (iii), the left-hand side of the equation increases from the case of the optimal solution, whereas the right-hand side decreases from that case. Therefore, (A.15) does not hold (i.e., an under-saving occurs) and $s = s^*$ cannot be the second-best equilibrium. Note that this point holds true regardless of the value of $\bar{a}$.

Next, we will show that an over-saving occurs when ordinary saving perfectly compensates for the reduction in annuity saving. This property is shown to hold true when $\bar{a}$ stays in the neighbourhood of a^*. First, note that perfect substitution means that:

$$a^* + s^* = \bar{a} + s. \tag{A.16}$$

In this case, it is immediately known that: (i') c_1 remains c_1^*, and (ii') b_D increases due to the increase in ordinary saving. However, it holds that $\rho < \rho_a$ even under perfect substitution. Hence, as in the above case, the consumable resource in the second period decreases. Therefore, as in the case of (A.13) and (A.14), (iii') b_S decreases.

As is clear from the above properties, the right-hand side of (A.15) remains the same as the optimal solution, whereas the left-hand side of (A.15), in general, can either increase or decrease, reflecting the opposite movements of b_D and b_S. However, in the case where $\bar{a}$ stays in the neighbourhood of a^*, we can determine the direction of the movement of the left-hand side.

Regarding the left-hand side of (A.15) as a function of s, we take a Taylor expansion of the function around s^*. Then, taking up only the first-order term of the expansion, we obtain the following expression:

$$
\begin{aligned}
(1 - p) &\cdot v'(\rho s) + p \cdot v'(\rho s + \rho_a \bar{a} - c_2) \\
&= (1 - p) \cdot v'(\rho s^*) + (1 - p) \cdot v''(\rho s^*) \cdot \rho(s - s^*) \\
&\quad + p \cdot v'(\rho s^*) + p \cdot v''(\rho s^*) \cdot (\rho s + \rho_a \bar{a} - c_2 - \rho s^*) \\
&= v'(\rho s^*) + v''(\rho s^*) \cdot \{\rho(s - s^*) + p(\rho_a \bar{a} - c_2)\}.
\end{aligned}
\tag{A.17}
$$

The second term in $\{\}$ of the last expression can be rewritten as:

$$
\begin{aligned}
p(\rho_a \bar{a} - c_2) &= p(\rho_a a^* - c_2^*) + p\rho_a(\bar{a} - a^*) - p(c_2 - c_2^*) \\
&= \rho(\bar{a} - a^*) - p(c_2 - c_2^*).
\end{aligned}
$$

(The second equality is obtained from the perfect specialization condition of the optimal solution and the relation of $\rho = p\rho_a$.) Substituting this expression into (A.17) and further using the perfect substitution condition (A.16), we finally obtain the approximate expression of the left-hand side of (A.15):

$$(1 - p) \cdot v'(b_D) + p \cdot v'(b_S) = v'(\rho s^*) - p \cdot v''(\rho s^*) \cdot (c_2 - c_2^*).$$

As we have already seen, since in this case $c_2 < c_2^*$ and $c_1 = c_1^*$ it holds that:

$$(1 - p) \cdot v'(b_D) + p \cdot v'(b_S) < v'(\rho s^*) = \frac{1}{\rho} \cdot u'(c_1^*) = \frac{1}{\rho} \cdot u'(c_1).$$

This means that the perfect substitution gives rise to an over-saving. Thus it is known that the ordinary saving imperfectly substitutes for the annuity saving when the quantity constraint $\bar{a}$ stays in the neighbourhood of the optimal quantity a^*. (QED.)

The statement in the text will be obtained by considering this property in the opposite direction, i.e., in the direction of relaxing the quantity constraint $\bar{a}$.

4. The following analysis is a simplified two-period version of the intergenerational transmission model of Atkinson (1971*a*). The emerging patterns of dynamics and the conditions determining the classification are the same. Substituting first

$$u'(c_i) = c_i^{-\varepsilon} \quad (i = 1, 2)$$
$$v'(b_j) = b_j^{-\mu} \quad (j = D, S)$$

into the first-order conditions (A.6), (A.10), (A.11), and (A.12), and then substituting the results into the budget constraint of the first period and rearranging it, we obtain:

$$b_0 + y = \left\{ p \cdot \rho^{-1} + \rho^{-1/\varepsilon} \right\} b_s^{\mu/\varepsilon} + \frac{N}{\rho} b_s. \tag{A.18}$$

This relation is graphically expressed as the wealth transmission curve between generations. Although it is evident that b_S increases monotonically with b_0, the shape of the curve differs depending on whether ε/μ is larger than unity or smaller.

(a) When $\varepsilon/\mu > 1$, the first term of the right-hand side of (A.18) converges to zero with an increase in b_0 and thus,

$$b_s \to \frac{\rho}{N} \{b_0 + y\} \quad \text{when } b_0 \to \infty.$$

Therefore, the curve crosses the 45-degree line twice when $(\rho/N) > 1$, and once when $(\rho/N) \le 1$.

(b) When $\varepsilon/\mu = 1$, the curve is a straight line. It crosses the 45-degree line only if:

$$\frac{p}{\rho} + \left(\frac{1}{\rho}\right)^{1/\varepsilon} + \frac{N}{\rho} > 1.$$

This inequality is always satisfied when $\rho \le N$. The reverse inequality is obtained when ρ is sufficiently larger than N.

(c) When $\varepsilon/\mu > 1$, by (A.18):

$$\frac{d(b_0 + y)}{db_S} = \frac{\mu}{\varepsilon}(p \cdot \rho^{-1} + \rho^{(-1/\varepsilon)})b_S^{(\mu/\varepsilon)-1} + \frac{N}{\rho}$$

$$\rightarrow \infty \quad \text{(when } b_0 \rightarrow \infty\text{)}.$$

In other words, the slope of the wealth transmission curve eventually becomes horizontal. In this case, it crosses the 45-degree line once.

Although Case (b) is not graphically shown in these figures, the path diverges upward when ρ is sufficiently larger than N, otherwise (the case $\rho \leq N$ included) it converges to the unique long-run equilibrium, as is the case of Figure 7.3(B) (Case (a)).

5. With small changes to the argument in mathematical note 1, we can present, households' saving behaviour as:

$$\text{Maximize} \quad u(c_1) + (1 - p)N \cdot v(\omega_D) + p\{u(c_2) + N \cdot v(\omega_S)\} \qquad \text{(A.19)}$$

s.t.,

$$c_1 = \omega_0 + N(\delta - e)y(e) - a - s. \qquad \text{(A.20)}$$

$$N \cdot (\omega_D - y(e)) = \rho \cdot s. \qquad \text{(A.21)}$$

$$N \cdot (\omega_S - y(e)) = \rho \cdot s + \rho_a \cdot a - c_2. \qquad \text{(A.22)}$$

Eliminating s from both (A.21) and (A.22), and eliminating a also by using (A.20), we obtain the intertemporal budget constraint equation of the parents' generation as:

$$c_1 + \frac{pc_2}{\rho} + \frac{p}{\rho}N\omega_S + \frac{1-p}{\rho}N\omega_D = \omega_0 + N\left(\delta - e + \frac{1}{\rho}\right)y(e). \qquad \text{(A.23)}$$

This is the budget constraint equation which introduces the next generation's lifetime resources, mentioned in the text. In order to maximize (A.19) with the constraint (A.23), it is evident that the right-hand side of (A.23) should be maximized. That is the maximization of the joint resource pool of parents and children. The first-order condition for this problem is (7.10) in the text. The first-order conditions for other variables are omitted since they can be obtained just by replacing ω_D or ω_S by b_D or b_S respectively in the argument of mathematical note 1.

6. Let us consider the maximization of (A.19) with constraints (7.12) and (7.13) in addition to (A.23). In mathematical note 5, we explained the feature of the phase that constraints (7.12) and (7.13) are not effective. Introduce Lagrange multipliers: λ for (A.23), λ_D ($\lambda_D \geq 0$) for (7.12), and λ_S ($\lambda_S \geq 0$) for

(7.13), to obtain the Kuhn–Tucker conditions:

$$u'(c_1) = \lambda, \tag{A.24}$$

$$pu'(c_2) = \frac{\lambda}{\rho a}, \tag{A.25}$$

$$(1-p)N \cdot \left\{ v'(\omega_D) - \frac{\lambda}{\rho} \right\} + \lambda_D = 0, \tag{A.26}$$

$\lambda_D \geq 0$, $y(e) \leq \omega_D$, and $\lambda_D\{y(e) - \omega_D\} = 0$,

$$pN \cdot \left\{ v'(\omega_S) - \frac{\lambda}{\rho} \right\} + \lambda_S = 0, \tag{A.27}$$

$\lambda_S \geq 0$, $y(e) \leq \omega_S$, and $\lambda_S\{y(e) - \omega_S\} = 0$,

$$\lambda N \cdot \left\{ \left(\delta - e + \frac{1}{\rho} \right) y'(e) - y(e) \right\} - (\lambda_D + \lambda_S)y'(e) = 0. \tag{A.28}$$

The case of $\lambda_D = \lambda_S = 0$ has been already considered in mathematical note 5. Other possible cases are that both λ_D and λ_S are positive, and that either λ_D or λ_S is positive.

However, we can show that it is impossible that only one of λ_D and λ_S is positive. In fact, if $\lambda_D > \lambda_S = 0$, then:

$$(1-p)N \cdot \left\{ v'(\omega_D) - \frac{\lambda}{\rho} \right\} = -\lambda_D < 0 = pN \cdot \left\{ v'(\omega_S) - \frac{\lambda}{\rho} \right\}.$$

Thus, $v'(\omega_D) < v'(\omega_S)$ are satisfied and this means that $\omega_D > \omega_S$. Then, $\omega_S < y(e)$ by the assumption $\omega_D = y(e)$. This contradicts $\omega_S \geq y(e)$. Therefore, when one of the multipliers has a positive sign, another must have the same sign.

When $\lambda_D > 0$ and $\lambda_S > 0$, $\omega_D = \omega_S = y(e)$ by (A.26) and (A.27). That is, when constraints (7.12) and (7.13) are effective, the condition of perfect insurance is also realized.

In addition, by (A.25), we can obtain:

$$v'(\omega_S) - \frac{\lambda}{\rho} = v'(\omega_S) - u'(c_2) = -\frac{\lambda_S}{pN} < 0, \tag{A.29}$$

and by comparing (A.26) and (A.27) with the perfect insurance condition, we can get:

$$(1-p)\lambda_S = p\lambda_D. \tag{A.30}$$

Finally, (7.14) in the text is induced by substituting (A.29) and (A.30) into (A.28).

7. Although the ratio λ_w/λ can be affected by the rate of profits of the system and the rate of growth, as we have already seen, it cannot affect these variables. How, then, does the ratio depend on the rate of profits and the rate of growth? Here, we develop a strict comparative-static analysis of the share of wealth in steady-state growth.

First, with respect to the profit share, we obtain:

$$\text{sign}\,\frac{\partial(\lambda_w/\lambda)}{\partial R} = \text{sign}\,\partial\left\{\frac{R + \pi\psi(g)}{\pi}\right\} = \text{sign}\,\frac{\pi - \pi' \cdot R}{\pi^2} = \text{sign}\,\frac{\sigma}{\pi} \geq 0, \qquad (A.31)$$

where σ is the elasticity of the substitution of the production function. That is, the sign is positive as far as substitution between production factors is possible, even though the extent of substitution is small.

This evaluation of the sign concerns the case where the rate of profits varies endogenously in the phase of full employment, with the natural rate of growth given. When the elasticity of substitution exceeds unity, an increase in R brings about a large factor substitution of labour for capital and thus π decreases. Therefore, the transition of weight from wealth holders' saving to workers' saving raises λ_w. This is also intuitively understandable.

In fact, a variation of factor shares is a crucial factor for determining workers' share of wealth in the original Pasinetti model where money does not exist. This is because a condition corresponding to (7.32) in the model is:

$$s_c R(1 - \lambda_w) = s_w\left(\frac{1-\pi}{\pi}R + \lambda_w R\right). \qquad (A.32)$$

Thus, λ_w (note $\lambda \equiv 1$) is:

$$\lambda_w = \frac{s_w}{s_c - s_w}\frac{1-\pi}{\pi},$$

and thus satisfies:

$$\text{sign}\,\lambda_w'(R) = \text{sign}(\sigma - 1) \gtreqless \times 0 \Leftrightarrow \sigma \gtreqless 1.$$

However, the argument in our model including money does not end at this point, since there exists transfer income from the monetary sector to households. Moreover, variations in R and π simultaneously change the share-holding ratio λ (which is endogenous) in order to maintain the equilibrium of the product market. This is because an increase in π with other things being equal causes the household saving rate to exceed the necessary amount for investment and thus another endogenous variable λ must decrease.

In fact, considering the relation between λ and R by using (7.33') in footnote 28, we can find:

$$\lambda'(R) = \frac{\phi + \psi}{\{s_c(R + \psi) - \pi(\phi + \psi)\}^2} Z(R), \qquad (A.33)$$

where:

$$Z(R) = -\{s_c(1 - \pi) + \pi'(R)\{s_c(R + \psi) - (\phi + \psi)\}\}$$
$$= -s_c\left\{(1 - \pi) + \frac{(R + \psi)\pi}{R}(1 - \sigma)\left(1 - \frac{\phi + \psi}{s_c(R + \psi)}\right)\right\}. \qquad (A.34)$$

In addition, we can rewrite (7.33) to obtain:

$$\frac{\phi + \psi}{s_c(R + \psi)} = \lambda + (1 - \lambda)\frac{\lambda\pi}{1 - \pi + \lambda\pi} \le 1 \text{ (the equality holds when } \lambda = 1\text{),}$$

$$(A.35)$$

for any $0 \le \lambda \le 1$ and thus $Z(R) < 0$ only if $\sigma \le 1$. Therefore, $\lambda'(R) < 0$ is always satisfied when $\sigma \le 1$. The opposite relation arises only when σ is larger than unity by a sufficient amount.

Next, let us investigate the relation between λ_w and R. Denoting the term in $\{ \}$ of the right-hand side of (F.1) in footnote 28 by $Y(R)$, we get:

$$\lambda'_w(R) = -\frac{s_w}{s_c - s_w}\frac{1}{R + \psi}\left\{\left(\frac{\pi(1 - \sigma)}{R} + \frac{1 - \pi}{R + \psi}\right)Y(R)\right.$$

$$\left. -(1 - \pi)\left(\frac{\sigma}{\pi} - \frac{(\phi + \psi)Z(R)}{\{s_c(R + \psi) - \pi(\phi + \psi)\}^2}\right)\right\}, \qquad (A.36)$$

where $Y(R)$ is always positive. In addition, $Z(R)$ has already been defined in (A.34) and shown to be negative unless σ is sufficiently larger than unity. When $\sigma \le 1$, the first and second terms in $\{ \}$ of the right-hand side of (A.36) are positive and negative, respectively. The former represents the effect of an increase in the profit share (already mentioned), which decreases λ_w. The latter reflects the effect of a decrease in λ, which enlarges a tax rebate shared with wage income and increases λ_w. The net effect, that is, which dominates, is not conclusive. Thus, in general, the relation between λ_w and R is not monotonic. However, as (A.31) has shown, the ratio λ_w/λ increases with R even if $\sigma \le 1$. This is because an effect that reduces the denominator operates sufficiently.

The above argument does not consider how variations in the exogenous variables cause a rise in the endogenously determined profit share. If the rise is brought about by variations in parameters included in the right-hand side of (7.34), we should consider the effect at the same time. In the discussion that follows, in the main text, we refer to the effects of changes in s_c and s_f. Since s_f is not included in the right-hand side of (7.34), an increase in R by that in s_f, which will be mentioned later in the text, is the case to which the above argument can be exactly applied. In contrast to this, since an increase in s_c decreases R, which will also be mentioned later in the text, a decreasing effect of R on s_w is added to the direct effect on λ_w caused by an increase in s_c. (Although the direction of the latter effect is unclear, it is thought to reduce λ_w usually.) On the other hand, an increase in the natural rate of growth g directly forces λ_w to go down, as (A.37) shows. However, it raises the endogenously determined profit share R as is usually expected (as in the neo-classical phase), and the opposite force which increases λ_w will also rise. (In our model, however, it is not evident whether an increase in the natural rate of growth raises r or R.) In this case, after all, we cannot generally conclude the direction of the movement of λ_w caused by the net effect. The same argument as that given above can be applied to the relation between λ_w/λ and the natural rate of growth. As a result, we obtain:

$$\text{sign}\,\frac{\partial(\lambda_w/\lambda)}{\partial g} = \text{sign}\,\frac{\partial\left\{\dfrac{R + \pi\psi(g)}{\phi(g) + \psi(g)}\right\}}{\partial g}$$

$$= \text{sign}\left\{-\frac{\phi'(R + \pi\psi) + \phi''g(R - \pi\phi)}{(\phi + \psi)^2}\right\} < 0. \tag{A.37}$$

This corresponds to (A.31). We can confirm that a numerator of the last expression is positive by the strict convexity of the ϕ-function and $R > \phi$ from (7.19). That is, an increase in the rate of growth, with other things being equal, decreases the ratio of wealth holding of workers. It is necessary to use this property with care, depending on the two cases: the case of endogenous g and the case of exogenous g. This point is the same as in the case of the profit share.

8. The proof is simple. Call the difference between the true value and the predicted value the 'prediction error', and denote it by e_i. By substituting (7.38) into (7.44) and taking note of $E(\varepsilon_i \,|\, P_1) = 0$, we obtain:

$$E(e_i \,|\, P_1) = \frac{1}{1 + \theta_i\sigma^2}(P_1 - \underline{P}_1).$$

Hence, if $P_1 > \underline{P}_1$, then it overstates (on average) the true value. Furthermore, because for any i, j such that $\theta_j > \theta_i$:

$$E(e_j - e_i \,|\, P_1) = \frac{(\theta_i - \theta_j)\sigma^2}{(1 + \theta_i\sigma^2)(1 + \theta_j\sigma^2)}(P_1 - \underline{P}_1).$$

The degree of under or overstatement is the less, the higher the quality of information. To take a numerical example, if

$$\underline{P}_1 = 21, \quad \sigma^2 = 4, \quad n = 2, \quad \theta_1 = 3/2, \quad \theta_2 = 1/2,$$

then:

$$E(e_1) = \tfrac{1}{7}(P_1 - \underline{P}_1) \qquad E(e_2) = \tfrac{1}{3}(P_1 - \underline{P}_1),$$

and we have:

$$E(e_1 - e_2) = -\tfrac{4}{21}(P_1 - \underline{P}_1).$$

Therefore, except for the case where by chance $P_1 = \underline{P}_1$, there is about 20 per cent difference over the amount of divergence between P_1 and $\underline{P}_1$.

9. The proof of this proposition is the same as Grossman's except that we have extended it to the case where the variance of each individual's information error is different (i.e., heteroscedastic). Although Danthine (1978: 90), in discussing a model similar to Grossman's, once remarked that a sufficient statistic did not exist when investors' information errors were heteroscedastic, such a comment is not correct, at least not in the original Grossman model.

We define x_i as the product of an individual's information y_i and the level of informational power θ_i. Because θ_i is known to the individual, y_i and x_i are equivalent information. The variable $\bar{x}$ defined in the text is a simple arithmetic average of x_i's.

In the following discussion we adapt Grossman's proof to the case of heteroscedastic variances to show that so long as individuals all come to know $\bar{x}$, each individual's intrinsic information, x_i, becomes redundant in forming the expectation of P_1. This is precisely the meaning of the proposition that there exists a sufficient statistic of the information vector $(y_1, y_2, \ldots, y_n)$ with respect to the unknown parameter, P_1.

First we derive the joint distribution of $(x_i, \bar{x})$ conditional on an arbitrary given P_1. Using the definition (7.47), (7.38), and the normalization assumption (7.39), we can verify that:

$$E(x_i \mid P_1) = E(\theta_i(P_1 + \varepsilon_i) \mid P_1) = \theta_i P_1$$

$$E(\bar{x} \mid P_1) = \frac{P_1}{n} \sum_{i=1}^{n} \theta_i = P_1$$

$$\mathrm{Var}(x_i \mid P_1) = \theta_i^2 E(\varepsilon_i^2 \mid P_1) = \theta_i$$

$$\mathrm{Var}(\bar{x} \mid P_1) = \frac{1}{n^2} E\left\{ \left(\sum_{i=1}^{n} \theta_i \varepsilon_i \right)^2 \mid P_1 \right\}$$

$$= \frac{1}{n^2} \sum_{i=1}^{n} \theta_i = \frac{1}{n}$$

$$\mathrm{Cov}(x_i, \bar{x} \mid P_1) = E\{(x_i - E(x_i))(\bar{x} - E(\bar{x}))\}$$

$$= E\left\{ \theta_i \varepsilon_i \cdot \frac{1}{n} \sum_{i=1}^{n} \theta_i \varepsilon_i \right\}$$

$$= \frac{\theta_i}{n}.$$

Hence, if we denote the probability density function by $h_i(x_i, \bar{x} \mid P_1)$ we can express it by:

$$h_i(x_i, \bar{x} \mid P_1) = (2\pi)^{-1} \cdot \begin{vmatrix} \theta_i & \theta_i/n \\ \theta_i/n & 1/n \end{vmatrix}^{-1/2}$$

$$\times \exp\left\{-\frac{1}{2}\begin{bmatrix} x_i - \theta_i P_1 \\ \bar{x} - P_1 \end{bmatrix}' \begin{bmatrix} \theta_i & \theta_i/n \\ \theta_i/n & 1/n \end{bmatrix}^{-1} \begin{bmatrix} x_i - \theta_i P \\ \bar{x} - P_1 \end{bmatrix}\right\}. \quad \text{(A.38)}$$

By evaluating the determinant as well as the quadratic form inside the bracket { }, $h_i(x_i, \bar{x} \mid P_1)$) can be rewritten as:

$$h_i(x_i, \bar{x} \mid P_1) = (2\pi)^{-1} \cdot \frac{n}{\sqrt{\theta_i(n - \theta_i)}} \times \exp\left\{-\frac{1}{2}\frac{n}{\theta_i(n - \theta_i)}(x_i^2 - 2\theta_i x_i \bar{x})\right\}$$

$$\times \exp\left\{-\frac{1}{2}n\left[(P_1 - \bar{x})^2 - \frac{(n - 1 - \theta_i)\bar{x}^2}{n - \theta_i}\right]\right\}. \quad \text{(A.39)}$$

Because the first exponential term does not involve P_1, the product of the constant term and the first exponential function can be expressed as $g_1(x_i, \bar{x})$. Similarly, because the second exponential term does not involve x_i, the second exponential function term can be summarized as $g_2(P_1, \bar{x})$. Then $h_i(x_i, \bar{x} \mid P_1)$ is rewritten as:

$$h_i(x_i \bar{x} \mid P_1) = g_1(x_i, \bar{x}) \cdot g_2(P_1, \bar{x}). \quad \text{(A.40)}$$

The reason why $h_i(x_i, \bar{x} \mid P_1)$ can be separated into two expressions, one involving x_i and $\bar{x}$ only, $-(\theta_i P_1 x_i/n)$ and $(\theta_i P_1 x_i/n)$, the other involving P_1 and $\bar{x}$, is that the two cross terms of x_i and P_1, that appear when the quadratic form inside the bracket { } of (A.38) is expanded exactly cancel each other. Were we to have made a statistic of $(y_1, y_2, \ldots, y_n)$ with any other weights than θ_i, we would not have had the property in question.

Our major proposition is that the distribution of P_1 conditional on $\bar{x}$ and x_i, and the distribution of P_1 conditional on $\bar{x}$ only, and identical. (In such a case, individual information x_i surely becomes redundant.) Denote the former density function by $m_i(P_i \mid \bar{x}, x_i)$ while denoting the latter density function by $m(P_1 \mid \bar{x})$. The former is defined by:

$$m_i(P_1 \mid \bar{x}, x_i) = \frac{g(P_1)h_i(x_i, \bar{x} \mid P_1)}{\int_{-\infty}^{\infty} g(P_1)h_i(x_i, \bar{x} \mid P_1)\,dP_1},$$

using Bayes's Theorem. If we substitute (A.40) into the above expression and take the expression $g_1(x_i, \bar{x})$ which does not contain P_1, out of the operand of integration, then we obtain:

$$m_1(P_1 \mid \bar{x}, x_i) = \frac{g(P_1)g_2(P_1, \bar{x})}{\int_{-\infty}^{\infty} g(P_1)g_2(\bar{x} \mid P_1)\, dP_1}. \tag{A.41}$$

On the other hand, in order to obtain the expression of the latter density function we first define the marginal distribution of $\bar{x}$ on the basis of $h_i(x_i, \bar{x} \mid P_1)$ as follows:

$$f(\bar{x} \mid P_1) = \int_{-\infty}^{\infty} h_i(x_i, \bar{x} \mid P_1)\, dx_i.$$

By substituting (A.40) into the right-hand side of this expression and noting that $g_2(P_1, \bar{x})$ does not contain x_i, we can rewrite $f(\bar{x} \mid P_1)$ as:

$$f(\bar{x} \mid P_1) = g_2(P_1, \bar{x}) \int_{-\infty}^{\infty} g_1(x_i, \bar{x})\, dx_i. \tag{A.42}$$

Now the density function of P_1 conditional on $\bar{x}$ only is defined as:

$$m(P_1 \mid \bar{x}) = \frac{g(P_1)f(\bar{x} \mid P_1)}{\int_{-\infty}^{\infty} g(P_1)f(\bar{x} \mid P_1)\, dp_1}.$$

Substituting (A.42) into $f(\bar{x} \mid P_1)$ and cancelling out the expression both from the numerator and the denominator, we arrive at the expression:

$$m(P_1 \mid \bar{x}) = \frac{g(P_1)g_2(P_1, \bar{x})}{\int_{-\infty}^{\infty} g(P_1)g_2(P_1, \bar{x})\, dp_1}. \tag{A.43}$$

By comparing (A.41) and (A.43), we observe that the two density functions are indeed identical. Hence, $\bar{x}$ is the sufficient statistic of the market information vector $(y_1, y_2, \ldots, y_n)$.

10. It is obvious that $m(P_1 \mid \bar{x})$ defined in (A.43) follows a normal distribution. Its mean and variance can be derived as follows. First, by looking at the numerator of (A.43), we see:

$$
\begin{aligned}
g(P_1)g_2(P_1, \bar{x}) &= \frac{1}{\sqrt{2\pi}\sigma} \exp\left\{ -\frac{1}{2} \cdot \frac{1}{\sigma^2} (P_1 - \underline{P}_1)^2 \right\} \\
&\quad \times \exp\left\{ -\frac{1}{2} n \left[(P_1 - \bar{x})^2 - \frac{(n - 1 - \theta_i)}{n - \theta_i} \bar{x}^2 \right] \right\} \\
&= \frac{1}{\sqrt{2\pi}\sigma} \exp\left\{ -\frac{(P_1 - \underline{P}_1)^2}{2\sigma^2} - \frac{n}{2}(P_1 - \bar{x})^2 + \frac{n(n - 1 - \theta_i)}{2(n - \theta_i)} \bar{x}^2 \right\}.
\end{aligned}
$$

By expanding the expression inside { }, and after rearrangement, the expression inside { } can be rewritten as:

$$-\frac{1}{2}\frac{\left(P_1 - \dfrac{P_1 + n\sigma^2 \bar{x}}{1 + n\sigma^2}\right)^2 + \dfrac{\sigma^2}{1 + n\sigma^2}\left(\dfrac{P_1^2}{\sigma^2} + \dfrac{n\bar{x}^2}{(n - \theta_i)}\right) - \dfrac{(P_1 + n\sigma^2\bar{x})^2}{(1 + n\sigma^2)^2}}{\dfrac{\sigma^2}{1 + n\sigma^2}}.$$

Note that in the above expression the integrant variable P_1 in the denominator of (A.43) appears only in the first term of the numerator, while the remaining terms are cancelled out from both the numerator and the denominator of (A.43). Hence $m(P_1 \,|\, \bar{x})$ is a normal distribution, with:

$$E(P_1 \,|\, \bar{x}) = \frac{P_1 + n\sigma^2\bar{x}}{1 + n\sigma^2};$$

$$Var(P_1 \,|\, \bar{x}) = \frac{\sigma^2}{1 + n\sigma^2}.$$

This proves the expressions (7.48) and (7.49) in the text.

8

Conclusion

In this book, I have surveyed the economic theories on the distribution of income and wealth. I have focused mainly on the principles of comparative advantage and equalizing difference in relation to labour supply, human capital accumulation, competition for employment opportunities or quota places, and incentives for higher productivity. Also, in relation to the distribution of wealth, I discussed the creation of wealth within a generation and the transfer of wealth between generations, determinants of the rates of return on assets and the segmentation of wealth holders, and the fluctuations of asset prices and the importance of being able to obtain information on future changes. Furthermore, I have surveyed empirical studies on those issues, focusing on those that stimulated new theoretical developments. This is an area in economics which arguably enjoys the most fruitful interactions between theoretical and empirical lines of research.

The new contribution of this book is that it systematically reviews the two contrasting views of the labour market, the neo-classical competitive labour market and the dual labour market, and unifies them theoretically as the theory of employment and income determination. I have argued that the two competing views should not be considered as mutually exclusive, but rather as different regimes that are the outcome of the same institutions, or organization. That means that, in one regime, market competition will be dominant, achieving full employment, and in the other, the institutional labour allocation mechanism will dominate, leading to involuntary employment or involuntary unemployment. In the latter regime, we will see inequalities in employment opportunities, and income inequalities that cannot be explained by compensating differentials. On casual inspection, this may look similar to Keynes's claim of downward wage rigidity. But the new insight that I provide here is that I have clarified the mechanism and conditions of downward wage rigidity. Which of the two regimes is realized depends not only on the relative importance of the demand and supply factors in the market, but also on socio-institutional factors such as those determining the motivation of the workers, and the inherent willingness of the workers to co-operate and share costs with the employer.

The integrated theory of the labour market implies that, given that other factors are the same, during the regime in which there is accelerated capital accumulation by the firm, the earned income of individuals becomes more equal, and, during the regime with stagnant capital accumulation or capital decumulation within the firm, income inequality worsens. Basically, economic growth and greater income equality can coexist. Therefore, generally, economic growth works positively on income distribution. On the other hand, if capital accumulation is constrained by factors other than entrepreneurs' long-run revenue expectations, such as the supply of savings or outside factors such as depletion of resources or environmental concerns, then the distribution of income becomes a policy issue. In that case, in addition to the policies advocated conventionally, such as public job creation, worker retraining, etc., I have shown that, by improving the quality of jobs to improve the workers' inherent willingness to work and also by accelerating structural changes of the labour process (if necessary, through policies of guidance), we can eliminate job rationing, which is an important reason for income inequality.

Also, through the empirical studies on the entrance fee and the bonding effect, I have demonstrated that our integrated labour market theory is an effective tool in understanding the current Japanese labour market (section 6.2). I concluded by claiming that during the high-growth period, from the early 1960s to the early 1970s, the Japanese labour market operated as a neo-classical competitive regime, and that during the low-growth period of the mid-1970s to the mid-1980s, the Japanese labour market operated as a dual labour market regime with involuntary unemployment and job rationing, both of which are characteristics of that regime. It is well known that during the high-growth period, Japanese income distribution dramatically equalized, and the major reason behind that occurrence is that the Japanese labour market at that time operated as a neo-classical competitive labour market. Labour demand induced by rapid capital accumulation raised general labour income relative to other incomes, and the new high income opportunities for the educated and the skilled induced a vigorous human capital investment, reducing labour income inequality. On the other hand, it is said that the trend for more income equality stalled or reversed itself from the mid-1970s. This fact accords well with our claim that the labour market at that time was in a regime with involuntary unemployment and job rationing. Of course, the empirical studies in this book are rather preliminary, and leave more elaborate analyses including analysis of the dynamic process of short-run fluctuations of employment and income to future research.

There still are aspects of the dual labour market hypothesis whose implications for income distribution I have not discussed sufficiently. I refer here to the issue of how the system of division of labour is determined, not the issue of employment determination given the production function, but how the production function itself is chosen. In particular, if we consider how the number of jobs, the scope of each job, and the accompanying learning opportunities are determined, there are factors that we cannot explain simply by taking into account the benefits of specialization and the division of labour, as Adam Smith did in his analysis of the production of pins. This also has a lot to do with how the employer wants to share incomes with workers and with the employer's management needs (section 5.2). Clearly, a different division of labour will result in a different distribution of power and responsibility during work and, hence, a different distribution of income.

On the job, both the givers of orders and their receivers are humans. Hence there inevitably develops a power structure. The issues that I mentioned earlier, such as the inherent motivation of workers towards their work, or the necessity of an external incentive and its economic cost, are closely related to the depth of the learning opportunities on the job, and to the way in which authority and responsibilities are distributed. If jobs are repetitive and simple, and require no decision making by workers, then it is natural that the workers' objectives would be income, leisure, and low intensity of work. Thus, we have a world which may be characterized as the Incentive Hypothesis, where an external incentive is introduced, with a high wage at one end and the possibility of dismissal at the other end. The argument that the bonding system is effective in eliminating distortions in the allocation of resource and involuntary income differences has been made on the presumption that we cannot change the content of work.

As has been shown in various experiments in relation to job reorganization in Europe and the USA, reorganization of the workplace to give more power to workers, such as expanding the job content of individual workers, and letting individual workers and groups manage the production operation themselves, dramatically increases productivity both quantitatively and qualitatively. If that is true, then it can be said that throughout our history up to now, we have not been able to create a production system that is both efficient and humane.

It has been pointed out that, in Japan, junior core workers (lower-tier workers in the internal labour market) obtain relatively broad on-the-job training by moving between various job ladders. That could be interpreted as an example of being ahead of the movement towards the above mentioned yet-to-be-achieved production system. In fact, the high productivity of those workers and their flexible attitude towards the introduction of new technologies, which has attracted international attention, could be largely due to inherent work motivation supported by a wide variety of job contents and the existence of broad opportunities for learning on the job.

Yet, as the situation stands at present, we could not say that the possibilities for other divisions of labour have been fully tested, or that real changes have been made to ranks of authority or to the structure of the allocation of responsibilities. The problem of how to construct a system of division of labour that is both efficient and in harmony with workers' motivation remains as a task for others to tackle in earnest.

At the same time, we should not forget that, at present, the people that can experience jobs with broad job categories and on-the-job training are only in the minority, namely, core workers in large companies. The results of various empirical studies show that in medium to small-sized firms, learning opportunities are fewer than in large firms and, moreover, only a limited number of workers can experience those opportunities (section 6.1). As I pointed out at the beginning of the book (section 1.2), in Japan, the over-whelming majority of workers work in medium to small-sized firms. Further-more, employers have recently become increasingly dependent on external workers, such as housewives working part-time, who have in general very few learning opportunities. Even though the external workforce provides various job opportunities and additional income to people who inherently have a low commitment to labour force participation, it is probably not only this author who has reservations about the desirability of this change. The length of working hours and the quality of jobs should be and can be treated as separate issues.

As the above summary indicates, one of the characteristics of this book is that I have focused not only on the income differences that are the consequence of the labour process but also on the labour process itself and its content, as this is the process of income generation. That is the author's modest answer to the issues of social justice put forward by the philosopher Rawles. Let us recall that Rawles called role and job position social status goods, and postulated that, together with income and wealth, which are economic goods, they are part of the basic social goods of a person (section 2.4). I expect that more equal distribution of social status goods enhances the self-respect of indivi-duals, and induces them to increase their work efforts. Furthermore, individual self-respect is the foundation for mutual respect and understanding. It is in this way, I think, that the motivation for comforting other people during their distress and sharing one's happiness with others is strengthened. It can even be said that this is the foundation underlying the analysis of income redistribution, which is outside the scope of our analysis. I think that the strength of mutual emotional ties depends on how they were generated.

Next, let us turn to the generation and distribution of wealth. I have dis-cussed, using three separate time horizons, how household wealth is accumu-lated. I discussed wealth accumulation within a single generation first, intergenerational transfers of wealth second, and, third, fluctuations in the level of wealth over a short period.

In the first type, wealth is held as the means to intertemporally allocate consumption, or to guarantee the household its minimum living standard. That is, this type of wealth is used as the continued source of the minimum income necessary to maintain the household's livelihood, as savings laid down for future spending anticipated in the course of the life cycle such as post-retirement spending, or as a buffer against unanticipated economic hardships. This type of wealth can be called 'life-cycle wealth'. The second type of wealth holding occurs when the parental generation leaves wealth (bequests) inten-tionally or unintentionally. This is called 'the wealth for bequests'. It includes not only tangible assets, financial assets, and physical assets such as real estate and housing, but also intangible assets such as education for the children.

Also, the wealth can be transferred once (bequest) or given on many occasions before death. The third type of wealth is generated through rises in the price of assets, which occur in spurts. This is called 'wealth generated by capital gain'. Investors' formation of price expectation is an important component in market price determination, and since the expectation itself has the potential to exhibit self-fulfilling movements termed bubble and bandwagon effects, the amplitude of price fluctuations is further magnified. The asset market inherently harbours instability.

In this book, we have discussed the implications of the various reasons for asset accumulation on the distribution of wealth. Since the economy at any one time includes households at various stages of the life cycle, the level of life-cycle wealth holdings will naturally be different among households. And those life-cycle-type wealth holdings will also be significantly affected by factors such as the existence of a public pension system. Therefore, it is not without reason that it has been suggested that wealth distribution can be explained mainly by differences in life-cycle wealth holdings among households. If that is true, then the difference in wealth holdings can be explained by differences in the (permanent) income of individuals, and thereby ceases to be an issue by itself. But there are clear inconsistencies between the above interpretation and reality. In fact, the distribution of wealth shows as great a degree of inequality after controlling for the age of the household head as without any control for the age of the household head (Section 1.2). That, more than anything else, tells us convincingly that the other types of wealth are very important factors in the inequality of wealth holdings.

Wealth holdings by non-accidental bequest can be classified into two groups, one created by the one-sided altruistic behaviour of the parent generation, and the other by the risk-sharing motive among the parents and children of the family, which is based on trust within the family. If we consider the long-run distribution of wealth, it is important to notice that in both cases, there will be similar transfer relationship between the wealth of the parents and that of the children. If the personal consumption of the children is the necessary good relative to the parents' consumption (the elasticity of the bequest is less than one) or if the consumption of the children is a luxury good (the elasticity of the bequest exceeds one) but the parents' wealth is below some threshold, then over generations, wealth holdings will display mean reversion. That means, over the long run, that economic forces will work towards equalizing wealth distribution. But, in the latter case, when the parents' wealth exceeds the threshold value, then over the generation, unlimited wealth is going to be accumulated. In that case, we will see a clear segmentation of wealth holders into different groups according to the amount of wealth holding (sections 7.1 and 7.2).

We also found out that in the macroeconomy, which is the aggregate of the above households, there are two possible equilibrium growth paths: one with clear stratification of wealth holders into distinct groups, and one with a single homogeneous working class through the mean reversion of wealth holdings (Section 7.3).

We do not need to say much to explain the importance of wealth by capital gain, to those who observed the explosive growth of land and stock prices in the Japanese economy during the late 1980s. In the capital market, the effort to predict future prices more accurately is sometimes rewarded by excess profits. In this book, we have demonstrated this point, along with the rigorous discussion of the efficient capital market hypothesis. We are not so surprised to see the surge in various types of money games, such as investment in financial information gathering, and gains from arbitrage through cleverly choosing the timing of transactions (Section 7.4).

Empirical studies of US bequest behaviour show that the average elasticity of bequests among wealthy parents exceeds one by a large margin. That evidence indicates the existence of a social class for which the forces towards mean reversion of wealth holdings do not work. The above micro evidence is consistent with the significant skewness of the distribution of wealth and the clear stratification of wealth holders in the USA.

We do not need to try to explain wealth accumulation behaviour characterized by high elasticity of bequests, by models of either the altruistic motive or intra-family risk sharing. Rather than using those models, we could interpret the data by claiming that the accumulation of wealth over generations becomes a motive in its own right. Wealth which is held for its own sake not only has a tendency towards self-preservation, but also has a natural tendency towards self-expansion, while exercising considerable influence in various political and economic arenas. Needless to say wealth itself has no (social) influence, but the more wealth is held by a person who has ambitions to exercise influence over other peoples' actions, the easier it will be for him to do so (Harsanyi 1962). In that sense, wealth can be the basis for power. There are abundant examples of money entering the political process, thereby distorting it.

In Japan, the published statistics provide no evidence for segmentation of asset holders. Even though the distribution of asset holdings in fact is more skewed than that of annual income, the degree of concentration of wealth is much more moderate than in the UK and the USA (see section 1.2, where I pointed out that the published statistics have some shortcomings).

Historic events such as the post-Second World War agricultural land reform or the Zaibatsu dissolution, which resulted in artificial equalization of wealth, and the Dodge line, which decreased drastically the value of financial assets through inflation, have clearly contributed to the formation of such distribution. Later, from the late 1950s to the early 1970s, throughout the high-growth period other factors have been involved: (i) earnings have significantly increased and differences in earnings have decreased; (ii) demand for housing and other durable goods has increased due to the increase in the youth population and the massive migration of the population to urban areas; (iii) increased demand for financial asset holdings has not only kept up with the increase in income, but even exceeded its pace, due to households' buffer stock motives safeguarding a certain minimum standard of living; (iv) because of the delay in the full implementation of the Social Security system (in particular, the post-retirement income maintenance programme), households have had additional motives for further accumulating financial assets. All of these factors contributed to exceptionally high savings rates in Japanese households, compared to other countries. And I think that they also gave rise to the economic situation that fits the model of the single labour class economy.

On the other hand, during the 1970s, well before the late 1980s' explosive appreciation of land and stock prices that led to the rapid increase in the gap in wealth holdings among people, there were signs that the inter-household gap in wealth holdings between the upper and the lower tail of the distribution had been increasing (Section 1.2). If this trend and the occasional burst of the asset prices continue in the future, it is not unlikely that we will (again) find ourselves in a class society similar to those of pre-war Japan or Europe or the USA, where there is clear segmentation of people into the working class and the wealth holder class. Therefore, if we are in favour of the equal distribution of wealth, we need to try to keep a close watch on those developments.

Throughout our theoretical analyses, I have been assuming that households are the only agents that hold assets in the private sector. That is, the premise was that the net assets (net wealth) of the firm, which are the asset values net of the value of the stocks issued by the firm, always remain zero because the asset holdings of the firm are incorporated in the value of households' stock holdings. But in reality, those assumptions are not met. If we look at the aggregate asset statistics, at the end of 1985 the Japanese corporate sector had wealth holdings that were as much as 30 per cent of the wealth in the household sector. Furthermore, it is pointed out that, in Japan, managers avoid shareholder control through the closely knit system of mutual shareholding among companies. Therefore, (at least) the wealth accumulated within a firm is effectively controlled by its manager. Also, this is the typical case of wealth held for its own sake. It is needless to say that the degree of concentration of corporate wealth is very high (see Ishikawa 1990).

How should we evaluate the fact that huge amounts of wealth are held by the managerial class? If we consider managerial know-how, talent, and innovative ability as scarce human resources, then it makes sense for a society to give managers greater control over wealth. By allowing firms to pursue the accumulation of wealth, the private sector economy expects, in effect, maximum usage of the above managerial resources. At the same time, increases in knowledge and new opportunities for innovation favour the injection of fresh blood into management, and hence no single individual or social class can hold on to managerial positions and control. We can expect this system to enhance social equality by encouraging high mobility among the social classes over time.

It is true that, because managers in large corporations freed themselves from shareholder control and acquired broad control over their firms, they were able to give workers jobs with broad training opportunities, which resulted in employment stability and high productivity. On the other hand, it is also true that, backed by huge wealth holdings, they have repeatedly exercised their political power and influence to protect their vested interests. Nowadays, there has been increasing criticisms, both in Japan and from abroad, pointing out that, compared to its high income and wealth, its democracy is disproportionately immature. We need to critically examine whether the concentration of wealth among a small class of people, and the lack of effective countermeasures was one of the reasons for this. Those points, however, are beyond the scope of this book and await future research.

Let us now conclude this book by pointing out areas that I did not discuss. Inequalities of income and wealth among nations and redistribution of wealth including allocation of the costs and benefits of public goods are clearly important distributional issues. Those topics, however, require approaches that are different from those in our book. Hence, I leave the analysis and examination of those issues for future consideration.

Bibliography

Abel, Andrew B. (1985), 'Precautionary Saving and Accidental Bequests', *American Economic Review*, 75 (September): 777–91.

Adams, James D. (1980), 'Personal Wealth Transfers', *Quarterly Journal of Economics*, 95 (August): 159–79.

Akerlof, George A. (1970), 'The Market for "Lemons": Qualitative Uncertainty and the Market Mechanism', *Quarterly Journal of Economics*, 84 (August): 488–500.

—— (1982), 'Labor Contracts as Partial Gift Exchange', *Quarterly Journal of Economics*, 97 (November): 543–69.

—— and Yellen, Janet (1985), 'A Near-Rational Model of the Business Cycle, with Wage and Price Inertia', *Quarterly Journal of Economics*, 100 (Supplement): 823–38.

Alchian, Armen, and Demsetz, Harold (1972), 'Production, Information Costs, and Economic Organization', *American Economic Review*, 62 (December): 777–95.

Altonji, Joseph (1982), 'The Intertemporal Substitution Model of Labor Market Fluctuations: An Empirical Analysis', *Review of Economic Studies*, 49 (Special Issue): 783–824.

Aoki, Masahiko (1980), 'A Model of the Firm as a Stockholder–Employee Cooperative Game', *American Economic Review*, 70 (September): 600–10.

—— (1982), 'Equilibrium Growth of the Hierarchical Firm: Shareholder–Employee Cooperative Game Approach', *American Economic Review*, 72 (December): 1097–1110.

Arrow, Kenneth J. (1963a), *Social Choice and Individual Values*, 2nd edition. New Haven: Yale University Press.

—— (1963b), 'Uncertainty and the Welfare Economics of Medical Care', *American Economic Review*, 53 (December): 941–73.

—— (1972), 'Models of Job Discrimination', in Anthony H. Pascal (ed.), *Racial Discrimination in Economic Life*. Lexington, Mass.: D.C. Heath: 83–102.

—— (1973a), 'Some Ordinalist-Utilitarian Notes on Rawls' Theory of Justice', *Journal of Philosophy*, 70 (May): 245–63.

—— (1973b), 'Higher Education as a Filter', *Journal of Public Economics*, 2 (July): 193–216.

Asako, Kazumi, Kanoh, Satoru, and Sano, Hisashi (1990), 'Stock Price and Bubble', (in Japanese), in K. Nishimura and Y. Miwa (eds.), *Stock and Land Price in Japan*. Tokyo: University of Tokyo Press: 57–86.

Ashenfelter, Orley, and Card, David (1982), 'Time Series Representations of Economic Variables and Alternative Models of Labour Market', *Review of Economic Studies*, 49 (Special Issue): 761–81.

Atkinson, Anthony B. (1970), 'On the Measurement of Inequality', *Journal of Economic Theory*, 2 (September): 244–63.

—— (1971a), 'Capital Taxes, the Redistribution of Wealth and Individual Savings', *Review of Economic Studies*, 38 (April): 209–27.

—— (1971b), 'The Distribution of Wealth and the Individual Life-Cycle', *Oxford Economic Papers*, 23 (July): 239–54.

——and Harrison, Alan J. (1978), *Distribution of Personal Wealth in Britain*. Cambridge: Cambridge University Press.

Aumann, Robert J., and Kurz, Mordecai (1977), 'Power and Taxes', *Econometrica*, 45 (July): 1137–60.

Averitt, Robert (1968), *The Dual Economy: The Dynamics of American Industry Structure*. New York: Norton.

Banfield, Edward C. (1968), *The Unheavenly City: The Nature and the Future of Our Urban Crisis*. Boston: Little Brown.

Barro, Robert J. (1974), 'Are Government Bonds Net Wealth?', *Journal of Political Economy*, 82 (November/December): 1095–1117.

——and Friedmann, James (1977), 'On Uncertain Lifetimes', *Journal of Political Economy*, 85 (August): 843–9.

Becker, Gary S. (1962), 'Investment in Human Capital: A Theoretical Analysis', *Journal of Political Economy*, 70, Supplement (October): 9–49.

——(1964), *Human Capital: A Theoretical and Empirical Analysis, with Special Reference to Education* (2nd edition, 1975). New York: Columbia University Press.

——(1967), 'Human Capital and the Personal Income Distribution: An Analytical Approach', Woytinski Lecture No. 1. Ann Arbor: University of Michigan Press. Reprinted in *Human Capital* (2nd edition, 1975): 94–144.

——(1974), 'A Theory of Social Interactions', *Journal of Political Economy*, 82 (November/December): 1063–93.

——and Stigler, George (1974), 'Law Enforcement, Malfeasance, and Compensation of Enforcers', *Journal of Legal Studies*, 3 (January): 1–18.

——and Tomes, Nigel (1979), 'An Equilibrium Theory of the Distribution of Income and Intergenerational Mobility', *Journal of Political Economy*, 87 (December): 1153–89.

Behrman, Jere R., and Taubman, Paul (1976), 'Intergenerational Transmission of Income and Wealth', *American Economic Review*, 66 (May): 436–40.

Ben-Porath, Yoram (1967), 'The Production of Human Capital and the Life Cycle of Earnings', *Journal of Political Economy*, 75 (August): 352–65.

Bernheim, B. Douglas, Shleifer, Andrei, and Summers, Lawrence H. (1985), 'The Strategic Bequest Motive', *Journal of Political Economy*, 93 (December): 1045–76.

Blau, Peter M., and Duncan, Otis D. (1967), *The American Occupational Structure*. New York: John Wiley.

Blaug, Mark (1972), *An Introduction to the Economics of Education*. Baltimore and Middlesex: Penguin.

——(1976), 'The Empirical Status of Human Capital Theory: A Slightly Jaundiced Survey', *Journal of Economic Literature*, 14 (September): 827–55.

Blinder, Alan S. (1973), 'A Model of Inherited Wealth', *Quarterly Journal of Economics*, 87 (November): 608–26.

——(1988), 'Comments on Chapter 1 and Chapter 2', in Denis Kessler and Andre Masson (eds.), *Modelling the Accumulation and Distribution of Wealth*. Oxford: Clarendon Press: 68–76.

——and Weiss, Yoram (1974), *Human Capital and Labor Supply: A Synthesis*. Princeton: Princeton University Press.

Blumenthal, Tuvia (1968), 'Scarcity of Labor and Wage Differentials in the Japanese Economy', *Economic Development and Cultural Change*, 17 (October): 15–32.

Bodmer, Walter F. (1972), 'Race and IQ: The Genetic Background', in K. Richardson and D. Spears (eds), *Race and Intelligence: The Fallacies Behind the Race-IQ Controversy*. Baltimore: Penguin.

Boorman, Scott A. (1975), 'A Combinatorial Optimization Model for Transmission of Job Information through Contact Networks', *Bell Journal of Economics*, 6 (Spring): 216–49.

Bowles, Samuel (1972), 'Schooling and Inequality from Generation to Generation', *Journal of Political Economy*, 80 (May/June): S219–S251.

—— and Gintis, Herbert (1976), *Schooling in Capitalist America, Educational Reform and the Contradictions of Economic Life*. New York: Basic Books.

—— and Nelson, Valerie (1974), 'The Inheritance of IQ and the Intergenerational Reproduction of Economic Inequality', *Review of Economics and Statistics*, 56 (February): 39–51.

—— Gintis, Herbert, and Meyer, Peter (1975), 'The Long Shadow of Work: Education, the Family, and the Reproduction of the Social Division of Labor', *Insurgent Sociologist*, 5 (Summer): 3–22.

—— Gordon, David, and Weisskopf, Thomas (1983), *Beyond the Waste Land: A Democratic Alternative to Economic Decline*. New York: Anchor Press.

Braverman, Harry (1974), *Labor and Monopoly Capital: The Degradation of Work in the Twentieth Century*. New York: Monthly Review Press.

Bray, Margaret (1981), 'Futures Trading, Rational Expectations, and the Efficient Markets Hypothesis', *Econometrica*, 49 (May): 575–96.

Brenner, Marshall H. (1968), 'Use of High School Data to Predict Work Performance', *Journal of Applied Psychology*, 52 (February): 29–30.

Brittain, John A. (1978), *Inheritance and the Inequality of Material Wealth*. Washington, D.C.: The Brookings Institution.

Brown, Charles (1980), 'Equalizing Differences in the Labor Market', *Quarterly Journal of Economics*, 95 (February): 113–34.

Buchanan, Allen (1975), 'Revisability and Rational Choice', *Canadian Journal of Philosophy*, 5 (November): 395–408.

Bulow, Jeremy, and Summers, Lawrence H. (1986), 'A Theory of Dual Labor Market with Application to Industrial Policy, Discrimination and Keynesian Unemployment', *Journal of Labor Economics*, 4 (July): 376–414.

Cain, Glen (1976), 'The Challenge of Segmented Labor Market Theories to Orthodox Theory: A Survey', *Journal of Economic Literature*, 14 (December): 1215–57.

Calvo, Guillermo (1979), 'Quasi-Walrasian Theories of Unemployment', *American Economic Review*, 69 (May): 102–7.

—— and Wellisz, Stanislaw (1978), 'Supervision, Loss of Control, and the Optimum Size of the Firm', *Journal of Political Economy*, 86 (October): 943–52.

———— (1979), 'Hierarchy, Ability and Income Distribution', *Journal of Political Economy*, 87 (October): 991–1010.

Carmichael, Lorne (1985), 'Can Unemployment Be Involuntary?: Comment', *American Economic Review*, 75 (December): 1213–14.

Chamberlin, Gary, and Griliches, Zvi (1975), 'Unobservables with a Variance-Components Structure: Ability, Schooling, and the Economic Success of Brothers', *International Economics Review*, 16 (June): 422–49.

—————(1977), 'More on Brothers', in Paul Taubman (ed.), *Kinometrics: Determinants of Socioeconomic Success Within and Between Families*. Amsterdam: North-Holland: 97–124.

Champernowne, David G. (1953), 'A Model of Income Distribution', *Economic Journal*, 63 (June): 318–51.

Clower, Robert (1965), 'The Keynesian Counter-Revolution: A Theoretical Appraisal', in F. Hahn and F. Brechling (eds.), *The Theory of Interest Rates*. London: Macmillan: 103–25.

Coase, Ronald (1937), 'The Nature of the Firm', *Economica* (New Series), 4 (November): 386–405.

Cootner, Paul H. (ed.) (1964), *The Random Character of Stock Market Prices*. Cambridge, Mass.: MIT Press.

Cootner, Robert, and Rappoport, Peter (1984), 'Were the Ordinalists Wrong about Welfare Economics?', *Journal of Economic Literature*, 22 (June): 507–30.

Daniels, Norman (1975), *Reading Rawls: A Critical Study of 'A Theory of Justice'*. Oxford: Basil Blackwell.

Danielsen, Albert L., and Okachi, Katsuji (1971), 'Private Rates of Return to Schooling in Japan,' *Journal of Human Resources*, 6 (Summer): 391–7.

Danthine, Jean-Pierre (1978), 'Information, Futures Prices and Stabilizing Speculation', *Journal of Economic Theory*, 17 (February): 79–98.

Dasgupta, Partha (1974), 'On Some Criteria for Justice between Generations', *Journal of Public Economics*, 3 (November): 405–23.

Davidson, Paul (1972), *Money and the Real World*. New York: John Wiley.

Davies, James (1981), 'Uncertain Lifetime, Consumption, and Dissaving in Retirement', *Journal of Political Economy*, 89 (June): 561–77.

Davis, Louis E., and Trist, Eric L. (1974), 'Improving the Quality of Work Life: Sociotechnical Case Studies', in James O'Toole (ed.), *Work and the Quality of Life: Resource Papers for Work in America*. Cambridge, Mass.: MIT Press: 246–80.

Denison, Edward (1967), *Why Growth Rates Differ: Postwar Experience in Nine Western Countries*. Washington, D.C.: The Brookings Institution.

Diamond, Peter, and Hausman, Jerry (1984), 'Individual Retirement and Savings Behavior', *Journal of Public Economics*, 23 (February/March): 81–114.

Dickens, William, and Katz, Lawrence (1987), 'Inter-Industry Wage Differences and Industry Characteristics', in Kevin Lang and Jonathan Leonard (eds.), *Unemployment and the Structure of Labor Markets*. Oxford: Basil Blackwell.

——and Lang, Kevin (1985*a*), 'A Test of Dual Labor Market Theory', *American Economic Review*, 75 (September): 792–805.

—————(1985*b*), 'Testing Dual Labor Market Theory: A Reconsideration of the Evidence', *NBER Working Paper* 1670 (July).

Doeringer, Peter, and Piore, Michael (1971), *Internal Labor Markets and Manpower Analysis*. Lexington, Mass.: D.C. Heath.

Donaldson, David, and Eaton, B. Curtis (1976), 'Firm-Specific Human Capital: A Shared Investment or Optimal Entrapment?', *Canadian Journal of Economics*, 9 (August): 462–72.

Duncan, Otis D., Featherman, David L., and Duncan, Beverly (1968), 'Socioeconomic Background and Occupational Achievement: Extensions of A Basic Model', Final

Report Project No. 5-0074(EO-191), Bureau of Research, Office of Education, U.S. Department of Health, Education, and Welfare (May).

Dworkin, Ronald (1975), 'The Original Position', in N. Daniels (ed.), *Reading Rawls*. Oxford: Basil Blackwell: 16–53.

Eaton, B. Curtis, and White, William (1982), 'Agent Compensation and the Limits of Bonding', *Economic Inquiry*, 20 (July): 330–43.

Eckstein, Zvi, Eichenbaum, Martin S., and Peled, Dan (1985), 'The Distribution of Wealth and Welfare in the Presence of Incomplete Annuity Markets', *Quarterly Journal of Economics*, 100 (August): 789–806.

Economic Planning Agency (1975), *Facts and Problems about Income and Wealth Distribution: A Report on Studying Group of Income Distribution* (in Japanese). Tokyo: Economic Planning Agency.

Edwards, Richard C. (1977), 'Personal Traits and "Success" in Schooling and Work', *Educational and Psychological Measurement*, 37 (Spring): 125–38.

——(1979), *Contested Terrain: The Transformation of the Workplace in the Twentieth Century*. New York: Basic Books.

—— Gordon, David M., and Reich, Michael (1982), *Segmented Work, Divided Workers: The Historical Transformation of Labor in the United States*. Cambridge: Cambridge University Press.

Eichenbaum, Martin S., and Peled, Dan (1987), 'Capital Accumulation and Annuities in an Adverse Selection Economy', *Journal of Political Economy*, 95 (April): 334–54.

Fägerlind, Ingemar (1975), *Formal Education and Adult Earnings: A Longitudinal Study on the Economic Benefits of Education*. Stockholm: Almqvist and Wiksell International.

Fallon, Peter, and Layard, Richard (1975), 'Capital-Skill Complementarity, Income Distribution, and Output Accounting', *Journal of Political Economy*, 83 (April): 279–301.

Fama, Eugene F. (1970), 'Efficient Capital Markets: A Review of Theory and Empirical Work', *Journal of Finance*, 25 (May): 383–424.

——(1976), *Foundations of Finance: Portfolio Decisions and Securities Prices*. New York: Basic Books.

Figlewski, Stephen (1978), 'Market "Efficiency" in a Market with Heterogeneous Information', *Journal of Political Economy*, 86 (August): 581–97.

Foley, Duncan K. (1975), 'On Two Specifications of Asset Equilibrium in Macro-economic Models', *Journal of Political Economy*, 83 (March/April): 303–24.

Friedman, Benjamin M., and Laibson, David I. (1989), 'Economic Implications of Extraordinary Movements in Stock Prices', *Brookings Papers on Economic Activity*, 2: 137–89.

Friedman, Milton (1953), 'Choice, Chance and the Personal Distribution of Income', *Journal of Political Economy*, 61 (August): 277–90.

——(1962), *Capitalism and Freedom*. Chicago: University of Chicago Press.

Friend, Irwin, and Blume, Marshall E. (1975), 'The Demand for Risky Assets', *American Economic Review*, 65 (December): 900–22.

Funahashi, Naomichi (1983), *Japanese Employment and Wages* (in Japanese). Tokyo: Hosei University Press.

Gibrat, R. (1931), *Les Inégalités Economiques*. Paris.

Gintis, Herbert (1971), 'Education, Technology, and the Characteristics of Worker Productivity', *American Economic Review*, 61 (May): 266–79.

—— and Ishikawa, Tsuneo (1986), 'Wages, Work Intensity and Labor Hoarding under Uncertain Demand: A State Contingent Recontracting Model', *Discussion Paper 86-F-4*, University of Tokyo (October).

—— —— (1987), 'Wages, Work Intensity and Unemployment', *Journal of the Japanese and International Economies*, 1 (June): 195–228.

Goode, William J. (1964), *The Family*. Englewood Cliffs, N.J.: Prentice Hall.

Granovetter, Mark S. (1974), *Getting a Job: A Study of Contracts and Careers*. Cambridge, Mass.: Harvard University Press.

Green, Jerry, and Stokey, Nancy (1983), 'A Comparison of Tournaments and Contracts', *Journal of Political Economy*, 91 (June): 349–64.

Griliches, Zvi (1969), 'Capital-Skill Complementarity', *Review of Economics and Statistics*, 51 (November): 465–8.

—— (1977), 'Estimating the Returns to Schooling: Some Econometric Problems', *Econometrica*, 45 (January): 1–22.

—— (1979), 'Sibling Models and Data in Economics: Beginnings of a Survey', *Journal of Political Economy*, 87 (October): S37–S64.

—— and Mason, William M. (1972), 'Education, Income, and Ability', *Journal of Political Economy*, 80 (May/June): S74–S103.

Grossman, Sanford (1976), 'On the Efficiency of Competitive Stock Markets Where Traders Have Diverse Information', *Journal of Finance,* 31 (May): 573–85.

—— and Shiller, Robert J. (1981), 'The Determinants of the Variability of Stock Market Prices', *American Economic Review*, 71 (May): 222–7.

—— and Stiglitz, Joseph E. (1980), 'On the Impossibility of Informationally Efficient Equilibrium', *American Economic Review*, 70 (June): 393–408.

Hammond, Peter J. (1976), 'Why Ethical Measures of Inequality Need Interpersonal Comparisons', *Theory and Decision*, 7 (October): 263–74.

Hanoch, Giora (1967), 'An Economic Analysis of Earnings and Schooling', *Journal of Human Resources*, 2 (Summer): 310–29.

Hansen, Lee (1963), 'Total and Private Rates of Return to Investment in Schooling', *Journal of Political Economy*, 71 (April): 128–40.

Harbury, C. D. (1962), 'Inheritance and the Distribution of Personal Wealth in Britain', *Economic Journal*, 72 (December): 845–68.

—— and Hitchens, D. M. W. N. (1976), 'The Inheritances of Top Wealth Leavers: Some Further Evidence', *Economic Journal*, 86 (June): 321–6.

—— and McMahon, P. C. (1973), 'Inheritance and the Characteristics of Top Wealth Leavers in Britain', *Economic Journal*, 83 (September): 810–33.

Harris, John R., and Todaro, Michael P. (1970), 'Migration, Unemployment and Development: A Two Sector Analysis', *American Economic Review*, 60 (March): 126–42.

Harris, Milton, and Holmstrom, Bengt (1982), 'A Theory of Wage Dynamics', *Review of Economic Studies*, 49 (July): 315–33.

Harsanyi, John C. (1953), 'Cardinal Utility in Welfare Economics and the Theory of Risk-taking', *Journal of Political Economy*, 61 (October): 434–5.

—— (1955), 'Cardinal Welfare, Individualistic Ethics and Interpersonal Comparisons of Utility', *Journal of Political Economy*, 63 (August): 309–21.

Harsanyi, John C. (1956), 'Approaches to the Bargaining Problem before and after the Theory of Games: A Critical Discussion of Zeuthen's, Hicks's and Nash's Theories', *Econometrica*, 24 (January): 144–57.

—— (1962), 'The Dimension and Measurement of Social Power', *Behavioral Science*, 7: 67–80.

Hashimoto, Masanori (1975), 'Wage Reduction, Unemployment and Specific Human Capital', *Economic Inquiry*, 13 (December): 485–504.

—— and Raisian, John (1985), 'Employment Tenure and Earnings Profiles in Japan and the United States', *American Economic Review*, 75 (September): 721–35.

Hayashi, Fumio, Ando, Albert, and Ferris, Richard (1988), 'Life Cycle and Bequest Saving: A Study of Japanese and U.S. Households Based on the 1984 NSFIE Data and Data from the Survey of Consumer Finances', *Journal of the Japanese and International Economies*, 2 (December): 450–91.

Hayek, Friedrich A. (1960), *Constitution of Liberty*. London: Routledge & Kegan Paul.

Helpman, Elhanan (1981), 'International Trade in the Presence of Product Differentiation, Economies of Scale and Monopolistic Competition: A Chamberlin–Heckscher–Ohlin Approach', *Journal of International Economics*, 11 (August): 305–40.

Hicks, John (1970), 'Elasticity of Substitution Again: Substitutes and Complements', *Oxford Economic Papers*, 22 (November): 289–96.

Higuchi, Yoshio (1989), 'Japan's Changing Wage Structure: The Impact of Internal Factors and International Competition', *Journal of the Japanese and International Economies*, 3 (December): 480–99.

Hindle, Brooke (1981), *Emulation and Invention*. New York: Norton.

Horioka, Charles (1990), 'Why is Japan's Household Saving Rate So High?: A Literary Survey', *Journal of the Japanese and International Economies*, 4 (March): 49–92.

Hutchison, Terrence W. (1964), *'Positive' Economics and Policy Objectives*. London: Allen and Unwin.

Inada, Ken-ichi (1977), *Economics for the Disadvantaged* (in Japanese). Tokyo: Toyo Keizai Shinposha.

Ishikawa, Tsuneo (1974), 'Imperfection in the Capital Market and the Institutional Arrangement of Inheritance', *Review of Economic Studies*, 41 (July): 383–404.

—— (1975), 'Family Structures and Family Values in the Theory of Income Distribution', *Journal of Political Economy*, 83 (October): 987–1008.

—— (1980), 'Corporation Saving, the Financial Market, and Macro Distribution of Income' (in Japanese), *Keizaigaku Ronshu*, 46 (July): 20–48.

—— (1981a), 'The "Emulation" Effect as a Determinant of Work Motivation' (in Japanese), *Keizaigaku Ronshu*, 47 (April): 2–15.

—— (1981b), 'Dual Labor Market Hypothesis and Long-Run Income Distribution', *Journal of Development Economics*, 9 (August): 1–30.

—— (1984), 'Learning Opportunity and Job Hierarchy', paper presented at the American Studies Seminar, Doshisha University, Kyoto, August.

—— (1987), 'Structural Elements in Household Saving and Financial Taxation' (in Japanese), in K. Hamada, A. Horiuchi, and M. Kuroda (eds.), *A Macro-economic Analysis of the Japanese Economy*. Tokyo: University of Tokyo Press: 177–210.

—— (1988a), 'On the Conceptualization of the Cost of Human Investment and the National Income Accounting' (in Japanese), in Y. Onitsuka and

K. Iwai (eds.), *Studies in Modern Economics*. Tokyo: University of Tokyo Press: 328–46.

——(1988*b*), 'Saving and Labor Supply Behavior of Aged Households in Japan', *Journal of the Japanese and International Economies*, 2 (December): 417–49.

——(1989), 'A Theoretical Re-examination of the Dualistic Wage Structure' (in Japanese), in M. Tsuchiya and Y. Miwa (eds.), *Small and Medium Size Firms in Japan*. Tokyo: University of Tokyo Press: 117–40.

——(1990), 'Household Wealth and Corporate Wealth—On the Concentration of Wealth in Japan' (in Japanese), in Y. Miwa and K. Nishimura (eds.), *Stock and Land Prices in Japan*. Tokyo: University of Tokyo Press: 231–62.

——and Genda, Yuji (1989), 'Rationing in the Labor Market and the Seniority Wage' (in Japanese), *Discussion Paper 89-J-9*, Faculty of Economics, University of Tokyo, September.

Ishizaki, Tadao (1983), *The Distribution of Income and Wealth in Japan* (in Japanese). Tokyo: Toyo Keizai Shinposha.

Ito, Mitsuharu (1962), 'Evaluation of the Dual Labor Market Theory' (in Japanese), in H. Kawaguchi, M. Shinohara, K. Nagasu, K. Miyazawa, and M. Ito (eds.), *The Basic Structure of the Japanese Economy*. Tokyo: Shunjyusha: 169–212.

Jencks, Christopher (1972), *Inequality: A Reassessment of the Effect of Family and Schooling in America*. New York: Basic Books.

Jensen, Arthur R. (1969), 'How Much Can We Boost IQ and Scholastic Achievement?', *Harvard Educational Review*, 39 (Winter): 1–123.

Johnson, William R. (1978), 'A Theory of Job Shopping', *Quarterly Journal of Economics*, 92 (May): 261–77.

Johnston, John (1972), *Econometric Methods* (2nd edition). New York: McGraw-Hill.

Jones, Ronald W. (1965), 'The Structure of Simple General Equilibrium Models', *Journal of Political Economy*, 73 (December): 557–72.

Jorgenson, Dale W., and Griliches, Zvi (1967), 'The Explanation of Productivity Change', *Review of Economic Studies*, 34 (July): 249–83.

Jovanovic, Boyan (1979), 'Job Maching and the Theory of Turnover', *Journal of Political Economy*, 87 (October): 972–89.

Kaizuka, Keimei, Ishida, Yuko, Ishiyama, Yukitada, Hara, Takahiro, and Ono, Hiroko (1979), 'A Research for Income Distribution among Working Households: Human Capital Theory and Income Distribution by Life Stage' (in Japanese), *Economic Research Series* 34, Economic Planning Agency.

Kaldor, Nicholas (1966), 'Marginal Productivity and the Macro-Economic Theories of Distribution', *Review of Economic Studies*, 33 (October): 309–20.

Kalecki, Michal (1945), 'On the Gibrat Distribution', *Econometrica*, 13 (April): 161–70.

Kanbur, S. M. Ravi (1979), 'Of Risk Taking and the Personal Distribution of Income', *Journal of Political Economy*, 87 (August): 769–97.

Kant, Immanuel (1785), *Groundwork of the Metaphysic of Morals*, translated by H. J. Patton. New York: Harper.

——(1793), 'Über den Gemeinspruch: Das mag in der Theorie richtig sein, taugt aber nicht für die Praxis', *Die Berlinische Monatsschrift* (September).

Keynes, John M. (1936), *The General Theory of Employment, Interest and Money*. London: Macmillan.

Killingsworth, Mark R. (1983), *Labour Supply*. Cambridge: Cambridge University Press.

King, Melvyn A., and Dicks-Mireaux, L-D. L. (1982), 'Asset Holdings and the Life-Cycle', *Economic Journal*, 92 (June): 247–67.

Knight, Frank H. (1923), 'The Ethics of Competition', *Quarterly Journal of Economics*, 37 (August): 579–624. Reprinted in *The Ethics of Competition*. Chicago: University of Chicago Press, 1935.

Kohn, Melvin L. (1969), *Class and Conformity: A Study in Values*. Homewood, Illinois: Dorsey.

——and Schooler, Carmi (1973), 'Occupational Experience and Psychological Functioning: An Assessment of Reciprocal Effects', *American Sociological Review*, 38 (February): 87–118.

Koike, Kazuo (1971), 'Wage Level' (in Japanese), in Rodo Mondai Bunken Kenkyu-kai (ed.), *Readings: Japanese Labor Problem*. Tokyo: Sogo Rodo Kenkyu-sho: 112–29.

——(1977), *Labor Union in Workplace and Participation* (in Japanese). Tokyo: Toyo Keizai Shimposha.

——(1981*a*), *Skill Formulation in Small and Medium-sized Firms* (in Japanese). Tokyo: Dobunkan.

——(1981*b*), *Skill in Japan* (in Japanese). Tokyo: Toyo Keizai Shimposha.

Kotlikoff, Laurence, and Spivak, Avia (1981), 'The Family as an Incomplete Annuities Market', *Journal of Political Economy*, 89 (April): 372–91.

——and Summers, Lawrence (1981), 'The Role of Intergenerational Transfers in Aggregate Capital Accumulation', *Journal of Political Economy*, 89 (August): 706–32.

————(1988), 'The Contribution of Intergenerational Transfers to Total Wealth: A Reply', in Denis Kessler and Andre Masson (eds.), *Modelling the Accumulation and Distribution of Wealth*. Oxford: Clarendon Press: 53–67.

Krueger, Alan, and Summers, Lawrence H. (1988), 'Efficiency Wages and the Inter-industry Wage Structure', *Econometrica*, 56 (March): 259–93.

Landes, David S. (1972), *The Unbound Prometheus: Technological Change and Industrial Development in Western Europe from 1750 to the Present*. Cambridge: Cambridge University Press.

Lazear, Edward (1979), 'Why Is There Mandatory Retirement?', *Journal of Political Economy*, 87 (December): 1261–84.

——and Rosen, Sherwin (1981), 'Rank-Order Tournaments as Optimum Labor Contracts', *Journal of Political Economy*, 89 (October): 841–64.

Leibowitz, Arleen (1977), 'Family Background and Economic Success: A Review of the Evidence', in Paul Taubman (ed.), *Kinometrics: Determinants of Socioeconomic Success Within and Between Families*. Amsterdam: North-Holland: 9–33.

Leigh, Duane (1976), 'Occupational Advancement in the late 1960s: An Indirect Test of the Dual Labor Market Hypothesis', *Journal of Human Resources*, 11 (Spring): 155–71.

LeRoy, Stephen F. (1973), 'Risk Aversion and the Martingale Property of Stock Prices', *International Economic Review*, 14 (June): 436–46.

——and Porter, Robert D. (1981), 'The Present-Value Relation: Tests Based on Implied Variance Bounds', *Econometrica*, 49 (May): 555–74.

Levhari, David, and Weiss, Yoram (1974), 'The Effect of Risk on the Investment in Human Capital', *American Economic Review*, 64 (December): 950–63.

Levitan, Sar A., and Werneke, Diane (1984), 'Worker Participation and Productivity Change', *Monthly Labor Review*, 107 (September): 28–33.

Lillard, Lee A. (1977), 'Inequality: Earnings vs. Human Wealth', *American Economic Review*, 67 (March): 42–53.

Lindbeck, Assar, and Snower, Denis (1986), 'Wage Setting, Unemployment, and Insider-Outsider Relations', *American Economic Review*, 76 (May): 235–9.

Lucas, Robert E., and Rapping, Leonard (1969), 'Real Wages, Employment and Inflation', *Journal of Political Economy*, 77 (September/October): 721–54. Reprinted in R. E. Lucas, *Studies in Business Cycle Theory*. Cambridge, Mass.: MIT Press, 1981.

Malinvaud, Edmond (1977), *Lectures on Microeconomic Theory* (2nd edition). Amsterdam: North-Holland.

Mandelbrot, Benoit (1962), 'Paretian Distributions and Income Maximization', *Quarterly Journal of Economics*, 77 (February): 57–85.

——(1963), 'The Variation of Certain Speculative Prices', *Journal of Business*, 36 (October): 394–419.

Marglin, Stephen A. (1974), 'What Do Bosses Do? The Origins and Functions of Hierarchy in Capitalist Production', *Review of Radical Political Economics*, 6 (Summer): 60–112.

Marris, Robin (1964), *The Economic Theory of 'Managerial' Capitalism*. London: Macmillan, reprinted with corrections, 1967.

Marshall, Alfred (1920), *Principles of Economics* (8th edition). London: Macmillan.

Marx, Karl (1867), *Das Kapital: Kritik der politischen Oekonomie, I*. Hamburg.

——(1875), *Critique of the Gotha Programme, with Appendices by Marx, Engels and Lenin*. New York: International Publishers, 1938.

Mayer, Thomas (1972), *Permanent Income, Wealth and Consumption: A Critique of the Permanent Income Theory, the Life-Cycle Hypothesis and Related Theories*. Berkeley: University of California Press.

Meade, James E. (1964), *Efficiency, Equality, and the Ownership of Property*. Cambridge, Mass.: Harvard University Press.

——(1966), 'The Outcome of the Pasinetti Process: A Note', *Economic Journal*, 76 (March): 161–5.

Medoff, James, and Abraham, Katherine (1980), 'Experience, Performance and Earnings', *Quarterly Journal of Economics*, 95 (December): 703–36.

————(1981), 'Are Those Paid More Really More Productive? The Case of Experience', *Journal of Human Resources*, 16 (Spring): 186–216.

Menchik, Paul L. (1979), 'Intergenerational Transmission of Inequality: An Empirical Study of Wealth Mobility', *Economica*, 46 (November): 349–62.

——(1980), 'Primogeniture, Equal Sharing, and the U.S. Distribution of Wealth', *Quarterly Journal of Economics*, 94 (March): 299–316.

——and David, Martin (1983), 'Income Distribution, Lifetime Savings, and Bequests', *American Economic Review*, 73 (September): 672–90.

Metzler, Lloyd A. (1951), 'Wealth, Saving and the Rate of Interest', *Journal of Political Economy*, 59 (April): 93–116.

Mill, John S. (1863), *Utilitarianism* (7th edition, 1879). London: Longmans, Green, Reader & Dyes: 459–528.

Mill, John S. (1848), *Principles of Political Economy* (9th edition, 1885). London: Longmans.

Mincer, Jacob (1958), 'Investment in Human Capital and Personal Income Distribution', *Journal of Political Economy*, 66 (August): 281–302.

—— (1974), *Schooling, Experience and Earnings*. New York: Columbia University Press.

—— and Higuchi, Yoshio (1988), 'Wage Structures and Labor Turnover in the United States and Japan', *Journal of the Japanese and International Economies*, 2 (June): 97–133.

Ministry of Labour, Japan (1985), *Basic Survey on Wage Structure 1985*, Tokyo: Ministry of Labour.

Mirer, Thad (1979), 'The Wealth–Age Relation among the Aged', *American Economic Review*, 69 (June): 435–43.

Miyazaki, Hajime (1977), 'The Rat Race and Internal Labor Markets', *Bell Journal of Economics*, 8 (Autumn): 394–418.

Mizoguchi, Toshiyuki, and Takayama, Noriyuki (1984), *Equity and Poverty under Rapid Economic Growth: The Japanese Experience*, Tokyo: Kinokuniya.

Modigliani, Franco (1988), 'Measuring the Contribution of Intergenerational Transfers to Total Wealth: Conceptual Issues and Empirical Findings', in Denis Kessler and Andre Masson (eds.), *Modelling the Accumulation and Distribution of Wealth*, Oxford: Clarendon Press: 21–52.

Moggridge, Donald (1976), *Keynes*, London: Macmillan.

Moore, Basil J. (1975), 'Equities, Capital Gains, and the Role of Finance in Accumulation', *American Economic Review*, 65 (December): 872–86.

Morishima, Michio (1988), 'Wage Differentials in Japan: 1958–85', a paper presented at Japan–Italy Workshop, 11–12 October.

Mortensen, Dale T. (1978), 'Specific Capital and Labor Turnover', *Bell Journal of Economics*, 9 (Autumn): 572–86.

Nash, John F. (1950), 'Bargaining Problem', *Econometrica*, 18 (April): 155–62.

Negishi, Takashi (1989), *History of Economic Theory*, Amsterdam: North-Holland.

Noguchi, Yukio (1989), *Economics of Land* (in Japanese). Tokyo: Nihon Keizai Shimbunsha.

Nozick, Robert (1974), *Anarchy, State and Utopia*, Oxford: Basil Blackwell.

Odaka, Konosuke (1984), *Labor Market Analysis: Transition of the Dual Structure in Japan* (in Japanese) Tokyo: Iwanami Shoten.

Ohashi, Isao (1978), 'Imperfect Information, Quasi-fixed Labor, and Selection within Firms' (in Japanese), *Economic Studies Quarterly*, 29 (August): 97–108.

Oi, Walter (1962), 'Labor as a Quasi-Fixed Factor', *Journal of Political Economy*, 70 (December): 538–55.

Okun, Arthur M. (1973), 'Upward Mobility in a High-Pressure Economy', *Brookings Papers on Economic Activity*, 1: 207–61.

—— (1975), *Equality and Efficiency: The Big Tradeoff*. Washington, D.C.: The Brookings Institution.

Ono, Akira (1973), *Wage Determination in Post-war Japan* (in Japanese). Tokyo: Toyo Keizai Shimposha.

—— (1989), *Japanese Employment Practices and the Labor Market* (in Japanese). Tokyo: Toyo Keizai Shimposha.

Oster, Gerry (1979), 'A Factor Analytic Test of the Theory of the Dual Economy', *Review of Economics and Statistics*, 61 (February): 33–9.

Osterman, Paul (1975), 'An Empirical Study of Labor Market Segmentation', *Industrial and Labor Relations Review*, 28 (July): 508–23.

——(1977), 'Reply', *Industrial and Labor Relations Review*, 30 (February): 221–4.

——(1980), *Getting Started: The Youth Labor Market*. Cambridge, Mass.: MIT Press.

O'Toole, James (ed.) (1974), *Work and the Quality of Life: Resource Papers for Work in America*. Cambridge, Mass.: MIT Press.

Oulton, Nicholas (1976), 'Inheritance and the Distribution of Wealth', *Oxford Economic Papers*, 28 (March): 86–101.

Parsons, Talcott (1959), 'The School Class as a Social System: Some of Its Functions in American Society', *Harvard Educational Review*, 29 (Fall): 297–318.

Pasinetti, Luigi (1962), 'Rate of Profit and Income Distribution in Relation to the Rate of Economic Growth', *Review of Economic Studies*, 29 (October): 267–79.

Pazner, Elisha A., and Schmeidler, David (1974), 'A Difficulty in the Concept of Fairness', *Review of Economic Studies*, 41 (July): 441–3.

————(1976), 'Social Contract Theory and Ordinal Distributive Equity', *Journal of Public Economics*, 5 (April–May): 261–8.

Phelps, Edmund S. (1970), 'Introduction', in *Microeconomic Foundations of Employment and Inflation Theory*. New York: Norton: 1–23.

——(1972), 'The Statistical Theory of Racism and Sexism', *American Economic Review*, 62 (September): 659–61.

Pigou, Arthur C. (1932), *The Economics of Welfare*. London: Macmillan.

Piore, Michael J. (1973), 'Fragments of "Sociological" Theory of Wages', *American Economic Review*, 63 (May): 377–84.

——(1975), 'Note for a Theory of Labor Market Stratification', in Richard C. Edwards, Michael Reich, and David M. Gordon (eds.), *Labor Market Segmentation*. Lexington, Mass.: D.C. Heath: 125–50.

——(1980a), 'Dualism as a Response to Flux and Uncertainty', in Michael Piore and Suzanne Berger, *Dualism and Discontinuity in Industrial Societies*. Cambridge: Cambridge University Press: 15–54.

——(1980b), 'The Technological Foundations of Dualism and Discontinuity', in Michael Piore and Suzanne Berger, *Dualism and Discontinuity in Industrial Societies*. Cambridge: Cambridge University Press: 55–81.

——and Sabel, Charles F. (1986), *The Second Industrial Divide: Possibilities for Prosperity*. New York: Basic Books.

Polanyi, Karl (1968), 'Aristotle Discovers the Economy' (1957), in George Dalton (ed.), *Primitive, Archaic and Modern Economies: Essays of Karl Polanyi*. Boston: Beacon: 78–115.

——(1977), *The Livelihood of Man*, ed. Harry W. Pearson. New York: Academic Press.

Poterba, James M., and Summers, Lawrence H. (1986), 'The Persistence of Volatility and Stock Market Fluctuations', *American Economic Review*, 76 (December): 1142–51.

Psacharopoulos, George, and Layard, Richard (1979), 'Human Capital and Earnings: British Evidence and a Critique', *Review of Economic Studies*, 46 (July): 485–503.

Raisian, John (1979), 'Cyclic Patterns in Weeks and Wages', *Economic Inquiry*, 17 (October): 475–95.

Rasmusen, Eric (1989), *Games and Information: An Introduction to Game Theory.* Oxford: Basil Blackwell.

Rawls, John (1971), *A Theory of Justice.* Cambridge, Mass.: Harvard University Press.

—— (1972), 'Reply to Lyons and Teitelman', *Journal of Philosophy*, 69 (October): 556–7.

—— (1980), 'Kantian Constructivism in Moral Theory', *Journal of Philosophy*, 77 (September): 515–72.

Reder, Melvin (1955), 'The Theory of Occupational Wage Differentials', *American Economic Review*, 45 (December): 833–52.

Riley, John G. (1975), 'Competitive Signalling', *Journal of Economic Theory*, 10 (April): 174–86.

—— (1979), 'Informational Equilibrium', *Econometrica*, 47 (March): 331–59.

Robbins, Lionel (1932), *The Nature and Significance of Economic Science.* London: Macmillan.

Rosen, Sherwin (1972*a*), 'Learning and Experience as Joint Exchange', *Quarterly Journal of Economics*, 86 (August): 366–82.

—— (1972*b*), 'Learning by Experience in the Labor Market', *Journal of Human Resources*, 7 (Summer): 326–42.

—— (1974), 'Hedonic Prices and Implicit Markets', *Journal of Political Economy*, 82 (January/February): 34–55.

—— (1977), 'Human Capital: A Survey of Empirical Research', in Ronald G. Ehrenberg (ed.), *Research in Labor Economics*, Vol. 1. Greenwich, Conn.: JAI Press: 3–39.

—— (1978), 'Substitution and Division of Labour', *Economica* (New Series), 45 (August): 235–50.

Rosenberg, Nathan (1976), 'The Direction of Technological Change: Inducement Mechanisms and Focusing Devices', in *Perspectives on Technology.* Cambridge: Cambridge University Press: 108–25.

Rothschild, Michael, and Stiglitz, Joseph E. (1976), 'Equilibrium in Competitive Insurance Markets: An Essay on the Economics of Imperfect Information', *Quarterly Journal of Economics*, 90 (December): 629–49.

Roy, A. D. (1951), 'Some Thoughts on the Distribution of Earnings', *Oxford Economic Papers*, 3 (June): 135–46.

Sabel, Charles F. (1982), *Work and Politics: The Division of Labor in Industry.* Cambridge: Cambridge University Press.

Salop, Joanne, and Salop, Steven (1976), 'Self-Selection and Turnover in the Labor Market', *Quarterly Journal of Economics*, 90 (November): 619–27.

Samuelson, Paul A. (1965), 'Proof That Properly Anticipated Prices Fluctuate Randomly', *Industrial Management Review*, 6 (Spring): 41–50.

—— (1973), 'Proof that Properly Discounted Present Values of Assets Vibrate Randomly', *Bell Journal of Economics and Management Science*, 4 (Autumn): 369–74.

—— and Modigliani, Franco (1966), 'The Pasinetti Paradox in Neoclassical and More General Models', *Review of Economic Studies*, 33 (October): 269–301.

Sato, Ryuzo, and Koizumi, Tetsunori (1973), 'On the Elasticities of Substitution and Complementarity', *Oxford Economic Papers*, 25 (March): 44–56.

Sawyer, Malcolm (1976), 'Income Distribution in OECD Countries', *OECD Economic Outlook Occasional Studies* (July): 3–36.

Schultz, Theodore W. (1960), 'Capital Formation by Education', *Journal of Political Economy*, 68 (December): 571–83.

—— (1971), *Investment in Human Capital: The Role of Education and Research*. New York: Free Press.

Schwartz, Adina (1973), 'Moral Neutrality and Primary Goods', *Ethics*, 83 (July): 294–307.

Scitovsky, Tibor (1976), *The Joyless Economy: An Inquiry into Human Satisfaction and Consumer Dissatisfaction*. Oxford: Oxford University Press.

Sen, Amartya (1970), *Collective Choice and Social Welfare*. San Francisco: Holden Day.

—— (1973), *On Economic Inequality*. Oxford: Basil Blackwell.

—— (1975), 'Rawls versus Bentham: An Axiomatic Examination of the Pure Distribution Problem', in N. Daniels (ed.), *Reading Rawls*. Oxford: Basil Blackwell: 283–92. Originally published in *Theory and Decision*, 4 (February/April, 1974): 300–9.

—— (1977), 'On Weights and Measures: Informational Constraints in Social Welfare Analysis', *Econometrica*, 45 (October): 1539–72.

—— (1979), 'Personal Utilities and Public Judgements: Or What's Wrong with Welfare Economics?', *Economic Journal*, 89 (September): 537–58.

Sewell, William H., and Hauser, Robert M. (1975), *Education, Occupation, and Earnings: Achievement in the Early Career*. New York: Academic Press.

Shapiro, Carl, and Stiglitz, Joseph E. (1984), 'Equilibrium Unemployment as a Worker Discipline Device', *American Economic Review*, 74 (June): 433–44.

Sheshinski, Eytan, and Weiss, Yoram (1981), 'Uncertainty and Optimal Social Security Systems', *Quarterly Journal of Economics*, 96 (May): 189–206.

Shiller, Robert J. (1981), 'Do Stock Prices Move Too Much to be Justified by Subsequent Changes in Dividends?', *American Economic Review*, 71 (June): 421–36.

—— (1984), 'Stock Prices and Social Dynamics', *Brookings Papers on Economic Activity*, 2: 457–98.

Shimada, Haruo (1974), 'Earnings Structure and Human Investment: A Comparison between the United States and Japan', Ph.D. Dissertation, University of Wisconsin, 1974. Published Tokyo: Kogakusha, 1981.

Shinohara, Miyohei (1970), *Structural Changes in Japan's Economic Development*. Tokyo: Kinokuniya.

Shionoya, Yuichi (1984), *The Structure of Value Concept: Utility and Right* (in Japanese). Tokyo: Toyo Keizai Shimposha.

Shorrocks, Anthony F. (1975), 'The Age–Wealth Relationship: A Cross-Section and Cohort Analysis', *Review of Economics and Statistics*, 57 (May): 155–63.

—— (1988), 'Wealth Holdings and Entrepreneurial Activity', in Denis Kessler and Andre Masson (eds.), *Modelling the Accumulation and Distribution of Wealth*. Oxford: Clarendon Press: 241–56.

Shoup, Carl S. (1966), *Federal Estate and Gift Taxes*. Washington D.C.: The Brookings Institution.

Simon, Herbert (1951), 'A Formal Theory of the Employment Relationship', *Econometrica*, 19 (July): 293–305. Reprinted in *Models of Man, Social and Rational: Mathematical Essays on Rational Human Behavior in a Social Setting*. New York: John Wiley, 1957: 183–95.

Smith, Adam (1904), *An Inquiry into the Nature and Causes of the Wealth of Nations*, Volumes I and II, ed. Edwin Cannan. London: Methuen (originally published 1776).

Smith, James D. (1988), 'The Concentration of Wealth in the United States: Trends in the Distribution of Wealth among American Families', Joint Economic Committee, United States Congress, July.

Smith, Robert (1979), 'Compensating Wage Differentials and Public Policy: A Review', *Industrial and Labor Relations Review*, 32 (April): 339–52.

Solow, Robert (1979), 'Alternative Approaches to Macroeconomic Theory: A Partial View', *Canadian Journal of Economics*, 12 (August): 339–54.

—— (1985), 'Insiders and Outsiders in Wage Determination', *Scandinavian Journal of Economics*, 87 (2): 411–28.

Spence, Michael (1973), 'Job Market Signalling', *Quarterly Journal of Economics*, 87 (August): 355–74.

—— (1974), 'Competitive and Optimal Responses to Signals', *Journal of Economic Theory*, 7 (March): 296–332.

Stiglitz, Joseph E. (1969), 'Distribution of Income and Wealth among Individuals', *Econometrica*, 37 (July): 382–97.

—— (1974), 'Wage Determination and Unemployment in L.D.C.'s', *Quarterly Journal of Economics*, 88 (May): 194–227.

Stoikov, Vladimir (1973), 'Size of Firm, Worker Earnings, and Human Capital: The Case of Japan', *Industrial and Labor Relations Review*, 26 (July): 1095–1106.

Stone, Katherine (1974), 'The Origins of Job Structures in the Steel Industry', *Review of Radical Political Economics*, 6 (Summer): 113–73.

Summers, Lawrence H. (1986), 'Does the Stock Market Rationally Reflect Fundamental Values?', *Journal of Finance*, 41 (July): 591–602.

Suzumura, Kotaro (1982), *Theory of Economic Planning* (in Japanese). Tokyo: Chikuma Shobo.

Tachibanaki, Toshiaki (1975), 'Wage Determinations in Japanese Manufacturing Industries—Structual Change and Wage differentials', *International Economic Review*, 16 (October): 562–86.

—— (1982), 'Further Results on Japanese Wage Differentials: Nenko Wages, Hierarchical Position, Bonuses, and Working Hours', *International Economic Review*, 23 (June): 447–61.

—— (1984), 'Youth Unemployment Problems' (in Japanese), *Nihon Rodo Kyokai Zasshi*, 307: 12–22.

—— (1988), 'Youth Employment and Labor Problems' (in Japanese), in Ministry of Labor (ed.) *The Long-run Prediction of the Labor Demand and Supply* (June): 1–29.

—— (1989), 'Variation of Wealth Prices and Inequality of the Wealth Distribution' (in Japanese), *Nihon Keizai Kenkyu* 18 (March): 79–91.

Takayama, Noriyuki (1980), *Economic Analysis of Inequality* (in Japanese). Tokyo: Toyo Keizai Shimposha.

—— Funaoka, Fumio, Ohtake Fumio, Sekiguchi, Masahiko, and Shibuya, Tokiyuki (1989), 'Household Assets and the Saving Rate in Japan' (in Japanese), *Keizai Bunseki* 116 (September): 1–93 (Economic Planning Agency).

—————————Ueno, Masaru, and Kubo, Katsuyuki (1990), 'Annual Movements of Household Asset Holdings and the Two Point Analysis of the Household Saving Rate' (in Japanese), *Keizai Bunseki*, 118 (March): 75–121 (Economic Planning Agency).

Tawney, Richard H. (1920), *The Acquistitive Society*. New York: Harcourt, Brace and World.

—— (1931), *Equality*; 4th edition, London: Unwin, 1952. Reprinted New York: Barnes and Noble, 1964.

Teitelman, Michael (1972), 'The Limits of Individualism', *Journal of Philosophy*, 69 (October): 545–56.

Thurow, Lester C. (1973), 'Toward a Definition of Economic Justice', *Public Interest*, 31 (Spring): 56–80.

—— (1975), *Generating Inequality: Mechanisms of Distribution in the U.S. Economy*. New York: Basic Books.

—— (1983), *Dangerous Currents: The State of Economics*. New York: Random House.

Titmuss, Richard M. (1952), 'Introduction', to R. H. Tawney, *Equality* (4th edition). London: Unwin. Reprinted New York: Barnes and Noble, 1964: 9–24.

Tobin, James (1972), 'Inflation and Unemployment', *American Economic Review*, 62 (March): 1–18.

—— (1980), *Asset Accumulation and Economic Activity: Reflections on Contemporary Macroeconomic Theory*. Chicago: University of Chicago Press.

Togashi, Mitsutaka (1979), 'Research on Wealth Distribution among Working Households in Japan' (in Japanese), *Hitotsubashi Ronso*, 81 (June): 767–77.

Tomes, Nigel (1981), 'The Family, Inheritance, and the Intergenerational Transmission of Inequality', *Journal of Political Economy*, 89 (October): 928–58.

Ueda, Kazuo (1990), 'Are Japanese Stock Prices Too High?', *Journal of the Japanese and International Economies*, 4 (December): 351–70.

Ujihara, Shojiro (1954), 'Characteristics of Workers in Large Factories in the Keihin Kogyo Area' (in Japanese). Reprinted in *Japanese Labor Research*. Tokyo: Tokyo University Press, 1966.

United States Department of Health, Education, and Welfare (1973), *Work in America*, Cambridge, Mass: MIT Press.

Ure, Andrew (1835), *The Philosophy of Manufactures: An Exposition of the Scientific, Moral, and Commercial Economy of the Factory System of Great Britain*: London: Charles Knight.

Uzawa, Hirofumi (1961), 'On the Two-Sector Model of Economic Growth', *Review of Economic Studies*, 29 (October): 40–7.

—— (1968), 'The Penrose Effect and Optimum Growth', *Economic Studies Quarterly*, 19 (March): 1–14.

—— (1969), 'The Preference and the Penrose Effect in a Two-Class Model of Economic Growth', *Journal of Political Economy*, 77 (July/August): 628–52.

Varian, Hal R. (1974), 'Equity, Envy and Efficiency', *Journal of Economic Theory*, 9 (September): 63–91.

—— (1975), 'Distributive Justice, Welfare Economics, and the Theory of Fairness', *Philosophy and Public Affairs*, 4 (Spring): 223–47.

Vickrey, William S. (1945), 'Measuring Marginal Utility by Reactions to Risk', *Econometrica*, 13 (October): 319–33.

—— (1960), 'Utility, Strategy, and Social Decision Rules', *Quarterly Journal of Economics*, 74 (November): 507–35.

Vickrey, William S. (1964), *Microstatics*. New York: Harcourt, Brace and World.

Wachtel, Paul (1975), 'The Effect of School Quality on Achievement, Attainment Levels, and Lifetime Earnings', *Explorations in Economic Research*, 2 (Fall): 502–36.

Wachter, Michael (1974), 'Primary and Secondary Labor Market: A Critique of the Dual Approach', *Brookings Papers on Economic Activity*, 3: 637–93.

Weiss, Andrew (1980), 'Job Queues and Layoffs in Labor Markets with Flexible Wages', *Journal of Political Economy*, 88 (June): 526–38.

Weitzman, Martin (1982), 'Increasing Returns and the Foundations of Unemployment Theory', *Economic Journal*, 92 (December): 787–804.

—— (1983), 'Some Macroeconomic Implications of Alternative Compensation Systems', *Economic Journal*, 93 (December): 763–83.

White, Betsy B. (1978), 'Empirical Tests of the Life Cycle Hypothesis', *American Economic Review*, 68 (September): 547–60.

White, Harrison C. (1970), *Chains of Opportunity*. Cambridge, Mass.: Harvard University Press.

Williamson, Oliver (1975), *Markets and Hierarchies*. New York: Free Press.

Willis, Robert J. (1986), 'Wage Determinants: A Survey and Reinterpretation of Human Capital Earnings Functions', in Orley Ashenfelter and Richard Layard (eds.), *Handbook of Labor Economics*, Vol. I. Amsterdam: North-Holland: 525–602.

—— and Rosen, Sherwin (1979), 'Education and Self-Selection', *Journal of Political Economy*, 87 (October): S7–S36.

Wilson, Charles (1977), 'A Model of Insurance Markets with Incomplete Information', *Journal of Economic Theory*, 16 (December): 167–207.

Wolff, Edward N. (1987), 'Estimates of Household Wealth Inequality in the U.S.', *Review of Income and Wealth*, 33 (September): 231–56.

Yaari, Menham (1965), 'Uncertain Lifetime, Life Insurance, and the Theory of the Consumer', *Review of Economic Studies*, 32 (April): 137–50.

Yellen, Janet (1984), 'Efficiency Wage Models of Unemployment', *American Economic Review*, 74 (May): 200–5.

Young, Allyn (1928), 'Increasing Returns and Economic Progress', *Economic Journal*, 38 (December): 527–42.

Zeuthen, Frederik (1930), *Problems of Monopoly and Economic Warfare*. London: Routledge & Kegan Paul.

Index